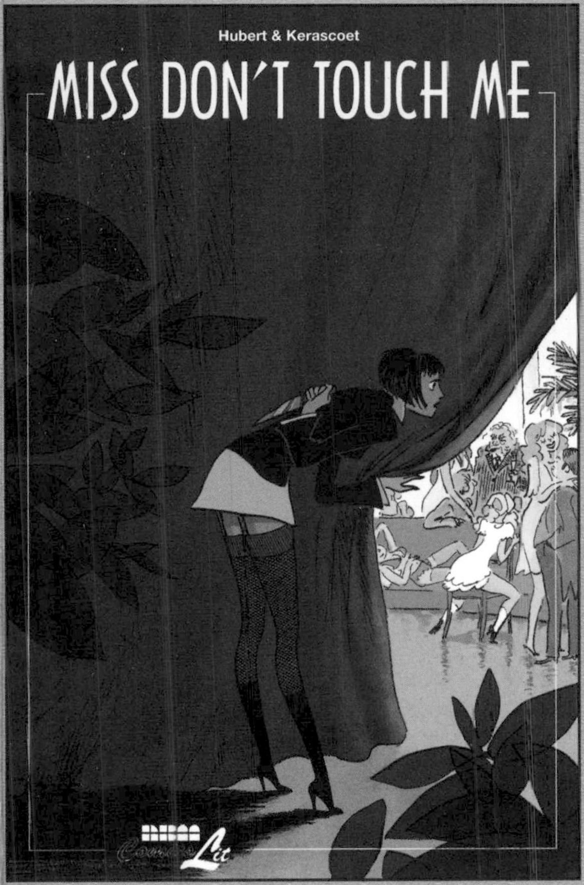
Hubert & Kerascoet
MISS DON'T TOUCH ME

MISS DON'T TOUCH ME
Hubert & Kerascoet

It's the turn of the XXth century. T
'Butcher of the Garden Cafes' is
the prowl for young loose wom
Florence has no family and works
a maid. Her only friend and th
family is her fellow maid, fun-lovi
Agatha, and Florence loses her to what she saw was murder but others only see as suicide. She decides to take matters into her own hands. In her pursuit, she ends up a servant in a luxury house of call-girls. She even becomes quite good at certain lascivious practices while still remaining a virgin! But she also doesn't lose sight of her goal: find the Butcher.

A suspenseful spicy tale as only the French could so lightly get away with, yet deceptive in its depth and realism.

61/2 x 9, 96pp. full color trade pb., $14.95, ISBN 978-1-56163-544-3

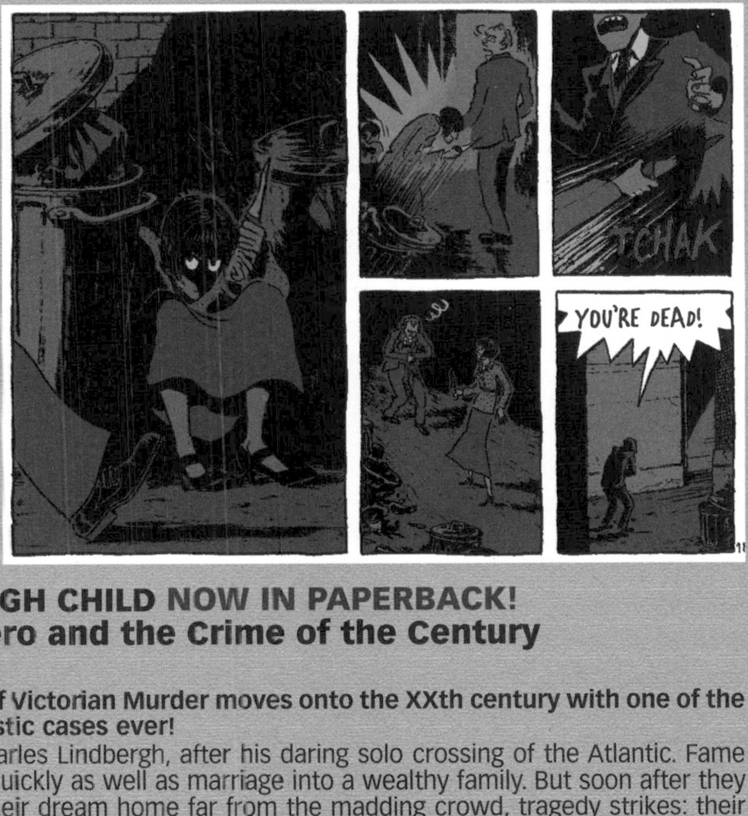
TCHAK
YOU'RE DEAD!

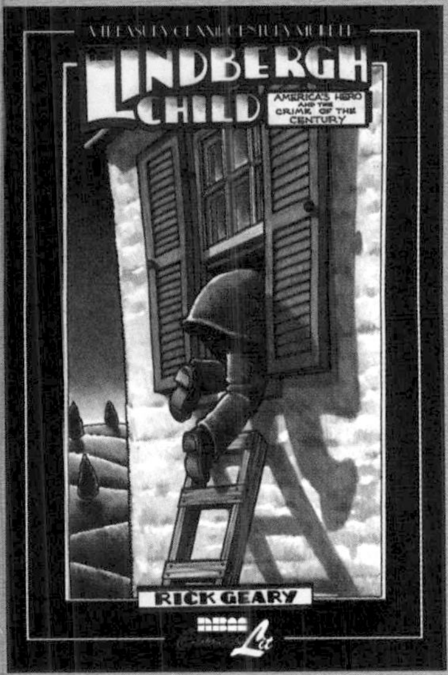
LINDBERGH CHILD
AMERICA'S HERO AND THE CRIME OF THE CENTURY
RICK GEARY

THE LINDBERGH CHILD NOW IN PAPERBACK!
America's Hero and the Crime of the Century
Rick GEARY

Geary's Treasury of Victorian Murder moves onto the XXth century with one of the most sensationalistic cases ever!

All was well for Charles Lindbergh, after his daring solo crossing of the Atlantic. Fame and fortune came quickly as well as marriage into a wealthy family. But soon after they build themselves their dream home far from the madding crowd, tragedy strikes: their baby is abducted! Geary retraces all the different highly publicized events, blackmail notes, false and otherwise, as well as the string of colorful characters wanting to 'help,' some of which actually successfully snookered the beleaguered hero. A fascinating story, of course without a fully satisfactory conclusion, replete with savory details and unsavory people as only Geary can masterfully relate with his understated dark humor.

"Rick Geary is one of cartooning's unsung treasures. Highly recommended, topnotch stuff." -Heidi McDonald, ***THE BEAT***

*"This thoughtful retelling of one of the century's most notorious crimes deserves several readings." -**Publishers Weekly starred review***

6x9, 80pp., B&W, trade pb., $9.95, ISBN 978-1-56163-530-6

NBM, 40 Exchange Place, Ste. 1308, New York, NY 10005, 1-800-886-1223

MC, VISA, Amex accepted, add $4 P&H for 1st item, $1 each additionall.

www.nbmpublishing.com SEE PREVIEW PAGES REVIEWS, INTERVIEWS...

$151,534

$41,264

$11,550

$19,898

$10,350

NOW'S THE TIME TO CONSIGN YOUR POP CULTURE COLLECTIBLES!

40 YEARS OF EXPERIENCE IN THE POP CULTURE MARKET AND THE BEST PRICES MAKES HAKE'S THE PLACE TO CONSIGN!

TIME IS RUNNING OUT! CONTACT ALEX WINTER AT 866-404-9800 EXT 1632 TO CONSIGN!

A DIVISION OF

HAKE'S AMERICANA & COLLECTIBLES
P.O. BOX 12001 • YORK, PA 17402 • WWW.HAKES.COM

ENTERTAINMENT
GEPPI'S
PUBLISHING &
AUCTIONS

On the cover: A Las Musketeer illustration by Jason. [©2008 Jason]

THE COMICS JOURNAL #294 (ISBN: 987-1-56097-984-5) Dec. 2008. Published monthly in Jan., Feb., Apr., May, July, Aug., Oct., Nov. by Fantagraphics Books, Inc., from the editorial and business offices at 7563 Lake City Way N.E., Seattle, WA 98115. *The Comics Journal* is copyright © 2008 by Fantagraphics Books, Inc. All images/photos/text © Their respective copyright holders. Unauthorized reproduction of any of its contents is prohibited by law. Periodicals postage paid at Seattle, WA, and at additional mailing offices. POSTMASTER: Please send address changes to The Comics Journal, 7563 Lake City Way N.E., Seattle, WA 98115. PRINTED IN SINGAPORE.

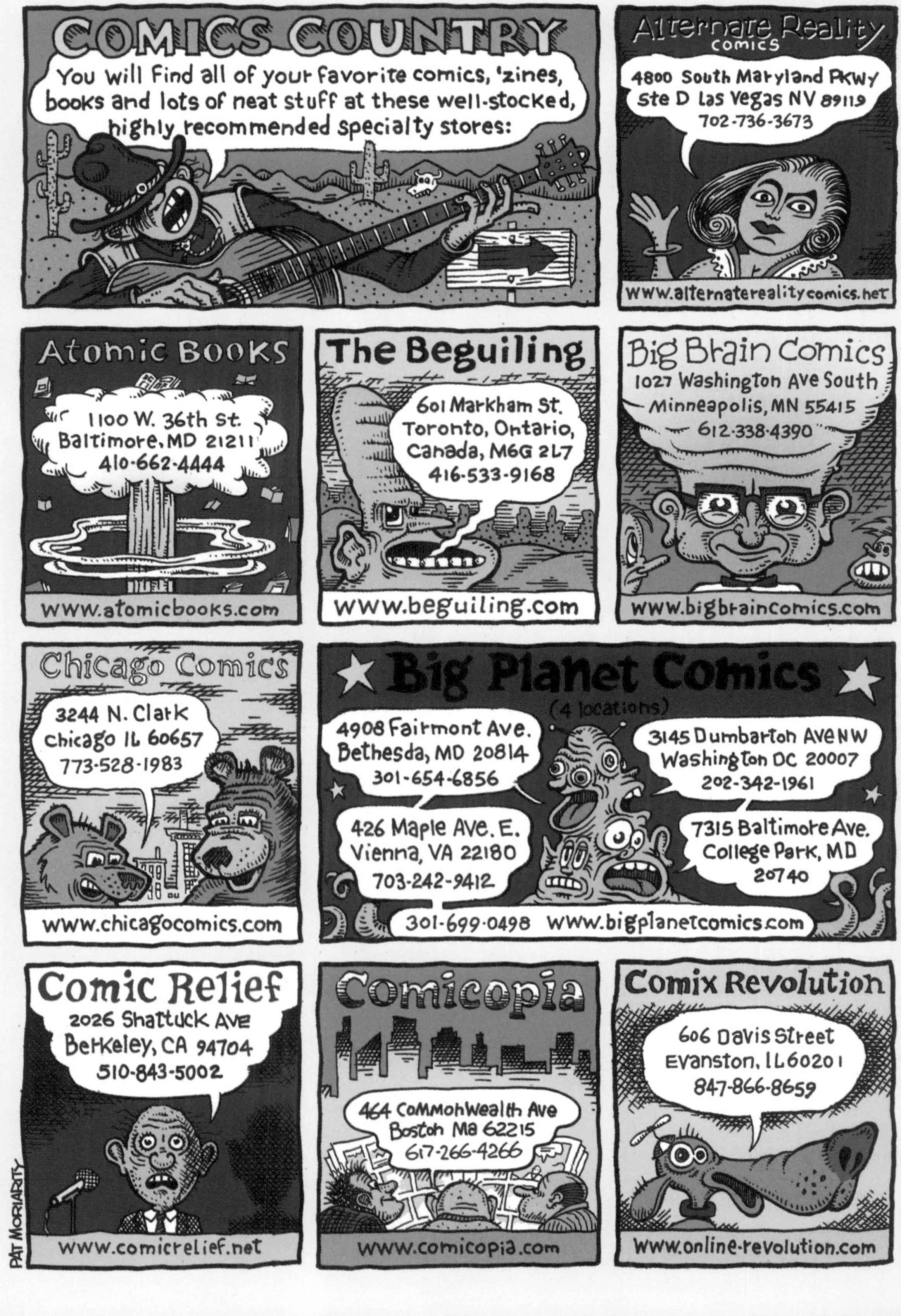
COMICS COUNTRY
You will find all of your favorite comics, 'zines, books and lots of neat stuff at these well-stocked, highly recommended specialty stores:
Alternate Reality COMICS
4800 South Maryland PKWY Ste D Las Vegas NV 89119 702-736-3673
www.alternaterealitycomics.net
Atomic Books
1100 W. 36th St. Baltimore, MD 21211 410-662-4444
www.atomicbooks.com
The Beguiling
601 Markham St. Toronto, Ontario, Canada, M6G 2L7 416-533-9168
www.beguiling.com
Big Brain Comics
1027 Washington Ave South Minneapolis, MN 55415 612-338-4390
www.bigbraincomics.com
Chicago Comics
3244 N. Clark Chicago IL 60657 773-528-1983
www.chicagocomics.com
Big Planet Comics
(4 locations)
4908 Fairmont Ave. Bethesda, MD 20814 301-654-6856
3145 Dumbarton Ave NW Washington DC 20007 202-342-1961
426 Maple Ave. E. Vienna, VA 22180 703-242-9412
7315 Baltimore Ave. College Park, MD 20740
301-699-0498 www.bigplanetcomics.com
Comic Relief
2026 Shattuck Ave Berkeley, CA 94704 510-843-5002
www.comicrelief.net
Comicopia
464 Commonwealth Ave Boston Ma 62215 617-266-4266
www.comicopia.com
Comix Revolution
606 Davis Street Evanston, IL 60201 847-866-8659
www.online-revolution.com
PAT MORIARITY

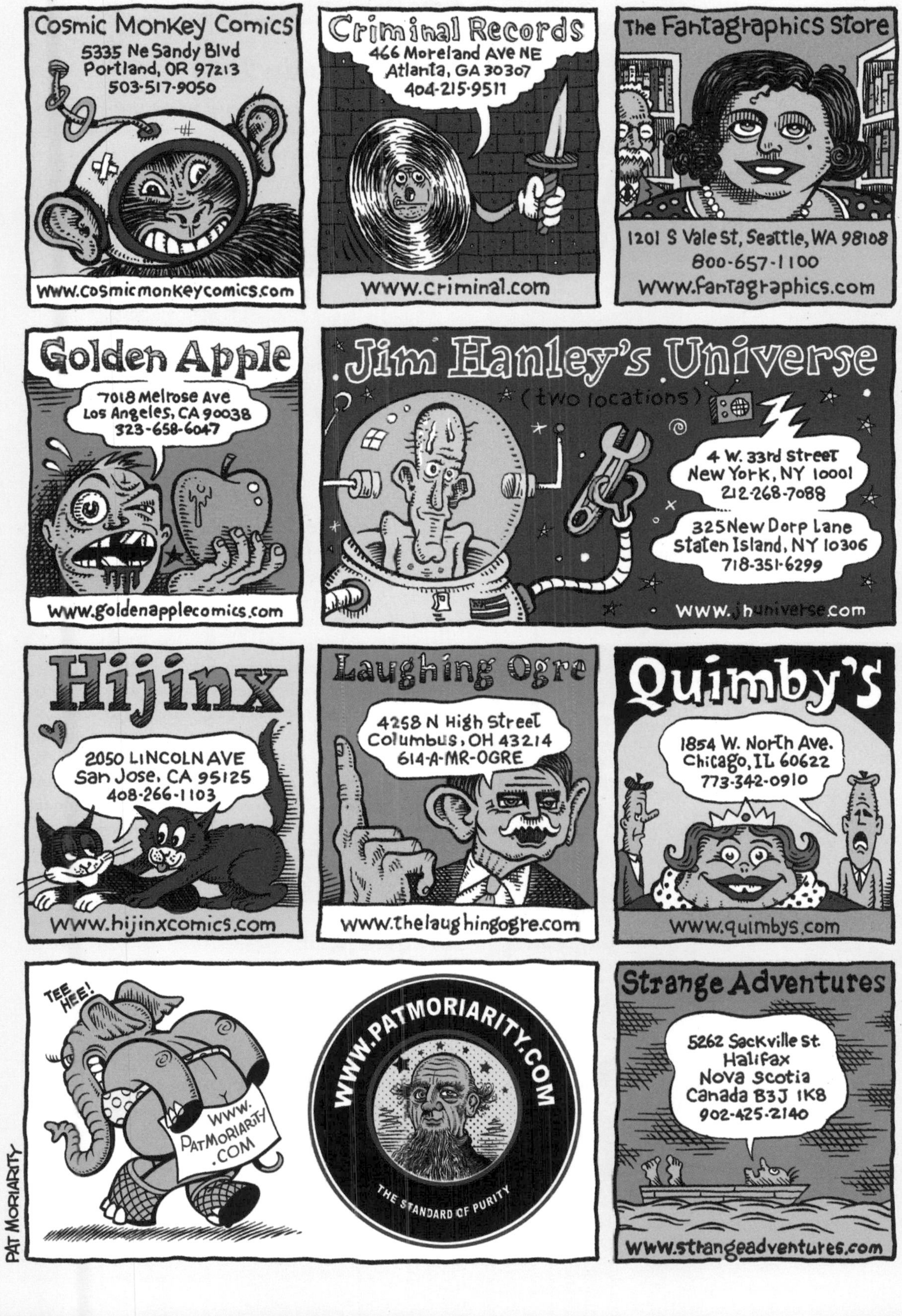
Cosmic Monkey Comics
5335 Ne Sandy Blvd
Portland, OR 97213
503-517-9050
www.cosmicmonkeycomics.com
Criminal Records
466 Moreland Ave NE
Atlanta, GA 30307
404-215-9511
www.criminal.com
The Fantagraphics Store
1201 S Vale St, Seattle, WA 98108
800-657-1100
www.fantagraphics.com
Golden Apple
7018 Melrose Ave
Los Angeles, CA 90038
323-658-6047
www.goldenapplecomics.com
Jim Hanley's Universe
(two locations)
4 W. 33rd Street
New York, NY 10001
212-268-7088
325 New Dorp Lane
Staten Island, NY 10306
718-351-6299
www.jhuniverse.com
Hijinx
2050 LINCOLN AVE
San Jose, CA 95125
408-266-1103
www.hijinxcomics.com
Laughing Ogre
4258 N High Street
Columbus, OH 43214
614-A-MR-OGRE
www.thelaughingogre.com
Quimby's
1854 W. North Ave.
Chicago, IL 60622
773-342-0910
www.quimbys.com
TEE HEE!
WWW.
PATMORIARITY
.COM
WWW.PATMORIARITY.COM
THE STANDARD OF PURITY
Strange Adventures
5262 Sackville St.
Halifax
Nova Scotia
Canada B3J 1K8
902-425-2140
www.strangeadventures.com
PAT MORIARITY

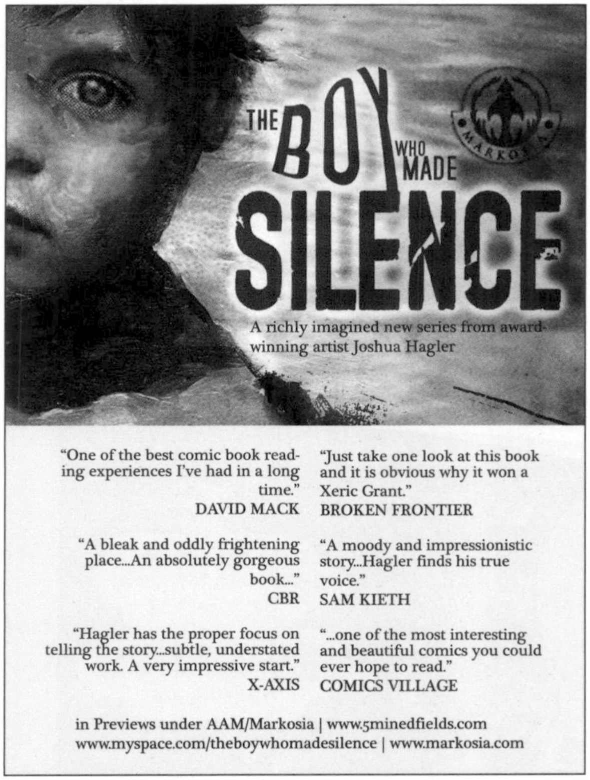
THE BOY WHO MADE SILENCE
MARKOSIA
A richly imagined new series from award-winning artist Joshua Hagler
"One of the best comic book reading experiences I've had in a long time." DAVID MACK
"Just take one look at this book and it is obvious why it won a Xeric Grant." BROKEN FRONTIER
"A bleak and oddly frightening place...An absolutely gorgeous book..." CBR
"A moody and impressionistic story...Hagler finds his true voice." SAM KIETH
"Hagler has the proper focus on telling the story...subtle, understated work. A very impressive start." X-AXIS
"...one of the most interesting and beautiful comics you could ever hope to read." COMICS VILLAGE
in Previews under AAM/Markosia | www.5minedfields.com
www.myspace.com/theboywhomadesilence | www.markosia.com

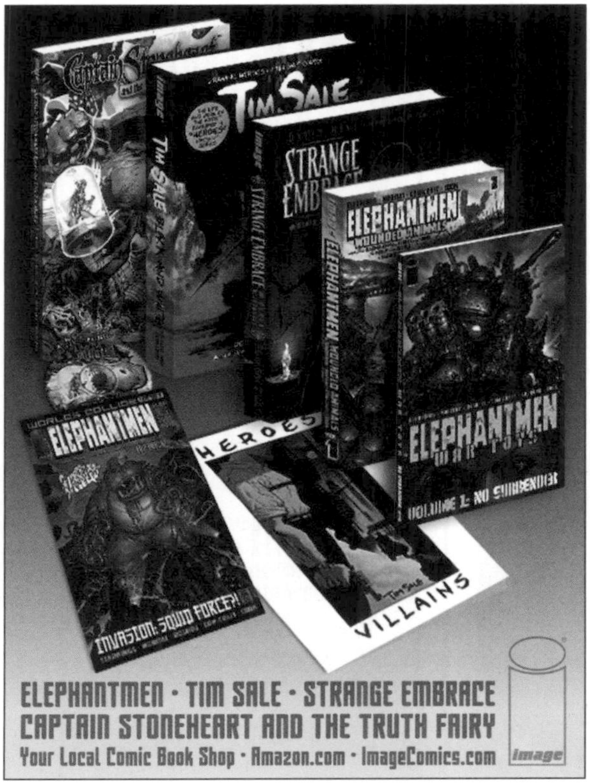
TIM SALE
STRANGE EMBRACE
ELEPHANTMEN
HEROES
VILLAINS
ELEPHANTMEN · TIM SALE · STRANGE EMBRACE
CAPTAIN STONEHEART AND THE TRUTH FAIRY
Your Local Comic Book Shop · Amazon.com · ImageComics.com
image

TCJ Gift Guide 2008

We know just what you so desperately want this holiday season: help figuring out what gifts to get your loved ones. We asked some *Journal* contributors and comics pros, including some 2008 Xeric Grant winners, for ideas and invited publishers to tell us what books they're pushing for this year's gift-buying season. To top it off, we interviewed James Kochalka, author of the holiday-season release *American Elf*. You're welcome.

Josh Simmons, Cartoonist:

"***Fluffy*** (Simone Lia) — Perfect for: The girlfriend, Ma, Sis. Fluffy the bunny is tiny, adorable, lovable and totally, totally annoying. This book is hilarious and sweet and gets at the frustrations and gratifications of relationships like few I read this year. ***Where Demented Wented, The Art and Comics of Rory Hayes*** (edited by Dan Nadel and Glenn Bray) — Perfect for: The family pervert/drug fiend/funny uncle. A beautifully assembled collection of and tribute to the late Hayes. Deranged, obsessive and inspired, these are some of my favorite comics of recent memory. ***Bottomless Belly Button*** (Dash Shaw) — Perfect for: The whole family. This is kind of an incredible comic, both because Shaw cranked out a 720-page book over the course of a couple of years in his early 20s, but more surprisingly, that it's pretty great. What family can't relate to the plain-jane blues, aging anxieties, the nightmare of familial interpersonal dynamics, the first love jitters and mom freaking out on Ecstasy. Bonus points for all the formal tricks enhancing rather than suffocating the reading experience. Big spender: Show you're the caring-est family member of them all. Get one of these giant, deluxe, $100+ fancy comic-art books; ***Many More Splendid Sundays***, ***Windsor McCay's Little Nemo in Slumberland*** (edited by Peter Maresca), ***Gary Panter*** (edited by Dan Nadel), and ***Kramers Ergot*** 7 (edited by Sammy Harkham). Hell, buy all three. Why not? What are you, a sissy?"

Steve Lieber, Artist:

"***Skim***, a terrific graphic novel written by Mariko Tamaki and illustrated by Jillian Tamaki is one of those rare collaborations that present an utterly unified vision, with a strong story and gorgeous, expressive art. It's listed as a Young Adult title, but I think its appeal goes way beyond the target market. ***The Great Outdoor Fight*** by Chris Onstad is a hardback collected edition of an insanely entertaining story arc from the Web-comic *Achewood*. I usually don't care much for reading comics on a monitor, but I never, ever miss this strip. ***X-Men First Class* Vol. 2: *Mutant Mayhem***. Written by Jeff Parker. Illustrated

by Roger Cruz, Kevin Nowlan, Paul Smith, Mike Allred, Nick Dragotta and the great Colleen Coover. This collection of stand-alone stories is perfectly constructed superhero fun, with delightful art and no continuity or angst. It's hard to believe a book this enjoyable is even allowed on the stands."

Jeffrey Brown, Cartoonist:

"The new *Kramers Ergot* will make a perfect stocking stuffer, full of huge, new beautiful comics from some of the most talented artists working today. Of course, you'll have to get one of those huge, jokey stockings. Or make one. I guess you could just track down some minicomics for your stocking gifts, there's lots coming out from students at **CCS** and **SCAD**. Or you could forgo the stocking idea; maybe you're buying for someone who already has the new *Kramers*, the Sunday Press *Nemo* books, Brian Chippendale's *Ninja* book ... in that case, you should buy them a special **bookcase** that can accommodate all those."

Richard Starkings, Letterer, Writer:

"Those awfully nice chaps at Comicraft have put out a cornucopia of classy publications in the past year — aside from the two *Elephantmen* trades, be sure and stick a copy of *Tim Sale: Black and White* or *Captain Stoneheart and the Truth Fairy* or Dave Hine's *Strange Embrace* (Now in full color hardcover format) in your loved one's stocking. And the 1000 piece *Elephantmen* **jigsaw puzzle** featuring the art of Ladrönn is still available for those wet and wintry Sunday afternoons!"

Dave Kiersh, 2008 Xeric Award Recipient:

"I highly recommend the book *Skitzy: The Story of Floyd W. Skitzafroid* by Don Freeman (Drawn & Quarterly). This is a rediscovered classic book for adults by the famous children's book author. I wrote the afterword. Also *My Brain Is Hanging Down* by David Heatley (Pantheon). This is a raw, honestly personal book with an insanely detailed and beautifully developed style. If you have dreamed of a cartoonist who exists somewhere between Robert Crumb and Gary Panter, this is the book that will make you blush. *Beetle Bailey by Mort Walker: The First Years 1950-1952* (Checker Book Publishing). Features the earliest strips by Mort Walker before Bailey was enlisted in the Army. A treasure trove of great cartooning and far more detailed than Mort's later work: A beautiful collection! And I have to recommend my own books as well: *Neverland* (2008) and *A Last Cry For Help* (2006) both available from bodegadistribution.com."

Jason Hoffman, 2008 Xeric Award Recipient:

"One of my absolute favorite books, one that I always suggest to anyone who is interested in comics is *God's Man* by Lynd Ward. It was published in 1929, weeks before the Stock Market crashed and it tells the story of an artist trying to make his way through life. The story itself is wordless and each of its 140 pages is illustrated with amazingly rich wood engravings. Ward created six other pictorial narratives, including *Mad Man's Drum* and *Vertigo*, but *God's Man* holds a special place in my heart because of how influential it has been to my work. I would definitely suggest this book to anyone who makes art either as a profession or a hobby, or anyone who is interested in the history of American graphic novels."

Jack Hsu, 2008 Xeric Award Recipient:

"If I had to make one, rather obvious, recommendation, I would push for the first five volumes of *Blade of The Immortal* from Dark Horse. Volume 2, *Dreamsong*, is my favorite. The story has a great premise and as usual is built around multi-faceted characters. Samura's deft pacing and cinematic staging are only topped by his breath-taking action sequences. It's such a highly immersive read to me that I endearingly call it "a poor man's movie" — and a masterful one at that."

Stef Lenk, 2008 Xeric Award Recipient:

"I find myself often to be biased in favor of wordless comics, so in that genre, I highly recommend *Cinema Panopticum* by Thomas Ott and *The Ticking* (nearly silent) by Renée French. In the independent genre, Shannon Gerard's *Hung* comics series is gorgeous (as are her crochet projects and sundry other books, available via shannongerard.etsy.com). *Arkham Asylum* by Dave McKean and Grant Morrison and *Mr. Punch* by Mckean and Neil Gaiman are favorites in the more mainstream lineup. Also the beyond sublime *Little Nemo in Slumberland* by Winsor McCay. The one you want is the oversized book (like, 2ft tall?), that'll make you feel the same age as Nemo when you're reading it."

Justin Murphy, 2008 Xeric Award Recipient:

"*Korgi*. These Welsh dogs are at the height of their popularity so it is fitting that they should have their own comic book. What makes *Korgi* such a delight to read is the artwork, which is reminiscent of Disney films like *Fox and the Hound*. A great gift for any Korgi lover! *Cleburne: A Graphic Novel*. Black soldiers in the Confederate Army! *Cleburne* is the true story of a General during the Civil War and his plan to enlist free slaves to fight for the

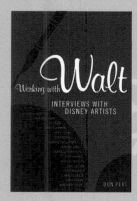

South. Winner of the Xeric Award and featured on the cover of *Publishers Weekly*. A great gift for history buffs or anyone interested in compelling stories."

Eroyn Franklin, 2008 Xeric Award Recipient:
"Tom Gauld's ***Three Very Small Comics*** come in multiple volumes that are perfect for all ages. The sets contain posters, panoramas and stapled minis. His irreverent tales about monsters, robots and war are articulated with enthusiasm for both the somber and silly. ***Pamplemoussi*** by Genevieve Castree is a nonlinear collection of nightmarish landscapes inhabited by intricately inked animals and children. The story is told without text but is coupled with a record by the artist of breath taking French songs that wander between the eerie, ethereal and erratic. It may be hard to get your hands on, so plan ahead. ***Bottomless Belly Button*** is a massive book by Dash Shaw that unravels like a dream. The setting is not burdened by time and there are hints of the absurd in what sometimes feels like a diary. It is in part about family, isolation and the inability to connect. What could be better to celebrate the holidays!"

Mark Bennett, 2008 Xeric Award Recipient:
"There are so many amazing comics about history! I like ***Satchel Paige*** By James Sturm and Rich Tommaso, ***Journey into Mohawk Country*** by Harmen Meyndertsz Van Den Bogaert and George O'Connor, ***A People's History of American Empire*** by Zinn, Konopacki and Buhle and ***Barefoot Gen*** by Keiji Nakazawa. I also recommend the self-published ***Marie of Montmartre*** by Alexis Frederick-Frost, and the fairy tales of ***Tragic Relief*** by Colleen Frakes. For year-'round gifts, try subscriptions to ***Phase-7*** by Alec Longstreth or ***High Maintenance Machine*** by Matthew Reidsma."

Gary Beatty, 2008 Xeric Award Recipient:
"***Action Philosophers*** — A series by Evil Twin Comics that presents philosophy in an understandable and entertaining form, something no college teacher ever accomplished for me. ***Age of Bronze: The Story of the Trojan War***, by Eric Shanower — The graphic-novel collections are incredible reads for history buffs. ***Castle Waiting*** by Linda Medley, the hardcover — A set of linked nouveaux fairy tales, interesting conflict without bloody resolution. ***Kabuki*** by David Mack. ***V for Vendetta*** by Alan Moore (or ***Swamp Thing*** by Alan Moore) — The movie was only 10 percent of the plot and little of the insight. ***Fables*** by Bill Willingham: Contemporary activities of characters from children's stories now living as secret refugees in New York. These graphic novels do feature bloody resolution but are smartly written. ***Y: The Last Man*** by Brian K. Vaughan: wherein a plague kills all the males but one. Not the party you envision. ***Alias*** by Brian Michael Bendis — Mysteries that hover just outside of Marvel's universe of superheroes, film noir with a fairly disturbed heroine. ***Sandman*** —Girls like these, too, but that doesn't mean they're 'girly.'"

Rich Kreiner, Comics Journal critic and columnist:
"I stopped writing about comics for total strangers about 10 years ago, abandoning local newspapers and regional magazines in favor of addressing fellow travelers exclusively through this magazine. Accordingly, the idea that I might suggest any comic-related gifts for the folks that *you* know and esteem seems pretty alien to me. So instead of my focusing on *them*, let me address you, acting as a memory aid, on the wealth of funnybook potential suitable for any season of giving.

Best, of course, is the stuff that you can personally vouch for (or, at worst, *explain*). Then there are the comics that need no explanation beyond gift-wrap. Let's call them canonical: Spiegelman's ***Maus***. McCloud's ***Understanding Comics***. Moore and Gibbons' ***Watchmen***. ***The Smithsonian Collection of Newspaper Comics***, should that still be available. Ware's ***Jimmy Corrigan***. (Hey, *there's* a ray of holiday sunshine!) **Your choice with Clowes**.

Ours is the golden era for newspaper reprints. Ruthless canonizing begins with Schulz's ***Peanuts***. King's ***Gasoline Alley*** (as ***Walt and Skeezix*** volumes) is really far better than you could otherwise believe. There's Segar's ***Thimble Theatre***, a.k.a. *Popeye* and did I mention that *Smithsonian* volume? All benefit from having some terrific production values and attractive packaging. Waterson's ***Calvin & Hobbes*** and Larson's ***The Far Side*** have those outstanding comprehensive collections. Ditto the Don Martin compilation. Caniff's ***Terry and the Pirates*** and Gould's ***Dick Tracy*** and Gray's *Little Orphan Annie*. Herriman's *Krazy Kat* reprints are gorgeous and ***The Kat Who Walked In Beauty*** would please the effetest of aesthetes. Gurewitch's ***The Trial of Colonel Sweeto*** probably wouldn't, but I'm sure glad I've got my copy. McDonnell's ***Mutts*** comes in a number of consumer-friendly packages sure to please any budget.

Comic reprints are scarcely less lustrous. Stanley's ***Little Lulu*** from Dark Horse, ***Mad*** from DC's Archive series, something of Gonick's ***Cartoon History of the Universe***. **Any Carl Barks ducks** anytime, anywhere. The Brothers Hernandez, with the ***Palomar*** and ***Locas*** whoppers preeminent. Don't overlook the recent sizable reprints of

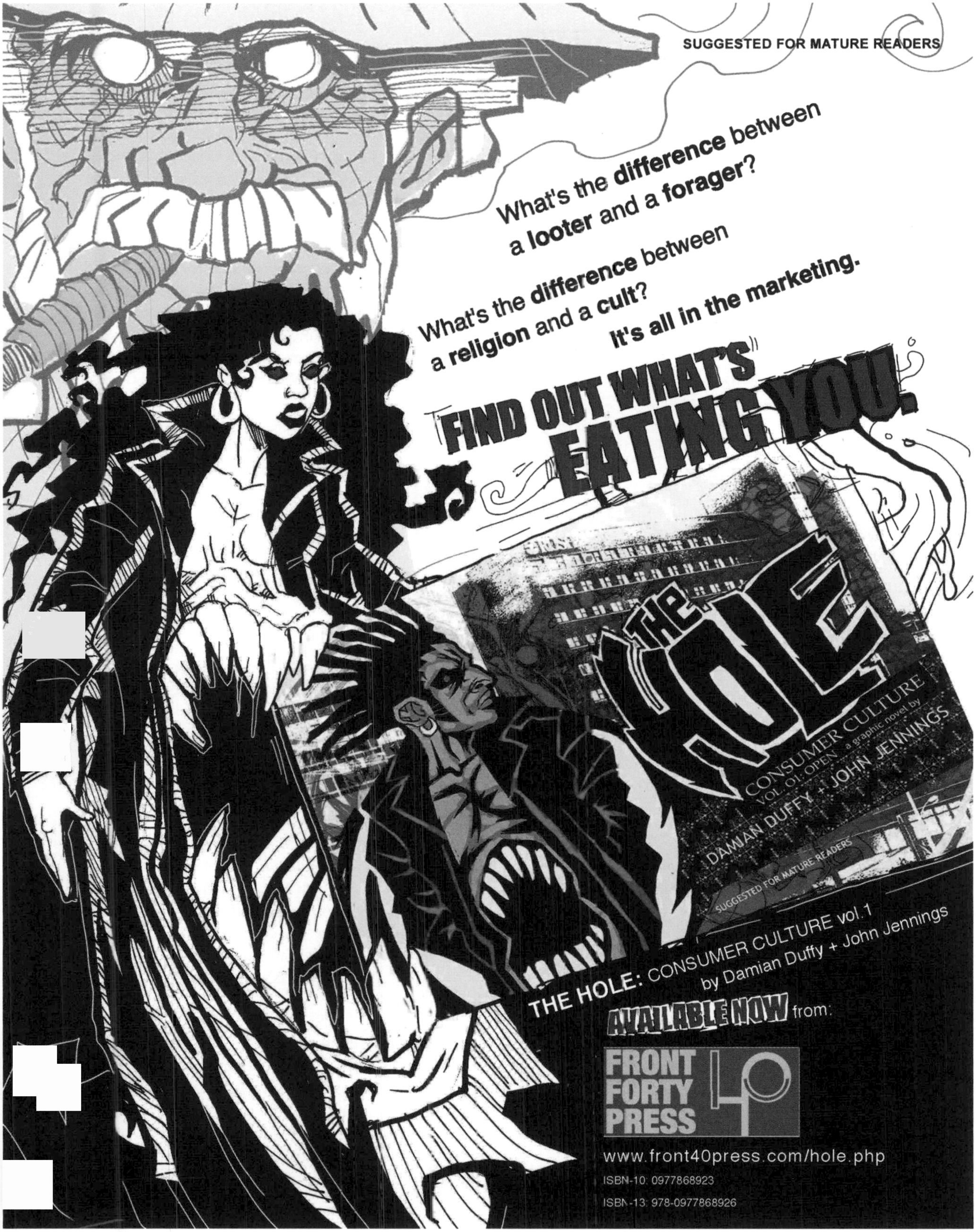
SUGGESTED FOR MATURE READERS
What's the difference between a looter and a forager?
What's the difference between a religion and a cult?
It's all in the marketing.
FIND OUT WHAT'S EATING YOU.
THE HOLE
CONSUMER CULTURE
VOL. 01: OPEN a graphic novel by
DAMIAN DUFFY + JOHN JENNINGS
SUGGESTED FOR MATURE READERS
THE HOLE: CONSUMER CULTURE vol.1
by Damian Duffy + John Jennings
AVAILABLE NOW from:
FRONT FORTY PRESS
www.front40press.com/hole.php
ISBN-10: 0977868923
ISBN-13: 978-0977868926

McCloud's collected **Zot!** and Messner-Loebs' **Journey**. Moore and Campbell's **From Hell** for that special someone. Huizenga's **Curses**. Or Chaykin's **American Flagg**?

Books qua books? Karasik and Mazzucchelli's adaptation of Auster's **City of Glass** and/or `most anything by Briggs (**Gentleman Jim** being the most recent release, **When the Wind Blows** my personal fave with **Ethel and Earnest** having perhaps the widest appeal). David B.'s *Epileptic*. I've had good luck giving scattershot volumes like the annual **Best American Comics** for the year and the perennial **An Anthology of Graphic Fiction, Cartoons, and True Stories** edited by Ivan Brunetti. Yeah, their excerpts are sometimes agonizingly brief, but you don't make a meal out of a chocolate sampler, either. Painful brevity is avoided in **A Smithsonian Book of Comic-Book Comics** and if this isn't in print any longer it's our collective loss.

Of course the longer I go on, the more this canon looks like provincial heresy. If you've been playing along at home, you've noticed how even a memory aid can play tricks, all forgetful, astigmatic, truncated and blinkered. (Proof? Take a random letter of the alphabet and see how many rich veins have been left out. Try "K," for example: Ben Katchor. Bernie Krigstein. The bulk of Kurtzman. Jack Kirby. Walt Kelly.)

So belatedly my point: rather than take a list of good books and great authors (Barry! Crumb! Sacco! Seth! Brown! Millionaire! Nilsen!) to a full-service comic shop (Pekar! Panter! McCay! Trondheim! Jason! Woodring! Feiffer! Lat! More if I can get my deadline delayed again!), go instead to that store with your roster of potential recipients fixed in your mind. With *those* folks front and center, with *their* likes and interests foremost, chances are excellent that you'll be able to scan the shelves and find a match of comic to their taste, sensibility and maturity (For instance, with many it's now possible to get a *Doonesbury* volume that cues up thematically to some ceremonious moment in your recipient's life or that correspond to some period during your relationship — a kind of "Funny The Year You Were Born" volume, or maybe "What Was Laughable When We First Had Sex." Or something.)

It wasn't always as good as this. Happy to you and yours."

Terry Nantier, Publisher, NBM:
"Four of the latest books from NBM make great Xmas gifts: the new beautiful **Happy Hooligan** collection in full color; the first new David B since *Epileptic*: **Nocturnal Conspiracies**; **Why I Killed Peter**, a deeply moving topical rendition of the author's youthful experience with

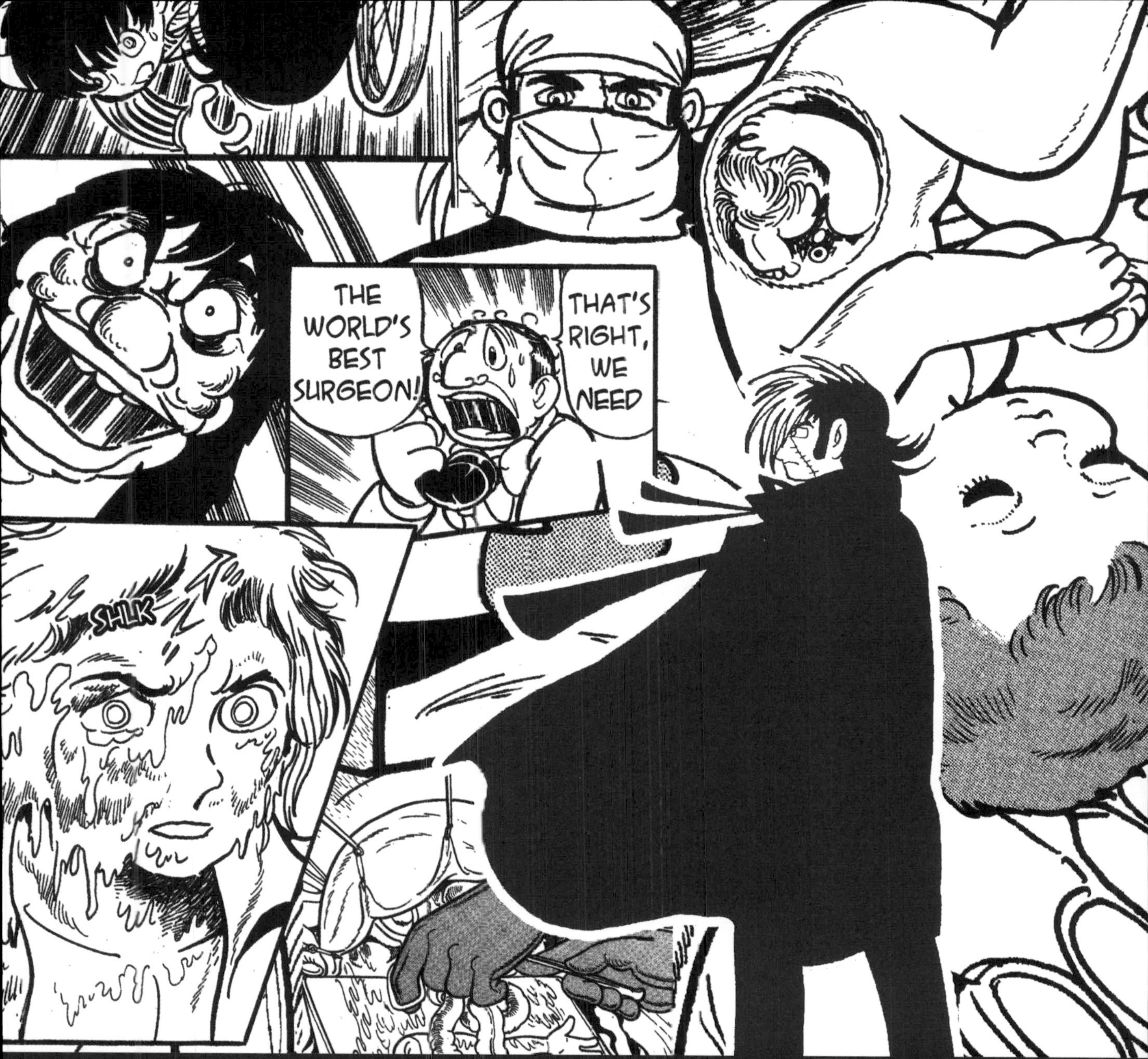
THAT'S RIGHT, WE NEED
THE WORLD'S BEST SURGEON!
SHLK

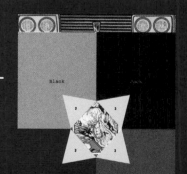

abuse at the hands of a priest who was a close friend, and *Miss Don't Touch Me*, a much lighter, spicier murder mystery tale in a high-class house of pleasure at the turn of the 20th century."

Stephen Vrattos, Vertical, Inc.:

"I must recommend *Black Jack* Vol. 2 by Osamu Tezuka. This beautiful hardcover volume sports an original cover and features an exclusive 20-page story recently approved for re-release after decades out of the public eye! And it's limited to a scant 1,200 copies!"

Brett Warnock, Publisher, Top Shelf:

"*American Elf* Vol. 3 by James Kochalka, *Veeps: Profiles in Insignificance*, by Bill Kelter and Wayne Shellabarger, *Swallow Me Whole*, by Nate Powell, and *Sulk* Vol.'s 1 & 2, by Jeffrey Brown."

Dave Marshall, Dark Horse Comics:

"Featuring some of the earliest work of Los Bros. Hernandez, as well as the debut and formative years of Seth, *Mister X: The Archives* contains more than a couple of watershed moments of '80s comics inside its hardcover. The brain child of Dean Motter, whose eye-catching book designs still look innovative 25 years after they hit comicshop shelves, *Mister X* was not only a previously unseen amalgamation of film noir, science fiction, and German Expressionism, it was a springboard for a generation of new talent, including a pre-*Violent Cases* Dave McKean. This deluxe, re-mastered volume collects the influential first series in its entirety, along with half a dozen short stories, reams of supplemental material, and a foreword by Warren Ellis."

John Fleskes, Flesk Publications:

"*William Stout: Prehistoric Life Murals* is an astonishing look at dinosaurs and their primeval worlds. This lavishly illustrated 144-page volume contains all of Stout's stunning murals for The Houston Museum of Natural Science, Walt Disney World's Animal Kingdom and the San Diego Natural History Museum. Stout's detailed commentary guides readers through his creative process. Included are preliminary drawings, color studies and one-quarter-scale oil paintings, guiding the reader through Stout's meticulous step-by-step methodology from initial design to finished masterpiece. The introduction is by Ray Harryhausen. This 10" x 12" hardcover book runs $39.95."

Karen Baliff Ornstein, Rutgers University Press:

"A lively, interdisciplinary collection of essays, *The Jewish Graphic Novel* addresses critically acclaimed works in this subgenre of Jewish literary and artistic culture. Featuring insightful discussions of notable figures in the industry — such as Will Eisner, Art Spiegelman and Joann Sfar — the essays focus on the how graphic novels are increasingly being used in Holocaust memoir and fiction, and to portray Jewish identity in America and abroad."

Tom Mayer, Associate Editor, W. W. Norton and Company:

"This fall and winter, Norton will roll out four new titles in our Will Eisner library: *The Dreamer*, *The Name of the Game*, *To the Heart of the Storm* and *The Will Eisner Reader*. These books had been incorporated in *Life In Pictures*, the last of the three major Eisner compilations we put together with Will and his agent, Denis Kitchen. We've got three more individual paperbacks coming in the Will Eisner Library in addition to the launch of Eisner's three beloved drawing textbooks this summer. A few other GNs are in the works but I hesitate to tell you about them now as they're probably not going to be ready until the fall of 2009."

Ellie Graham, Press Officer, Titan Books:

"Titan is launching a fantastic range of new *Watchmen* titles, starting in October with *Watching the Watchmen* [$39.95, 9781848560413], a phenomenal art book that companions the original graphic novel. Written by *Watchmen*'s artist, Dave Gibbons, this deluxe hardback features page upon page of imagery, from early character designs to thumbnail pages, sketches, posters, early script and correspondence. Designed by Chip Kidd and Mike Essl, this is a unique inside account of the genesis of the graphic novel that changed the industry. Then, kickstarting the new year, come three books to tie in to the new *Watchmen* movie, directed by Zack Snyder. *Watchmen: The Official Film Companion* [$19.95, 9781848560673] takes viewers inside this colossal movie with photographs and exclusive cast and crew interviews, while *Watchmen: The Art of the Film* [$40, 9781848560680] explores the movie's design, with production designs, set photos, costume sketches, storyboards and conceptual art in a lavish celebration of a comic book made real. To complete the deluxe set is *Watchmen: The Film Portraits* [$50, 9781848560697], a stunning collection of photographs by Clay Enos, who documented the making of the film with black-and-white portraits of every member of the cast and crew, offering a unique look behind the scenes of this highly anticipated release." ∎

An Interview With *American Elf* Author James Kochalka

Conducted by Michael Jewell

James Kochalka is a superstar. Says who? Says James Kochalka, that's who. For the past 10 years, he has brought his life and his art together in stories and a personal diary strip published by Highwater Books, Alternative Comics, Top Shelf Productions, and online at his website, americanelf.com. Each strip can be taken on its own merits, as silly, profound, confessional, dumb, or unimportant, but the real beauty is in the *body* of work, especially that first big collection from Top Shelf, where his whole life can be pieced together from a moment here, a moment there. With *American Elf*, Kochalka has brought a clarity of purpose to his life, and given the well-worn field of "journal comics" perhaps its most enduring masterpiece. *TCJ* sits down with the veteran artist to discuss his work.

— Michael Jewell

Michael Jewell:
Ten years! When the idea came to you on that plane to San Diego, did you have any idea how huge your journal project would become?

James Kochalka:
By the end of the week, I was pretty sure I had the beginning of an amazing idea. I was becoming frustrated with the limitations of the "graphic novel" format. For me, as an artist trying to explore what it means to be a human being alive in the world, the beginning-middle-end format that graphic novels tend to naturally fall into just didn't strike me as very real-feeling. Our lives are not stories in that sense. Our lives are thousands of interconnected threads, wrapping and looping around each other. Certain things happen again and again and again. Some threads of the story stop very suddenly, seemingly unresolved, only to be taken up again later.

I just felt that if I were to make a long-term project of

this, interesting patterns would emerge, and I might be able to gain a greater understanding of the human condition and to express who I am more completely. Also, as a young and ambitious cartoonist, the idea of doing a long-term "masterwork" was pretty appealing. But it also seemed like a crushing amount of work. I thought I'd try it for a year and then reassess. Actually, during the second year it all got to be too much for me and I quit. But I couldn't get the idea out of my mind, and after a few months, I started in again.

After 10 years of this, to what extent can a reader say they know you without having met you?
They certainly know me better than someone who has met me but never read the strip!

Your friends and neighbors take the form of Cyclopses, monsters and little robot dogs. What is the intent of introducing fantastical elements like Magic Boy and his elf family into a daily journal?
It's an iconic form of symbolism. The form of the characters I choose is an expression of some aspect of who these people are, or more importantly for my work, who these people are in relationship to me. Drawing characters as different non-human creatures helps me to express something about the person that would be difficult to achieve in any other way. Also, I very firmly believe that the realm of the imagination and landscape of our minds is as real as the physical realm we live in, and perhaps even more important. For instance, if someone wrongs me in a dream, I am angry at them in real life. I can't help it.

Do you ever cheat, cover up, embellish details of real experiences in your strips?
No. I do selectively edit my experience, of course. Sometimes I paraphrase. But I always try to do it to reveal

rather than obscure.

I don't have super-strict rules. Sometimes I'll pencil the strip at night and wait till morning to ink and color it. I don't consider that cheating. Sometimes I'll do more than one strip a day. Sometimes the strip will be a single-panel drawing. Sometimes the strip will have photos or collage elements.

You freely document tantrums, illness, mood swings and cat puke on the carpet. Is there a limit to your honesty? Do you sometimes regret what you reveal?

There have been moments in my life that the diary strip has made more difficult. For instance, between the birth of Eli and the birth of Oliver, my wife had a pregnancy that ended in miscarriage. It's not fun to mourn in public. But still, there was a part of me that was excited to make art from the experience. My life has still not yet really experienced any great tragedy, this was a minor one. But I know that every life will experience some tragedy, and when mine does, I want to be ready to fully experience it and write about it. I'm not going to let my embarrassment get in the way of my art.

However the strip is not some kind of a dare to see how many secrets I can reveal. There is much that I approach from a sideways manner ... addressing some aspect of my experience without explicitly explaining what it is I'm addressing. There are certain things that I'm still building up the courage to explore.

If every day is precious, how do you choose which moment to capture for your strip? Have you developed a system by now that distinguishes noteworthy moments, or are you entirely spontaneous?

There are thousands of moments every day worth exploring. But it's not so much the moment itself, but what I can say about that moment, or what that moment might reveal in relation to other moments that I've written about on other days. I certainly don't always pick the biggest, most important moment of the day. Nor do I necessarily try to choose the smallest moment of the day. Mostly, my choices are intuitive, with a periodic reminder to push myself to dig a little deeper and not play it safe.

At a certain point, you said "The last 10 years have been awesome ... but do I want the next 10 years to be the exact same thing? No way!" And sure enough, with the thrill and frustration of being a parent, your strip underwent a shift in tone. How is being a dad affecting your work?

I DRAW AND DRAW AND DRAW, AND STILL THE DAYS GO BY AT THE SAME UNSTOPPABLE PACE.

From *James Kochalka"s Sketchbook Diaries* Vol. 4.
[©2004 James Kochalka]

Being a dad has made my life more intense. I think it's made the work more intense too. It's definitely made my work more accessible, in some sense. Having children is pretty central to the human experience. I'm not doing a cute-kid family-type strip, though.

For better or for worse, your work has spawned a multitude of cartoonists drawing journals of their own, hoping to capture something worthwhile. Could this journaling be a good tool for everyone?

Many find drawing a daily diary strip to be an exhilarating experience. It certainly makes your life seem more meaningful, to make art from it. And drawing every day can't be a bad thing, for anyone. It definitely tests your discipline.

If craft is the enemy, what is your friend?

Will power. Imagination.

If art is a way of making sense of our world, can you say you've learned anything big from this comics experience?

It's made my life and art merge more closely, I think. There's no longer any separation between play and work, no separation between life and art, no separation between family and self. It turned out to be less about learning about who I am, and more about defining who I am. ∎

Letters from our readers.

Jules Feiffer:

Gene Deitch's explanation of the argument that led to the end of our friendship requires a response. I'm sorry he found it necessary to bring it up, but here's what actually happened. As Gene states, my children's book *I Lost My Bear* was based on my daughter Halley when she was 4 or 5. Gene and Weston Woods bought the story for animation. I was delighted. From the beginning, I thought it obvious that Halley who was now a college girl and a working actress should do the first-person narration.

Halley herself was dubious. She wondered, as Gene did, that she might sound too old for the part. I hoped that she might raise her voice an octave or two, an idea she scorned as unworthy of the serious actress she was determined to be. (Within a couple of years she would appear in five off-Broadway plays and five films including the memorable *The Squid and the Whale*.)

Halley had done a book-on-tape reading of *I Lost My Bear* and it went to Gene in Prague. I heard nothing for almost two weeks and then, returning home one afternoon, I found a seven minute long voicemail. Gene was calling from San Francisco. He started off expressing his sympathies for me as a father wanting to cast my daughter in the part. But on the basis of the CD, he thought that Halley was not right, lacked the proper feeling. He had a younger, more age-appropriate Czech girl that he had found at an acting school in Prague. He would work with her. She would be just what we needed. He then went into a brief lecture on the nature of collaboration to a writer of twelve plays and four films and wound up expressing his affection for me and our long association and hoped that I would not be too disappointed. He hung up without leaving a phone number for me to return so that we might collaborate.

I cooled off long enough to suggest to Paul Gagne that as much as I hated the idea, let's be fair and hear the girl that Gene was about to cast. Have Gene send us an audition CD so that we could make a judgment. If she was really better than Halley, I'd have no choice but to cast her.

Two weeks went by. Gene kept delaying sending the CD. By e-mail to Gagne he stated that other deadlines prevented him from doing the final edit on the audition. I exploded. "It's an audition, goddamnit, an audition! You don't pretty it up before you send it!" At my insistence, the audition CD arrived in two days. And I discovered Gene's Czech girl was mimicking Halley on the CD we had sent him; her inflections, her timing, her pauses. Clearly Gene had given her Halley's "inadequate" CD to prepare herself.

That's the part of the story Gene neglected to tell, the part that ended what had been a long, fond and rewarding association.

Too bad. But we'll always have Terrytoons.

Gene Deitch:

The Comics Journal #292 arrived on Friday, and even though I had to do time at hard labor at our mountain work camp over the weekend, I still managed to read the entire "Deitch Dynasty" set of interviews. I have no idea how many other people will be interested in this, but *I had the feeling that this book was put out just for me!* I devoured it; I was catching up with the doings & feelings of my sons. The questions you asked, Gary, and how you led the three phone interviews with me caused me to let it all hang out, and afterwards I had some trepidations about how the boys would react. I assumed you also successfully drew out their true feelings, and I was braced for possible hostility from them. None of us, I assume, knew anything of what any of the others would say; there could easily have been conflicting versions regarding the overlapping events. After all, I did leave my sons with each at a critical stage of their development. Yet I was delighted and relieved to find no real hostility, and a close convergence of recall in all of the interviews!

Some of it is quite amazing. I learned a great deal of the peripatetic adventures of Kim especially. How he got together with Paul Bartel was one of most incredible coincidences! Bartel was just a young twerp/dilettante/rich-kid/hanger-on at UPA-NY when I was the Creative Director there. It was amazing enough, when I read in later years that he actually had some success as a movie director, but much more amazing to read that he crossed paths with Kim!

It's a relief to me that Kim will not take offense at my comments about his classic drawing abilities, as he actually agrees with me about it and confirms my assessment that he has overcome any shortcomings with his overall brilliance as a unique decorative artist and, above all, as a master storyteller. Now I know that he is also a thorough researcher, interviewer, reporter, speaker and teacher! His experience with the old woman, Lucy Finkel, at the Park La Brea apartment house is something I knew about, as my mother and my uncle Eli lived there, and I met Lucy myself and knew about Kim's living with her.

Simon's recounting of my visit to him at the Tombs prison in New York, is also basically accurate; doubtless the most painful experience of my life as well as his. Just one point of divergence in our memory of this disastrous meeting: I do not believe I said,"You gotta learn your lesson."

What I said was, "Your mother says you gotta learn your lesson." That's what she instructed me to say to him. I was totally, painfully helpless in that miserable situation. I was on a two-day working trip to New York and vehemently instructed by Marie **not** to get Simon out! *"You can come in like a rescuing superhero, get him out of prison and then fly off into the sunset, leaving me to deal with him!"* I have never felt more helpless and inadequate in my life.

I was humbled as well as gratified, that each of my sons expressed how they missed me and my input into their lives. I strived mightily to continue my input and whatever inspiration I could give them, within the limitations of communication that existed in the early years of my time in Prague. But I well knew that it could not be the real thing of an in-house father.

Seth was the hardest for me to leave. I loved him dearly as a small, brilliant and charming boy. I constantly dreamt of him. My heart was full of regret and miserable feelings, mainly about him. I missed any reference in his interview to his role in our Oscar-winning film *Munro*, but, of course, how many of us can remember anything we did at the age of 3?

Also, when Gary asked Seth, "Your father and your brothers — how has your relationship evolved over your adult life?" I wished for a fuller answer to that. He doesn't mention me at all, yet I believe that of the three, Seth and I now have the closest and most frequent communication. I feel he is a superb, not nearly enough recognized fantasy writer. I hope that your other "Deitch Book," [*Dietch's Pictorama*], will go some way to showcase Seth's talents. I haven't yet received a copy.

I would like to do whatever I can to spread the word about this edition of *The Comics Journal*, so Gary, please let me know when it will be on your website, so I can refer people to order it.

Whoever else may find it interesting, this edition of *TCJ* is a treasure for me! Many, many thanks to all of you and especially my sons for their contribution to it. ∎

Correction:
On the contents page of issue #293, the imminent historian John Benson was incorrectly listed as the interviewer of S. Clay Wilson. As correctly identified in the interview itself beginning on page 28, the equally imminent Bob Levin actually conducted the interview. Apologies to Mr. Levin and Mr. Benson. Paycheck solely to Mr. Levin. ∎

The Comics Journal
http://www.tcj.com

Publisher: Fantagraphics Books

Editor in Chief: Gary Groth

Managing Editor: Michael Dean

Art Director: Adam Grano

Scanmaster: Paul Baresh

Assistant Editor: Kristy Valenti

Online Editor: Dirk Deppey

Interns: Eric Buckler, Suzy Chen, Michael Jewell, Alexa Koenings, Benjamin Neusius

Columnists:
Bart Beaty, Tom Crippen, R. Fiore, Steven Grant, R.C. Harvey, Rich Kreiner, John Lent, Tim O'Neil, Donald Phelps, Bill Randall, Kenneth Smith

Contributing Writers:
Simon Abrams, Jack Baney, Noah Berlatsky, Bill Blackbeard, Robert Boyd, Christopher Brayshaw, Ian Brill, Gabriel Carras, Michael Catron, Gregory Cwiklik, Alan David Doane, Austin English, Ron Evry, Craig Fischer, Jared Gardner, Paul Gravett, David Groenewegen, Charles Hatfield, Jeet Heer, John F. Kelly, Megan Kelso, Tim Kreider, Chris Lanier, Bob Levin, Ana Merino, Chris Mautner, Ng Suat Tong, Jim Ottaviani, Leonard Rifas, Trina Robbins, Larry Rodman, Robert Sandiford, Seth, Bill Sherman, Whit Spurgeon, Frank Stack, Greg Stump, Matthew Surridge, Rob Vollmar, Dylan Williams, Kristian Williams, Kent Worcester

Proofreader: Rusty McGuffin

Transcriptionists: Carol Gnojewski, Kristy Valenti

Advertising: Matt Silvie

Publicity: Eric Reynolds

Circulation: Jason T. Miles

"You say, "Where do you stand on the war?" Well, you stand right where you stood before, as far from the bullets and bombs as they fall." — Spiritualized

For advertising information, e-mail Matt Silvie: silvie @fantagraphics.com.

Contributions: *The Comics Journal* is always interested in receiving contributions — news and feature articles, essays, photos, cartoons and reviews. We're especially interested in taking on news correspondents and photographers in the United States and abroad. While we can't print everything we receive, we give all contributions careful consideration, and we try to reply to submissions within six weeks. Internet inquiries are preferred, but those without online access are asked to send a self-addressed stamped envelope and address all contributions and requests for Writers' and/or Editorial Guidelines to: Managing Editor, The Comics Journal, 7563 Lake City Way N.E., Seattle, WA 98115.

The Comics Journal *welcomes all comments and criticism. Send letters to Blood & Thunder, 7563 Lake City Way N.E., Seattle, WA 98115. E-Mail: tcjnews@tcj.com*

May 19, 2008 – July 25, 2008
by Greg Stump & staff

Ballantine to publish *Garfield Without Garfield* but with Garfield

Aug. 1: Ballantine announced this summer that it would be publishing a book edition of Dan Walsh's Internet phenomenon Garfield Without Garfield. Walsh began his Web project in 2007, using Photoshop to eliminate all the characters in the Jim Davis strip save for Garfield's owner Jon. The result was an absurd series of strips that portrayed its main character struggling with insanity and existential despair. Davis, who called the project "an inspired thing to do," will provide the foreword to the book.

The *Garfield Without Garfield* strips will be printed with the original comics appearing on the same page, which arguably deflates the entire effect. *Journal* readers are hereby advised to buy the book and find someone who can saw it in half.

Fujio Akatsuka dies

Aug. 2: Fujio Akatsuka, the influential Japanese cartoonist whose humorous and wildly popular works made him a revered figure, died of pneumonia at the age of 72 on Aug. 3.

Born in Manchuria, Akatsuka moved to Tokyo at the age of 19 and worked in a chemical factory while honing his cartooning skills off the job. His sensibilities were shaped in part by Western influences that included *Mad* magazine and Buster Keaton. Early in his career, the artist moved into an apartment in Tokyo that became something of a minor legend for serving as a hub and meeting ground for notable and emerging manga creators.

Akatsuka entered the field as a *shoujo* artist, creating manga aimed at young girls, but made a much bigger splash in 1962 with *Osomatsu-kun*, a series launched in a boys' magazine. His fame spread wider with the follow-up series, *Tensai Baka-bon*, which further solidified his status

From "Tateshi no Kensaku" ("Tateshi the Builder").
[©1978 Jirō Gyū and Fujio Akatsuka]

as a grand figure in the country's tradition of gag humor. Both features celebrated absurd characters whose punch lines came to be adopted as pop-culture catch-phrases. From a visual standpoint, Akatsuka's style was strikingly clean and cartoony, with a clarity and universal appeal not always evident in the work of other successful manga artists. In the genre known as "magical girl" comics, the cartoonist carved out a notable niche with the series *Himitsu no Akko-chan*. In addition to making his mark in the world of manga, many of the cartoonist's more popular features were translated into television properties.

Akatsuka was named a recipient of the Shogakukan

Manga Award in the mid-'60s and won the Literary Giant Award in 1997. He himself has an award in his name, given out semi-annually since 1974 by the Shueisha publishing house to humorous manga cartoonists.

In 1998, Akatsuka was diagnosed with esophageal cancer, although he continued to contribute features to various magazines with some regularity until a brain hemorrhage left him bedridden a few years later. His wife, Machiko, who had been caring for the artist, died in 2006. He is survived by a daughter, Rieko.

EC great Jack Kamen dies
Aug. 5: See Datebook Focus on page 23.

Doug Wright winners announced
Aug. 8: The results of the 2008 Doug Wright Awards, created to honor the best English-language comics from Canadian cartoonists, were announced Aug. 8 at the Toronto Reference Library. *For Better or For Worse* creator Lynn Johnston was on hand to receive recognition for being newly inducted into the Canadian Cartoonists Hall of Fame as a "Giant of the North." Inductees are chosen by a committee of cartoonists, writers and critics, which also nominates candidates for the other categories. Winners are chosen from the nominees by a separate five-member jury panel representing a range of cultural media.

In the category of Best Book, Ann Marie Fleming won for *The Magical Life of Long Tack Sam*, published by Riverhead Books. Fleming beat out Julie Doucet (*365 Days*), Joe Matt (*Spent*) and Laurence Hyde (*Southern Cross*), all of whom were nominated for work published by Drawn & Quarterly. For Best Emerging Talent, Jeff Lemire was chosen for his work published by Top Shelf over the self-published artists Ethan Rilly, Jason Kieffer and Nick Maandag. And, in the first awarding of the Pigskin Peters Award, created to honor work that falls "outside the bounds of traditional storytelling," Julie Morstad was recognized for the D&Q release *Milk Teeth*.

Watchmen print run for 2008 to top 1 million
Aug. 14: The interest in Alan Moore and Dave Gibbon's perennial best-seller *Watchmen*, increasing among consumers along with awareness of the movie adaptation of the property, has led DC Comics to ramp up production of the original book. According to Icv2.com, the company ordered 900,000 additional copies of the book in August after a previous increase of 300,000 copies proved too small a number to satisfy the heightened demand brought on by the *Watchmen* film trailer, which was shown in theaters along with the hit Batman movie

The Dark Knight. *Watchmen*, which according to *The New York Times* sold 100,000 copies in 2007, has been the top-selling graphic novel in bookstores according to the lists provided by Bookscan, *USA Today*, and Amazon.com, which are typically dominated by manga like *Naruto* and *Full Metal Alchemist*. The movie version of the property, which creator Moore has long disavowed any interest in, opens in March 2009.

The success of *Watchmen* helped boost overall GN sales for July 2008 by 19 percent over the previous year, according to *Icv2*, while sales of comic books have been declining for several months. Still, the site reported, overall sales of comics in 2008 are up compared to the same months as reported in 2006.

Virgin Comics goes dormant
Aug. 26: Virgin Comics, the publishing venture between Virgin Group and the India-based Gotham Entertainment, has closed its doors and laid off its eight employees in New York, according to a report in *Publishers Weekly*. The company released a statement in August that the venture's New York offices were closed and that "restructuring" would lead to new offices opening up in Los Angeles.

Virgin Comics was launched in 2006 with a stable of high-profile contributors (including Deepak Chopra, and later on Guy Ritchie, Jenna Jameson and Nicholas Cage) and aiming in part to use Hindu mythology as a foundation for a global pop-culture franchise. In all, Virgin produced 17 comic series, 18 trade collections and three hardcover collections, but the visibility of the Virgin contributors did not translate into notable commercial success. The NY closing does not affect Gotham Entertainment, which produces comics for Asian markets.

For Better or For Worse wraps up as strip starts over
Aug. 31: After several months of shifts and changes of direction, Lynn Johnston concluded *For Better of For Worse*, her long-running chronicle of the Patterson family. The text-heavy final installment of the strip gave a synopsis of the continued path of each major character's life — with Anthony and Elizabeth starting a family, Michael becoming a successful author and screenwriter, etc. — and ended with a statement of gratitude and a drawing of the cartoonist herself.

The resolution of *FBoFW* was clearly a complicated matter for Johnston, who changed her mind about how she would handle it multiple times. At one point, Johnston considered handing over the strip to another artist, and later floated the idea of freezing the character's ages in time but continuing their story in stand-alone graphic novels. She eventually settled on a hybrid version of the strip that featured some repeats of storylines mixed in with brand-new material — a compromise that the artist said confused some readers. The final verdict on the strip seems to be that it will be offered to papers again, starting from the beginning, but the cartoonist will be redrawing and tinkering with her storyline (a direction Johnston has called "new-runs").

In an interview with *Editor & Publisher*, Johnston explained that "everything in September is new — the punch lines, the drawing, all are new. The only thing retro is the way I'm drawing everything. I want it to flow into the classic material seamlessly." She added that the real-life dissolution of her marriage played a major role in keeping her from settling on a conclusion to her long-running work.

"At this time in my life I thought I would be on a cruise ship to Panama or the Mediterranean," she told *E&P*, "but I'm a single lady now, and I want to keep working. Because I don't have to work 365 days of new material into a year, I can still take time off to paint and travel." She added that "I'm a better storyteller now" than when the strip made its debut, "and I want to improve the storyline or take a piece of art and make it better ... I want this to be the best thing I've ever done."

Not all of Johnston's approximately 2,000 clients will be staying with the strip. A few cartoonists have fretted that Johnston's decision to keep offering her work sets a bad precedent for preventing other strips to develop and emerge at a time when newspapers are cutting the amount of space they devote to comic strips.

Animator Bill Melendez dies
Sept. 2: Bill Melendez, the animator whose work on a variety of *Peanuts* adaptations helped turn those television specials into huge hits, died Sept. 2 in Santa Monica, Calif. He was 91 years old. Born in Mexico in 1916 as José Cuauhtémoc Melendez, he moved to Arizona with his family at the age of 12. He worked as a laborer until convinced by a friend to submit his portfolio of drawings to the Walt Disney Company, which hired him in 1938, following a brief stint studying at the Chouinard Art Institute.

Among the features Melendez worked on at Disney were *Fantasia* and *Pinocchio* before he left the company in 1941 when the animators went on strike, a movement that Melendez helped organize. In the late '50s, he worked with Charles Schulz on an advertisement for the Ford Motor Company; according to *The New York Times*,

Schulz was reluctant to allow his characters to be utilized for the spot until he got a look at Melendez's rendition of his cast, and how the animator was able to keep the integrity of Schulz's artwork intact as it was adapted into another medium.

Melendez won six Emmy awards in his career, the first of which came in 1965 with *A Charlie Brown Christmas*, the landmark first adaptation of Schulz's comic strip produced by Melendez and his collaborator Lee Mendelson. Several more such features followed, including two more Emmy winners: 1975's *You're a Good Sport, Charlie Brown*, and 1980's *Life is a Circus, Charlie Brown*. The sped-up, nonsensical "speech" emitted by Snoopy in the specials was also Melendez's creation, for which he received residuals throughout the rest of his life. Melendez also won Emmys for two non-*Peanuts* animiated specials, *Garfield on the Town* in 1983 and *Cathy* in 1987.

Melendez is survived by his wife Helen, whom he married in 1940, two sons, and several grandchildren and great-grandchildren.

Borgman takes severance package from *Enquirer*
Sept. 3: Jim Borgman, the co-creator of *Zits* and the Pulitzer-prize winning editorial cartoonist for the Cincinnati *Enquirer*, is leaving his home-base newspaper after 32 years. Borgman was one of 60 employees (a self-reported approximate six percent of the *Enquirer*'s workforce) who applied for and received severance packages at the paper, which cited declining advertising revenue as the motivating factor behind the decision to shrink its payroll.

Borgman's departure from the *Enquirer* may be entirely voluntary, as the cartoonist has said that he wished to reduce the heavy workload necessitated by doing double duty on the comics and editorial pages. But the backdrop of his decision is the instability in his field. Many other cartoonists — such as another Pulitzer winner, Michael Ramirez — have been squeezed out of major dailies in recent years. Other papers, like the *Chicago Tribune*, simply fail to replace staff cartoonists lost to attrition, and the *Enquirer* has given no sign that it intends to replace Borgman.

Borgman isn't leaving the paper entirely; in addition to keeping on with *Zits*, he will continue to contribute to the *Enquirer* on a weekly basis with a featured cartoon on the cover of the paper's *Sunday Community Forum* section.

Best American Comics Vol. 3 ships to stores
Oct. 8: See Datebook Focus next issue. ∎

■ DATEBOOK FOCUS

EC Artist Jack Kamen Dies at 88

by Grant Geissman

Noted EC comics and advertising illustrator Jack Kamen, 88, died Tuesday evening, Aug. 5 at his home in Boca Raton, Fla. The cause of death was given as cancer.

Jack Kamen was born on May 29, 1920 in Brooklyn, N.Y. Kamen recalled "always drawing pictures," but he had no formal art training until high school, where he was enrolled in the Art Students League in New York City. His first paying job was as an assistant to a sculptor who was doing a heroic statue of Texas Governor P.H. Bell for the Texas Centennial. He paid for his classes at the Art Students League and the Grand Central Art School by sculpting, painting theatrical scenery, decorating fashion manikins and doing window displays. Kamen was actually more interested in fine art, but he had lost his father at age 14 and went into comic books strictly as a way to help out with the family finances. He spent a few years cutting his teeth in the Harry Chesler comic-art shop and then decided to try his hand at freelancing. He found work at Fawcett and Harvey Comics and also did some black-and-white illustrations for Better Publications, working in their Western and detective pulp magazines. He ultimately landed at S. M. "Jerry" Iger's shop.

Kamen was drafted in 1942, and he spent four years in the Army serving in the Pacific Theater. Upon his discharge, he went back to see Iger. "Jerry Iger was very glad to see me again and hired me immediately," Kamen told Ken Smith in a 2002 *Comics Journal* interview. "I stayed with him a couple of years, and that's where I met Al Feldstein." For Iger, Kamen regularly worked on *Blue Beetle*, *Jo-Jo Congo King*, *Rulah* and on the various romance titles the shop was turning out for Fox.

In 1950, Kamen was brought into the EC fold by artist/writer/editor Al Feldstein, who was very happy to have his old Iger-shop buddy working for the company. For his part, Kamen said "I was delighted, because Bill Gaines

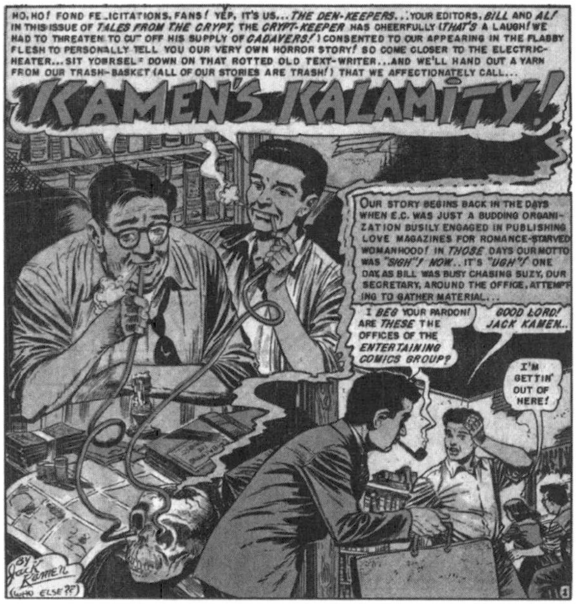
HO, HO! FOND FELICITATIONS, FANS! YEP, IT'S US... THE DEN-KEEPERS... YOUR EDITORS, BILL AND AL! IN THIS ISSUE OF TALES FROM THE CRYPT, THE CRYPT-KEEPER HAS CHEERFULLY (THAT'S A LAUGH! WE HAD TO THREATEN TO CUT OFF HIS SUPPLY OF CADAVERS!) CONSENTED TO OUR APPEARING IN THE FLABBY FLESH TO PERSONALLY TELL YOU OUR VERY OWN HORROR STORY! SO COME CLOSER TO THE ELECTRIC-HEATER... SIT YOURSELF DOWN ON THAT ROTTED OLD TEXT-WRITER... AND WE'LL HAND OUT A YARN FROM OUR TRASH-BASKET (ALL OF OUR STORIES ARE TRASH!) THAT WE AFFECTIONATELY CALL...
KAMEN'S KALAMITY!
OUR STORY BEGINS BACK IN THE DAYS WHEN E.C. WAS JUST A BUDDING ORGANIZATION BUSILY ENGAGED IN PUBLISHING LOVE MAGAZINES FOR ROMANCE-STARVED WOMANHOOD! IN THOSE DAYS OUR MOTTO WAS "SIGH"! NOW... IT'S "UGH"! ONE DAY, AS BILL WAS BUSY CHASING SUZY, OUR SECRETARY, AROUND THE OFFICE, ATTEMPTING TO GATHER MATERIAL...
I BEG YOUR PARDON! ARE THESE THE OFFICES OF THE ENTERTAINING COMICS GROUP?
GOOD LORD! JACK KAMEN..
I'M GETTIN' OUT OF HERE!

From *Tales from the Crypt* #31, Aug.-Sept. 1952. Drawn by Jack Kamen, written by Bill Gaines and Al Feldstein. [©2007 William M. Gaines, Agent]

was always Bill Gaines, and Al was my friend. So I got the work. I was glad to get it." Quickly seeing that Kamen was a very useful asset, Gaines offered to up Kamen's rates and make him exclusive to the company, to which Kamen readily agreed. About Kamen's art for EC, Bill Gaines said, "His pristine qualities lent a delightful contrast to the dreadful things that were going to happen!"

Common EC lore is that Kamen was initially brought in to work on the company's soon-to-be-defunct romance comics, but Kamen's first work for the company actually appeared in the first issues of the two science-fiction magazines, *Weird Science* and *Weird Fantasy* (cover dated May–June 1950). Over the next few months Kamen would also appear in *Modern Love* (the final two issues, cover dated June–July 1950 and August–September 1950), *The Vault of Horror, Tales from the Crypt, The Haunt of Fear* and *Crime SuspenStories*. Feldstein said of Kamen that "Jack was a professional. He had no qualms about being an 'artist,' or having a cult following, or anything like that. He was a dependable artist that did a good job on whatever he was assigned."

Kamen became almost immediately famous among EC fans for what came to be called "Kamen babes": women who were beautiful, voluptuous and, all too often, cold and calculating. Interestingly, Kamen's art was not initially a favorite among many of the readers. His pristine, slick style was markedly different from Wally Wood's or Graham Ingels's, artists who could readily inspire rabid hero worship. Gaines elaborated in *EC Lives!*: "To many people, he was not their favorite artist, but I think Jack was a good workman-like artist; he was a real pro. Jack was almost as fast as Davis. He never missed a deadline and was there when we needed him. I always felt that Jack was a very important cog in the EC machinery, and I'm glad we had him." With the continued reprinting of the EC comics — most notably in Russ Cochran's *Complete EC Library* series — Kamen's body of work grew to be much more appreciated in later years.

When Gaines and Feldstein would plot their stories each morning, they would always do so with a specific artist in mind. Feldstein said in *EC Lives!* that "When we sat down to do a Jack Kamen script, we did a story that was slick, modern and up-to-date to fit his style, which was a slick, modern, 'cold' style. His style was slick and controlled, and yet personally he was a very loose, free, wild guy." With Kamen, Gaines told *The Comics Journal* in 1983, "you're looking for something light, humorous, pretty women, a little sex, a little double-entendre." Gaines called the types of stories they gave to Kamen "Buster stories," because oftentimes the femme fatale would get fed up with her hapless suitor or philandering husband and exclaim something like, "Look, Buster!"

Unlike the other EC artists, Kamen rarely traveled into New York City to go to the EC offices. Because Kamen and Feldstein lived just one stop apart on the Long Island Railroad, Kamen would journey only as far as Feldstein's house. "What he would do is bring the script home and we would discuss it," Kamen told Smith. "I would pencil it and give him the pencils. He would take it back to the city and get it lettered. It was always a rotation. I'd be going to Al's house and reading the script, or getting my work back to ink."

When *Shock SuspenStories* was added to the EC line, Kamen had stories in every issue of that title; he also contributed covers for issues #10, #13 and #15, as well as for the final three issues of *Crime SuspenStories*: #25, #26 and #27.

Kamen drew most of the installments of the *Grim Fairy Tale!* feature that was sprinkled around various EC comics between 1952 and 1954. These fairy tales were tongue-in-cheek send-ups of various classic children's stories, done with an EC twist ending.

When EC dropped its horror and crime comics, Kamen drew the covers and all the stories in all four issues of one of EC's more unusual New Direction offerings, *Psychoanalysis*. Gaines and Feldstein were both in analysis at the time, so they got the idea to do a comic book of stories following people's progress in their analysis. "We had this idea that we were gonna put out this proselytizing comic book called *Psychoanalysis* and tell people what it was all about," Feldstein has said. "I don't know why we ever thought it would sell, when I think about it!"

Unusual as the book was, Kamen did some fine work in *Psychoanalysis*, including what many people consider his best cover, done for issue #3. Work on *Psychoanalysis* segued directly into EC's next experiment, the Picto-Fiction magazines. What would have appeared in comic-book form as *Psychoanalysis* #5 was reworked by Gaines and Feldstein into the first issue of the new magazine-sized Picto-Fiction title *Shock Illustrated*, which was drawn entirely by Kamen. And harkening back to his "romance comic" roots, Kamen also had stories in another Picto-Fiction title, *Confessions Illustrated*. Kamen adapted well into the more illustrative, black-and-white demands of the Picto-Fictions, and he was sorry to see them not succeed. Of the Picto-Fiction experiment, Kamen told Smith, "If it had continued and caught on, I would have stayed with it because I loved doing that stuff. If you look at it, you'll see a lot of pen work and atmosphere. To me, that was the most enjoyable time. I was so sorry to see that go."

Toward the end of EC, Gaines, Feldstein and Kamen tried to offer a syndicated strip based on *Psychoanalysis*. They worked up samples of the strip and even a précis of the storyline, shopping it around to King Features and United Features, but they never succeeded in placing the strip.

About the final days of EC, Kamen said in the EC fanzine *Horror from the Crypt of Fear* that "I knew the bad publicity was preventing distribution of the books, but Bill felt a responsibility to a family man with four children like myself, and paid me for three months of [Picto-Fiction] art that would probably never get print-

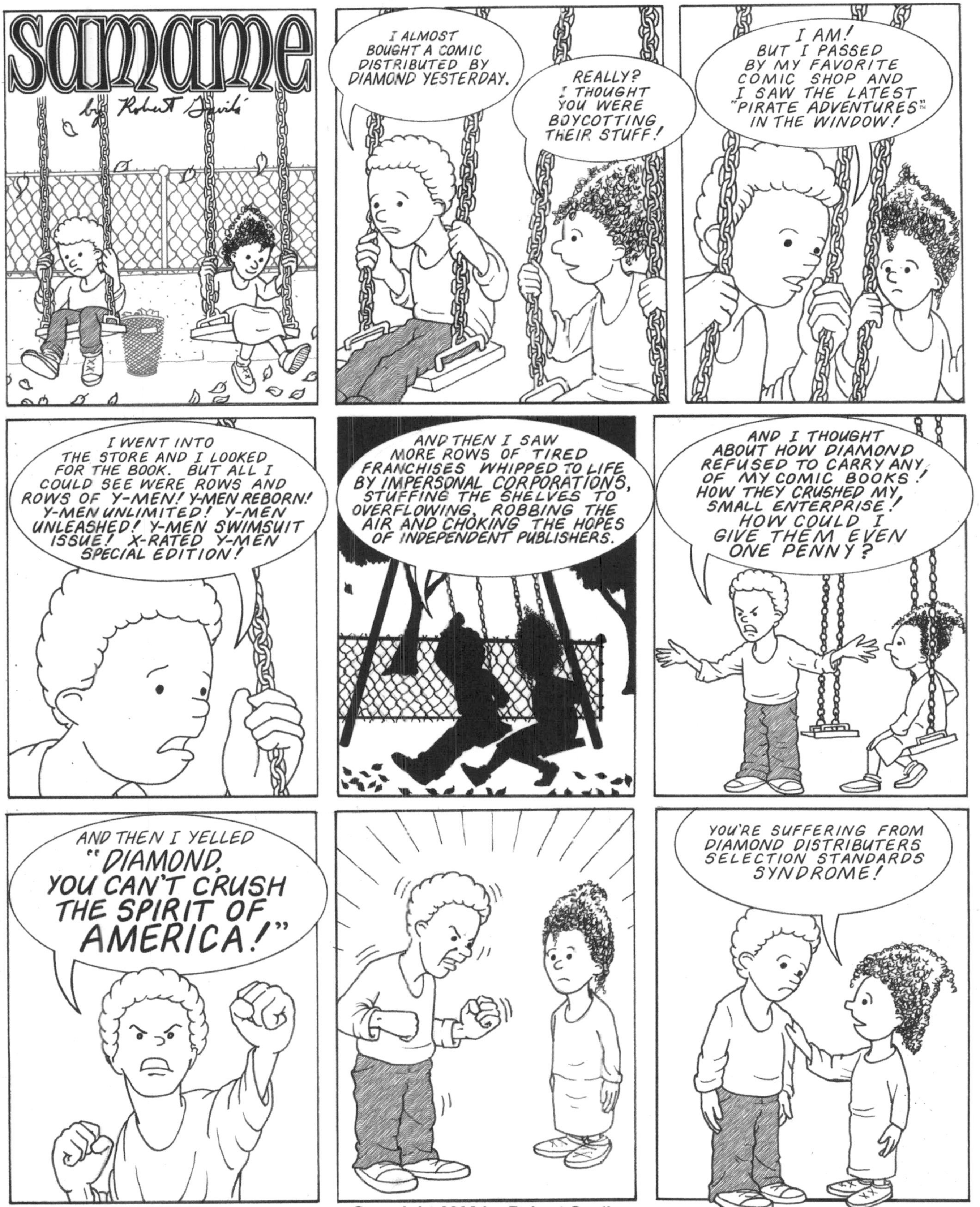
samame
by Robert Gavila
I ALMOST BOUGHT A COMIC DISTRIBUTED BY DIAMOND YESTERDAY.
REALLY? I THOUGHT YOU WERE BOYCOTTING THEIR STUFF!
I AM! BUT I PASSED BY MY FAVORITE COMIC SHOP AND I SAW THE LATEST "PIRATE ADVENTURES"™ IN THE WINDOW!
I WENT INTO THE STORE AND I LOOKED FOR THE BOOK. BUT ALL I COULD SEE WERE ROWS AND ROWS OF Y-MEN! Y-MEN REBORN! Y-MEN UNLIMITED! Y-MEN UNLEASHED! Y-MEN SWIMSUIT ISSUE! X-RATED Y-MEN SPECIAL EDITION!
AND THEN I SAW MORE ROWS OF TIRED FRANCHISES WHIPPED TO LIFE BY IMPERSONAL CORPORATIONS, STUFFING THE SHELVES TO OVERFLOWING, ROBBING THE AIR AND CHOKING THE HOPES OF INDEPENDENT PUBLISHERS.
AND I THOUGHT ABOUT HOW DIAMOND REFUSED TO CARRY ANY OF MY COMIC BOOKS! HOW THEY CRUSHED MY SMALL ENTERPRISE! HOW COULD I GIVE THEM EVEN ONE PENNY?
AND THEN I YELLED "DIAMOND, YOU CAN'T CRUSH THE SPIRIT OF AMERICA!"
YOU'RE SUFFERING FROM DIAMOND DISTRIBUTERS SELECTION STANDARDS SYNDROME!

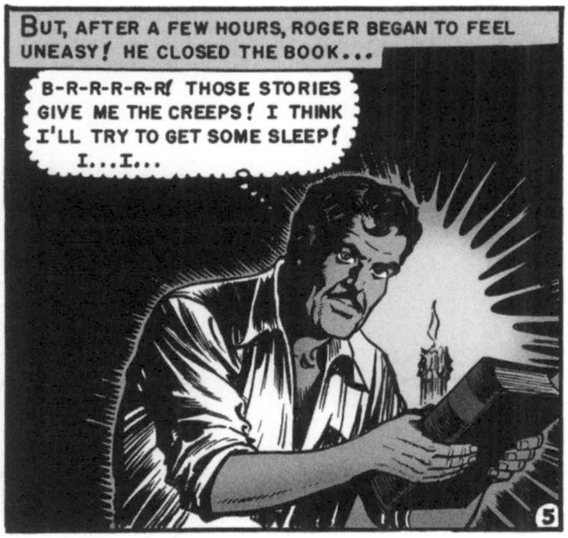
BUT, AFTER A FEW HOURS, ROGER BEGAN TO FEEL UNEASY! HE CLOSED THE BOOK...
B-R-R-R-R-R! THOSE STORIES GIVE ME THE CREEPS! I THINK I'LL TRY TO GET SOME SLEEP! I...I...
5
From "The Grave Wager" in *Vault of Horror* #16, Jan.-Feb. 1951.
[©2007 William M. Gaines, Agent]

ed." Gaines and Feldstein also had Kamen do two stories for the early *Mad* magazine, "Make Your Own Love-Story Comic" and a panel in "Real Estate Ads" (*Mad* #29, September–October 1956). In reality, Kamen's art didn't possess the right humorous touch for *Mad*. It was just as well, for in the interim Kamen had been finding work in the much higher-paying field of advertising.

"At that time, my [advertising] rates were exceedingly higher than comic-book pay, but I shall never forget that they tried to tailor material for me that could fit the format," Kamen said in *Horror from the Crypt of Fear*. He hooked up with an agency, and began illustrating black-and-white print ads for such companies as Vicks (doing ads for their cough drops), Playtex, U.S. Steel and Reynolds Aluminum. As the years went on, Kamen became very successful in advertising, and he did color paintings that advertised such high-profile products as Esquire shoe polish, Kent cigarettes, Mack trucks and Smith Corona typewriters.

Around 1961, Kamen was approached to be the art director of a children's encyclopedia. According to Kamen, every page was designed to look like a *Ripley's Believe It or Not* panel. There were two editions of it, one published by Harwyn (*Harwyn Picture Encyclopedia*), and another endorsed by Art Linkletter, entitled *Art Linkletter's Picture Encyclopedia for Boys and Girls*. Kamen immediately asked several of his fellow former EC artists to contribute, and the series is filled with full-color illustrations by the likes of Wallace Wood, George Evans and Al Williamson.

In 1982, Stephen King (a longtime EC fan) contacted Bill Gaines to try to get an EC artist to illustrate the movie poster for King's feature film *Creepshow*, an homage to the EC horror comics. King's first choice was Graham Ingels, who immediately refused. The assignment then went to Kamen; Kamen's art appeared on the one-sheet movie poster, and also on the cover of the graphic-novel version of *Creepshow*.

One of Kamen's sons, Dean (who was just a baby during the time of the EC comics), grew up to be a very successful inventor of various medical devices, specializing in remaking them in a much smaller, portable size for home use. "Dean has 60 patents in the medical field. Every one of them is operating today, and every one of them pays a royalty. Needless to say, he's a very wealthy young man," Kamen told Smith. At Dean's request, Kamen would help in the product design by working up renderings of Dean's various inventions, even doing detailed diagrams for the Patent Office. Kamen also invested in some of Dean's early patents, mortgaging his house to come up with the money. Dean was only 16 or 17 years old at the time. "Everybody said I was crazy," Kamen said. "We hocked everything. As it turned out, it was one of the best investments we ever made." More recently, Dean has received tremendous media coverage as the inventor of the Segway and the iBOT Mobility System. Dean is also perhaps the biggest collector of Kamen's original art, and owns the artwork to many of Jack's EC stories and covers. Kamen's oldest son, Dr. Barton Kamen, is a noted oncologist, and is now the Chief Medical Officer of the Leukemia & Lymphoma Society. When Barton was a child, he "played artist" on the splash page to "Killed in Time" (*Weird Science* #5, Jan.—Feb. 1951), which his father had to then paint over and correct. Gaines asked what all that was, and when he heard the story, he insisted that Jack sign it "Jack and Bart Kamen."

In later years, Kamen was basically retired from art as a profession, except for what Dean Kamen might ask him to do, and he painted for his own enjoyment. As Kamen told Smith in 2002: "You're looking at a very happy man."

Kamen is survived by his wife of 62 years, Evelyn; four children, Barton, Dean and twins Mitch (a musician) and Terri (a businesswoman); and his granddaughter, Libby. Memorial Services were held Aug. 8, 2008 at The Gardens Memorial Park in Boca Raton. ■

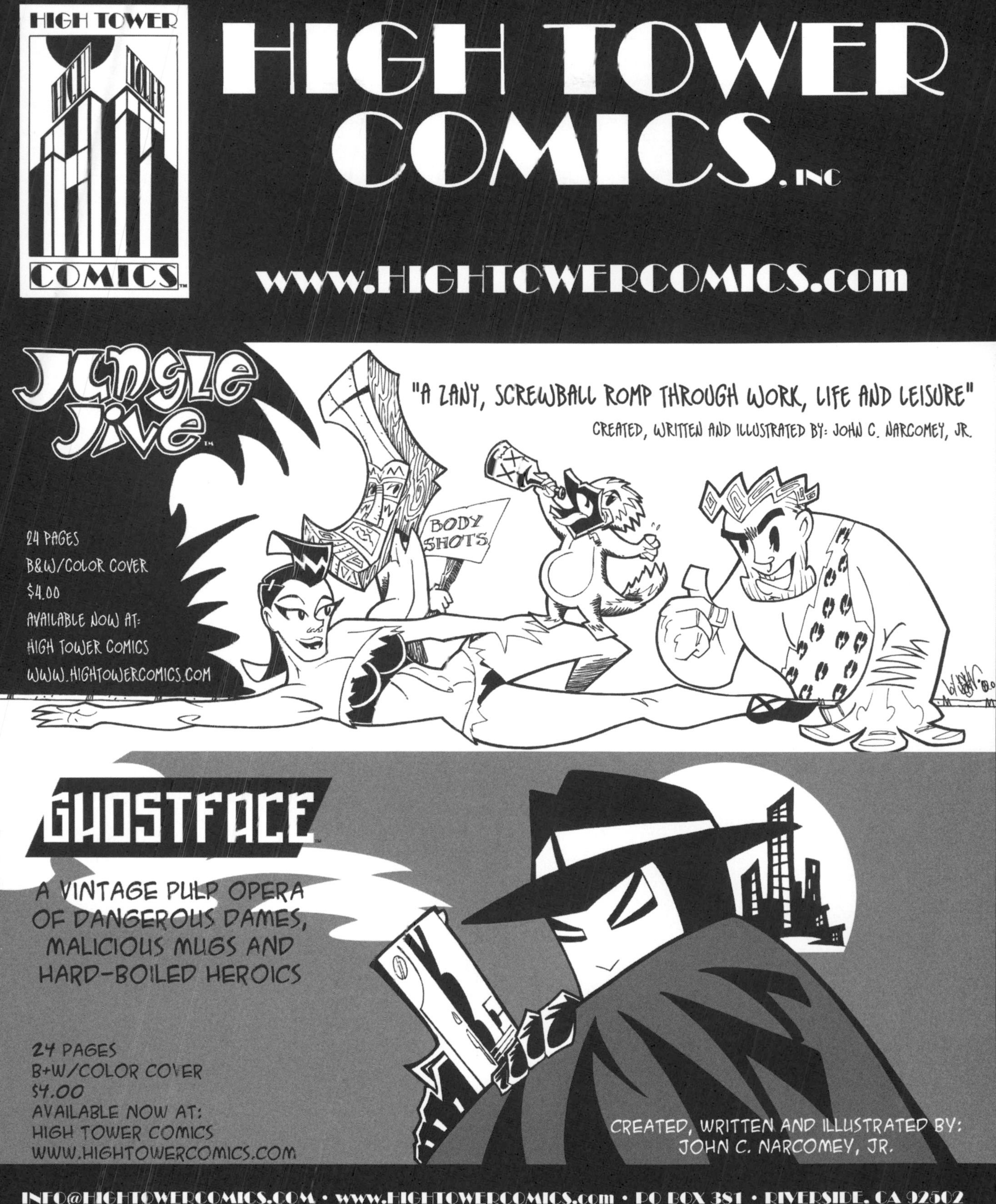
HIGH TOWER COMICS
HIGH TOWER COMICS.INC
www.HIGHTOWERCOMICS.com
JUNGLE JIVE™
"A ZANY, SCREWBALL ROMP THROUGH WORK, LIFE AND LEISURE"
CREATED, WRITTEN AND ILLUSTRATED BY: JOHN C. NARCOMEY, JR.
BODY SHOTS
24 PAGES
B&W/COLOR COVER
$4.00
AVAILABLE NOW AT:
HIGH TOWER COMICS
WWW.HIGHTOWERCOMICS.COM
GHOSTFACE™
A VINTAGE PULP OPERA OF DANGEROUS DAMES, MALICIOUS MUGS AND HARD-BOILED HEROICS
24 PAGES
B+W/COLOR COVER
$4.00
AVAILABLE NOW AT:
HIGH TOWER COMICS
WWW.HIGHTOWERCOMICS.COM
CREATED, WRITTEN AND ILLUSTRATED BY:
JOHN C. NARCOMEY, JR.
INFO@HIGHTOWERCOMICS.COM • www.HIGHTOWERCOMICS.com • PO BOX 381 • RIVERSIDE, CA 92502

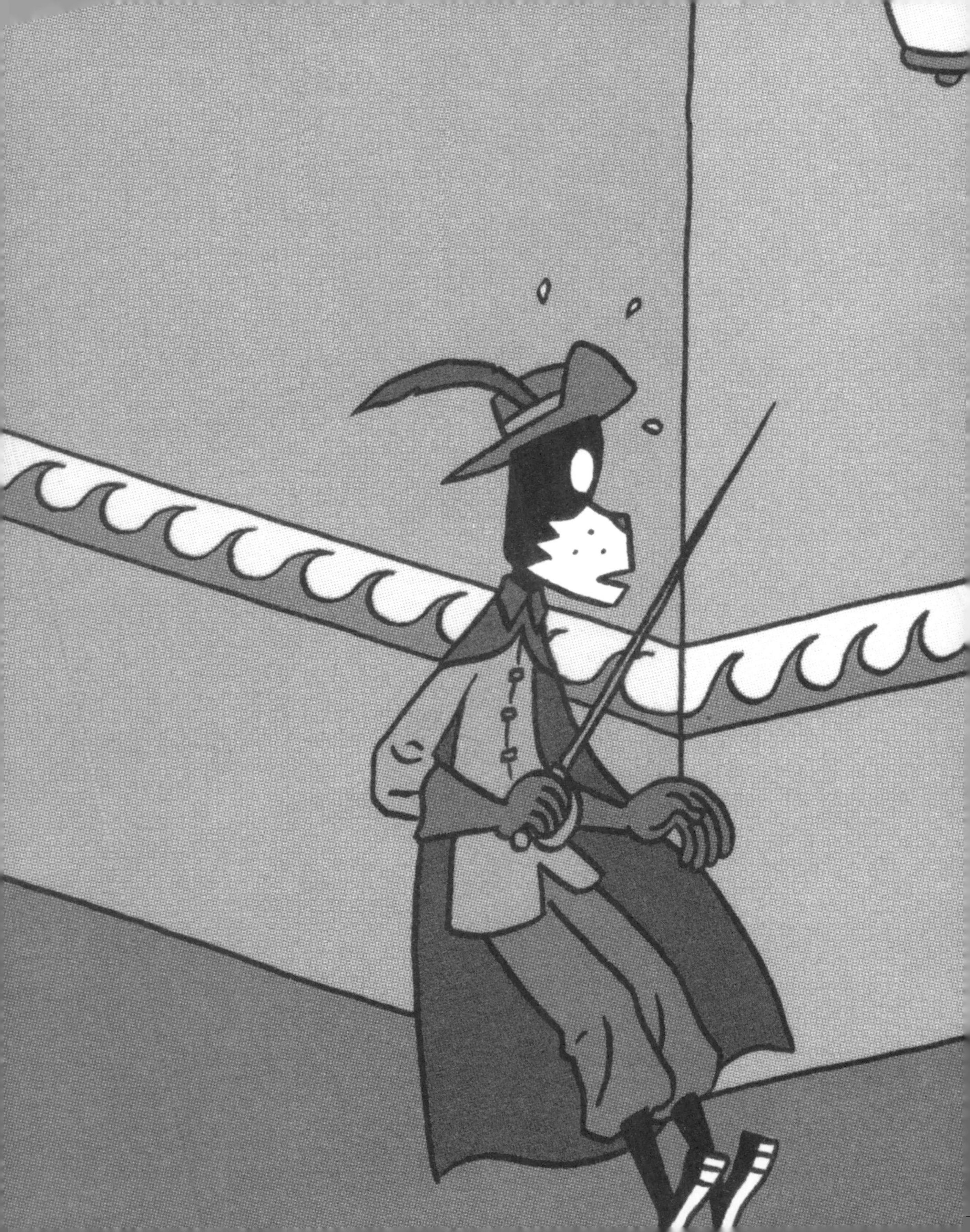

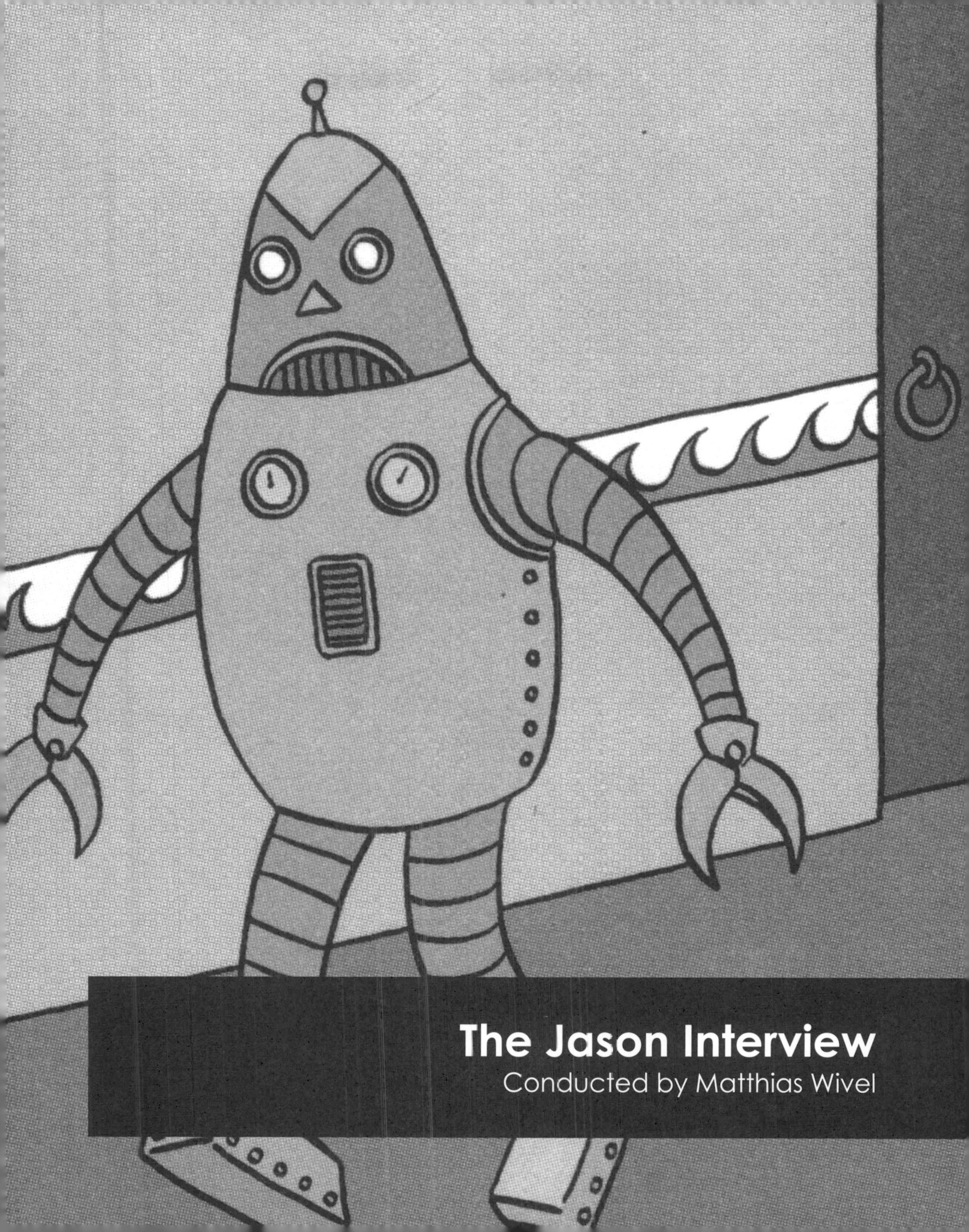

The Jason Interview

Conducted by Matthias Wivel

HEY PUSSYCATS, I AM KOJAK!

Jason's childhood drawings: courtesy of Jason. [©2007 Jason]

The Norwegian cartoonist Jason — born John Arne Sæteroey in 1965 — is something of a phenomenon in Scandinavian comics. By dogged discipline and distinct talent, he has successfully attained what was previously the exclusive province of artists working in the genres and formats of industrial comics — international stature and food on the table from comics. And he has done it by developing and refining the auteurial vision he arrived at early into a remarkable body of work.

Instantly recognizable, his comics combine pop-cultural cliché with minimalist slice-of-life, lived on paper in cartoon blank-face. He deals at once in subversion and pastiche, not so much undermining time-honored genre tropes as letting them resonate by playing them straight. If at times slight, his stories never fail to provide a perspective, a deadpan examination of life as lived now. Concerns with purpose and transience provide subtext to the fun on the page.

This approach works to cumulative effect across his *oeuvre*. And in his strongest work, the muted but determining underlying structure comes to loom with uncanny potency for the attentive reader. From his early short stories published in his personal comics magazine *Mjau Mjau* (1997-2001) and the critically acclaimed international breakthrough *Hey, Wait*... (1999) to his more recent color work created initially for the French market (from 2004 onwards), Jason has maintained his focus.

In addition to providing what is hopefully an illuminating look back at his career, the present interview is also an inquiry into his art and the influences that shape it. Established for some years now in Montpellier, France, the formerly errant cartoonist also discusses his current work and the steps he may be taking to carry his work beyond middle age.

—Matthias Wivel

Previous: From *The Last Musketeer*. [©2008 Jason]

MATTHIAS WIVEL:

Tell me a little about your background. I understand that you grew up in Molde on the coast. Can you give the readers an impression of the place?

JASON:

Molde is on the west coast of Norway. It's a small city, about 20,000 inhabitants. I grew up around three kilometers outside of the center of the city. It was a quiet place, not too much happening, a pretty safe place to grow up, I guess. This was in the '70s, so there was only one TV channel. Every Monday, they showed a feature film, on Wednesday there was a sitcom, and then on Friday a detective show. In the whole city there was only one cinema, with one single screen. Every Sunday, they had some movie for kids, either some new movie like *Olsenbanden*, that I guess you also know from Denmark *[*The Olsen Gang*, a classic Danish crime-comedy series that saw national versions produced in both Norway and Sweden]*, some Disney animation movie, or even some old black-and-white Tarzan film with Johnny Weissmuller. Thinking back upon it now, it seems like growing up in Russia or something.

I assume you drew as a child, like everyone else. What were your first experiences with comics?

Comics always seemed to be around. Everybody read them. A lot of *Donald Duck*, of course, that was very popular in Norway. There was a magazine called *Tempo* that was the Norwegian version of the French *Pilote*, which had stories like *Asterix*, *Bernard Prince* or *Blueberry*. Just five or six pages of each story, then you had to wait a month for the continuation. *Fantomet*, or *The Phantom*, was very popular. It was a monthly comic, made on license for the Scandinavian countries. My older sister had a collection of *Sølvpilen*, or *Silver Arrow*, a Western comic that I believe maybe was produced in Germany *[by the Belgian cartoonist Frank Sels]*, not very well drawn. It was about this Kiowa chief called Sølvpilen; a white guy, Falk, who also lived there; a young woman called Månestråle, or Moonbeam; and finally this puma cub called Tinka. They had these different adventures together. At the town library they had this small shelf of comics. More *Donald Duck* albums, but there were also some *Tintin* albums. I remember reading those.

In third grade, a new pupil, Håkon, started in my class, and he had a collection of Batman comics. He was the one who got me interested in superhero comics. We started a Batman club, just the two of us. And he was a very good artist — he made these really amazing drawings for a 10-11-year-old kid. He could copy pretty much everything. And that's when I also started to draw, drawing panels from *Batman* or some other comics, but nowhere near as good as he was. I hadn't really drawn that much before.

How would you describe your upbringing? What did your parents do? Any siblings?

I had a normal middle-class upbringing, I'd say. My dad was a carpenter, my mom a housewife. Later, she had a few different jobs. I have two sisters, one five years older, one five years younger. Because of the age difference, there was not that much of a bond in those days. They had their friends, and I had mine.

In *The Left Bank Gang* you have a scene where your cartoonist versions of Joyce and Hemingway discuss why they do comics, saying that it's because they read them as kids and implying that they would have had a normal, healthy childhood — and indeed life — if they hadn't. This, of course, is a common sentiment amongst cartoonists, but how autobiographical would

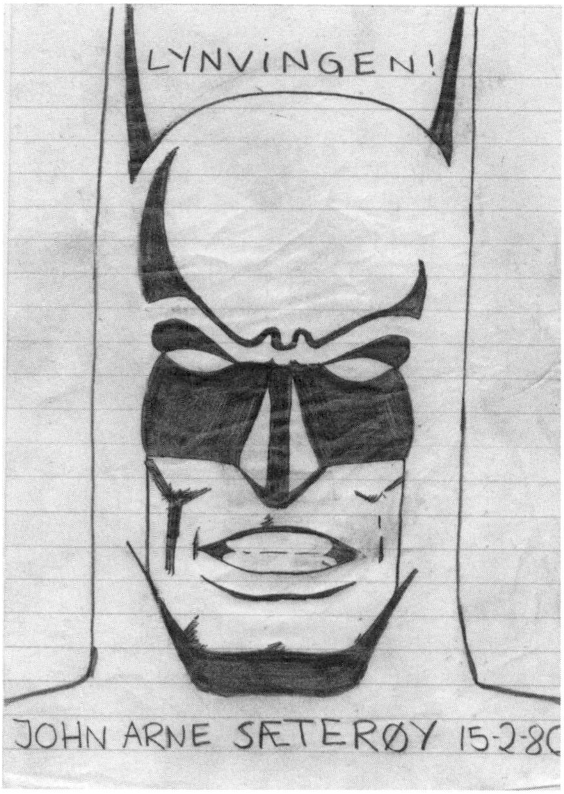
LYNVINGEN!
JOHN ARNE SÆTERØY 15-2-8C

Courtesy of Jason. [©2007 Jason]

you say it is?

Actually, I'd say I had a pretty happy childhood. I didn't mean to indicate that I only sat indoors, reading comics all day long. We did lots of outdoor stuff, playing soccer, climbing trees. That scene is about a specific time in my life, my mid-30s, when my career as an illustrator was going nowhere and I wasn't making much money from doing comics. I could only afford a small one-room apartment. I started wondering what I was doing with my life. Would it be like this always? Always having to worry about paying rent and never being able to buy a decent apartment? But the last five or six years, I've had an OK income from comics. And I can't really think of another job where I'd be happy. I don't know what I'd do today if I hadn't read comics as a kid. I'd probably be washing dishes somewhere.

Would you say that you were into the kind of fantastic manifestations of pop culture that are such a presence in your comics more than the average kid back then? How rooted in your childhood is your fascination with them?

I'm not sure if I was necessarily more into comics or movies than anybody else at that time. There was the Batman club that I had with Håkon. We used to buy the same comics and talk about our favorite artists and so on. That might be a more than average interest in comics, I guess. After sixth grade he moved away. The change came in junior high, I think, when everybody else stopped reading comics and I continued. But movies were just as important to me as comics, I think. A lot of the films I saw on TV on Monday evenings made a big impression on me. Movies like *Twelve Angry Men, Sabrina, Charade, A Bridge On the River Kwai*, Fred Astaire and Ginger Rogers films, French comedies. French movies were always exciting to watch because there might be some nudity. There are bits and pieces of other movies that I still remember, scenes that have stuck for some reason or another.

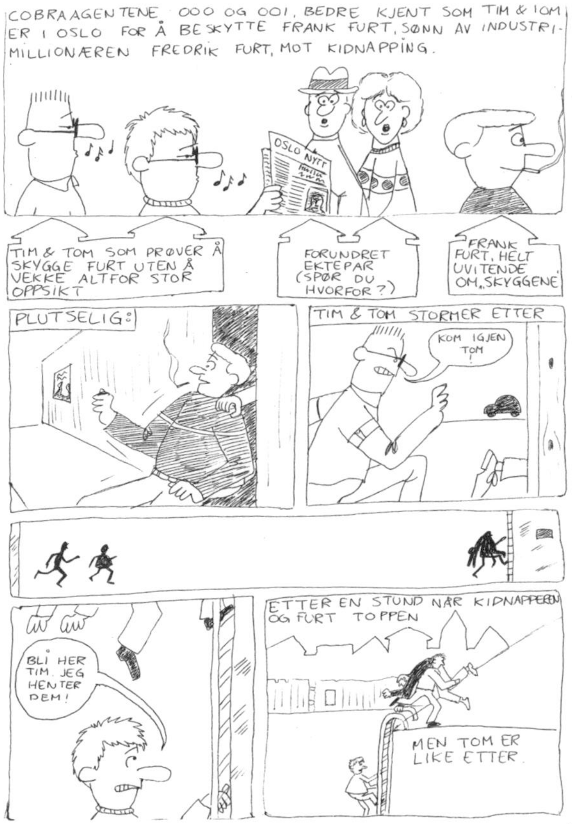

COBRAAGENTENE 000 OG 001, BEDRE KJENT SOM TIM & TOM ER I OSLO FOR Å BESKYTTE FRANK FURT, SØNN AV INDUSTRI-MILLIONÆREN FREDRIK FURT, MOT KIDNAPPING.
OSLO NYTT
TIM & TOM SOM PRØVER Å SKYGGE FURT UTEN Å VEKKE ALTFOR STOR OPPSIKT
FORUNDRET EKTEPAR (SPØR DU HVORFOR?)
FRANK FURT, HELT UVITENDE OM „SKYGGENE"
PLUTSELIG:
TIM & TOM STORMER ETTER
KOM IGJEN TOM!
BLI HER TIM. JEG HENTER DEM!
ETTER EN STUND NÅR KIDNAPPEREN OG FURT TOPPEN
MEN TOM ER LIKE ETTER.

From Jason's first effort at a comic: *The Adventures of Tim and Tom*. [©2008 Jason]

I assume that this was about the time you drew your first comics? What kind of comics did you draw?

For a long while I was just doing drawings, copying panels or creating my own superheroes. The first comic I made must be from '79 or '80, "Tim og Tom på eventyr" — 'The Adventures of Tim and Tom' — drawn with a ballpoint pen. In earlier interviews I've always said that this comic was inspired by reading *Tintin*, but I found a couple of pages from it recently, and it looks more like *Flipp og Flopp*, or *Clever and Smart* [the German title, of all things]. I don't know if this series has ever been translated into English, but it's Italian, I believe. An album series about these two bumbling secret agents.

Ah, *Mortadelo y Filemón*, I remember those! It's Spanish, by Francisco Ibañez — an endless series that was really funny in small doses, because of the crazy drawing, but rather repetitive in the long run. Would you say that you were gravitating towards humor from the beginning, despite your interest in superheroes?

I still read and enjoyed superhero comics in this period. *Spider-Man* was probably my favorite. I especially remember the Ross Andru issues. I would copy panels or make single drawings, but I would never have tried to make comics in that style at age 14 or 15. The European album series like *Flipp og Flopp* or *Tintin* had much simpler drawings that seemed like something you could try. You could tell a story in that style. It would look clumsy, sure, but you would eventually have a finished story, something complete. A few years later, I tried drawing in a more real-

istic style, a superhero/science-fiction type story, but after a page or two I just lost interest. It was just too difficult. I never finished.

When did you realize that you wanted to be a cartoonist?

I've already told this story, but that first comic I made was a pretty profound experience. I had trouble sleeping at night, just lying there thinking about what was going to happen next in the story, almost like in a fever, and then waking up early the following morning to continue drawing. The fact that I'm a cartoonist today is, I'm sure, very much because of that first experience. Like a drug addict I've been trying to re-experience that first high. Which almost never happens, of course. But this was at a time that becoming a cartoonist was not much of an option in Norway. I'm sure there were one or two, but I had no serious plans of becoming one. It was just a hobby.

At some point I must have bought a nib and a bottle of ink and started to ink my drawings. There was a magazine in Norway called *Western* that also had a few cartoons. I sent one in. They accepted it and invited me to participate in their humor magazine *Konk*, which I did. This must have been around '80, '81. All through high school I kept selling cartoons and one-page strips to them. I didn't really have any plans at all of continuing my education. It was only after working with my dad for a year, doing my service in the military, and then working in a furniture factory for nine moths, that I started thinking, 'hmmm, going back to school might not be such a bad idea after all.' I considered becoming a librarian, but finally chose art school, not to become a cartoonist but to become an illustrator, believing that was a profession I could make a living from.

What kind of magazine was *Konk*? Since they were paying you, I'm assuming it wasn't underground, but how widely distributed was it? Who else did they publish? Tell us a bit about your first experiences being published.

It was a bit like *Mad* magazine, I guess. A mix of articles, cartoons and short comics stories, mostly just a page or two. It was distributed to newsstands, so it was pretty easy to find. There is almost a *Konk* generation in Norway. A lot of people my age who do comics today got their start in *Konk*, both 'alternative' cartoonists and those who work in a more commercial style, doing strips for newspapers. You would be given a theme for the next issue and a deadline, usually around a month, and then you could send in as much as you wanted. What they kept they paid for, what they didn't want was returned to you. Mostly I got about half my stuff in return. One time I got everything back. But just to be a 16-year old kid being paid for your drawings and then seeing them printed in a nationally distributed magazine was an amazing experience. Of course, my earliest stuff wasn't very good, but they took some of it anyway. It was just a great source of inspiration and an important contribution to me being a cartoonist today.

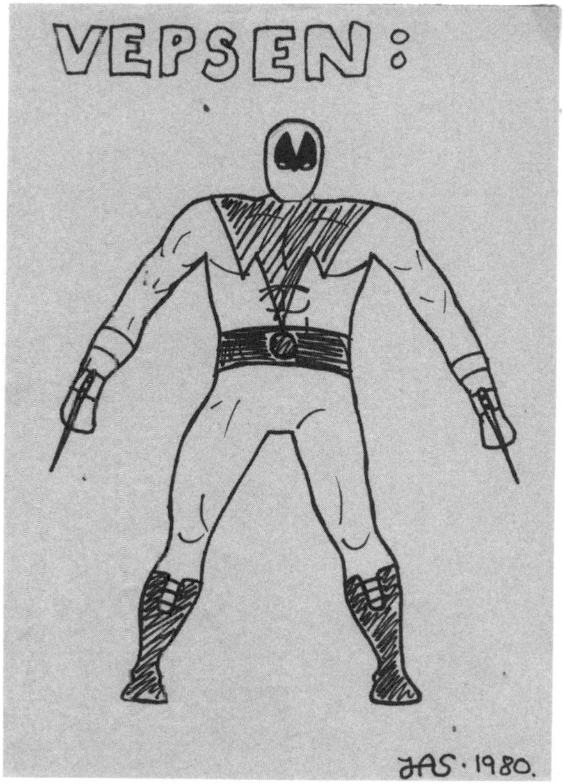
VEPSEN:
JAS · 1980.
Courtesy of Jason. [©2007 Jason]

For how long did you work for them?

Konk folded in '85, so that was that.

You subsequently went to Statens Håndverk- og Kunst–industriskole i Oslo. When was this? And how would you describe the school in terms of focus and such.

Well, first I went to a private art school called Strykejernet for two years, '87 to '89. SHKS was a government-funded, public art school, so attendance was free but it was difficult to get in. Only about 10 percent of the applications were accepted. It was only in my second year at Strykejernet that I felt I had learned enough that maybe

The first strip Jason sold: courtesy of Jason. [©2008 Jason]

I could submit an application. SHKS lasted four and a half years. First you were given fundamental instruction in form, light and shadow, anatomy and stuff like that, after which you could choose between assignments in illustration or graphic design, or even alternate between the two. In the fourth year you had to choose between them. Design didn't interest me at all at the time, so I only chose the illustration assignments. For the practical exam of the last semester, in '93, I did a 12-page comic-book version of the early chapters of *Jernvognen*, *The Iron Wagon*, by Stein Riverton. Later I redrew those and finished the book, but with animal characters.

Creating and being interested in comics was accepted at school. In the third year there was a three-week course on comics. The director of the department for graphic design and illustration, Peter Haars, had actually done a sort of pop-arty graphic novel in the '60s. However, you were told — wisely — that comics as a profession in Norway was difficult and would probably lead you to the poorhouse.

How was the experience of starting a more formalized education in art?

The main thing was moving to Oslo and meeting other people who had the same interests as me. I had only worked in black and white, so to suddenly start painting in color and in larger formats, at Strykejernet, was a big change. I had no interest in fine art, but learning how to mix colors was useful in itself, and to draw from life, to draw models. I'm not sure how much I learned at

SHKS. I didn't really listen to my professors that much — I should have, I guess. My big idol in those days was Dave McKean, and I just tried to copy him on every assignment I was given. I even broke apart watches and glued the wheels onto my illustrations, just like he did. Of course, as soon as I finished art school that style didn't really appeal to me that much any more, and I had to start all over. My biggest regret about art school was not learning how to use a computer and do graphic design. Computers were pretty primitive back then, but still... I'm completely computer-illiterate today. I don't know how they work and figuring it out just seems like too much work. I don't even own one.

Can you describe the cartooning scene in Oslo when you arrived? Whose acquaintance did you make, initially?

I don't know if there was much of a cartooning scene in Oslo at that time. There must have been some cartoonists living there, but I didn't know any of them. One of the first people I met at Strykejernet was Kaj Claussen who, it turned out, had also done some stuff for *Konk*. I think we were pretty much the only ones there who were into comics and that's probably why we became friends. After two years at Strykejernet both of us were accepted at SHKS. There wasn't really anybody else who did comics either. Kaj quit school after the third year and eventually moved more in the direction of graphic design, but we would still meet every once in a while to draw together.

I finished school in '94 and tried to get a career as an illustrator going, but without much luck. I didn't quite know what to do with the comic I had done for my practical exam, "The Iron Wagon." It was only 12 pages and I didn't want to do the rest of the story. I'd rather do a story of my own. Still, I sent the pages to this magazine on comics, *Tegn*, hoping that they would be interested in publishing it. And they did. This is how I met Erik Falk, who would eventually become my first publisher. He interviewed me for the magazine, and I showed him the first couple of pages of the new story I was working on. He found it interesting and wanted to publish it as an album. *Tegn* had already published one album by another Norwegian cartoonist. So I spent the next year and a half finishing the story, called *Lomma full av regn* — *Pocket Full of Rain*.

Right. This is a fascinating first book. It merges slice-of-life with a kind of early *Love and Rockets* approach to the fantastic, with distinctly surreal elements. Can you describe the thought process that went into its ba-

sic concept and feel?

There's almost never any thought process, really. It all just happens. It was all improvised. I knew there was going to be a couple on the run and the ex-boyfriend hired killer, but the fairy-tale element, the wolf and the hunter, that came later. There is definitely a Jaime Hernandez influence in there, but mostly in the drawings, I think. The early *Love and Rockets* also had SF elements, robots and superheroes, but I'm not sure if that was the primary inspiration. It's something that just felt very natural to me, to have the normal everyday stuff and then include fantastic elements. And having the characters behave and talk as if they're in a story by Raymond Carver. That mix, I just find it intriguing, I guess.

It already has the preoccupation with death, the fatalist streak that runs through your work. Since you so often employ genre conventions to capture this feel, I wondered whether you might have some thoughts on where your initial interest in this approach came from.

No, not really. I'm afraid these are things I never think about. It's also why I feel like such a phony in interviews — when I'm being asked why my comics are the way they are, I don't really have any good explanation. You feel that you can't just shrug your shoulders; you have to say something, and it's usually just the first thing that pops into your mind. But I don't really find it that interesting to know why. Yes, I can see there is a preoccupation with death. People are killed all the time. Dead people walk around. Where does this come from? I don't know. Nobody close to me has died. I'm sometimes asked if the death at the end of the first chapter of *Hey, Wait ...* is autobiographical. It's not. There's a recurring image in my comics: people digging graves. It's in a lot of my stories — it's in the opening of *Pocket Full of Rain*. What does it mean, this image? Does it mean anything? If it means something and I find out what it means, what does that mean? I don't know. Who knows? Maybe Freud. Get him on the phone!

From the titular story in the graphic novel *Pocket Full of Rain and Other Stories*. [©2008 Jason]

Sure, I understand the problem of analyzing your own stories. I wasn't thinking so much along those lines, as I was attempting to close in on your choice of certain genre tropes as the framework for most of your comics — something that is already apparent in *Pocket Full of Rain* with its hard-boiled crime elements. I guess I'm asking why you gravitated toward these more down-to-earth themes, dressing them in genre trappings, instead of doing more outright genre material.

But where's the fun in that? To do a straight crime story that's already been done a million times? And what do I know about being a criminal? I've never stolen anything in my life. Well, some erasers and stuff like that when I was a kid, but leave that aside. If you're going to do a genre story you should bring something new to the table. At the same time, doing straight social realism doesn't interest me either — the Mike Leigh/Ken Loach approach, telling stories of unemployed coalminers. If I catch one of those movies on TV, I turn it off after five minutes. I find it boring. It's bringing those two worlds together — juxtaposing them — that's interesting.

I'm working on a story now; it's about this couple who are arguing. He hasn't cleaned up the apartment like he was supposed to. It was his turn, and she's coming home from work, she's tired and the place is a mess. They argue, and this goes on for a while, very normal, everyday

From "Pocket Full of Rain." [©2008 Jason]

stuff, and then a '50s sci-fi monster walks in, picks her up and runs off. That's the thing, that meeting between the everyday and the fantastic that I find interesting, or at least fun.

What do you feel that this monster adds, apart from a funny non sequitur? What does the hero falling from his bike because he sees Krypto the Superdog flying through the air above him do for the narrative that an old lady stepping in front of his bike wouldn't? It certainly makes the reader take notice, so I wonder whether it's also something that allows you to capture the kind of emotion that you're going for more easily.

I'm not sure if I want to talk about a story that's not finished yet, but it's definitely meant to be more than just a funny gag. The rest of the story is about this incident, how it affects both the man who is left behind and their son. It's a story about divorce, I guess. But it's such a dreary thing. A '50s space monster is more fun than a divorce procedure, no? But the ending is the same as if it had been a divorce, the way it haunts them. I guess the ending of the story will have more weight like this, if you give the impression in the beginning of the story that it's going to be some sort of absurd comedy. Which it still is. I don't see any contradiction in doing that. Growing up in the '70s, everything was so political. All the books you were given to read at school were about unemployment, racism, women's lib or subjects like that. They were all a drag to read and even worse to write a paper about. There didn't seem to be much room for imagination or fantasy.

Why does he see Krypto? I don't know. I'm not sure if I was going for some particular kind of emotion. Visually it works better, I guess. It says something about him as a character — seeing a stupid dog from old superhero comics, rather than having an old lady step in front of his bike.

When I mentioned the emotional effect of it, I was also thinking about the portrayal of the killer as this faceless force of death. This adds to the sense of menace and fear of death in the story.

The killer was never meant to be a realistic ex-boyfriend of the girl; he was meant to be more of a menacing force, a cloud over their heads. Probably he was just a variation of the bounty hunter from *Raising Arizona*.

This makes me think of the first strip I read by you, namely the short story in *Comix 2000*, where the main character is transported from a fantastic environment to a mundane one while he sleeps. He wakes up, brushes his teeth, has his coffee, puts on his tie and is off to work. And for just a brief moment stops short, sensing something is off, before he continues on his way. To me, this is one of your most affecting strips — the momentary sense of normality being askew seems to reach for something irrational or an imaginary truth we all might at times sense behind things as they appear. I don't know; I was wondering whether you had any thoughts on this, or — failing that — could perhaps talk about that feeling of truth something imagined

can have for you?

Damn, this is going to be a tough interview! No, I don't have any particular deep thoughts on this. Did you ever, when you were a kid, believe that the whole world, everything around you, was somehow staged for your benefit? I never seriously did, but I would sometimes play with the idea. I'm not sure if that's a common thing or not.

Your interest in surrealism seems to tie into that. There's of course the big panel with the hats in *Pocket Full of Rain*, which is clearly an homage to Magritte, but generally I find the ominous silences and deadpan characters in your work broach the surreal.

I'm a big fan of Magritte, of any surrealism really. Buñuel, *The Discreet Charm of the Bourgoisie*. David Lynch. I still remember the big impression the dream sequence in the third episode of *Twin Peaks* made on me. I lay awake half the night just thinking about what I had seen. The first appearance of the giant, in the ninth episode. I'm not sure if Monthy Python could be called surrealism. They were an influence on the Sam Space stories I did, one of which is published in *Pocket Full of Rain*. There is something very appealing about surrealism. Some of my favorite writers are Hemingway, Bukowski, John Fante, Raymond Carver and Tobias Wolf — the whole dirty-realism genre, but if I do a story in that style, if I'm drawing something really ordinary, everyday stuff — people on a pavement, a couple in a kitchen — my mind almost automatically goes hmm ... what would happen if I had a monster walking in here, or a dinosaur flying by there? What possibilities would that give me, at least visually? Surrealism might work better in a photorealistic medium, like film, it might lose some of its power in a story with cats and dogs walking around, dressed as humans, I don't know.

How was *Pocket Full of Rain* received?

It got a couple of good reviews, but it didn't really sell that much. It just sort of disappeared. It was pretty disappointing, actually. I had spent 18 months on the goddamned thing. I was about to give up on cartooning and focus on my illustration career, which was also going nowhere. The thing about being an illustrator is that there are almost no full-time jobs, just freelance assignments, and if you don't get those you are pretty much fucked. Six years of school down the drain. I think one of the problems with my portfolio was that it had too many different styles. The people I showed it to at publishing houses and advertising agencies were just confused. They didn't know what to do with it. Nobody called me. I had to start

taking other jobs for short periods just to be able to pay the rent.

But what happened at this time was that Erik and some other young cartoonists started meeting on weekends to draw and talk about comics, and eventually I joined them. That was the first time I felt I was part of a cartooning scene, and that really was the beginning of Jippi comics. They started publishing this anthology, *Forresten* [By the Way], and then later solo comics, of which my own, *Mjau Mjau*, was one.

I have only seen a few of the early issues, and not the earliest ones, so I don't have much of an idea — was there a guiding principle of *Forresten*? Did you consciously try to promote a certain kind of approach to comics in opposition to whatever Norwegian "mainstream" existed at the time?

There's not really any tradition for albums in Norway; there were a few attempts, but the market is just too small. Pretty much the only way to make a living doing comics in Norway is to do strips for the newspapers. So yes, I guess *Forresten* was meant to be an alternative, that comics could be something else than epic, historical albums, or strips with a more-or-less funny punch line in the last panel — that there could be stories trying to say something about the present, or offer something you could relate to. So you would have lots of stories about guys sitting in cafés, in heavy overcoats and Doc Martin boots,

From "Pocket Full of Rain " [©2008 Jason]

drinking and talking about being dumped by their girlfriends or whatever.

Was there anybody in particular amongst your Norwegian colleagues whose work was inspirational?

There was another anthology that was started around the same time as *Forresten*, called *Fidus [*Trick *or* Con*]*. It was done by cartoonists about five to 10 years older than most of the cartoonists in *Forresten*. Age-wise I belonged more in that group, but somehow I ended up in *Forresten*. The main cartoonist appearing in *Fidus* was Christopher Nielsen. He's sort of a Norwegian Robert Crumb, not only in terms of his drawing style, but because he started doing comics quite young and was one of the first people to do alternative comics in Norway. In this sense, he's been a source of inspiration for the rest of us. There were two other cartoonists in *Fidus*, Steffen Kvernland and Lars Fiske, who did interesting work. Both of them, incidentally, got their start in *Konk*. Of the more commercial cartoonists, I'd say Frode Överli was the best. He does a newspaper strip, *Pondus*, that has become very popular both here and abroad. The collections of his strip top the best-seller lists in Norway. He, too, is an old *Konk* guy.

Apart from the age of the cartoonists, what distinguished *Forresten* and *Fidus*?

The content of *Forresten* and *Fidus* wasn't all that different; it was mostly the age thing — they were slightly older. No Comprendo, the publisher of *Fidus*, has changed a bit since then. They still publish their main cartoonists — Christopher Nielsen, Lars Fiske and Steffen Kverneland — but *Fidus* doesn't exist any more. They've also started publishing some foreign cartoonists. They did the Norwegian editions of *Persepolis* and *Ghost World*. Lately Jippi and No Comprendo have cooperated on *Angst*, an English-language anthology of their best comics, with two issues so far.

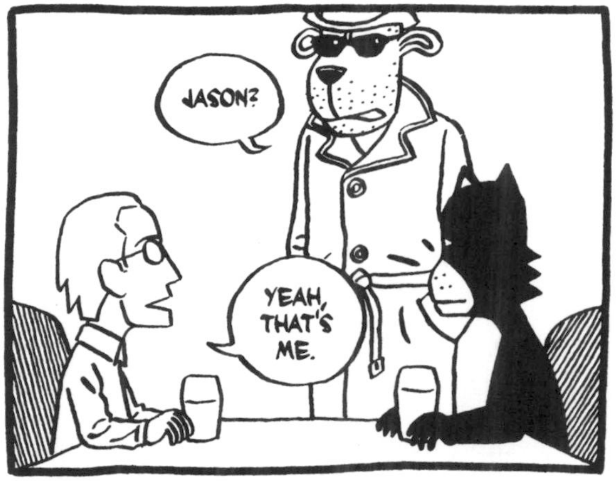
JASON?
YEAH, THAT'S ME.

From "What Time Is It?" in *Pocket Full of Rain and Other Stories*. [©2008 Jason]

Was *Mjau Mjau* an immediate addition to *Forresten* for Jippi? How did it come about?

I'm not sure when the first issue of *Forresten* was published, maybe '96. The first issue of *Mjau Mjau* came out in '97. It was not the first solo comic they published. Jens K Styve did the first one, called *Finn Finn Finn*. We shared a studio at the time. Actually, what happened was that another cartoonist, Tore Olsen, came back to Oslo after having lived in Copenhagen for a couple of years, working in a studio there — the Gimle studio — and he wanted to start something similar in Oslo. He found a place and invited other cartoonists. It was myself, him and Styve, as well as some other people: a writer, a translator and a graphic designer. It was an exciting period, after having worked alone for a long time. And seeing Styve's comic book was an inspiration. I'd already had an album out, but seeing his comic, with more personal stories, made me want to do something like that. *Eightball* by Dan Clowes was also sort of a model, inspiring me to do different kinds of short stories in different styles.

Who was involved in the day-to-day running of Jippi?

The two main people in Jippi would be Erik and then Per Jörgen Olsen, who handled the financial side. For *Forresten* there was an editorial board, which included some other people. But we all participated. You could subscribe to both *Forresten* and the solo comics, so for each new issue we'd all meet at the studio, stuff envelopes, and then schlep it over to the post office. Now, of course, I have nostalgic feelings about that period!

The first issues of *Mjau Mjau* were entirely short stories, right?

The two first issues of *Mjau Mjau* are pretty much me looking for a style, and then ending up with the animal characters. *Pocket Full of Rain* was such a drag to draw, it took so long — it was just frustrating having to work so slowly, to only have a panel or maybe two done by the end of the day. Basically, the early issues include stories in two different styles: stories like "Chalk" or "Glass," drawn in a McKean/*Cages* style, and stories featuring animal characters. I had already tried out that style earlier; I did a few drawings and strips in *Konk* in that mode, influenced by seeing some Tex Avery films. But I only stuck with it for

From "Bus" in *Pocket Full of Rain and Other Stories*. [©2008 Jason]

a short time. I'm not sure why. In *Mjau Mjau,* I returned to it. Initially, it's stories about me as a character talking to an animal character; later there are stories with no human characters at all. And I think it just fit. They were easier to draw, the animal characters, it was less of a pain in the ass than the realistic style. I actually drew the first couple of pages of *Hey, Wait ...* in the McKean style, but I gave it up and started over with animal characters. And I'm pretty sure I made the right decision. That was the third issue of *Mjau Mjau.*

There's a decent amount of straight, or rather thinly veiled autobiography in a lot of your early, short strips. Was this a case of following the lead of independent cartoonists across the pond, with autobio being the most obvious entrance point into the kind of comics you were interested in doing?

There are some stories with me as a character, but that doesn't necessarily mean they're autobiographical. There might be autobiographical elements, but then you invent stuff or change things around for it to work as a story. I've done very little straight autobio — it's not something I'm too comfortable with. I could never be as revealing about myself as someone like Joe Matt or Chester Brown.

Some of your early short strips — such as "Bus" or the one with the two nuns, are short lyrical pieces. To

me, these are really well done and foreshadow some of the elements you would soon develop into longer stories. Can you talk a little about composing such short pieces and what it may have meant for your cartooning sensibilities when doing longer stories?**

It's just trying out stuff. Like drawing somebody waiting for the bus, something that you would ordinarily spend one panel on, to drag that out to three pages. It could even have been longer, I think. I guess I learned something from it. Not having something new happen in every panel or changing the camera angle for no reason, to dare to be boring. *I Killed Adolf Hitler* is the album where I played around with that the most, especially the second half where they just stand around, waiting. Also, using conversation that doesn't really mean anything, just everyday chatter that is not about the plot, that doesn't move the story forward. Often that stuff is what you can relate to. Like in *Stranger than Paradise* where John Lurie is telling a joke but then can't remember the punch line, or the scene where they're at the movies, which goes on forever. It's truer to life than Tom Cruise cutting the blue wire of the bomb three seconds before it blows up.

Following directly from that, I wondered how important an influence Hugo Pratt was. You did an homage to him, "Corto Meowtese," and many of your strips have the same kind of lyrical qualities as his strips do.

From *The Iron Wagon*. [©2003 Jason]

I'm a big fan of Hugo Pratt, especially *The Ballad of the Salt Sea*, *Corto Maltese in Siberia* and the short Corto Maltese stories. I'm sure some of that has rubbed off on me. I like the way Pratt used silence, before it became a mannerism. There are some really great sequences in *Ballad* and also at the end of *Siberia*, when he says goodbye to the girl. He lets the story breathe a bit. I tried it a couple of times in *The Iron Wagon*. There's a sequence without words towards the end, where the main character is finally figuring out what is going on and making a decision about what to do. I like those quiet moments in a comic. I don't understand the old principle that there has to be some text in every panel, like in the *Blake and Mortimer* albums. Pratt was also very good at using the white of the page, to not fill every inch of every panel, to give the eye a bit of a rest once in a while.

Let's talk about *Hey, Wait …* This was your first long-form story since *Pocket Full of Rain*. You said you started drawing it in your McKean style. Can you explain how the story came about and how you arrived at drawing it the way it's drawn?

Hey, Wait... is very much influenced by Chester Brown's *I Never Liked You*. I think that's a really amazing book, one of the best graphic novels out there. It really captures childhood and early adolescence. Despite being autobio, it has a real ending. It's a complete story, something that doesn't always happen with autobiographical books. The first couple of pages of *Hey, Wait …* were drawn in the McKean style. I think I did four or five pages that way maybe. But they stayed half finished, and I finally gave up and started over with the animal characters. But again, it's something that just happened. It's not something you intellectualize too much while you're doing it.

Were you also influenced by Chester Brown's way of using negative space, silent panels and creating images that have that quiet, indeterminable resonance he is so good at? Your work in some ways reminds me of these aspects of his work.

Mostly it was just making me want to use my own childhood as basis for a story, but yes, I'm sure some of his images were also an inspiration. The quiet panels of him just sitting there eating crackers or lying in bed just looking at the ceiling. It's hard not to feel some sort of connection to those panels.

You said earlier that the story isn't autobiographical, but did you deliberately choose an approach that connoted autobio?

Actually, there are a lot of autobiographical elements in the book. The two main characters are very much based on myself and my best friend at the time, Håkon. There's even the Batman club. There are some changes. He was actually sort of the leader, and in the story it's more my character who dominates. Even the second chapter is partly autobiographical. It's based on the nine months I was working at the furniture factory. The main difference is the end of the first chapter, where Björn dies in an accident. That never happened. Håkon moved to another city. There was a cliff nearby. There was the tree with the branch sticking out, but I never tried to jump out to catch it.

I had finished about half the childhood part of the story and I needed something to happen. And a death is something profound, even more so if you're partially responsible — it will change you as a person I assume. I didn't really have anything to say about my teenage years so I decided to jump ahead to him being an adult, mostly,

I guess, to create a contrast, a before and after.

The two sections of the book contrast very well, the former is very observed and downplayed in its storytelling, while the second is more constructed, making more obvious use of dramatic storytelling strategies. You say you needed something to happen when you had just about finished the childhood part — so the dramatic turn of events wasn't planned?

It's very seldom that I have the whole story in my head when I start working. I knew I wanted to do a story based on my childhood, and that this would serve as the beginning of the story. I think I was about halfway into the first chapter when I knew what direction the story would go. But I don't remember in what order the decision was taken, if the accident and death of Björn came first and the second chapter followed, or if it was the other way round. It's a very organic — in the best cases sort of magical — thing, the way a story develops. You just have to let it happen.

How did you go about making the storytelling choices for the second part? I'm thinking of the disintegrating panels, the off-screen action, all that stuff — were you very conscious of approaching this differently than the first part, to play up the contrast, or did it also just come naturally?

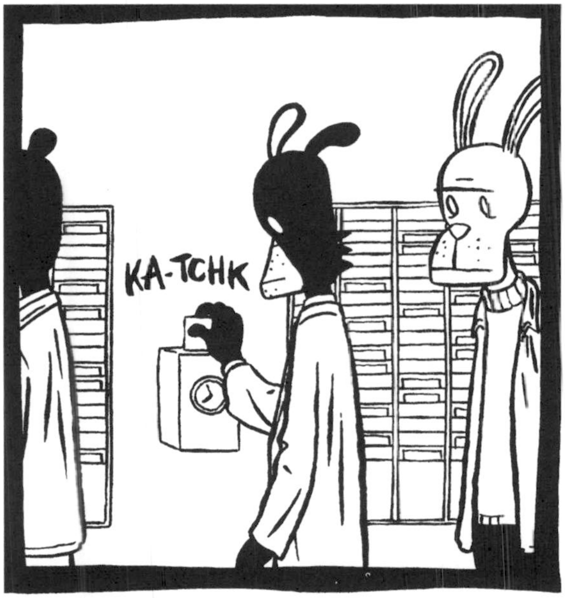
KA-TCHK

Jason drew on his time working in a furniture factory for *Hey, Wait ...* [©2001 Jason]

I knew the more fantastic elements would only happen in the first part, the adults on stilts, the flying dinosaur snatching the kite, and so on, and that the second part, the adult part, would be more realistic. I didn't make any conscious decision about changing the storytelling.

Hey, Wait ... is a book I have mixed feelings about today. It's not a book I reread. I haven't looked at it in a long time. It's pretty dark. I don't even know where the story is coming from any more. The drawings look clumsy to me. And the storytelling choices you talk about, I don't think I would have made them today. I find them a bit too much like showing off, a bit too much "Oohhh, look at this clever effect over here!" But it's a common thing when you're starting out, wanting to show off.

What do you mean when you call it dark? Is the kind of oppressive tone of the second half something you don't feel works for you any more?

I've had people tell me the book made them cry, so I must have achieved something with it. I don't regret doing it, but at the same time, had it been done by somebody else, I'm not sure if it's the kind of book I would have enjoyed. I find it just a bit too dark and gloomy now. It's not a very fun book.

It seems to have been the book that got noticed more broadly, but that was perhaps only later? In any case, it gets singled out a lot, even today — did it feel like some kind of creative breakthrough at the time, or like just another step on the road?

It's a breakthrough in the sense that it's the first longer story I did with animal characters. It's a more mature book than *Pocket Full of Rain*, I guess. I'm not sure if it was a creative breakthrough, because it's a kind of story I've stayed away from since then. But it's the first book I did that was translated into French and English. It may still be the book that I'm best known for. It sometimes comes up in reviews of my later books: Pretty good, but not quite as good as *Hey, Wait ...*

I'm one of the readers who really found it affecting and have been looking for something similar in your subsequent work, I guess unfairly to an extent, because I recognize that so many other things are going on in your more recent books, and presented more subtly. Is it because it's so up front about its weighty subject matter that you're not that fond of it?

I don't know. I guess I'm too close to it. It's based partly on my own life. The second part is based on those nine months I worked in a furniture factory, and it really wasn't

From *Hey, Wait ...* [©2001 Jason]

the happiest time in my life.

You mentioned fun, and even if certain of your books, like *The Iron Wagon*, are not all that humorous, it is something of a constant. To what extent is it a priority for you these days?

I don't think I have any priorities before starting a story. But I hope that the later books, the color albums and the zombie book [*The Living and the Dead*], are entertaining. They're not trying to be art. Even *The Iron Wagon*. It's a murder mystery. Those are entertaining, no? Fun is probably the wrong word. I don't necessarily mean they have to be all jokey. The color albums still have some sort of melancholy quality. It's more about the concepts, I guess. Mixing different genres, moving things around, trying to create something new.

When you say, "They're not trying to be art," you make it sound like that would be a bad, or at least very dull thing. Are you generally resistant to elitism?

When comics get too arty, I lose interest; when the drawings become more important than the story. Often the more arty elements just get in the way. You almost get the feeling of the cartoonist not trusting the story. I guess my taste in comics has changed a bit. Some of the comics I read in my early 20s, in art school, I find almost unreadable now. My heroes in cartooning today are people like Hergé, Schulz, Franquin or Harold Gray. These cartoonists didn't try to make art, they just told stories. It's the same with movies. I'd rather see some silly Fred Astaire film than something by Peter Greenaway or Lars von Trier.

But surely Hergé, Schulz, Gray, Franquin or Fred Astaire is also great art, no? I get what you mean, but do you find it useless to think of your work in terms of art?

Art is such a meaningless term. It's only when it comes to things that don't really have anything to do with the actual comics that it's a concern. Yes, comics are art, so that the state can give grants to cartoonists. Yes, it's art, so that libraries will put comics on their shelves. Yes, it's art, so that comics will be reviewed in newspapers. But when you're sitting with a comic in your hands, reading, is it art or not? Who cares?

Around this time, you also did a newspaper strip for while, some of which is reprinted in *Pocket Full of Rain*. How did this come about? Was it a daily?

It was not a daily. I had discovered the *Steven* comics by Doug Allen and had really enjoyed those. I wanted to try to do something similar as a strip and see if I could get it sold somewhere. *Peanuts* was also an inspiration — the more minimalist ones with Snoopy just watching leaves fall and so on. The strips were published in a Norwegian newspaper. I did about 50 strips, all in all, but I ran out of ideas pretty quickly. Also, it has its limitations, the strip form. You can't really tell a story. It's just two or three panels to set up the punch line in the last panel.

You worked a lot with pantomime in this period. It's a form that suits your approach very well, I think. What was the appeal of it for you?

It's something that happened gradually. *Hey, Wait ...* has less and less text the further it goes. I was never all that good at writing dialogue. In *Pocket Full of Rain* I found that to be the most difficult part. The drawings often came first and then I would have to come up with something for the characters to say while I was drawing. And then I discovered the work of Jim Woodring, and later Fabio, his vagabond cat stories. And it was a revelation. No text at all! I found it easier to work that way and it was also easier to improvise when there was no text. The first longer story was the one with the bird guy, where he's standing on the bridge, dropping a rock in the water and finding a girlfriend. I didn't know how it was going to end, and then the end came to me, with him back on the bridge, dropping in a new rock; there's no one. It fit together as if it had been planned that way from the beginning. It's very gratifying when that happens. The same with the second story, where he gets a son in the mail. I find these stories to be more of a breakthrough than *Hey, Wait ...*

This was a period when I was on the dole. It wasn't really that difficult to find work in Oslo at the time, but I chose to stay unemployed in order to be able to just sit and draw all day. And my production increased a lot, from one or two pages a week to three or four. In two years, I did seven or eight issues of *Mjau Mjau*, from issue 5, the first all-silent one, to *The Iron Wagon* in issue 11 and 12.

A notable thing about your animal characters — especially noticeable in your pantomimes — is their relative lack of facial expression, even for simple cartoon characters. This approach contributes immensely to the signature "silent" and poignantly eerie feel of your comics. How did you arrive at this, and what are your thoughts on it?

When I drew the first bird-guy story, the first seven or eight pages, I originally had him show emotions, but then I went back and changed it so that he had no expression at all. It just seemed right. Rationalizations came later, when I started getting that question from journalists, and my standard answer would be that if the characters show no emotion, the readers are encouraged to invest their own emotions in them. Also, somehow it makes sad scenes sadder and funny scenes funnier. Those are all good reasons, but it wasn't really something I was thinking of when I first did it.

Buster Keaton might be an inspiration, the deadpan thing. Aki Kaurismäki also — he doesn't allow his actors to show any emotions. I almost find it a bit embarrassing to watch overemotional films, like *Husbands and Wives*, *Festen* or *Magnolia*. Paul Thomas Anderson always gives his actors at least one scene where they get to *act!* For the most part it's just hysterical. It doesn't work at all for me. It just takes you out of the film.

Does the silent approach encourage more simple, "universal" stories for you?

Yes, I think using no text makes the stories more universal. They become fables. You don't hit the reader on the head with all the answers. It's more up to each reader to interpret the story — he has to fill in some of the answers himself. It's more of a meeting between the artist

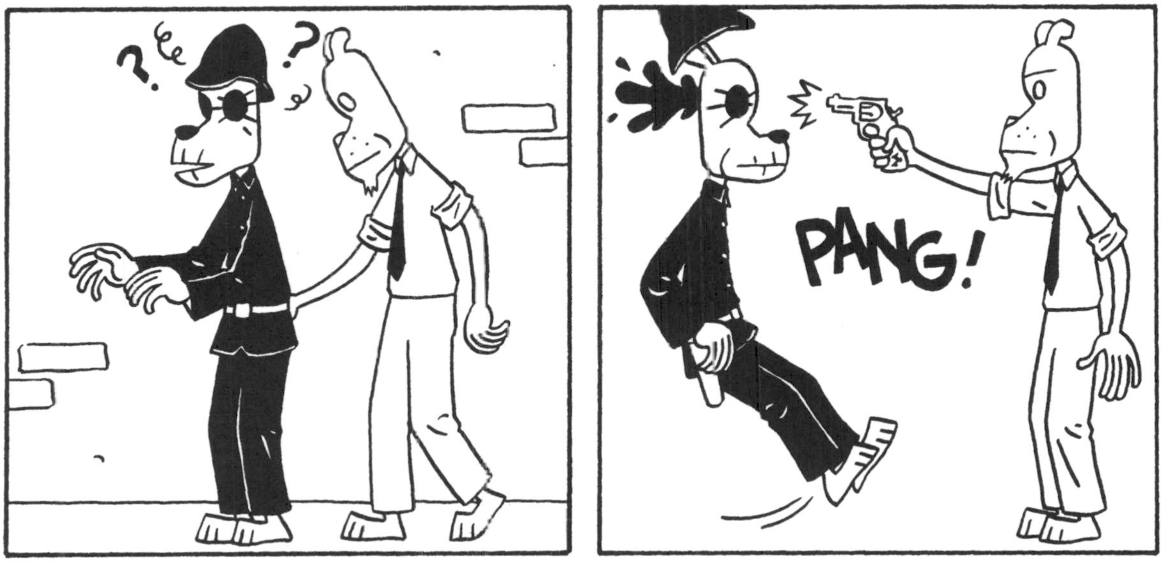
PANG!

Zombie slapstick: from *The Living and the Dead*. [©2006 Jason]

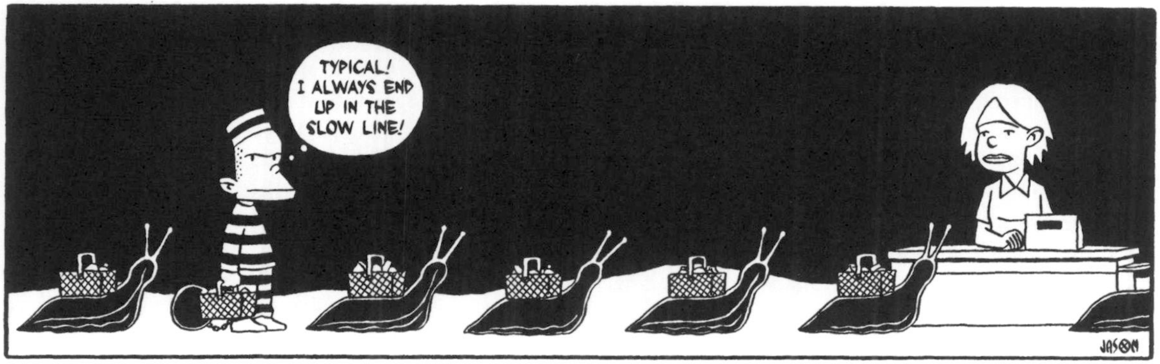
TYPICAL! I ALWAYS END UP IN THE SLOW LINE!
JASON

An example of Jason's newspaper strip, collected in *Pocket Full of Rain and Other Stories*. [©2008 Jason]

and the reader.

To me, the silence seems to suit the tenor of your stories well — there is that quiet, at times fatalistic streak to them. What are your thoughts on this silence on a more general level?

I don't really have any further thoughts on this. You want me to make stuff up or what? To not use text in a story you lose an important part of your storytelling devices, but at the same time you gain something, a more unexplainable element, a feeling of mystery, maybe.

I may be oversimplifying, but the general feeling of your work is that anything can happen. This is not a Cosmos overseen by God. Would you agree? How would you say the comics reflect your deeper view of the world?

They're mostly just stories, but I guess some of them might express my view of the world, if there is one. They show a healthy pessimism, I think, without being nihilistic. I don't think there is a God, or at least a God that can interfere. You just need to look at the world today, or pick up any book from the history shelf. Or read the paper. You can read about some kid whose clothes got stuck in the door on the way out of a car and was dragged along by it as it was speeding away until the driver realized what happened, at which point it was too late. How can there be a God? You can hope that if you lead a good life, life will be fair to you, but there are no guarantees of that. The opposite might happen, and probably will. But I think I'm a closet optimist, actually. If you're not, how can you get out of bed in the morning?

Your characters appear to somewhat make up for what they may lack in their faces by their body language, which I guess is a classic way of doing comics. Is this something you pay a lot of attention to?

Body language? No, not really. My characters stand straight with their hands hanging down a lot, and sometimes you want to break that. I guess it's all about choosing the right moment. If the character looks down or lowers his head it should mean something.

Silent film seems like an important inspiration. Your next, longer story, *Tell Me Something*, is obviously an homage to that era of film. How did that come about?

Tell Me Something was a culmination of the silent comics I did. It was the most ambitious story I could tell without words. Having no words at all wasn't a challenge any more. I felt I could actually use some in a couple of places to tell the story more clearly. The story takes place in two different levels of time, the present and the '20s. The scenes in the '20s are very much influenced by silent film. The few pieces of dialogue are given in white on black panels just like in silent film. A lot of the humor is based on slapstick: people running into each other, falling over, and so on. I like a lot of the old silent films, especially Buster Keaton, Harold Lloyd and Laurel and Hardy. There's something strange about seeing those films today: to know that these people are all in the grave and have been for a long time, but you're able to watch and enjoy their films. It's kind of touching, actually.

Both in *Tell Me Something* and *You Can't Get There from Here*, as well as a number of your shorter strips, you largely stick to the pantomime but insert the silent film inter-titles. In the latter, there's a clear distinction made between visual and the verbal humor. Can you talk about these choices and what, to you, are the limitations of pantomime?

Well, the obvious limitation is that in real life people talk. You lose complexity by not having any text. But at the same time, words often just get in the way. You can think back on a conversation you've had with someone and try to remember what you talked about and find out it was all about nothing. How often do you say something that actually means something? Not that often. I sometimes wonder if I lost the ability to talk, if I became mute, would I miss it that much? Maybe. Probably. A bit at least. When I started using more text in the color albums, it was mostly because of the challenge of writing dialogue. It was something I had stayed away from and had found difficult. I wanted to face that problem and try to overcome it.

I don't remember if I had the structure in my head when I began *You Can't Get There from Here*, to have the second chapter be full of action intercut with conversations between the two hunchbacked assistants. It might be something that just happened. Some of it is done for the sake of humor. The fact that it's the two assistants, who are usually never given anything to say in these kinds of films, that talk. And when they talk about their old classmate dying in a lab accident, as if they had all gone to a college for hunchbacked assistants. But of course, the conversation also mirrors the main story: the scientist and the Frankenstein monster, their loneliness and longing for someone else. I'm not sure if the dialogue was strictly necessary. It could probably have worked without.

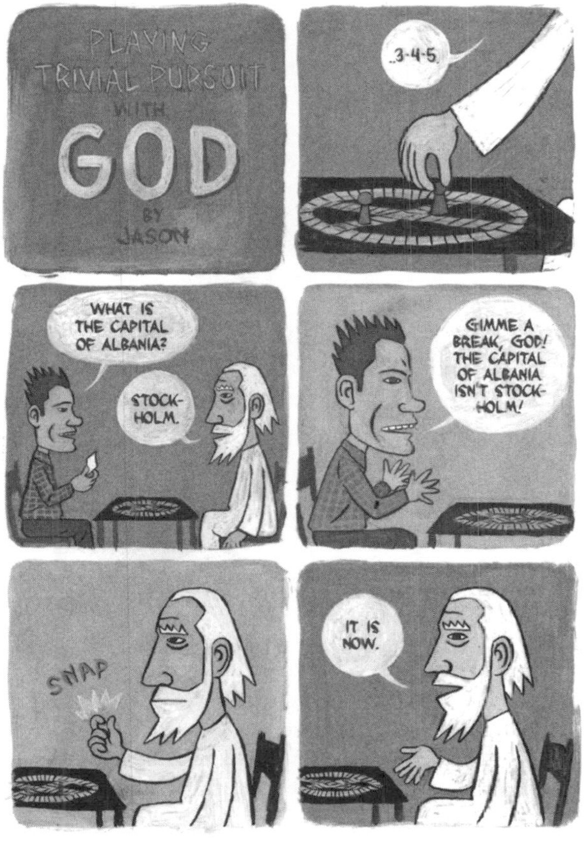
PLAYING TRIVIAL PURSUIT WITH
GOD
BY JASON
3-4-5
WHAT IS THE CAPITAL OF ALBANIA?
STOCK-HOLM.
GIMME A BREAK, GOD! THE CAPITAL OF ALBANIA ISN'T STOCK-HOLM!
SNAP
IT IS NOW.

From "Playing Trivial Pursuit with God": collected in *Pocket Full of Rain and Other Stories*. [©2008 Jason]

Why are you particularly interested in the time between the wars? You've set a number of your stories in that era.

It's mostly a visual interest. Things looked better then, and things are so ugly now. I don't like to draw cars, I try to avoid it, but at least the old Fords of the '20s had character. And somehow the clothes of that period look good on my animal characters. The sixpence, the straw hat, the fedora, the three-piece suit and the hats women wore in the '20s. Modern clothes are pretty boring. If you're inspired by old silent films, it's logical to set the stories in that period. Silent-film humor wouldn't work as well in a story set in the present. And of course, that period had an innocence that is lost today.

What do you mean?

There seems to have been a belief in progress and human opportunity that you find expressed, at least, in the popular entertainment at the time. The Harold Lloyd character can be seen as sort of a manifestation of that optimism. The stock market crash and the Depression took care of some of that, but it's still there in the '30s and the '40s. A film like *It's a Wonderful Life* — there is no way that could have been made today, without looking totally fake and ridiculous.

Even though you know life is not as easy as it is portrayed in those films, it's still very tempting to deceive yourself and believe so, just for a minute or two. I don't think people were that different then from what they are today. I don't think life back then was better. Maybe less complicated, but not better. But it's easy to feel nostalgic for a period when you weren't even born. You only see what you choose to see. In *Pocket Full of Rain* the two main characters have a conversation about how magical it would have been to travel by steam train, but of course that is only true from a modern perspective. I'm sure that in real life those things were slow, cold in the winter, and you couldn't open the windows in the summer because of the smoke. Just to mention one insignificant example,

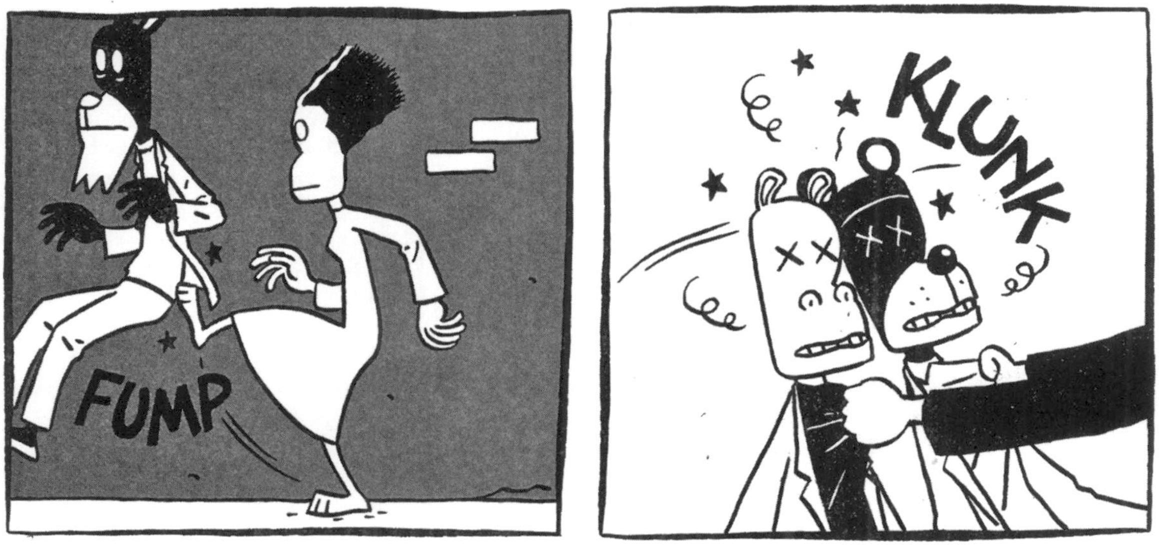
FUMP
KLUNK
Frankenstein's monster and the Bride engage in a slapstick brawl in *You Can't Get There From Here*. [©2004 Jason]

without even getting into human rights and such. I'm not sure if I would have liked to live in that period. Well, unless I had a lot of money, of course!

The kind of nostalgia for a period where you weren't born, and particularly the early 20th century and the period between the wars, seems rather prevalent in comics, at least amongst American cartoonists: Chris Ware, Seth, Kim Deitch, Tony Millionaire (OK, he's more into the late 19th century) and so on. Do you think your fascination is related to theirs through your profession — that period being, in many ways, the golden age of newspaper comics, animation and illustration — or do you think there are other common traits uniting you in this?

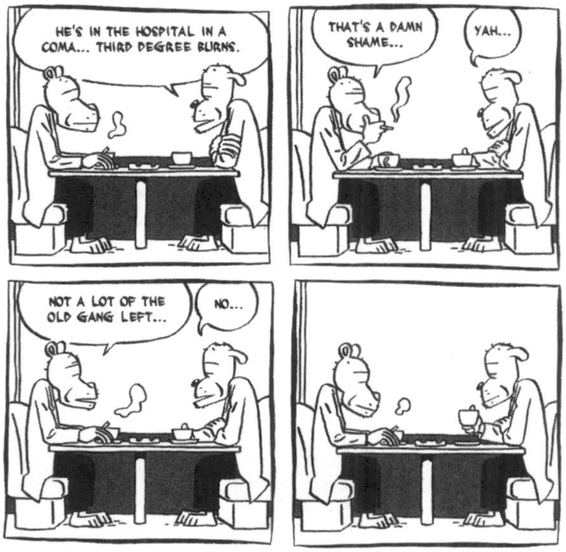
HE'S IN THE HOSPITAL IN A COMA... THIRD DEGREE BURNS.
THAT'S A DAMN SHAME...
YAH...
NOT A LOT OF THE OLD GANG LEFT...
NO...
The hunchbacks get all the lines in *You Can't Get There From Here*. [©2004 Jason]

For me, it's very much founded in the movies. The silent films, the musicals, the screwball comedies. I was buying a lot of film noir for a while. I think a lot of those hold up pretty well, at least the best of them, like *Asphalt Jungle, The Big Combo, Out of the Past.* They're not dated. They have a more cynical and pessimistic attitude than the other films of the period.

It's only quite recently that I've started to buy the strip collections. *Walt & Skeezix* I enjoy a lot, they're pretty amazing books. I've bought the new *Terry and the Pirates* and *Little Orphan Annie*. There is a French collection of *Polly and her Pals* with Sunday pages from 1929 and 1930; I really liked that book, just the exuberant quality of the cartooning. There are some collections that I don't care for. I tried one of the *Dick Tracy* books, but I found the plots to be kind of silly. The drawings didn't appeal to me too much. *Krazy Kat*: I have to admit I don't get that strip. I can see why it's a unique strip and a masterpiece, but I just find it hard to read more than a couple of pages at a time. *Popeye* I haven't tried yet. I'm not particularly into design of the '30s. I don't buy and surround myself with stuff from that period. It's mostly just the images — the films, the comics, photographs.

So those blank eyes and simple, black figures of yours that so recall classic strips are only related to them by proxy, so to speak?

There was the Tex Avery influence when I first tried out the animal characters, in the mid-'80s. *Little Orphan Annie* was not an inspiration even though you find the same blank eyes there. In the beginning all the animal characters had black skin, so they'd have white eyes. Later, when I started giving some of the characters white skin, just for the sake of variation, it seemed right to also give them blank circles for eyes.

While working in pantomime, or near-pantomime, around the turn of the millennium, you returned to your old adaptation of Stein Riverton's *Jernvognen*. Could you explain why you decided to return to it, and why were you interested in this novel in the first place?

After *Tell Me Something*, I was a bit afraid of starting to repeat myself, of using the same images over and over, doing silent comics. I wanted to do something with dialogue, and *The Iron Wagon* seemed to be a way of doing that. As mentioned, I had already drawn the first 12 pages in a realistic style. I still felt a bit bad about not completing the story. I wanted to do the whole thing, but in the animal-character style.

I first came across *The Iron Wagon* as a radio play, when I was about 15. It made a big impression on me, the moodiness of the story. I read the novel by Stein Riverton that the radio play is based on — it's a really well-written book. It's more than just a whodunnit by Agatha Christie. It's a lot more psychological, more Edgar Allan Poe. It's the kind of story that you remember, the kind that sticks with you, even after the identity of the killer has been revealed. It was a challenge to see if I could capture just a tiny part of that in a comic.

I haven't read the novel, so I was wondering how closely you followed the plot and what procedure you used in adapting it?

The comic is very faithful to the novel. I didn't change any major things. I made the choice to not include the narrative voice used in the book. In the first, realistically drawn version I kept it, but not in the animal-character version. I took it out. An important part of the ending of the book is lost by that, but it's still clear who the main character is.

While there's a good deal of exposition in places, revealing the "literariness" of the source, I still think it's an immensely visual story — your most visually rich comic up until that point. What were your thoughts in visualizing the story?

There are some great passages in the book, descriptions of nature that create a very dark, haunted atmosphere. These were painful not to include, but they had to go. The story had to work visually, as a comic, and not just be illustrations to the text. The comic having greater visual richness than the earlier work might be due to it being the first I actually did research for. I borrowed books with photographs from the period. I studied the clothes and the fashions. And I went out to Hvaler, where the story took place, and took a lot of photographs. A lot of modern buildings had come up of course, but the woods and the beaches were the same.

NOT TOO FAR BACK, DEFINITELY NOT THE MIDDLE AGES IN ANY EVENT, BUT SOME ROUND NUMBER, TURN OF THE CENTURY, OR LATE IN THE 1800S. IMAGINE BEING ABLE TO TRAVEL WITH A STEAM LOCOMOTIVE OR WITH A HORSE AND CARRIAGE. THAT MUST'VE BEEN SOMETHING...
THAT BAS-TARD HENRY FORD SPOILED EVERYTHING!
WELL YEAH, BUT IT'S TRUE, BACK THEN, TRAVEL WAS ALWAYS AN ADVENTURE.

From "Pocket Full of Rain." [©2008 Jason]

The Iron Wagon, to me, seems to make a lot of use of its Spartan, suggestive imagery — the dark pine silhouettes, the barren daylight landscape with solitary birch trees, the simple, clear-lined interiors with landscape pictures on the walls, etc. — to convey the inner life of its main character. You even have the dreamlike imagery of Miss Hilde with the mirror — to what extent were you going for a kind of psychological portraiture with your drawings?

I didn't really think about that too much. The landscapes in the comic are very much from the photographs I took. I didn't really change anything to give them a more expressionistic look. Originally, I might have been thinking about that. *The Iron Wagon* was the practical part of my exam at SHKS, while the written one was about expressionism in comics. But I'm no Muñoz or Baudoin. It's not how I see the world. A more restrained, naturalistic look is what appeared on the pages as I was drawing. The dream sequences are where I get closest to expressionism, I guess. He has dreams in the novel. I haven't read it in a while, so I don't remember exactly what they were. The naked woman holding the mirror was my invention — Magritte might have been an inspiration there. It expresses the desire of the main character. The image of himself in the mirror, decaying into a dead man, was supposed to express his state of anxiety and guilt.

One criticism pertaining to *The Iron Wagon* that I've heard expressed a lot is that the central conceit is obvious almost from the beginning. Now, I don't regard this as a problem at all, as it isn't a traditional whodunnit, but were you at all concerned about this, or did you rather try to foreground it? To me it seems you do in the way you call attention to the main character in the drawings, especially when Asbjørn Krag talks to him.

It's not the most difficult thing in the world to guess who the killer is. There are no second suspects, really. The ghost outside the window is more of a mystery, really. But it didn't worry me too much. It was more important for me to elicit empathy for him, and understanding of his actions, why the killer did what he did. It's not a condemning portrayal, I hope. In the flashback to the murder, we see the triumphant smile of the forest ranger. How would you have reacted in a similar situation? Who knows? We're all potential killers. One mad impulse you can't control, and it's done.

Concerning the leaving out of the narrator's voice, you almost seem to be withholding it till the very end, where it comes in to great effect. This must be a rather strong departure from the book?

The text at the end is taken from the novel. It's the ending of the novel as well. I thought it might work in the comic to finally give him that narrative voice, since he's writing in his journal. And it's a great passage too, very poetic. The one touch I gave it was the eyes looking at him through the hole in the door, but without showing

A surreal moment in *The Iron Wagon*. [©2003 Jason]

And soon I shall journey surrounded by stillness and quiet

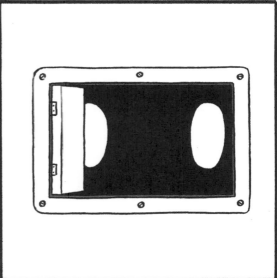

Mysterious eyes from the conclusion of *The Iron Wagon*. [©2003 Jason]

who it is.

Your mention of the mystery of the "ghost" makes me think of that brilliant Barks story where Gyro Gearloose has a machine that accidentally renders a wolf intelligent, whereupon the wolf dresses up as a (dog-snouted) human, while in the meantime Donald has dressed up as a wolf. The kinds of transformative disguises you see in comics, and the way they can be used for great visual effect and sight gags as well as explorations of the characters' identities.

I assume Asbjørn Krag is also disguised in the novel, but when drawn as a funny animal in your "blank" style, the device works at a different level. Would you say you foreground this aspect in the comic, and do you have any thoughts on how cartooning works in this respect?

Umm ... no. Sorry! I'm often asked if my characters are cats or if they are dogs, and I don't really know what to say to that. Is it important? If they have pointy ears, they're cats and if they have floppy ears they're dogs, I guess. Asbjørn Krag is the one example, an exception really, where I chose for him to be a dog. It just seemed the right thing, since he's a detective, but besides that it's not something I think about.

I'm not so much talking about anthropomorphism, but about the way a mask looks just like a "real" face in

a cartoony, Funny Animal comic — allowing characters to switch their identities totally, both in the story and to the reader. I think this adds something to *The Iron Wagon* that might not be there to the same extent in the novel. I suppose I just wanted to ask you about what you think about these things...

Your thoughts about this are probably more interesting than mine. I think I understand what you're talking about. It's an interesting aspect of the cartoony style, the mask/face thing, the added dimension it gives. I've never used it for comedic effect, like in that Barks story. In *Tell Me Something*, I have a dog character put on a beak and bird's feet to pose as the birdman in a series of photographs, set up by the female character's father, to separate the two. In "Secret of the Mummy," the longer story in *Meow, Baby!*, there is a play of gender and identity: the main character — a man — wakes up as a woman. But there are no philosophical answers. In the case of "Secret of the Mummy," the whole thing started by me reading 12 *Allan Faik* albums — that is, *Ric Hochet*, the old Franco-Belgian series — in a row. There were certain repeated clichés, and I wanted to put as many of them as possible into one story.

***The Iron Wagon* has a little of that unsettling feel you find in some surrealism, like David Lynch, and *Pocket Full of Rain* did too. But most of your work doesn't, concentrating as it does more on humor and the jux-**

From "The Mummy's Secret," a short collected in *Meow, Baby!*.
[©2005 Jason]

taposition of the ordinary and the fantastic. Did you ever consider moving more in the direction of the unsettling or horrific?

In *The Living and the Dead* I have a zombie eating a baby. That's not good enough for you? I'm not sure if a *ligne claire* animal-character style is the best place to tell horror stories. It could be a challenge, though. Maybe it's possible: Something like *The Tenant* or the film with Catherine Deneuve and the skinned rabbit by Polanski [*Repulsion*]. But if I were to do horror, it would probably always be with an ironic or comedic distance. The most unsettling story I've ever done is probably "Glass," from *Pocket Full of Rain*, a two-page story. I don't think I'd be interested in doing a whole album like that.

Why did you decide on the rust-red second color? I believe the installments as they ran in *Mjau Mjau* were pure black and white?

Yes, originally it was published in black and white. The extra color was added to create a bit more mood, especially for the night scenes, which seemed too bright. I had seen several books like that, in black and white plus one color, and wanted to try that myself. It was a time-consuming process because I didn't have a computer. I had to take copies of all the pages and indicate with a colored pen which parts I wanted colored. It took a bit longer to do than it was worth really. I tried it again for *You Can't Get There from Here*, but chose not to for *The Living*

and the Dead.

The Iron Wagon ran in issues 11-12 in 2001. Those were the last issues. Why did you decide to suspend the magazine?

I got a new publisher, Schibsted. They published hard-cover collections of *Hey, Wait ...* and *The Iron Wagon*. For *You Can't Get There from Here*, I chose to publish it directly as a book. *Mjau Mjau* had played out its part. Maybe, some day, if I try to do a longer story, I might serialize it in *Mjau Mjau* first.

Summing up, how would you describe your development as a cartoonist between *Mjau Mjau* issues 1 and 12?

I guess the difference between the first and the last issue of *Mjau Mjau* is looking for something and finding it. The early issues are drawn in a crude style. I deliberately worked with cheap brushes on cheap paper. If the line bled, fine, no problem, I tried to worry less about having a perfect line. By issue 12 my style is pretty much set. It's a return to a more controlled line. It's back to the pen nib, back to a clear line, and it's the style I still work in.

The problem with *ligne claire* is that it's not a fun style to work in. It's all about a steady hand and a precise line. It doesn't really give me any pleasure to draw, and that worries me a bit actually. With a bit of luck, I might be doing this comic-book thing for another 20 years. Or, who knows if comics will even be around in 2028? But anyway, the thought of sitting down at my drawing table every day for the next 20 years and not to enjoy drawing is a bit scary. Lately, I've been thinking about going back to the brush, to work more freely, to do less penciling first and to ink directly. I'm not sure if it will happen, though. I might be stuck with the style I have.

Why did you decide to adopt this clear, pen style? And what does it give you today?

It's not so much that I chose the *ligne claire* style, as it was the style that chose me. It's all because of that damn *Tintin*, I tell ya! The simplicity of the drawings appealed to me as a 13-year old kid, the clear storytelling. I could read and enjoy the *Asterix* and *Gaston* albums, but I would never have tried to draw in that style. It just seemed too difficult.

For me there are nine perfect *Tintin* albums, the first being *The Blue Lotus* and the last being *The Seven Crystal Balls*. The later albums don't appeal to me, the drawings just got too perfect; everything had to be logical. It lost its charm. The two Moon-travel albums must be the most boring albums ever made. Even *Tintin in Tibet,* which some consider a masterpiece, I find hard to read. The last album, *Tintin and the Picaros,* I never even bought. I don't want to read an album where Tintin wears bellbottoms! It's just wrong. But pick up one of the better albums, like *The Shooting Star* or *King Ottokar's Sceptre,* and it's simply great cartooning, you just want to step into the panels and live there.

Today, one of my favorite cartoonists would be Christophe Blain. Looking at his pages you get an impression that the guy just loves to draw. That is not something you get from *ligne claire.* And he's a terrific storyteller. But even though I admire his style, I'm not sure it's something I could do myself. I'm not sure whether your style, once you have one, is something you can change. It's who you are.

Were you working full-time on comics at the time when you finished *The Iron Wagon*? And where were you based?

I was still in Oslo at this point, at the studio I shared with the other cartoonists. I had been three months in Copenhagen, at the Gimle studio, around '99 probably, but ended up going back.

How was Denmark, and Gimle? And why did you go?

Denmark had a longer tradition for comics publishing than what you'd find in Norway. The market was bigger. In the '80s I'd buy a lot of Danish albums that were not published in Norway. There would be translations of a lot of the Franco-Belgian albums, cartoonists like Moebius, Bilal, Comès, Bourgeon, and so on. I'd order these albums from Fantask in Copenhagen and read them in Danish. There were also the albums by Danish cartoonists, like the *Valhalla* series by Peter Madsen.

I had heard about the Gimle studio from Tore Olsen who had been there, and I met Teddy Kristiansen and Peter Snejberg during one of the festivals in Bergen. They

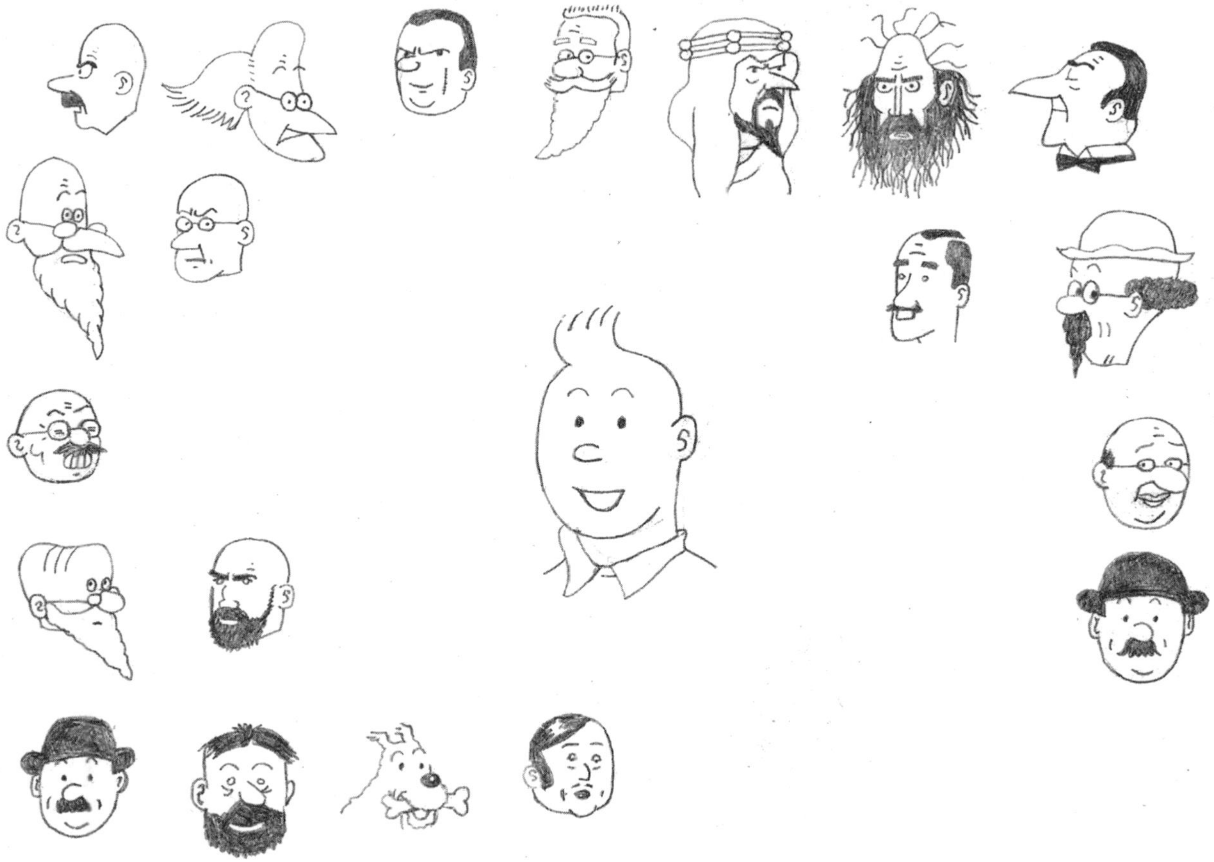

Another one of Jason's childhood drawings: courtesy of Jason. [©2008 Jason]

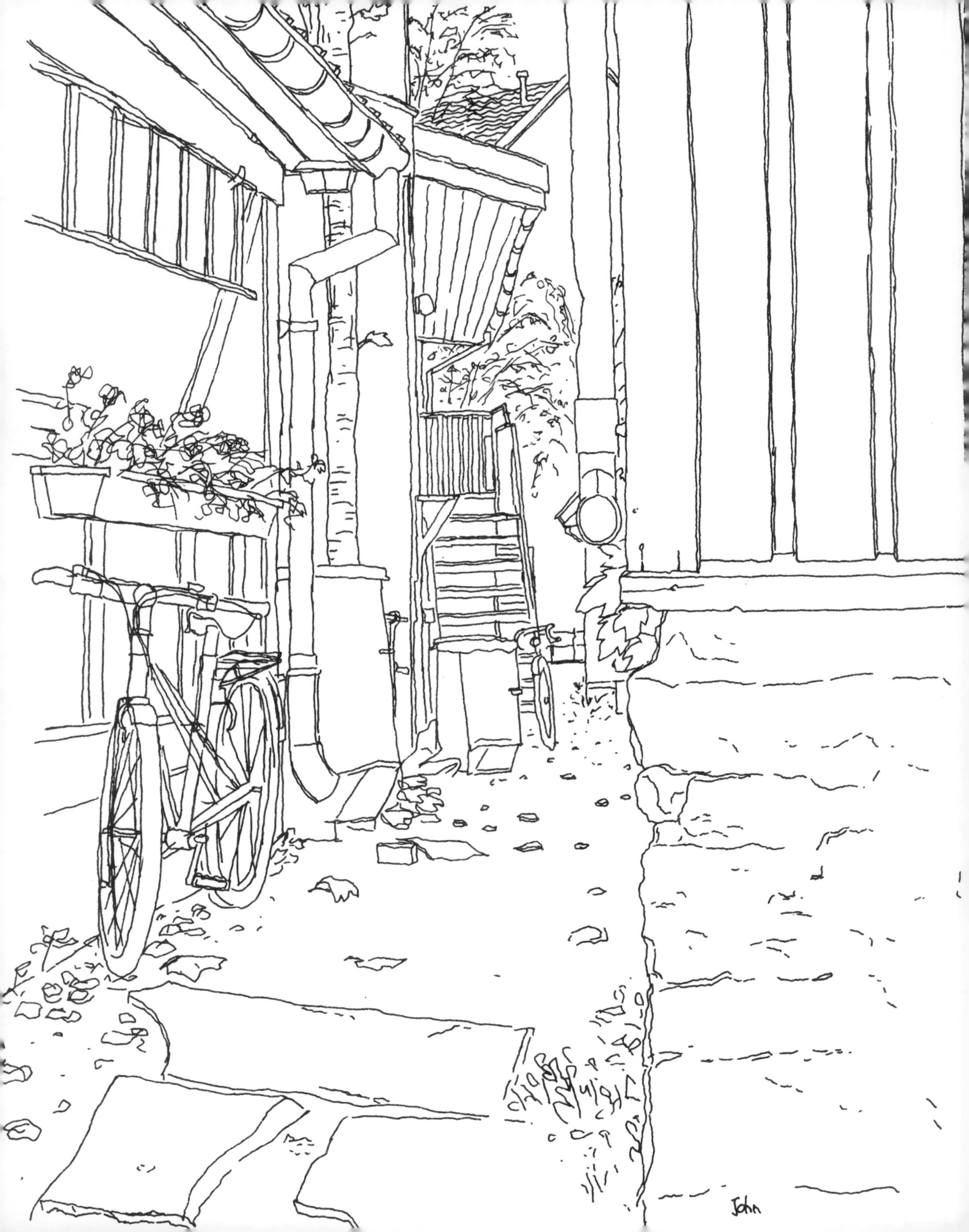
John

gave me a guest place at the studio for three months and I sublet a room in an apartment. I couldn't stay any longer, since I didn't really have a secure income at the time. But I enjoyed my stay in Copenhagen. It had more of a big-city pulse than Oslo. And I find the city to be more of a European, continental city, while Oslo and Stockholm seem to have their eyes set more towards America.

So you returned to Oslo. What kind of work were you doing at the time?

As I said, the two last years of *Mjau Mjau*, I was doing comics pretty much full-time. I had started getting a few illustration assignments by then. I had done a series of animal illustrations, in a realistic style, for a lexicon. I put a few of those in my portfolio, and that seemed to be the only thing the art directors noticed. I did some more for different school textbooks and books for kids. It was not something I particularly enjoyed doing. It's not very creative, just copying photos. But there are worse jobs, and I had to pay the rent. I was still feeling a certain frustration, both with the illustration work and with not making much money from comics.

What was the cartooning scene in Oslo like at the time?

The weekend meetings where we'd draw and talk about comics didn't happen any more. People had day jobs and worked in the evenings, and I was at the studio with the other two cartoonists. At this time Jippi was publishing five or six different solo comics series plus *Forresten*, the anthology, which came out twice a year. There would often be release parties at some pub or café, with one or two bands. Included in the price of admittance would be a copy of the comic. They were fun, those parties. I miss them.

Also, once a year there would be a comic-book festival in Bergen, and pretty much everybody would go there. The festival itself would be kind of commercial and family-oriented; they'd invite some Donald Duck artist or some guy inking *Batman*. Those of us who were into more alternative comics never really felt included in that part of the festival and were rather a bit embarrassed by it. It was mostly an opportunity just to meet other cartoonists who didn't live in Oslo and to get drunk.

***You Can't Get There from Here* was published by Schibsted? How did that happen?**

Eivor Vindenes, who had a room at the studio, started working for Schibsted, so it made sense for me to follow her. We already knew each other. Jippi was good at getting newsstand distribution for the *Mjau Mjau*s, but had trouble getting the collections into the bookshops. Jippi was two guys with day jobs publishing comics in their free time; Schibsted was a real publisher. I still haven't severed all my ties with Jippi. They published *The Living and the Dead*. I might do other books with them in the future.

Were the strips in *Meow, Baby!* all earlier material, or did you continue doing shorter strips at his point?

Meow, Baby! is a mix of silent comics from *Mjau Mjau* and strips I did for different newspapers and magazines. Eivor was the editor of *Larson*, a monthly magazine of the Gary Larson cartoons that also had other strips in the back. I had a page in each issue. And later she was the editor of a short-lived magazine of exclusively Norwegian comics. I had one or two pages an issue there. Also, some of the strips in *Meow, Baby*! ran in the newspaper *Dagbladet*.

Hold on, did you say *Mjau Mjau* was newsstand-distributed? That's amazing — would never happen in Denmark, I'm sad to say. How broad an audience do you reckon you were reaching by this point, both with the last issues of *Mjau Mjau* and your first books with Schibsted?

No too broad. We're not talking about best sellers here. I think the general conception of me was this guy who did these strange and melancholy comics, and why didn't I cheer up? The strips I did for *Larson* and for the newspapers were probably more important in bringing in an audience and creating at least a certain curiosity about my work.

Was there a growing sense of an alternative scene in Norwegian comics at this point?

I wouldn't say that there was a growing sense of an alternative scene. There wasn't much of a tradition of making comics in Norway, so what would we have been an alternative to? There were still basically two camps, the *Fidus* gang and the *Forresten* gang. It's only in the last four or five years that there has been a new generation, cartoonists in their 20s. *Fidus* doesn't exist any more, so mostly the cartoonists associated with it publish their work at Jippi.

What were the possibilities for living off comics in Norway at this point?

It was possible if you didn't mind working in a commercial style. In the late '80s and '90s there was a maga-

Opposite: A sketch of Montpellier: courtesy of Jason. [©2008 Jason]

This spread: Samples of Jason's more successful illustration efforts: courtesy of Jason. [©2008 Jason]

zine called *Python*, a sort of *Mad* magazine, but less adult, more geared towards adolescents. Several cartoonists worked there and they all made a living from it. The magazine eventually folded, and some of those cartoonists started doing newspaper strips. Something happened in the late '90s: The Norwegian newspapers, which for the most part had carried American strips, started publishing Norwegian ones. The most popular of these was *Pondus* by Frode Øverli. Later came strips like *M* by Mads Eriksen and *Nemi* by Lise Myhre. All these strips have their own monthly magazines. If you were doing more alternative comics, it was harder to make a living. Most of us did illustrations to earn money. Another thing that has happened in the last couple of years, by the way, is that the mainstream publishers are beginning to pick up the cartoonists that got their start at No Comprendo and Jippi. It's the same old story, I guess.

I guess it was also around this time that you started being published abroad. What were your earliest experiences with international publishing?

I started sending out stories to different foreign anthologies, like *Stripburger*, and getting some stuff published. I had that three-page story in *Comix 2000* from L'Association. One of the reasons I started doing the silent

strips was to avoid the whole language problem, to create something that could be understood anywhere. In 2001 I went to the festival in Angoulême for the first time, handing out issues of *Mjau Mjau* to different publishers there. One of them was Atrabile, and they contacted me about doing a book. I had already been translated and published in Sweden, but *Attends …* was the first book outside of Scandinavia. Then Kim Thompson told me Fantagraphics would be interested in doing the English-edition *Hey, Wait …* And that was the beginning.

As far as I remember you also moved abroad sometime in the early naughts? What made you decide to move?

I started traveling abroad while finishing *The Iron Wagon*. At this point I had lived 14 years in Oslo. My life seemed to consist of going to the studio in the morning and going back the same way in the evening, and to stop by the comic-book shop once a week. I was getting a bit fed up. I was in my mid-30s, but hadn't really traveled anywhere. I just couldn't afford it. I had been to the Scandinavian capitals, there had been a class trip to Italy when I was in art school, and I had been to Paris, Caen and Angoulême in France. But that was it. You can do comics anywhere — all you need is pen and paper, so why stay in Oslo? You can draw and see some of the world at the same time. I wanted to get closer to the French comics market since that seemed to be a way to actually make a living from drawing. I first went to Lyon and took a three-month French course. Then I went to Belgium, first Liège and then Brussels, where I had a table at the studio Employé du moi …

How was that?

It was very nice working at the studio Employé du moi. There were around eight or nine cartoonists there. Most of them had day jobs or were on the dole. I got to practice my French. When somebody had a birthday we would all go eat at a restaurant. What I remember best is that when they arrived at the studio in the morning they would each go and *faire la bise*, kiss each other on the cheek. As a reserved Scandinavian that was pretty strange, and something I found hard to get used to. Mostly I got away with just shaking hands. Greeting rituals are different. In Norway when you meet somebody you say hi, and that's it. Here [in France] you say hi, plus the name of the person you meet, plus you ask how they're doing: *"Salut, Claude, ça va?"*

"Oui, ça va, et toi?" And you also shake hands or kiss on the cheek. The handshake is fine, but I still find it hard to do the kiss without feeling self-conscious.

What's the chronology here? Did you finish *The Iron Wagon* while in Belgium, or before?

I don't really remember. I don't think I did much drawing in Lyon. A couple of pages maybe. I'm pretty sure I finished *Mjau Mjau* 12, the second half of *The Iron Wagon*, in Liège. I remember drawing the scene of the main character shooting the "ghost" of the forest ranger, because one of the guys at the studio where I worked lent me a book of guns. Then I heard of an apartment for rent in Paris, and that's an offer you cannot say no to. So I stayed five months in Paris, then went back to Brussels for seven months ...

Did you get into the cartooning when you were there? There are so many things going on, so I am curious about your early impressions of working there.

No, I didn't really know anybody there. I met Charles Berberian a couple of times. I'm not really the most social person in the world. For the most part, I'd work at home in the apartment or I'd go to the movies. There are several repertory cinemas in the 5th and the 6th District of Paris, and I would see lots of old American films: Ford, Hawks, Capra, Hitchcock and so on. After three months, Paris kind of lost its charm. All you'd notice was the crowds when you took the subway. And I felt like a foreigner there. I felt more at home in Brussels. It was closer to the Nordic, protestant culture. There were more people with blond hair. Brussels is a grayer city, it has less obvious charm, but I still prefer it to Paris.

You also lived in New York, right?

Yeah, I went there after Brussels. I had already been to [the San Diego] Comic-Con and SPX in the US, and had met some cartoonists there, so I was able to sublet an apartment in Brooklyn for three months. I didn't have a Green Card, so that was the time limit.

Where in Brooklyn were you? How was your stay, cartooning-wise?

I don't remember the name of the part of Brooklyn I was in. It was on the G Line, I think, a pretty much all-black neighborhood. I had gotten the apartment through Peggy Burns and Tom Devlin. There were a couple of parties and pub nights, and I met some cartoonists. Megan Kelso didn't live too far away. She and her husband took me to a baseball match and tried to explain the rules to me. It's still a mystery to me. The apartment I was subletting didn't have a good table for working, so I didn't get any cartooning done. Also it was in the middle of the summer and pretty hot. Most days I'd take the subway into Manhattan and just walk around. I'd go to the Strand bookstore or go to the parks to watch the squirrels. There was a big blackout while I was there. I was sitting in Tompkins Square Park when it happened, and had to walk home to Brooklyn.

I enjoyed my stay in New York, but at the same time found it to be too big and noisy. I think I got my dose of big-city life while I was there. Now I'd rather live in small cities. After that I returned to Oslo for one year, got restless again, and went to Seattle for three months.

I'm guessing that would be due to the Fantagraphics connection? How was it?

I liked Seattle. The country around the city is very close to what I grew up with in Norway. There are lots of great bookstores there. Thanksgiving was celebrated at Gary Groth's house, so I got to experience that part of American culture. The presidential debates between Kerry and Bush were happening at that time, and that was interesting to watch. I still can't believe they chose Bush. And I got hooked on *Lost* — they were broadcasting the first episodes at the time. I got some cartooning done while I was there. I had brought reference books and photographs from Paris with me and finished the first half of *The Left Bank Gang* there.

What made you decide to move to Montpellier and settle there?

I got tired of moving around all the time. I wanted to settle down somewhere for a longer stay, a smaller city in France. I had already been to Montpellier once, during a book tour for my first French color album, *Why Are You Doing This?* Montpellier was the city with the least people showing up for the signing, and it was raining the whole time I was there, but it was still sort of a magical experience. The local comic-book shop, Opera Comix, is one of the nicest bookshops I've been to. Lewis Trondheim showed up. After the signing, we all went to have dinner at this tiny pizzeria with only three tables. The owner of the comic-book shop had gotten me a very nice hotel room, with a view of the rooftops, and the next morning he walked me down to the train station. We walked by this big statue of Jesus on the Cross. The whole thing was just a memorable experience.

I had two French cities in mind for moving to, Montpellier and Rennes. I checked on the Net for French courses in those two cities, and I could start the one in Montpellier right away. I called them on a Friday and started on the Monday.

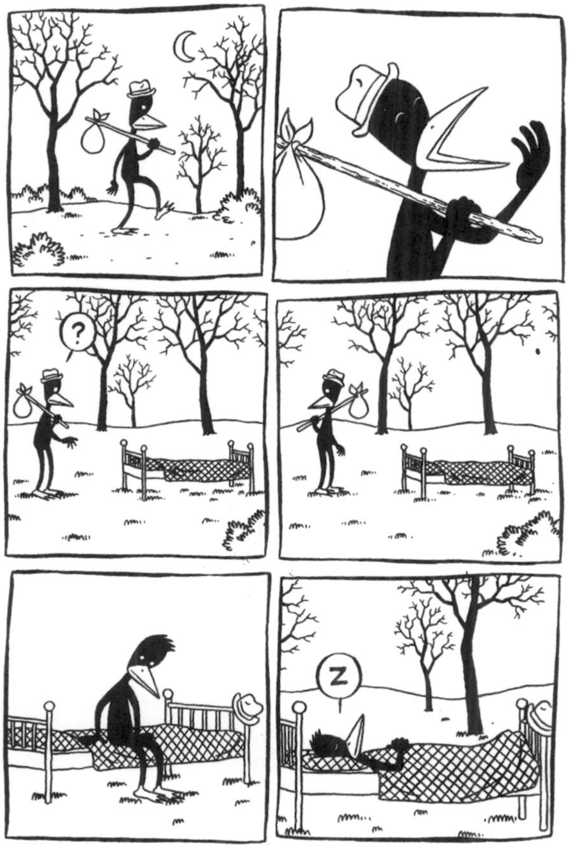
?
Z

A page from Jason's contribution to L'Association's *Comix 2000* anthology. [©1999 Jason]

Backtracking a bit here, I wanted to ask you how you first got in touch with Tournon Carabas, your French publisher?

I wanted to try the traditional 48-page hardcover color album, and my first French [Swiss] publisher, Atrabile, didn't do those — they mostly publish black-and-white books — so I had to find someone else. I had drawn the first 10 pages of *Why Are You Doing This?* and written the script for the rest of the story. I wrote it in English and a friend of mine in Brussels did the translation. I sent the thing to a couple of French publishers but didn't get any response. Then, at Comic-Con, I met Jérôme Martineau, the publisher at Carabas, and he was looking for projects. I gave him the pages and script and he accepted it. So I had to go to San Diego to find a French publisher.

The album shows a certain amount of development when compared with your previous work. It's denser, more classic in its storytelling, which I'm guessing is your way of adapting to the classic Franco-Belgian album format, and it's in color. Can you talk about the decision to make this album and the challenges involved?

It's me trying to do a *Tintin* album, basically. The pages are layered in four strips, like the *Tintin,* albums and the storytelling is more traditional than my previous work, more commercial, I guess. It's more of a typical thriller, very much influenced by Hitchcock, the whole innocent-man-on-the-run thing. The opening of the story, the first

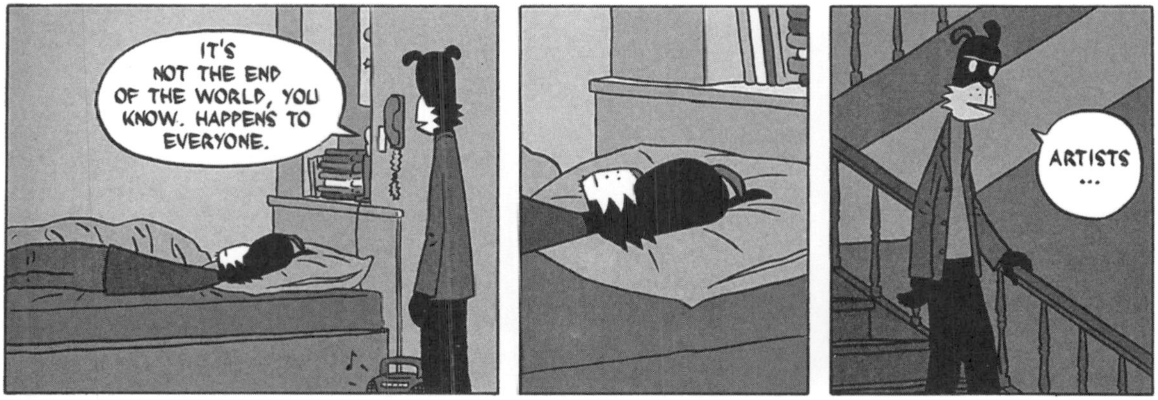
IT'S NOT THE END OF THE WORLD, YOU KNOW. HAPPENS TO EVERYONE.
ARTISTS ...

From Jason's first color album: *Why Are You Doing This?* [©2005 Jason]

10 pages, I'd had in my head for a long time. When I decided to do a traditional French album, it seemed a fitting story. Since I lived in Brussels, I chose to set the story there. I didn't want to include the best-known, touristy places, but rather tried to capture the particular architecture of Brussels. The café at the end, the Greenwich, where Alex goes to meet the killer, is an actual café in Brussels.

It was sort of a nostalgic project for me. I had grown up with the classic Franco-Belgian albums — *Tintin, Spirou, Lucky Luke* — and here I was, trying to make such an album myself. But by the next album, *The Left Bank Gang*, I already started questioning that. Why am I changing my style? Why do I try to copy that older, traditional-type storytelling? I think I pretty much got it out of my system with that first album. I think the later color albums are closer to the black-and-white books I had done before.

I immediately thought of Hitchcock, before even opening the book; the cover is very much in the vein of his storytelling. So much promise in that simple image — seeing somebody in the window across the street. Can you perhaps talk about what you've taken away, as a storyteller, from watching Hitchcock?

I'm not that big a fan of Hitchcock. There are five or six of his films I like. There's something a bit stale and lifeless about his films, maybe from storyboarding the whole thing and not allowing any improvisation or accidents. My favorite Hitchcock film is probably *Charade*, which is not by Hitchcock, but by Stanley Donen, I think. But it's more fun than the Hitchcock films, and Audrey Hepburn is a lot more appealing than the stuck-up blondes that Hitchcock liked. I haven't really studied his storytelling that closely — I just have a general idea of the tricks he uses to create tension. The whole bomb-on-the-bus thing: that the audience is aware of the bomb, but the people riding on the bus aren't. There is one scene like that in the book, where the main character is searching Vandoren's apartment while he's out, and then it starts to rain, so Vandoren turns around and comes back to the apartment.

A staging device you make increasing use of here, but which goes all the way back to *Pocket Full of Rain*, is the superimposition of dialogue on detailed long shots of buildings or streets in the city. How does the relative richness of detail of the *ligne claire* approach help this kind of punctuation of conversation scenes?

It's just to give visual variation to long conversation scenes. There are different ways to do this. You can have the characters do things, like lighting a cigarette, or you can have exterior shots with word balloons superimposed. The last device will, of course, give an impression of where the story takes place, but also, hopefully, create some sort of mood, if, let's say, it's a night scene. There's something cinematic about it, I guess, whether it's *ligne claire* or not.

I also think the book makes use of color to rather distinctive effect. How was working for color different from your earlier work, and what was the process like — how much did you supervise the coloring?

I don't think my drawing style changed much because of the color. The one thing I learned is to close all the lines to make it easier for the colorist to fill in the colors in Photoshop. Also, *ligne claire* often looks better in color anyway. I think I was very lucky in getting Hubert as colorist. I asked him to do flat, muted colors, and that seems to fit with what he wants to do. In the first album,

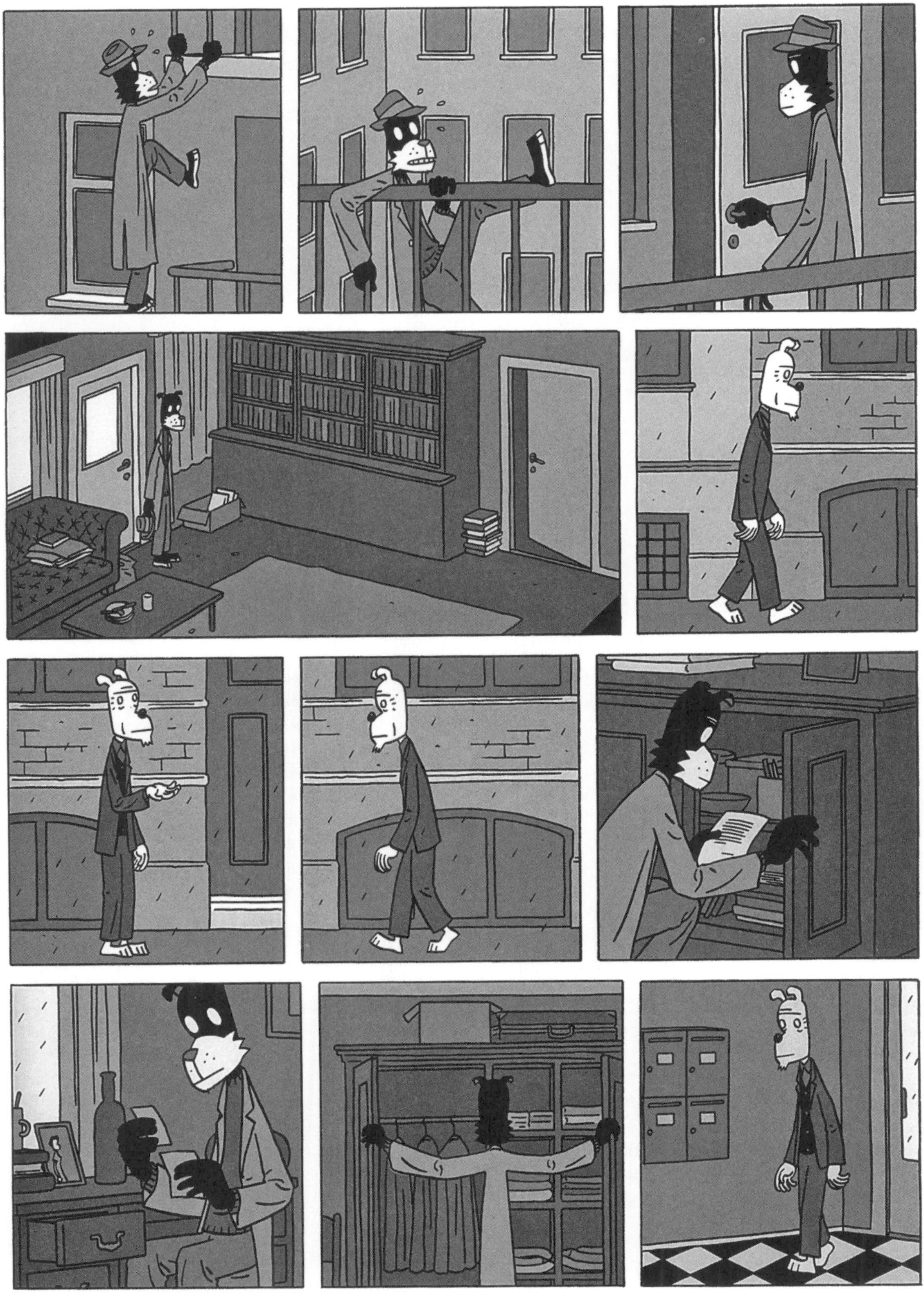

Opposite: Jason tries his hand at Hitchcockian suspense in this sequence from *Why Are You Doing This?* [©2005 Jason]

I asked for some changes, but I've pretty much learned to stay out of his way. There have been changes I've asked for, but then looking at the printed book I've realized that his choice was better and that I should have shut up. It's only when there are direct mistakes that I let him know.

I'm assuming he was brought in by Carabas. What's his background? Is he also a cartoonist?

I've met him a couple of times, but we haven't talked that much. The comments I have about the coloring go through my publisher. I don't know what kind of background he has, but I know that he's also a successful scriptwriter for other cartoonists.

***Why Are You Doing This?* is a rather somber story — along with *Hey Wait ...* and *The Iron Wagon* probably your most somber. What made you decide to go in this direction with your first color album, rather than do something more, I don't know, humorous — like your classic models, and a lot of the work you'd been doing previously?**

I don't really find the story to be that somber. There is humor, like in the dinner scene. The story itself is somewhere between a pastiche and a parody. It's not completely straight. It's a collection of all the clichés I could think of from that kind of movie. To have the main character wake up next to a dead body — it has nothing to do with reality; it's a movie thing. That's a fun scene to me. And the female character, to trust the main character just from looking at his eyes and to bring him, a suspect of murder, home to her daughter, I mean, come on! These characters don't behave like they would in real life — they behave as if they're in a movie. The villain is obviously a movie villain. You shouldn't take the story too seriously. Some of the things they talk about are more serious, I guess. Remembering and the power of memories — are painful memories better than no memories at all? The ending goes in a darker direction, but I think it's also the most satisfying ending, more than a traditional happy ending would have been.

Yeah, I was just going to ask about Geraldine's rather surprising behavior. It seems to me that her actions, if rather unrealistic, are essential to the point the story makes about being human. It's clearly a Hollywood-type narrative turn, but you make it contrast clearly with the killer's actions at the end. It seems to me that you often subvert these kinds of clichés to a certain extent — in this case by making it a story about memory and love with moments of rather stark reckoning. What are your thoughts on the use of clichés in this way?

I like using clichés. There's one I didn't get to use in *Why Are You Doing This?*: somebody opening a drawer and there's a gun there. Something you've seen in a million films and TV series. I think there's something very powerful in an image like that. It creates certain expectations that you can choose to fulfill or not.

Right, and you end up with something that seems to me quite stark and rather moving. How can I not take it seriously?

Well, let me say I want you to take the characters seriously, and not necessarily the story. I want you to take Athos in *The Last Musketeer* seriously, even though he breathes air on Mars, and I want you to take the main characters in *I Killed Adolf Hitler* seriously, even though they travel in a time machine that takes 50 years to charge. As I said earlier, I don't necessarily see any contradiction in having serious characters, or for them to talk about serious things, but having a story full of silliness. I didn't care too much for Begnini's *Life Is Beautiful*, but I thought it was a brave attempt to look at a serious subject from a different angle.

Another thing you do in the book is to make use of a rather clichéd plot points and then leaving them hanging — I'm thinking of Vandoren's crisis of conscience when he goes to the police, but also of the ending, where we suddenly jump ahead and Geraldine makes a somewhat ambiguous remark. At other times you're very clear about what happens. What are your thoughts about ambiguity versus clarity in storytelling?

That was a conscious choice, to leave that ambiguity.

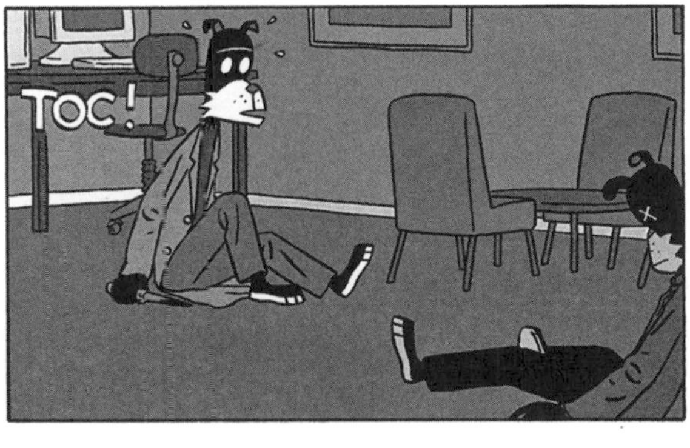
TOC!

Jason plays with clichés in *Why Are You Doing This?* [©2005 Jason]

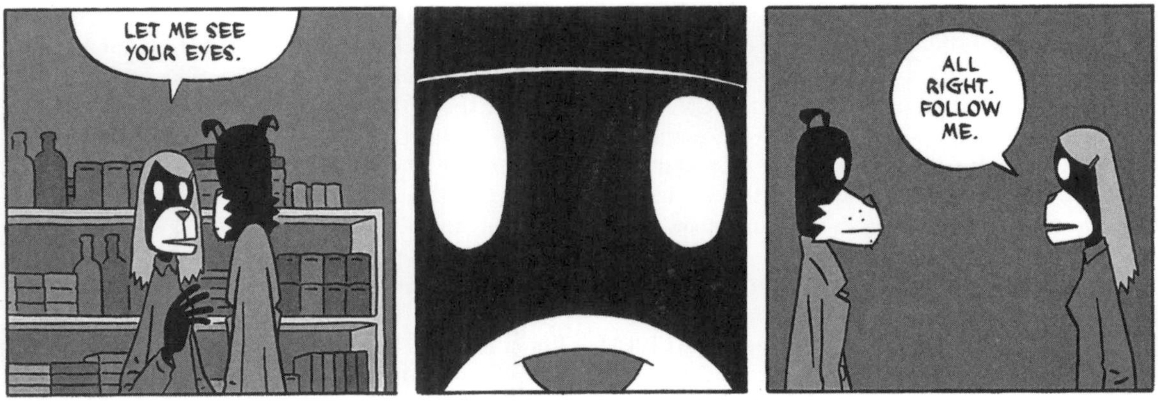
LET ME SEE YOUR EYES.
ALL RIGHT. FOLLOW ME.

From *Why Are You Doing This?* [©2005 Jason]

Does Vandoren talk to the police or not? It's not clear. It's up to each reader to decide. I'm sometimes asked what happened at the end of *Hey, Wait ...* Usually I prefer not to say anything, but there was this guy once who was really insistent, so I told him and he was almost upset: "Really? That's what happened?"

"Umm ... yeah. Well, you asked!" That's a part of the modern mindset that I find hard to understand, wanting to be told everything. Movies in the '70s often had ambiguity. That seems to be gone today. The screen-test audiences just don't allow it. They don't want have to figure things out for themselves. Is this a bad guy or a good guy? Well, maybe he's a bit of both.

The story seems to be addressing the deeper problem of whether we live in an ordered universe that we touched upon earlier. Geraldine's humane action is a central turning point in the story and is motivated by compassion, or even love. It is mirrored in the killer's action at the end, where he seems to me the same kind of character you had in *Pocket Full of Rain* — that Coen Brothers-derived unstoppable, Agent of Fate-type killer, who lately found his perhaps most compelling portrayal in their *No Country for Old Men*. Alex suggests that he acts as he does because he has never loved anyone, indicating that, if he had, he would realize he didn't have to do this, while Geraldine actually acts out of love and explains this to Alex when he asks her. You seem to be questioning whether love is what makes us free agents, or whether it is merely what seems to order the fabric of things as they are. Are we closer to some kind of Order here than in your previous books?

Nah.

All right, I thought as much. But would you say the characters are entirely free agents?

I'm glad you see all these themes in the book, and at least some of it was intended from my side. But I don't really want to say too much about it. It's not my job to explain what the book is about.

Fair enough. Having brought up the killer, I guess this is as good a point as any to talk about your literary influences. Having mentioned *No Country for Old Men*, I wondered whether there's a Cormac McCarthy influence there?

I hadn't read anything by McCarthy when I did *Why Are You Doing This?* I read *No Country for Old Men* last year, before seeing the movie. It's a great book, of course. I thought *The Road* was amazing. Incredibly bleak, but with some hope at the end. I had one problem — I couldn't help seeing in my head the villains from *Mad Max*. *The Border Trilogy* is one of the books on my bedside table; I haven't started it yet.

He seems to me to bring this cosmological perspective to his stories. He deals to an extent in archetypes, making things almost mythological. Is this something that appeals to you, specifically?

No, I don't think that's the appeal of his stories, not for me at least. My taste goes more in the direction of someone like Hemingway, even though *The Old Man and the Sea* also has that mythical quality. But McCarthy forces you to look at darkness, and there is something fascinating about that. Like the character of Chigurh in *No Country*. There is evil in this world, in human beings, and it should be reflected in literature, I guess.

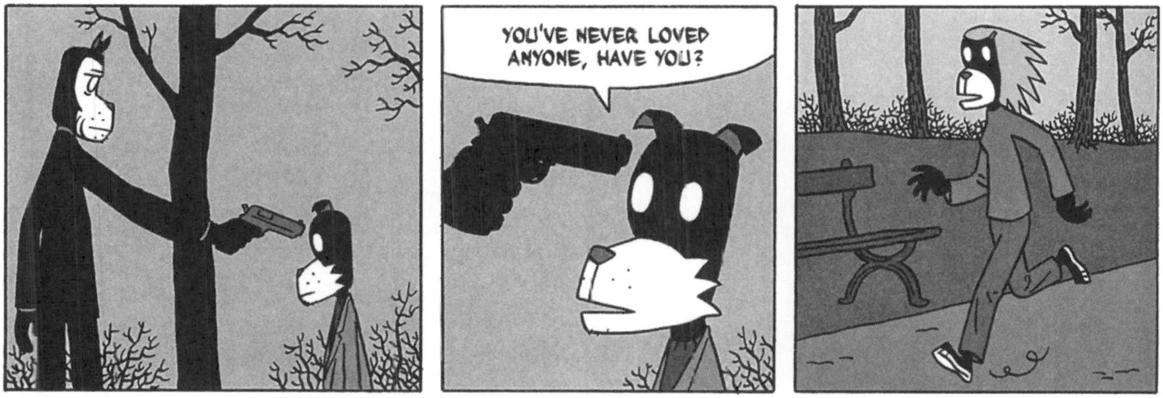
YOU'VE NEVER LOVED ANYONE, HAVE YOU?

From *Why Are You Doing This?* [©2005 Jason]

You mentioned Raymond Carver earlier. How would you describe his importance for you as a reader and writer?

I discovered his books in my early 20s, and he was an important inspiration mostly in making me realize that I didn't have to do stories about heroes and villains — I could talk about ordinary people and it would still be interesting: more interesting, even, that I could use events from my own life as basis for stories. It's obvious now, but it was a revelation then. I like his language. Just as with Hemingway, it's a very basic, meat-and-potatoes type language. I try to do the same in my comics, to avoid unnecessary effects and just tell the story as simply as possible.

I really hated the movie *Short Cuts*. The point where you stop is very important in a short story, but in the movie you'd reach that point, but then continue. One of Carver's most powerful stories is the one about this guy who kills two women with a rock. It's a big shock, and there is no explanation. Altman tried to explain it, and the explanation he came up with, that his wife is a sex phone operator, was just ridiculous. The characters Altman added who had nothing to do with Carver, the nightclub singer and her daughter, were pretty annoying. But I think what really made me react unfavorably towards the film was something Altman said in an interview, that this, the film, is the novel Carver never wrote. I'm sure that if Carver had ever written a novel it would have been much better than *Short Cuts*.

Do you also take exception to Altman's famed cynicism? Carver doesn't strike me as cynical, just stark at times.

I think that's a good point. There is nothing cynical at all about Carver. I haven't really seen enough Altman movies to talk about his view. Certainly the ending in *The Long Goodbye* was pretty cynical. But it was mostly his specific choices in *Short Cuts*, the changes he made, that bothered me.

Carver has this precision of description and evocation that he shares with Hemingway, whom we'll get to in a minute. As you say, he gets to the point, avoiding digressions or elaborations and the like. Do you have more specific thoughts on the mechanics of constructing your stories in this light?

I don't remember the name of the story, but it's the one with the baker and the cake, the one where the child is run over by a car. The parents are in the waiting room, waiting for news, and as you say, it's a very precise description of their behavior, the way they sit there, how he squeezes her hand and so on. Hemingway did the same thing, his whole tip-of-the-iceberg theory, about not showing what's under the surface. I find it to be very effective. I hope to achieve some of that by keeping the characters expressionless and not giving them thought balloons: to show only what's essential and to avoid unnecessary details. Doing things this way, having one character bow his head slightly can be pretty expressive, more so than knowing exactly what his thoughts are.

Are there any other writers who are especially important to you that you want to address?

There is a Norwegian writer, Ragnar Hovland, that I like and that I'm sure was an inspiration early on. His books are very laconic, dryly funny and he'd occasionally use surrealism. He would talk about a summer day and say it made the skeletons rise up, sit on their gravestones, tilt their heads towards the sun and wiggle their toes. That kind of writing made a big impression on me. There are scenes in his books that I've pretty much stolen and used directly in my comics. I like Paul Auster. I probably prefer his earlier books, *The New York Trilogy, Moon Palace, The Invention of Solitude. Squeeze Play*, his detective novel, is great.

He strikes me as kind of an odd man out here, writing as he does very cerebral stories. What in his work appeals to you, more specifically?

I'm sorry. I'm not really very good at explaining why I like something. I either like it or I don't. To me, his stories are sort of fairy tales. Auster has his characters go through extreme situations, but at the same time it's written in this cool, very precise language. And there is mystery in his books, not only in *The New York Trilogy* where he plays around with the detective genre, but also in a book like *Moon Palace*. The main character starves himself half to death and later walks across half of America, towards the sea, without knowing why. I found the ending of that book to be very powerful.

Would his way of approaching a story — creating a mystery founded in questions of identity and, often, rather philosophical issues — appeal to you as a possibility of writing a story in the future?

I don't know. Then it would pretty much be a Paul Auster story. I just don't think that's something I could do. For one thing, I never choose a theme before starting a story. That's like starting at the wrong end. I was thinking once of doing a story that would be Paul Auster meets Jane Austen: Jane Auster! A woman is looking for a husband and through a series of coincidences finds one who happens to be her long-lost brother. It seemed like a fun idea for a couple of seconds, but I'm sure it will remain in my notebook.

Any others?

The last couple of years I've been reading some of the old pulp guys who went on to write novels, like Charles Willeford and David Goodis. They can be kind of downbeat, a lot of those books. I just feel a connection to their work, that worldview.

Could you say a bit more about their work and why you find an affinity there?

The first books I read by them were *Down There/Shoot the Piano Player* by Goodis and *Pick Up* by Willeford. I still think those are their best. I've read some other books; not everything is brilliant. Willeford's Hoke Moseley books are very good, but they are more traditional crime novels. Apparently Goodis was not the happiest person in the world, and you can feel that in his books. There is a despair that seeps through. The same with someone like Cornell Woolrich. These are genre books meant to be cheap paperbacks, but they're also expressions of deeply personal visions, whether that was their intention or not. Probably not.

Anyway, the list of people I've never read is pretty long. Kafka, Camus, Joyce, and on and on. I feel a bit bad about it. I wish I had more time to read.

Let's talk about Hemingway. When did you first encounter his work, and what did you like about it?

I discovered Hemingway through *Corto Maltese*. In one of the stories, taking place in Italy in World War I, there is a character named Hernestway. It's not a realistic portrayal of Hemingway, but I became curious and started reading his books. He burned out pretty fast, Hemingway — he did his best stuff before turning 30. His later stuff is uneven; his style changed a bit. I prefer the early short stories, the first two novels, *The Sun also Rises* and *A Farewell to Arms*, just the sparseness of the writing. I find him to be intriguing as a person too. A complete opposite of me, Hemingway actually went out and did stuff. By the time he was 25, I'm sure he'd experienced more than I will in my whole life. And as I've talked about in *Why Are You Doing This?* and other places, I find it interesting what it means when somebody leads a rich life, but then commits suicide. Does the person with the most anecdotes win? I still don't know the answer to that.

What's your take on Hemingway's later work?

His best known later books, *For Whom the Bell Tolls* and *The Old Man and the Sea,* don't really appeal to me that much. I read *Islands in the Stream* a long time ago and seem to remember that it was uneven but with some very good parts. *Across the River and Into the Trees* is on my bedside table; I hope to get to it soon. *Garden of Eden*, published after his death, I thought was very interesting, showing a new side of him as a writer. And *A Moveable Feast*, his Paris memoirs, I think is a terrific book. Who knows how much of it is true, but it's got some great writing in it. The first half of *The Left Bank Gang* is pretty much based on it. These memoirs were written at a time when he had long ago broken his friendships with most of the people he writes about. He's being unfair and condescending to Scott Fitzgerald. Like the story of Fitzgerald worrying about his penis size and wanting Hemingway to check it out. It probably never happened, but it's such a great story that I had to include it in the comic.

I was going to ask about this macho persona Hemingway is so famous for cultivating. As you say, it is very unlike what you do. What's your take on it, and how would you describe your interest in it?

Hey, for all you know I could be involved in bar brawls all the time! I just don't make comics about it. Wouldn't be fair to the people who lost. I was reading his collection of letters and somewhere in his late 30s something happened to Hemingway, he changed. His letters are all about who he punched out, or how many animals he shot, or how many fish he caught. It's a less attractive side of Hemingway, but at the same time, you got to admire someone who manages to build a myth around himself like that. It's sort of a lost art form.

Also, there's a distinctly romantic feel to some of his writing, which I find not uncongenial to some of your work. Is this something you appreciate in him?

Sure. *A Farewell to Arms* must be one of the most romantic books ever written. People say Hemingway can't write women, but I thought Catherine in the book is just as credible as Frederic. A bit idealized maybe. And the ending was just perfect. First the newborn baby dies, then she dies, he leaves the hospital, and ... it's raining! It doesn't get any better than that.

Yeah, that ending is harrowing, and very moving too. He even dips into stream of consciousness at times, but without it taking over. It's rather impressionistic in a way, conveying the emotional turmoil the protagonist is going through by way of what he sees, hears, smells, tastes, etc. To me, Hemingway is best in these impressionistic passages, like when he describes the motionless, dark baby — it's just deeply unsettling — or more mutedly, the way the entire book seems drenched in rain. Do you give any thought to this kind of sensory or atmospheric suggestion when drawing your pages?

There is a great stream-of-consciousness monologue towards the end. "What if she dies? Nobody dies in childbirth any more. What if she dies? She won't die. But what if she dies?" It goes on and on. It's very effective. So you can choose some specific moments and go into people's heads. And then, after she dies, he's again very objective and restrained.

If I've learned anything from that particular book, it's not to be afraid of sad endings. It's just clearly the right choice. The whole book is about war and death. They try to run away from it, but they can't. I'm sorry to keep bringing up movies all the time, but it's what comes to mind — *War of the Worlds* by Spielberg: If you use images from 9/11 in a movie there should be a price. You can't have everybody survive in the end. OK, save the little girl, but at least kill off the son. There is something false in saying that everything will be all right in the end. That's not how life is. And a sad ending is just more memorable — it sticks with you for longer. A happy ending is telling the reader to forget everything he has read up till now, to not think about it.

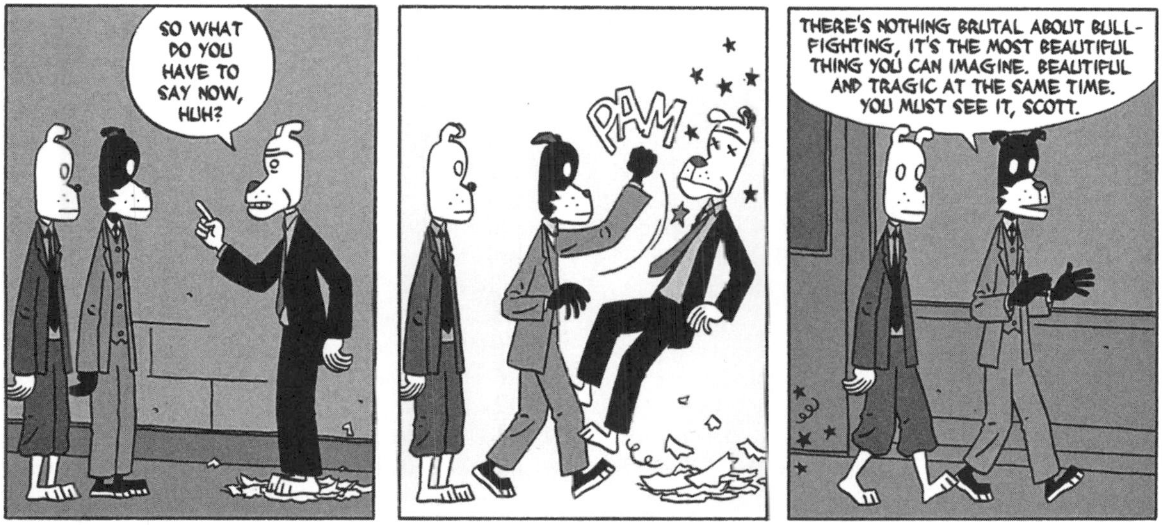
SO WHAT DO YOU HAVE TO SAY NOW, HUH?
PAM
THERE'S NOTHING BRUTAL ABOUT BULL-FIGHTING, IT'S THE MOST BEAUTIFUL THING YOU CAN IMAGINE. BEAUTIFUL AND TRAGIC AT THE SAME TIME. YOU MUST SEE IT, SCOTT.

Jason's characterization of Hemingway: from *The Left Bank Gang*. [©2005 Editions de Tournon/Jason]

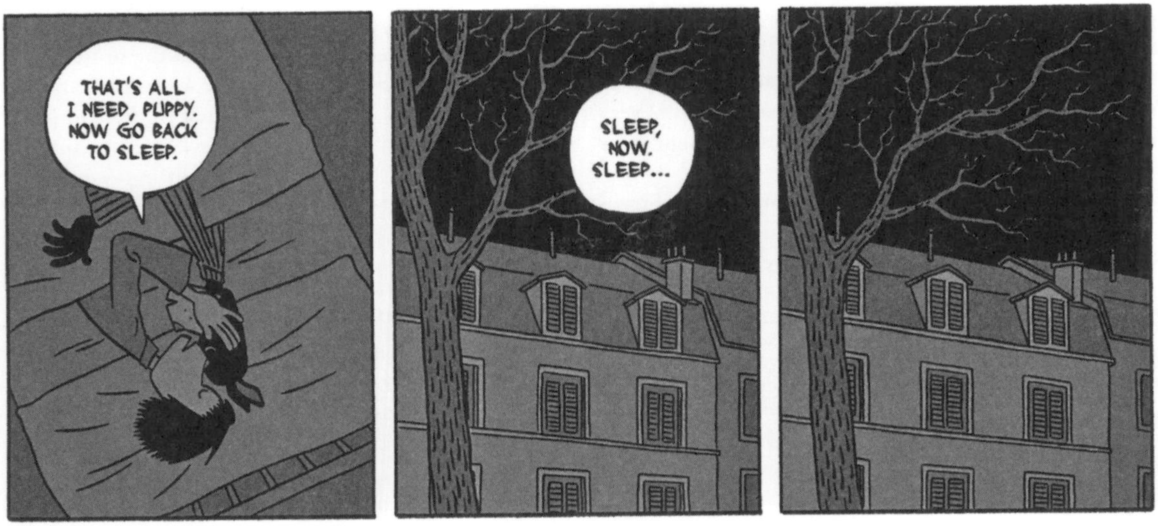
THAT'S ALL I NEED, PUPPY. NOW GO BACK TO SLEEP.
SLEEP, NOW. SLEEP...

Hemingway and Hadley: from *The Left Bank Gang*. [©2005 Editions de Tournon/Jason]

In talking about impressionism, I was thinking about sensory evocation on the page. Your general approach to *ligne claire* leaves things very bare and understated, but every once in a while you have pages such as the one adapted from *A Moveable Feast* where Hemingway sits at a café, drawing a girl. I find this page very atmospheric, and in a different way from the effective but often very sparse understatement of your work. What's your thinking about this kind of evocation on the page?

I was happy with that page, and yes, it's taken almost directly from *A Moveable Feast*. There is a scene there where Hemingway sits in a café, writing, and notices a girl. I'm not sure if it means anything, it doesn't push the plot forward, it's mostly, as you say, for the atmosphere. In some ways, it's another little homage to Hugo Pratt. He was very good at creating scenes like that, to stop the story and have everybody look at the moon or something. It's something that should be done carefully, to find the right place for it. If you overdo it, it will lose its impact.

You said you hadn't read Joyce, but have you read any of the other authors in Hemingway's Parisian circle — Scott Fitzgerald, Ezra Pound?

I've read a couple of books by Fitzgerald. *The Great Gatsby* and *Tender Is the Night*. They're both fine, but the sort of exquisite prose that Fitzgerald writes doesn't appeal to me in the same way as Hemingway. Ezra Pound I've never read. Hemingway is clearly the main character in *The Left Bank Gang*. We see the main story through his eyes — the other characters had to fit certain parts, so I didn't bother learning too much about them.

I'm assuming that *The Left Bank Gang* grew out of a deeper fascination with these authors in this setting at this particular point in time, but at the same time it seems pretty high-concept: "Hemingway and Co. as cartoonists in Paris, pulling a heist *Reservoir Dogs* style." How did this angle suggest itself?

I had read a lot of books about Hemingway, different biographies. There is a series of five books by Michael Reynolds going through the whole of Hemingway's life. They're very well written, and especially one of them, *The Paris Years*, was an inspiration. Also, *A Moveable Feast* and the collection of Hemingway's letters. It just struck me as a great place for a story, Paris in the '20s. It was a very exciting period, and lots of memorable individuals walking around. I didn't have the guts to try to do a true biography about Hemingway.

The idea of making him a cartoonist gave me a lot more freedom. I could use certain facts, but I could also invent things. So I had the concept for a long time, but not the story. Then I watched *The Killing* by Stanley Kubrick one night, really enjoyed it, and wanted to do something in that style — to have one event seen from different perspectives. Those two ideas folded into one. I don't remember if it was an instant thing or if it happened slowly. But I couldn't help seeing how my characters fit into the plot of the movie. Hemingway in the Sterling Hayden part,

Fitzgerald as Elisha Cook, Jr., and Zelda as Marie Windsor. Ezra Pound seemed to fit as the traitor since later, in World War II, he ended up on the side of Mussollini and the fascists.

So the idea was to split the album in two, to have the Paris in the '20s stuff and then have the heist in the second part. Looking back on it now, I think that might have been a mistake. I think the first half of the book worked out better than expected. It's funnier than I thought it would be. So the heist in the second part that was meant to be the climax is almost anticlimactic. I wish I had kept up what was going on in the first half, the comedy part, and maybe actually skipped the heist part, and then rather have had the whole group go down to Pamplona, like in *The Sun also Rises*. But I don't know. They talk about not having money, and it's building up to something, so the heist is maybe necessary.

Your portrayal of Hemingway is rather sympathetic; basically you present him as a balanced, responsible man who makes a bad choice. It seems obvious that he would be the one to come up with the plan, but he's much less gung ho about it than one might have expected. How did you arrive at this portrayal?

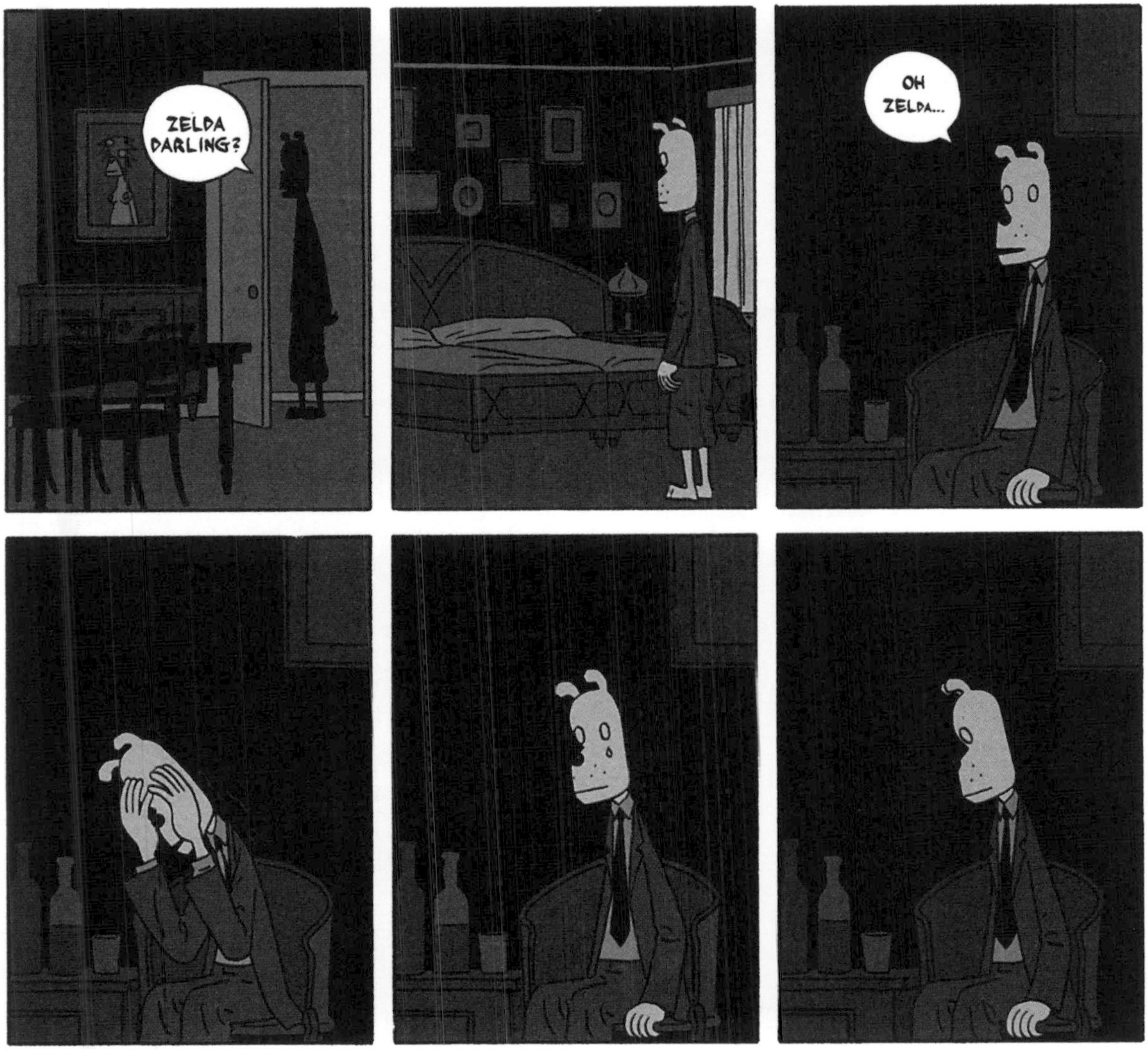
ZELDA DARLING?
OH ZELDA...

Jason's Fitzgerald registers one of his many betrayals in *The Left Bank Gang*. [©2005 Editions de Tournon/Jason]

Well, my characters are just not very gung ho. The ending of the book is bittersweet if you know what actually happened. Hemingway left Hadley for another woman. It's Scott and Zelda that stuck together, almost all the way. Zelda ended up in an asylum and Scott went to Hollywood where he eventually met someone else. I tried to leave small hints in the comic. Scott Fitzgerald became an alcoholic. Zelda died in a fire. And Pound ended up as a traitor.

But since the comic is mostly based on *A Moveable Feast*, Hemingway is necessarily the hero. His memoirs were written 30 years after the events he writes about, and you can feel he has kind of an agenda. At that time, there had been a re-evaluation of the work and significance of Fitzgerald, the opinion being that it had been underestimated. At the same time, a lot of Hemingway's later work had been met with lukewarm criticism. That might explain the condescending portrayal of Scott and Zelda Fitzgerald in the book. Zelda and Hemingway never liked each other. Hemingway thought Zelda ruined Scott's gift as a writer. On the other hand, Hadley comes off as almost angelic in the book. He clearly has regrets about what happened, him leaving her. So you end up realizing that Hemingway was just human, like everybody else, having both good and bad sides.

So, can *The Left Bank Gang* be described as a kind of magnanimous validation of Hemingway's self-representation in *A Moveable Feast*? A way of accepting and perpetuating the truth in his sentiments, if not the events, as he tells it?

You might be reading too much into it. Actually, another inspiration for the comic was the film *The Moderns*, by Alan Rudolph. It's also set in Paris in the '20s and Hemingway appears as a character. I didn't really care too much for the film, but I liked that it didn't even try to give a realistic portrayal of the period. It's clearly a fantasy. Even the characters: Hemingway is presented almost like a buffoon, if I remember correctly, walking around and spouting these quasi-philosophical statements. But that's fine. You can't recreate somebody's life anyway — you weren't there. You might as well use your imagination and run with it. Sometimes that might bring you closer to the truth.

By the way, have you read Dave Sim's idiosyncratic takes on Hemingway/Mary and Scott/Zelda in *Cerebus*?

No, I haven't.

All right, I think it's better left alone then. At the beginning of the interview, we talked about the scene with Joyce and Hemingway discussing their vocation as cartoonists. To what extent would you say that choosing to make the characters cartoonists was a way of discussing your own vocation?

Not too much. It's not a big part of the story. That would be interesting for maybe five people. There was the

This'll give you something to dream about tonight.

An example of Jason's silent-movie-intertitle technique from *The Living and The Dead*. [©2006 Jason]

Jason felt that black and white was the most suitable medium with which to tell the story of *The Living and The Dead*. [©2006 Jason]

conversation between Hemingway and Joyce about the financial insecurity involved in cartooning. And in another scene, Joyce talks about not filling in every inch of every panel, to let it breathe, something I agree with. But that's pretty much it. I'm a bit suspicious of novelists who only write about novelists, like that is all they know. I hope I don't end up cartooning about cartooning.

The next thing you did was The *Living and the Dead*. How did that come about, and why the shift in format, style and publisher?

In many ways it's a follow up to *Tell Me Something*. It has the same silent film text plates as that story, so it made sense to have it published by my first publishers, Jippi and Atrabile. I got the idea the last time I lived in Brussels. They have a silent movie cinema there, with live piano music, so I would be watching lots of films there, especially Buster Keaton. My apartment was in the middle of the prostitution district. The girls would be standing on the pavement right in front of my building. They would often proposition me when I came home from the studio in the evening, and I would have to say, "Thank you, that's very tempting, but no, I live here." That's where the female character in *The Living and the Dead* came from. The whole concept of the story was: What would a silent zombie film have looked like? I kept thinking it would be a great idea for some movie director to shoot the film in black and white, scratch it and make it look like it had

been made in the '20s. But I don't know any movie directors, and I don't know if there are any producers today who would spend money on a black-and-white, silent film, so I made it myself as a comic.

Which are your zombie favorites and what's the appeal of the genre for you?

My favorite zombie film would be *Return of the Living Dead* by O'Bannon. To me it has the right mix of horror and comedy. Of Romero, I like *Night of the Living Dead*. *Dawn of the Dead* doesn't appeal to me at all; I find it to be an ugly and unpleasant film. I prefer the remake, especially the opening and the ending. The use of the Johnny Cash song is brilliant. The whole part at the mall is maybe more uneven. I haven't seen any of Romero's other films. *Shaun of the Dead* I didn't like. I didn't find it particularly funny. And it's shot in a style that already looks dated. I thought the beginning of *28 Days Later* was good, but then later at the army base, it gets pretentious, when they start having philosophical debates. There should be a rule: Don't make a pretentious zombie film. To me there is something silly about the zombie genre. How can you take it seriously? When they start trying to squeeze political massages into these movies, I just don't get it. Who wants to see a zombie film and learn something?

In terms of getting your work out there and getting reactions, how is it different to publish a black-and-white book with Atrabile and Jippi, compared to the color albums? I'm asking partly because except for dialogue, your approach doesn't seem either more or less "commercial" or broad for either. Do you make any distinction based on perceived audience?

Why Are You Doing This? was an attempt at a more commercial album, drawn in the traditional Franco-Belgian style, but I don't really see any big differences between the later color albums and the black-and-white books. I have the same freedom. My editor at Carabas doesn't approve storylines in advance. He has never said, "No, you can't do that." It depends on the story: some should be in color and some, like *The Living and the Dead*, should be in black and white. A color album will automatically appeal to a wider audience and I have to admit I have that in mind. I thought France would be like heaven for comics, that everybody would read everything, but there are still readers who are just not interested in picking up a black-and-white book.

Your next color album was *I Killed Adolf Hitler* ...

I had the opening scene in my head a long time: the

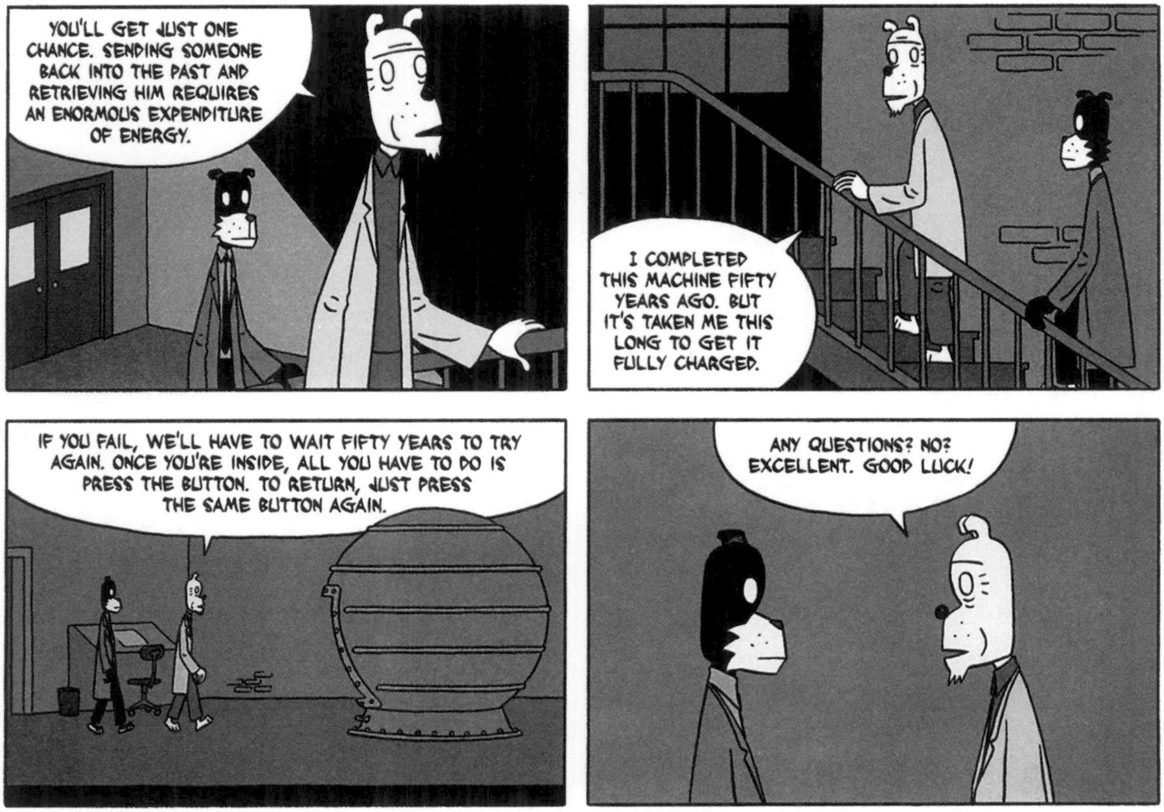
YOU'LL GET JUST ONE CHANCE. SENDING SOMEONE BACK INTO THE PAST AND RETRIEVING HIM REQUIRES AN ENORMOUS EXPENDITURE OF ENERGY.
I COMPLETED THIS MACHINE FIFTY YEARS AGO. BUT IT'S TAKEN ME THIS LONG TO GET IT FULLY CHARGED.
IF YOU FAIL, WE'LL HAVE TO WAIT FIFTY YEARS TO TRY AGAIN. ONCE YOU'RE INSIDE, ALL YOU HAVE TO DO IS PRESS THE BUTTON. TO RETURN, JUST PRESS THE SAME BUTTON AGAIN.
ANY QUESTIONS? NO? EXCELLENT. GOOD LUCK!

From *I Killed Adolf Hitler*. [©2007 Editions de Tournon/Jason]

hired killer in a hotel room with a rifle out the window, waiting for the victim to appear, and a woman lying on the bed. She was supposed to say, "I'm bored," and have this long monologue, but then I used that in *The Left Bank Gang*, so I had to change it. So instead she says, "I'm horny," and has this long monologue. I just thought it was an intriguing opening. I also wanted to do a story with a time machine, to see what opportunities that would bring. And to go back in time to kill Adolf Hitler — it's such an obvious idea. I hoped I could have some fun with it. Originally, the story was meant to be longer; the time machine would have been used several times and brought back Abraham Lincoln and John F. Kennedy. Hitler would have an army of Martian Nazis. But I lost interest in that and chose to focus on the killer and the woman. What would happen if they didn't find Hitler?

It's another genre romp with a love story at its heart. This seems very much to have become your signature kind of story. We've already discussed your interests in pop cultural genres, but what attracts you to the love story, apart from the obvious fact that it's a universal theme?

I don't really have any explanation for that. It makes a good story, I guess. Those are often very idealized love stories, like in the movies I grew up watching. It's not about the everyday relationship stuff that you've already seen a million times on *Seinfeld*. I find that to be a bit tedious in comics. But it's something I'm moving away from a bit. There's the danger of starting to repeat yourself. I want to try to explore other storylines.

To what extent do you worry about this? How do you keep things interesting for yourself?

How many times can you tell a boy meets girl-type story and have one of them die at the end before it becomes a formula? There is a definite danger there. Three of the

Opposite: These panels are from *I Killed Adolf Hitler*'s opening sequence. [©2007 Editions de Tournon/Jason]

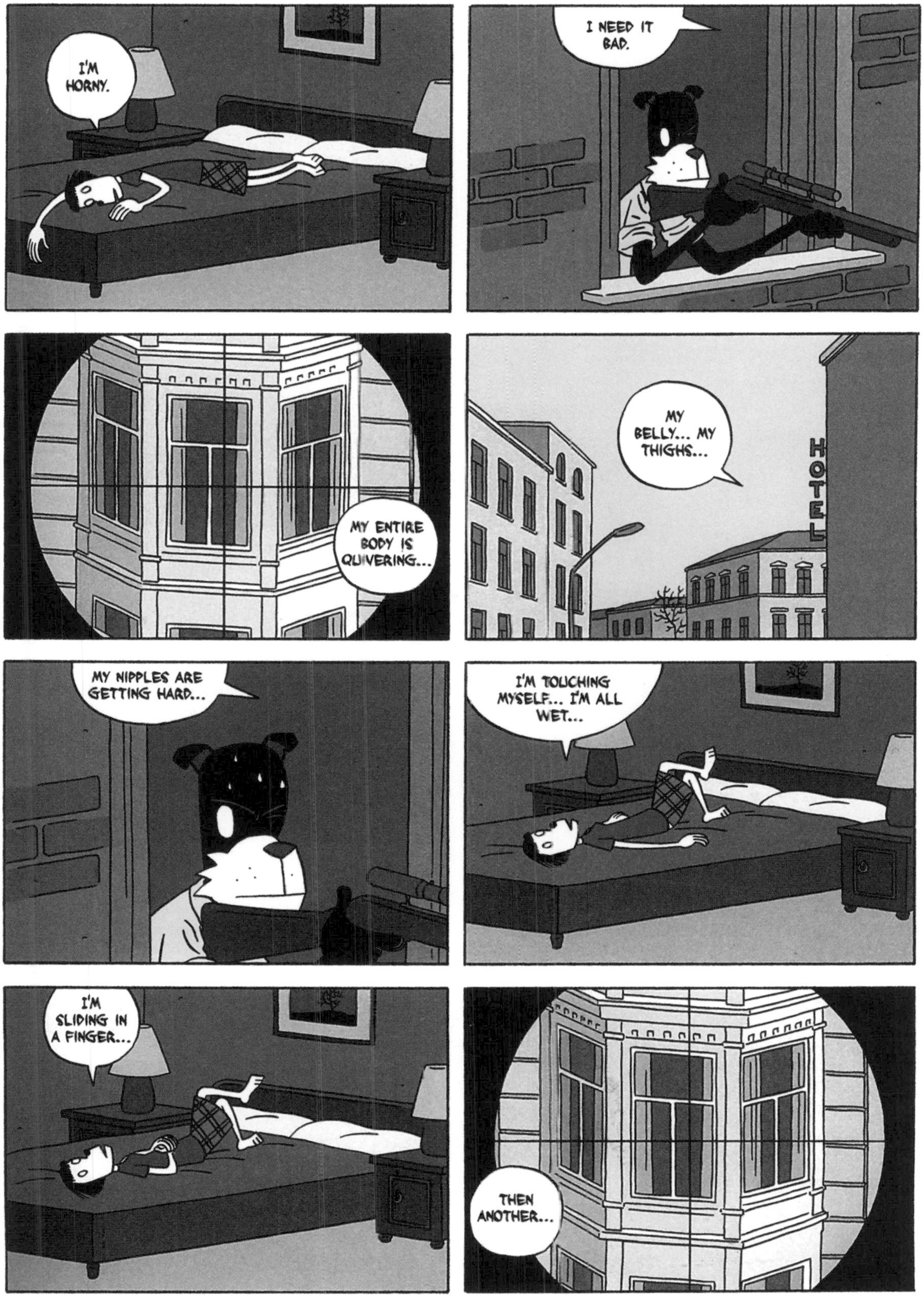
I'M HORNY.
I NEED IT BAD.
MY ENTIRE BODY IS QUIVERING...
MY BELLY... MY THIGHS...
HOTEL
MY NIPPLES ARE GETTING HARD...
I'M TOUCHING MYSELF... I'M ALL WET...
I'M SLIDING IN A FINGER...
THEN ANOTHER...

color albums have ended with the main character dying. It's a great way to end a story, of course, to have someone die, but it shouldn't be predictable. It's something I have to be careful about in the future.

One reason I'm asking is that you're relatively prolific, producing at least one book a year. Is speed of production ever a concern, both in terms of coming up with good ideas and making a living, or does it just come naturally?

I do about two, 2 1/2 pages a week. That's not too prolific, at least compared with a lot of the French cartoonists. But I don't do much illustration work, and I have rent to pay, so one album a year is the minimum. For the moment, coming up with ideas is not a problem, but I'm sure it will happen some day. When that happens, I might regret not taking better care of the old ideas, and not having made a book like *The Left Bank Gang* a 200-page graphic novel. I will probably go in that direction, and try to do longer work, but at the same time, what do you do if you spend five years on a book, and end up not liking it? If I don't like a given 48-page album, at least I've only wasted five or six months.

Right. Let's look at *I Killed Adolf Hitler*. The pages seem to me very sparse, even less adorned than the other color albums. It makes for a bleak atmosphere. Was this a conscious choice?

No, it wasn't conscious. It was mostly that the story took place in Berlin and I was somewhere else. I had some photographs to look at, but mostly exteriors. I had almost no interiors, except for a bar where I took some photos. I repeat the same angles over and over, that might create a bleaker, more claustrophobic atmosphere.

Why's the story set in Berlin?

Hitler was in Berlin. I thought it made sense to set the story there. And I had this idea that each album should take place in a new city. I'd already done Brussels and Paris. It may have been a mistake — I had never been to Berlin before. I went there for five or six days, walking around taking photographs, but the architecture is less typical than in Brussels and Paris. I found it to be harder to capture on paper, and towards the end of the album I just gave up, and buildings in the background just became nondescript buildings.

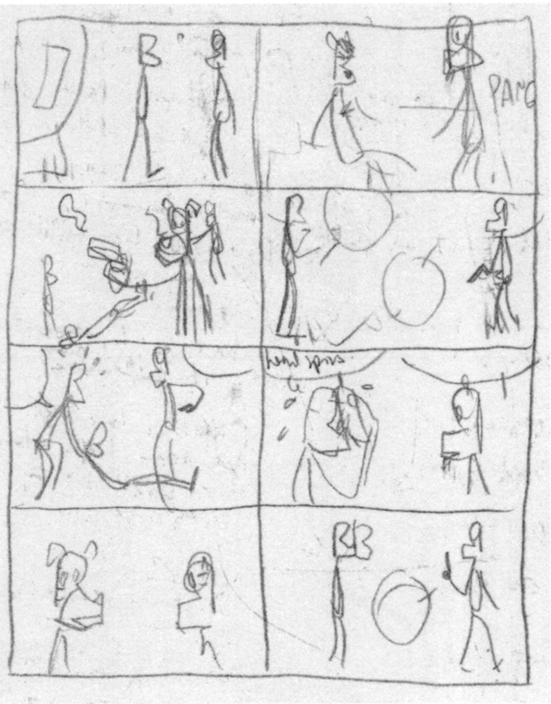

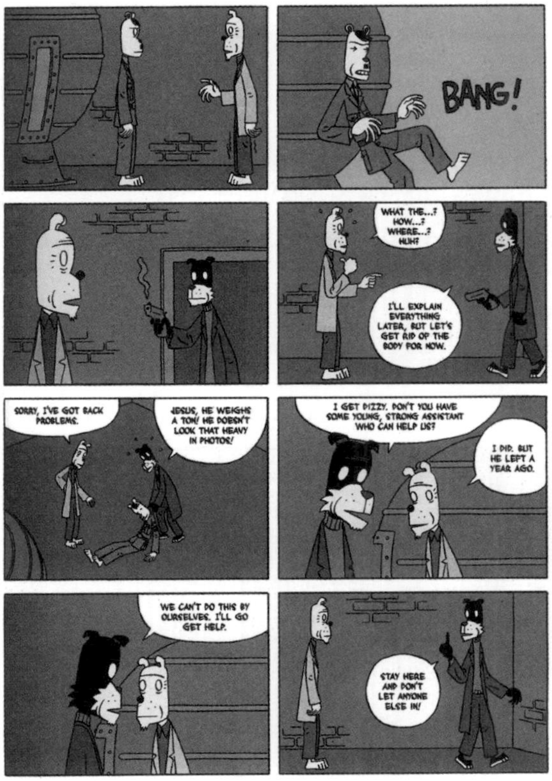
BANG!
WHAT THE...? HOW...? WHERE...? HUH?
I'LL EXPLAIN EVERYTHING LATER, BUT LET'S GET RID OF THE BODY FOR NOW.
SORRY, I'VE GOT BACK PROBLEMS.
JESUS, HE WEIGHS A TON! HE DOESN'T LOOK THAT HEAVY IN PHOTOS!
I GET DIZZY. DON'T YOU HAVE SOME YOUNG, STRONG ASSISTANT WHO CAN HELP US?
I DID. BUT HE LEFT A YEAR AGO.
WE CAN'T DO THIS BY OURSELVES. I'LL GO GET HELP.
STAY HERE AND DON'T LET ANYONE ELSE IN!

Some samples of Jason's process: thumbnails versus the completed page in *I Killed Adolf Hitler*. [©2007 Editions de Tournon/Jason]

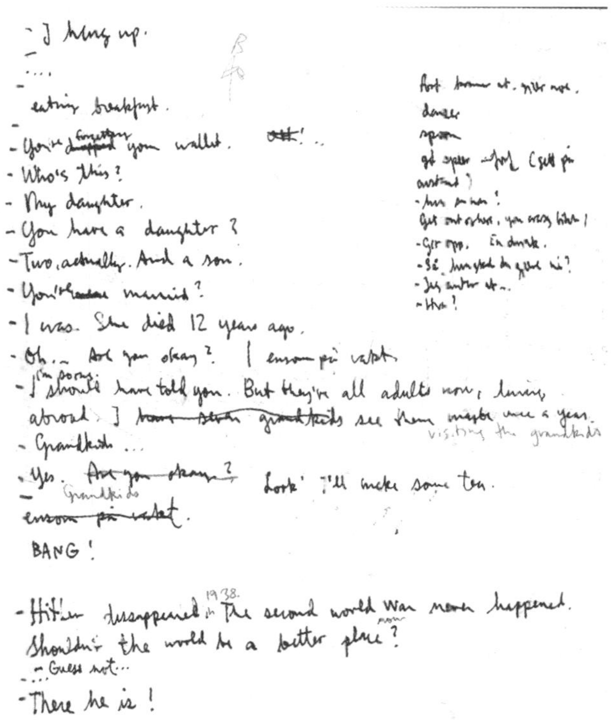
- I hung up.
eating breakfast.
- You've forgotten your wallet.
- Who's this?
- My daughter.
- You have a daughter?
- Two, actually. And a son.
- You're married?
- I was. She died 12 years ago.
- Oh... Are you okay?
- Grandkids...
Look! I'll make some tea.
BANG!
- Hitler disappeared in 1938. The second world war never happened. Shouldn't the world be a better place?
- Guess not...
- There he is!

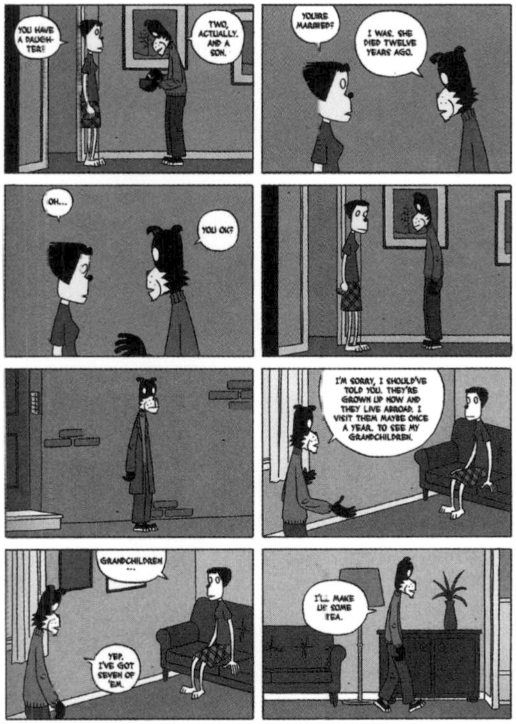
YOU HAVE A DAUGH-TER?
TWO, ACTUALLY. AND A SON.
YOU'RE MARRIED?
I WAS. SHE DIED TWELVE YEARS AGO.
OH...
YOU OK?
I'M SORRY, I SHOULD'VE TOLD YOU. THEY'RE GROWN UP NOW AND THEY LIVE ABROAD. I VISIT THEM MAYBE ONCE A YEAR. TO SEE MY GRANDCHILDREN.
GRANDCHILDREN...
YEP. I'VE GOT SEVEN OF 'EM.
I'LL MAKE UP SOME TEA.

Courtesy of Jason: a script, for comparison against the completed *I Killed Adolf Hitler* page. [©2007 Editions de Tournon/Jason]

Each color album has a distinct tone to its color, with this one — again — being the harshest. Is this entirely Hubert's doing, or do you have rather specific color schemes in mind when you're drawing your stories?

No, that was all Hubert. I was very happy with his job, the bluish tone he kept for a lot of the book. He has freedom to do what he wants, to adjust his style to the particular story in each album. For *The Last Musketeer*, he was influenced by the coloring in the old *Flash Gordon* comics, and used considerably stronger colors than he usually does, and I thought that was very effective, the contrast between the French sequences and the ones taking place on Mars.

One thing the sparseness of especially this comic, and 'naturalistic' elements such as the swans on the last page made me think of is whether you spend much time drawing from life or whether you focus more exclusively on cartooning? It would seem to me the latter, from this look your comics have: rather simple decor and efficient, suggestive storytelling.

The swans are based on a photograph. I do very little drawing from life. Lewis Trondheim encouraged me to get a sketchbook, and I kept one for a month or two, but now it's gathering dust on a shelf somewhere. I feel a bit bad about it. If you're an artist you should have a sketchbook, right? But as I said, I don't really derive any pleasure from drawing. When I pick up a pencil or a pen it's for work: for comics or for illustration assignments. The thing is, I enjoy looking at sketchbooks, by people like Robert Crumb, Chris Ware or Dupuy and Berberian, but I find it hard to keep one myself.

Yeah, I was actually thinking of Lewis, because he described it to me as something of a revelation for him when he started sketching from life, and it has certainly changed his art in interesting ways.

Lewis Trondheim has showed me how he works now: no penciling, just drawing directly in a sketchbook. I'd like to try something like that. He has been an inspiration a long time, Lewis. I had already started trying out animal characters when I discovered his work, but it was like sign that I was going in the right direction. He was sort of a Moses coming down from the mountain with the Ten Commandments.

If the drawing just feels like work, what are the parts to creating comics you enjoy the most?

My favorite part of cartooning is the early penciling, placing the characters, trying to create rhythm and balance on the page and solving the storytelling problems. My least favorite part is drawing the backgrounds. My method of drawing is pretty much postponing drawing the backgrounds for as long as possible. I usually work on eight or 10 pages at the same time, drawing the characters, often standing around in nothing. I ink that, and then finally I will have to start on the backgrounds. In the beginning, I might have had some grand ideas about, say, drawing a complicated street scene, but at the end I'm just sick and tired of the whole thing, and go, "Eh! I'll just make it a brick wall," and draw in some bricks.

In your color albums, you make use of the same characters in different roles, a bit like Tezuka's so-called "Star System." The same guy is cast in starring roles in *Why Are You Doing This?*, *The Left Bank Gang*, *I Killed Adolf Hitler* and *The Last Musketeer*. Like the bird guy earlier. What made you decide to do this, and what do you think it adds to the comics?

Originally, when I started the second album, *The Left Bank Gang*, Hemingway was supposed to look different, but I was happy with the design of the main character from *Why Are You Doing This?*, so I just kept him. My characters are basically five or six different types. I may do variations on the noses and ears, but they look like each other anyway. So I thought, "Why not keep the same characters from album to album?" It will be like the stock company of actors in the John Ford films. Here's the John Wayne character, and there are the Ward Bond and Ben Johnson characters.

Your next book was *The Last Musketeer*, which as you said takes off old *Flash Gordon* comics and other classic SF and mixes in the Alexandre Dumas musketeers. This would seem to me the wildest of your mix-and-match of pop-culture stock elements yet, with less of a realistic aspect to it than the previous books.

I got the initial idea from watching old film serials like *Rocketmen on the Moon* and *Flash Gordon*. Visually the emperor in the book is based on Ming, but actually the one in *Undersea Kingdom* was more of an inspiration. He would keep saying things like, "Nothing will stand in the way of my conquering the world!" "How dare you question my demands?!" and so on. That was the beginning of the book, wanting to write dialogue like that. "Look, the Earthman is getting away! Stop him, you fools!" How can you not love dialogue like that? I'm sure it would be easy to make fun of old science-fiction films and serials, with their clumsy special effects and women with '40s hairdos, but to me that is part of the charm. I would never want to do a parody of something like that. This is more of a pastiche.

I'm not quite sure where the musketeer came from. He came later. I had to read *The Three Musketeers* to figure out how he should talk. My characters don't talk much, but Athos is the exception, and I had a lot of fun writing his monologues. In some ways I consider the book a failure. I think I teamed him up with the princess and the general too quickly. He had to shut up around them and became less interesting. I shouldn't have killed off the robot so soon. They should have had more adventures together, and Athos could have kept up his monologue. At the end they win over the emperor too easily. It should have been more difficult. I had marked off three pages for the confrontation between Athos and Rochefort, thinking that it would be enough, but I should have had at least one more, to give the fight a more epic feel. That's the problem with the French 48-page albums — they can't

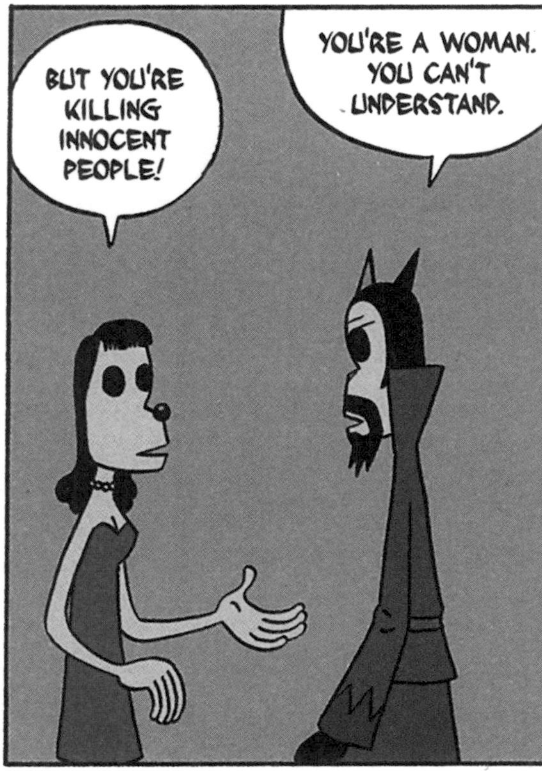
BUT YOU'RE KILLING INNOCENT PEOPLE!
YOU'RE A WOMAN. YOU CAN'T UNDERSTAND.

From *The Last Musketeer*. [©2007 Jason]

be 49 pages.

The book has made me question the way I work: Improvising the story and not writing a full script. There will always be small things you wish you had done differently. It's a bit like writing a novel and then to not do any rewrites. Comics are very hard to edit once they are finished. If there are two panels on page 36 you'd like to take out, you can't do it without putting in something else. I think writing a full script would bore me, but perhaps I could at least sketch out the rest of the story when I was halfway or two thirds into the book. It would probably make a better, less uneven album. Or maybe not. Every time I start an album I think, "OK, this is the one. This is the album that will be perfect." And for a while I thought *The Last Musketeer* would be it — I'm very happy with the first 15 pages. But it never happens. When you're drawing the last couple of pages, you're usually just sick and tired of the whole thing and just want to finish it, so you can start on the next one.

Would you say that working in the album format feels constricting in terms of developing your work, or does the format's relative rigidity help you focus on more important things, creatively?

So far it hasn't felt constricting. I'm not much of a writer, really. 48 pages or around 70 pages of the six-panel grid feel about the right length for me. It's kind of the equivalent of a 75-minute movie, not a 300-page novel. It's very seldom that I find myself thinking, "Ooh, I wish I had more pages." But obviously, doing a longer story is the next challenge, after writing dialogue.

Would a long-form comic, or other formats, be viable options at the moment?

I have a couple of more ideas for 48-page albums, in the same series as the other ones, but I feel it's time for me to move on. The next book, *Low Moon*, a collection of the story in *The New York Times Magazine* and four other short stories, will be of a smaller size, with four panels per page. "Low Moon" itself will be edited so that what was one page of 12 panels in the magazine will be three pages of four panels in the book. I had that in mind when I was drawing. I really like the smaller book size — it's more intimate somehow, and I want to do other books in that style.

How have you found working in the French market? How does it compare to what you know elsewhere? Are there some limitations to go with all the obvious advantages it has over almost any other market?

The biggest problem with the French market is over-production. A lot of new albums come out each week. You might be exhibited on display for a week or two, but then there will be new albums to take your place. If you are Bilal or Tardi you don't have a problem, people will always know you have a new book out, but for everybody else it's a difficult to stay visible. It's very easy for your book to just drown and disappear. Luckily, I also have the Norwegian and the American markets. Those are the three markets where I make money. There are some translations into other languages, but that's more like a bonus.

I've become a bit disillusioned with French comics since I moved here. Considering their long history and tradition for comics, it's easy to believe that all the publications here are of high quality, but frankly there is a lot of crap. Genre stuff with half-naked girls on the covers. I look at some of these books when I visit the comic-book stores, and there are just so many of them with ugly drawings and ugly computer coloring. I find it hard to imagine who buys these things. You have to search to find the good stuff.

Returning to the concerns you mentioned you have about being able to write, Athos definitely seems like an example of you working on that, and rather successfully so, I think. What are your thoughts in terms of further developing this part of your comics vocabulary?

Of all the characters I've created, Athos is probably my favorite. I enjoyed writing his dialogue and creating this figure that is both a bit pathetic and endearing at the same time — the way he refuses to acknowledge reality. I had that voice in my head right from the beginning. So I'm a bit bummed that I wasn't happier with the book as it ended up.

I find any kind of exposition hard to write. There is a lot of it in *Why Are You Doing This?* and most of it sounds clumsy. There's that whole cliché of characters who write themselves. Sometimes that happens and it is very gratifying when it does — when you write a piece of dialogue, read it and wonder, 'Where did that come from?' But this doesn't happen all the time. I still consider myself to be more of a drawer than a writer. So it will be a challenge to try longer narratives and more complex characters.

So far, I've mostly played around with clichés and archetypes: the villain, the misunderstood monster, the mad scientist. A longer story requires more rounded, three-dimensional characters — someone you can recognize and identify with, someone you will care about. I'm not talking about going all Bergman or Dostoevsky. I will probably continue working within some genre, but maybe do

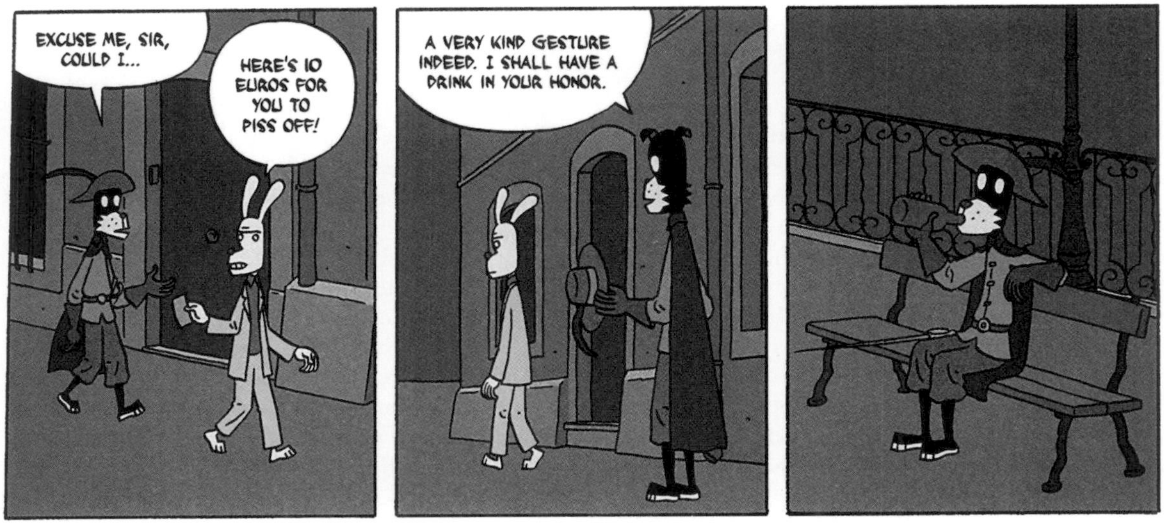
EXCUSE ME, SIR, COULD I...
HERE'S 10 EUROS FOR YOU TO PISS OFF!
A VERY KIND GESTURE INDEED. I SHALL HAVE A DRINK IN YOUR HONOR.

Jason enjoyed Athos' "voice." [©2007 Jason]

something less playful, more for real.

***The Last Musketeer* — and to an extent *The Living and the Dead* and *I Killed Adolf Hitler*, I suppose — seem more concerned with physical action than your earlier stories. Though action is natural in an adventure story, much of what you've done has tended to subvert that aspect of the genres you were working with. You seem to be enjoying it, especially with the funny punch-outs that constantly occur. Does this make sense?**

No, I don't think there has been a development towards more physical action in my books. *You Can't Get There from Here* had a lot of action: slapstick and fight scenes. I like doing those, to avoid the talking heads for a while, to have things move. *I Killed Adolf Hitler* on the other hand had very little action, and very static storytelling. People would stand around and do nothing. *The Last Musketeer* was done as a reaction to that book in fact. I wanted to do a book with more energetic storytelling, to change the angles more, for it to have a more cinematic feel, I guess. Then "Low Moon" was a return to not very much happening. People would just sit, talk, drink coffee, play chess. It depends on the story how it should look.

OK, the physical action I saw in *I Killed Adolf Hitler* was mostly the brains being blown out here and there, but other than that it is quite static, that's true. In any case, *The Last Musketeer* seems to be the most epic in scope, with the chase scene across the Martian landscape and so on, so I guess that's what prompted my question. It seems "bigger" in some ways than most of your earlier books, which are more intimate and subdued, even if several of them have lots of action. I was wondering whether that is something that would attract you further in the future — expanding the scope of your stories. I guess it would invariably involve more background drawing though.

I'd like to do another story like that, with bigger scope. I didn't really mind doing the backgrounds for the French part, since that part of the story takes place in Montpellier and I had taken a lot of photographs. Or for *The Iron Wagon*, where I had done a lot of research. What I find boring to draw is mostly the stories taking place in the present, with modern apartments or street scenes with modern cars.

One idea I've been thinking about doing is a version of *Around the World in 80 Days*. I was watching the Jackie Chan version on TV and it's pretty awful. I kept coming up with gags they should have put in there. The '50s version with David Niven isn't that great either. The Passepartout character is obviously meant to be comic relief, but he's not that funny, really. My take on it would be a very free adaptation, the concept being how it would look if it had been a Harold Lloyd film. It would be very influenced by silent film or by the early *Tintin* albums that carried that influence. You can find variations of gags by Buster Keaton in those early *Tintins*. It would mean a lot of research, the whole Victorian era — not the least on how things looked back then, not only in London, but in Paris, India, America, all over. It would be a lot of work.

It's not the next album, but maybe some day.

By the way, where's D'Artagnan in the story? I know he died in *Ten Years Later*, but so did Athos...

They died in one of the later books? I didn't know that. I read half of *The Three Musketeers*, but I found it to be a bit hard to get through. If Dumas could use five words where one was enough, he would. In my version, in this particular universe, there is no D'Artagnan, there was no room for him. I thought it worked better for the story to have three musketeers, for one of them to die, and then for the other two to have a falling out. I didn't specify exactly what had happened. I wanted to leave that to the reader's imagination. And how come Athos and Aramis are still alive in the present? Who knows? I didn't find it necessary to give any explanation for that.

Before proceeding, I wanted to ask you about what is obviously a recurring inspiration for you: film. Could you talk a bit about what it is in cinema that attracts you, and how it affects your cartooning?

On one hand, I like directors like Jim Jarmusch, Hal Hartley and Aki Kaurismäki. The way the bird guy is dressed in *Sshhhh!* I pretty much stole directly from *Stranger than Paradise*, the kind of hat and jacket that John Lurie and Richard Edson wear in that film. I learned from Hal Hartley that dialogue doesn't necessarily have to be naturalistic. If I ever went to the theater, I might have picked up on that earlier, but it was sort of a revelation, and a big help when I started to work more with text. There are dialogue scenes in *Why Are You Doing This?* that are quite inspired by him. I've stolen some of his gags too. In *Trust* there is a scene of Martin Donovan coming out of a TV store where he just turned down a job, and on the pavement outside there is a long line of people, standing there with busted TVs in their arms. In *I Killed Adolf Hitler* I had a client come out of the office of the main character, the hired killer, and there is a long line of people in the waiting room. Hartley would often have his characters, especially the male ones, push each other. I started having my characters punch each other in the stomach.

The Kaurismäki films are probably the biggest influence. They can be kind of melancholy, but very funny too. His use of the camera is very minimalist. Mostly it moves only if the characters move. There is a brilliant sequence in *Ariel* where somebody robs a bank. We see them running into the bank, but we never see what happens there — the camera just stays on the outside, half a minute passes, and then they come running out again, with money in their hands. It's a style that translates well to comics.

On the other hand, I can watch all kinds of films. In France there is a chain called Gibert Joseph that sells CDs, DVDs and books, but also second-hand stuff, and you can buy DVDs for six or seven Euros, sometimes for as little as three or four. That way, you can take a bit more of a risk buying films. For a time, I was buying five or six films every week, but I've calmed down a bit now. You get hooked on different things. I was watching a lot of young Al Pacino films for a while, then John Carpenter movies, then Westerns, then Audrey Hepburn films, then Dean Martin/Jerry Lewis. At the moment I'm watching a lot of Italian *giallo* [crime] movies. It doesn't matter if they are good or bad. Bad can often be better — old black-and-white monster films, rather than the literary films in good taste that win the Oscars. Often ideas for stories come from just one little scene in one of those films. Or from thinking, "What would have happened if the story had gone in this direction rather than in that direction?" Sometimes it's from reading a totally unrelated book at the same time, and then those two worlds meet somewhere in your brain.

"Low Moon" is the most recent thing you've had published. I assume it was commissioned directly by *The New York Times*?

Yes, they contacted me. I kept waiting for them to say, "Sorry, we changed our minds; we were only kidding," but that never happened. I had this idea for a story lying

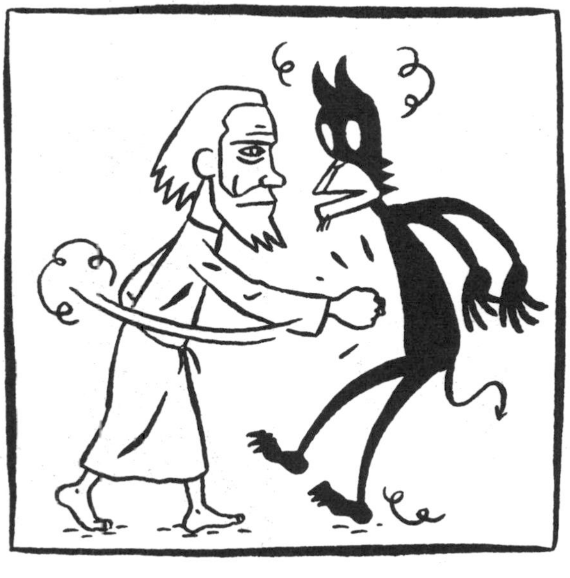

Jason often depicts stomach-punches: from *Meow, Baby!*.
[©2005 Jason]

around that was basically *High Noon*, but with a game of chess instead of a duel at the end. I had been thinking that you can't drag that out to a 48-page album, but it could work as a shorter story. I tried to come up with other ideas, thinking, "Are you crazy? *The New York Times* asks you for a story and you're giving them a Western?!" But in the end I thought, "Yes! Because it's *The New York Times*, it *should* be a Western!' They asked for a synopsis and I panicked for a while, thinking, "It's *The New York Times*, it can't just be a story. It has to be *about* something." So for the first time I actually thought about themes before starting the story, something I usually never do.

It seems to me to be about the time in your life when you're no longer young and have to make serious long-range decisions about your future. I can identify! Is it in any way autobiographical?

It's autobiographical in the sense that I'm a middle-aged man now. In seven years I'll be 50. I'm not making enough money to buy a Porsche, but who knows, maybe I'll start running marathons? There are just certain facts

you have to face and decisions you have to make. You can't keep jumping from city to city. You will have to settle down somewhere. And as the barber talks about in the strip, the girls you look at may be in their 20s, but if you hook up with a woman, it's more likely that she will be closer to your age. She will probably have some lines in her face. It's not necessarily a sad thing. There are also opportunities that are perhaps clearer to you than when you were young. That's why the prostitute leaves at the end of the strip. There's no future for her in that town. That's what her story about the pawns was about. I don't think the chess-as-metaphor-for-Life is the most elegant thing I've done, it's probably a bit pretentious, but anyway ...

It also appears to subtly address your fascination with earlier periods, the notion we discussed earlier that things seemed simpler way back when we weren't around. The Western town almost seems like a set, with anachronisms such as the high-wheeler and the cell phone popping up. Again, this seems to me to tie in with some kind of self-reflection on the part of the artist.

This sequence is from the 13th chapter of Jason's "Low Moon" serial, which ran May 18, 2008 in *The New York Times*. [©2008 Jason]

The story talks about the idea of progress and about feeling out of step with the present. Those are not uncommon themes for Westerns, at least not for the Peckinpah ones. There are no flying cars or robots walking around, but the one thing in modern society that I find to be a bit science fiction-like is the cell phone — everybody walking around with it stuck to their ears. How much it's taken for granted now. I remember a time when people seemed to get by fine without it. I have one myself, but I keep it in my apartment in place of a regular phone. I never have it on me when I go out — I just hate talking on the damn thing in public. It's funny, I sometimes feel as if I'm already a grumpy old man, talking about how much better things were before. I should probably complete the act and move into a hut deep in the forest somewhere.

You mention four other stories to be collected along with it. I've been sent photocopies of two shorter stories — one with a hired killer and one with a caveman — which I assume are two of them? They seem quite different in tone from "Low Moon," though — darker, more oppressive somehow, but also funny of course. Will there be an overarching principle to this collection or not?

No, there is no common theme or principle. They are just ideas I had for shorter stories. The two stories you've seen are influenced by film noir; I was watching a lot of that for a while. They're more surreal takes on it, though. One is pretty much *The Postman Always Rings Twice*, but with cave people. The other one is about the character of the *femme fatale*, but it's also an exercise — to have the whole story take place in a room, but still try to keep it interesting. The third story is also a bit noir, but it's a return to the humor of silent films, more in the direction of Laurel and Hardy this time. The last story is the one I talked about earlier, about the couple arguing and the woman being kidnapped by a space monster. We follow the husband and the son dealing with this and trying to find her again. The whole book should be around 200 pages. In Europe there is a tradition for the 48-page album, but in the U.S. I've seen some criticism that my books are too short, so I wanted to do something with more pages this time.

As I said, I find the story about the assassin and the woman almost nightmarish, perhaps darker than anything else you've done. And the "Postman" story is also like some kind of nightmare, but more lighthearted about it. Do you agree, and is this a direction you could see yourself moving in with some of your

A fight is interrupted: from one of the shorts to appear in Jason's next collection. [©2008 Jason]

future work?

No, I don't find that story to be so dark. Any story where a guy kills someone just so he can sniff a pair of panties is funny to me. But I keep most of the characters expressionless, so when the woman, the *femme fatale*, smiles, it's probably the creepiest thing I've drawn. I don't really see myself going in just one direction. I'd like to do a story that is a more serious examination of the noir style. I've already mentioned the Jules Verne book, and there's another novel I'd like to do an adaptation of, but less faithfully than with *The Iron Wagon* — to read the book but then put it back on the shelf and do it from memory instead of line for line. I'd also like to do a detective story, a war story, a werewolf story. A Russ Meyer type story would be fun to do. There are lots of things I'd like to try. I hope to stick around for a while. ∎

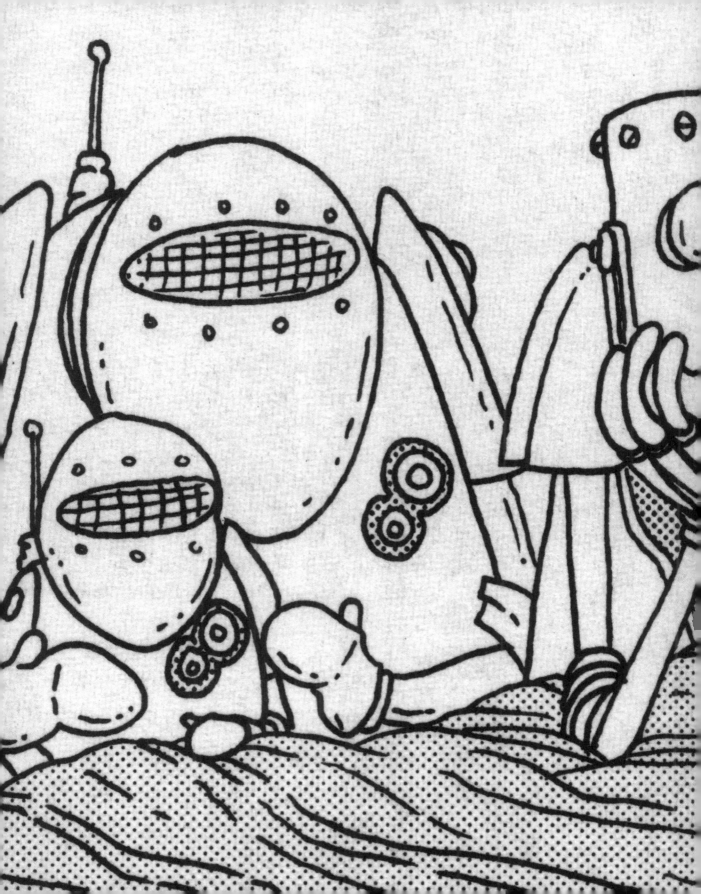

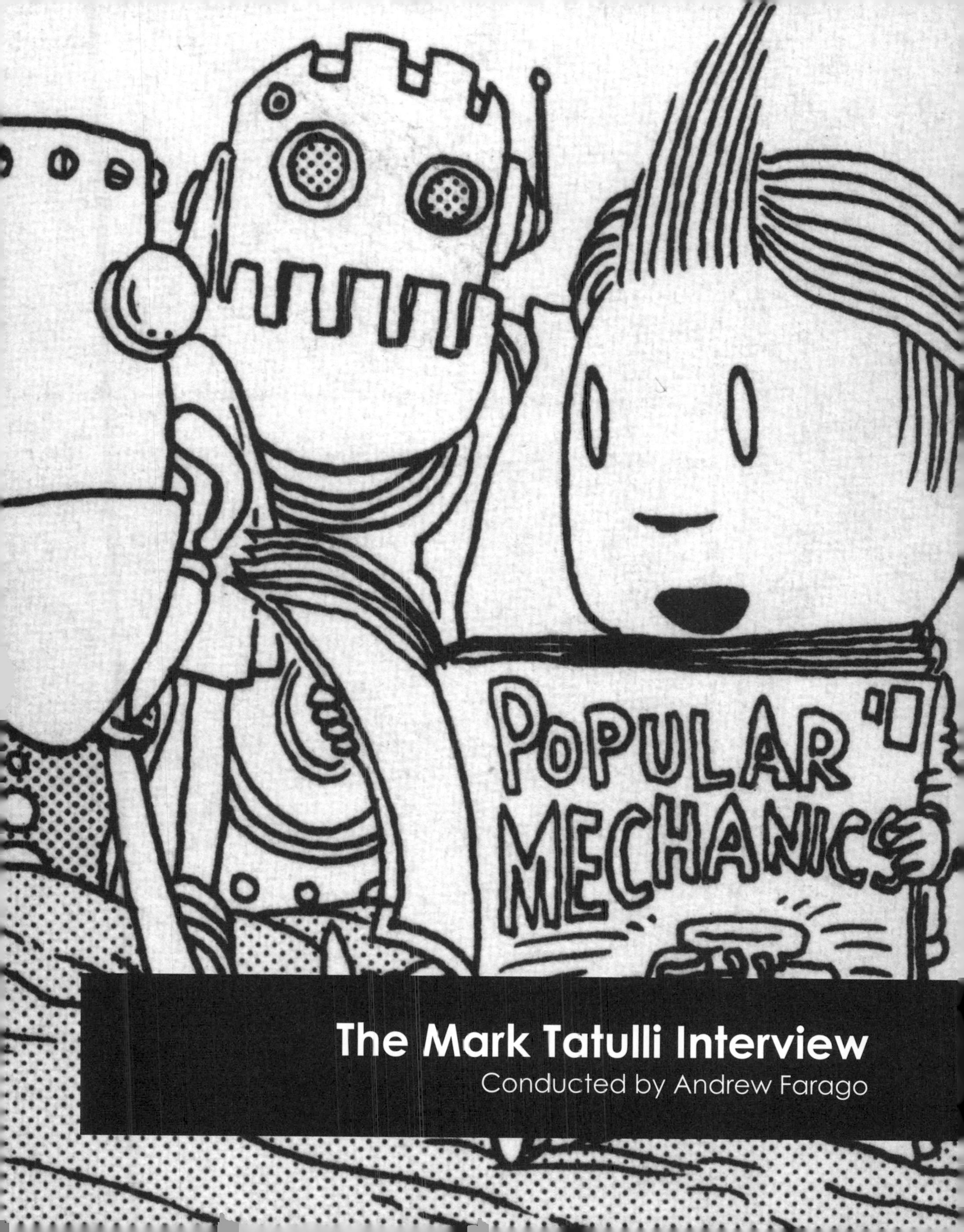
POPULAR
MECHANICS

The Mark Tatulli Interview

Conducted by Andrew Farago

Mark Tatulli photo courtesy of the Universal Press Syndicate.

Ever since Bill Watterson's retirement in 1996, observers have been predicting the death of the newspaper comic strip. Syndicates rarely launch more than three strips a year, new strips often appear in 30 newspapers or less, and it's increasingly difficult for a cartoonist to make a decent living off of a strip within two years of launch. Mark Tatulli's *Liō*, however, launched in over 100 newspapers and quickly gained traction in an increasingly uncertain business. His other daily strip, *Heart of the City*, hit its peak around the 100-paper mark, and faces many of the same difficulties as other "new" strips in an ever-shrinking market.

It's hard to find two more disparate strips in the modern newspaper comics section than *Heart of the City* and *Liō*. *Heart* is a charming, dialogue-driven, often sentimental, family strip starring a sunny, adorable little girl, while *Liō* is an odd, pantomime, often wince-inducing comic starring a disturbing, sociopathic little boy. The strips are so different in tone that it's not uncommon for readers to assume that there are two different Mark Tatullis on the comics page, each with a different art style, sense of humor, and signature (which is just one of many ways that he keeps the two strips at arm's length from each other).

I met Tatulli at the first of about 20 cocktail mixers over the course of the National Cartoonists Society Reuben Awards Weekend in New Orleans. Within minutes, we were bonding over our Sicilian heritage, trading sausage recipes and making arrangements to meet up a couple of days later to conduct a pre-interview for this feature. Following Tatulli's career-spanning presentation on Sunday afternoon, we sat down in the Ritz-Carlton courtyard and I gathered the background information for the *actual* interview, which took place two months later, in July. My biggest challenge was making sure to get Mark to repeat all of the best stories that I'd heard in New Orleans, and, fortunately, I caught him in a talkative mood.

Previous: From the second collection: *Liō: Silent But Deadly*.

[©2008 Mark Tatulli]

ANDREW FARAGO:
What am I interrupting right now, which strip are you working on?

MARK TATULLI:
Today, I am working on *Liō*, I am working on *Liō* Sunday.

OK, so you're one of the rare comic-strip artists that actually has two ongoing syndicated strips.

I don't know how rare it is any more. It seems like a lot of cartoonists are doing two or three. Bill Hinds, he does *Cleats* and he also does *Tank McNamara*, and there's Darren Bell, who does *Rudy Park* and *Candorville*, and the list goes on. I think I'm one of the few who actually does the writing and drawing of both strips. Brian Bassett does two strips where he writes and draws both. He does *Red and Rover* and also *Adam @ Home*.

I guess, as the newspaper market shrinks, more and more people are going that route.

Yeah, it seems like you have to. Also, in addition to the newspaper market shrinking, the wages of what newspapers pay for a comic has not gone up since the '70s, so what would have been a good salary in the '70s and '80s now just ain't enough. You could have made a good living doing one strip back in the '70s and '80s if you add 50 papers, and now that's just not the case. Plus, like you said, the market's dwindling, so even if you *do* get 50 papers, you're lucky. Believe me, it's tough out there.

How many papers do you have covered between your two strips?

Let's see ... *Heart of the City* is in about 88 newspapers and *Liō* is in just under 300, so it's a good number between the two, but keep in mind that *Heart of the City* is celebrating 10 years this November. So, it took 10 years to build up to that. I peaked at about 113, 114 papers with *Heart*, and it has since dwindled to about 88.

So, not pushing *Garfield* numbers just yet.

No, no, no, no. Not even close.

You mentioned the '70s and '80s, so that will be a good opening for talking about how you got into the newspaper market in the first place.

Well, I was always interested in doing comics — also interested in doing animation — so while I was trying to get syndicated — and now we're talking in the mid-to-late '80s — I was also working a full-time job in the advertising industry. That's where I learned to do computer graphics and 3D animation and that kind of stuff, and that's how I made my living. But on the side, I was always trying to get syndicated.

My *first* comic strip that ever got into newspapers was called *Mr. Fipps*. It's about a schoolteacher that taught in junior high. That actually was the replacement strip for *Bloom County* back in 1989 at the *Burlington County Times*, our local paper, which, at the time, had a circulation of about 55,000. Lord knows what it is now. So, that was my first foray into actually doing a strip on a daily basis. I didn't do Sundays; I just did dailies. It was my first real professional cartooning job. They paid me like a columnist. So, I did that for six months. It was just *so* much work for just one newspaper, and so what I decided to do was continue trying to get syndicated with something else that I felt had stronger appeal, so I started submitting to syndicates again and I caught the attention of a small syndicate out of Bisbee, Ariz., called Lew Little Enterprises.

Back then, Lou Little did something like an internship program, where you would basically send your strips to him, and he would decide if you were qualified for the internship, and if you did, he would rate your comic. You'd send him a month's worth of comics and for $50, he would rate your comic and then send them back with a letter grade, like A, B, C, D — D being unusable, and the rest being excellent, good or fair. So, I was a member of an internship program with another strip I had back in the mid-'80s and I stopped doing that with him after about a year, but I kept submitting strip concepts to him, because he did manage to get a few strips off the ground. One of them being *Sibling Revelry* — I don't know if you remember *that* strip, but that's going back in the late '80s — and also, *The Fusco Brothers* was his. He turned around and sold them to Universal Press once he'd got them in a couple of papers and got them going.

So I submitted a strip to him called *Bent Halos,* which was about a couple of rambunctious angels with attitude — you know, how they come to earth and try to do things their own way. He syndicated that, which means that he basically walked around and sold it to a bunch of newspapers — not that many. The big one that I had was *The Philadelphia Inquirer*, daily and Sunday. But, I had some papers in California and the Midwest: *Rocky Mountain News*, Long Beach *Press-Telegram*, a couple of others. It did not make that much money, but I did that for 18 months, and I just couldn't do it any more after 18

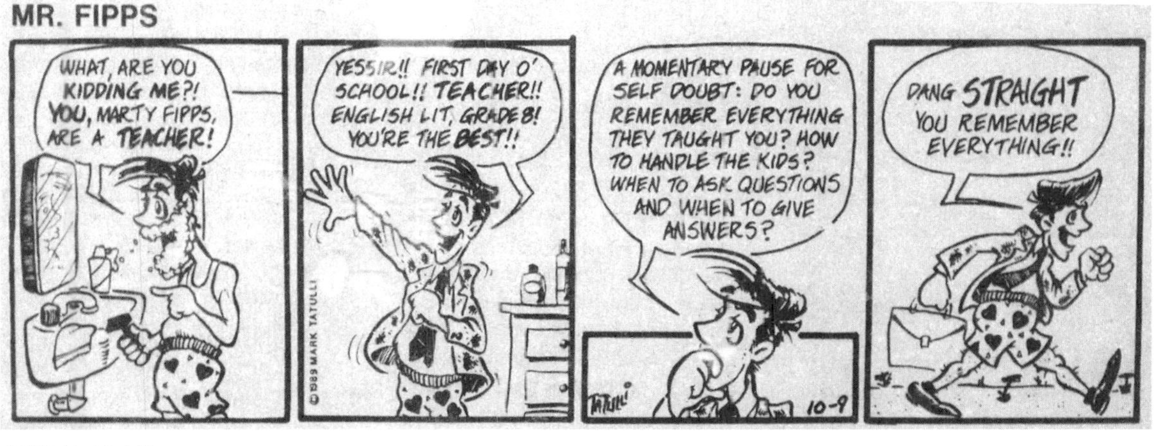
MR. FIPPS
WHAT, ARE YOU KIDDING ME?! YOU, MARTY FIPPS, ARE A TEACHER!
YESSIR!! FIRST DAY O' SCHOOL!! TEACHER!! ENGLISH LIT, GRADE 8! YOU'RE THE BEST!!
©1989 MARK TATULLI
A MOMENTARY PAUSE FOR SELF DOUBT: DO YOU REMEMBER EVERYTHING THEY TAUGHT YOU? HOW TO HANDLE THE KIDS? WHEN TO ASK QUESTIONS AND WHEN TO GIVE ANSWERS?
TATULLI
10-9
DANG STRAIGHT YOU REMEMBER EVERYTHING!!

[©1989 Mark Tatulli]

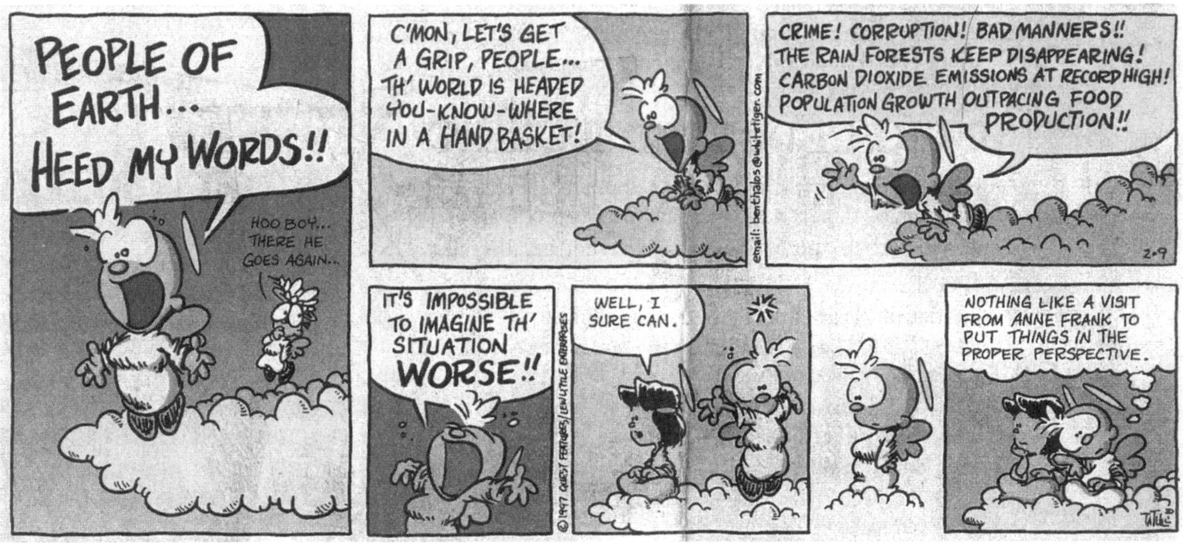
PEOPLE OF EARTH... HEED MY WORDS!!
HOO BOY... THERE HE GOES AGAIN...
C'MON, LET'S GET A GRIP, PEOPLE... TH' WORLD IS HEADED YOU-KNOW-WHERE IN A HAND BASKET!
CRIME! CORRUPTION! BAD MANNERS!! THE RAIN FORESTS KEEP DISAPPEARING! CARBON DIOXIDE EMISSIONS AT RECORD HIGH! POPULATION GROWTH OUTPACING FOOD PRODUCTION!!
2-9
IT'S IMPOSSIBLE TO IMAGINE TH' SITUATION WORSE!!
WELL, I SURE CAN.
NOTHING LIKE A VISIT FROM ANNE FRANK TO PUT THINGS IN THE PROPER PERSPECTIVE.

Feb. 9,1997 *Bent Halos* strip.

months, daily and Sunday. It made about $200 a month, and that just wasn't enough.

I told my wife, "I just can't do this any more. This is too much work." I said, "I'm just gonna try to get with a *real* syndicate and see if I can't make something happen." So I stopped doing *Bent Halos* and I started drawing *Heart of the City*, and I guess this is about now 1996, and I started drawing *Heart of the City* the next day and started coming up with the concept, putting it all together. I sent it out to the syndicates, and I had positive feedback from King Features and Universal Press, but Universal Press moved the fastest and incidentally, they were the syndicate I wanted to be with anyway, because they were *Calvin and Hobbes* and *For Better or for Worse*, and they now had *Garfield* — So, that was a big syndicate, and of course, Lee Salem, who is head of editorial was *the* man that every cartoonist wanted to work with, because he had developed *Calvin and Hobbes.* So we signed a contract and I went into development for about four months, and then we picked a launch date of about April of 1999 — I knew I just had to get myself ready for that.

Then about June of '98, they said to me, "Listen, the guy that we were gonna launch in November, he just isn't gonna be ready, and we think that *Heart of the City*'s ready to go. So, are you ready to do it and launch early?"

And I said, "Sure, I can do that." So, I had to rush and get a bunch of stuff done for the sales kit, and we started the sales campaign in September and then we launched in newspapers in November of 1998 with about 56 clients.

Do you know which strip was dragging its feet?

Yeah, *The Boondocks. [Laughs.]* But, that's OK. Back then, they were launching three or four strips a year, so I had a small window to build a client base. It was between September and December, four months where they really hit hard with *Heart of the City*, and then they started the sales campaign of January of '99 for *The Boondocks,* and *The Boondocks* did really well and just sucked all the air out of the room. So, any momentum I had was just kinda squashed. I had sold a bunch of papers too that had *Heart of the City* waiting in the wings. They bought it with the idea that as soon as the space opened up, they'd drop in *Heart of the City*. Well, *Boondocks* came in, and it sold to over a hundred newspapers right away, and they put it *right in*. So it just kind of bumped me out of the way. Over the years, I had a pretty decent client base with *Heart of the City.* It made good money, but it just wasn't enough to live on; not with a family of five.

So, I did my full-time job working in the advertising industry — and the television industry, eventually, doing design, graphics, opens for reality shows — and I did that all the way up until 2005 where there was a real slowdown in the reality-television business. We had a whole bunch of shows that were really big. We had *Trading Spaces* and *Wedding Story*, and a whole bunch of shows on Fox, and then they all dried up. The networks were taking their shows and spreading them out over a whole bunch of different companies, so we lost a lot of our shows. We were down to basically just *Trading Spaces,* and so I got laid off with a whole bunch of other people in 2005. I had a little bit of time before I had to really start to panic, because I had some savings. So I decided to develop another strip.

I figured, "Lemme use the time to develop another strip and see what I can do with that." I always wanted to do a strip that was silent. I thought it would be a good complement to *Heart of the City*. *Heart of the City* was script-driven, so it seemed like a good idea to do something that was completely different, so there would be no confusion in my own mind about how to write for them. If I had two script-driven strips, I think I would have a problem with overlap in character, and so forth. So I wanted to do something that was just what I call a pantomime strip, and I wanted to rework the concept into something that was dark and appealing to a younger, more hip crowd. Actually, to as many ages as I can get, because I figured, "Kids are gonna love to look at monsters and stuff like that. They don't even have to get the joke." I know when I was looking at comics as I kid, I just liked looking at pictures, even if I didn't get the joke.

And so I came up with the idea of this dark little boy who lives in this fantastical world of his own creation — it could be real, it may not be. Who knows? The idea being that when you're afraid of things when you're a kid, they're very real to you, even though the light of day makes those things as they really are. When you're a kid, you're really, really afraid of things, so they're very real to you. Liō's world is very real to him, and that's what I wanted to do.

I pitched it to Lee Salem — actually, first I showed it to the head of sales, John Vivona, when we were at the Reubens in Arizona because I figured "if *he* can't get excited about it, I'm not even gonna bother with it." Because if you don't have the salesmen behind you, it's just not even worth it. You know, it's *all* about sales. Doing what you love first, but if you have a product that they can't sell in this tough market, it's just not worth going through all the effort because it is a *huge* amount of effort. And the other reason for making it pantomime was that I could appeal to international audiences. It would be a lot easier than something that's written in American slang with American pop-cultural references. I don't do that with *Liō*, and so I figured, "Well, that'll just open our ability to sell it."

He really liked it, and he said, "Yeah, I think I can sell this, I *know* I can sell this, let's do it."

And I said, "OK, lemme show it to Lee Salem and make sure *he* signs off on it." So, the next day at about 8 o'clock in the morning, I met with Lee Salem and pitched it to him, and he said, "Yeah, I like it." I only had done seven daily samples and one Sunday sample, and he said, "I can't give you a contract based on these samples; I'll need to see more," so the next three weeks I turned about 30 roughs and they gave me a development deal. That was May of 2005. We went to development. They liked everything and said "We can fast-track this and start selling it in January of 2006," which they did, and we launched in newspapers in May of 2006 with over a hundred clients.

And hardly any strips launch with that number, right? That's a pretty high…

Hardly any strips launch with over 30. Nowadays, launching with 20 clients is a good start.

Had *Foxtrot* and *The Boondocks* left papers?

Not yet. I got the 100 just on the strength of the strip, and then when *Foxtrot* left — *Boondocks* first announced he wasn't coming back in November of that same year and I got some of his papers — and then in December, *Foxtrot* announced that *he* wasn't going to do dailies any more, so I got some of those papers, too. So I got real, real lucky with the timing on those. By January of 2007,

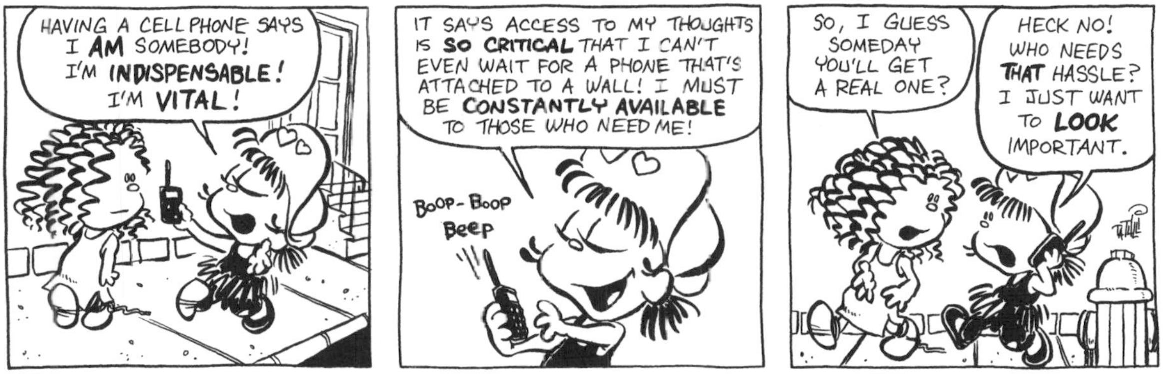
HAVING A CELL PHONE SAYS I AM SOMEBODY! I'M INDISPENSABLE! I'M VITAL!
IT SAYS ACCESS TO MY THOUGHTS IS SO CRITICAL THAT I CAN'T EVEN WAIT FOR A PHONE THAT'S ATTACHED TO A WALL! I MUST BE CONSTANTLY AVAILABLE TO THOSE WHO NEED ME!
BOOP-BOOP BEEP
SO, I GUESS SOMEDAY YOU'LL GET A REAL ONE?
HECK NO! WHO NEEDS THAT HASSLE? I JUST WANT TO LOOK IMPORTANT.

[©2000 Mark Tatulli]

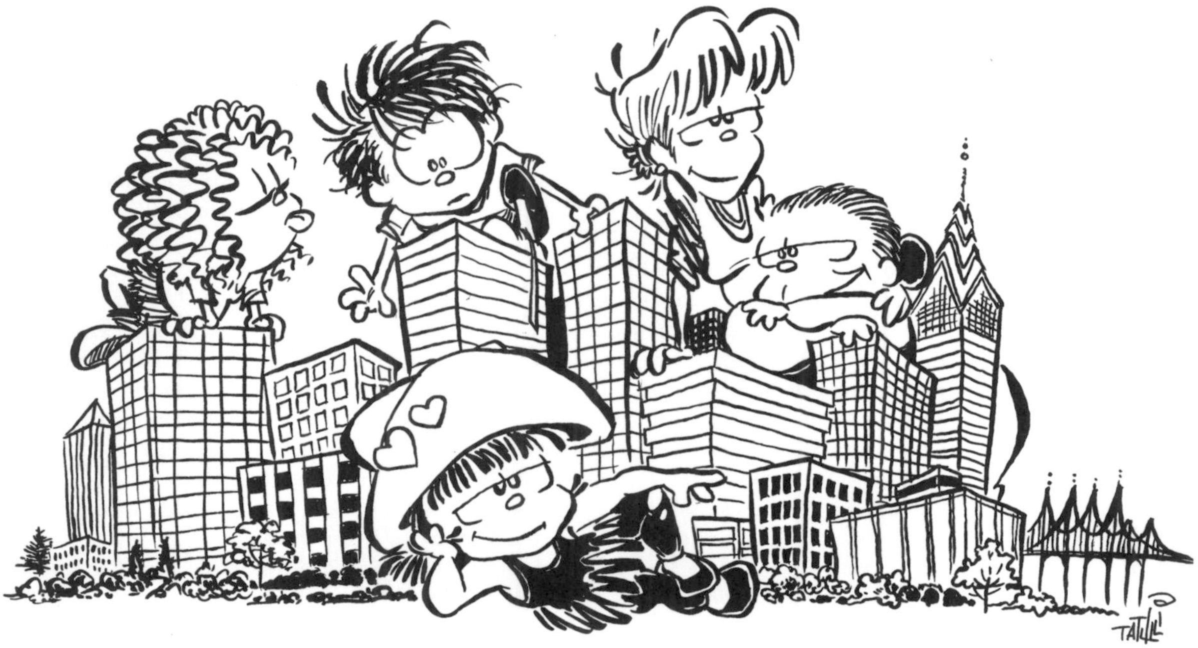

[©2000 Mark Tatulli]

I had 250 clients.

It seems like every newspaper has certain categories they have to fill — and *Boondocks* and *Foxtrot* were the edgy category, right?

Yeah, you would hope that newspapers would function that way. I mean, I don't like to think of an African American strip that way; I'd still think of them as a people strip, but you would think that they'd have something for the older people, something for the younger people, something for people who trend to dark, different tastes in humor. I think a lot of them do, so I was trying to fill that niche. But there are other strips out there that are really popular in that — notably, *Pearls before Swine* and *Get Fuzzy* — I definitely had to turn over some papers to them when *Boondocks* and *Foxtrot* quit.

Let's backtrack a little bit to your day job, which was in animation. You actually have some Emmy awards, is that right?

Yeah, I won three Emmy awards for my work as — I designed show opens for — one of them I won for a show I had done for Flyers hockey, when I know nothing about hockey. One I had done on a music-video show. I can't even remember what the other one was for, but it was for show opens for cable television.

So did you go to college to learn computer animation?

No, I got into the business in 1982. Instead of going to college, I got a job at a film production company. And back then, there was no computer graphics, there were no computers back in '82. It was all film, and we were doing film and slide shows: Sophisticated slideshows, but slideshows nonetheless. That segued into video, and then that turned into computer graphics for video, and I just basically taught myself.

What city were you getting started in?

Philadelphia. It all happened in Philly.

Is that where you're from, originally?

No, I grew up in New Jersey, but Philadelphia was the closest city, and that's where all the production was.

And that's also the setting of *Heart of the City*. I was wracking my brain, and I really couldn't think of any other strips set in Philadelphia, and most of them aren't even set in specific cities.

That's correct. I mean, that's one of the things I wanted to do that was different. Every strips seems to be set in this mythical suburb, *Liō* included. So, I wanted to do something that was in the city, and I wanted to do a realistic city, because I felt that it made the characters more real if they had a real environment that they were in, you know? I worked in the city every day, so I knew it like the back of my hand, so I thought that would be fun. You know,

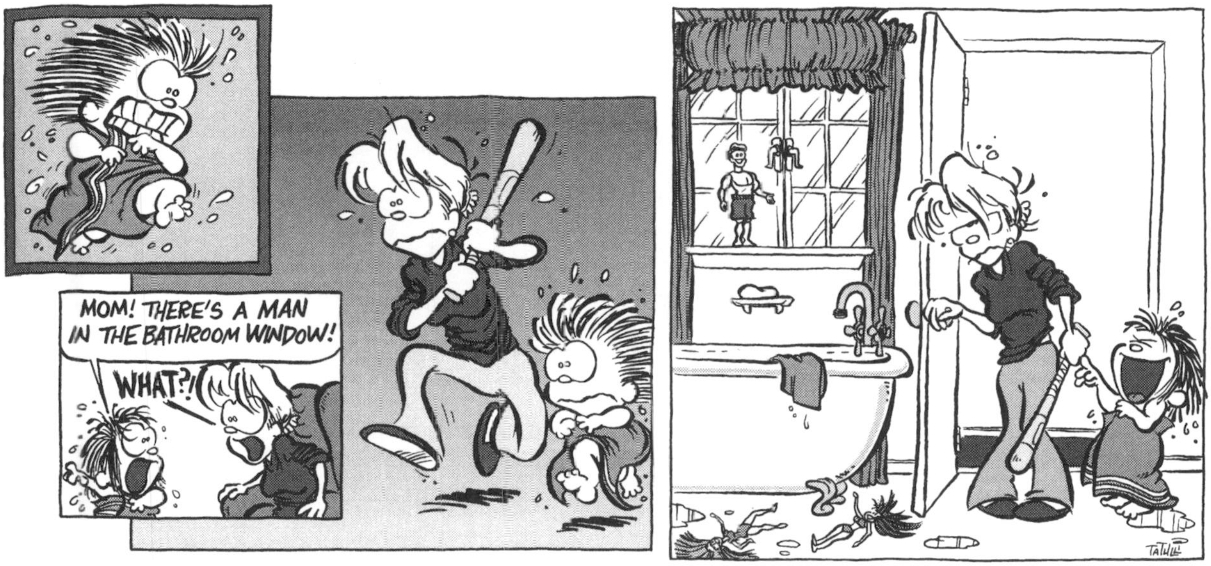
MOM! THERE'S A MAN IN THE BATHROOM WINDOW!
WHAT?!

Heart's mom is a single parent. [©2000 Mark Tatulli]

they say, "Write what you know." So that's what I did, and I thought it would be different.

You know what I was really motivated by, honestly? I always liked the *Madeline* books, and how they showed real pictures of France, and she wasn't just walking around in some generic French situation, there were actually scenes — you walked by the Arc de Triomphe, and there are different Paris street scenes that are real places Madeline occurred in front of. I always liked those whimsical illustrations of Paris, so I kind of wanted to do that with Philadelphia. Philadelphia, as you know, is the Paris of the Americas.

Heart's family situation: I don't know that I would say it's controversial exactly, but there aren't a lot of single-parent strips.

Yeah, the whole thing I wanted to do with *Heart of the City*, too, was to focus on the relationship between the mother and the daughter. I didn't want them necessarily to be adversarial. That would become parents against the kid. So, Heart and her mother are kinda in this together, and the nanny figure of Mrs. Angelini, who is an Italian American nanny from South Philadelphia, is the older generation. So we get three generations of women, in all, doing it on their own and successfully — having a successful family existence, helping each other in their

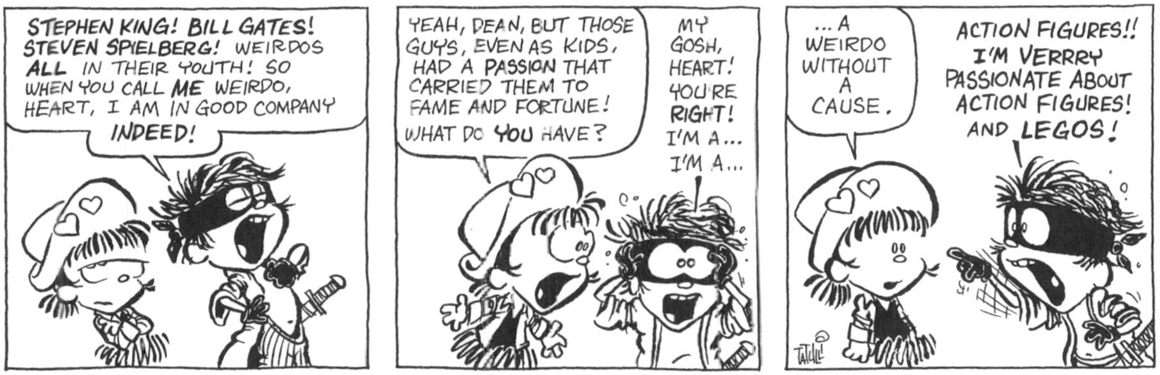
STEPHEN KING! BILL GATES! STEVEN SPIELBERG! WEIRDOS ALL IN THEIR YOUTH! SO WHEN YOU CALL ME WEIRDO, HEART, I AM IN GOOD COMPANY INDEED!
YEAH, DEAN, BUT THOSE GUYS, EVEN AS KIDS, HAD A PASSION THAT CARRIED THEM TO FAME AND FORTUNE! WHAT DO YOU HAVE?
MY GOSH, HEART! YOU'RE RIGHT! I'M A... I'M A...
... A WEIRDO WITHOUT A CAUSE.
ACTION FIGURES!! I'M VERRRY PASSIONATE ABOUT ACTION FIGURES! AND LEGOS!

Dean is based on Tatulli's son. [©2000 Mark Tatulli]

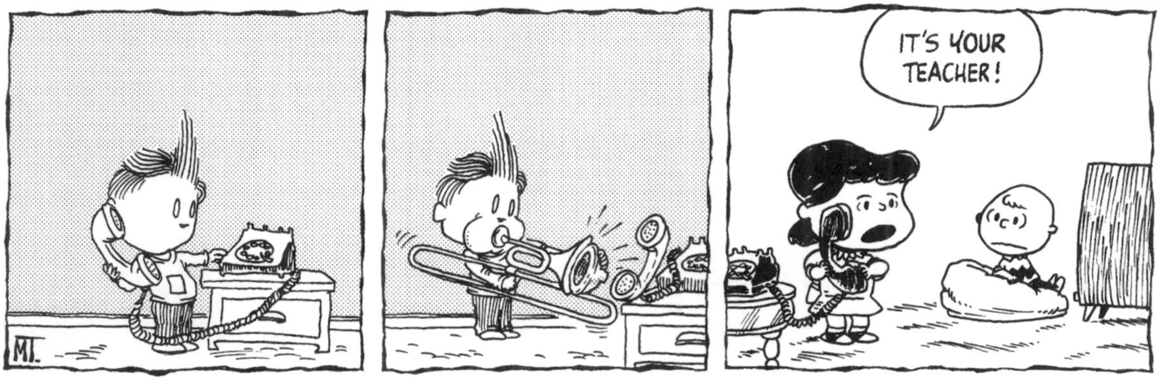
IT'S YOUR TEACHER!

[©2007 Mark Tatulli]

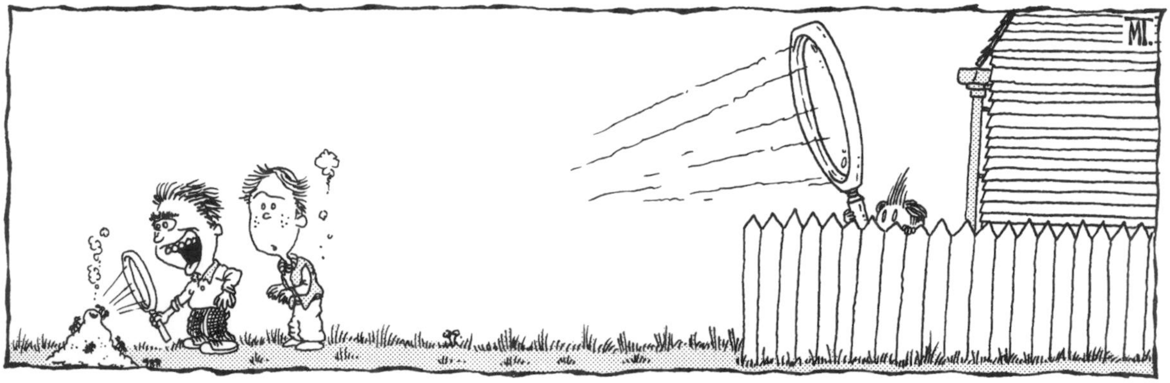

[©2007 Mark Tatulli]

own way.

I guess another hard sell is having a female lead, or actually multiple female leads, in your comic.

Well, the other thing that I noticed in the paper is there aren't a lot of female leads. They're all primarily male. And at the time when I launched *Heart of the City*, it was right after King Features had launched a strip called *Claire and Weber,* which was about a little girl and a frog, then United launched a strip called *Meg!* about a little girl who's a soccer freak, and then Creators launched *Agnes*, so this all happened within a year. And right now, the only two that are left standing are me and *Agnes.* But at the time, there was nothing that I can think of. *One Big Happy*, maybe? I don't know, I can't think of any other strong female leads, can you?

Blondie is the title character in her strip?

Yeah, but that's not a little girl; that's a woman.

***Peanuts* always had prominent girl characters.**

Which were ensemble. That's more ensemble with the lead being Charlie Brown. So, I felt that it was time to have a little girl in there, and I wanted her to have a strong relationship with her mother. It's one thing I always admired about my wife and my kids. I mean, as close as I am with my kids and as a good a father as I think I am, I was never ever gonna come close to the relationship that my kids have with their mother. So, maybe in a way it was me grabbing at that. And because Heart doesn't age, I'll always have that relationship. No matter how old *my* kids get.

Are there any specific kids you drew on when you were creating Heart?

She is a real mix of me and my two daughters and my son. Now, there's the Dean character who is actually based on my son, Dean. The Dean character is a mix of me and my son. All of the characters have me in them, or an aspect of my personality, but I've also drawn my family for personalities, but I don't go outside the family for any kind of inspiration.

I just read the first book collection, and right away, she felt like a real little girl. I've got nieces and I grew up with lots and lots of cousins back home, and she didn't feel like this was a corporate idea of what a "sassy little girl" in the strip was going to be.

Yeah. Well, my daughters were big on — God, they're always putting on *some* show. When my kids were little, when this strip was launched, the Spice Girls were big, and Britney Spears and all that stuff, which has now been replaced by other things, because that changes. But you know, those things are big, and that's what *Heart* was about: wanting to be a movie star, and wanting to be on the stage, and the Heart character's a lot more tenacious than my kids ever thought of being, but I also thought that was understandable as a city girl. It would be more acceptable from a kid that's in the city, because they seem to grow up faster.

There are a lot of non-generic references in there, so there are things like, for example, she seems to be obsessed with *Gone with the Wind.*

See, I loved *Gone with the Wind* growing up — it was like, the first real book that I ever read. I wanted to make the relationship between her and Mrs. Angelini like the relationship between Scarlett O'Hara and Mammy — that same kind of dynamic where they work each other, but at the same time they've got a relationship that is totally different than the relationship that Mom and Heart have. They've got their own private little things, and Heart may screw up, but Mrs. Angelini keeps it to herself, because she's working her angles on her, and those little things like that. They all are a part of shaping who Heart is.

What kind of fan reaction do you get to Heart?

I get a lot of fan reaction that was interesting — especially in the beginning. People were surprised that it was written by a man. People just love her. I'm still surprised 10 years later that I get the reaction that I do. People say, "Oh my God, this is my niece, this is my nephew, this was me, I grew up with *Heart of the City* and now I'm pinning them up on the wall in college." That kind of reaction is always great to get.

How long had you been doing *Heart of the City* when you came up with the idea for *Liō*?

Let's see, I launched *Heart* in '98, so I'd been working on it since '97. I would say I'd been working on *Heart* eight years by the time I'd started actually working on *Liō*. There's a lot of work that goes into it before it actually hits the paper, so I started working on *Liō* in about March of 2005, and it didn't actually get into papers until May of 2006.

And the impetus for starting the second strip: How much of it was financially based? How much of it was just wanting to try something different?

Well, I had lost my job. I had got laid off, and I was half-looking for another job, and I thought to myself, "Maybe this is a good opportunity," because suddenly I had time to develop another strip concept. So in order to not have to go back to work, and to have my dream of finally working at home as a professional cartoonist, I developed another strip.

Visually, he really stands out: the little blank eyes …

The idea behind that was: He's supposed to be kind of remorseless. At first it was a much darker figure. My syndicate said, "Yeah, that's fine, and we like it, but you're

MT.
L'IL GUILLOTINE! MODEL KIT
Really works!

[©2007 Mark Tatulli]

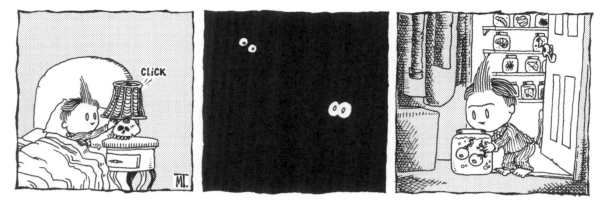

[©2007 Mark Tatulli]

gonna have to lighten it up a little bit, or they're just going to get nothing but complaints." So I had to reel it
back a little bit. And, you know, make him softer. He
could never be a type of character that could torture little
animals, not that I would ever condone that anyway, but
anything that even hinted that he might be doing that. It
always had to be someone who had it coming to them. If
you'll notice, the ones that he's usually getting are bullies
or people that are rude or hunters who are shooting little
animals, which makes them the bad guy. So you know …
even though he has dark and twisted intentions, it's usually tuned for good.

**Yeah, I think that's one of the roles that the creators
established for Bugs Bunny: that he shouldn't be ini-
tiating schemes against people. He should be wronged
first. I guess you have that same thing going on with
Liō. He's the…**
The "dark knight."

So the eyes are remorseless and …
That was the original concept behind it, but you know,
I've since made him not so remorseless. He's nonchalant.
He's nonchalant pretty much about the darkness that goes
on around him.

**That's a good way to put it. Where did the hairstyle
come from?**
The hairstyle: I wanted something that would stand out
and make him obvious. Because it's in a pantomime strip,
we couldn't have people calling his name or anything like
that, so he had to be very recognizable from the front and
the back. Part of that is his shirt with the square on it. His
outfit is always pretty much the same, so that's part of his
identity. But a major part of his identity is the eyes, which

are like nobody else's in the comic, and also the hair, because whether he's coming or going, the hair is poking up,
so it makes him instantly recognizable, instantly discern-
able from the other characters in the strip.

**Was there anything unusual that went into the design?
Odd references, or…**
Well, I actually looked up pictures of Hitler youth on
the Internet, just to see what kind of hairstyles they had,
because I wanted a dark look to his hair. And they all had
these slicked down, very Hitler-ish kind of hair-dos, and
the only difference is that I pulled Liō's up in the front just
to give it that extra … It's very stylized, slicked-down hair
otherwise, except for the tuft in the front that just pokes
straight up.

Liō, the traditional spelling is L-E-O.
I wanted it to have a foreign look to it. When somebody
opened the paper, they'd say "Oh, this is really odd, this
may be something that's produced in France or Germany
or something like that," with the interesting spelling L-
I-O, with that little mark over the top of the "O," you
know, that long "O" sound? I don't know what you call
that. I just wanted to have a different, foreign look to it.

**The NCS presentation that I saw, you mentioned that's
helped you on Google, as well, right?**
That's the other thing. If you do a Google search on
"Liō," you're going to get *my* strip, or you're gonna get this
hotsy totsy French singer, the French Madonna. When
I was originally doing Google searches, I didn't see any-
thing about this French singer, and then all of a sudden,
I'm like, "What? Where did *she* come from?"

I'd say probably the most obvious influences I see

when reading through the strip would be Gahan Wilson.

Yeah.

So I take it you're a big fan of his work.

Yeah. I still love his stuff in the *National Lampoon.* My dad used to buy *National Lampoon*, and he would hide it in the organ bench, you know, with the sheet music? "Keep it away from the *kids.*" But you know, I always knew to look there. The *National Lampoon* was great, because they had these really dark, adult-oriented comics, and one of them was *Nuts* by Gahan Wilson. And of course, there were spot illustrations here and there, but I just loved how he drew monsters and people with really odd-shaped heads. Just, you know, weird-looking stuff. He had that really fine point on his pen, very detailed illustrations. That was a big influence.

Yeah, and talking to Gahan, something that came up in conversation with him is he seems to remember every single horrible thing that ever happened to him in his childhood.

Yep, me too. That's exactly right. And, it's funny to meet people that you knew when you were kids, and you'll see them years later, and whatever the situation is, they won't remember any of that. "I don't know what you're talking about, dude?"

I'm like, "Don't you remember? My God! You shook my life to the core, you know?" So yeah, it's funny, and those things, I'll tell you, they stay with you, the little scares that you had when you were a kid, things you were afraid of, and that's why I kinda like, have Liō. He definitely deals with the same kind of fears I had, but he's at peace with it.

Yeah, I think Gahan said something like, "If you remember childhood as this completely happy, blissful time, then you're just fooling yourself."

That's totally correct. It's constant fear. Of course, whenever you didn't have anything to be afraid of that day, you could always fall back on the old "Oh, what happens if my mother dies during the night?" That was always in the background, you know?

What were some of your other recurring fears?

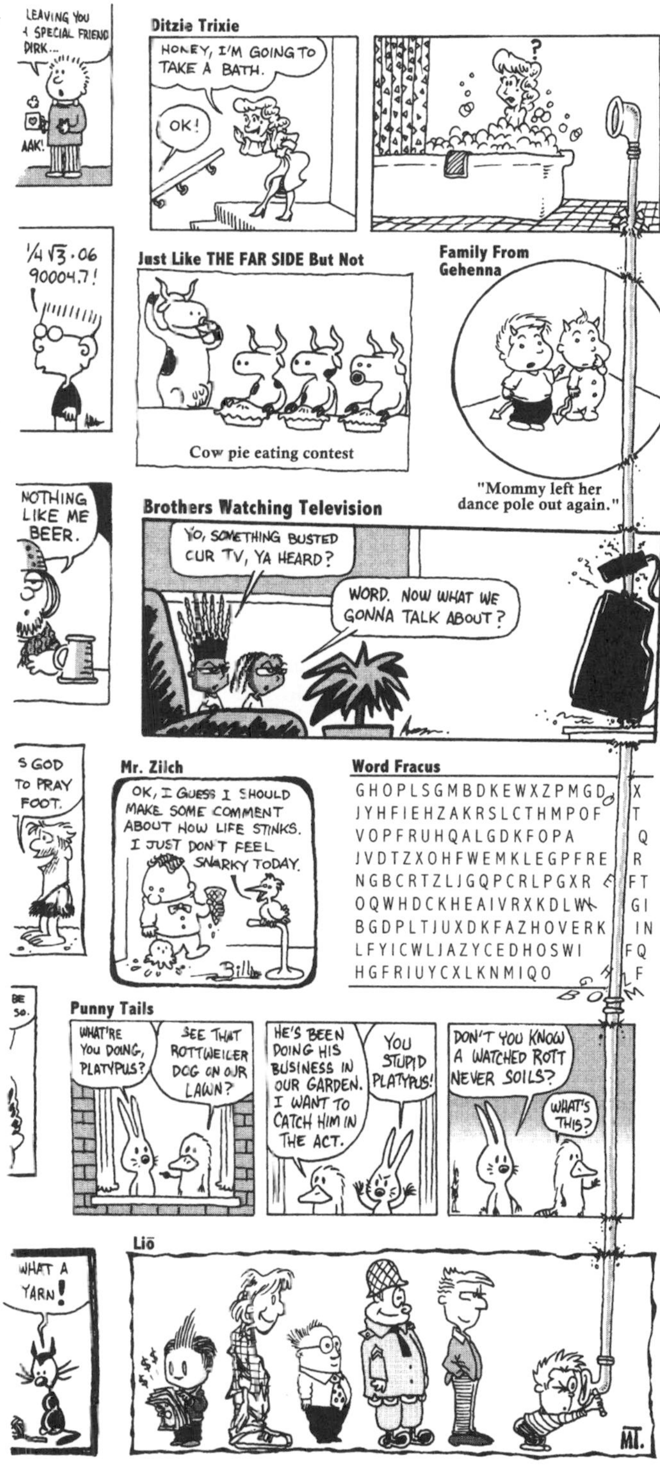
LEAVING YOU A SPECIAL FRIEND DIRK...
AAK!
Ditzie Trixie
HONEY, I'M GOING TO TAKE A BATH.
OK!
?
1/4 √3 · 06 90004.7!
Just Like THE FAR SIDE But Not
Cow pie eating contest
Family From Gehenna
"Mommy left her dance pole out again."
NOTHING LIKE ME BEER.
Brothers Watching Television
YO, SOMETHING BUSTED OUR TV, YA HEARD?
WORD. NOW WHAT WE GONNA TALK ABOUT?
S GOD TO PRAY FOOT.
Mr. Zilch
OK, I GUESS I SHOULD MAKE SOME COMMENT ABOUT HOW LIFE STINKS. I JUST DON'T FEEL SNARKY TODAY.
Word Fracus
GHOPLSGMBDKEWXZPMGD
JYHFIEHZAKRSLCTHMPOF
VOPFRUHQALGDKFOPA
JVDTZXOHFWEMKLEGPFRE
NGBCRTZLJGQPCRLPGXR
OQWHDCKHEAIVRXKDLW
BGDPLTJUXDKFAZHOVERK
LFYICWLJAZYCEDHOSWI
HGFRIUYCXLKNMIQO
X T Q R FT GI IN FQ F
BOOM
Punny Tails
WHAT'RE YOU DOING, PLATYPUS?
SEE THAT ROTTWEILER DOG ON OUR LAWN?
HE'S BEEN DOING HIS BUSINESS IN OUR GARDEN. I WANT TO CATCH HIM IN THE ACT.
YOU STUPID PLATYPUS!
DON'T YOU KNOW A WATCHED ROTT NEVER SOILS?
WHAT'S THIS?
WHAT A YARN!
Liō
MT.

From *Liō: Happiness is a Squishy Cephalopod.* [©2007 Mark Tatulli]

Oh God, the biggest one was nuclear war. I grew up during, let's see … I was born in '63. That always overshadowed everything. And they were always talking about it on television, and of course, you know, the second world war was only 20 years before I was born, and you'd always see the movies like *Tora! Tora! Tora!* And I was certain that the Japanese were gonna come and bomb us. Nobody ever even thought to tell me that that was never going to happen. It was just a fear I kept, and whenever I heard the drone of planes, I was sure this was *it*, the Japanese were coming to bomb us now. So those were definitely fears, and certainly monsters. I didn't worry about monsters in my closet or under my bed. They were definitely roaming around downstairs, though, in my house.

I was talking to [King Features President] Rocky Shepard and he was telling us about how many people are trying to get in.

Are as many people trying to get in?

He said they still get a few hundred submissions a year, and maybe three of them are worth looking at, and maybe one of those will get launched in a given year.

I'd say that Universal is pretty much down to one or two a year. I don't know how many they have in development. But development can stretch three years now easily. They wanna be sure that what they're putting in is something that's got a chance. So it's really more difficult than it's ever been. I would say it's on the verge of impossible to make a living doing it now. I mean, I'd say that *Liō* is definitely the exception, not the rule.

For a while, it looked like *Boondocks* was gonna be the last successful comic strip, but now it looks like *Liō* is currently wearing that crown.

Yeah, it's not easy out there, man. I used to recommend it as a great way to make a living, but you can't. I mean, you know what it costs to live, but you actually don't. With the mortgages and college, as a stay-at-home cartoonist, or a stay-at-home-stripper as I call it, we have to pay our own health insurance. And for me, for a family of five, it's $1,200 dollars a month, just for health insurance. Most of these new comics don't even make *that.* In fact, they'd be lucky if they made that. So, it's not an easy thing these days, and I don't know what the answer is. I mean, I think the answer is the Internet. The problem with the Internet is that anybody can get on there and post a comic strip, and I don't care how bad or crappy it is, it'll get *some* fans. The audience has become so watered down by all these different choices that it's hard to make a living. So, let's see where that leads.

In addition to the strip, you have one collection out already for *Liō*. Is the second one on the way, or is that out?

Yeah, it's coming out in about two weeks.

How have book sales done?

Good. In fact, we're in the process of doing three more books: a treasury and two more regular collections. Again, in this market, that doesn't happen unless they have faith.

Are you gonna be doing any director's commentary or anything like that?

Yes. In the new treasury, I'm gonna do an origins thing. I don't know if you knew Stan Lee's *Origins* books? It's like the origins of all the superheroes? Well, I was gonna do origins of *Liō*. You know, just show the illustrations that led up to his actual creation —some of the things that I

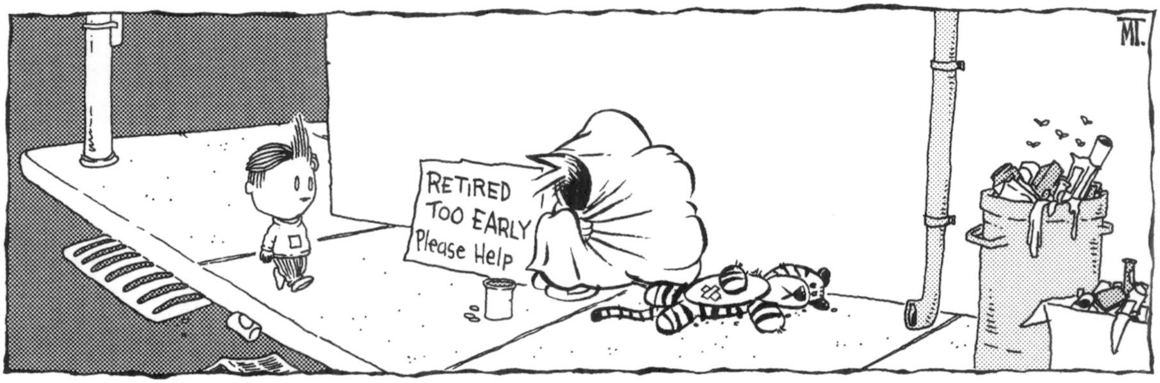
MT.
RETIRED
TOO EARLY
Please Help

Calvin and Hobbes is a fruitful source of humor for *Liō*. [©2007 Mark Tatulli]

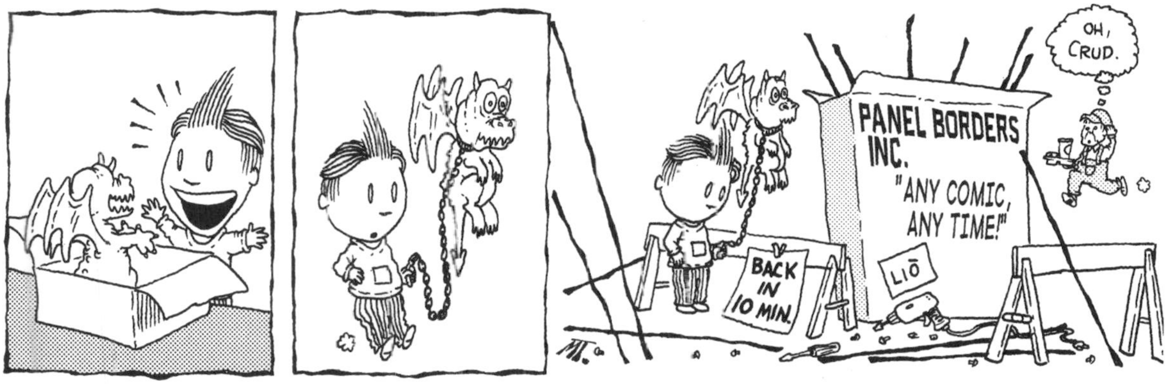
OH, CRUD.
PANEL BORDERS INC.
"ANY COMIC, ANY TIME!"
BACK IN 10 MIN.
LIŌ

[©2007 Mark Tatulli]

showed in the slide presentation that you saw at the Reubens. I think that's fun stuff. It adds value to the treasuries too: It's not just a retread of what's already in collections.

Yeah, most of my favorite collections go along those lines, like the *Calvin and Hobbes Tenth Anniversary* book, I reread that one all the time just to get Watterson's thoughts.

It's hard for me to fathom that anybody would care what I was thinking when I drew a strip, but I may do something like that, eventually. I just can't imagine somebody caring about them; Watterson, yeah, I can see. And by 10 years, everybody's interested, so maybe 10 years from now, I'll be something like that. Well, not 10 years. I've already been doing *Liō* for two, two and a half? God, time goes fast, huh?

You probably do have a lot of readers trying to figure out what's going on in your head when they're reading *Liō*.

I think to have an origin section is a good way to start. Show 'em how *Liō* came to be, and then go through that process and say "Here's what I was thinking, here's what I wanted to do, and here are all the different manifestations of Liō and the changes." You know, originally, his eyes were gonna be black. They were gonna be larger and black, and when I looked at it, it's like, he's a *really* dark figure. He looks like a murderer. I didn't wanna go *that* far. I wanted him to have a blank look, but I also wanted a mixture of nonchalance and innocence.

I mentioned readers, and I'm gonna go out on a limb here and guess that *Liō* generates quite a bit more mail than *Heart of the City*.

You know, it's funny, they take turns.

Really?

Well, here's the thing. I don't post an e-mail address on my *Liō* strip because I don't necessarily want to know what readers are thinking. I know that's counterintuitive to what the modern-day Web cartoonist thinks, that a Web comic is more about community than it is about comics. It's about creating a community and then entertaining them with the comic, and then there's a lot of reader input into what happens in that comic. And I know just from my experience of doing *Heart*, that it can shape how you move forward with your strip when you have people responding to different things, and I don't necessarily want to do that. I want it to grow in a very natural way that comes completely from what *I* think. So for that reason, I didn't put an e-mail address on my strip.

But interestingly enough, I do get a lot of snail-mail, and some people have found out — people don't look that deep into it, but you'd be surprised that people don't know that I do the two strips. But some have found out and get my e-mail address from *Heart of the City* and that's how they write me.

Well, the strips are drawn in completely different styles. There's a different signature for each strip.

For that reason: I wanted them to be completely separated. One thing that always bothered me was when a cartoonist did two strips and then he did them in the same style, just different characters. And to me, I'm still looking at more of the same. I don't feel like I'm getting anything new. And that's just me personally. That's just how I felt about it. So I didn't want that at all. It's also part of keeping an interest in both strips, because when I shifted from one to another, it felt like I was doing something different. It wasn't like I was doing 14 strips a week; it was like I was doing two sets of seven. And it makes it more bear-

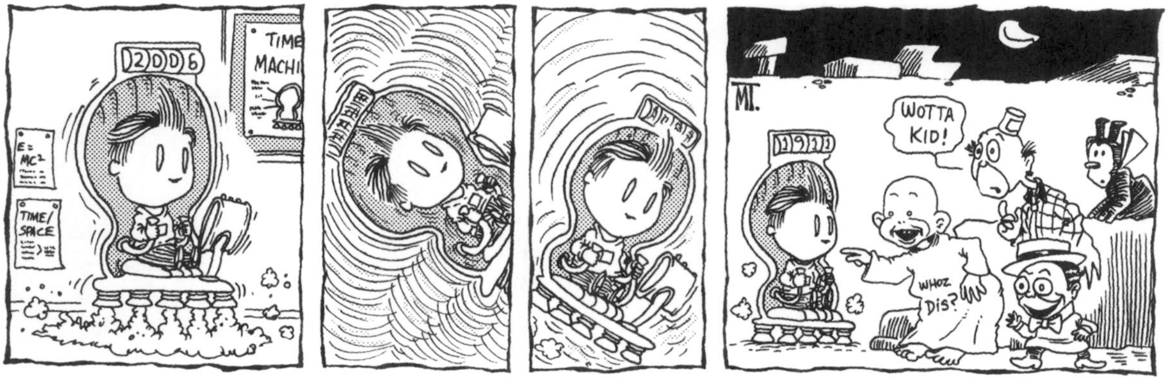
2006
TIME MACHI
E= MC2
TIME/ SPACE
MT.
WOTTA KID!
WHOZ DIS?

[©2007 Mark Tatulli]

able, believe it or not.

And so how do you get into the mindset to do each strip? What do you do that keeps them from intruding on each other?

Well, they have to be separated by days. I will wake up, and what I'm gonna do that day is *Liō* strips, or I'll wake up, and what I'm gonna do that day is *Heart* strips. And so, I immediately slide into that mode. And like I said, *Heart* is script-driven, so I'll start writing strips. *Liō* is visually motivated, so I will go through my old *Liō* strips and I have tons of reference books, and lately I've been going to the library and just looking at old *Creepshow* comics and stuff like that, just to get into the mindset. It starts to happen.

What's the split on how much time you spend on each strip.

I said about 70/30 — but it's more like 50/50 honestly. It depends on who needs more help that week. Some weeks *Heart of the City* will just flow right out of my pen, and some weeks it'll be more of a struggle, and vice versa. It's like teaching math to a class. You can't divide the class in half and say "I spend more time on this half of the class than that half of the class." Every week it's going to be different.

Do you use a brush on *Heart of the City*?

Yes. I use a brush dipping into ink, and with *Liō* I draw with Micron pens, all different sizes.

Are you the colorist on your Sunday strips?

Yes, I do everything.

***Liō* occasionally will use computer fonts, right?**

Yeah, because, again, it separates it from *Heart*. I use some goofy fonts I get online that have kind of a weird look to them; an edgy look. My handwriting doesn't change between *Heart* and *Liō*, so I try to keep my handwriting to a minimum in *Liō*.

It looks like you use tones in *Liō*, but I don't really see any, flipping through the first *Heart* collection.

No, back then, I didn't. Like I said, that was back in '98, so I wasn't doing anything on the computer. I was drawing it, I was doing everything the old-fashioned mechanical way and not scanning or anything, just sending the originals right to my syndicate. They would take it from there and ship them back to me. It wasn't until I started incorporating the computer and scanning that I started adding grayscales and Zipatone and that kind of stuff.

Do you still hand-letter *Heart*?

Yes.

That's good to hear. That seems to be one of the fastest dying aspects of comic strips.

Yeah, I don't like computer fonts. I use them in *Liō*, but they're usually for signage. But I don't use it for any kind of word balloons, only because I think that it has a very mechanical look — it just feels inappropriate within a drawn strip.

One of the things you touched on when you gave your presentation in New Orleans is the notion that maybe comic strips shouldn't go on forever and ever.

Yeah, I think they have a natural lifespan, because you start to repeat yourself so much. Yeah, I would never tell anybody when they should walk away. I'm only talking for myself. It seems to me that like a sitcom, after a while, it's like "OK, how much shit can this person do?" Comic strips to me seem to have a natural lifespan too, and I don't know what it is. I think it's between 10 and 15 years. It's just like, you say everything you *can* through those characters.

You're around the 10-year mark for *Heart*?

Yeah, exactly, but again, I don't speak for anybody else. People don't *want* it. They want to see the strips because they're used to seeing them, like when you get die-hard fans. I'm not saying that's a bad thing, I think that's great. I certainly appreciate any fans that *Heart* has, but after a while, you wonder, "Gee, if I just did a week where it was nothing but black frames with eyeballs floating around and dialogue," and just said "oh, there's a blackout," and just had the characters say whatever. I wonder how long you can get away with that, or you can have your characters sitting there and not making jokes, but just talking to each other in a very dialogue-y kind of way, but without any punch lines, I wonder how long you can get away with that, too. Just because people are happy to see their characters that they're used to seeing every day. Is it a habit? Yeah, I think it is. Part of it is habit, thank God, or I wouldn't have a job. I don't know. What's that point where a comic strip starts to overstay its welcome? We all know where it is when it comes to sitcoms on television, right? Everybody says, "Oh, well now it's starting to get old," or "They really jumped the shark, because they brought in a baby," and everyone seems to know that. It's not the same, though, with comic strips.

People are resistant to any sort of change. I remember when they changed the hairstyle in *The Family Circus* about a decade ago, maybe more at this point. But the mother got a haircut, and this is big news: or Blondie starting her catering job.

That *is* big news. Blondie going to work for sure is big news. And the mother in *Luann* changed her hairstyle, and characters get cancer, these are all big-news things. It's breaking the routine.

Which *Liō* strips have generated the most mail, either positive or negative?

Oh, definitely the *Calvin and Hobbes* strip that I had done got the most reader reaction. What I did was I took the final *Calvin and Hobbes* strip, where he goes sledding off, "It's a great big beautiful world, Hobbes. Let's go exploring." And he goes sledding off. For readers, the strip never *ended,* we just can't see what he's doing now. We're just not allowed to see what Calvin's up to. He kept going on, we just can't see it.

So what I did with *Liō* was I had him walking through the same kind of forest and discovering the sled and there's the skeleton of Calvin and the Hobbes doll, and he's thinking in his head "Boy missing since '95," the implication being that he never made it farther that day than when we saw him sledding off. He just died. Which is pretty sick, but I thought it was *funny,* because I consider — I love *Calvin and Hobbes*, but it's like a sacred cow — and of course, I want to skewer that. Yeah, I got a lot of reaction to that. A lot of people thought it was funny, and a lot of people thought it was just *sick*, and how dare I touch *Calvin and Hobbes* with my dirty fingers. But that got the strongest reaction. Chats popped up out of nowhere to discuss it.

Has that encouraged you to do more strips along that line?

Yeah, I think I'm gonna name one of my collections

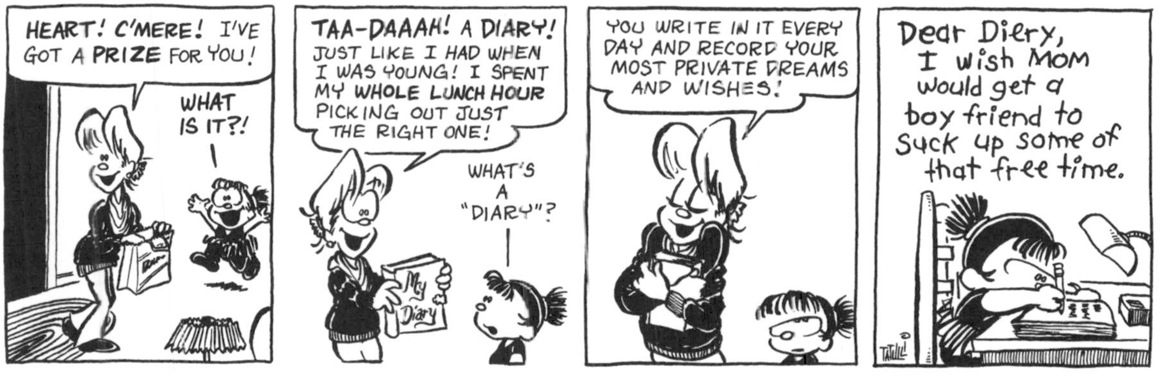
HEART! C'MERE! I'VE GOT A PRIZE FOR YOU!
WHAT IS IT?!
TAA-DAAAH! A DIARY! JUST LIKE I HAD WHEN I WAS YOUNG! I SPENT MY WHOLE LUNCH HOUR PICKING OUT JUST THE RIGHT ONE!
WHAT'S A "DIARY"?
My Diary
YOU WRITE IN IT EVERY DAY AND RECORD YOUR MOST PRIVATE DREAMS AND WISHES!
Dear Diery,
I wish MOM would get a boy friend to suck up some of that free time.
TATULLI

[©2000 Mark Tatulli]

after a *Calvin and Hobbes* collection. There's a *Calvin and Hobbes* collection called *There's Treasure Everywhere*, and it has him digging a hole with Hobbes, and he's pulling out a worm or something. So I was gonna do a *Liō* collection called *There's Corpses Everywhere*, and have Liō in the hole with a squid nearby, and he's pulling out the Calvin skull. And of course, the Hobbes doll will by lying nearby too. I think that would be funny.

Yeah, I like it. So why the squid in *Liō*?

It's the dynamic of the boy and his dog. They go off together and do their thing, and nobody understands them, kind of like *My Dog Skip*. Except that it's Liō's world, so it's a squid, and to me there is nothing more bizarre than — crustaceans and cephalopods, they're probably the least approachable type of creatures, something you wouldn't think of as cuddly or something you wanna get in bed with, getting cozy with like a dog or a cat. So it seems perfect for Liō, a squid.

Some of my favorite *Liō* strips along the lines of the Calvin and Hobbes ones are the strips where he interacts with other cartoon characters, and it seems like that happens a lot more frequently on today's comic page.

Yeah, that's why I've been walking back from that, because a lot of cartoonists are doing it; crossovers they call them. I do them from time to time, but I kind of step back from doing it as much. I think it's also not a bottomless pit. You can't keep going to that well. I think the last thing I did, Dick Tracy popped up in there and Liō stole his hat and started his own detective agency.

They seem like very casual things and I think you mentioned Stephan Pastis earlier, and he's one of the biggest culprits.

Yeah, he has *The Family Circus* popping up every now and then. Never does anything with Charlie Brown, did you notice that?

He knows who signs his checks.

Well, he works at Creative Associates, the *Peanuts* organization. I would love to see what would happen if he did that.

Yeah, Jeannie [Schulz] knows where he lives. *[Laughter.]*

So yeah, I've noticed there's a definite sort of camaraderie among these guys. Are you tight with any other cartoonists who came up around when you did?

Yes. I talk to Stephan more than any of them. We talk about once a week, maybe twice a week. But I talk to Rob Harrell too, who used to do *Big Top*. We're good friends. I'll talk to different guys from the NCS from time to time. Whoever, Jeff Keane every now and then. We're kind of an antisocial group. You wouldn't know it when we get together at the NCS, but other than that, we're pretty antisocial and we kind of are loners and stick to ourselves. But it's always good to do those things, like when I went out to the book expo in Los Angeles, actually the week after the Reubens, and I was hanging out with — Scott Adams was there, and Jerry Scott, and Tom Wilson Jr., who does *Ziggy*. So, it's kind of cool to hang out with those guys, and just chit-chat about the business.

Has the old guard been pretty supportive of you?

How do you mean supportive of me? You mean, when I take stabs at other strips? That kind of thing, or just what I'm doing?

I guess, first of all, nobody's taking offense when you use their characters?

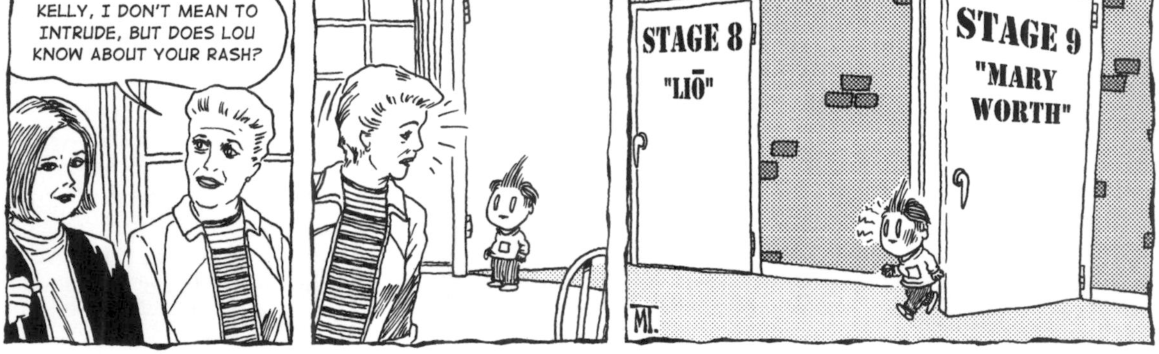
KELLY, I DON'T MEAN TO INTRUDE, BUT DOES LOU KNOW ABOUT YOUR RASH?
STAGE 8
"LIŌ"
STAGE 9
"MARY WORTH"
MT.

One example of a *Liō* comic-strip crossover with *Mary Worth*. [©2007 Mark Tatulli]

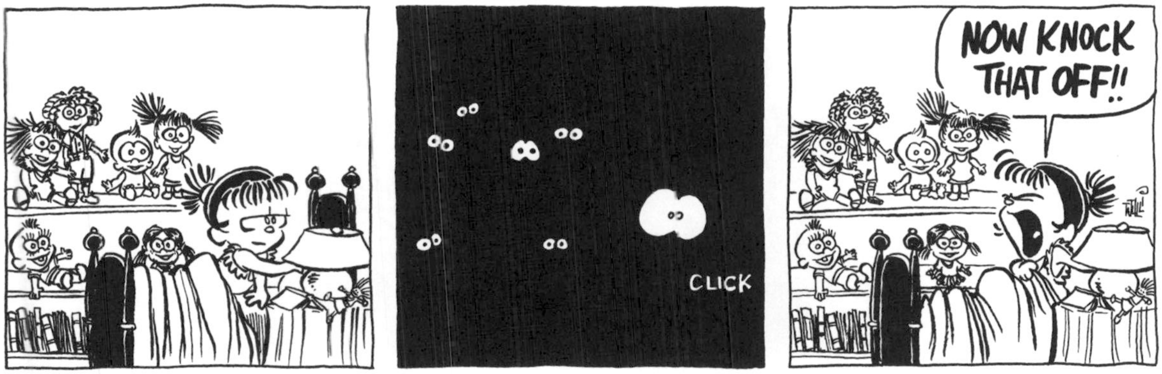
CLICK
NOW KNOCK THAT OFF!!

[©2000 Mark Tatulli]

Not to me, they haven't said anything. But I don't ask for permission; I just do it. Because I consider them to be — first of all, in every case, they're homages. Secondly, if you were getting made fun of in another comic strip, that means you're successful enough that you can be used as a comic figure and that people will understand. I mean, that's a *good* thing. It's nothing to get upset about. I don't do anything that is nasty. I really don't do anything that's really nasty. It may be dark, but I'll never do anything that's mean-spirited to other comics.

One of the other things I was getting at is: Are there any cartoonists who — I guess right when *Heart* was starting out — who were the first artists that you heard from? Are there any longtime supporters or fans who —

I didn't go to my first Reubens until 2000. Like I said, I launched in '98, but I didn't go to Reubens until 2000, and I guess that's when I started meeting the cartoonists. Up to then, it was mostly just talking to the syndicate people. But I had written letters to cartoonists; this was before e-mail and stuff. I had written to Berkeley Breathed and Jim Davis, and I had gotten responses from both of them, and Cathy Guisewite, and it was interesting. I had written to Cathy, oh God, back in the late '80s, and she wrote back to me in the early '90s, and then when we were in Chicago at the Reubens, I produced the letter, and I said, "Look, this is the letter you wrote to me back in the early '90s, and I just wanted to say I really appreciated it at the time, and now we're both syndicated by the same syndicate." Because she wrote on there "Maybe some day you'll have a contract, you'll see. You never know," and lo and behold.

One of the things you mentioned at your presentation was that a *Liō* movie is a possibility now.

Yes, there's an executive producer attached to it, and he's driving the ship at this point. Actually, his production company, that's David Kirschner, did the Chucky movies, you know, the *Child's Play* movies, and he did *Martian Child* that just came out, and oh God, *Fievel goes West* and *An American Tail* and those kinds of things. He's got quite an eclectic slate: also *Miss Potter*. Did you see that movie?

Yeah.

Secondhand Liōns, yeah, those were his movies. So, right now, we're developing a story to go with this thing. And it's not as easy as it may sound. You might think, "Ah, this is going to lend itself perfectly to that," but it's difficult coming up with a linear storyline for something that is not linear in its telling every day in the newspapers. It may look like Liō is dead one day, and then the next day, he's back in action. So we don't have that same kind of luxury within the linear storytelling that movies afford us.

On that note, do you find it really difficult to write *Liō* in that every day has to be a self-contained joke?

Do I find it difficult? I find it difficult pleasing myself, but I think that's natural, I think that's part of the process. Everywhere I look, there's a potential for a gag. Everything is potentially funny. Everything can be turned into what Liō's world is. It's looking at things that normally happen within your life, and then putting them into the context of *Liō* and monsters and robots, and a pizza delivery man comes to be a completely different thing when it comes to the concept of Liō's world. I think that there's jokes everywhere, and like I said, I have a hard time pleasing myself some weeks. But other than that, it's a great job.

So getting back to the *Liō* movie, visually, what do you

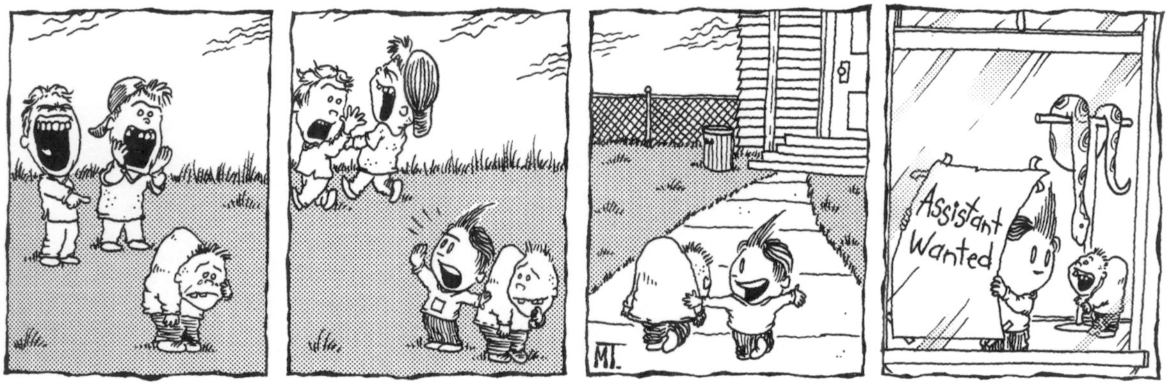
Assistant Wanted

[©2007 Mark Tatulli]

see this —

I think what they're talking about doing, at least right now, is a combination of live action and CGI. Liō would be a real boy, and his squid and his snakes and all that stuff, his menagerie would be 3D computer graphics. You know, kind of like the *Alvin and the Chipmunks* movie that came out last year.

So, on the subject of movies — you already mentioned *Gone with the Wind* — but what kind of movies just really got you excited when you were growing up?

Oh, anything Disney because I was just blown away by the high detail of the animation, the real cinematic quality to cartoons. When I saw *The Sword in the Stone*, I said "oh my God, Disney's got to do *The Lord of the Rings*, they could do a great job with that." Of course, that was before computer graphics and everything. And *Fantasia* just blew me away. So anything Disney, anything by Mel Brooks — there's a combination for ya — I guess that's the essence of *Liō*.

***Young Frankenstein*'s probably my favorite movie of all time.**

Yeah, and I love *Blazing Saddles* too, I gotta tell ya. *Young Frankenstein* is an exceptionally stylish movie. It's the old-style horror black and white done to perfection. They didn't miss a beat. Even the music was perfect, just everything. The makeup, spot on.

OK, so Mel Brooks, Disney, and you mix that all together. What sort of books and comics were you reading?

Roald Dahl was always a favorite, *Charlie and the Chocolate Factory, James and the Giant Peach,* those kinds of things, and *Charlotte's Web*, you know, fantastical stuff: the comic books that I read — I didn't read superheroes. My brother was into the superhero stuff. That's how I ended up seeing [Stan Lee's] *Origins*, because he bought them, but he also bought *Creepy* and *Eerie*. Do you remember those? That's probably before your time. But you've heard of them, I'm sure. They were horror tales. They were great. The greatest artists, and great stories. *Heavy Metal* magazine had really great artwork and scary stories and futuristic stuff. I also liked, of course, *Mad* magazine, and there was also something called *Plop!* in the '70s, which was primarily drawn by Sergio Aragonés. I loved *Plop!* But that's the kind of stuff that I read.

Sergio's probably one of the best-known practitioners of the pantomime cartoon.

Yes, he is. I can't think of anybody else that is even known for it. We all know *The Little King* and *Henry* and all, but I couldn't tell you who the artist was. *Ferdinand*, too, but Sergio is king.

Have you looked at *Henry* very much?

You know, I remember reading it when I was a kid, and *Ferd'nand* too. But there are no collections that I've ever seen. You'd have to go online, I guess, and do a Google search. But I doubt you'd get very much. I haven't seen a collection of *Henry* strips.

That mainly focused on one mute character.

In my estimation, the syndicate was a little worried about me doing something without dialogue from anybody, and they said, "Well, how about if you have Liō being the only one who doesn't talk," and I said "if I have Liō being the only one who doesn't talk, I have to have an explanation for why he doesn't talk," and that makes him a problem instead of everybody else is the problem. The world is bizarre. Liō lives in a very visual world. We don't need to explain things like that, like "Why isn't he talking?" There's no explanation needed if nobody else is talking.

Is Liō's father modeled on anyone in particular?

Yeah, actually he was modeled on me at the time. Like I said, I had lost my job in the great layoff of 2005, and I was feeling pretty useless, I mean, you just feel like a loser. You're not going to work, you're not shaving. I didn't actually lie around the house in my underwear and drink beer, but I felt that way. And you know, my kids certainly didn't help the situation. "Oh Dad, you're gonna be here all the time? You're gonna be watching everything we do?" So that's where he came from.

I met your kids at the Reubens, and they seemed really into the whole scene, which must be nice for you. They were probably the most courteous and polite kids I've met.

Yeah, there's lots of beatings to get them to that point. No, they're great kids. We love them to death, and they have absolutely no interest in comic books or comic strips. They have no interest in helping me at all in the business. They want to go off and do their own thing. That's fine.

Are they interested in the arts?

My son is studying filmmaking in college. He writes a lot, and occasionally he'll draw something, like a graphic novel-y type thing, but nothing where it's a passion.

Did you have anything else to say about them or family life?

Well, I wouldn't be able to do this if it wasn't for them. I mean, they're constant inspiration to me, my wife and my kids. They make you think in a way that you just don't think yourself, or they remind you to think like a kid or a teenager or whatever, to look at things a little differently. So being around them is definitely a plus, and I wouldn't be able to do this if I were on my own. I wouldn't. It just would get monotonous.

So, how did you meet your wife?

Well, I like to say to my kids, "We met at a dance." But it was a bar that had dancing at it. But it sounds better if you say, "We met at a dance." Something very *Back to the Future* about that.

So what does she do for a living?

She raises my kids. She does work at a tanning salon/hair salon every now and then, but she takes the summer off and my son works her hours.

Yeah, I think we talked about that. We're both from the Sicilian background, and my mom was stay-at-home until my little brother was old enough to start school.

It's definitely better that way. There was always somebody here with them. Even though it was difficult in the early years to make ends meet, you do. And my kids have

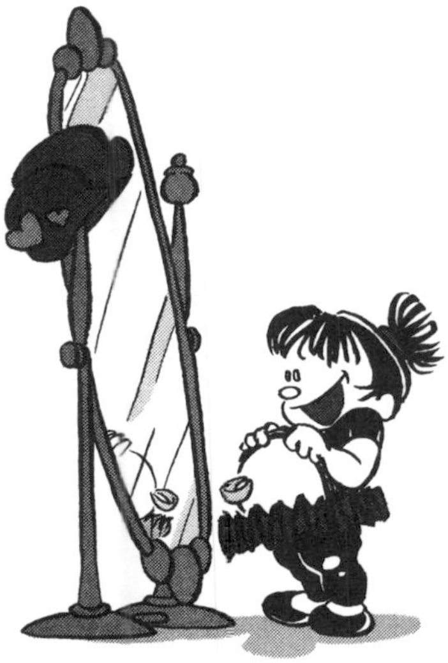

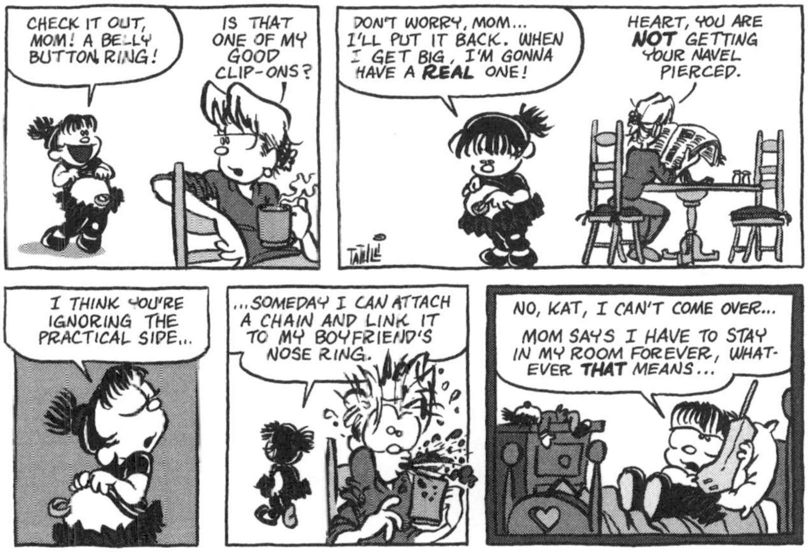
CHECK IT OUT, MOM! A BELLY BUTTON RING!
IS THAT ONE OF MY GOOD CLIP-ONS?
DON'T WORRY, MOM... I'LL PUT IT BACK. WHEN I GET BIG, I'M GONNA HAVE A REAL ONE!
HEART, YOU ARE NOT GETTING YOUR NAVEL PIERCED.
I THINK YOU'RE IGNORING THE PRACTICAL SIDE...
...SOMEDAY I CAN ATTACH A CHAIN AND LINK IT TO MY BOYFRIEND'S NOSE RING.
NO, KAT, I CAN'T COME OVER... MOM SAYS I HAVE TO STAY IN MY ROOM FOREVER, WHATEVER THAT MEANS...

[©2007 Mark Tatulli]

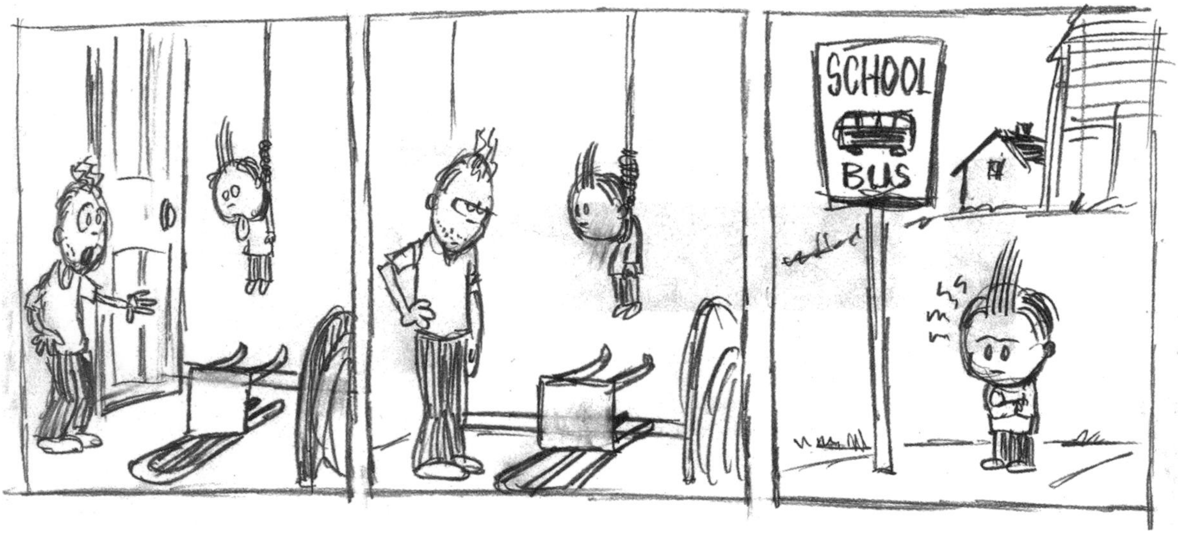
SCHOOL
BUS

Rejected *Liō* strip. © 2008 Mark Tatulli

definitely benefited from having a parent at home.

Who's the editor that you work with?

The editor at Universal Press that I work with is Greg Melvin.

I don't suppose *Heart* runs into too many problems, but is he sympathetic on *Liō*? He has a pretty good idea of what you're trying to do?

Oh yeah, and he tells me when I can't do things. Well, you saw *[at the Reubens]* the strips that got rejected, and I gave my reasons why the editors felt it just might garner too much complaint. It's all part of getting you ready to leave the nest, so to speak. I'm pretty good at editing myself — but in the beginning, it's hard to really get a sense of: We're playing it safe, because we're trying to get as many clients as we can so we can try to get it established. You're gonna get complaints no matter what, and especially in the case of *Liō* being so dark. We knew that there was gonna be complaints going in, but we hoped that we could build a fan base up fast enough that it wouldn't matter, and you have to be careful that you don't piss off the fan base by doing something that's wrong.

Like I said, I had done a strip where *Liō* walked by a pet store, and he sees the dogs jumping in the window, little puppies, and he begs his dad for one of the puppies, and dad lets him get a puppy, and then in the last panel is Liō with a present, and he's presenting it to his pet snake. And the present's jiggling, the assumption being that the puppy is now a present for the snake and the snake's gonna eat it. I didn't show that actually happening, that was just the assumption that you would have to make as the reader. Of course, all hell broke loose on that one. You can't show little boys giving puppies to snakes, even if you don't show it. You run the real risk of losing all your fans with that kind of stuff. But that's how you learn, sometimes. Even my editor didn't know it would get that kind of reaction.

Yeah, you seem to be very careful not to outright show death and destruction.

That's correct. It's better left in your own mind. There's only one logical way you could go, and it's pretty obvious what I intended, but it's much funnier in your head, for you to work that out. It's like the shark in *Jaws*. You don't need to see it; it's the idea that *it's coming*, and that we *know* it's coming. You know, your mind's gonna make it much worse than it really is.

That was one of the fun parts of your presentation that you'd show a *Liō* strip and you'd point out the happy ending that you could tell yourself.

Right. Here's the nice thing that really happened. What were *you* thinking? See, the darkness is coming from our own minds. That's what people have a hard time dealing with, too. That's what really aggravates some people, is they *know* that these dark thoughts are lingering in their minds, and that's just where their minds went. I mean, that's where I pointed them, but they didn't have to go there. ■

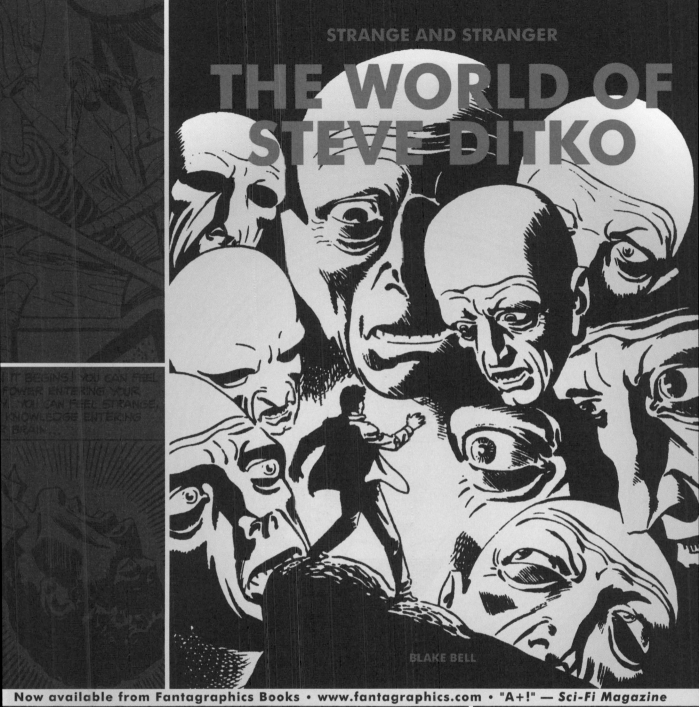

STRANGE AND STRANGER

THE WORLD OF STEVE DITKO

BLAKE BELL

As you read this, Christmas Muzak has probably already started wafting from elevators and grocery aisles and boughs of holly are likely dangling over the major intersections, but this issue was put together in the dog days of August. To put ourselves in a Yuletide spirit, however, all we had to do was open the boxes of holiday greeting cards received from comics friends and pros over the years by *The Comics Journal* and editor/publisher Gary Groth. Help yourself to a little holiday cheer by checking out the following gallery of images from those cards. ■

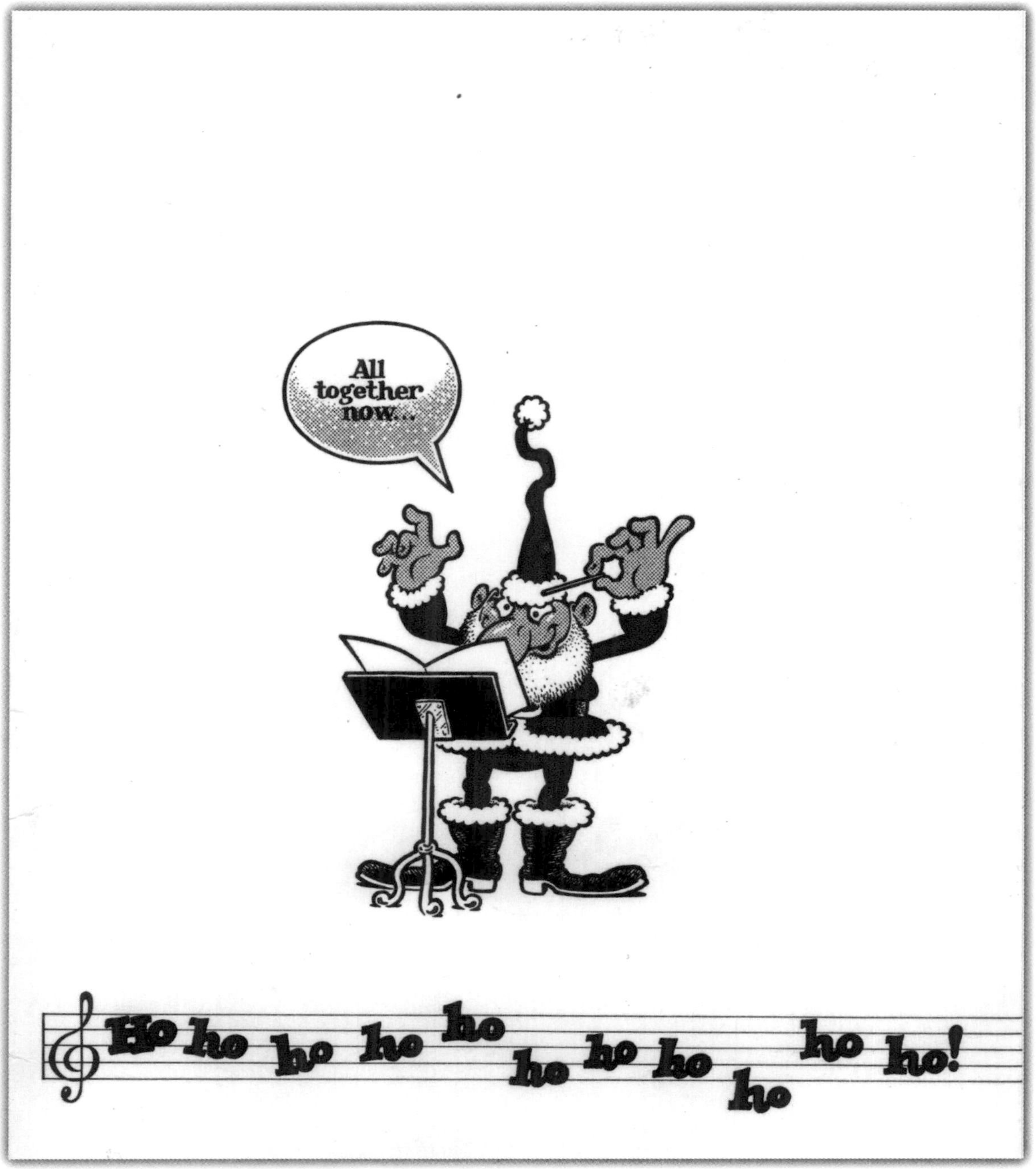
All together now...
Ho ho ho ho ho ho ho ho ho ho ho!

Howard Cruse

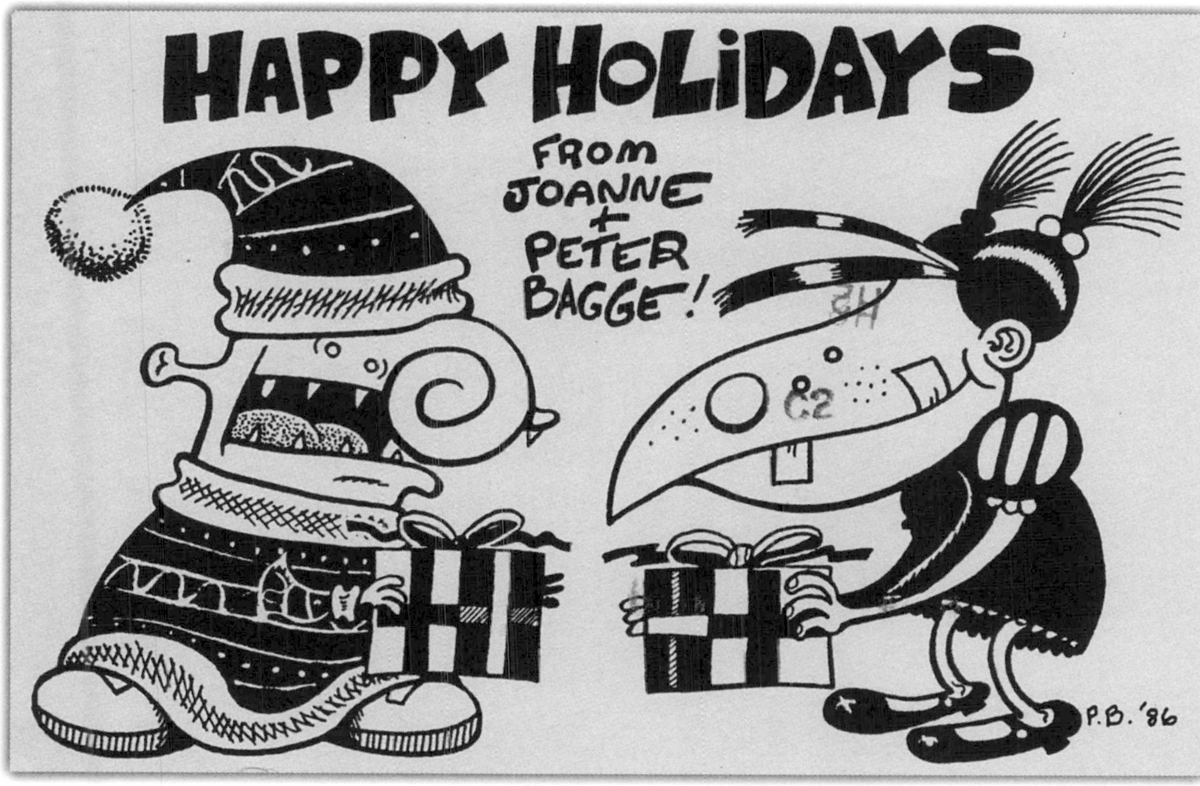
HAPPY HOLIDAYS
FROM JOANNE + PETER BAGGE!
P.B. '86

Peter Bagge

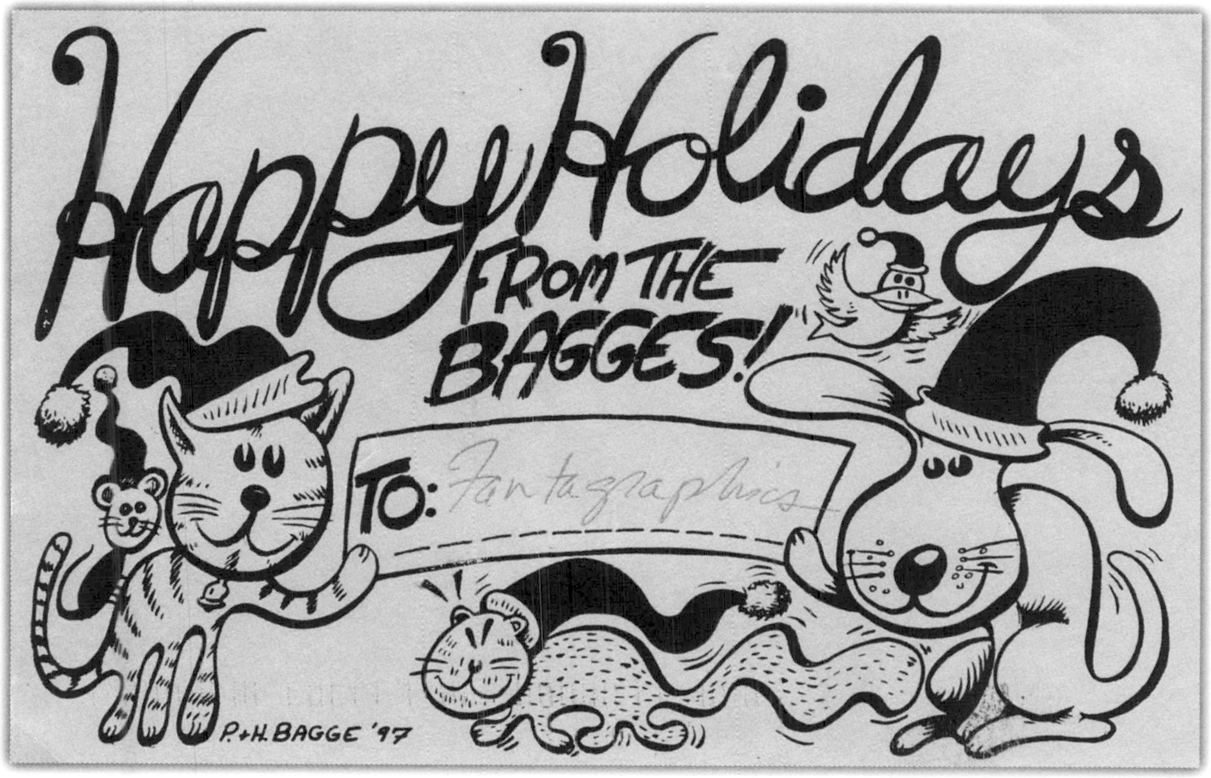
Happy Holidays
FROM THE BAGGES!
TO: Fantagraphics
P+H. BAGGE '97

Peter Bagge

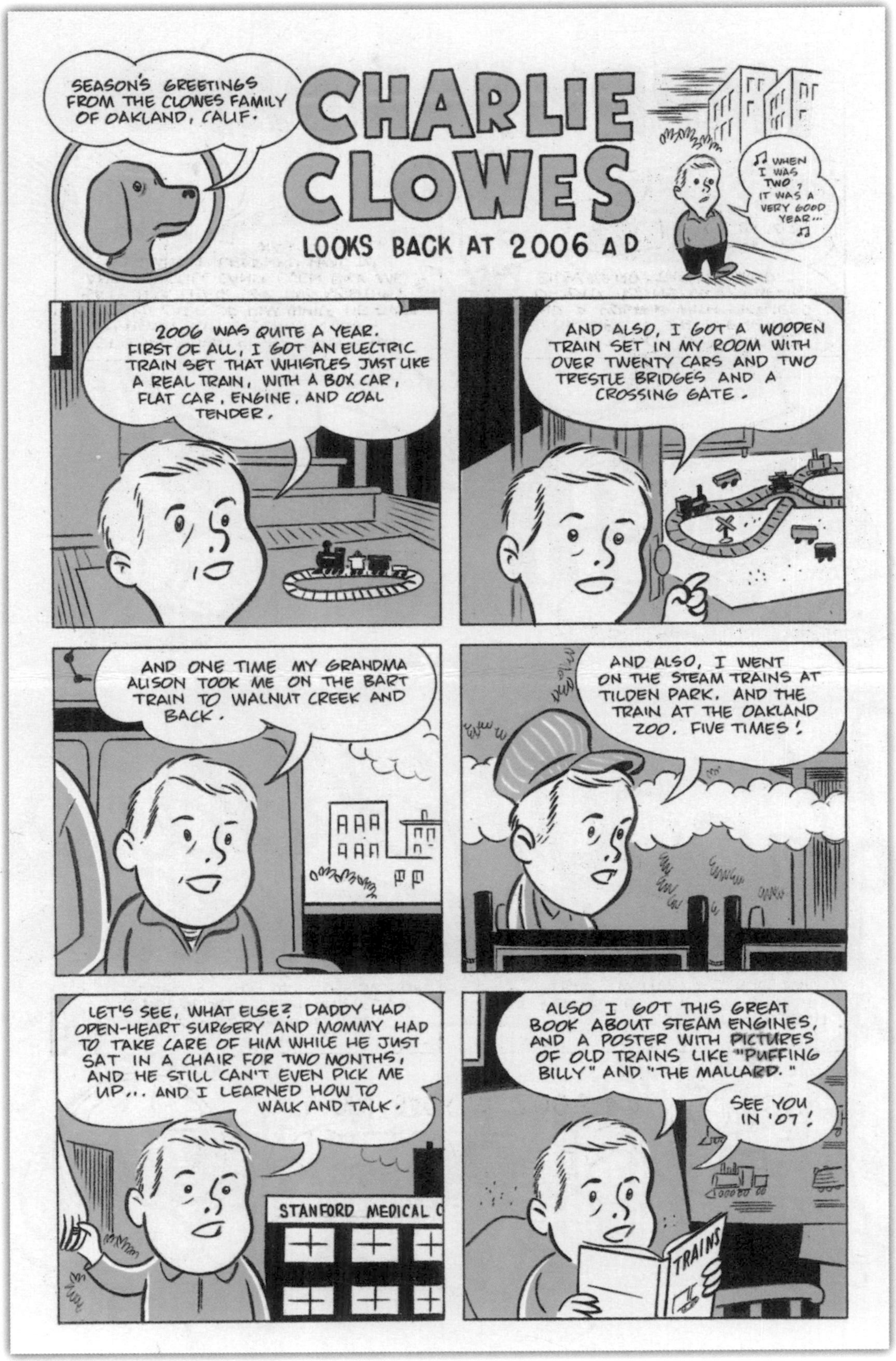
SEASON'S GREETINGS FROM THE CLOWES FAMILY OF OAKLAND, CALIF.
CHARLIE CLOWES
LOOKS BACK AT 2006 A D
♫ WHEN I WAS TWO, IT WAS A VERY GOOD YEAR... ♫
2006 WAS QUITE A YEAR. FIRST OF ALL, I GOT AN ELECTRIC TRAIN SET THAT WHISTLES JUST LIKE A REAL TRAIN, WITH A BOX CAR, FLAT CAR, ENGINE, AND COAL TENDER.
AND ALSO, I GOT A WOODEN TRAIN SET IN MY ROOM WITH OVER TWENTY CARS AND TWO TRESTLE BRIDGES AND A CROSSING GATE.
AND ONE TIME MY GRANDMA ALISON TOOK ME ON THE BART TRAIN TO WALNUT CREEK AND BACK.
AND ALSO, I WENT ON THE STEAM TRAINS AT TILDEN PARK. AND THE TRAIN AT THE OAKLAND ZOO. FIVE TIMES!
LET'S SEE, WHAT ELSE? DADDY HAD OPEN-HEART SURGERY AND MOMMY HAD TO TAKE CARE OF HIM WHILE HE JUST SAT IN A CHAIR FOR TWO MONTHS, AND HE STILL CAN'T EVEN PICK ME UP... AND I LEARNED HOW TO WALK AND TALK.
STANFORD MEDICAL C
ALSO I GOT THIS GREAT BOOK ABOUT STEAM ENGINES, AND A POSTER WITH PICTURES OF OLD TRAINS LIKE "PUFFING BILLY" AND "THE MALLARD."
SEE YOU IN '07!
TRAINS

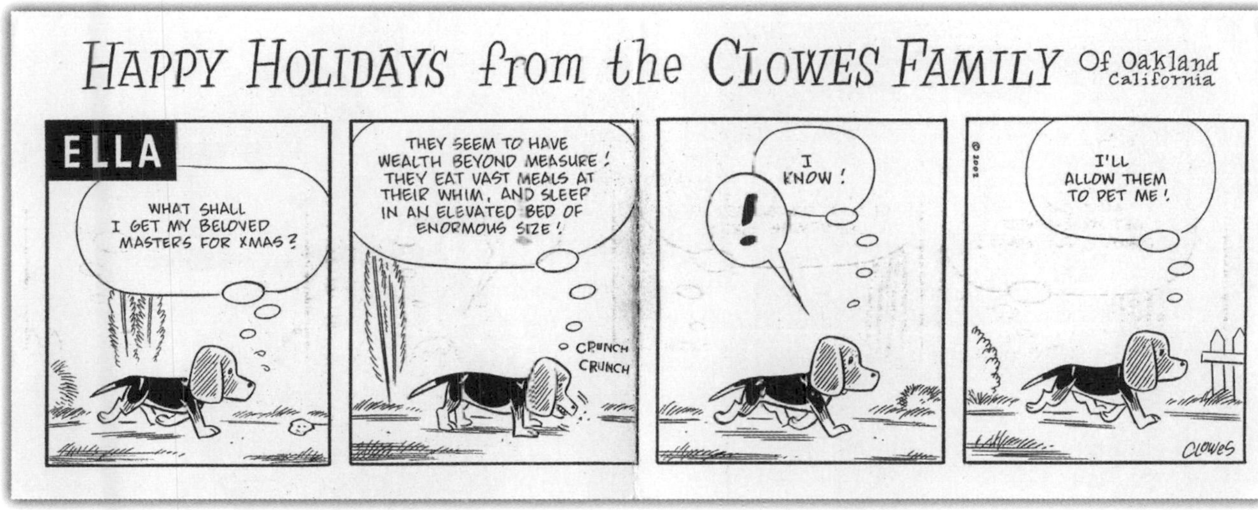
HAPPY HOLIDAYS from the CLOWES FAMILY Of Oakland California
ELLA
WHAT SHALL I GET MY BELOVED MASTERS FOR XMAS?
THEY SEEM TO HAVE WEALTH BEYOND MEASURE! THEY EAT VAST MEALS AT THEIR WHIM, AND SLEEP IN AN ELEVATED BED OF ENORMOUS SIZE!
CRUNCH
CRUNCH
I KNOW!
!
© 2002
I'LL ALLOW THEM TO PET ME!
CLOWES

Daniel Clowes

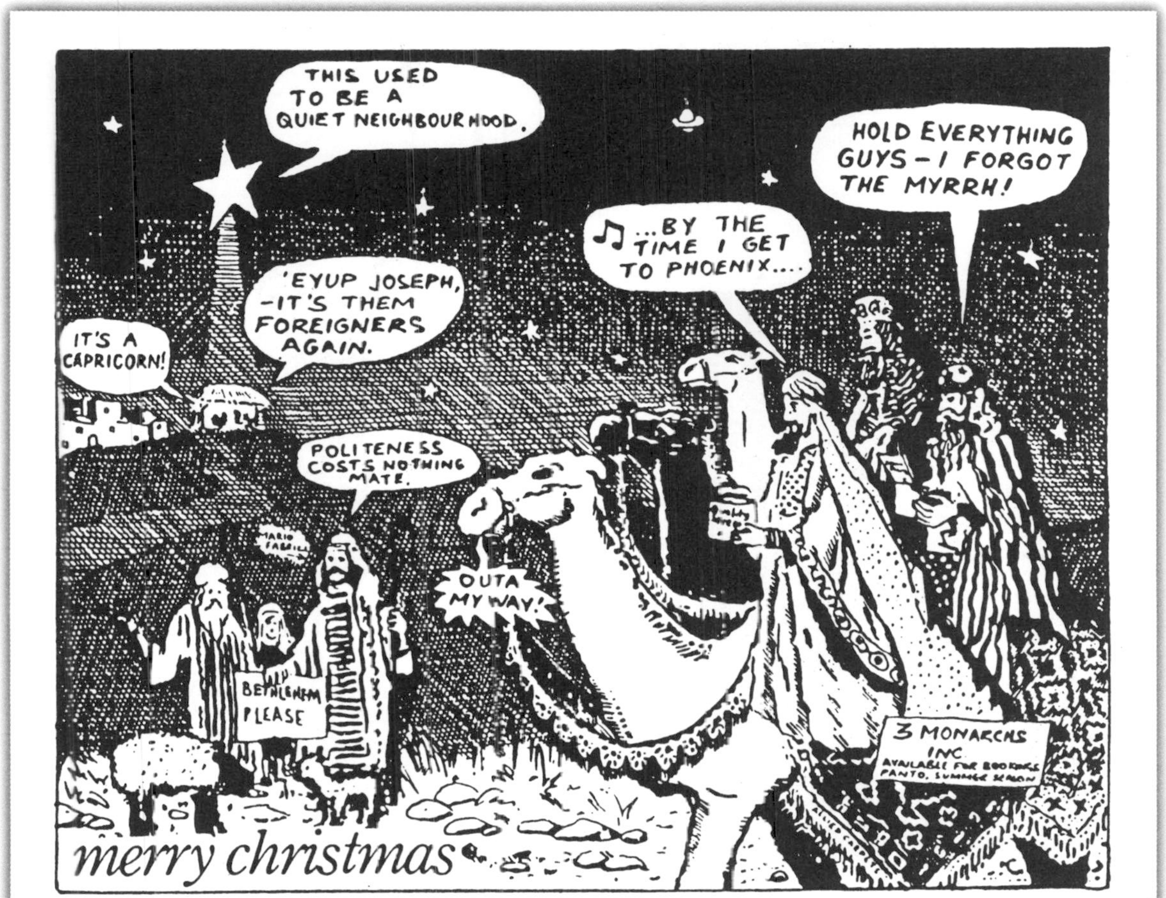
THIS USED TO BE A QUIET NEIGHBOURHOOD.
HOLD EVERYTHING GUYS - I FORGOT THE MYRRH!
♫ ...BY THE TIME I GET TO PHOENIX....
'EYUP JOSEPH, -IT'S THEM FOREIGNERS AGAIN.
IT'S A CAPRICORN!
POLITENESS COSTS NOTHING MATE.
OUTA MY WAY!
BETHLEHEM PLEASE
3 MONARCHS INC.
AVAILABLE FOR BOOKINGS PANTO, SUMMER SEASON
merry christmas

Carol Swain

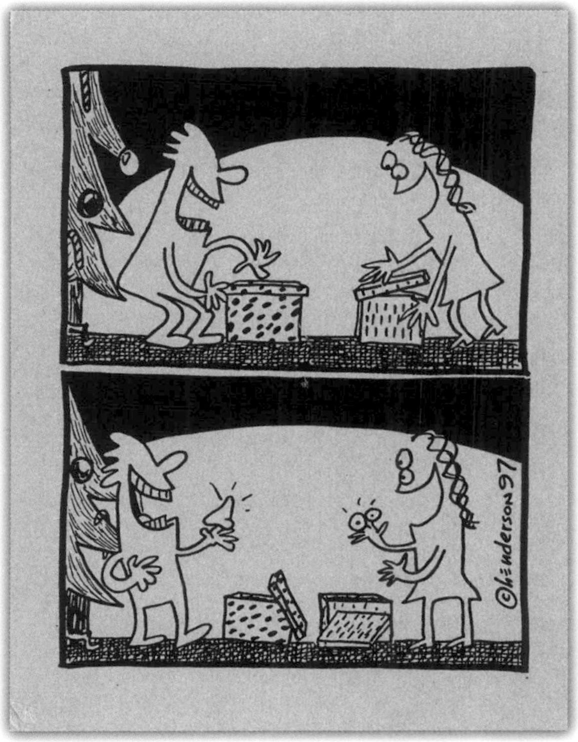
©henderson97
Sam Henderson

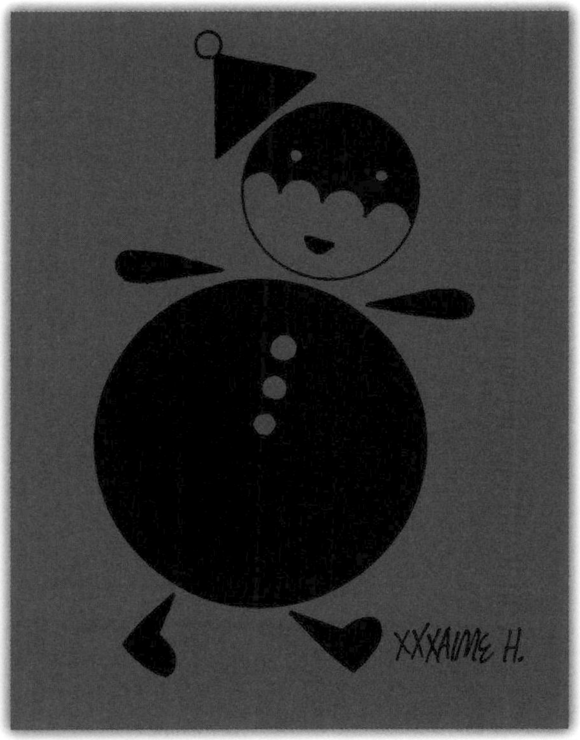
XXXAIME H.
Jaime Hernandez

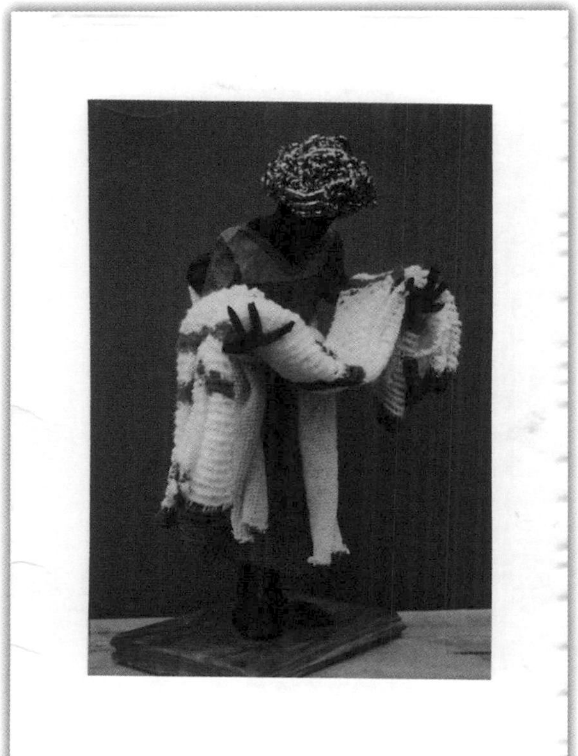
Ralph Steadman (Art by Anna Steadman)

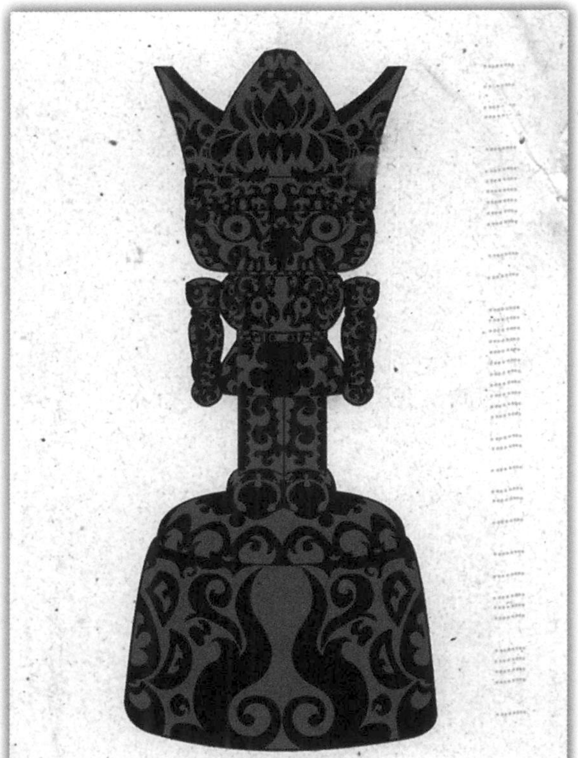
Jim Woodring

Bill Griffith

The HOLIDAYS are a BLUR of DREIDLS and MISTLETOE!
NOW PLAYING "IT'S A WONDER-FUL LATKE"
Bill & Diane
©2004 GRIFFY and DiDi

Bill Griffith

ZIPPY'S 12 days of Christmas

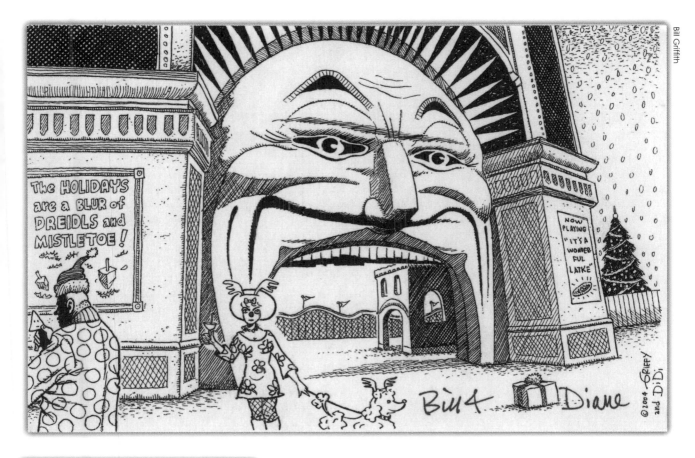

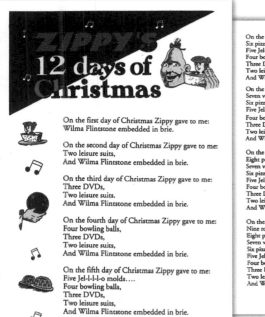

On the first day of Christmas Zippy gave to me:
Wilma Flintstone embedded in brie.

On the second day of Christmas Zippy gave to me:
Two leisure suits,
And Wilma Flintstone embedded in brie.

On the third day of Christmas Zippy gave to me:
Three DVDs,
Two leisure suits,
And Wilma Flintstone embedded in brie.

On the fourth day of Christmas Zippy gave to me:
Four bowling balls,
Three DVDs,
Two leisure suits,
And Wilma Flintstone embedded in brie.

On the fifth day of Christmas Zippy gave to me:
Five Jel-l-l-l-o molds….
Four bowling balls,
Three DVDs,
Two leisure suits,
And Wilma Flintstone embedded in brie.

On the sixth day of Christmas Zippy gave to me:
Six pizzas cooling,
Five Jel-l-l-l-o molds….
Four bowling balls,
Three DVDs,
Two leisure suits,
And Wilma Flintstone embedded in brie.

On the seventh day of Christmas Zippy gave to me:
Seven velvet paintings,
Six pizzas cooling,
Five Jel-l-l-l-o molds….
Four bowling balls,
Three DVDs,
Two leisure suits,
And Wilma Flintstone embedded in brie.

On the eighth day of Christmas Zippy gave to me:
Eight pre-teens primping,
Seven velvet paintings,
Six pizzas cooling,
Five Jel-l-l-l-o molds….
Four bowling balls,
Three DVDs,
Two leisure suits,
And Wilma Flintstone embedded in brie.

On the ninth day of Christmas Zippy gave to me:
Nine robots wrestling,
Eight pre-teens primping,
Seven velvet paintings,
Six pizzas cooling,
Five Jel-l-l-l-o molds….
Four bowling balls,
Three DVDs,
Two leisure suits,
And Wilma Flintstone embedded in brie.

On the tenth day of Christmas Zippy gave to me:
Ten tubs of topping,
Nine robots wrestling,
Eight pre-teens primping,
Seven velvet paintings,
Six pizzas cooling,
Five Jel-l-l-l-o molds….
Four bowling balls,
Three DVDs,
Two leisure suits,
And Wilma Flintstone embedded in brie.

On the eleventh day of Christmas Zippy gave to me:
Eleven surgeons surfing,
Ten tubs of topping,
Nine robots wrestling,
Eight pre-teens primping,
Seven velvet paintings,
Six pizzas cooling,
Five Jel-l-l-l-o molds….
Four bowling balls,
Three DVDs,
Two leisure suits,
And Wilma Flintstone embedded in brie.

On the twelfth day of Christmas Zippy gave to me:
Twelve twins a-twisting,
Eleven surgeons surfing,
Ten tubs of topping,
Nine robots wrestling,
Eight pre-teens primping,
Seven velvet paintings,
Six pizzas cooling,
Five Jel-l-l-l-o molds….
Four bowling balls,
Three DVDs,
Two leisure suits,
And Wilma Flintstone embedded in brie.

Bill & Diane

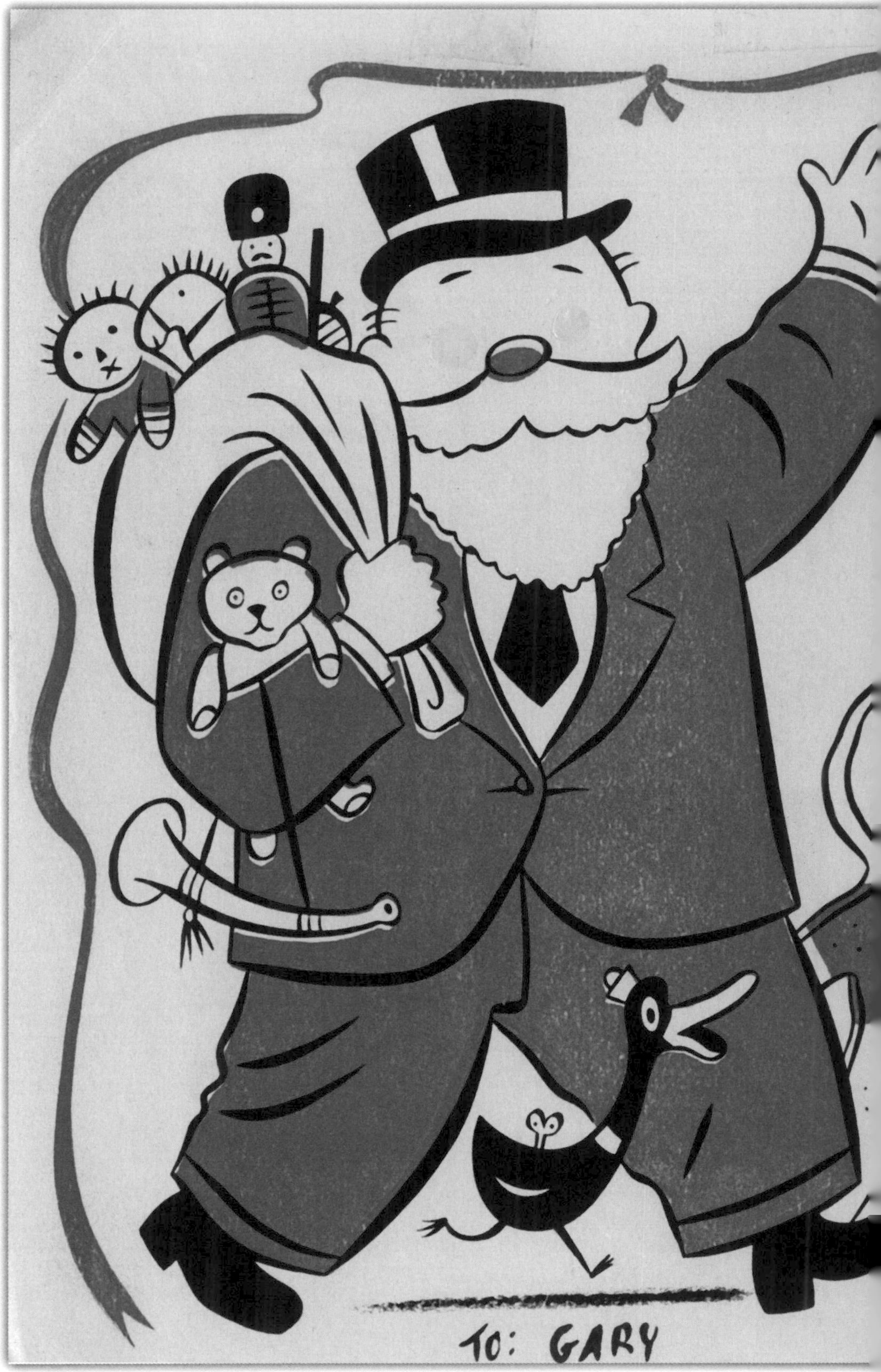
TO: GARY

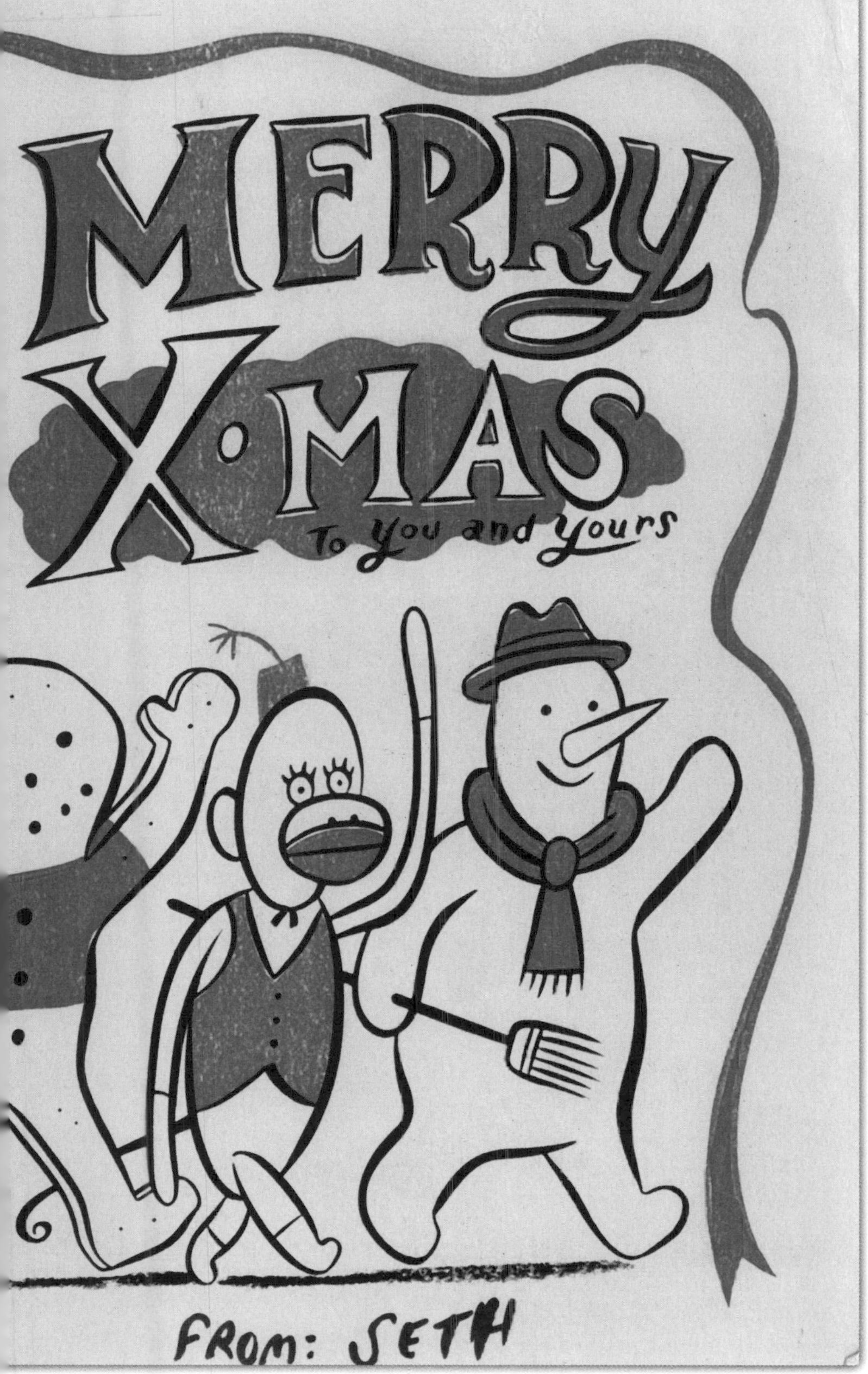
MERRY
X-MAS
To you and yours
FROM: SETH

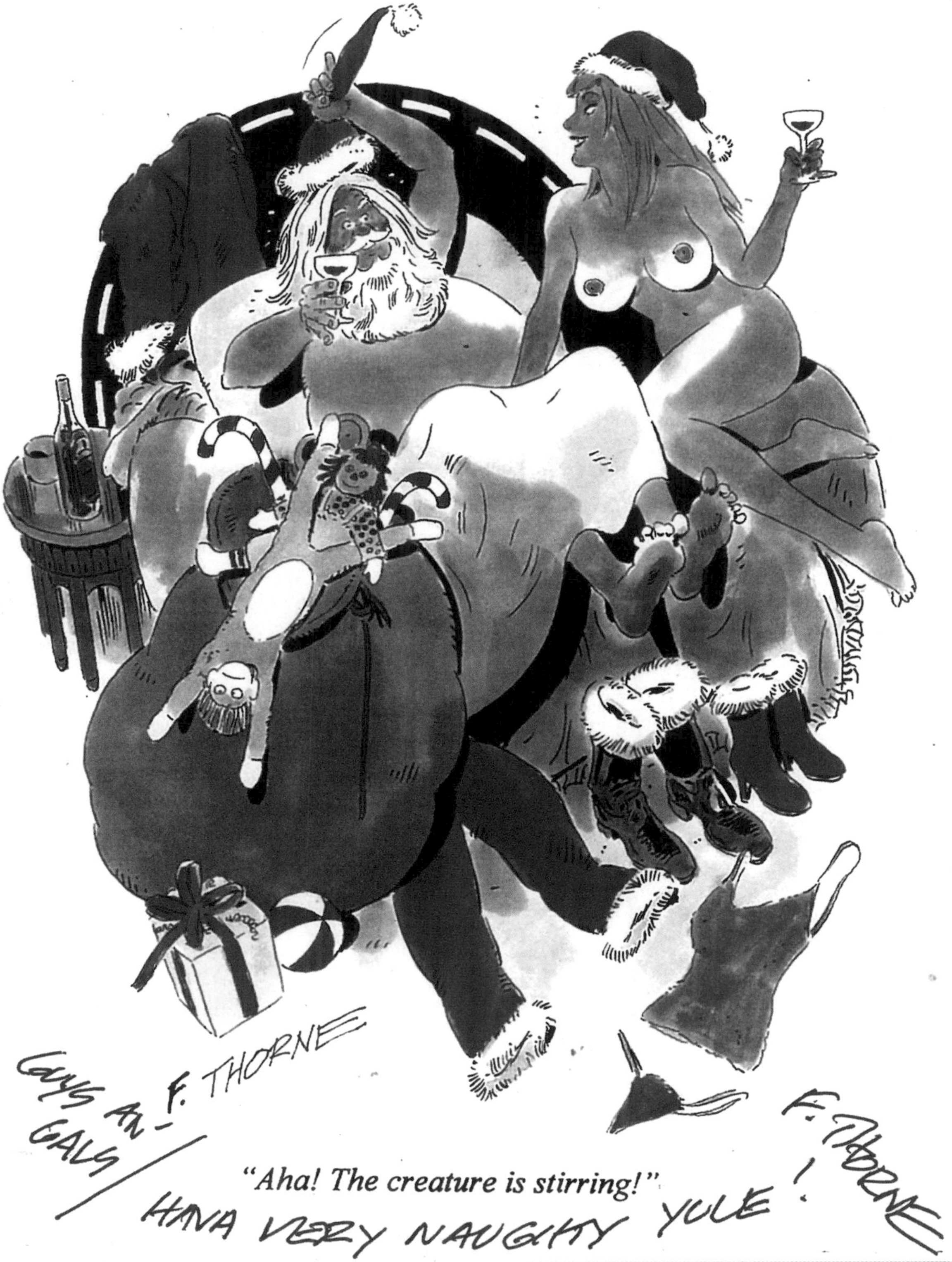
F. THORNE
GUYS AN' GALS
HAVA VERY NAUGHTY YULE!
F. THORNE

"Aha! The creature is stirring!"

Frank Thorne

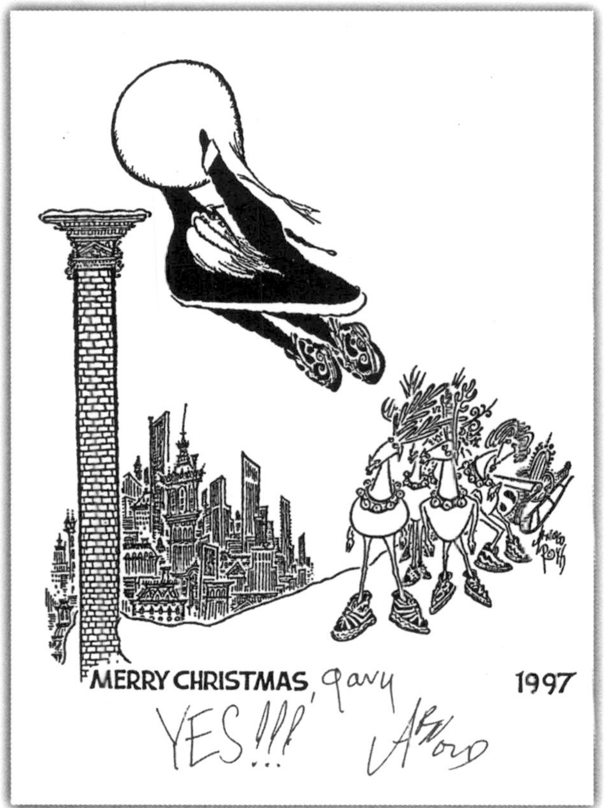
MERRY CHRISTMAS, gary 1997
YES!!!

Arnold Roth

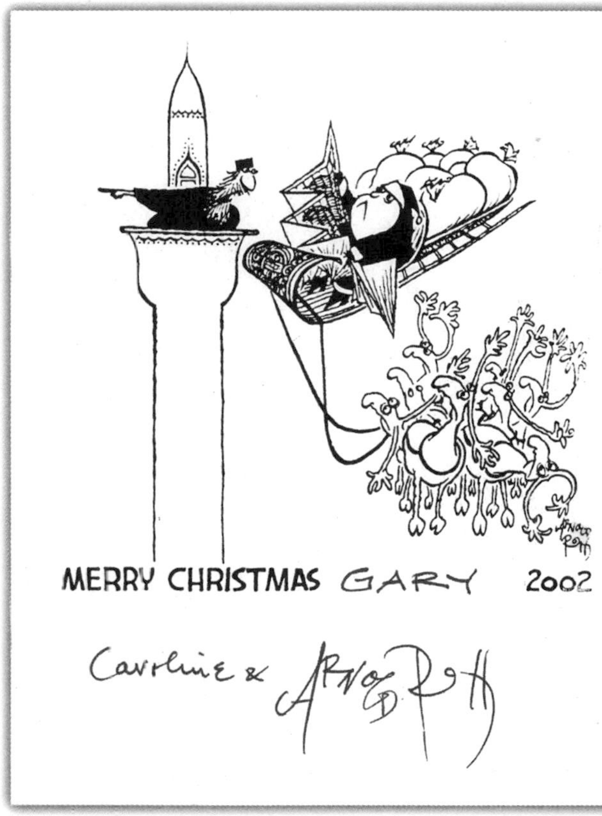
MERRY CHRISTMAS GARY 2002

Arnold Roth

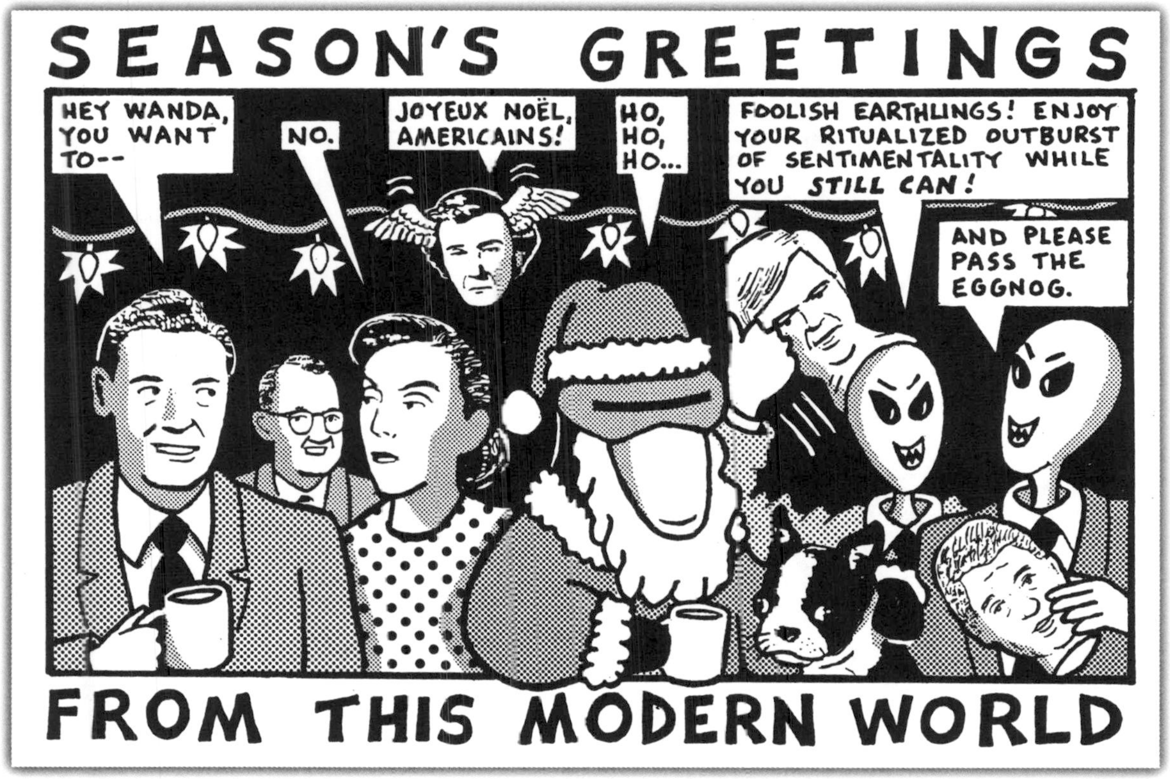
SEASON'S GREETINGS
HEY WANDA, YOU WANT TO--
NO.
JOYEUX NOËL, AMERICAINS!
HO, HO, HO...
FOOLISH EARTHLINGS! ENJOY YOUR RITUALIZED OUTBURST OF SENTIMENTALITY WHILE YOU STILL CAN!
AND PLEASE PASS THE EGGNOG.
FROM THIS MODERN WORLD

Tom Tomorrow

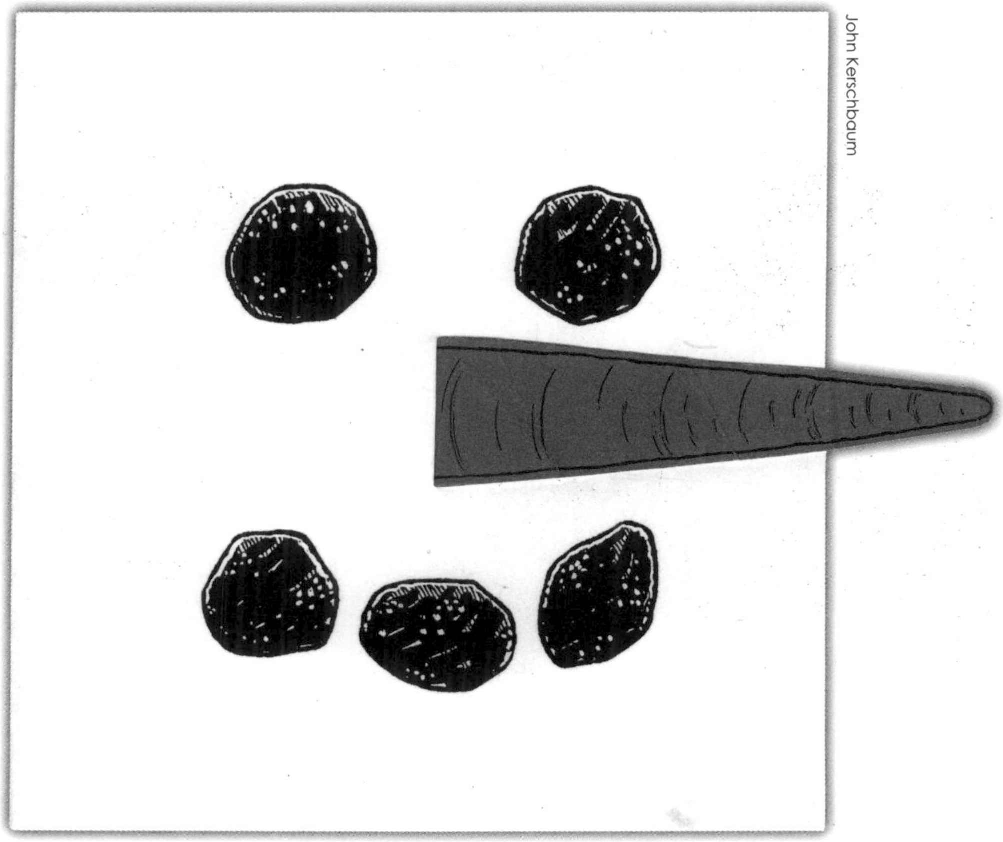

John Kerschbaum

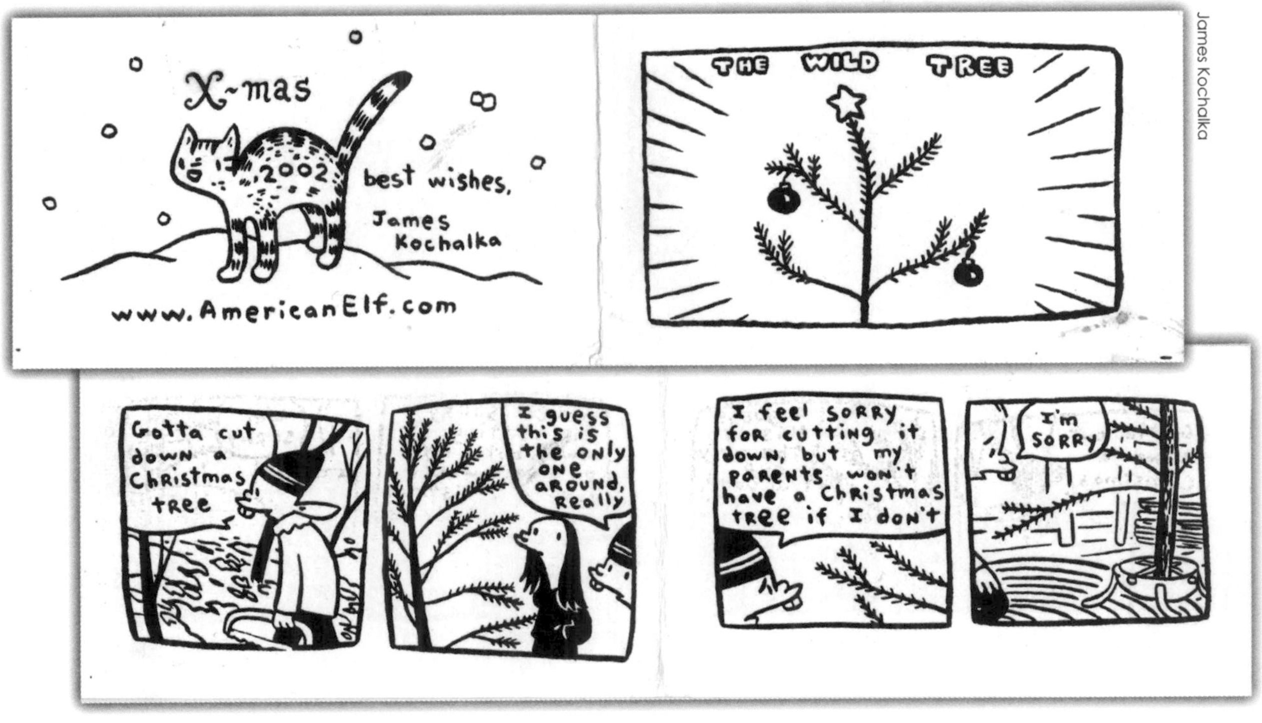
X~mas
2002
best wishes,
James Kochalka
www.AmericanElf.com
THE WILD TREE
Gotta cut down a Christmas tree
I guess this is the only one around, Really
I feel sorry for cutting it down, but my parents won't have a Christmas tree if I don't
I'm sorry

James Kochalka

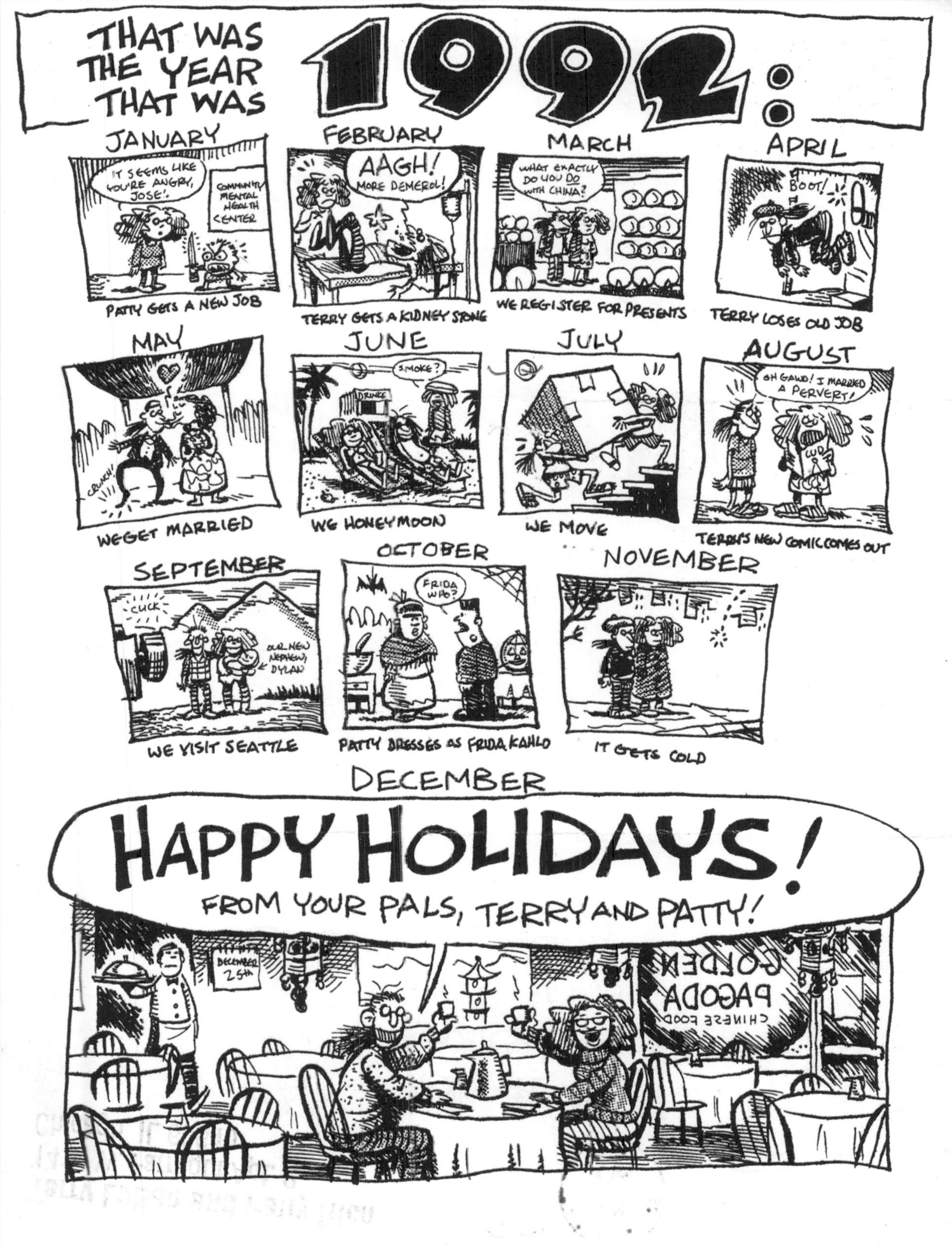

THAT WAS THE YEAR THAT WAS 1992:
JANUARY
IT SEEMS LIKE YOU'RE ANGRY, JOSE!
COMMUNITY MENTAL HEALTH CENTER
PATTY GETS A NEW JOB
FEBRUARY
AAGH! MORE DEMEROL!
TERRY GETS A KIDNEY STONE
MARCH
WHAT EXACTLY DO YOU DO WITH CHINA?
WE REGISTER FOR PRESENTS
APRIL
BOOT!
TERRY LOSES OLD JOB
MAY
CRUNCH!
WE GET MARRIED
JUNE
SMOKE?
DRINKS
WE HONEYMOON
JULY
WE MOVE
AUGUST
OH GAWD! I MARRIED A PERVERT!
CUD
TERRY'S NEW COMIC COMES OUT
SEPTEMBER
CLICK
OUR NEW NEPHEW, DYLAN
WE VISIT SEATTLE
OCTOBER
FRIDA WHO?
PATTY DRESSES AS FRIDA KAHLO
NOVEMBER
IT GETS COLD
DECEMBER
HAPPY HOLIDAYS!
FROM YOUR PALS, TERRY AND PATTY!
DECEMBER 25th
GOLDEN PAGODA CHINESE FOOD

Terry LaBan

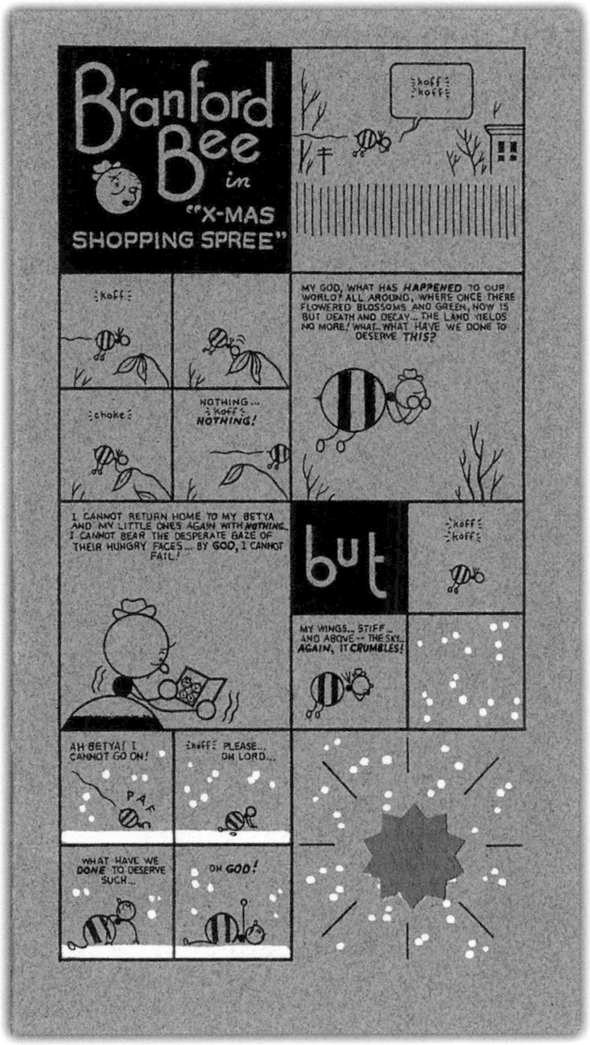
Branford Bee in
"X-MAS SHOPPING SPREE"
koff koff
koff
choke
NOTHING... koff NOTHING!
MY GOD, WHAT HAS HAPPENED TO OUR WORLD? ALL AROUND, WHERE ONCE THERE FLOWERED BLOSSOMS AND GREEN, NOW IS BUT DEATH AND DECAY... THE LAND YIELDS NO MORE! WHAT... WHAT HAVE WE DONE TO DESERVE THIS?
I CANNOT RETURN HOME TO MY BETYA AND MY LITTLE ONES AGAIN WITH NOTHING... I CANNOT BEAR THE DESPERATE GAZE OF THEIR HUNGRY FACES... BY GOD, I CANNOT FAIL!
but
koff koff
MY WINGS... STIFF... AND ABOVE -- THE SKY... AGAIN, IT CRUMBLES!
AH BETYA! I CANNOT GO ON!
PAF
koff PLEASE... OH LORD...
WHAT HAVE WE DONE TO DESERVE SUCH...
OH GOD!
Chris Ware

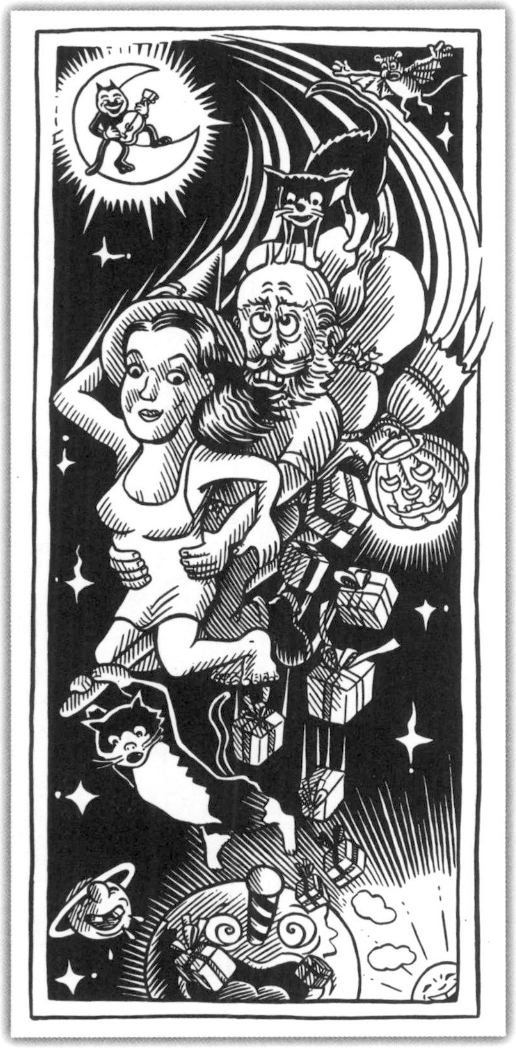
Kim Deitch

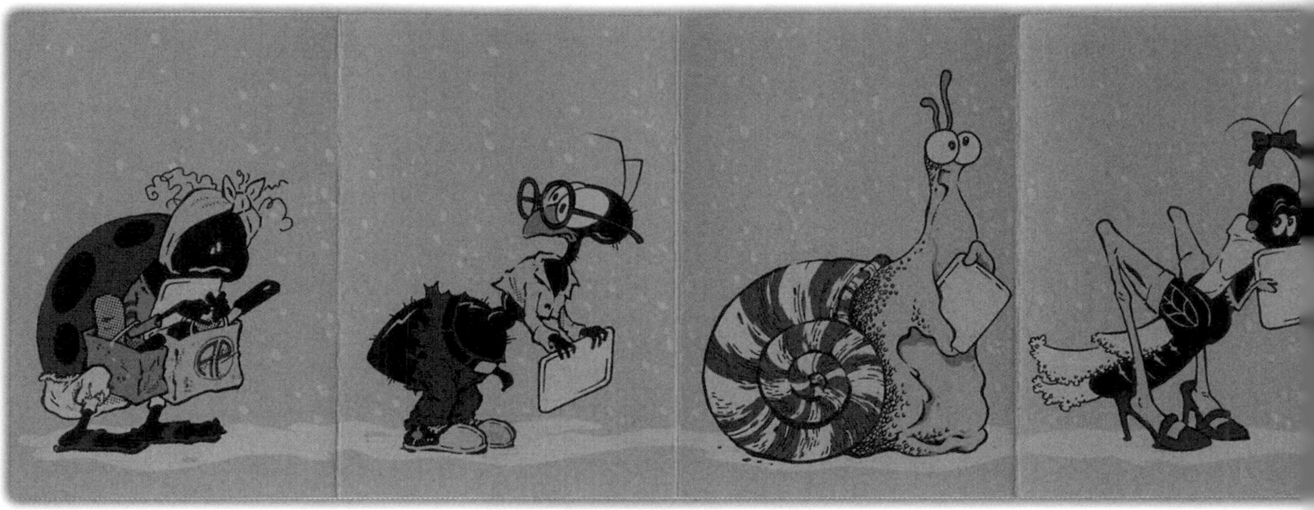

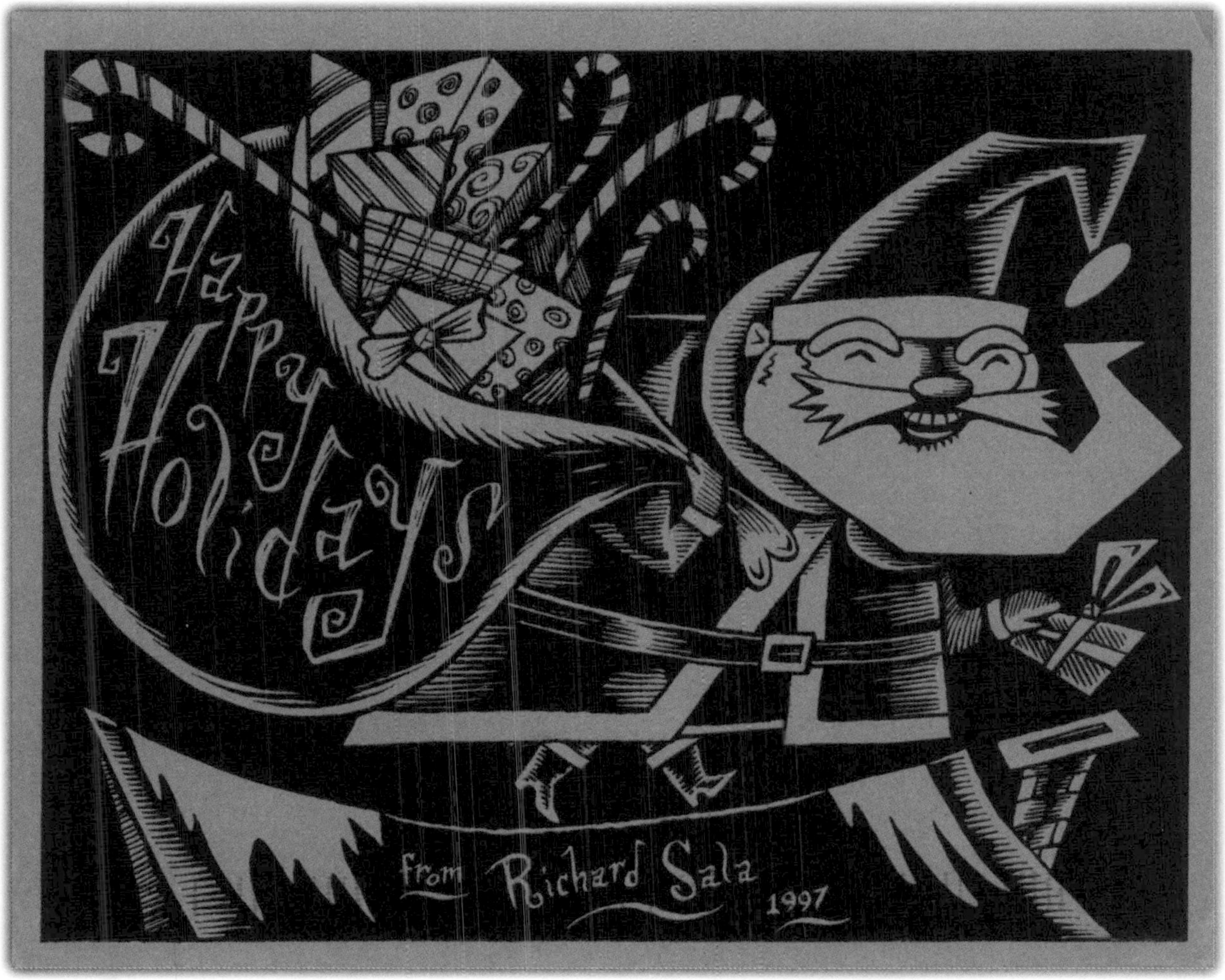
Happy Holidays
from Richard Sala
1997
Richard Sala

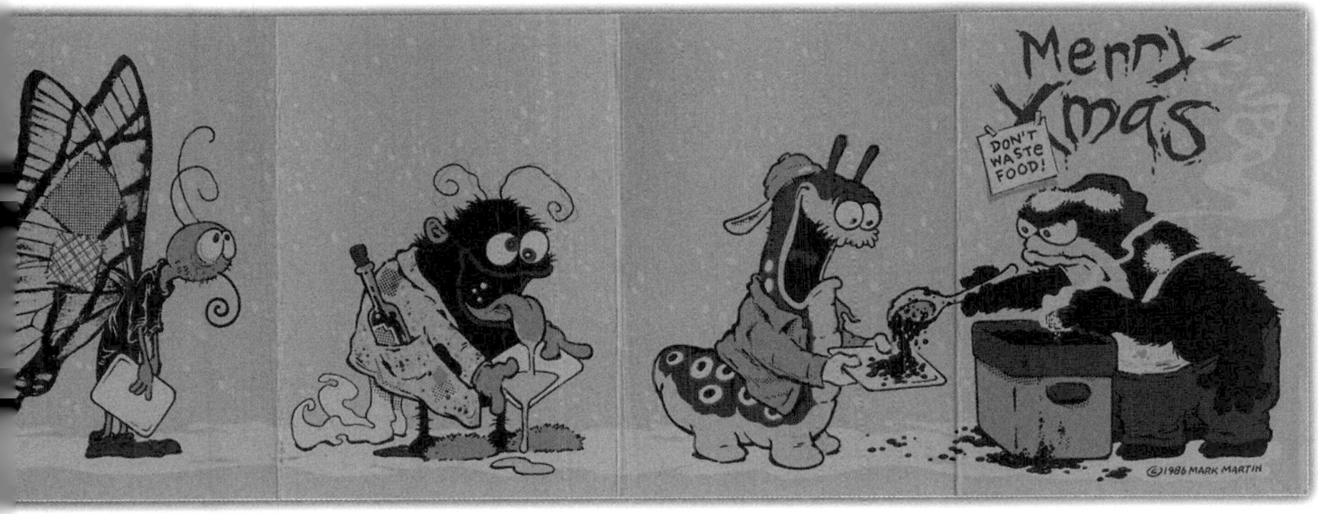
Merry Xmas
DON'T WASTE FOOD!
©1986 MARK MARTIN
Mark Martin

Skip Williamson

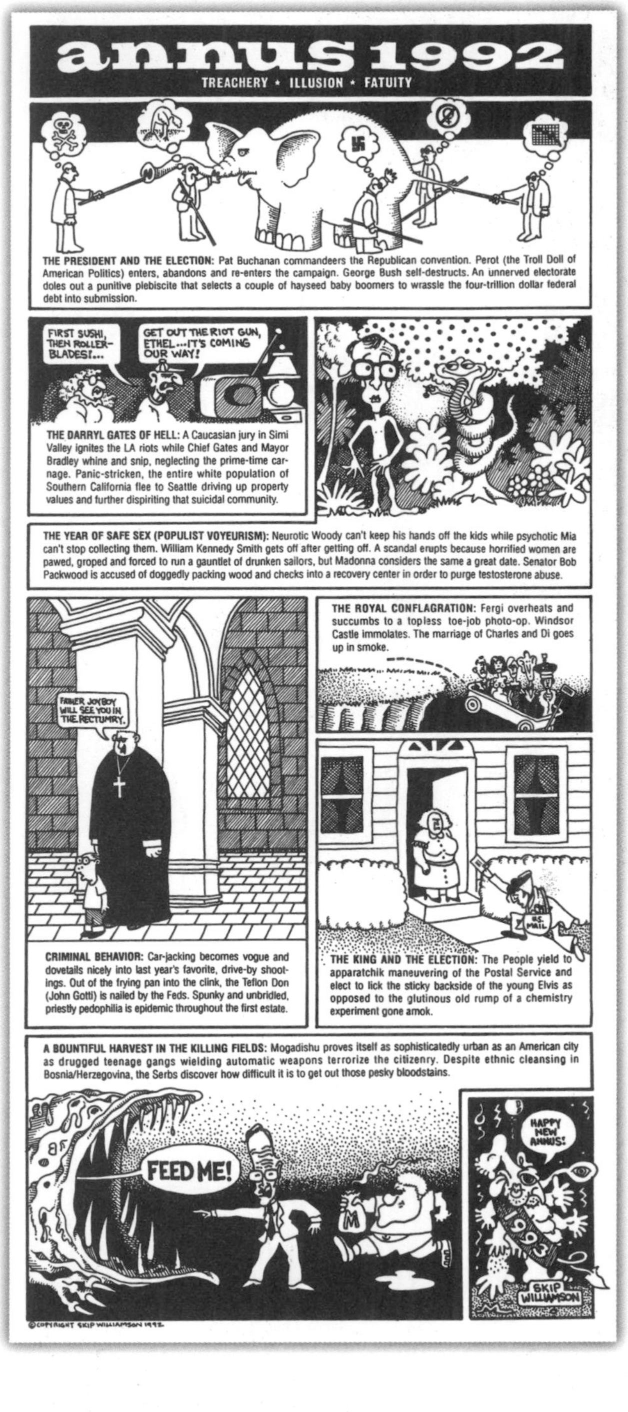
annus 1992
TREACHERY ★ ILLUSION ★ FATUITY
THE PRESIDENT AND THE ELECTION: Pat Buchanan commandeers the Republican convention. Perot (the Troll Doll of American Politics) enters, abandons and re-enters the campaign. George Bush self-destructs. An unnerved electorate doles out a punitive plebiscite that selects a couple of hayseed baby boomers to wrassle the four-trillion dollar federal debt into submission.
FIRST SUSHI, THEN ROLLER-BLADES!...
GET OUT THE RIOT GUN, ETHEL...IT'S COMING OUR WAY!
THE DARRYL GATES OF HELL: A Caucasian jury in Simi Valley ignites the LA riots while Chief Gates and Mayor Bradley whine and snip, neglecting the prime-time carnage. Panic-stricken, the entire white population of Southern California flee to Seattle driving up property values and further dispiriting that suicidal community.
THE YEAR OF SAFE SEX (POPULIST VOYEURISM): Neurotic Woody can't keep his hands off the kids while psychotic Mia can't stop collecting them. William Kennedy Smith gets off after getting off. A scandal erupts because horrified women are pawed, groped and forced to run a gauntlet of drunken sailors, but Madonna considers the same a great date. Senator Bob Packwood is accused of doggedly packing wood and checks into a recovery center in order to purge testosterone abuse.
FATHER JOYBOY WILL SEE YOU IN THE RECTUMRY.
CRIMINAL BEHAVIOR: Car-jacking becomes vogue and dovetails nicely into last year's favorite, drive-by shootings. Out of the frying pan into the clink, the Teflon Don (John Gotti) is nailed by the Feds. Spunky and unbridled, priestly pedophilia is epidemic throughout the first estate.
THE ROYAL CONFLAGRATION: Fergi overheats and succumbs to a topless toe-job photo-op. Windsor Castle immolates. The marriage of Charles and Di goes up in smoke.
U.S. MAIL
THE KING AND THE ELECTION: The People yield to apparatchik maneuvering of the Postal Service and elect to lick the sticky backside of the young Elvis as opposed to the glutinous old rump of a chemistry experiment gone amok.
A BOUNTIFUL HARVEST IN THE KILLING FIELDS: Mogadishu proves itself as sophisticatedly urban as an American city as drugged teenage gangs wielding automatic weapons terrorize the citizenry. Despite ethnic cleansing in Bosnia/Herzegovina, the Serbs discover how difficult it is to get out those pesky bloodstains.
FEED ME!
M
HAPPY NEW ANNUS!
1993
SKIP WILLIAMSON
©COPYRIGHT SKIP WILLIAMSON 1992

Gilbert Hernandez

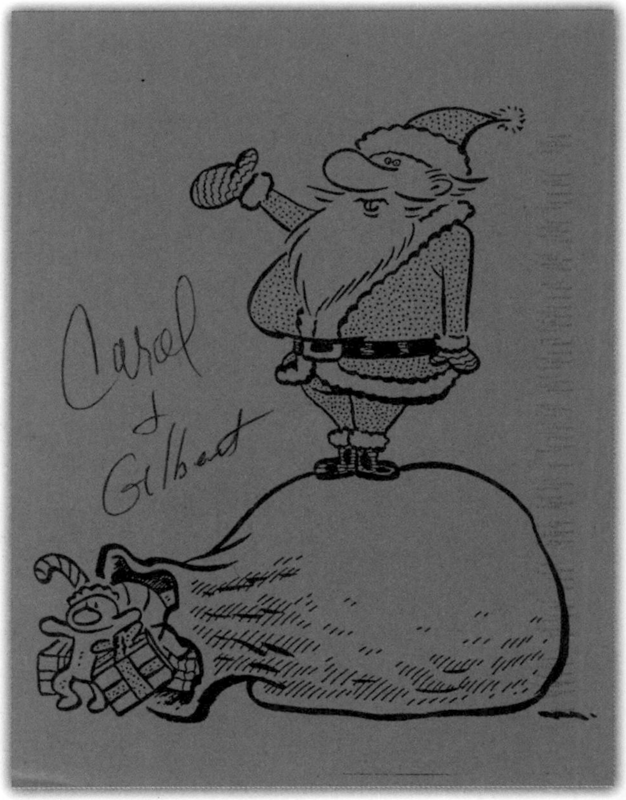
Carol
&
Gilbert

Gilbert Hernandez

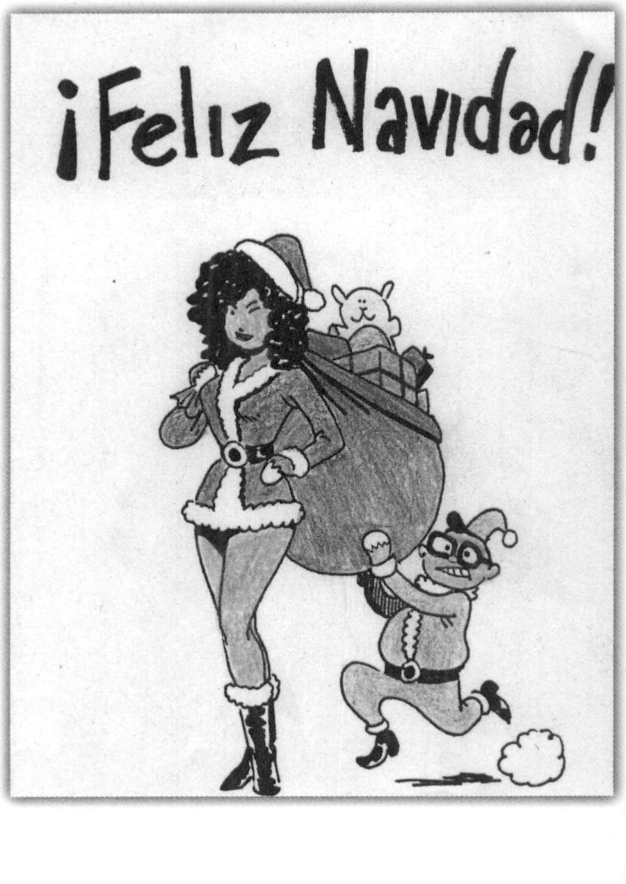
¡Feliz Navidad!

Jaime Hernandez

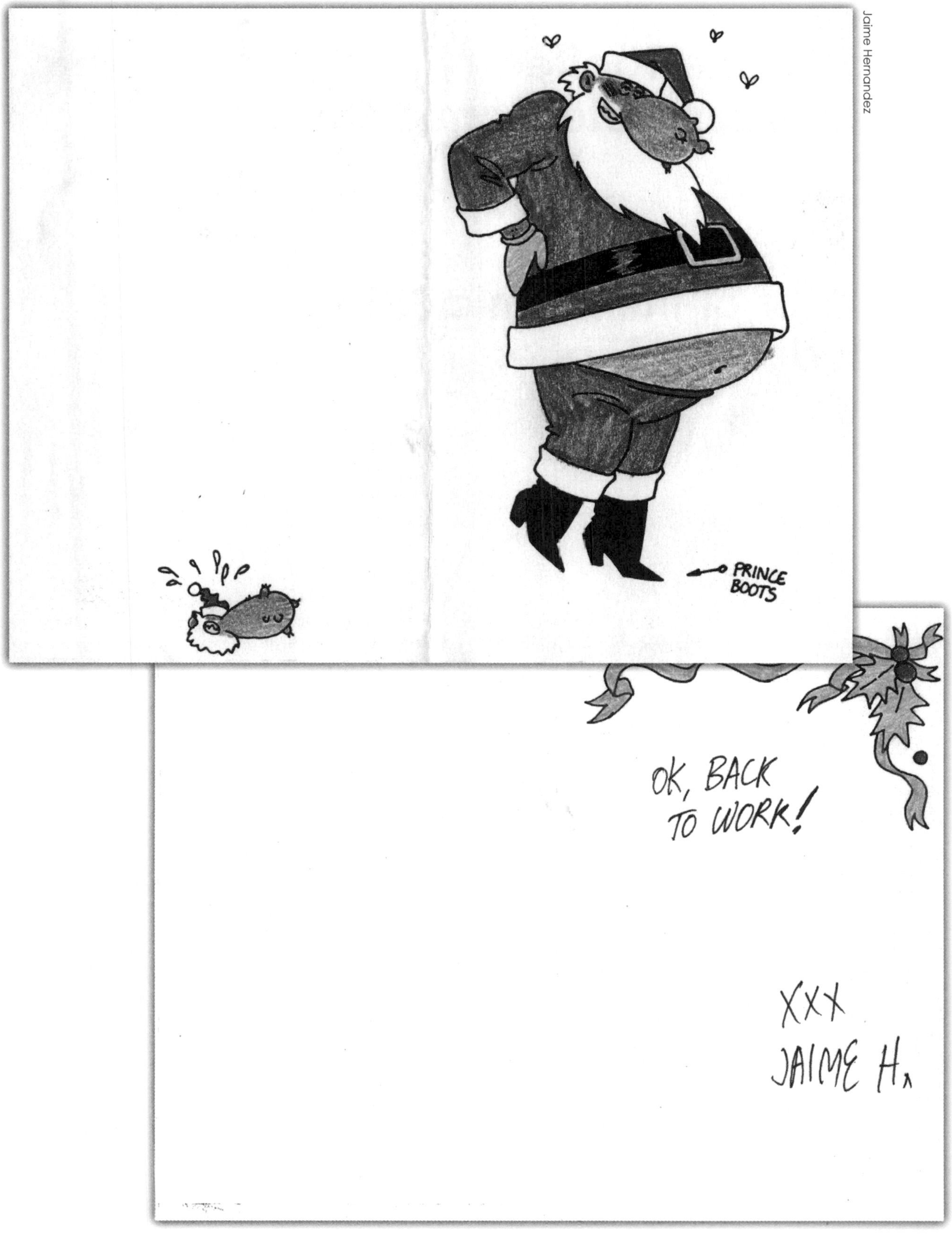
PRINCE BOOTS
OK, BACK TO WORK!
XXX
JAIME H.

Rodolphe Töpffer: The Complete Comic Strips

David Kunzle, Translator and Complier
University Press of Mississippi
650 pp., $65.00
B&W, Hardcover
ISBN: 9781578069460

Father of the Comic Strip: Rodolphe Töpffer

David Kunzle
University Press of Mississippi
207 pp., $25.00
B&W, Hardcover
ISBN: 9781578069484

Review by Chris Lanier

The University Press of Mississippi has brought out the first comprehensive English-language collection of Rodolphe Töpffer's comics, translated and annotated by David Kunzle, along with an excellent companion monograph by Kunzle, "Father of the Comic Strip: Rodolphe Töpffer." Paternity is hard to establish in the arts; it's impossible to call Töpffer the inventor of the comic strip, but he essayed a number of insights and approaches that were crucial to its development. Despite the patina of historical significance, there's nothing taxidermic about Töpffer's comics; it would be a challenge to find contemporary work that can keep pace with Töpffer's effortless display of sophistication and wit.

To delve into any of the eight narratives that make up the bulk of *The Complete Comic Strips* is to be swept up by a breakneck caprice, conducted through the nervous wire of Töpffer's line. The restlessly imaginative stories are filled with incident, slapstick, inversions, switchbacks, the fantastic. Kunzle does a good job of pointing out how much of future comics lies looped in his scribbles, in embryonic form, committed to paper in the mid-1800s. One can find elements of the adventure comic and the science-fiction comic and prototypes of such reliable characters as the errant schoolchildren who do their part to upend civilization or the animal sidekick who mutely comments

on the story's main action. And above all this, Töpffer maintains a wry sensibility that remains entirely his own.

THE TWO REVOLUTIONS

From a superficial glance, his work might seem to share much in common with his predecessors; for centuries, artists had been creating images in sequence, using captions to explain the storyline. Töpffer didn't even push forward to adopt the last piece of the formal puzzle that would make his work unarguably "comics," the leap into speech balloons (or at least not in his published work — he toyed with them in a notebook and then abandoned the approach). But there are two crucial differences in his method — differences that were in fact innovations — which keep his work feeling "modern," functioning as stories rather than specimens of graphic history.

The primal innovation was the injection of speed into the graphic narrative, both in the execution of the drawings themselves and in the time that exists between the images. He's not drawing scenes, but moments. His images don't languish in a buffer of time, adrift in temporality like islands at sea — they flow one after the other with a kind of ticking impatience. The sort of time he captures is unthinkable without the metronomic guillotine of the clock. There's a bit of a conundrum in this, in that each image seems to have a lesser duration (each panel sticks in the eye less than the framed quasi-theatrical dioramas of a typical broadsheet) — and yet more images are needed to elaborate the full circumference of an event, to feed the impatience of time.

Töpffer's other major innovation was his realization that the text and image need not support each other in a kind of explicatory unity (or redundancy), where one converges with the other toward a mutual vanishing point of agreed-upon meaning. Rather, text and image can exist on fundamentally parallel tracks, supporting each other in contradiction.

Text and image perform a dance of mutual commentary, not explanation. Two cohabitating modes of expression are yoked in one singular medium, producing a space where the primary mode of meaning is divergence: in short, a universe defined by irony.

THE ENGINE OF IRONY

If I could hazard a guess, this ironical mode might have emerged from Töpffer's position as a teacher. When he drew his first picture story, he was running a boarding school for boys in Geneva. Apparently, his first audience for the picture stories was his students (the clearest traces of that adolescent peanut gallery are some fart jokes that exist in Töpffer's manuscipt versions, which were omitted when they were finally printed for a wider audience).

There is always a disjunction between pedagogy and reality, where the ideal is set in counterpoint to actuality. Education proposes how things should be in contrast to how things are. If you're predisposed to see this gap as tragedy — then you probably won't last as a teacher. It's far healthier for an educator to see it as comedy.

If Töpffer's sense of counterpoint didn't come from his experience as a teacher, it certainly finds persuasive expression in *M. Crépin*, Töpffer's spoof on educational systems. The central problem of the story is Monsieur Crépin's search for a teacher who can properly educate his unruly brood — a conglomeration of nearly identical boys, most often depicted splayed in various iterations of mischief, a jumble of puzzle pieces continually in the act of not fitting together.

ayant appris qu'Albert est établi à Bordeaux, Mangini Pacini et Carabini viennent l'y voir, et ils se plaisent à boire à sa santé.
Et aussi à la santé de la liberté!
de l'Égalité !!
de la fraternité !!!
de la vertu !!
à la haine des Tyrans !!
des fonctionnaires !!
du clergé !!!!
de la presse soudoyée !!!!
de l'autocrate !!!
des Rotschilds !!!!!
de Metternich !!!..
24.

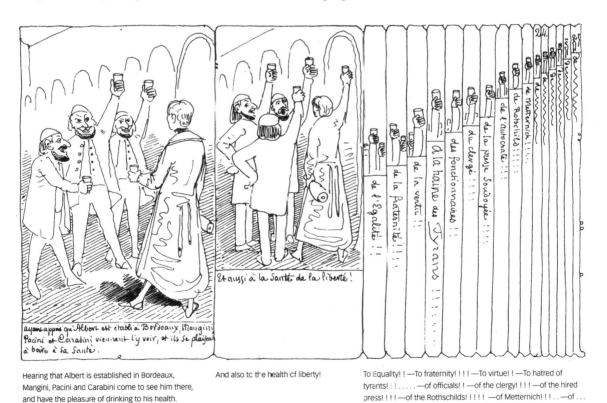

Hearing that Albert is established in Bordeaux, Mangini, Pacini and Carabini come to see him there, and have the pleasure of drinking to his health.

And also to the health of liberty!

To Equality! ! —To fraternity! ! ! ! —To virtue! ! —To hatred of tyrants! ! ! . . . . . —of officials! ! —of the clergy! ! ! ! —of the hired press! ! ! ! —of the Rothschilds! ! ! ! ! —of Metternich! ! ! . . —of . . . —of . . . —of . . . —of . . . —of . . . —of . . .

From "Histoire d'Albert" in *Rodolphe Töpffer: The Complete Comic Strips*: translation by David Kunzle. [©2007 University of Mississippi]

Crépin runs through a whole series of ineffectual tutors, each of which has some system for organizing knowledge. The first tutor's system is to "proceed from the general to the particular" — when he asks one of Crépin's boys what eight pounds of lard would cost at five florins a pound, the boy replies that "lard is in the totality of things, which includes the universe, which includes the three kingdoms, which includes the animal kingdom, which includes the pig, which includes lard." Subsequent tutors employ methods derived from physics, fractions, etiquette and phrenology. What they have in common is that they serve, at best, as a gloss on the irrepressible destructive instincts of the children.

Töpffer actually inserts himself into the story as the one effective tutor, whose method is "to do as one can and for the best" — in other words, the system of no system. Any system that smacks of ideology spurs on Töpffer's sense of dissonant dialectic: the split between word and image becomes roughly the split between theory and practice. The world of ideas is sustained in the narration, but it must always be seen in relation to the actual world, which exists stubbornly on its own terms in the pictures.

THE SPEED OF THOUGHT

Those pictures were rendered with a novel technique — a form of lithography that allowed for the reproduction of quickly executed line-work. A sense of rapidity permeates the drawings, but is most evident in the shading, which often looks like it's made up of a tangle of coiled springs. Töpffer's drawing speed is so quick, in fact, it leaps off the page and collapses decades, nearly centuries — linking himself, Thurber, Gross, Steig, Blechman and Porcellino with the velocity of a flying nib (Blechman has the closest squiggle to Töpffer, the one with the flutter of daydream). All these cartoonists understand the principle of "just enough" — just enough drawing to get the thought across — the images discharged from the pen like puffs of thought.

Töpffer demonstrated, in a much-reproduced sequence from "Histoire d'Albert," that an incomplete drawing could be perfectly understandable if previous drawings had prepared the way for it. Here, the final panels are barely squiggles, time is sliced thin as a razor, and the text liquefies to a dangling corkscrew — and yet we understand those panels as repetitions of a toast, echoes trapped in a chamber ad infinitum.

It reminds me of some of John Porcellino's comics, where people and objects wink out of existence as soon as they're unnecessary for the narrative flow. He establishes a room and some characters, and once that's done, it's possible to dispense with most of it — even the bodies of people who are still talking vanish, and a character is left as a little blip of a head, stranded like a balloon in a panel of open sky.

Töpffer was probably the first to understand comics as a state of permanent synecdoche. His framing often cuts off limbs, or sometimes even the greater part of the figure, admitting only a gesturing arm or a kicking foot. Working on his stories roughly the same time as the daguerreotype was appearing, Töpffer's invention proved more precocious than this new technique of fixing images, which was still restrained by the necessary slowness of the exposure, making the daguerreotype plate a zone of stillness, of stasis. Toward the dawn of photography, Töpffer is already, in flashes, anticipating the compositional attack of the snapshot.

Precociousness is a kind of speed. Töpffer's characters are often in a rush. In "Monsieur Cryptogame" there's a perfectly Töpfferian chase. ("Cryptogame" is an adventure story that, looking backwards, calls to mind Baron Munchausen, attuned as it is to the essential absurdity of derring-do; looking forward, it glancingly suggests Roy Crane, who of all the adventure strip artists understood best that adventure is really a category of farce.) Monsieur Cryptogame and his romantic pursuer, Elvire, have been kidnapped, and are taken prisoner on a Moorish ship. Cryptogame, in an attempt to escape (not from the Moors, but from Elvire), dashes across the page. And Elvire dashes after him. Both run in a bodily rictus, their legs sprung open like the blades of scissors, cutting through space. Cryptogame's friend the Abbée chases after Elvire, and then the Moors chase after the Abbée — which sets the shipboard domestic animals racing, and then the shipboard rats, until the boat itself is spurred on in its own rotations (as the caption scientifically notes, at "eight revolutions a second"). At this point, the world of all these characters and objects has been reduced to the energetic vortex of a scribble.

THE SPEED OF SLAPSTICK

It was such lithographic speed that allowed Töpffer to catch up with the spasms of slapstick. The haystack, which would go on to provide a punch-line repository for the airborne pratfalls of countless silent comedians, was already a handy device for Töpffer, deployed as a loosely hatched cushion in both "Monsieur Pencil" and "Le Docteur Festus." "Monsieur Trictrac" provides an extended set piece with a ladder that gets hung around the necks of two policemen, who proceed to mow down unlucky pedestri-

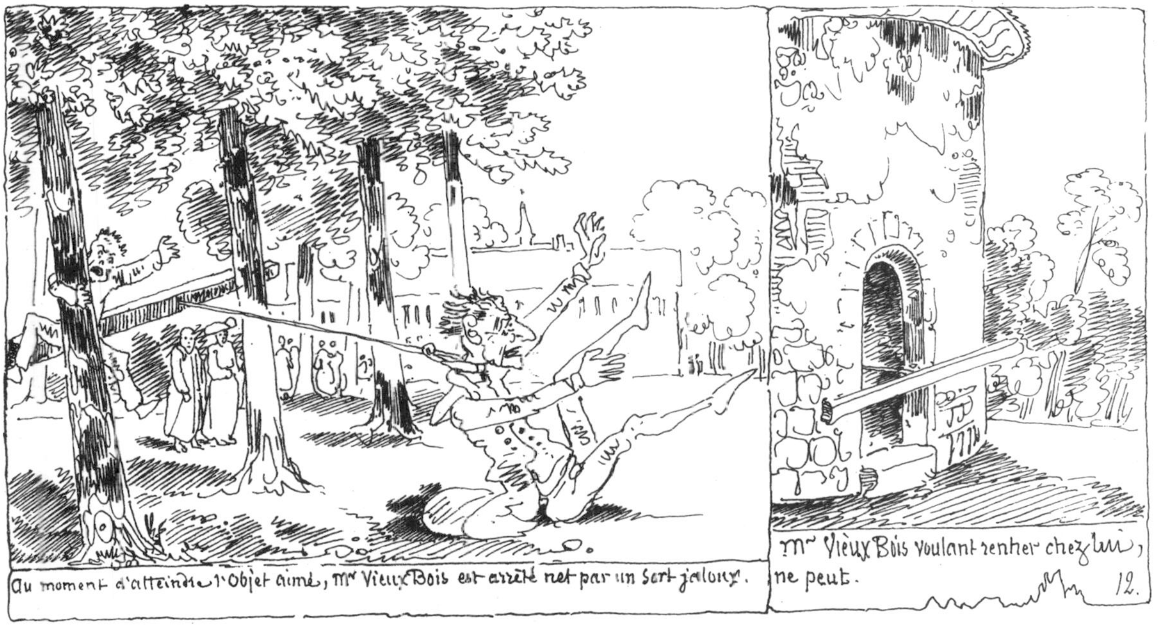
Au moment d'atteindre l'Objet aimé, Mr VieuxBois est arrêté net par un Sort jaloux.
Mr VieuxBois voulant rentrer chez lui, ne peut.
12.

At the moment of catching the Beloved Object, Mr. Vieux Bois is stopped short by a jealous fate.

Mr. Vieux Bois trying to return home, fails.

From "Monsieur VieuxBois." [©2007 University of Mississippi]

ans in their fruitless attempts to extricate themselves.

The more impossible his slapstick gets, the better. In "Monsieur Pencil," a man is boxed up in a crate, quite against his will. There are two holes cut for his eyes, and at a certain point he manages to extend his arms through the box, so that he can drag himself along, and even assault his antagonists — though he can't manage to free himself. Finding himself alone in the woods, he succumbs to despair. He tries to hang himself, but since he's denied access to his neck by the intervention of the crate, the best he can make of it is to hang by the arm. When this fails to prove fatal, in a gesture of black optimism he tries the other arm. (A nice throwaway touch — when this poor encoffined man is subdued in a fight with someone wielding a club, the eye-holes bored into the crate close up into unconscious slits.)

FUNNY UNFUNNY DRAWING, AND OTHER FORMAL TRICKS

"Monsieur VieuxBois" contains what might be my favorite single panel in comics. The story involves the romantic travails of Mr. VieuxBois as he pursues the object of his affection — who is at first resistant to his effusions, and who finally succumbs to them, while maintaining in both dimensions the equipoise of a mute bovinity. Before her acquiescence, however, VieuxBois responds to every rejection with a suicide attempt. He tries hemlock ("fortunately it is herb soup"), jumping out of a window ("fortunately Mr. VieuxBois is caught on the index of a Sundial"), impalement ("fortunately the sword passes under his arm").

In one attempt, VieuxBois tries to hang himself from a beam ("fortunately the rope is too long"). But hearing the voice of his beloved coming through his window, he is revived, and rushes after her, the beam dragged behind him — like a reluctant dog yanked by a leash. The beam, in its travels, wreaks havoc in the street (VieuxBois is oblivious to the disaster caused in his wake) — but at the point where he is almost upon his beloved, the beam gets wedged between two trees, finally arresting his headlong sprint.

Defeated, he dejectedly does an about-face, and as the caption has it "trying to return home, fails."

On its own, this drawing seems like a vague study of an eccentric architectural detail. It's a completely non-funny drawing, made funny by its place in a sequence. We can "see" the surprise of VieuxBois, suddenly choked — perhaps we can hear an off-panel crash — the indignity of VieuxBois no less indelible for being occluded.

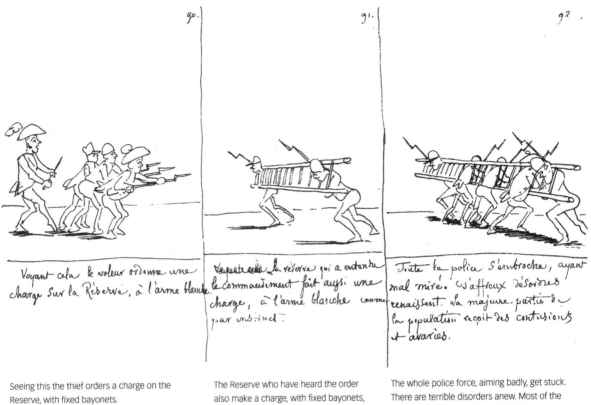

90. 91. 92.

Voyant cela le voleur ordonne une charge sur la Réserve, à l'arme blanche.

La réserve qui a entendu le commandement fait aussi une charge, à l'arme blanche comme par instinct.

Toute la police s'embroche, ayant mal miré. D'affreux désordres renaissent. La majeure partie de la population reçoit des contusions et avaries.

Seeing this the thief orders a charge on the Reserve, with fixed bayonets.

The Reserve who have heard the order also make a charge, with fixed bayonets, as if by instinct.

The whole police force, aiming badly, get stuck. There are terrible disorders anew. Most of the population suffers bruises and injuries.

From "Histoire de Monsieur Trictrac." [©2007 University of Mississippi]

The vivid invisibility of the humiliation indicates a formal knowingness on the part of the author. Töpffer had an extraordinary self-awareness about his effects, most explicitly laid out in his "Essay on Physiognomy" (which to my knowledge is only available in the out-of-print *Enter the Comics*, edited and translated by Ellen Wiese). In it, Töpffer makes very interesting distinctions between the attributes of painting and the attributes of drawing, and delves into the typology of caricature. In his description of how drawn features indicate traits of character, one can find hints of Eisenstein and his theory of "typage" (as Wiese points out). That Töpffer believed this strategy was a fact of aesthetics and not science is indicated by his attack on phrenology in "Mr. Crépin": one of the fraud teachers in Crépin is a phrenologist, continually fixated on skull palpation.

Töpffer pioneered other techniques that are more usually associated with "cinematic" innovations (which of course makes them "supra-cinematic" techniques — techniques that derive from a visual or conceptual system of which cinema is but one extension). In "Mr. Crépin," he employs a version of the "split screen," stacking one panel on top of another to suggest two activities happening at once — separated in space but conjoined in time.

And in "VieuxBois" he uses cross-cutting, over half a century before D. W. Griffith's famous/notorious use of the technique in *Birth of a Nation*. (It would be interesting to know if this technique has any antecedents in prose — certainly it would be possible to switch back and forth from one scene to another in alternating paragraphs, but perhaps that kind of zig-zagging is more readily suggested by systems of images.)

The cross-cutting in "VieuxBois" occurs when Vieux-Bois finally makes off with his beloved, after having vanquished a romantic rival. The rival, set adrift in a river, gets caught up in a waterwheel. As VieuxBois indulges in the pastoral life with his beloved — playing the flute, milking a cow, executing "bucolic dances" — each of these tableaux is alternated with scenes of the rival, getting dunked over and over again at every turn of the waterwheel.

By the time the rival has gotten to shore and dried himself out, VieuxBois' beloved has gone from scrawny to plump, fattened by the pastoral life (she must have drunk a lot of milk). It's not enough that Töpffer has developed cross-cutting, he's actually gone one better, seeing the humor not just in cutting across simultaneous time, but in cutting across two distinct modes of temporality, two types of duration. Töpffer was most likely the first artist to grasp that sequentiality is the perfect technique to render time a plaything.

THE BITE OF WHIMSY

The figures that stand as artistic innovators are fascinating, in part, because they provide windows into the sorts of pressures that exert themselves on systems of representation. Every formal innovation suggests a need that was previously unrealized, a notion that demanded a form. In the development of comics, the primary source of its inventions has been the pressure for sequentiality. Why, in the process of visual thinking, would it be necessary to draw more than one image? Or put another way — what sorts of ideas demand multiple images for their expression?

William Hogarth, another potential "father" of comics, was an acknowledged inspiration for Töpffer. In the mid-1700s, Hogarth created several print cycles, the most famous of which are probably his "Progresses" — "A Harlot's Progress" and "A Rake's Progress." These "Progresses" are actually more like regresses, or at least devolutions. In the case of the Harlot, we begin with a fairly innocent woman, who step by step goes down the drain, suffering exploitation, arrest and disease. In the case of the Rake, his money is squandered by degrees, landing him at first in debtor's prison, and finally in Bedlam. These characters' bad choices and flimsy morality lead to their downfall, degradation and eventual death. For Hogarth, there's a moral impetus for sequence. A single image of a diseased prostitute or a ne'er-do-well locked up in Bedlam is not enough; it omits the trajectory of moral instruction. Sequentiality gives him access to the principles of cause and effect.

Töpffer was no doubt admiring of Hogarth's visual syntax of cause and effect, and uses the construction of one thing leading to another, but he completely inverts its import. Cause and effect are made absurd. In "Monsieur Pencil," there is a scientist who is continually trying to explain phenomena and unravel causal relationships — and he's always spectacularly wrong. The notion of cause and effect reveals nothing of the true nature of the world to him — it merely provides a pseudo-rationalist excuse for jumping to wild conclusions.

The scientist is a figure of satire, but making leaps is what Töpffer loved to indulge. His storylines jump unpredictably from one incident to another. In "Le Docteur Festus," the title character's voyage on an "educational tour" precipitates a series of mistaken arrests, an erroneous sighting of the devil run amok, the evacuation of a commune and an astronomical frenzy based on the misidentification of an unidentified flying object. "Monsieur Pencil" begins with an artist making a bucolic landscape drawing, and quickly escalates to a series of events that include the imprisonment and study of a faux extraterrestrial visitor, mobilization of the national guard due to misfiring telegraph cables, and mass panic at a purported cholera outbreak.

The ruling spirit of "Pencil" is a wind, a zephyr, personalized as a sort of cherubic figure that goes about blowing objects and characters into the air (the zephyr can be read as the imp of Töpffer's own imagination, pushing along the plot with digressive zeal). Throwing his characters into the air, sometimes for pages at a time, was something he enjoyed — the image recurs in many of his stories. In "Le Docteur Festus," a giant telescope, made airborne by an explosion of steam, remains suspended in the sky long enough for three disgruntled astronomers to have a prolonged fistfight atop it. One of Töpffer's best throwaway gags is to have eight pigs thrown into the air by a furiously revolving windmill blade — three weeks later they fall back to earth, "twenty-eight in number, for the females have brought forth young in flight." There's something about a lack of gravity that appealed to Töpffer.

For Töpffer, the motive behind sequentiality isn't moral or pedagogic: it's the motive of whimsy, of transformation. More concretely, one could say the motive stemmed from a desire to entertain his students, to be playful with them, to speak to them in a language other than that of instruction and textbooks. Truly, I suspect he drew his stories primarily to amuse himself, and his students gave him an excuse to indulge that fancy.

Again, the style itself is tied to that quality of digression, or the provisional — the style of "just enough" is a notional style, an edifice built on squiggles. Töpffer's panel borders are completely non-emphatic, apt to be brushed aside by coattails flung by an obsequious bow, or by the extended toes of a foot. He doesn't hide that he's rethinking things on the spot — sometimes in the caption a scrapped word remains crossed out, or he leaves in lines whose fiddling purpose has been discarded: should the elbow go here, or here? Every now and again, in the skies, there is a flock of decorative birds that look more like handwriting — marginalia in some other, more serious book. Töpffer proposes that a doodle is something sufficient unto itself, alive as an aviary. His world is made of a looping string that could be pulled straight, and everything would vanish.

The plotlines and the drawn lines are in the thrall of a daydream — they can go this way or that. In Hogarth, the outcome is determined from the first. Sequence is inexorable. In Töpffer, you look at one scene, and the next, and you think: if he'd been in a slightly different mood — if a branch had brushed the window and distracted him for a couple more moments, his pen suspended above the page — something else might've occurred to him, and the story might've gone elsewhere.

The pleasing freedom of his stories is a freedom of inconsequentiality. Which is not to say Töpffer's sense of absurdity is entirely toothless. There's an unnerving undertone to how arbitrary the fates of his characters are — and to the way people can be whipped up into frenzy and riot by occurrences they perpetually fail to understand. It's significant that Alfred Jarry, creator of *Ubu Roi* and a patron saint of the surrealists, was inspired by Töpffer's work, writing a play based on "VieuxBois." Jarry pushed absurdity farther into cruelty and malevolence than Töpffer ever would; Ubu Roi stands a literary pre-

le chapeau étant tombé, la force armée se jette contre terre et demande quartier.

The hat having fallen, the armed force throws itself on the ground and demands quarter.

Also from "Histoire de Monsieur Trictrac." [©2007 University of Mississippi]

cursor for the dictators who would be unleashed on the 20th century, who made life-and-death decisions based on the seemingly arbitrary moods of their egos. For Töpffer, absurdity is often conjoined with authority, but is just as likely to undermine or unravel it — authority is, by alternations, absurdity's arbiter and its victim. One gets the sense that anarchy will ultimately get the better of it, because it's closer to the functioning principles of the universe. Was Töpffer himself — schoolteacher, bourgeois, patriot — on the side of anarchy? Certainly not. But his imagination was.

PATHETIC HUMANISM

All of his picture stories are pegged on the names of their instigating characters — "Monsieur Vieuxbois," "Histoire d'Albert," "Le Docteur Festus," and so on. But who are his characters, really? Though they tend to go through all sorts of dramatic events, they experience no character development, per se — Töpffer's world is populated by a series of "types." And yet there's more personality to them than in the figures found in broadsheets, and they exhibit more independence of action than the models in Hogarth's print cycles, where characters are expressions of social conditions or states. For Töpffer, there's something illusory about these social states.

"Monsieur Trictrac," Töpffer's last (and uncompleted) picture story, is predicated on an uneasy fluidity between social types. A thief sneaks into the bed of an upstanding citizen, while the citizen is out; the citizen is then mistaken for a thief, and the thief for the upstanding citizen. The thief later dons the uniform of the chief of police (who himself gets thrown in jail, mistaken as a thief), but the adoption of authority ends up doing the thief no favors — the general populace has, through a series of circumstances, turned against the police force, and apprehends the police-clothed thief with the intention of having him hanged. In jail, yet another transfer takes place between thief and police chief, social stations swapped via the exchange of uniforms.

Töpffer understands the importance of a uniform — in "Le Docteur Festus," a Mayor's martial uniform commands the obedience of two dim members of the armed forces; as in Trictrac, the uniform is donned by a series of imposters, but the armed forces pay no attention to the fluctuations in the inhabitants of it — whoever happens to be in it, they follow behind in march step. At one point the uniform is hung on a tree branch, so its most recent tenant can take a swim, and as the wind twists the arms of the costume, it sets the armed forces on a series of chaotic drills. The uniform is a powerful talisman —

Et elle s'accroche aux autres ailes pour le rattraper.
Le vent ayant considérablement fraîchi, les ailes tournent avec tant de vitesse qu'elles ne sont déjà plus visibles. C'est ce qui fait que les huit cochons d'Irlande s'acheminent pour paître l'herbe qui a crû dessous.
Les huit cochons d'Irlande ne paissent pas l'herbe, mais ils sont lancés au plus haut des airs
35.

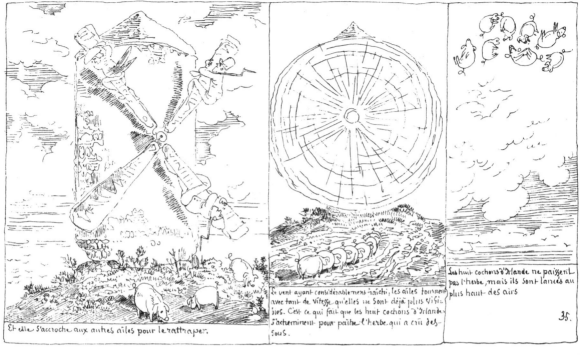

And hangs on to the other arms to catch up with him.

The wind having considerably freshened, the arms turn with such speed that they are already no longer visible. Which causes the eight Irish pigs to proceed to the grass that has grown beneath.

The eight Irish pigs do not get to graze, but are thrown high up into the air.

A variation of "when pigs fly" was an expression in use centuries before Töpffer depicted it in "Le Docteur Festus." [©2007 University of Mississippi]

and a fundamentally empty one. This is a perspective that is entirely consistent with a caricaturist who understands that physiognomic appearance is graphically potent and spiritually worthless.

One could say that Töpffer's whimsy provides an entrée for autonomy. It allows him to detach his characters for a while from their social destiny. They are not completely reducible to the place they take up in society. And the text/image split becomes the split between their image of themselves and how they actually appear to others. His "heroes" are mock heroes at best.

This could be related to the reason Töpffer didn't adopt the word balloon for his published work. It's difficult to imagine his characters narrating their own lives. If they did that, we'd have boring drama; since we're distanced from the blinkered view of their egos, we have farce. The Töpfferian mode is to have the story's point of view standing coolly outside the frenzy of the action. A satirist is always part anthropologist — an anthropologist who's invested in the moral dimensions of the subject culture.

There's no doubt that Monsieur Jabot — his first published and perhaps most typical character — is an ass. He relentlessly tries to climb the social ladder, and manages somehow to succeed while making a general botch of it — at a society ball, he cluelessly knocks drinks over, and eventually incapacitates an entire line of dancers, flattening them like dominoes. By the end of the evening, he's racked up appointments for several successive duels.

He wants to fit in and has no idea how ridiculous he is — and that's what endears him to us. Like most of Töpffer's principle characters (with the exception of Albert, whose delusions of grandeur are intended to be taken as outright villainy) we have an affection for him, but we never like him on his own terms. The stories engender a "double consciousness" — and it's the gap between who the characters think they are and who they actually are that makes them human. This is the point at which Töpffer's oppositional manner — hitched to the hybridity of the medium he was helping to invent — implies not only a logic of irony, but a logic of humanism as well. ■

The Complete Terry and The Pirates
Vol. 1: 1934-1936

Milton Caniff; edited by Dean Mullaney, with an introduction by Howard Chaykin
IDW
368 pp., $49.95
B&W + Color, Hardcover
ISBN: 9781600101007

Meanwhile ...
A Biography of Milton Caniff, Creator of *Terry and the Pirates* and *Steve Canyon*

Robert C. Harvey
Fantagraphics
952 pp., $34.95, Hardcover
ISBN: 9781560977827

Review by Tim O'Neil

Let's begin this review with a very banal and uncontroversial statement, and we can backtrack from there:

Terry and the Pirates is one of the most important and influential comic strips in the history of the medium. Although the series has seen numerous reprint projects come and go throughout the years, the present series from IDW is a welcome entry into our current crop of refurbished newspaper-strip archive collections. Given the resurgent interest in comics and comic art throughout the land, this current volume will probably be the one to find a permanent home on school and university library shelves across the country. This will probably remain the definitive volume for many, many years to come.

But I hesitate to say that at this late date *Terry* and Caniff are by no means as immediately familiar and central as they once were. To say nothing of the fact that Caniff's last installment of *Terry* ran over 60 years ago, it's hard to understand exactly why *Terry* was as important as it was, because there's really nothing quite like it any more. The field of continuity adventure strips is more or less dead, with just a handful of legacy properties left to continue their zombie runs: *The Phantom* and *Prince Valiant* are still around in one form or another, as are *Mark Trail* and *Spider-Man* (the newspaper version), but these are all pretty wretched. There aren't even many straight soap-opera strips left, just a few like *Apt 3-G* and *Mary Worth*. (And, of course, the last really important continuity strip, *For Better Or Worse*, is as I write this in the long process of tumbling out the door in a long, planned senescence.) While there are certainly many strip cartoonists working in the humor field who deserve credit for trying to keep the medium alive, the fact is that newspaper strips just aren't very good any more, and even at their best they no longer represent anything close to the vanguard of the medium. The evolutionary trail leading from modern comics back to *Terry* is obscured because the strip itself represents the fossilized remnant of a long-dead species.

This analogy becomes more telling when you put *Terry* up against other classic strips: *Krazy Kat, Gasoline Alley, Dick Tracy, Peanuts*. Each of these strips has found a receptive audience with modern readers because, on some level, they all reflect successful antecedents of current cartooning attitudes. *Krazy Kat* is formalistically revolutionary and pleasingly current in its sustained approach to ironic melancholy. Anyone familiar with Chris Ware's work, upon picking up a copy of Fantagraphics' *Krazy & Ignatz*, should be able to comprehend how and why the strip was so important, and furthermore be able to draw a connection between the strip and Ware's own *Acme Novelty Library*. (In this respect, the choice of Ware to provide design work for the series as well as Drawn & Quarterly's *Walt & Skeezix* remains an excellent and insightful choice, as is the choice of Seth for the *Complete Peanuts* project.

But it's harder to look at the modern cartooning landscape and see where Caniff's influence fits. Or rather, it's difficult to see where he fits because his influence is so primary that it's been almost entirely absorbed by subsequent generations of adventure cartoonists. And the field of adventure cartooning, at least in the English-speaking world, has evolved in a curiously isolated fashion. The foundation of modern superhero cartooning is built on the work of Caniff and Noel Sickles, in addition to Burne Hogarth and Hal Foster. But how to explain the layers of stylistic and formalistic attribution passed down throughout the years from the early years of *Terry* and on down through artists as disparate as Rob Liefeld and Darwyn Cooke? That requires an explanation by orders of magnitude more exhaustive than the relatively simple genealogy of Charles Schulz' direct and obvious influence on almost the entire field of modern "alt" cartooning. Most modern adventure strips — or, let's be honest, superhero books, because that's by far the lion's share of adventure material produced in America — could not be further removed from the work of those "literary" cartoonists whose work is currently enjoying such a renaissance of popular acclaim. Anyone arguing for Caniff's continued relevance has a hard task ahead: You would need to methodically retrace the genealogy of Caniff's influence for modern audiences for whom the implicit paternity has faded like footprints in the sand.

Harvey has his work cut out for him, and *Meanwhile* ... is as massive a book as you might expect given this brief. To his credit Harvey does not shirk from the enormousness of the task he presents himself: Far from being "merely" a cartoonist's biography, *Meanwhile* ... is also the history of an entire generation of cartoonists, their influences, their contexts, their lives and their world. If you want to understand why Caniff — unfashionable though he may be — is so damned important, this book will take you through the paces.

Thankfully, Harvey takes the time to discuss the intricate formalistic detail of how *Terry's* technique evolved.

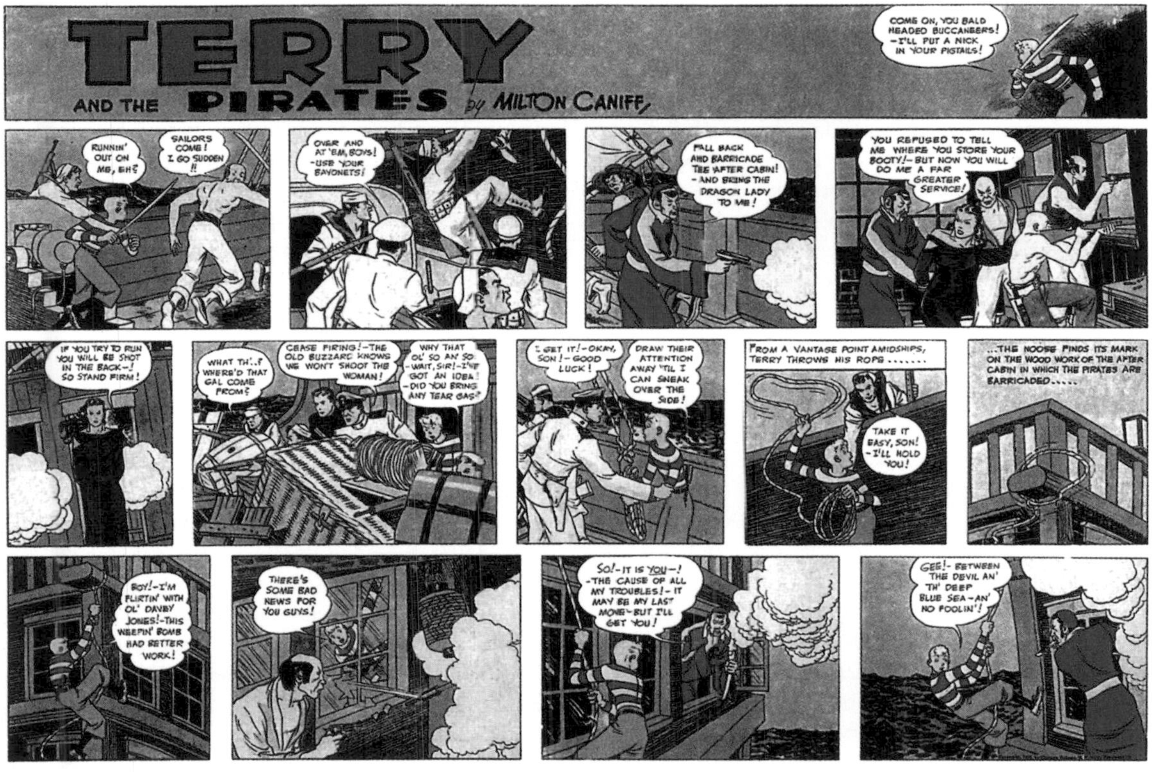
TERRY AND THE PIRATES by MILTON CANIFF
COME ON, YOU BALD HEADED BUCCANEERS! —I'LL PUT A NICK IN YOUR PIGTAILS!
RUNNIN' OUT ON ME, EH?
SAILORS COME! I GO SUDDEN!!
OVER AND AT 'EM, BOYS! —USE YOUR BAYONETS!
FALL BACK AND BARRICADE THE AFTER CABIN! —AND BRING THE DRAGON LADY TO ME!
YOU REFUSED TO TELL ME WHERE YOU STORE YOUR BOOTY!—BUT NOW YOU WILL DO ME A FAR GREATER SERVICE!
IF YOU TRY TO RUN YOU WILL BE SHOT IN THE BACK—! SO STAND FIRM!
WHAT TH'..? WHERE'D THAT GAL COME FROM?
CEASE FIRING!—THE OLD BUZZARD KNOWS WE WON'T SHOOT THE WOMAN!
WHY THAT OL' SO AN' SO —WAIT, SIR!—I'VE GOT AN IDEA! —DID YOU BRING ANY TEAR GAS?
I GET IT!—OKAY, SON!—GOOD LUCK!
DRAW THEIR ATTENTION AWAY 'TIL I CAN SNEAK OVER THE SIDE!
FROM A VANTAGE POINT AMIDSHIPS, TERRY THROWS HIS ROPE.......
TAKE IT EASY, SON! —I'LL HOLD YOU!
...THE NOOSE FINDS ITS MARK ON THE WOOD WORK OF THE AFTER CABIN IN WHICH THE PIRATES ARE BARRICADED.....
BOY!—I'M FLIRTIN' WITH OL' DAVBY JONES!—THIS WEEPIN' BOMB HAD BETTER WORK!
THERE'S SOME BAD NEWS FOR YOU GUYS!
SO!—IT IS YOU—! —THE CAUSE OF ALL MY TROUBLES!—IT MAY BE MY LAST MOVE—BUT I'LL GET YOU!
GEE!—BETWEEN THE DEVIL AN' TH' DEEP BLUE SEA—AN' NO FOOLIN'!

The March 3, 1935 strip, collected in *The Complete Tery and the Pirates* Vol. 1: *1934-1936*. [©2007 Tribune Media Services]

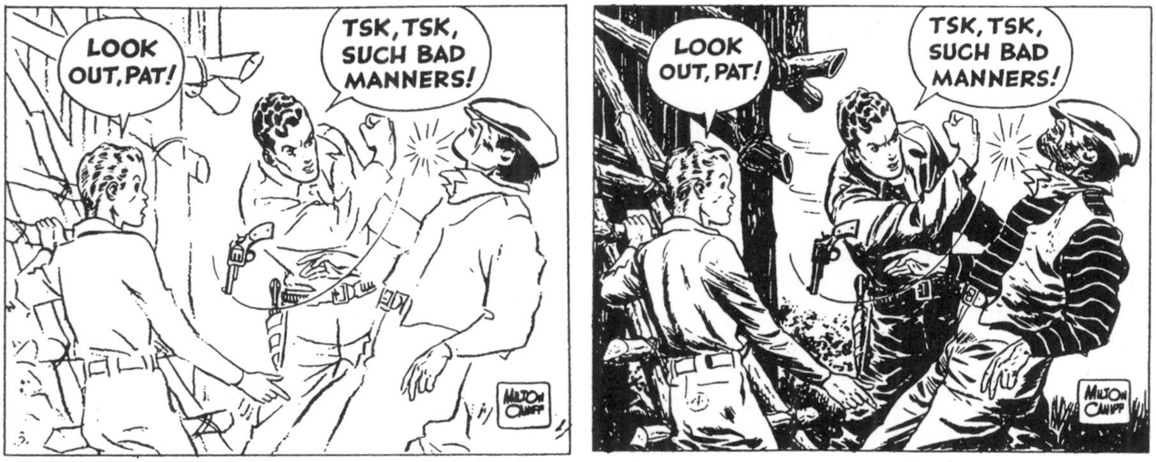
LOOK OUT, PAT!
TSK, TSK, SUCH BAD MANNERS!
MILTON CANIFF
LOOK OUT, PAT!
TSK, TSK, SUCH BAD MANNERS!
MILTON CANIFF

Harvey included a "how I draw *Terry and the Pirates*" sequence of panels by Caniff in *Meanwhile* ...[©2007 Estate of Milton Caniff]

The story of Caniff's evolution, and how the shifting of his personal technique swayed so many subsequent artists, is one of the most fascinating and informative stories in cartooning history. Harvey goes into exhaustive detail on the subject of just how Noel Sickles influenced Caniff and Terry (devoting a special appendix to the subject, even). While Sickles was undoubtedly the most significant influence on Caniff's growing skill, Caniff would never quite achieve the casual mastery enjoyed by his friend. Sickles is patently the better cartoonist, at least at the time of their collaborations, up to 1936. The crudeness of the strips from this period supposedly ghosted by Sickles makes a convincing argument against those who claim that Sickles' contributions to the strip were larger than has been historically accepted. The fact is that Caniff did start out pretty rough, and he did learn better, over time. It's why the strip is still fascinating. You can see the tangible, measurable progression of Caniff's skill over the course of the run. Caniff's ongoing education is one of the reasons why Terry is so significant: If you want to learn how to draw cartoons, there's no better way than to observe someone else's step-by-step progress.

Caniff improved his skills markedly over time, but he still never learned how to draw an attractive face. The one area in which he was clearly Sickles' superior was the field of storytelling — and this is why, weird faces notwithstanding — we remember Terry as one of the high points of the medium's history, and *Scorchy Smith*, while an important footnote in the evolution of cartooning, is still merely a footnote. Caniff may not have been able to draw a face to save his life, but he knew how to make the reader feel invested in those faces.

Is Harvey's ambition more than can reasonably be accommodated in the space of a single narrative? You'd have a hard time arguing that the book wasn't overstuffed. The really scary part is that the original manuscript apparently ran some 679,000 words, compared to the practically anorexic 425,000 presented in the finished product. Even given the tremendous cuts, there's still some repetition. Harvey's enthusiasm for the subject comes through in the copious detail on every page and in his willingness to pursue every opportunity for digression. In fact, I'm tempted to say that constant digression is so pervasive throughout the book as to be practically its *raison d'être*, a series of branching "meanwhiles" designed to illustrate a picture of the man and his times through an exhaustive catalog of detail.

At times, it's a hard book to read. The book's density — while at times frustrating — is part and parcel of its appeal, representing what will likely become a definitive text for comics historians of all stripes. Harvey writes like an essayist, however, and the book's major weakness comes from the stylistic decision to keep the full range of essayist's tics intact: the frequent digression, obviously, but also the presence of discursive conversational asides throughout the narrative to indicate shifting trains of thought. It's a technique that works wonderfully in the short form of an essay or a review (just like this, heh), but unfortunately has the effect of sapping momentum over the long haul of an extended subject, wherein following the intricate evolution of an author's thoughts is probably less important than the thoughts themselves. Also, the copious rehashing of plot-point minutiae, while in many places necessary to illustrate points, can seem excessively wonkish.

The book is written in such a way as seems to reward casual browsing, flipping through the volume at random and getting swept into Caniff's world for 20 minutes or two hours at a time. Just the fact that it exists in any form whatsoever is as warm a tribute to Caniff's talent as any conceivable, and for all its faults it deserves a place on the bookshelf of anyone who really and truly cares about the history of comics.

Unfortunately, anyone looking for the material evidence of Caniff's importance based on the work presented throughout *Meanwhile* ... will find unfortunately slim pickings in the first volume of IDW's *Terry and the Pirates*. Newspaper strips are almost unique in the world of art for being at a disadvantage when presented in strict chronological order. Whereas it always makes intrinsic sense to start at the beginning of any long narrative, the end result is that the vast majority of classic newspaper strips end up putting their worst feet forward with the first volumes of their reprints. Fantagraphics sidestepped the problem of presenting the early, Popeye-less *Thimble Theater* strips by merely picking up where Popeye joins the cast, jumping in near the point of the strip's zenith and forgoing years of Ham Gravy adventures. The saga of *Terry*, however, needs to start from the beginning by virtue of the complex continuity, so this first volume is filled with what are, in the context of the strip's later high points, essentially "Ham Gravy" stories. (To his credit, Howard Chaykin gives as good a warning as any in his introduction. It *does* start out pretty rough.)

When *Terry* began in 1934, the brief was simple: Caniff was to replicate the success of his earlier strip *Dickie Dare*, while adding a nominally more "adult" feel that would give the strip more potential for long-term growth than its predecessor. Captain Joseph Patterson, then editor for the Chicago Tribune-New York News Syndicate, grabbed Caniff from the Associated Press (for whom Caniff had created *Dickie Dare*), gave him the barest outline of a plot as well as the title and desired location (contemporary China). It didn't really matter that Caniff didn't know anything about China at the time. He checked some books out of the library and began drawing, filling in what he needed to know in hindsight and, at least in the beginning, not letting what he didn't know about China get in the way of producing seven strips a week.

The elements for *Terry's* later success are all present, but not quite as effective as they would later become. The *Dickie Dare* formula is replicated essentially verbatim: Terry Lee is a young orphan who accompanies fortune hunter/travel-writer Pat Ryan on his adventures throughout China, just as 12-year-old Dickie Dare traversed the globe in the company of adventurer Dan Flynn. The main difference from the start is that *Terry* is a far more sexualized universe than that of *Dickie Dare*, which was essentially kids' stuff through-and-through. Although Ryan's initial "love interest," Dale Scott, never takes off (I use scare quotes because she's about as lovely and interesting as a wet dishtowel), it wasn't long before the strip was flooded with dames: the well-heeled Normandie Drake, the wild (and quite lascivious) Burma, and of course the infamous Dragon Lady.

The problem is that the formula Caniff had been saddled with began very quickly to work at cross-purposes with the stories he wanted to tell. Very early in the strip's progression it becomes patently obvious that presenting Terry as anything other than a drag on the adventure sequences is a difficult proposition. Despite a few early cornball missteps with hidden temples and skull-clad mystics, the strip settles into a comfortable, fairly realistic milieu early on. But a number of times throughout the evolving storyline, whenever Caniff begins to build a head of steam on this or that narrative thread, it is interrupted by having to shoehorn Terry and Connie into the action, however incongruously. The kid's name *is* in the title, after all. I guess the idea of a 13- or 14-year-old kid bumming around one of the most dangerous countries in the world never stopped anyone's good time.

Later on, of course, Terry grew up and became less of a drag on the proceedings, eventually becoming the strip's central protagonist with the onset of World War II. But young as he is in these early strips, the character is only

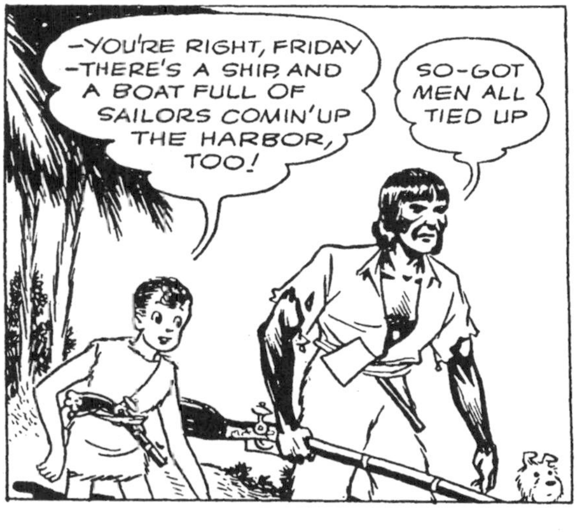
-YOU'RE RIGHT, FRIDAY -THERE'S A SHIP AND A BOAT FULL OF SAILORS COMIN' UP THE HARBOR, TOO!
SO-GOT MEN ALL TIED UP

A panel from Caniff's *Dickie Dare* strip.

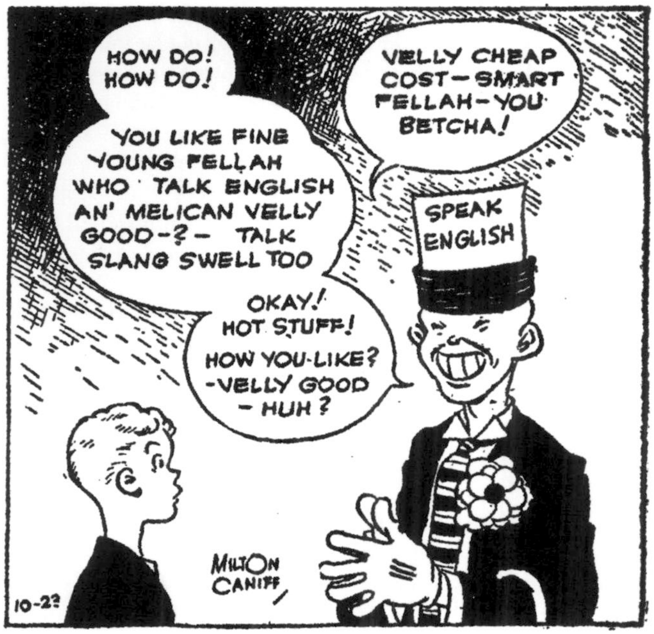
HOW DO! HOW DO!
VELLY CHEAP COST—SMART FELLAH—YOU BETCHA!
YOU LIKE FINE YOUNG FELLAH WHO TALK ENGLISH AN' MELICAN VELLY GOOD-?- TALK SLANG SWELL TOO
SPEAK ENGLISH
OKAY! HOT STUFF! HOW YOU-LIKE? -VELLY GOOD - HUH?
MILTON CANIFF
10-23

Connie's first appearance: Oct. 23, 1934. [©2007 Tribune Media Services]

ancillary to Pat Ryan's adventures. Ryan himself isn't really much of a character yet, either, but he still provides the main motor of the strip's forward momentum.

As the strip progresses, the canvas grows more and more broad. Whereas China appears initially to be nothing more than a series of loping hills teeming with benighted coolies, eventually Caniff's setting grows more intricate and unadulterated. Eventually — long after this first volume leaves off — *Terry* would attempt to encompass the full spectrum of China, from the poverty that forced peasants into piracy, to the depredations of civil war and Japanese imperialism. But then, there's only one mention of Japan throughout this entire book, and it's in passing — a regrettable sop to diplomacy that robs these early strips of a great part of their authority.

If all we had to remember *Terry* by was these early years, it'd stand as a pretty unforgivable strip. China here is little more than a playground for white colonialist powers, a setting for adventure and intrigue but of little intrinsic interest itself. And of course, there's the figure of Connie, Pat and Terry's Asian servant. Regardless of how well-rounded Connie eventually becomes, it's impossible to forgive the blatant caricature that stands as the basis of his character. Jaundiced yellow skin, buckteeth, huge ears and slanty eyes — no amount of cultural and temporal relativism can impel the reader to look beyond what is essentially inexcusable. (And as for the loathsome, sinister and clearly homosexual-coded bandit lord Papa Pyzon ... well, the less said the better.)

Eisner eventually came to recognize the sorrowful misfortune of Ebony White's despicable appearance in *The Spirit* — and Caniff came to a much more nuanced understanding and appreciation of China, as well. Harvey best illustrates this transformation — well, more like maturation — when he includes a fragment from Caniff's aborted *Terry and the Pirates* novelization, dated circa 1939. In the brief section Harvey includes, Ryan explains:

> Pirates are usually no more or less than farmers who've had a bad crop year, or who have been driven from their village by marauding parties or bandits or soldiers, and so take to pirating to make a living. It's sometimes difficult to tell when a Chinese is a pirate, or even when a pirate's a pirate.

In just a few short years, Caniff's attitudes toward the country he had undertaken to chronicle had evolved considerably. The China from these early strips is a pretty louche place, little more than an action-packed fun ride for Western adventurers. Eventually — not actually very long after the end of these 1936 strips — the series got serious. You can see inklings of this in a sequence where Pyzon's fearsome bandits are picked off by the Dragon Lady in the most ingenious manner: Reasoning that Pyzon's forces were desperate for female companionship, she sets up a whorehouse on the outskirts of Pyzon's territory with the promise of wives for any bandits who defect. People are fighting and plundering, not because they are essentially evil, but because they don't have a choice and are essentially after nothing more than a better life than what they have.

Regardless, the first couple of years of the strip, while certainly notable for the gradual evolution of Caniff's talent and artistic accomplishment, are still just a warm-up for the feast of later years. These early years, while a necessary part of the historical record, are only really palatable in the context of the strip's later success. Anyone reading through this first volume and wondering why the strip was so popular should remember, it *does* get better. ■

This Book Contains Graphic Language: Comics as Literature

Rocco Versaci
Continuum International Publishing Group
191 pp., $19.95
B&W illos, Softcover
ISBN: 9780826428516

Review by Kristian Williams

Why study comics? What makes you think these weird picture books are deserving of serious intellectual consideration or critical engagement?

These are the sort of questions Rocco Versaci tries to answer in *This Book Contains Graphic Language: Comics as Literature*. Versaci explains his efforts: "I have attempted to show that comic books are worthy subjects for literary study in that they are every bit as complicated, revelatory, and relevant as more acceptable types of art. By positioning different comic-book genres against the literatures of memoir, journalism, and film, I have attempted to show that comics creators can achieve artistic and political feats that are unique to the medium and thus unavailable to authors of these more respectable forms" (165). Versaci's approach is to take a genre of "serious" literature, present its defining characteristics and main virtues, and then show us how comics does everything that prose, photography or film can do — and sometimes does it better. So comics are more honest than straight memoir, journalism or history; more sophisticated and humane than war movies; and more semiotically complex than novels. There's a case to be made here, and many of the arguments will be familiar to readers of this magazine — so familiar, in fact, that one might be forgiven for wondering why we need a 191-page book to argue that comics should be taken seriously.

The real weakness of Versaci's approach is that it relies on comparisons between comics and respectable, canonical works. This effort is intended to loan comics some of the legitimacy of the established work, but the implicit suggestion is that comics are only worthy of serious consideration *because* they resemble the accepted literature. This is akin to arguing that scholars should study movies just because films are rather like plays. Versaci does try valiantly to show the unique properties of the comics form, but because it is framed by way of a comparison,

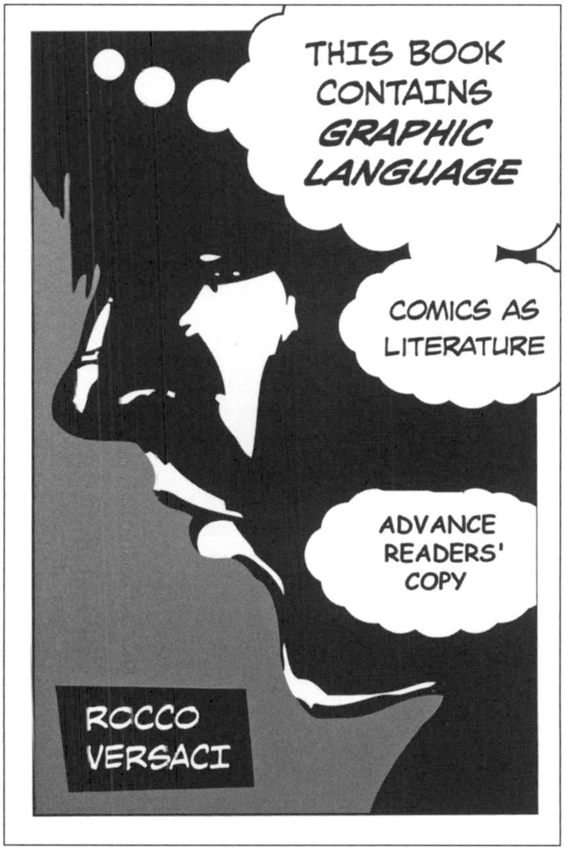
THIS BOOK CONTAINS GRAPHIC LANGUAGE
COMICS AS LITERATURE
ADVANCE READERS' COPY
ROCCO VERSACI

[© 2007 Continuum International Publishing Group]

the emphasis is always on the conventions inherent to the *genre* rather than the potential of the *medium*. So we end up with — to cite one case — a tedious, page-long examination of Lauren Slater's prose memoir *Lying* and just a paragraph on Alison Bechdel's *Fun Home*. Why is

Lying even in this book at all? For the sake of comparison, so we can see how *Fun Home* is "also" literary.

The underlying irony is that it wasn't that long ago that the items Versaci uses for his legitimizing comparisons would have been despised themselves. English literature only became a subject for serious study in the late 19th century. Before that, it was considered merely a shallow approximation of the Classics, "a subject fit for women, workers and those wishing to impress the natives" — as Terry Eagleton's masterful *Literary Theory: An Introduction* characterizes the dominant view of the time. Eagleton goes on:

> English was an upstart, amateurish affair as academic subjects went, hardly able to compete on equal terms with the rigors of Greats or philology; since every English gentleman read his own literature in his spare time anyway, what was the point of subjecting it to systematic study? ... [T]he definition of an academic subject was what could be examined, and since English was no more than idle gossip about literary taste it was difficult to know how to make it unpleasant enough to qualify as a proper academic pursuit. ... The only way in which English seemed likely to justify its existence in the ancient Universities [of Oxford and Cambridge] was by systematically mistaking itself for the Classics; but the classicists were hardly keen to have this pathetic parody of themselves around (29).

It's funny, then, to see comics following in the footsteps of English, attacking an establishment whose most sacred works were seen as shallow-minded and trivial barely a century ago. And it might not be enough for comics criticism to "systematically mistak[e] itself" for English lit.

In fact, Versaci highlights the multiple challenges that comics present for the canon:

> The work of comic book creators like Gaiman, Moore, and Sikoryak assault the canon, but the assault is less on the content of the canon than on the very idea of it. Or more specifically, on the assumptions of canon-makers that "literature" embodies only certain forms, and that comic books are certainly not one of them. But comic book creators who use the form with imagination and insight have the ability to complicate the very nature of how we award literary merit. All of the incarnations of the comic book that I have discussed ... help to upend the notion of "literature" as an inviolable model that

must adhere to certain dimensions. What we are in need of is a new model of the "literary" (188).

Yet despite this acknowledgement, his discursive strategy relies on the idea that literature exists as a more-or-less stable category, with established criteria for inclusion. In making his comparisons, Versaci tacitly accepts the values of the canon as it is presently construed, and thus is left trying to justify the inclusion of comics in terms of those values. His argument takes the form: We read X for such and such reasons; and those same reasons apply to Y; therefore we should read Y. What he fails to see is that the canon is inherently conservative, and its valuations are not in any sense impartial or objective. Expanding the canon doesn't depend on applying agreed-upon criteria to new media or to new literary forms — not least because there are no such criteria, and even if there were, the application would itself be contestable. So simply measuring *Blankets* against *A Separate Peace* does not get us very far — and wouldn't, even if we could agree about what the relevant points of comparison ought to be.

More to the point, Versaci's agenda of inclusion may be in some sense self-defeating. As he himself notes, comics can achieve a profound effect in part because it *is* a maligned medium. Comics can play against our expectations, insist on a level of ironic distancing, and point out their own "constructed-ness" and perspectivity — all because the reader approaches them with a certain set of assumptions about what the medium is and what it's for.

"While many of us comic book boosters lament this situation, it is also possible to see a power in such marginality," he concedes. "That is, so long as comics in general and comics journalism in particular are left on the margins of literature, they may continue to surprise readers and level powerful criticisms against corporate interests, including the mainstream media. More important, they may provoke us to think about the constructed nature of truth in all forms of journalism. The fact that most people will always see a contradiction between a 'juvenile' medium and 'adult' content is enough to ensure that comics journalists will be free to be as radical as they wish" (121).

But what happens when the medium finally overcomes its history and its reputation? Will it lose its edge? Does the comic book, like punk rock, rely on its position as a disreputable outsider to really achieve its full effect? If it does, then the entire battle for inclusion, for respectability, may be badly conceived. Perhaps we critics should desist from offering intellectual defenses for comics and stop fighting for their place among "serious" literature, and develop instead their sense of oppositional marginality. Rather than finding a place for comics in the "mainstream" of literature, maybe we should establish it as a foil to the canon.

What's needed is not a new application of the same criteria, but new criteria — not the values of a novel transposed onto a graphic novel, but values particularly suited to the understanding and evaluation of graphic novels. In short, rather than *arguing* that comics should be treated as literature, Versaci would be better advised just to *treat them as literature*. The justification comes in the execution. Either one can find interesting things to say about comics, or one cannot. Versaci can, and I only wish he had done more of it rather than trying endlessly to justify the effort in the first place.

There are moments of genuine insight and original analysis in *Graphic Language*. (For instance, Versaci offers an excellent study of self-representation in comics autobiography, with well-chosen examples from the work of Jeffrey Brown and Daniel Clowes.) But these are brief and scattered among the tiresome justifications for fitting comics into the canon. Perhaps this is exactly the sort of thing you need if, as a junior professor, you're trying to explain to the head of the English Department why *Two-Fisted Tales* appears on your syllabus alongside *The Armies of the Night* and *The Things They Carried*. But for the rest of us, arguments about the canon just seem pointless and boring. They're exactly as interesting as listening to teenage boys argue about the technical merits of Eric Clapton's guitar work.

And that's the problem with Versaci's book. When he talks about the *comics* — how they work, and what they do — he's quite readable and occasionally brilliant. But mostly the book is preoccupied with its justifications for talking about comics *at all*. And to explain why we should, he falls back on a stereotyped comparison with the already accepted body of work. Again, it's like suggesting that the best reason to read Kathy Acker is that one might possibly draw a favorable comparison to Baudelaire. Perhaps this is how a syllabus is developed, but it's no way to go through life.

A work of real literature must stand or fall on its own merits, not by analogy to some other work in some other medium. It makes no difference whether we're discussing *Heart of Darkness* or *The Killing Joke*. If it's worth reading, then no further justification is necessary. And if it's *not* worth reading, than no comparison to something else will possibly help it. Of course, Versaci is not just arguing that comics are worth reading, but that they're worth *studying*, and the criteria there are somewhat different.

But the best way to show that comics are worth studying is *to study them* and do a good job of it. Tell us something interesting about the form, or about some of its finest specimens. Comment on it smartly. Offer a penetrating analysis. Reveal something subtle about the work. Show us how it illuminates our lives, our culture, or our society, or how it subverts its genre, or deconstructs the medium itself. And, if you need to, relate it to other works in the same, or other, media. If the criticism is worth reading, then it's worth writing; if the study is worthwhile, then its object is worth examining. There may be other criteria in the physical, or even social, sciences, but it's hard to think of another standard of judgment in the humanities.

If there is a meta-level argument to be made, it would not address the reasons why comics should be accepted as literature — but the question of why, traditionally, they haven't been. I don't have anything like a full account of why this is so, and neither does Versaci, but the case he makes implies — in a negative sense, if you will — what he suspects the reasons might be. Mainly, it comes down to a cycle of ignorance: Serious people don't read comics because they don't know how good they can be; they don't know how good they can be because they don't read them. Versaci tries to break the cycle by demonstrating that comics can, by the standards suggested in the criticism of other literature, be very good. I don't know if "quality" is quite what's at issue, though. I'm not sure one can just put *Watchmen* on a sort of literary scale and weigh it against *The Lord of the Flies*, and I'm not sure what it would settle if you could.

Or: Perhaps these categories — inclusion and exclusion; mainstream and marginal; canon and apocrypha — are exactly backwards. It is, after all, only in an academic faculty meeting that *Gravity's Rainbow* could be considered more "mainstream" than *Spider-Man*. And I strongly suspect that the one perfectly valid ethical principle that most Americans can quote verbatim is not the Golden Rule or the Categorical Imperative, but "With great power comes great responsibility." Perhaps there is something significant in that. ∎

Kristian Williams also writes about comics for Mindbuck.com and is presently at work on a book about Oscar Wilde and anarchism. His first two books, *Our Enemies in Blue: Police and Power in America* and *American Methods: Torture and the Logic of Domination* are available from South End Press.

Thoreau at Walden

John Porcellino
Hyperion Books
112 pp., $16.99
B&W + Color, Hardcover
ISBN: 9781423100386

Review by Rich Kreiner

At first blush, this would seem a match made in counter-culture heaven.

Here's Thoreau, autobiographer and bootstrap philosopher, a staunch individualist who valued simplicity and straightforwardness and who revered nature in its less-tamed resplendence. And here's John Porcellino, a self-made autobiographical cartoonist whose own unceremoniously steadfast individualism is embodied in his distinctive style. He's an inadvertent philosopher who champions unconditional acceptance, who practices pragmatic simplicity and straightforwardness and who harbors a special regard for nature, first and foremost human nature, first and foremost his own.

Spiritually and methodologically, the pair are kin. Says the one on his woodsy retreat, "To be a philosopher ... is to solve some of the problems of life — not only theoretically — but practically." Says the other (and the only one of the two with his own *Journal* interview, back in issue #241): "The experiment was to find out, how can I live? How can I live in this world and stay true to myself, and do something I can feel good about? How do I do that?" Their collaboration — to borrow the words of Thoreau at the end of *Thoreau at Walden* — meets "with a success unexpected in common hours."

On second blush, though, the pairing of Thoreau and Porcellino would seem to have its share of potential bumps. A little prior knowledge of their oeuvres suggests, for one thing, that Thoreau is more formally and aesthetically exacting. From Porcellino's end, he had little track record dealing with stories not distinctly his own. Yet these complications wind up showing both creators in a somewhat different, flattering light, yielding surprises perhaps exactly when you think you were no longer capable of being surprised by either of them.

The book's magic begins mechanically. Its panels can be big, as big as or bigger than anything Porcellino has had in print before. Bigger than *King-Cat* covers. This makes his drawings, done as usual with a uniform line of unwavering thickness, big as well, blown up so that any blemish would be especially impressive. Big too are individual objects, enlarged so any weakness in proportion, construction, relationship or perspective would be glaring. Big, big, big.

Porcellino rises to scale. His line is confident, strikingly so, betraying no hesitation in hand or head. It is stolidly gestural, brawnily lyrical, unconsciously sublime. Here's a most flagrant example: Under the paper wrap of the hardcover, a portrait of Thoreau by Porecellino from the interior is reprinted to stretch across both front and back covers. The likeness owes nothing to the ol' transcendentalist to begin with, but here facial features are enlarged and cropped near to the point of abstraction. That great curling swoop, like a graceful skater's mark across fresh ice? Turns out it's his nose. The ribbed dot becomes the unblinking eye (the book will hold no other solid blacks). The narrow slash, as mouth, betrays no speech, no emotion, keeping its council and remaining unmoved by outer circumstance. This is fluent, minimalist calligraphy writ prodigiously, the unstudied product of prolonged preparation.

The line sets the mood and the mood is one of quiet resonance and sympathetic allowance. Porcellino's strength was never his draftsmanship, but here epresentation is not the point. Suggestion — transformational suggestion — is. Composition and execution broach mysteries deeper and more splendid than visual fidelity ordinarily traffics in. This sort of revelatory quest has been the foundation of relatively recent art movements and here Porcellino quotes one directly by constructing several cubist arrangements of objects and angles. They manage to be fully functional while avoiding that anxious art's dissociative jitteriness.

IT IS TO SOLVE SOME OF THE PROBLEMS OF LIFE — NOT ONLY THEORETICALLY —

Actual-size panel by Porcellino, with Thoreau's words: from *Thoreau at Walden*. [©2008 The Center for Cartoon Studies]

Other visual variances hold to no organized school. Anyone who studies the hand-drawn map of the Pond and its environs will know that the picket fence Thoreau surveys across the water is actually the tracks of the Fitchburg Railroad *à la* Porcellino. And who cares if what appears to be a work hat doffed for lunch on page 40 is later deciphered by its close resemblance to a mound of food (bread?) spread out (on a cloth?) on page 51? Who would even notice?

The second unusual feature employed by Porcellino (who experimented with Zipatone only tentatively) is the pervasive incorporation of an added color, a uniform, neutral beige. The shade fills a number of roles, as well as a great deal of two-dimensional space. It acts as color field. (Hmmm ... that makes four distinct artistic movements that have come to mind, none of which Porcellino

cultivates doctrinally.) Primarily, it offers contrast. It can be used to highlight, but often it is applied too evenly to convey special emphasis. It does not attempt to build in spacial depth with any degree of scientific or aesthetic accuracy. It often defines forms and fills in shapes, be they stand of trees. ridge of hills, or Thoreau's body in the form of a lump.

The color outlines. It suggests visual planes and even completes the momentum of lines when they simply come to a stop. The shade works best under two circumstances. One is when it slips from our conscious attention. The other is when Porcellino has a clear, artlessly practical reason for its presence, for instance when moving between day and night or exterior and interior. Or when throwing lamplight shadows. Or when brightening surfaces dressed in freshly fallen snow. On the flip side,

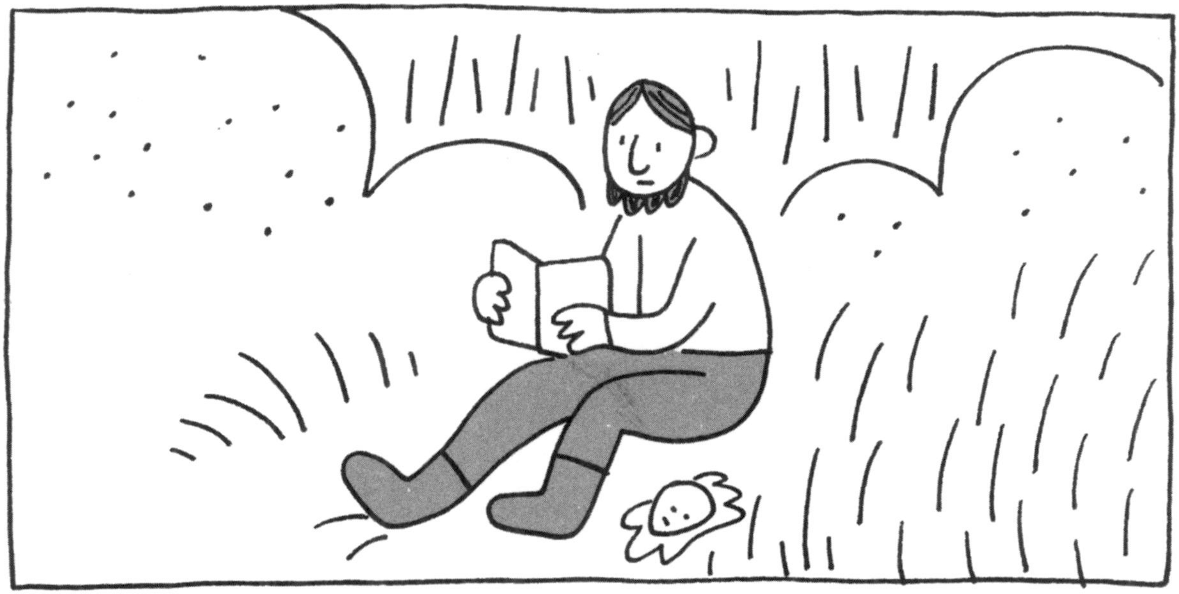

[©2008 The Center for Cartoon Studies]

the browning flatters least when it's noticed. Awkward exploitations are rare but can be singled out as design elements in general, or, in specific, as the pattern of windows in the unaccountably massive, penitentiary-like hoosegow of 19th-century Concord, Mass.

The book is organized soundly. A brief prologue shows Thoreau in Concord, observing its citizens and formulating his discontents with communal life. Part One escorts us to his newly hand-hewn homestead at Walden Pond, around house and grounds, sketching out the prospects that led him thither. Part Two revels in the rewards of life in the woods, from waking dawn till drifting dusk. Part Three covers Thoreau's arrest and overnight incarceration in Concord for nonpayment of its poll tax, an event that formed the basis of his famous essay "Civil Disobedience." The final part offers more reflective thoughts of his experiences, with the comic ending as it began: Thoreau walking along a path.

In the closing credits, Porcellino is listed as both artist and author of the book, exactly what you would expect from a book produced under the aegis of the Center for Cartoon Studies. Still, it also points up the poverty of language for our medium, at least in this case of clarifying creative chores, since the whole of the comic's text, right down to bird noises and sound effects, is taken from the written works of Thoreau. We know this thanks to a scrupulous, line-by-line listing of quoted material. (Textual sources number four. *Walden* dominates except for the relevant chapter where "Civil Disobedience" competes. Thoreau's journals provide three quotes, his essay "Walking," one.)

The comic has no balloons. Thoreau's thoughts are presented as a running but intermittent interior monologue, parceled out principally in heading or caption boxes. The sampling is catholic and far-ranging. It roams back and forth through Thoreau's texts with a brisk sense of purpose, sometimes weaving from one literary work to another on a single page. Yet its course remains steadfast. The monologue remains uniformly cogent and sympathetically arranged throughout.

Such delivery makes remarks necessarily short and on point. The concise commentary and succinct observation serves to reduce Thoreau to an aphorist ... but he makes a great aphorist! (See *Simplify, Simplify and Other Quotations from Henry David Thoreau*). I'm not sure Thoreau himself would be pleased with the streamlining of expression, the ruthless boiling-down of lofty thought, the savage truncation of rhetorical style ("Books must be read as deliberately and as reservedly as they were written"). There's no doubt some aspects of his beliefs are presented more compellingly than others: As it appears here, the foundation for "Civil Disobedience" would never have wowed Gandhi or Martin Luther King, Jr.. But what *is* here is presented honestly and framed winningly. Spirit

[©2008 The Center for Cartoon Studies]

remains true and on target.

So pruning and winnowing has its costs. On the plus side, this book will make Thoreau's thoughts and aspects of his life far more accessible and immediately comprehensible to a far wider range of readers, beginning with young adults and those who would otherwise encounter the author only as part of school curriculum. I am told (by *Approaches to Teaching Thoreau's* Walden *and Other Works*, as long as I'm name-dropping) that today's students believe *Walden* a difficult book, daunting and filled with fusty artifice, that it is found to be "all attitude, no sex, and too hard to read." (Well, it's like the man said: "The heroic books, even if printed in the character of our mother tongue, will always be in a language dead to degenerate times.")

It's true that Thoreau, for all his regard for simplicity, directness and clarity, could make his own passages and arguments ornate and elaborate, spiked with references and literary devices that are now hardly commonplace, let alone appreciated. No doubt Thoreau grew up and grew old with the belief that "deliberate reading" was dimly if irrevocably associated with the amount of effort he himself had to expend while reading the classics in their original Greek and Latin. ("To read true books in a true spirit, is a noble exercise, and one that will task the reader more than any exercise which the customs of the day esteems.") The benefit of Porcellino's *Thoreau at Walden* is that it

pares certain issues down to the barest bone without sacrificing essential marrow. (It does not, for instance, get mired down with the three quotes above.)

On other occasions, Porcellino proves fully capable of carving up the meat for his own expressive purposes: in the quiet concluding moments of Part Two, Thoreau is depicted drifting off to sleep in his cabin, listening to the calls of birds that had been introduced to us as readers during his sunlit hours. His last waking thought is "I rejoice that there are owls," as soothing and beatific a closing thought for a day as anyone could hope for. Now, in *Walden* proper, Thoreau would go on to write that "They represent the stark twilight and unsatisfied thoughts which all have." What does he mean by that and — cripes — who can get to sleep now?

Porcellino's respect for Thoreau is obviously not slavishly literal. Additionally, his drawings have an unusual relationship to Thoreau's words, unusual in a "medium-of-comics" sense. In comics we are habituated to pictures illustrating action. Here they illuminate *an* action — like hoeing, rowing, waking, walking, sitting, writing, bathing, splitting wood — motions born of repetition and potentially carried out without much in the way of conscious thought. Here they call attention to themselves. These common acts are offered as if they are in fact suspended, arrested and set aside at elevation, with *each* deserving of a moment's focus. They slip from strategic narrative roles and invite, either explicitly or implicitly, the reader's thoughtful consideration, as if they were unthreatening little spur-of-the-moment visual koans. They lightly but firmly insist that any "action" within an episode include its internal component, its listening, observing, weighing, Zen being. Many panels and whole scenes are quiet, wordless and voluble.

This sort of knotting of Thoreau's and Porcellino's sensibilities provide the richest of the unexpected successes in the book. *Thoreau at Walden* is not an illustrated text, not a translation or an abridged "version." It comes closest to interpretive homage. (The title of that Donovan album: *A Gift From a Flower To a Garden*.) Take the segment of the houseguest mouse ... it's handled much more affectionately by Porcellino than written by Thoreau. Yet it is in keeping with Porcellino's understanding of honored beasts (see *King-Cat*). Moreover, the segment is explicated with a sensitive quartet of quotes plucked from the length and breadth of *Walden* that serve to make his reading wholly defensible. And sometimes such perceptive reading is *all* Porcellino: Stepping out of jail onto the town streets, Thoreau realizes just how wide the gulf is that separates him from Concord's citizens, his clos-

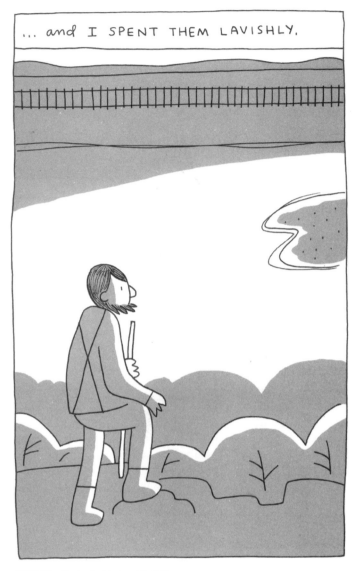

... and I SPENT THEM LAVISHLY.
[©2008 The Center for Cartoon Studies]

Porcellino for compensations, particularly capturing "the countless moments of silence that Thoreau experienced at Walden ... moments of quiet reverie."

Concluding features include an afterword from Porcellino, a short and practical if quirky bibliography (including *The Night Thoreau Spent in Jail: A Play*), that dutiful quote appendix and supplemental panel notes. Collectively the material is an important adjunct to the comic, expanding incidents and offering valuable perspective. (We'd otherwise not know from the comic alone that Thoreau spent a total of two years and two months at Walden.)

But the extras can be tricky to coordinate with the experience afforded by the comic. Overly diligent consultation of notes invariably works against the muted eloquence and focused integrity of Porcellino's story. In at least one instance, panel commentary can be faulted for too much information. It reports of Thoreau that "Mainstream members of Concord society considered him an oddball." This can be more or less intrusive depending on when it was read, as it invariably comes between Porcellino's Thoreau and readers by tainting our evolving relationship with him. Worse, it unavoidably interjects a distracting, superfluous issue, because, unless I'm reading Thoreau wrong, the estimation of others is not to be overvalued (see "Drummers, Different").

Regardless, as comic and as educational experience, this is a highly gratifying, highly successful, readily accessible distillation of some provocative, coordinated thinking. Along those lines, *Thoreau at Walden* already looks good in our local library. It's been placed in the Young Adult section which unfortunately

est neighbors. We come to realize it too, powerfully, eloquently, through a wordless, two paneled-page whereby the lumpen Thoreau moves past two female heads, floating bodiless in an otherwise empty frame.

The book's introduction by author and illustrator B.D. Johnson (*Henry Hikes to Fitchburg*) fleshes out Thoreau's life broadly, filling in both essential and irresistible details. (At the Pond, Thoreau cultivated the equivalent of a "seven-mile-long row of beans"!). Addressing the severe abridgements necessary for the comic, he rightly praises

belies its All Audience benefits. With Porcellino as the set-up man, this Thoreau has something vital and vibrant to say to just about anybody, irrespective of stage of life. By way of personal testimony: It's May as I write this, May following a winter — a *Maine* winter — so I perk up my ears when Thoreau mentions an attraction of living in the woods as being able to "see the spring come in." Spring! Oh, he's talking my kinda language right to my face. Porcellino? He opens up all the windows and lets the whole thing *breathe*. ■

Trains Are ... Mint
Oliver East
Blank Slate
120 pp., $24.99
Color, Hardcover
ISBN: 9781906653002

Oliver East walks. When he's done, he draws. In *Trains Are...Mint*, he walks and draws Manchester to Blackpool along the train tracks. It all seems terribly English, and quite refreshing.

England has already produced many fine walkers, from William Hazlitt, who wrote some great essays on the act, to the conceptual artist Richard Long, who chose the walk itself as his primary medium. A charity, the Ramblers' Association, even exists to keep the old rural pathways open. East contributes walking not as a rural idyll, but a meditation on the other side of the tracks. He focuses on train stations and apartment blocks, trash-strewn alleys and scrawled graffiti.

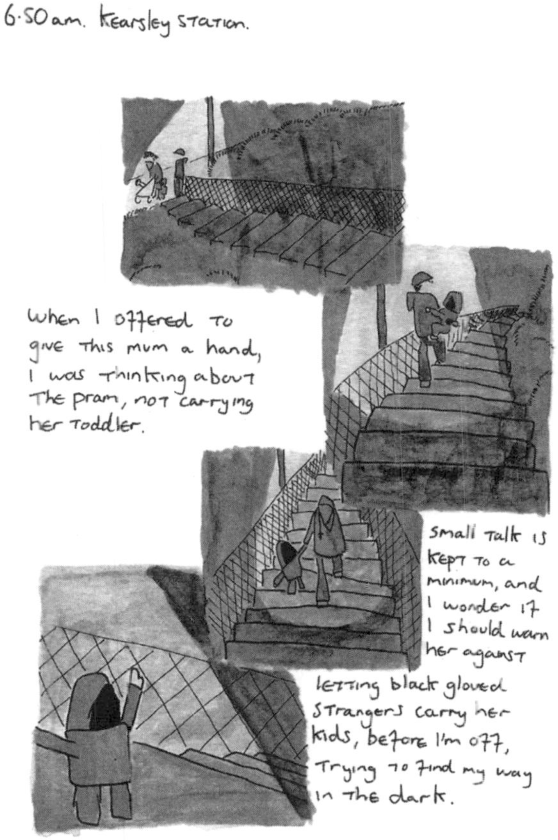
6.50am. Kearsley Station.
When I offered to give this mum a hand, I was thinking about the pram, not carrying her toddler.
Small talk is kept to a minimum, and I wonder if I should warn her against
letting black gloved strangers carry her kids, before I'm off, trying to find my way in the dark.

From Trains are ... Mint. [©2008 Oliver East]

The results are oblique and intoxicating. His first book reads not like most other comics, or even narratives. Because it centers on a journey, East has considerable freedom. He can omit transitions and motivation, instead focusing on small ironies. In fact, he even omits himself most of the time. In doing so, he follows Hazlitt, who wrote that we travel "to leave ourselves behind, much more to get rid of others." All walks are lonesome.

The trains and their routes tie it all together. He follows the tracks, putting his keen eye to the places around them. It is an England known by the people who live in it, considerably more dank and decayed than the postcard images on American public television. Yet he draws it in charming bulbous forms, a childlike style. People become buoyant lumps, and buildings look like toy blocks. His watercolors, subdued washes of green, brown and gray, make it pulsate with life. Though I've never seen Manchester and environs, *Trains* reminds me of Birmingham, which I have. It makes me want to go back and walk the same routes East did, if just to feel the grit of the tracks.

Though a few other cartoonists have attempted long-form travel comics, like K. Thor Jensen, I know of no one doing work like East. He has been known as a unique voice to minicomics readers and those of us who chanced on his online epic, *Trains Are... Mint* #4. Good news, then, that this hardcover edition will introduce him properly to new readers.

The better news is that East has a reprint of *Trains Are ... Mint* #4 in the works (one of my best books of 2007). Blank Slate will also release another book, called *Proper Go Well High*. To his publisher, my thanks for beginning an innovative new program of British comics. To Mr. East, I say: Keep walking.

— Bill Randall

Big Questions #10: The Hand That Feeds
Anders Nilsen
Drawn & Quarterly
42 pp., $6.50
B&W, Softcover
ISBN: 9781897299432

There are any number of stock settings in modern comics, from mean streets and futuristic worlds, to high-school classrooms and low-rent diners. I can't think of many comics — apart from *Big Questions* and the same author's *Dogs and Water* — that take place in and around the wreckage of small aircraft. Unless you count *Lost*, Anders Nilsen pretty much owns the surreal crash-site genre.

Frankly, *Big Questions* has more in common with experimental theater than with anything on prime time.

Nilsen's visually centered narrative moves at a carefully modulated pace, but he is in a hurry to get started. The story opens on the title page (which is also the inside front cover), and grinds to a halt on the inside back cover. There's drama and angst in these cardstock pages, but not much of a conventional plot. The story is centered around two nearly mute humans who appear disoriented and possibly a little insane, along with contending groups of crows and finches who keep watch on the mysterious strangers. One of the main characters wears the garb of a spiritual seeker, while the other is almost catatonic. The birds can talk, but the humans can't decipher their language. Simple communication seems beyond the reach of everyone involved, and the prospects for meaningful dialogue appear exceedingly slim, either between the two humans or the two groups of birds, or for that matter across the human/non-human divide.

Nilsen may be drawn to this unusual setting, at least in part, because it allows him to evoke an entire landscape of alienation and hopelessness. In this context, the plane wreckage could be understood as a metaphor for social decay and our collective estrangement from the natural world. But I suspect that Nilsen is more interested in achieving certain visual effects and emotional responses than he is in turning his comics into social commentary. The reader may feel deeply out of sorts, for whatever reason, and the characters in this book may feel profoundly alienated, but ultimately the two worlds are not destined to meet. The characters are unlikely to find their way into our reality, and their world is a little barren to be mistaken for ours. At the same time, in both our world and theirs, crows do not think much of the human form. "Man, he's ugly," says one. "That whole thing with the bare skin gives me the creeps."

— Kent Worcester

Welcome to the Dahl House: Alienation, Incarceration and Inebriation in the New American Rome

Ken Dahl
Microcosm Publishing
122 pp., $7.00
B&W, Softcover
ISBN: 9781934620021

This book gives every indication that the Ignatz-winning *Monsters* #1 did not exactly spring full-grown from the mind of Ken Dahl. As a sampler of some 25 strips from the past 12 years, the compilation suggests rather that his fêted funnybook on STDs was the healthy offspring of an anxious, sustained artistic gestation.

The pieces here range widely in subject from jail to Army recruitment, from adolescent sexuality to adult romance. (With luck, the day will come when Dahl's tale of air travel on the one-year anniversary of 9/11 will invoke laughter that is blithe and not bilious. But you can laugh at "Love: A Colossal Waste of Time" and his skateboarder's relapse *right now*.) An overriding theme is the indictment of pop and consumer cultures for their shallowness and hypocrisy while demonstrating the inability of alternatives — punk and zine cultures — to offer any serious competition. Dahl translates the snippets of the lives of others literally yet fancifully, but it is autobiography that earns his most thoughtful scrutiny, especially growing older without reparations.

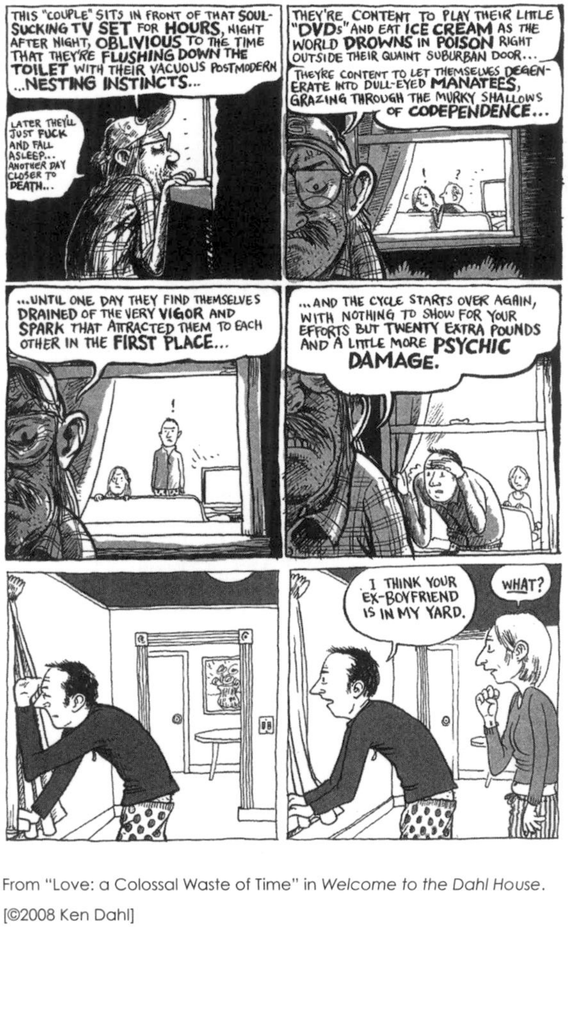
THIS "COUPLE" SITS IN FRONT OF THAT SOUL-SUCKING TV SET FOR HOURS, NIGHT AFTER NIGHT, OBLIVIOUS TO THE TIME THAT THEY'RE FLUSHING DOWN THE TOILET WITH THEIR VACUOUS POSTMODERN ...NESTING INSTINCTS...
LATER THEY'LL JUST FUCK AND FALL ASLEEP... ANOTHER DAY CLOSER TO DEATH...
THEY'RE CONTENT TO PLAY THEIR LITTLE "DVDs" AND EAT ICE CREAM AS THE WORLD DROWNS IN POISON RIGHT OUTSIDE THEIR QUAINT SUBURBAN DOOR...
THEY'RE CONTENT TO LET THEMSELVES DEGENERATE INTO DULL-EYED MANATEES, GRAZING THROUGH THE MURKY SHALLOWS OF CODEPENDENCE...
...UNTIL ONE DAY THEY FIND THEMSELVES DRAINED OF THE VERY VIGOR AND SPARK THAT ATTRACTED THEM TO EACH OTHER IN THE FIRST PLACE...
...AND THE CYCLE STARTS OVER AGAIN, WITH NOTHING TO SHOW FOR YOUR EFFORTS BUT TWENTY EXTRA POUNDS AND A LITTLE MORE PSYCHIC DAMAGE.
I THINK YOUR EX-BOYFRIEND IS IN MY YARD.
WHAT?

From "Love: a Colossal Waste of Time" in *Welcome to the Dahl House*. [©2008 Ken Dahl]

Dahl uses a number of visual styles, including streamlined minimalism, cartoon animation and selective realism. Settings and environments can be evocative and transporting. Dahl's stand-in, Gordon Smalls, is depicted nakedly, without self-pity, which is in keeping with the bulk of the book, as there's precious little pity to be had anywhere. This makes the tenor fairly consistent. Dahl is entirely persuasive at mining the horrible humor in everyday life. He finds himself as the (comparatively) clear-thinking misfit, the Jeremiah in unavoidable opposition to unassailable Powers That Be. Hence the book's subtitle.

Dahl's lengthier segments invariably gain in strength, clarity and impact, offering further supporting evidence of his skill and import. There's a distinct sense that *Welcome to the Dahl House* functions, in the words of the last panel of the last strip, as "clearing the wasteland for a passage towards better times."

Oh, two facts submitted not as critical commentary but as public service: The book's a bargain and *Monsters*, as a graphic novel, is slated for release in the fall of 2009.

— Rich Kreiner

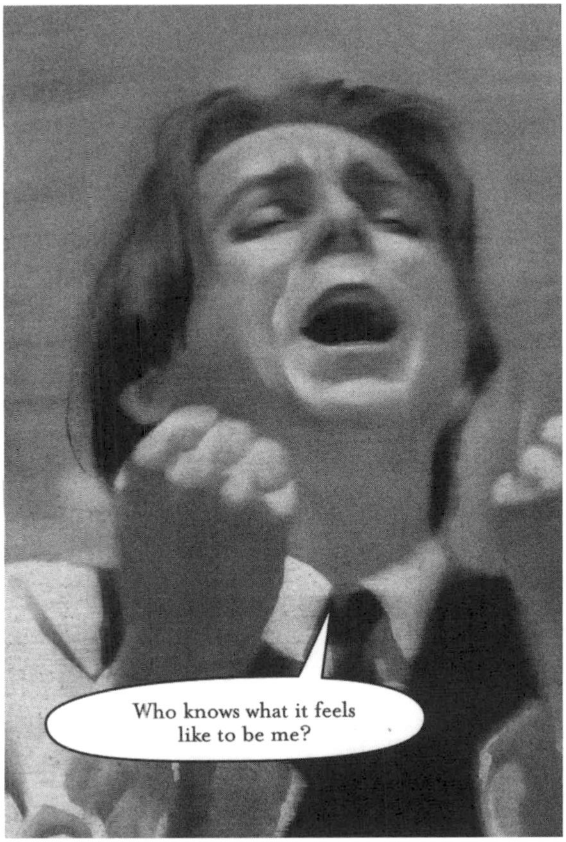
Who knows what it feels like to be me?

[©2008 Jon J. Muth]

M

Jon J. Muth
Harry N. Abrams
192 pp., $24.95
Color, Hardcover
ISBN: 9780810995222

Now that graphic novels have made inroads into bookstores, publishers have a chance to raid the vaults. Hidden there wait scores of forgotten masterpieces, eager to be dusted off by readers who want to develop their sense of history. It's good business: Movie studios have made a mint rereleasing old movies in new editions.

Such thinking explains the attractive new Abrams edition of Jon J. Moth's *M*. An adaptation of the 1931 German thriller by director Fritz Lang, it has a ready-made audience. Tellingly, the introduction, by a film critic, waxes about Fritz Lang, Peter Lorre and Jean-Luc Godard's *Contempt*. Jon J. Muth's comic, however, merits just a few short paragraphs of comparison. It is cited as an important early painted comic. Other merits receive only vague mention.

Chief among those merits, Muth can handle a brush. His hazy, mostly monochrome images look beautiful on the page. He uses silverpoint, oils and pastels, though a reliance on photo reference makes them less dynamic than a comic book demands. They echo the Bill Sienkiewicz of *Big Numbers*, from the same year, and are reminiscent of a time when "graphic novel" meant 48 perfect-bound pages with paintings of models in spandex.

Unfortunately, Muth's style distracts from the story. The detail in his paintings overwhelms the panel-to-panel flow. Worse, the intrusive typeset captions and word balloons make *M* a sterile hybrid, not unlike the comics version of a mule. Reading it offers little pleasure. I can't imagine imitating it. Other artists, like Sienkiewicz and Dave McKean, have shown more fruitfully how to integrate painting with the idioms of comics. Muth's *M* seems an artistic cul-de-sac.

However, it offers some grist for comparative criticism. Muth's pretty pictures entirely rob the film of its chief asset: Peter Lorre's clammy, taut face. By contrast, Muth's murderer recalls no one in particular. Thus, the mix of sympathy and loathing evoked by Lang's film has no place in the comic. And it should have no place on the shelf, at least not before other, better works appear. *M* was not the best comic yet uncollected from 1990 — start with the unfinished *Big Numbers* and go from there. At worst, it is a publishing mistake twice committed, an odd career footnote for an artist now happily working in children's books. At best, it is an excuse to dust off the original film, available in not one but two DVD editions.

— Bill Randall

The Twilight Zone: The After Hours
Created by Rod Serling, adapted by Mark Kneece, illustrated by Rebekah Isaacs
Walker Books
72 pp., Color
Softcover, $9.99, ISBN 9780802797179
Hardcover, $16.99, ISBN 9780802797162

The Twilight Zone: Walking Distance
Created by Rod Serling, adapted by Mark Kneece, illustrated by Dove McHargue
Walker Books
72 pp., Color
Softcover, $9.99, ISBN 9780802797155
Hardcover, $16.99, ISBN 9780802797148

It can be dangerous to try to transfer a story from one medium to another. Change too much and you lose the charm of the original. Offer too faithful a rendition and you forget to take advantage of the strengths of the new form.

The comics adaptation of *The Twilight Zone* makes the latter mistake.

Which is not to say that the comics fail. These two volumes are actually pretty good. "Walking Distance" offers a meditation on regret, loss, nostalgia and hope. "The After Hours" blurs the distinction between reality and representation and directly asks: "Just how normal are we? Just who are the people we nod our hellos to as we pass on the street?" In each case, the comic manages to keep the disorientating, uncomfortable, creepy feel of the original. The art is crisp, clean and somewhat understated. The pace is perfect — which is particularly important for the creation of suspense and must have been especially challenging with "The After Hours." And the overall effect is successful — these comics are deeply unnerving, with just enough mid-century conscience to also make them touching and a little bit sad. But what I really missed was the *sound* of the old shows — the signature music and Rod Serling's disconcerting, but oddly reasonable, voice.

The comics are fun, and even a little scary. But there's nothing here that shows what the medium can do, and I was reminded by comparison, not just how great the original shows were, but also how well suited to *television*.

— Kent Worcester

Crooked Little Vein
Warren Ellis
William Morrow (HarperCollins Publishers)
280 pp., $21.95
Prose Hardcover
ISBN: 9780060723934

Warren Ellis' first prose novel, *Crooked Little Vein*, is as worn-out as I am in trying to find a lead: It's filled with typical Ellisian fetishes (kinky sex, sex-fiend hypocrites, sex-fueled conspiracies and cities-cum-cesspools … drenched in sex) but none of the inspiration that makes them enjoyable. Ellis' world is a strange place because ours is, and even though his world is growing more exotic all the time, it already feels pretty bland. Ellis jokes in his acknowledgments that he only wrote the book to get his literary agent off his back and, if that's true, it's the most direct way of saying "Fuck off and die" I can think of, not because *Crooked* is incendiary, but because it's the most anti-explosive thing I've ever read by the former self-appointed prophet of "shock and awe" (for anyone keeping score, *Crooked* makes Ellis' run on *Ultimate Fantastic Four* seem like a shake-up of epic proportions).

Meet Mike McGill, a permanently down-on-his-luck "shit magnet" who finds himself at the apex of kookiness after he's contracted by a shadowy arm of the U.S. government to find the "real" Constitution, a book that can turn back the clock on American values and bring it back to "normalcy." McGill's nationwide hunt takes him everywhere from Godzilla bukkake movie marathons to the ranch of old man Roanoke, a sexually deviant cattle baron who seems to be part of one of the oldest families in America. (Roanoke was the first English colony in the New World, natch; the character, however, is a perverted version of *The Simpsons*' Mr. Burns, complete with his wimpy, gay assistant, Menlove). In other words, it's like Dashiell Hammett mixed with William S. Burroughs — but less subtle.

It has its moments of enjoyment — an encounter with a user named Muppet and an anecdote about Ozzy Osbourne and the Alamo, to name two brief ones — but as the story goes on, it becomes increasingly irrelevant as it revels in the absurdity of real-life pit stops like the hotel where the decor is slathered in caricatures of Christian iconography and American flags. (A toilet sings "Onward Christian Soldiers" when you open the lid.) It's basically a parade of entertaining freaks and dirty jokes so turn on, tune in and drop out.

While Ellis could've done a lot better, he knows how to make junk food appealing and seem fairly dynamic, filling you up on dialogue-heavy and sentence-long chapters. At the same time, if you refuse to check your brain at the door, expect to be disappointed — while giant, saline-injected testicles and serial killers on airplanes will still entertain you, realizing the icing is the best part of the cake is a real bitch.

— Simon Abrams

At A Crossroads

Kate T. Williamson
Princeton Architectural Press
140 pp., $19.95
Color, Softcover
ISBN: 9781568987149

Kate Williamson's autobiographical *At A Crossroads* is subtitled "Between a Rock and My Parents' Place." The loss of the "hard place" proves both frank and accurate: The family manse, as it appears here, seems a perfectly comfy, nurturing layover for the recent college grad fresh from a year abroad. Williamson's episodic observations provide an opportunity for some wry amusement, but greater involvement is hindered by, among other things, the author's implicit, earnest entreaty for our empathy regarding her privileged disquietude.

This visual diary of selected incidents over 23 months unfolds in mostly single-panel pages with frequent double-paged spreads. At this scale, Williamson's figuration is broad and stiff. Posture and facial expression are underdeveloped, offering little in the way of implication or depth. It is her watercolor skills that provide body to the material. She also has a focused sense of picture composition. Several of the double-page tableaux are strikingly rendered, offering a graceful, subtle emotional component that serves to emphasize the absence elsewhere.

Delivery and presentation owe a lot to that of children's books. Directness and guilelessness are valued. The problem remains content, with a two-page panoramic close-up of a dustpan filled with plant clippings being emblematic. The author never chooses to probe too deeply beyond the incidental, the inconsequential, the trivial and the innocuous. There's mention of instructional classes enrolled in, occasional jobs, Halloween costumes, acquaintances from the past. The thematic climax is pretty much when the author stumbles upon the title for this book, which is then wielded as a shorthand device to fend off potentially unwelcome lines of conversation. Genuine reflection or insight is not a priority. Instead of empathy, we catch the artist's contagious case of the blahs. (In one area, though, Williamson is ferocious in her self-disclosure; her most unguarded, devastatingly honest admissions have to do with her taste in rock and roll. Within the genre of autobiographical comics, this horrible fidelity reminds most immediately of the terrible demons that once drove Joe Matt and Chester Brown to depict their masturbation rituals. Chilling! Fearless!)

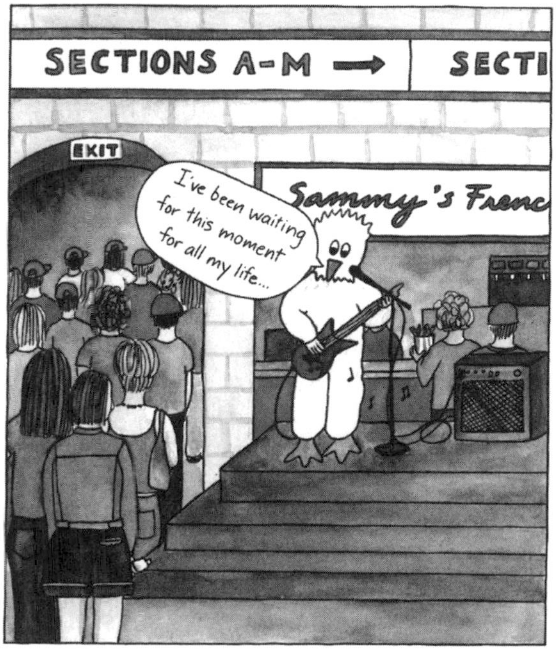
SECTIONS A-M →
SECTI
EXIT
Sammy's Frenc
I've been waiting for this moment for all my life...

I felt a certain kinship with the man in a chicken suit performing "In the Air Tonight" in front of the food stands as we left the ballpark.

[©2008 Kate T. Williamson]

The book does wrap up with a conclusion of sorts, but it arrives seemingly as a matter of unpersuasive happenstance and necessity. *At A Crossroads* might possibly be recommended for the woman- or manchild, freshly beached by an outgoing tide, who fret on the sand that they may never be afloat again ... recommended, that is, if you don't want to, you know, actually talk to them about it.

— Rich Kreiner

Barney Google:
The Early Years, 1919-1923
by Jared Gardner

In the world of the classic comic strip, if there were one character who should need no introduction, it would be Billy DeBeck's Barney Google. The star of one of the longest-running (and, in the opinion of many of us, the funniest) strips in the history of the form, in his heyday in the 1920s and '30s, Barney was one of the nation's most popular celebrities. But for most readers today, it is Snuffy Smith, the hillbilly moonshiner Barney met in North Carolina in 1934, who remains the face of DeBeck's masterpiece. The strip was retitled *Barney Google and Snuffy Smith* not long after Smith's character was introduced, but although Barney hung on to his titular importance, in the hands of DeBeck's masterful successor, Fred Lasswell, it was Snuffy's strip from then on.

Before Snuffy came on the scene, however, Barney had 15 years of adventures in a strip originally titled *Take Barney Google, F'rinstance*. Although Barney would be celebrated in the hit 1923 song as the man with "goo-goo-goo-ga-ly eyes" and "a wife three times his size," he originally appeared in 1919 as fairly long and lean, more like George Herriman's Baron Bean than the bug-eyed half-pint he would soon become. As he became more inventive (and unscrupulous) in his attempts to evade family values, the puritan work ethic and all related laws, written and unwritten, Barney shrank, his compressed height seemingly reemerging in his bulging eyes. Like *Mutt and Jeff*, *Barney Google* began in the sports pages and much of its rough-and-tumble sensibility comes from that milieu: a world of gambling, prizefights, petty cons and the fierce belief that there is, indeed, such a thing as a free lunch.

In an upcoming issue, the great Donald Phelps will introduce DeBeck's career better than I ever could, so I will keep my own introduction to this gallery of strips to a minimum. But some of the stories about DeBeck's early career suggest how closely he identified with his hero. As a young man, DeBeck apparently forged and sold Charles Dana Gibson illustrations. Before hitting it big with *Barney*, he operated a lucrative correspondence course entitled "How to Be a Cartoonist and Make Big Money." And to pad his meager income before being hired by Hearst, he created an alternate persona — "Tom Rover," a "cripple confined to his bed out on the South Side" — to submit additional strips to his art editor. Like Barney, DeBeck was a kid from the streets who knew how to hustle and who knew how to have a good time.

This identification between creator and character explains in large measure the profound bond between DeBeck and his readers. Unlike many of his contemporaries, DeBeck was not slumming in comics: He loved what he did, and he shared with his readers the joy of the form and its often low, physical humor. He was one of them, and he encouraged his readers to see Barney, no matter how unscrupulous some of his actions, as one of them as well — even when he abandoned his wife for life on the road with a racehorse.

The *Barney Google* comics featured in this gallery are all drawn from the first five years of the strip, 1919-1923. *Barney* went through many transformations during this period, as his size quickly diminished (and that of his "Sweet Woman" correspondingly increased) and his stories moved gradually toward longer continuities, culminating in the storyline that made him a true celebrity: his career as the owner of the unlikely racehorse, Spark Plug. But from the start, the rough-edged humor and keen insight into the darker secrets of the human soul were already fully articulated, and Barney immediately assumes his status as the hero of all those whose deepest ambition it is to take a pass on the American Dream.

Thanks to the Cartoon Research Library at the Ohio State University for providing examples of some of the earliest strips for this gallery. ■

Jared Gardner studies and teaches comics in Columbus, Ohio.

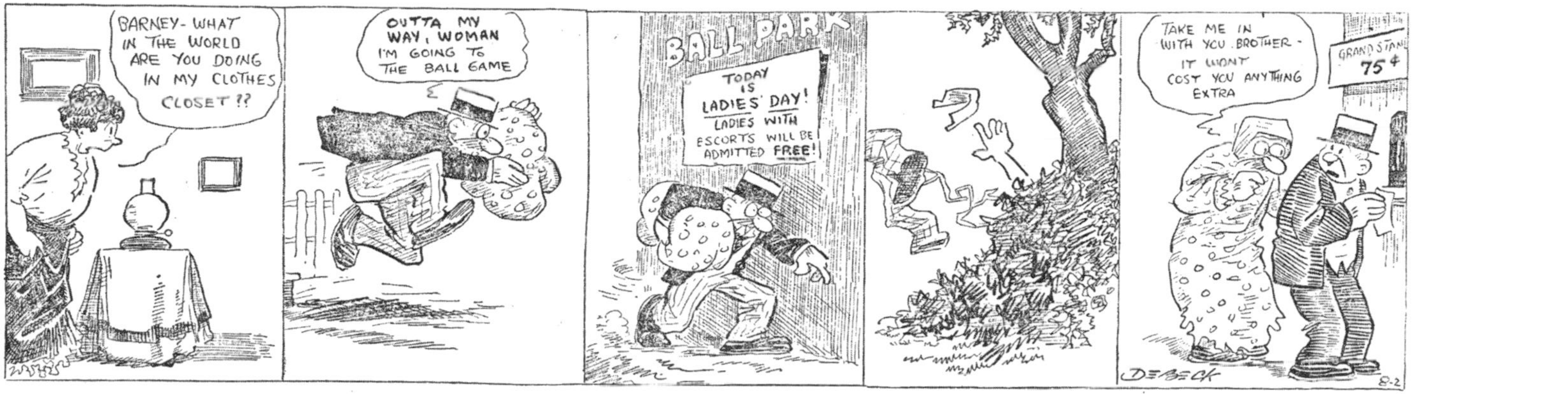
BARNEY - WHAT IN THE WORLD ARE YOU DOING IN MY CLOTHES CLOSET ??
OUTTA MY WAY, WOMAN I'M GOING TO THE BALL GAME
BALL PARK
TODAY IS LADIES' DAY! LADIES WITH ESCORTS WILL BE ADMITTED FREE!
TAKE ME IN WITH YOU BROTHER - IT WONT COST YOU ANYTHING EXTRA
GRAND STAN 75¢
DEBECK
8-2

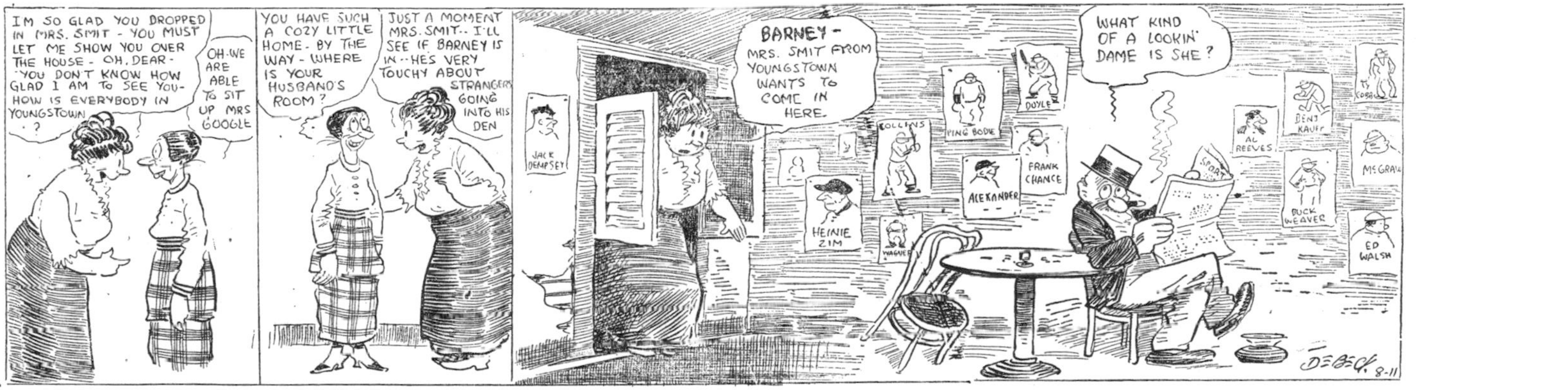
IM SO GLAD YOU DROPPED IN MRS. SMIT - YOU MUST LET ME SHOW YOU OVER THE HOUSE - OH, DEAR - YOU DON'T KNOW HOW GLAD I AM TO SEE YOU - HOW IS EVERYBODY IN YOUNGSTOWN ?
OH WE ARE ABLE TO SIT UP MRS GOOGLE
YOU HAVE SUCH A COZY LITTLE HOME - BY THE WAY - WHERE IS YOUR HUSBAND'S ROOM ?
JUST A MOMENT MRS. SMIT -- I'LL SEE IF BARNEY IS IN -- HE'S VERY TOUCHY ABOUT STRANGERS GOING INTO HIS DEN
JACK DEMPSEY
BARNEY - MRS. SMIT FROM YOUNGSTOWN WANTS TO COME IN HERE.
COLLINS
PING BODIE
DOYLE
HEINIE ZIM
WAGNER
ALEXANDER
FRANK CHANCE
WHAT KIND OF A LOOKIN' DAME IS SHE ?
AL REEVES
DENT KAUFF
TY COBB
McGRAW
BUCK WEAVER
ED WALSH
SPORT
DEBECK 8-11

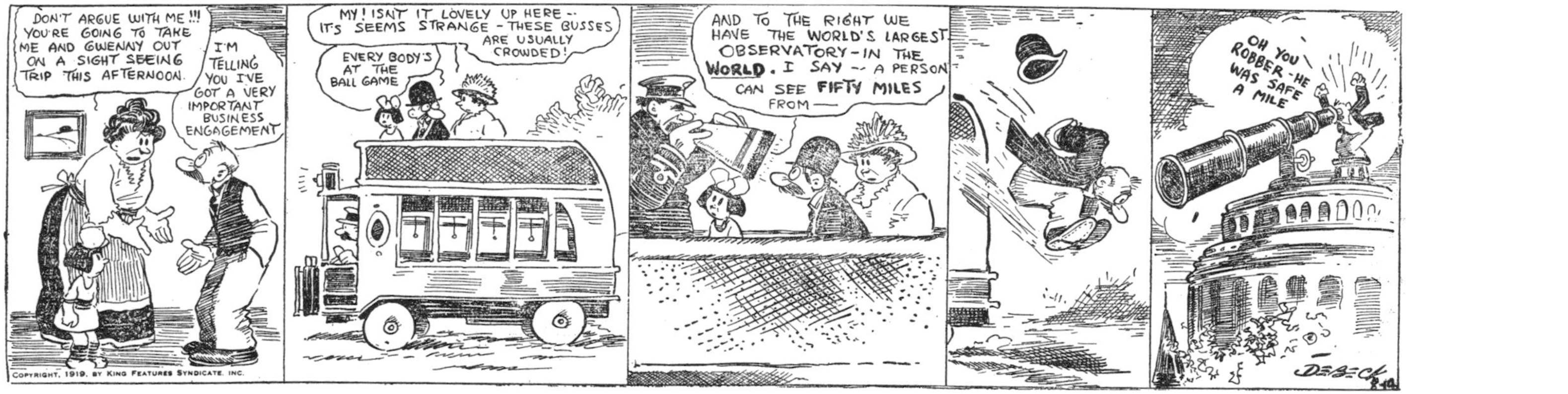
DON'T ARGUE WITH ME !!! YOU'RE GOING TO TAKE ME AND GWENNY OUT ON A SIGHT SEEING TRIP THIS AFTERNOON.
I'M TELLING YOU I'VE GOT A VERY IMPORTANT BUSINESS ENGAGEMENT
COPYRIGHT, 1919, BY KING FEATURES SYNDICATE, INC.
MY! ISN'T IT LOVELY UP HERE -- IT'S SEEMS STRANGE - THESE BUSSES ARE USUALLY CROWDED!
EVERY BODY'S AT THE BALL GAME
AND TO THE RIGHT WE HAVE THE WORLD'S LARGEST OBSERVATORY - IN THE WORLD. I SAY -- A PERSON CAN SEE FIFTY MILES FROM —
OH YOU ROBBER - HE WAS SAFE A MILE
DEBECK

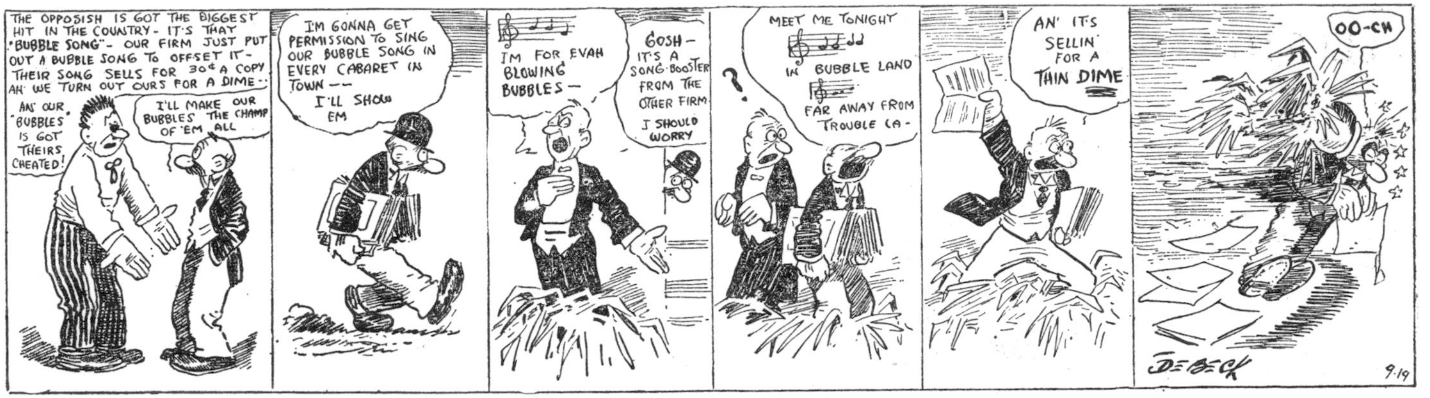
THE OPPOSISH IS GOT THE BIGGEST HIT IN THE COUNTRY - IT'S THAT "BUBBLE SONG" - OUR FIRM JUST PUT OUT A BUBBLE SONG TO OFFSET IT - THEIR SONG SELLS FOR 30¢ A COPY AN' WE TURN OUT OURS FOR A DIME -
AN' OUR "BUBBLES" IS GOT THEIRS CHEATED!
I'LL MAKE OUR BUBBLES THE CHAMP OF 'EM ALL
I'M GONNA GET PERMISSION TO SING OUR BUBBLE SONG IN EVERY CABARET IN TOWN -- I'LL SHOW EM
I'M FOR EVAH BLOWING BUBBLES -
GOSH - IT'S A SONG-BOOSTER FROM THE OTHER FIRM
I SHOULD WORRY
?
MEET ME TONIGHT IN BUBBLE LAND FAR AWAY FROM TROUBLE LA -
AN' IT'S SELLIN' FOR A THIN DIME
OO-CH
DE BECK
9·19

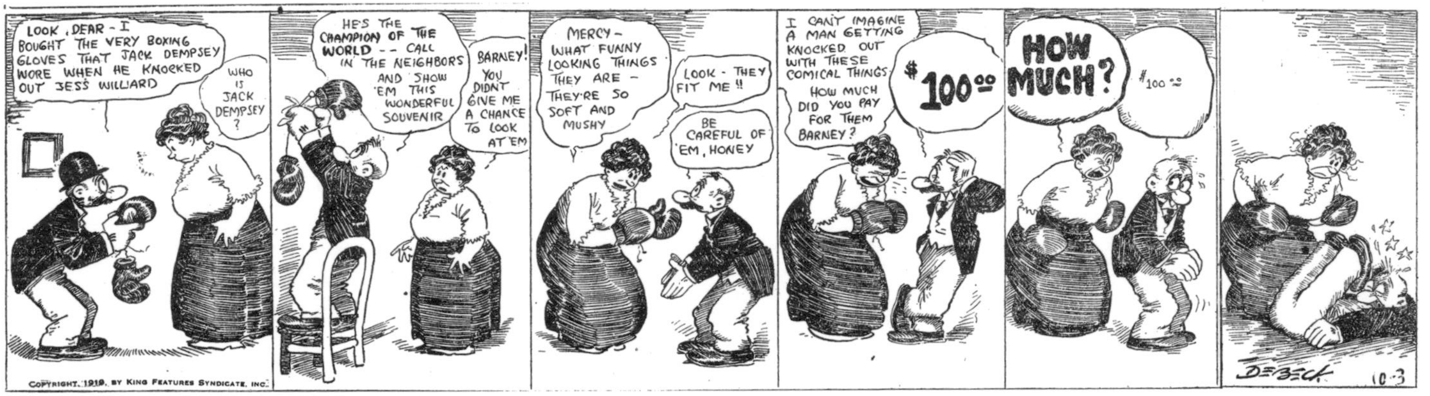
LOOK, DEAR - I BOUGHT THE VERY BOXING GLOVES THAT JACK DEMPSEY WORE WHEN HE KNOCKED OUT JESS WILLARD
WHO IS JACK DEMPSEY ?
HE'S THE CHAMPION OF THE WORLD -- CALL IN THE NEIGHBORS AND SHOW 'EM THIS WONDERFUL SOUVENIR
BARNEY! YOU DIDN'T GIVE ME A CHANCE TO LOOK AT 'EM
MERCY - WHAT FUNNY LOOKING THINGS THEY ARE - THEY'RE SO SOFT AND MUSHY
LOOK - THEY FIT ME !!
BE CAREFUL OF 'EM, HONEY
I CAN'T IMAGINE A MAN GETTING KNOCKED OUT WITH THESE COMICAL THINGS - HOW MUCH DID YOU PAY FOR THEM BARNEY?
$100.00
HOW MUCH?
$100.00
DE BECK
10·3
COPYRIGHT, 1919, BY KING FEATURES SYNDICATE, INC.

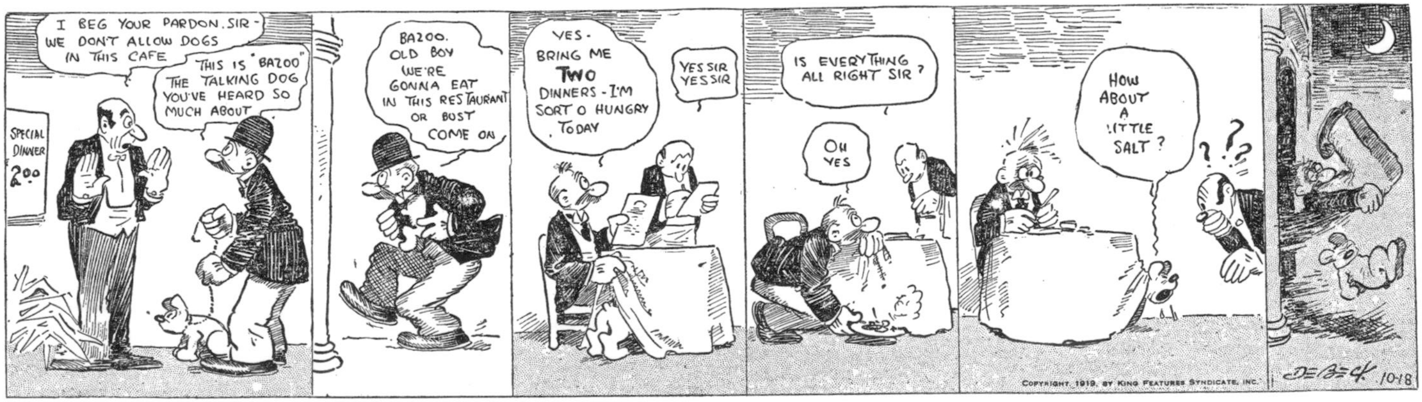
I BEG YOUR PARDON, SIR - WE DON'T ALLOW DOGS IN THIS CAFE
THIS IS "BAZOO" THE TALKING DOG YOU'VE HEARD SO MUCH ABOUT
SPECIAL DINNER 2.00
BAZOO. OLD BOY WE'RE GONNA EAT IN THIS RESTAURANT OR BUST COME ON
YES - BRING ME TWO DINNERS - I'M SORT O HUNGRY TODAY
YES SIR YES SIR
IS EVERYTHING ALL RIGHT SIR ?
OH YES
HOW ABOUT A LITTLE SALT ?
? ? ?
DE BECK
10·18
COPYRIGHT, 1919, BY KING FEATURES SYNDICATE, INC.

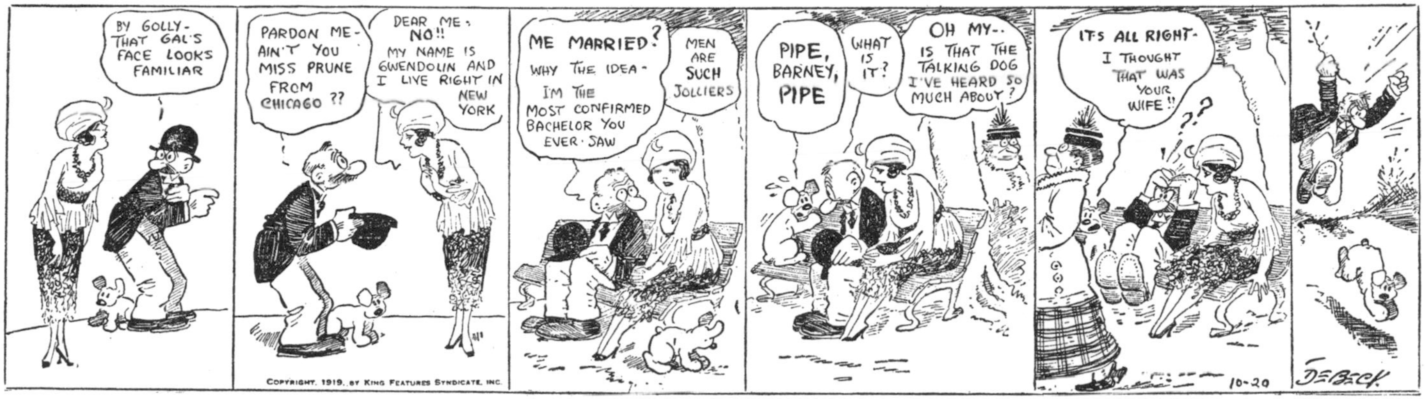
BY GOLLY- THAT GAL'S FACE LOOKS FAMILIAR
PARDON ME- AIN'T YOU MISS PRUNE FROM CHICAGO ??
DEAR ME - NO!! MY NAME IS GWENDOLIN AND I LIVE RIGHT IN NEW YORK
ME MARRIED? WHY THE IDEA - I'M THE MOST CONFIRMED BACHELOR YOU EVER SAW
MEN ARE SUCH JOLLIERS
PIPE, BARNEY, PIPE
WHAT IS IT?
OH MY-- IS THAT THE TALKING DOG I'VE HEARD SO MUCH ABOUT?
IT'S ALL RIGHT- I THOUGHT THAT WAS YOUR WIFE!!
??
COPYRIGHT, 1919, BY KING FEATURES SYNDICATE, INC.
10-20
DE BECK

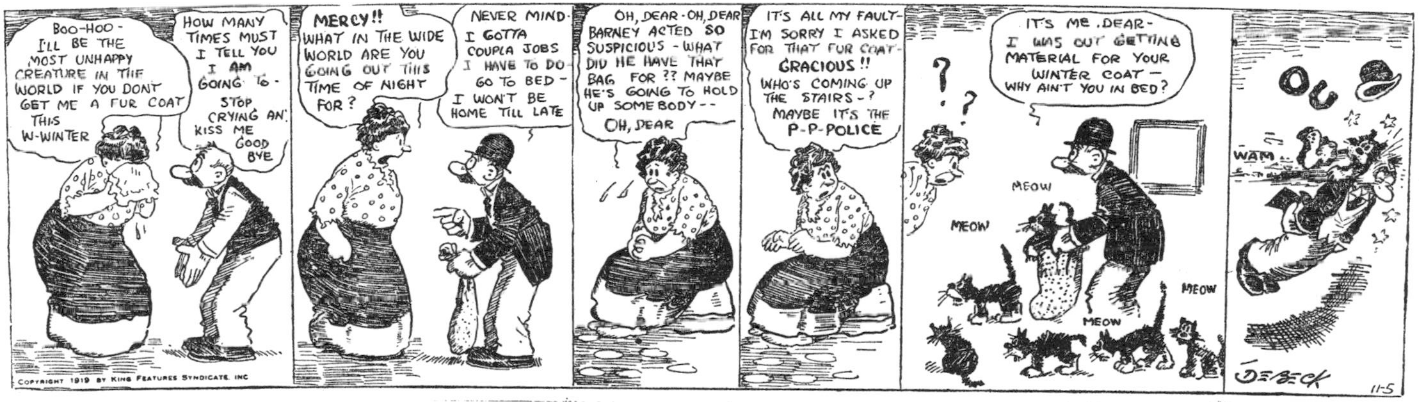
BOO-HOO- I'LL BE THE MOST UNHAPPY CREATURE IN THE WORLD IF YOU DON'T GET ME A FUR COAT THIS W-WINTER
HOW MANY TIMES MUST I TELL YOU I AM GOING TO - STOP CRYING AN' KISS ME GOOD BYE
MERCY!! WHAT IN THE WIDE WORLD ARE YOU GOING OUT THIS TIME OF NIGHT FOR?
NEVER MIND- I GOTTA COUPLA JOBS I HAVE TO DO - GO TO BED - I WON'T BE HOME TILL LATE
OH, DEAR - OH, DEAR BARNEY ACTED SO SUSPICIOUS - WHAT DID HE HAVE THAT BAG FOR ?? MAYBE HE'S GOING TO HOLD UP SOMEBODY--
OH, DEAR
IT'S ALL MY FAULT- I'M SORRY I ASKED FOR THAT FUR COAT-
GRACIOUS!! WHO'S COMING UP THE STAIRS-? MAYBE IT'S THE P-P-POLICE
??
IT'S ME, DEAR- I WAS OUT GETTING MATERIAL FOR YOUR WINTER COAT - WHY AIN'T YOU IN BED?
MEOW
MEOW
MEOW
MEOW
WAM
OU
COPYRIGHT 1919 BY KING FEATURES SYNDICATE INC
DE BECK
11-5

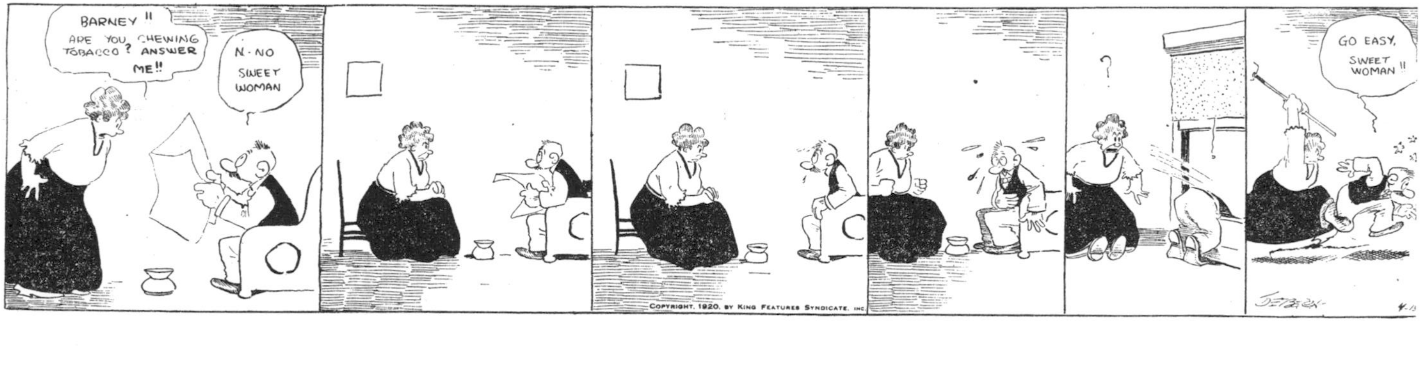
BARNEY !! ARE YOU CHEWING TOBACCO? ANSWER ME!!
N-NO SWEET WOMAN
?
GO EASY, SWEET WOMAN !!
COPYRIGHT, 1920, BY KING FEATURES SYNDICATE, INC.
DE BECK
4-13

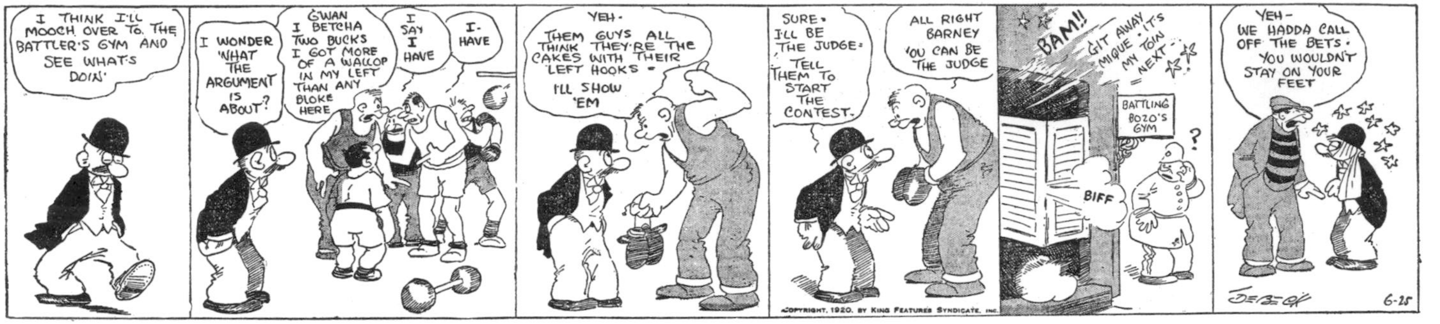
I THINK I'LL MOOCH OVER TO THE BATTLER'S GYM AND SEE WHAT'S DOIN'
I WONDER WHAT THE ARGUMENT IS ABOUT?
G'WAN I BETCHA TWO BUCKS I GOT MORE OF A WALLOP IN MY LEFT THAN ANY BLOKE HERE
I SAY I HAVE
I. HAVE
YEH. THEM GUYS ALL THINK THEY'RE THE CAKES WITH THEIR LEFT HOOKS = I'LL SHOW 'EM
SURE. I'LL BE THE JUDGE= TELL THEM TO START THE CONTEST.
ALL RIGHT BARNEY YOU CAN BE THE JUDGE
©COPYRIGHT, 1920, BY KING FEATURES SYNDICATE, INC.
BAM!!
GIT AWAY - IT'S MIQUE . MY TOIN NEXT
BATTLING BOZO'S GYM
BIFF
?
YEH - WE HADDA CALL OFF THE BETS. YOU WOULDN'T STAY ON YOUR FEET
DEBECK
6-25

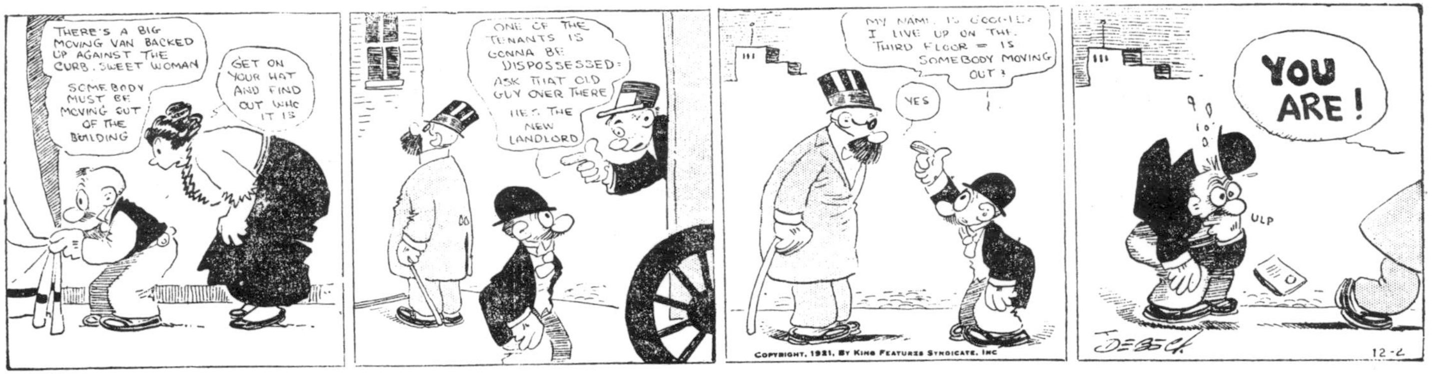
THERE'S A BIG MOVING VAN BACKED UP AGAINST THE CURB. SWEET WOMAN
SOMEBODY MUST BE MOVING OUT OF THE BUILDING
GET ON YOUR HAT AND FIND OUT WHO IT IS
ONE OF THE TENANTS IS GONNA BE DISPOSSESSED= ASK THAT OLD GUY OVER THERE HE'S THE NEW LANDLORD
YES
COPYRIGHT, 1921, BY KING FEATURES SYNDICATE, INC
YOU ARE!
ULP
DEBECK
12-2

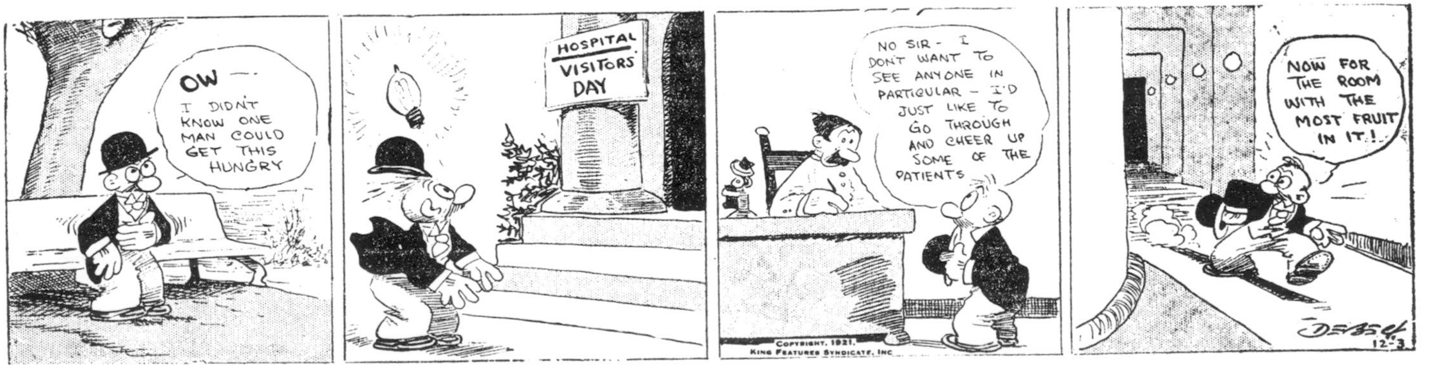
OW — I DIDN'T KNOW ONE MAN COULD GET THIS HUNGRY
HOSPITAL VISITORS' DAY
NO SIR - I DON'T WANT TO SEE ANYONE IN PARTICULAR - I'D JUST LIKE TO GO THROUGH AND CHEER UP SOME OF THE PATIENTS
COPYRIGHT, 1921, KING FEATURES SYNDICATE, INC
NOW FOR THE ROOM WITH THE MOST FRUIT IN IT!
DEBECK
12-3

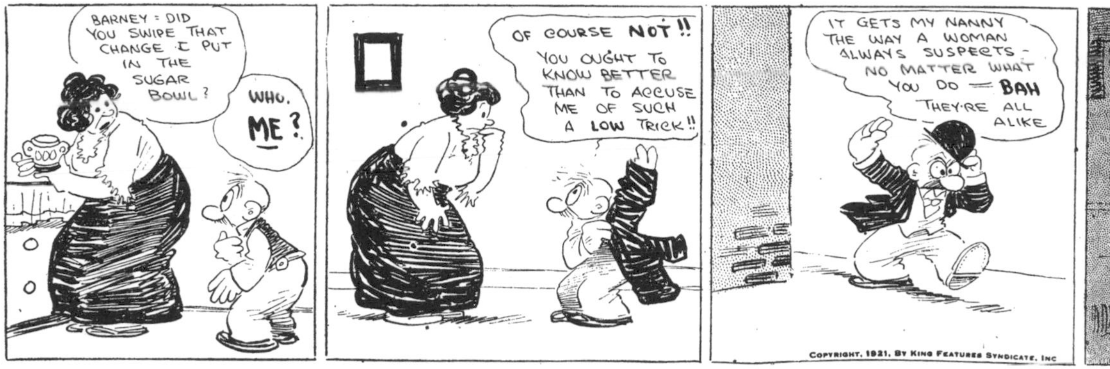
BARNEY = DID YOU SWIPE THAT CHANGE I PUT IN THE SUGAR BOWL ?
WHO, ME ?
OF COURSE NOT !!
YOU OUGHT TO KNOW BETTER THAN TO ACCUSE ME OF SUCH A LOW TRICK !!
IT GETS MY NANNY THE WAY A WOMAN ALWAYS SUSPECTS - NO MATTER WHAT YOU DO = BAH THEY'RE ALL ALIKE
COPYRIGHT, 1921, BY KING FEATURES SYNDICATE, INC
GOSH = I WISH I'D KNOWN SHE KEPT MONEY IN THE SUGAR BOWL
DEBECK
12-7

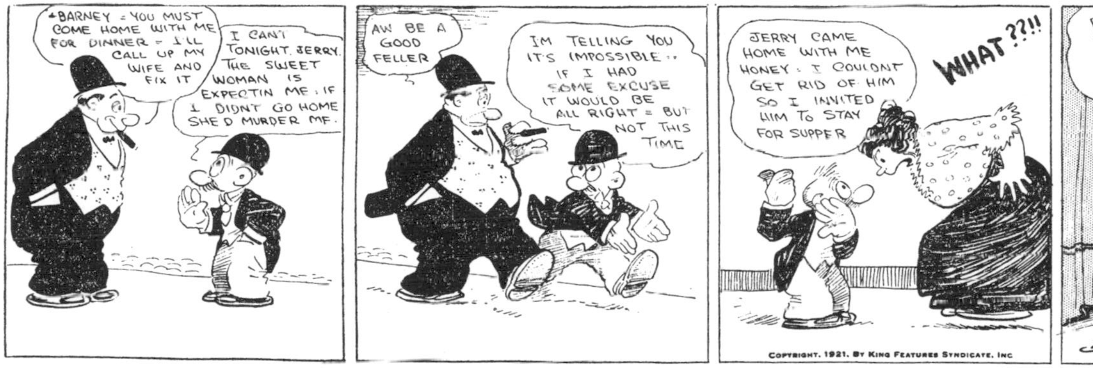
BARNEY = YOU MUST COME HOME WITH ME FOR DINNER = I'LL CALL UP MY WIFE AND FIX IT
I CAN'T TONIGHT, JERRY. THE SWEET WOMAN IS EXPECTIN ME = IF I DIDN'T GO HOME SHE'D MURDER ME.
AW BE A GOOD FELLER
I'M TELLING YOU IT'S IMPOSSIBLE . IF I HAD SOME EXCUSE IT WOULD BE ALL RIGHT = BUT NOT THIS TIME
JERRY CAME HOME WITH ME HONEY = I COULDN'T GET RID OF HIM SO I INVITED HIM TO STAY FOR SUPPER
WHAT ??!!
COPYRIGHT, 1921, BY KING FEATURES SYNDICATE, INC
PUT ON YOUR HAT, JERRY - I'M GONNA ACCEPT YOUR INVITATION!
?
DEBECK
12-9

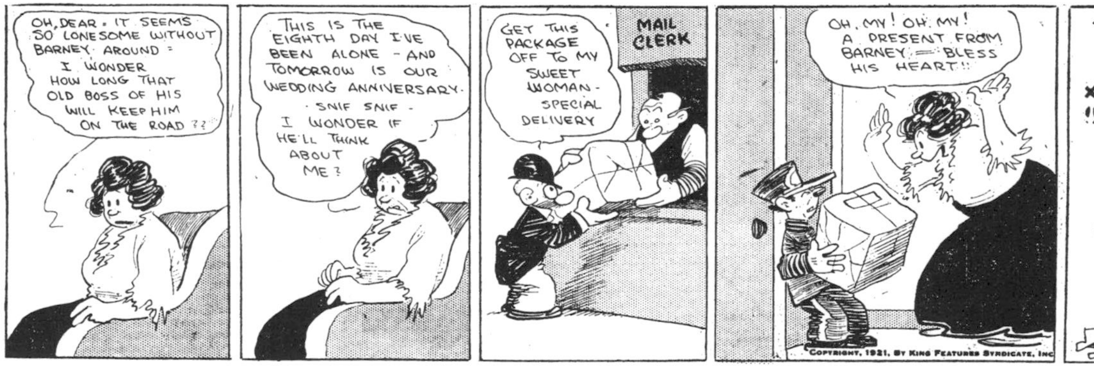
OH, DEAR = IT SEEMS SO LONESOME WITHOUT BARNEY AROUND = I WONDER HOW LONG THAT OLD BOSS OF HIS WILL KEEP HIM ON THE ROAD ??
THIS IS THE EIGHTH DAY I'VE BEEN ALONE - AND TOMORROW IS OUR WEDDING ANNIVERSARY. - SNIF SNIF - I WONDER IF HE'LL THINK ABOUT ME ?
GET THIS PACKAGE OFF TO MY SWEET WOMAN - SPECIAL DELIVERY
MAIL CLERK
OH, MY! OH, MY! A PRESENT FROM BARNEY = BLESS HIS HEART !!
COPYRIGHT, 1921, BY KING FEATURES SYNDICATE, INC
!!XXX!! !!!!! HIS WEEK'S WASH !! XX!! !!!!! ***! !!??
12-12
DEBECK

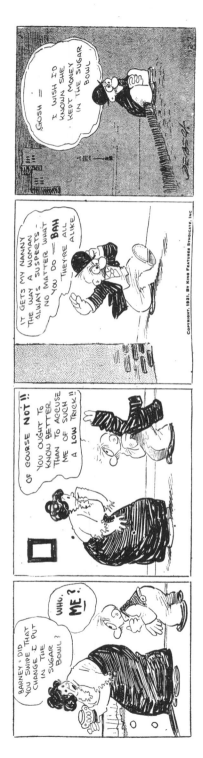

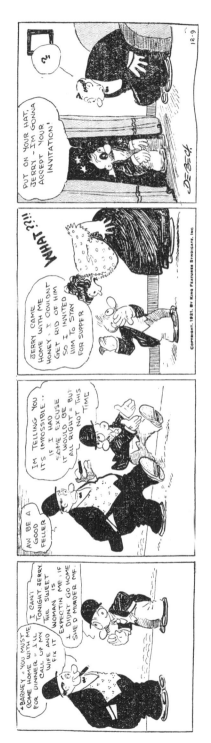

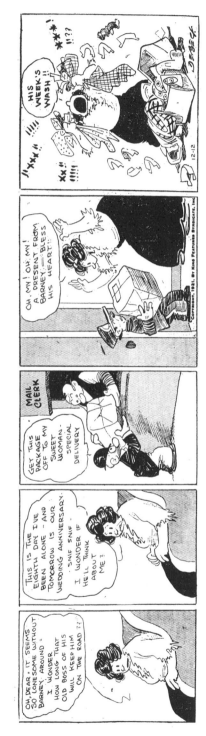

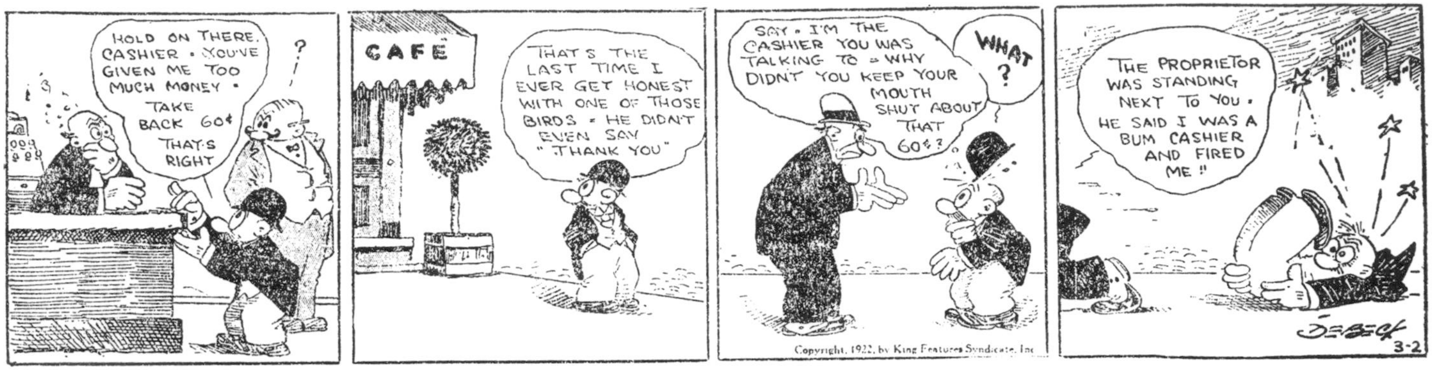
HOLD ON THERE. CASHIER • YOU'VE GIVEN ME TOO MUCH MONEY • TAKE BACK 60¢ THAT'S RIGHT
?
CAFE
THAT'S THE LAST TIME I EVER GET HONEST WITH ONE OF THOSE BIRDS • HE DIDN'T EVEN SAY "THANK YOU"
SAY • I'M THE CASHIER YOU WAS TALKING TO • WHY DIDN'T YOU KEEP YOUR MOUTH SHUT ABOUT THAT 60¢?
WHAT ?
Copyright, 1922, by King Features Syndicate, Inc
THE PROPRIETOR WAS STANDING NEXT TO YOU • HE SAID I WAS A BUM CASHIER AND FIRED ME !!
DEBECK
3-2

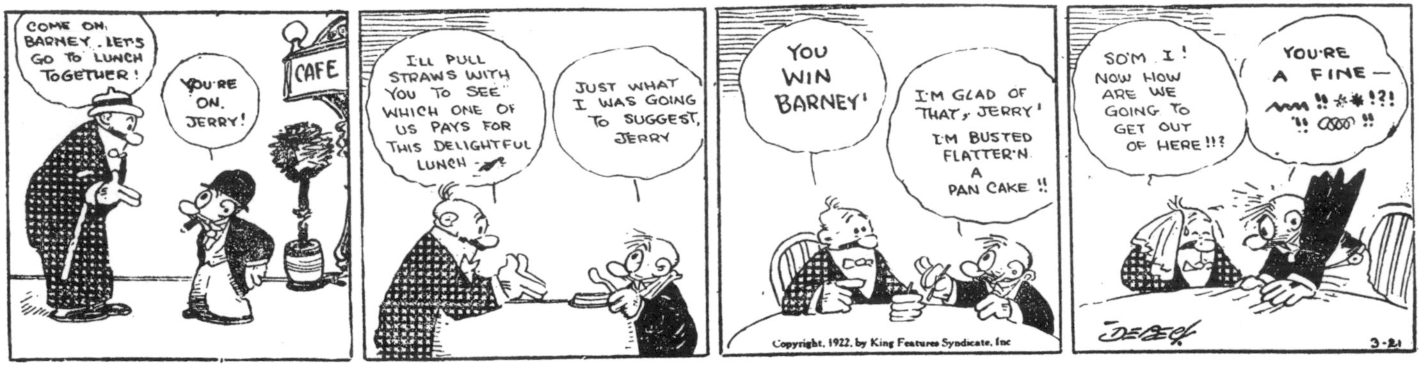
COME ON, BARNEY. LET'S GO TO LUNCH TOGETHER!
YOU'RE ON. JERRY!
CAFE
I'LL PULL STRAWS WITH YOU TO SEE WHICH ONE OF US PAYS FOR THIS DELIGHTFUL LUNCH
JUST WHAT I WAS GOING TO SUGGEST, JERRY
YOU WIN BARNEY!
I'M GLAD OF THAT, JERRY! I'M BUSTED FLATTER'N A PAN CAKE !!
Copyright, 1922, by King Features Syndicate, Inc
SO'M I! NOW HOW ARE WE GOING TO GET OUT OF HERE!!?
YOU'RE A FINE — !! * * !?! !! !!
DEBECK
3-21

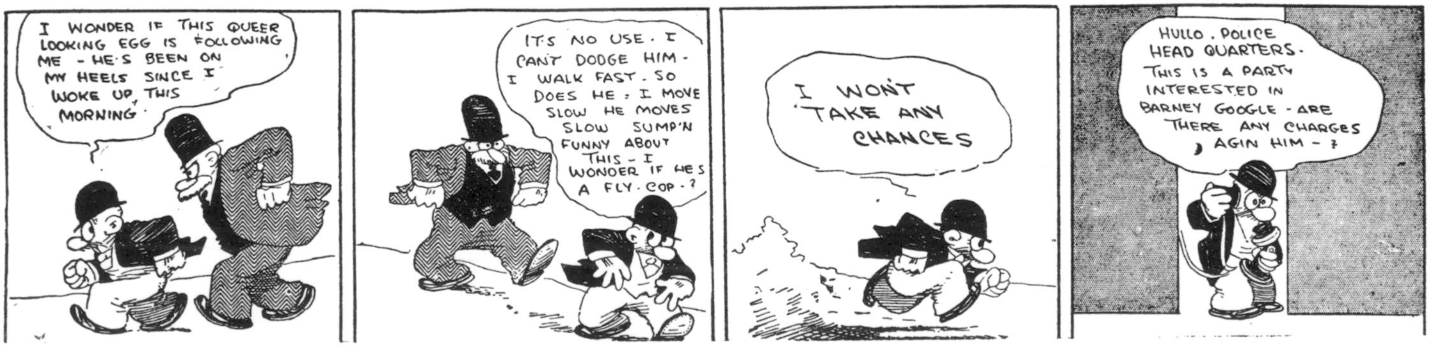
I WONDER IF THIS QUEER LOOKING EGG IS FOLLOWING ME - HE'S BEEN ON MY HEELS SINCE I WOKE UP, THIS MORNING.
IT'S NO USE - I CAN'T DODGE HIM - I WALK FAST. SO DOES HE: I MOVE SLOW HE MOVES SLOW SUMP'N FUNNY ABOUT THIS - I WONDER IF HE'S A FLY-COP - ?
I WON'T TAKE ANY CHANCES
HULLO. POLICE HEAD QUARTERS. THIS IS A PARTY INTERESTED IN BARNEY GOOGLE - ARE THERE ANY CHARGES AGIN HIM - ?

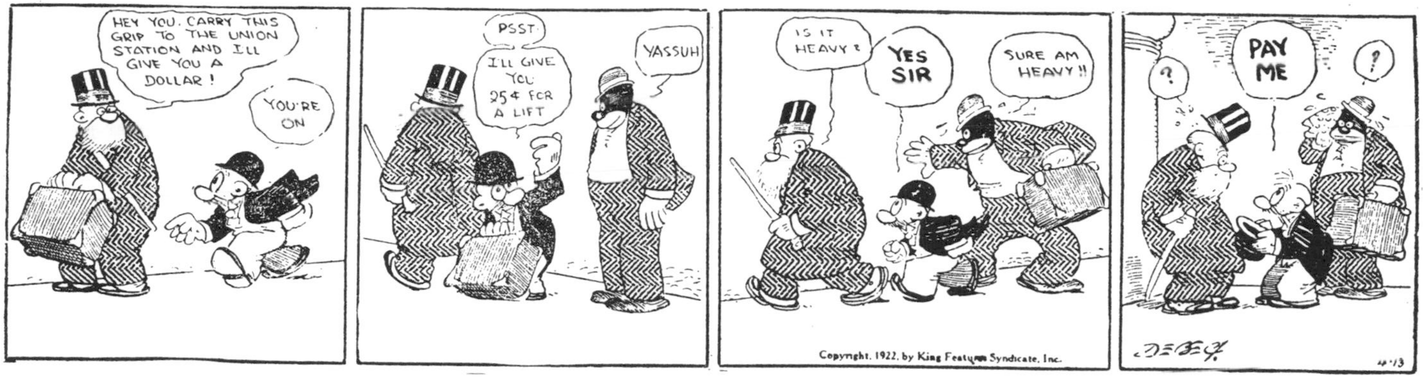
HEY YOU. CARRY THIS GRIP TO THE UNION STATION AND I'LL GIVE YOU A DOLLAR!
YOU'RE ON
PSST:
I'LL GIVE YOU 25¢ FOR A LIFT
YASSUH
IS IT HEAVY?
YES SIR
SURE AM HEAVY!!
Copyright, 1922, by King Features Syndicate, Inc.
?
PAY ME
?
DE BECK
4-13

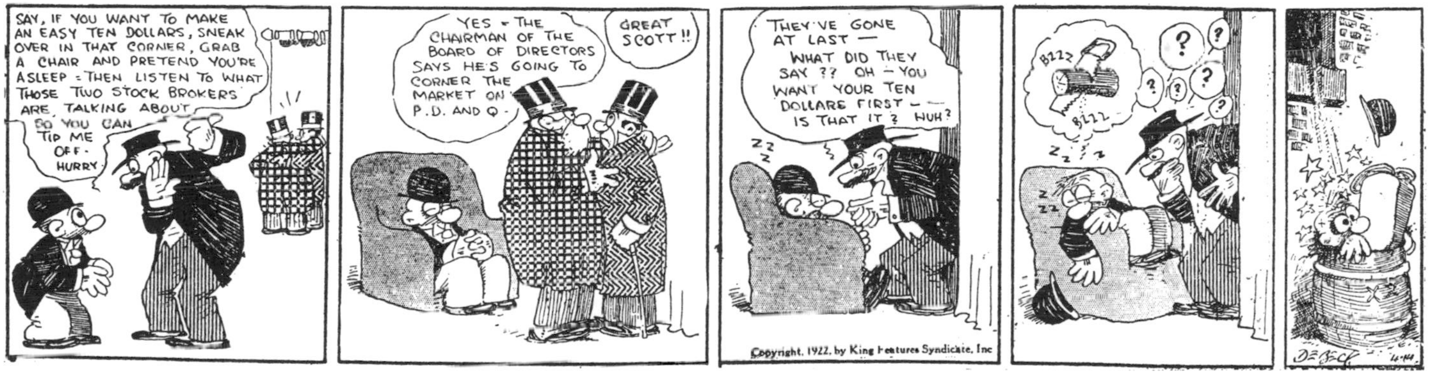
SAY, IF YOU WANT TO MAKE AN EASY TEN DOLLARS, SNEAK OVER IN THAT CORNER, GRAB A CHAIR AND PRETEND YOU'RE ASLEEP - THEN LISTEN TO WHAT THOSE TWO STOCK BROKERS ARE TALKING ABOUT SO YOU CAN TIP ME OFF - HURRY
YES - THE CHAIRMAN OF THE BOARD OF DIRECTORS SAYS HE'S GOING TO CORNER THE MARKET ON P.D. AND Q -
GREAT SCOTT!!
THEY'VE GONE AT LAST — WHAT DID THEY SAY ?? OH - YOU WANT YOUR TEN DOLLARS FIRST — IS THAT IT? HUH?
ZZZ
Copyright, 1922, by King Features Syndicate, Inc
BZZZ
BZZZ
DE BECK
4-14

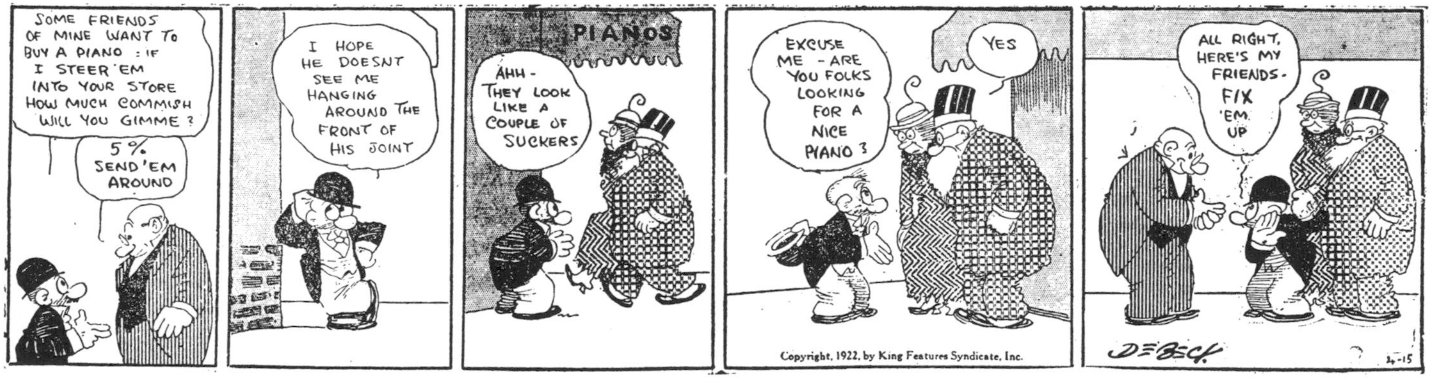
SOME FRIENDS OF MINE WANT TO BUY A PIANO - IF I STEER 'EM INTO YOUR STORE HOW MUCH COMMISH WILL YOU GIMME?
5% SEND 'EM AROUND
I HOPE HE DOESNT SEE ME HANGING AROUND THE FRONT OF HIS JOINT
PIANOS
AHH - THEY LOOK LIKE A COUPLE OF SUCKERS
EXCUSE ME - ARE YOU FOLKS LOOKING FOR A NICE PIANO?
YES
Copyright, 1922, by King Features Syndicate, Inc.
ALL RIGHT, HERE'S MY FRIENDS - FIX 'EM UP
DE BECK
4-15

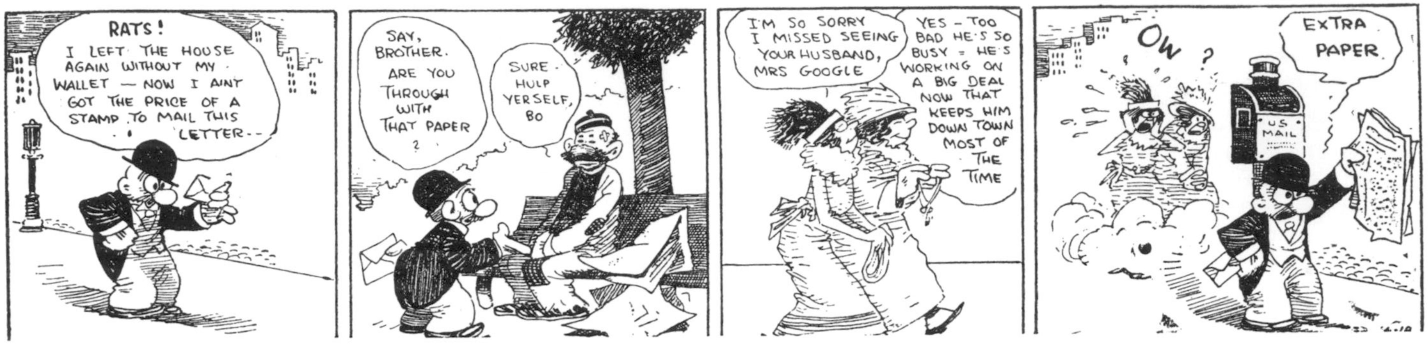
RATS! I LEFT THE HOUSE AGAIN WITHOUT MY WALLET — NOW I AINT GOT THE PRICE OF A STAMP TO MAIL THIS LETTER
SAY, BROTHER. ARE YOU THROUGH WITH THAT PAPER ?
SURE HULP YERSELF, BO
I'M SO SORRY I MISSED SEEING YOUR HUSBAND, MRS GOOGLE
YES - TOO BAD HE'S SO BUSY = HE'S WORKING ON A BIG DEAL NOW THAT KEEPS HIM DOWN TOWN MOST OF THE TIME
OW ?
U.S. MAIL
EXTRA PAPER
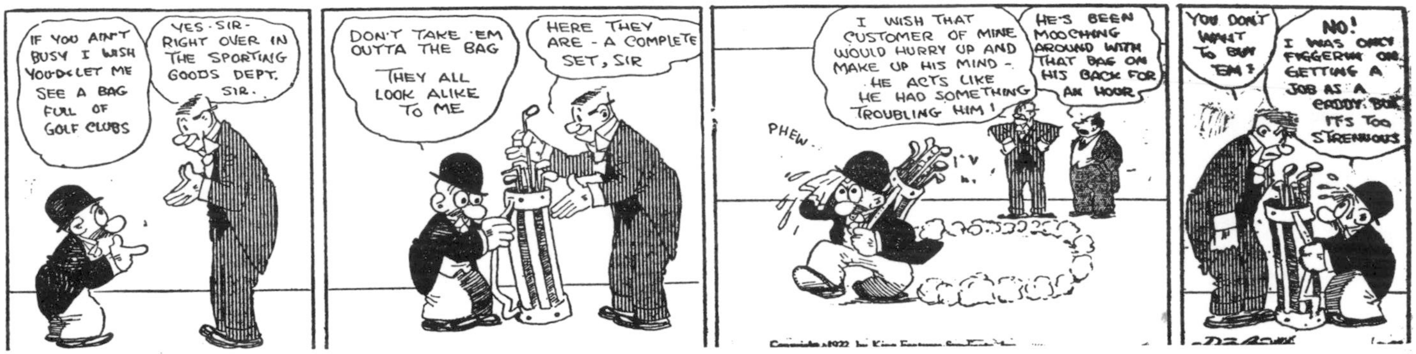
IF YOU AIN'T BUSY I WISH YOU-D LET ME SEE A BAG FULL OF GOLF CLUBS
YES-SIR-RIGHT OVER IN THE SPORTING GOODS DEPT. SIR.
DON'T TAKE 'EM OUTTA THE BAG
THEY ALL LOOK ALIKE TO ME
HERE THEY ARE - A COMPLETE SET, SIR
I WISH THAT CUSTOMER OF MINE WOULD HURRY UP AND MAKE UP HIS MIND - HE ACTS LIKE HE HAD SOMETHING TROUBLING HIM!
HE'S BEEN MOOCHING AROUND WITH THAT BAG ON HIS BACK FOR AN HOUR
PHEW
YOU DON'T WANT TO BUY 'EM ?
NO! I WAS ONLY FIGGERIN ON GETTING A JOB AS A CADDY. BUT IT'S TOO STRENUOUS
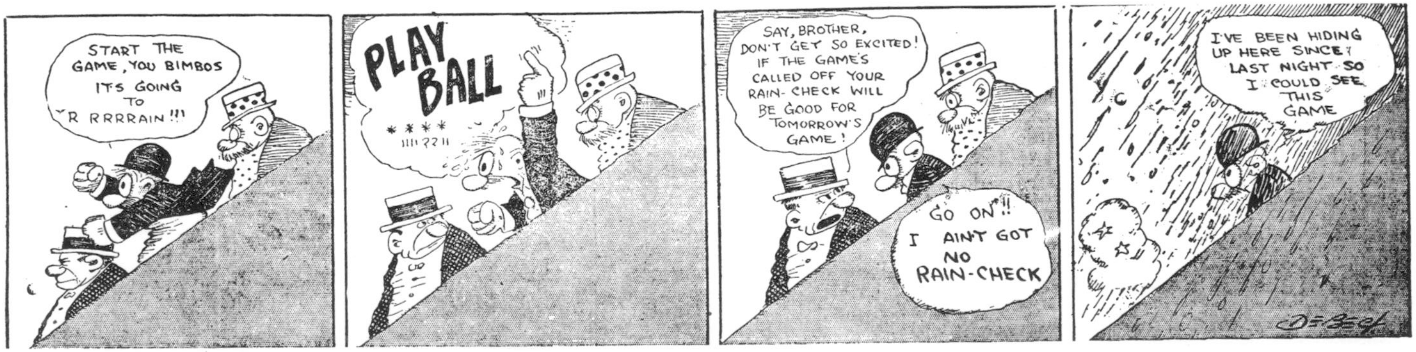
START THE GAME, YOU BIMBOS IT'S GOING TO 'R RRRRAIN!!!
PLAY BALL
SAY, BROTHER, DON'T GET SO EXCITED! IF THE GAME'S CALLED OFF YOUR RAIN-CHECK WILL BE GOOD FOR TOMORROW'S GAME!
GO ON'!! I AIN'T GOT NO RAIN-CHECK
I'VE BEEN HIDING UP HERE SINCE LAST NIGHT SO I COULD SEE THIS GAME

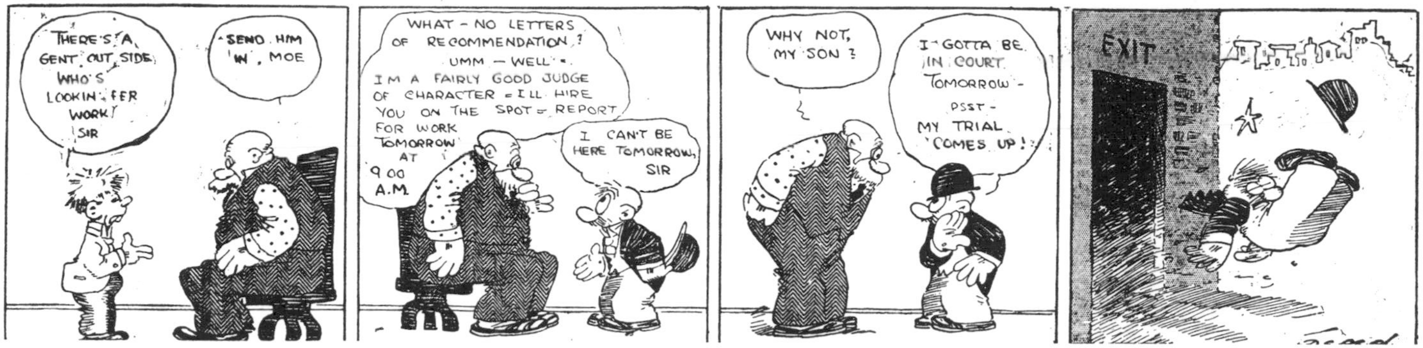
THERE'S A GENT OUT SIDE WHO'S LOOKIN' FER WORK! SIR
SEND HIM 'IN', MOE
WHAT - NO LETTERS OF RECOMMENDATION ? UMM — WELL = I'M A FAIRLY GOOD JUDGE OF CHARACTER = I'LL HIRE YOU ON THE SPOT = REPORT FOR WORK TOMORROW AT 9.00 A.M.
I CAN'T BE HERE TOMORROW, SIR
WHY NOT, MY SON ?
I - GOTTA BE IN COURT TOMORROW - PSST - MY TRIAL COMES UP !
EXIT

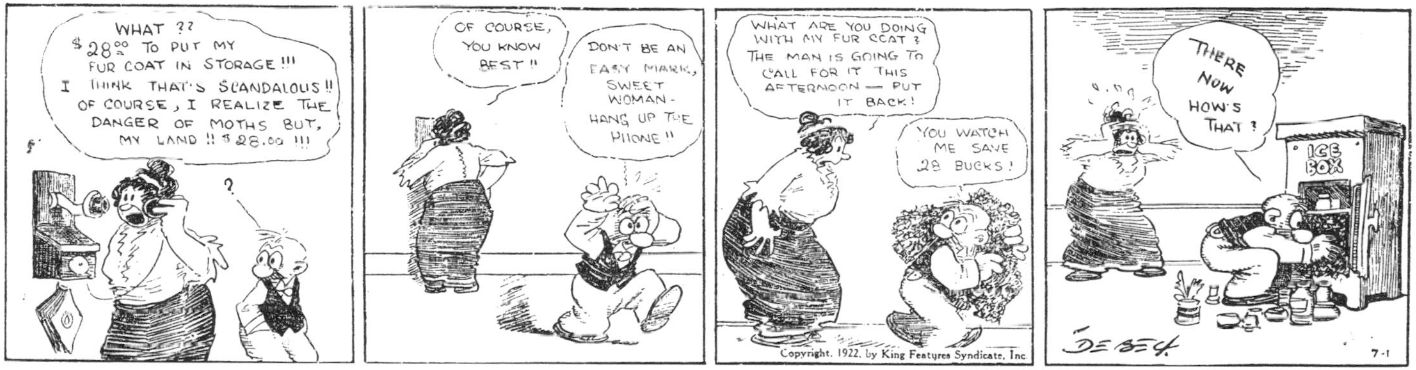
WHAT ?? $28.00 TO PUT MY FUR COAT IN STORAGE !!! I THINK THAT'S SCANDALOUS !! OF COURSE, I REALIZE THE DANGER OF MOTHS BUT, MY LAND !! $28.00 !!!
?
OF COURSE, YOU KNOW BEST !!
DON'T BE AN EASY MARK, SWEET WOMAN - HANG UP THE PHONE !!
WHAT ARE YOU DOING WITH MY FUR COAT ? THE MAN IS GOING TO CALL FOR IT THIS AFTERNOON — PUT IT BACK !
YOU WATCH ME SAVE 28 BUCKS !
Copyright, 1922, by King Features Syndicate, Inc
THERE NOW HOW'S THAT ?
ICE BOX
7-1

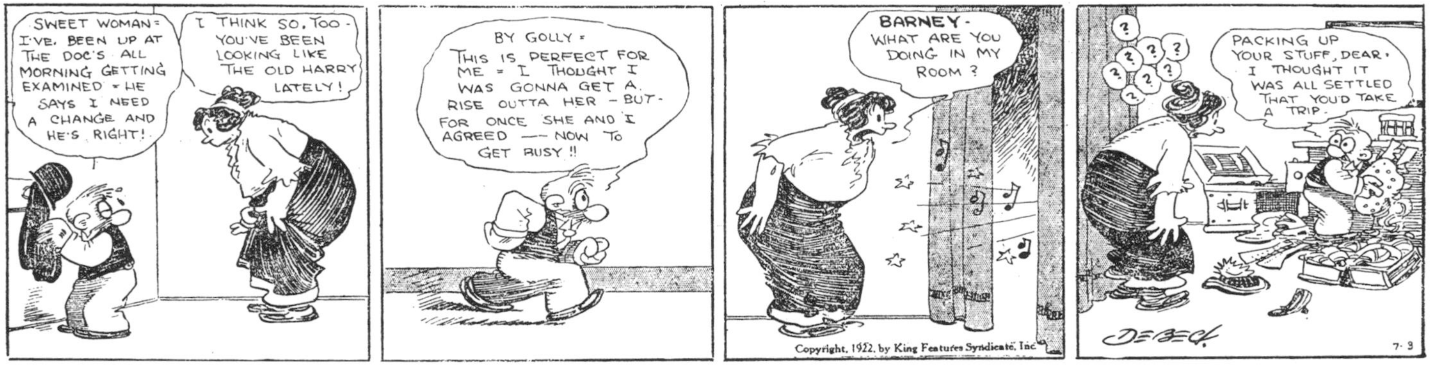
SWEET WOMAN = I'VE BEEN UP AT THE DOC'S ALL MORNING GETTING EXAMINED = HE SAYS I NEED A CHANGE AND HE'S RIGHT !
I THINK SO, TOO - YOU'VE BEEN LOOKING LIKE THE OLD HARRY LATELY !
BY GOLLY = THIS IS PERFECT FOR ME = I THOUGHT I WAS GONNA GET A RISE OUTTA HER - BUT - FOR ONCE SHE AND I AGREED —— NOW TO GET BUSY !!
BARNEY - WHAT ARE YOU DOING IN MY ROOM ?
Copyright, 1922, by King Features Syndicate, Inc
? ? ? ? ? ? ?
PACKING UP YOUR STUFF, DEAR. I THOUGHT IT WAS ALL SETTLED THAT YOU'D TAKE A TRIP.
7-3

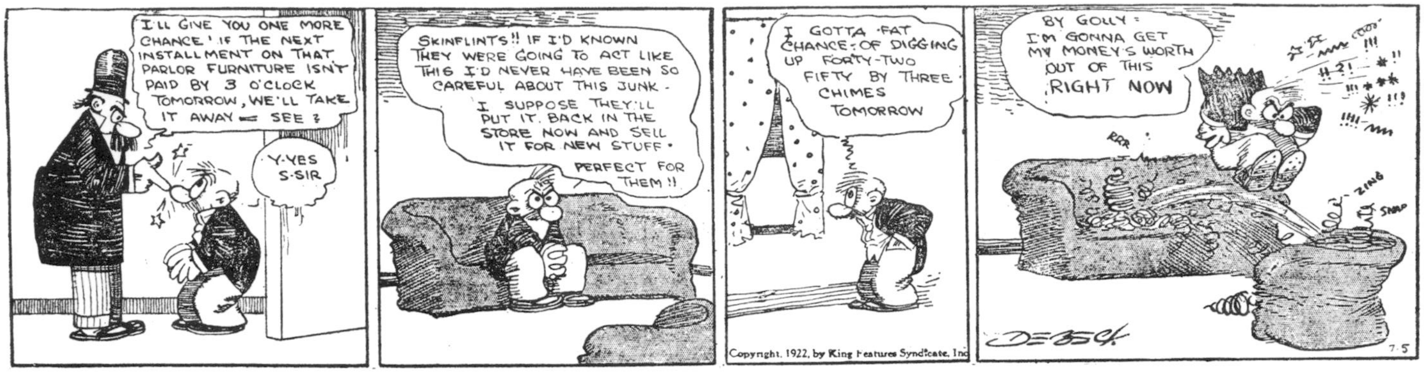
I'LL GIVE YOU ONE MORE CHANCE! IF THE NEXT INSTALLMENT ON THAT PARLOR FURNITURE ISN'T PAID BY 3 O'CLOCK TOMORROW, WE'LL TAKE IT AWAY — SEE?
Y-YES S-SIR
SKINFLINTS!! IF I'D KNOWN THEY WERE GOING TO ACT LIKE THIS I'D NEVER HAVE BEEN SO CAREFUL ABOUT THIS JUNK - I SUPPOSE THEY'LL PUT IT BACK IN THE STORE NOW AND SELL IT FOR NEW STUFF - PERFECT FOR THEM!!
I GOTTA FAT CHANCE OF DIGGING UP FORTY-TWO FIFTY BY THREE CHIMES TOMORROW
BY GOLLY: I'M GONNA GET MY MONEY'S WORTH OUT OF THIS RIGHT NOW
RRR
ZING
SNAP
DEBECK
7-5
Copyright, 1922, by King Features Syndicate, Inc

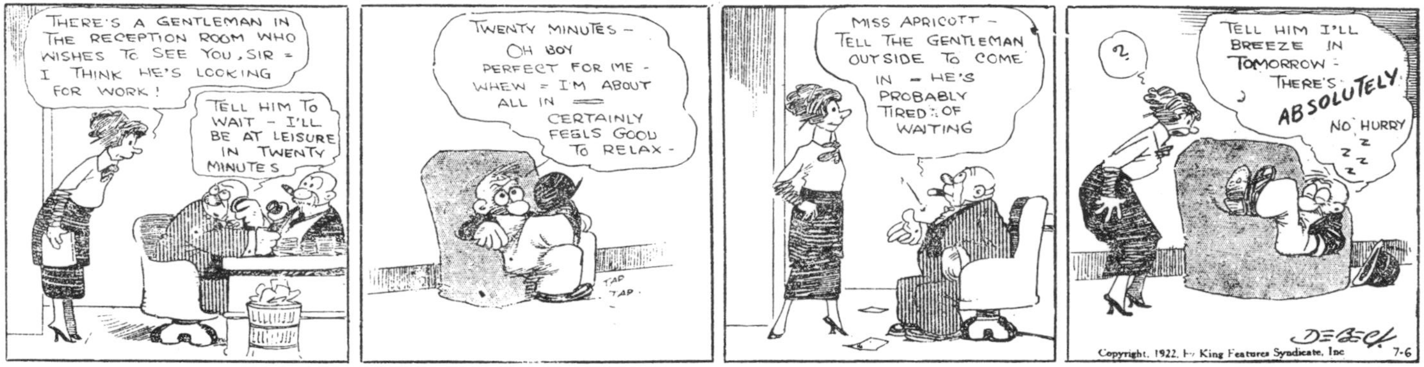
THERE'S A GENTLEMAN IN THE RECEPTION ROOM WHO WISHES TO SEE YOU, SIR = I THINK HE'S LOOKING FOR WORK!
TELL HIM TO WAIT - I'LL BE AT LEISURE IN TWENTY MINUTES
TWENTY MINUTES - OH BOY PERFECT FOR ME - WHEW = I'M ABOUT ALL IN — CERTAINLY FEELS GOOD TO RELAX -
TAP TAP
MISS APRICOTT - TELL THE GENTLEMAN OUTSIDE TO COME IN - HE'S PROBABLY TIRED OF WAITING
?
TELL HIM I'LL BREEZE IN TOMORROW - THERE'S ABSOLUTELY NO HURRY
Z Z Z
DEBECK
Copyright, 1922, by King Features Syndicate, Inc
7-6

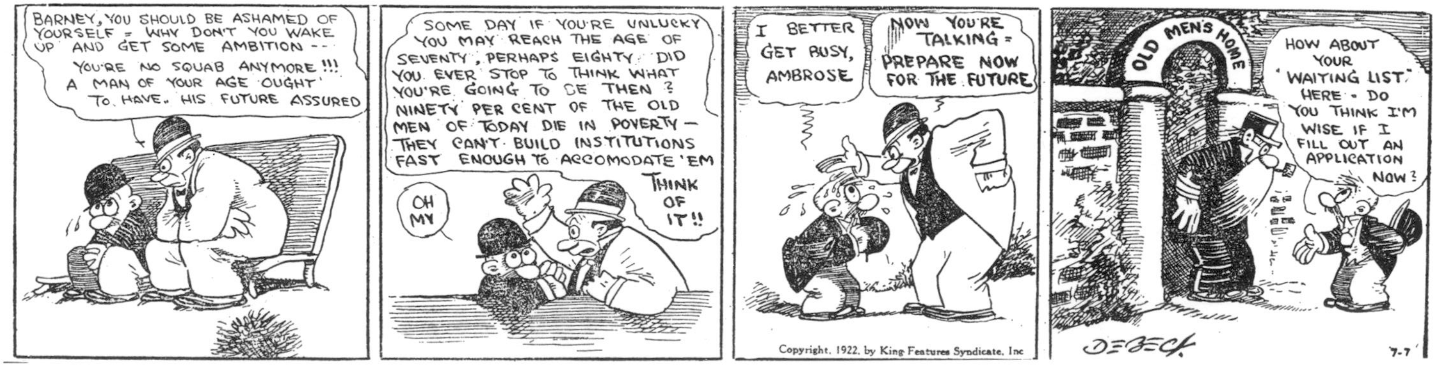
BARNEY, YOU SHOULD BE ASHAMED OF YOURSELF = WHY DON'T YOU WAKE UP AND GET SOME AMBITION -- YOU'RE NO SQUAB ANYMORE!!! A MAN OF YOUR AGE OUGHT TO HAVE HIS FUTURE ASSURED
SOME DAY IF YOU'RE UNLUCKY YOU MAY REACH THE AGE OF SEVENTY, PERHAPS EIGHTY. DID YOU EVER STOP TO THINK WHAT YOU'RE GOING TO BE THEN? NINETY PER CENT OF THE OLD MEN OF TODAY DIE IN POVERTY — THEY CAN'T BUILD INSTITUTIONS FAST ENOUGH TO ACCOMODATE 'EM
OH MY
THINK OF IT!!
I BETTER GET BUSY, AMBROSE
NOW YOU'RE TALKING = PREPARE NOW FOR THE FUTURE
Copyright, 1922, by King Features Syndicate, Inc
OLD MEN'S HOME
HOW ABOUT YOUR "WAITING LIST" HERE - DO YOU THINK I'M WISE IF I FILL OUT AN APPLICATION NOW?
DEBECK
7-7

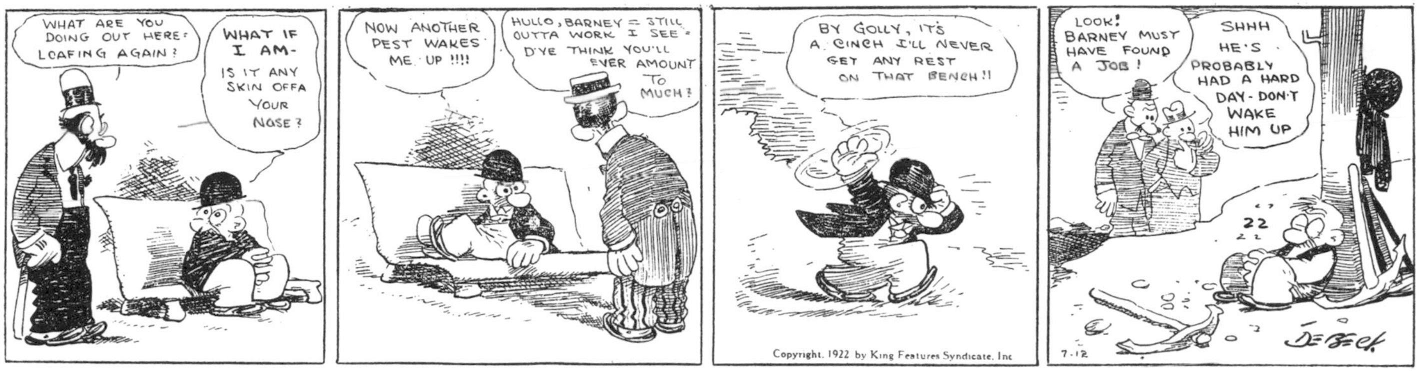
WHAT ARE YOU DOING OUT HERE: LOAFING AGAIN?
WHAT IF I AM- IS IT ANY SKIN OFFA YOUR NOSE?
NOW ANOTHER PEST WAKES ME UP !!!!
HULLO, BARNEY = STILL OUTTA WORK I SEE = D'YE THINK YOU'LL EVER AMOUNT TO MUCH?
BY GOLLY, IT'S A CINCH I'LL NEVER GET ANY REST ON THAT BENCH!!
Copyright, 1922, by King Features Syndicate, Inc
LOOK! BARNEY MUST HAVE FOUND A JOB!
SHHH HE'S PROBABLY HAD A HARD DAY-DON'T WAKE HIM UP
22
7-12
DE BECK

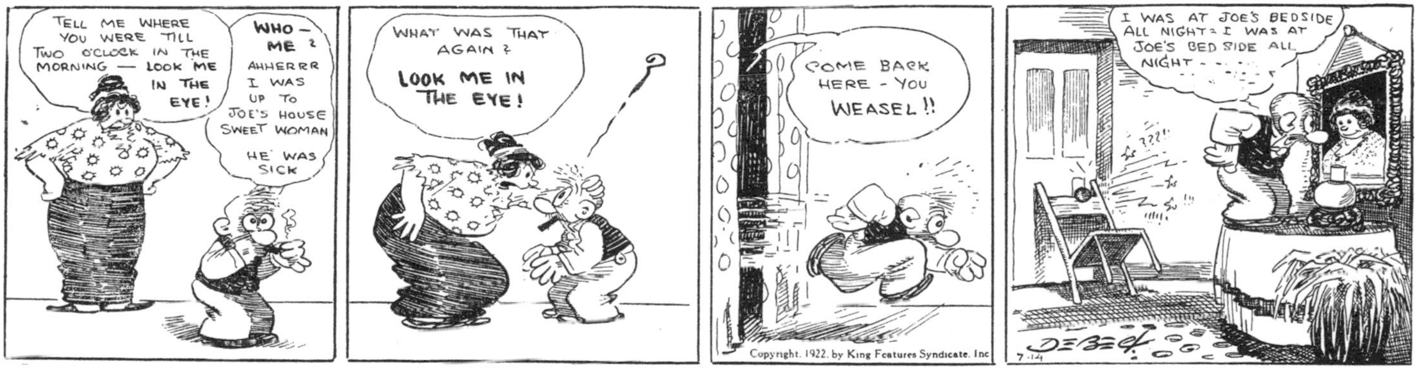
TELL ME WHERE YOU WERE TILL TWO O'CLOCK IN THE MORNING — LOOK ME IN THE EYE!
WHO — ME? AHHERRR I WAS UP TO JOE'S HOUSE SWEET WOMAN HE WAS SICK
WHAT WAS THAT AGAIN? LOOK ME IN THE EYE!
COME BACK HERE - YOU WEASEL!!
Copyright, 1922, by King Features Syndicate, Inc
I WAS AT JOE'S BEDSIDE ALL NIGHT = I WAS AT JOE'S BED SIDE ALL NIGHT - - - -
???!
DE BECK
7-14

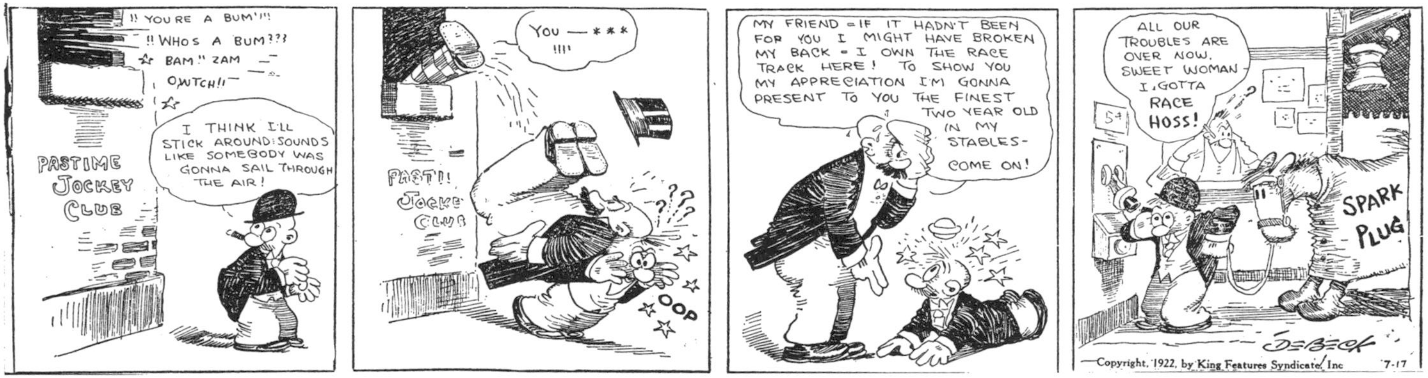
!! YOU'RE A BUM'!!!
!! WHOS A BUM???
BAM!! ZAM
OWTCH!!
I THINK I'LL STICK AROUND: SOUNDS LIKE SOMEBODY WAS GONNA SAIL THROUGH THE AIR!
PASTIME JOCKEY CLUB
YOU — * * * !!!
PASTI! JOCKE CLUB
OOP
MY FRIEND = IF IT HADN'T BEEN FOR YOU I MIGHT HAVE BROKEN MY BACK = I OWN THE RACE TRACK HERE! TO SHOW YOU MY APPRECIATION I'M GONNA PRESENT TO YOU THE FINEST TWO YEAR OLD IN MY STABLES- COME ON!
ALL OUR TROUBLES ARE OVER NOW, SWEET WOMAN I GOTTA RACE HOSS!
SPARK PLUG
DE BECK
Copyright, 1922, by King Features Syndicate, Inc
7-17

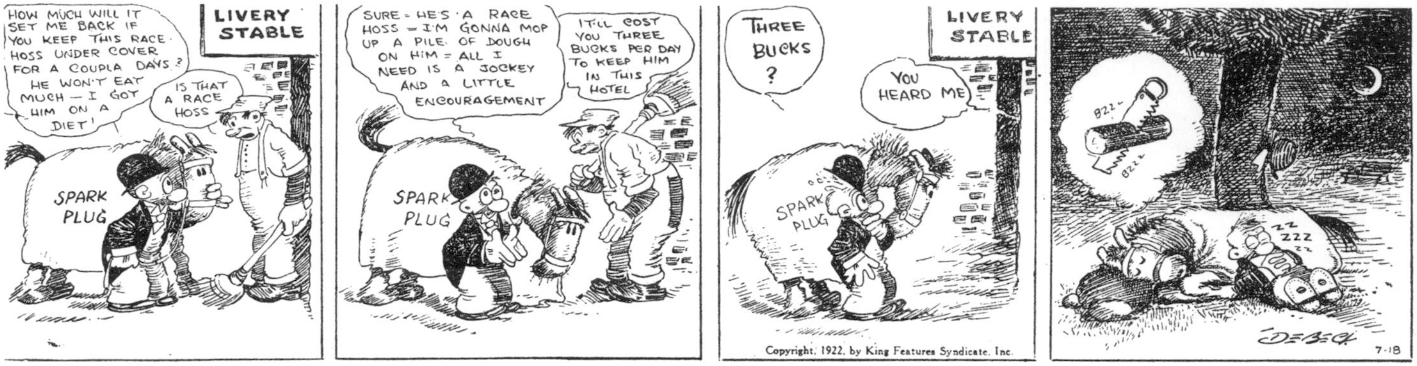
HOW MUCH WILL IT SET ME BACK IF YOU KEEP THIS RACE HOSS UNDER COVER FOR A COUPLA DAYS ? HE WON'T EAT MUCH — I GOT HIM ON A DIET !
LIVERY STABLE
IS THAT A RACE HOSS
SPARK PLUG
SURE = HE'S A RACE HOSS = I'M GONNA MOP UP A PILE OF DOUGH ON HIM = ALL I NEED IS A JOCKEY AND A LITTLE ENCOURAGEMENT
IT'LL COST YOU THREE BUCKS PER DAY TO KEEP HIM IN THIS HOTEL
SPARK PLUG
THREE BUCKS ?
LIVERY STABLE
YOU HEARD ME
SPARK PLUG
Copyright, 1922, by King Features Syndicate, Inc.
BZZ
BZZZ
ZZ ZZZ ZZ
DE BECK
7-18

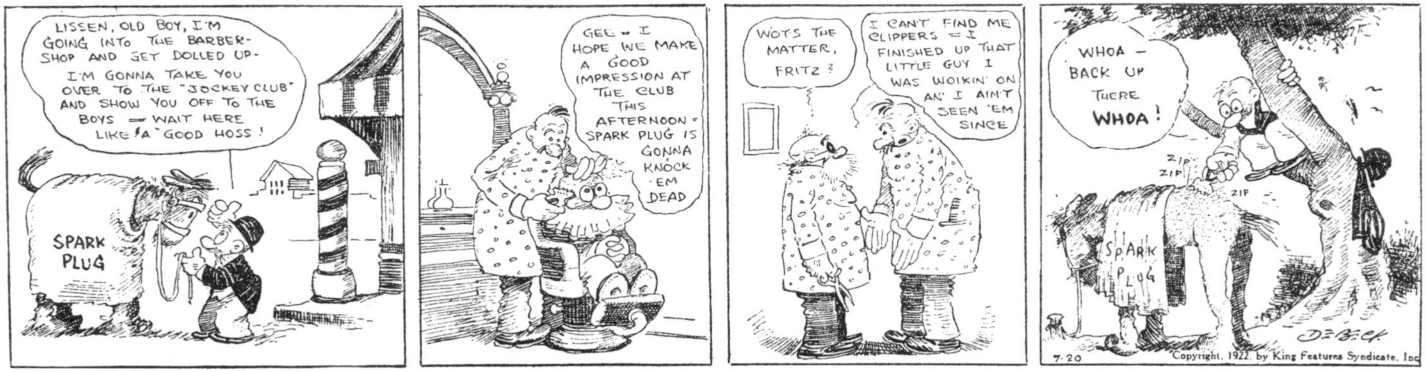
LISSEN, OLD BOY, I'M GOING INTO THE BARBER-SHOP AND GET DOLLED UP- I'M GONNA TAKE YOU OVER TO THE "JOCKEY CLUB" AND SHOW YOU OFF TO THE BOYS — WAIT HERE LIKE A GOOD HOSS !
SPARK PLUG
GEE = I HOPE WE MAKE A GOOD IMPRESSION AT THE CLUB THIS AFTERNOON = SPARK PLUG IS GONNA KNOCK 'EM DEAD
WOT'S THE MATTER, FRITZ ?
I CAN'T FIND ME CLIPPERS = I FINISHED UP THAT LITTLE GUY I WAS WOIKIN' ON AN' I AIN'T SEEN 'EM SINCE
WHOA — BACK UP THERE WHOA !
ZIP
ZIP
ZIP
SPARK PLUG
DE BECK
7-20
Copyright, 1922, by King Features Syndicate, Inc

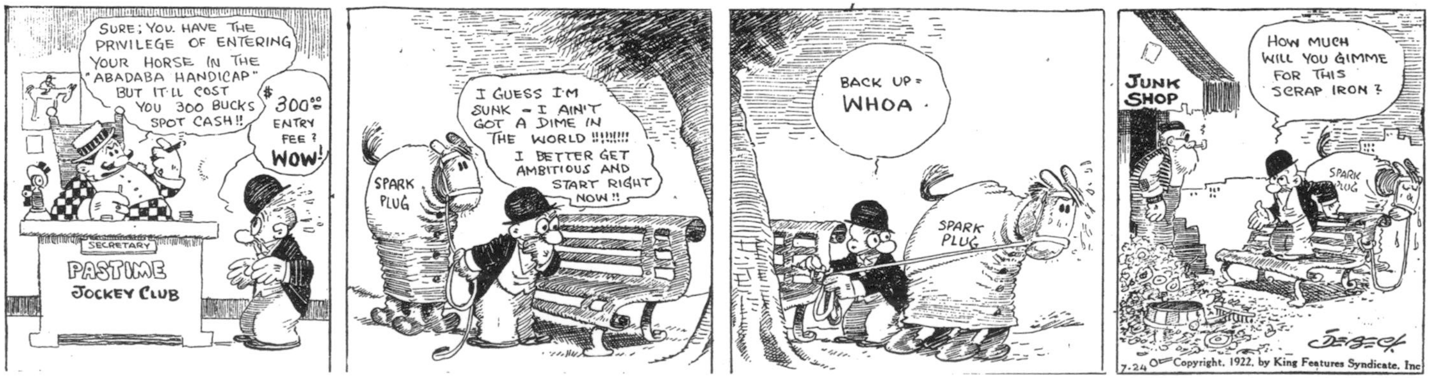
SURE; YOU HAVE THE PRIVILEGE OF ENTERING YOUR HORSE IN THE "ABADABA HANDICAP" BUT IT'LL COST YOU 300 BUCKS SPOT CASH!!
$300.00 ENTRY FEE ? WOW!
SECRETARY
PASTIME JOCKEY CLUB
SPARK PLUG
I GUESS I'M SUNK - I AIN'T GOT A DIME IN THE WORLD !!!!!!!! I BETTER GET AMBITIOUS AND START RIGHT NOW !!
BACK UP = WHOA .
SPARK PLUG
JUNK SHOP
HOW MUCH WILL YOU GIMME FOR THIS SCRAP IRON ?
SPARK PLUG
DE BECK
7-24
Copyright, 1922, by King Features Syndicate, Inc

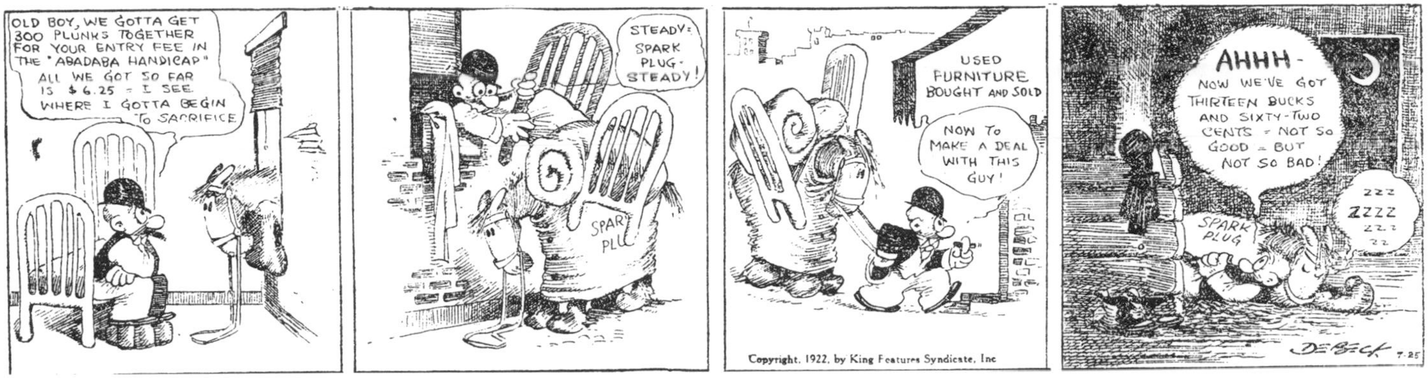
OLD BOY, WE GOTTA GET 300 PLUNKS TOGETHER FOR YOUR ENTRY FEE IN THE "ABADABA HANDICAP" ALL WE GOT SO FAR IS $6.25 = I SEE WHERE I GOTTA BEGIN TO SACRIFICE
STEADY = SPARK PLUG - STEADY!
SPARK PLUG
USED FURNITURE BOUGHT AND SOLD
NOW TO MAKE A DEAL WITH THIS GUY!
Copyright, 1922, by King Features Syndicate, Inc
AHHH - NOW WE'VE GOT THIRTEEN BUCKS AND SIXTY-TWO CENTS = NOT SO GOOD = BUT NOT SO BAD!
SPARK PLUG
ZZZ ZZZZ ZZZ ZZ
DEBECK 7-25
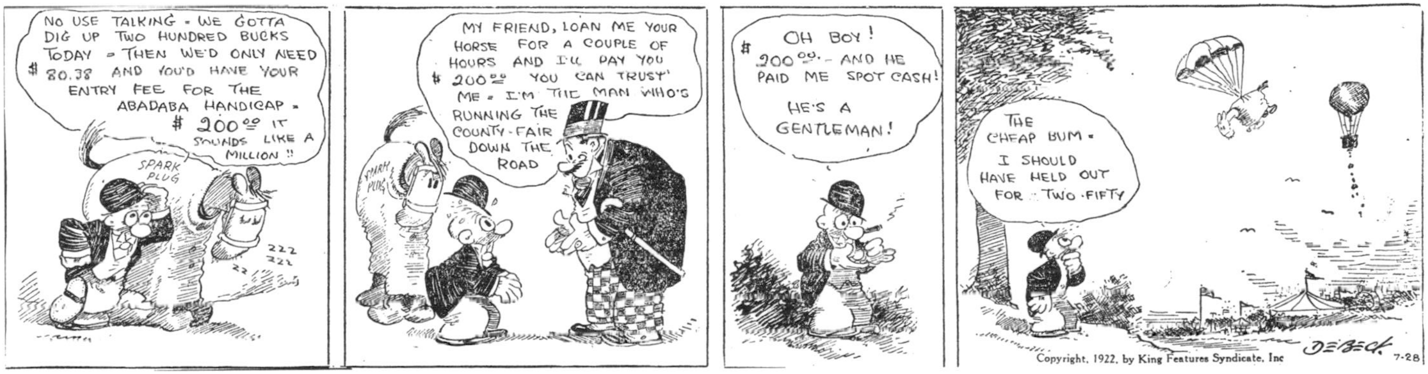
NO USE TALKING = WE GOTTA DIG UP TWO HUNDRED BUCKS TODAY = THEN WE'D ONLY NEED $80.38 AND YOU'D HAVE YOUR ENTRY FEE FOR THE ABADABA HANDICAP = $200.00 IT SOUNDS LIKE A MILLION!!
SPARK PLUG
ZZZ ZZZ ZZ
MY FRIEND, LOAN ME YOUR HORSE FOR A COUPLE OF HOURS AND I'LL PAY YOU $200.00 YOU CAN TRUST ME = I'M THE MAN WHO'S RUNNING THE COUNTY-FAIR DOWN THE ROAD
SPARK PLUG
OH BOY! $200.00 - AND HE PAID ME SPOT CASH!
HE'S A GENTLEMAN!
THE CHEAP BUM = I SHOULD HAVE HELD OUT FOR TWO-FIFTY
Copyright, 1922, by King Features Syndicate, Inc
DEBECK 7-28
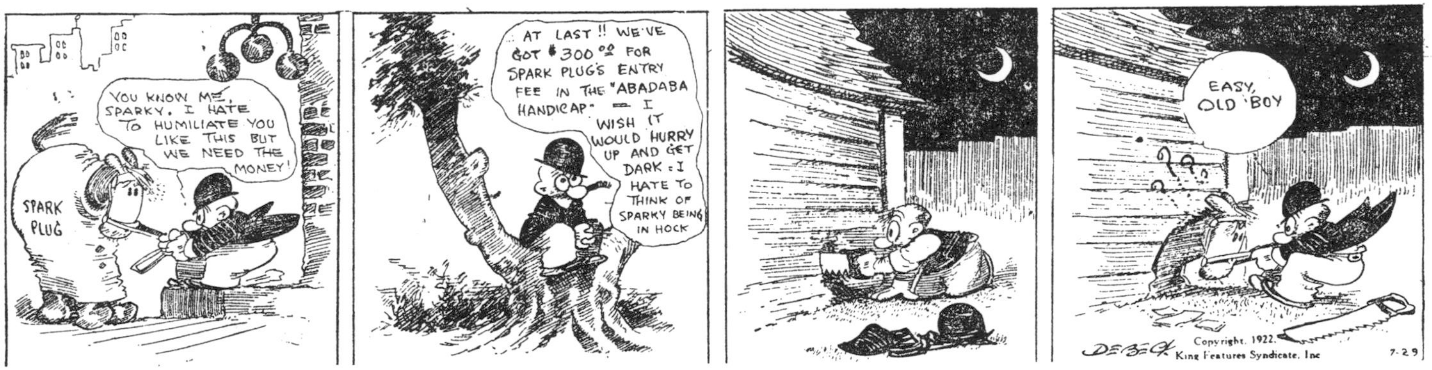
YOU KNOW ME, SPARKY. I HATE TO HUMILIATE YOU LIKE THIS BUT WE NEED THE MONEY!
SPARK PLUG
AT LAST!! WE'VE GOT $300.00 FOR SPARK PLUG'S ENTRY FEE IN THE "ABADABA HANDICAP" — I WISH IT WOULD HURRY UP AND GET DARK = I HATE TO THINK OF SPARKY BEING IN HOCK
EASY, OLD BOY
DEBECK
Copyright, 1922, King Features Syndicate, Inc
7-29

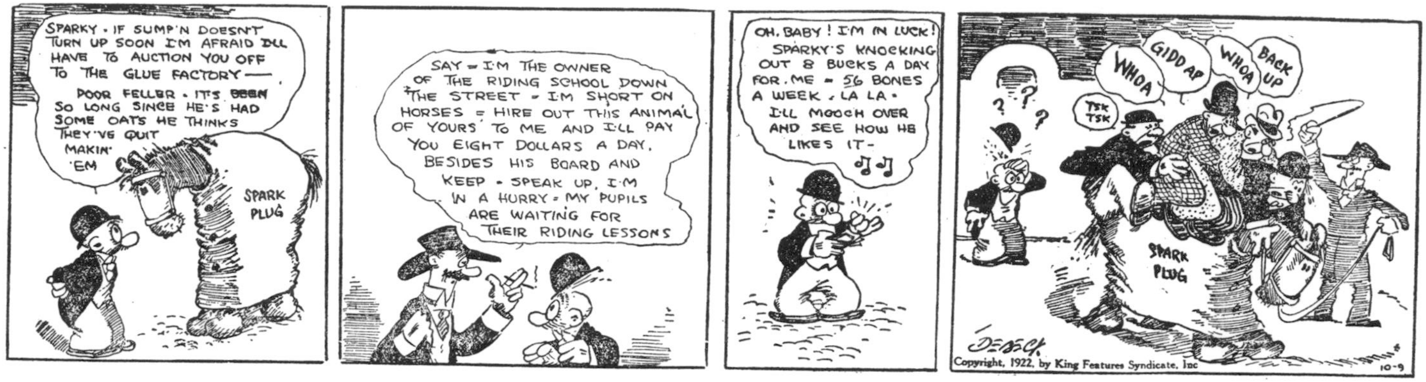
SPARKY - IF SUMP'N DOESN'T TURN UP SOON I'M AFRAID I'LL HAVE TO AUCTION YOU OFF TO THE GLUE FACTORY —
POOR FELLER - IT'S BEEN SO LONG SINCE HE'S HAD SOME OATS HE THINKS THEY'VE QUIT MAKIN' 'EM
SPARK PLUG
SAY - I'M THE OWNER OF THE RIDING SCHOOL DOWN THE STREET - I'M SHORT ON HORSES - HIRE OUT THIS ANIMAL OF YOURS TO ME AND I'LL PAY YOU EIGHT DOLLARS A DAY, BESIDES HIS BOARD AND KEEP - SPEAK UP, I'M IN A HURRY - MY PUPILS ARE WAITING FOR THEIR RIDING LESSONS
OH, BABY! I'M IN LUCK! SPARKY'S KNOCKING OUT 8 BUCKS A DAY FOR ME - 56 BONES A WEEK - LA LA - I'LL MOOCH OVER AND SEE HOW HE LIKES IT -
TSK TSK
WHOA
GIDD AP
WHOA
BACK UP
SPARK PLUG
DE BECK
Copyright, 1922, by King Features Syndicate, Inc
10-9

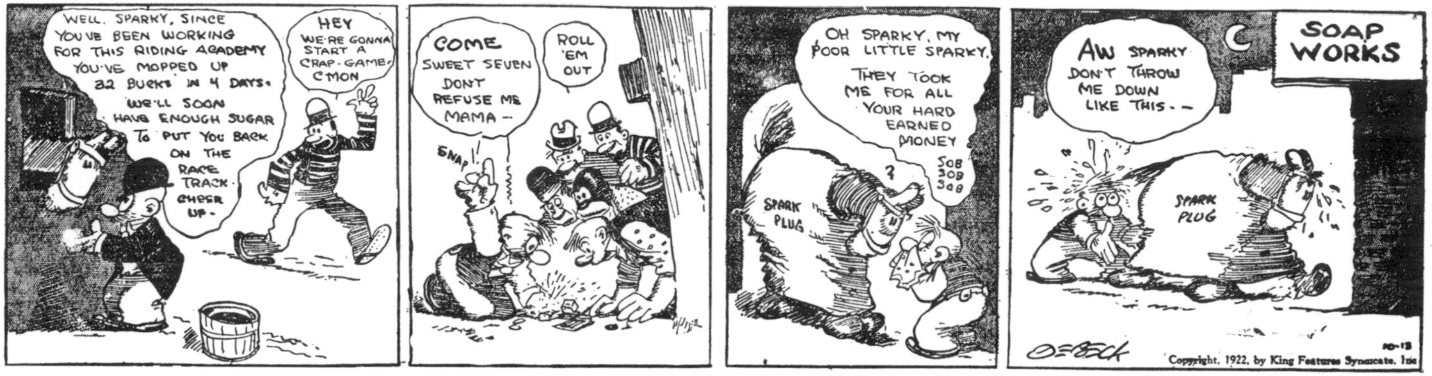
WELL, SPARKY, SINCE YOU'VE BEEN WORKING FOR THIS RIDING ACADEMY YOU'VE MOPPED UP 32 BUCKS IN 4 DAYS - WE'LL SOON HAVE ENOUGH SUGAR TO PUT YOU BACK ON THE RACE TRACK - CHEER UP -
HEY WE'RE GONNA START A CRAP-GAME - C'MON
COME SWEET SEVEN DONT REFUSE ME MAMA —
ROLL 'EM OUT
SNAP
OH SPARKY, MY POOR LITTLE SPARKY, THEY TOOK ME FOR ALL YOUR HARD EARNED MONEY
SOB SOB SOB
SPARK PLUG
AW SPARKY DON'T THROW ME DOWN LIKE THIS —
SOAP WORKS
SPARK PLUG
DE BECK
Copyright, 1922, by King Features Syndicate, Inc
10-13

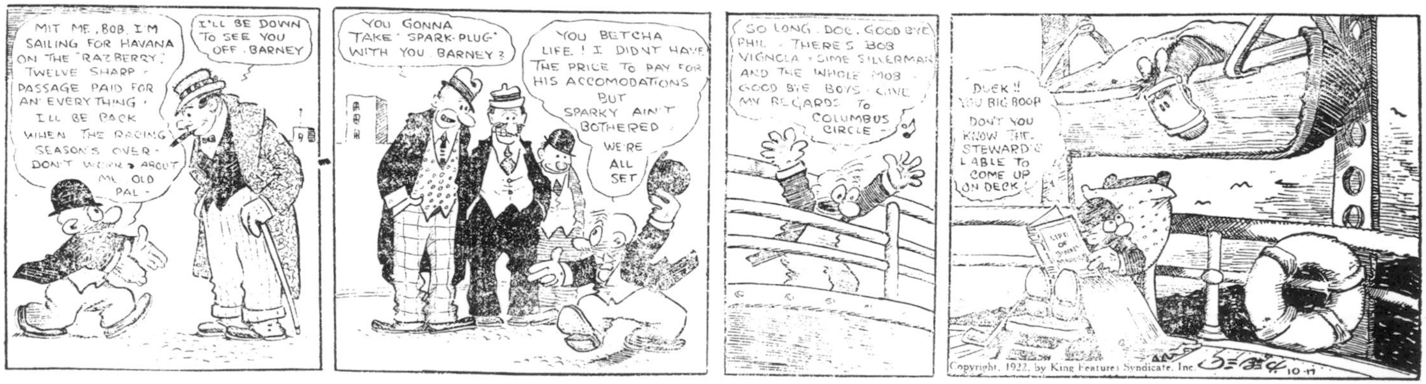
MIT ME, BOB, I'M SAILING FOR HAVANA ON THE "RAZBERRY," TWELVE SHARP - PASSAGE PAID FOR AN' EVERYTHING - I'LL BE BACK WHEN THE RACING SEASON'S OVER - DON'T WORRY ABOUT ME OLD PAL -
I'LL BE DOWN TO SEE YOU OFF, BARNEY
YOU GONNA TAKE "SPARK PLUG" WITH YOU, BARNEY?
YOU BETCHA LIFE! I DIDN'T HAVE THE PRICE TO PAY FOR HIS ACCOMODATIONS BUT SPARKY AIN'T BOTHERED
WE'RE ALL SET
SO LONG, DOC, GOOD BYE PHIL - THERE'S BOB VIGNOLA - SIME SILVERMAN AND THE WHOLE MOB - GOOD BYE BOYS - GIVE MY REGARDS TO COLUMBUS CIRCLE -
DUCK!! YOU BIG BOOB DON'T YOU KNOW THE STEWARD'S LIABLE TO COME UP ON DECK
Copyright, 1922, by King Features Syndicate, Inc
DE BECK
10-17

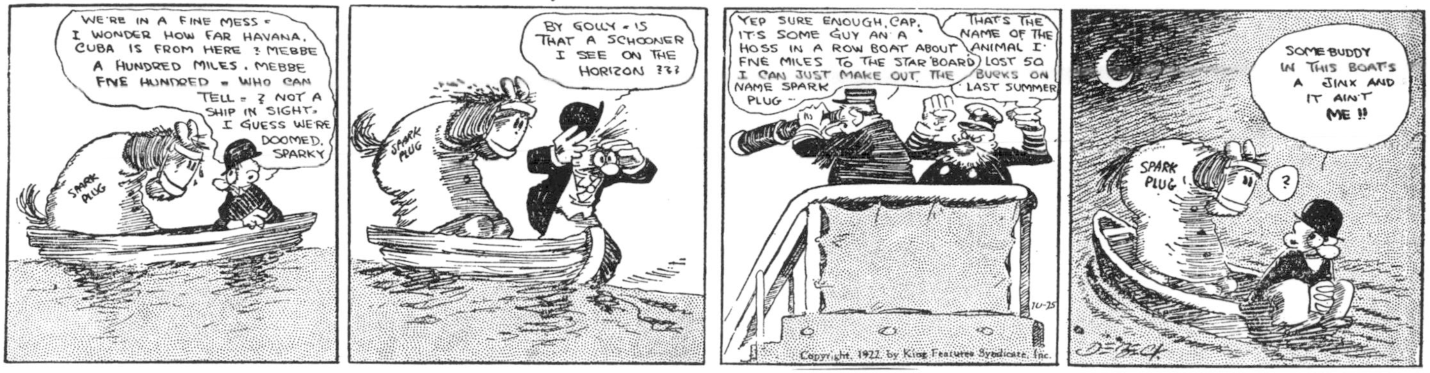
WE'RE IN A FINE MESS - I WONDER HOW FAR HAVANA, CUBA IS FROM HERE ? MEBBE A HUNDRED MILES. MEBBE FIVE HUNDRED - WHO CAN TELL - ? NOT A SHIP IN SIGHT. I GUESS WE'RE DOOMED, SPARKY
SPARK PLUG
BY GOLLY - IS THAT A SCHOONER I SEE ON THE HORIZON ???
SPARK PLUG
YEP SURE ENOUGH, CAP. IT'S SOME GUY AN' A HOSS IN A ROW BOAT ABOUT FIVE MILES TO THE STAR'BOARD I CAN JUST MAKE OUT THE NAME SPARK PLUG --
THAT'S THE NAME OF THE ANIMAL I LOST 50 BUCKS ON LAST SUMMER
Copyright, 1922, by King Features Syndicate, Inc.
SOMEBUDDY IN THIS BOAT'S A JINX AND IT AIN'T ME !!
?
SPARK PLUG

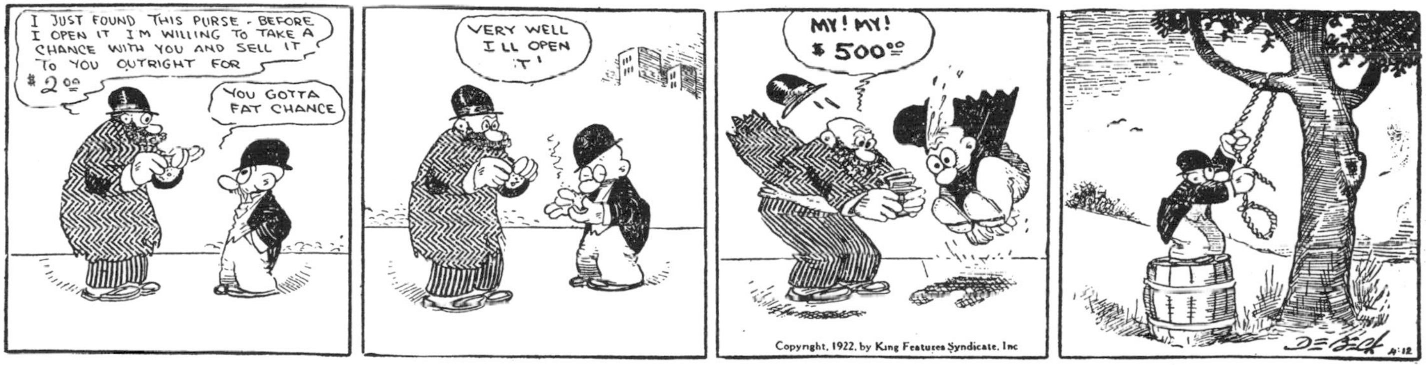
I JUST FOUND THIS PURSE - BEFORE I OPEN IT I'M WILLING TO TAKE A CHANCE WITH YOU AND SELL IT TO YOU OUTRIGHT FOR $2.00
YOU GOTTA FAT CHANCE
VERY WELL I'LL OPEN IT!
MY! MY! $500.00
Copyright, 1922, by King Features Syndicate, Inc

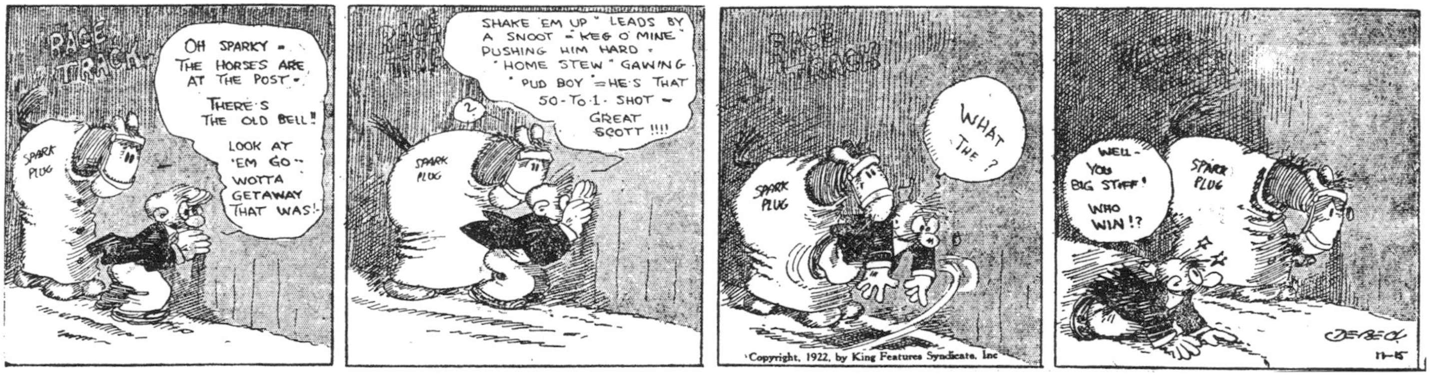
RACE TRACK
OH SPARKY - THE HORSES ARE AT THE POST -
THERE'S THE OLD BELL!!
LOOK AT 'EM GO -- WOTTA GETAWAY THAT WAS!
SPARK PLUG
SHAKE 'EM UP" LEADS BY A SNOOT - "KEG O' MINE" PUSHING HIM HARD - "HOME STEW" GAINING "PUD BOY" = HE'S THAT 50-TO-1 SHOT - GREAT SCOTT !!!!
?
SPARK PLUG
WHAT THE ?
SPARK PLUG
Copyright, 1922, by King Features Syndicate, Inc
WELL - YOU BIG STIFF! WHO WIN!?
SPARK PLUG

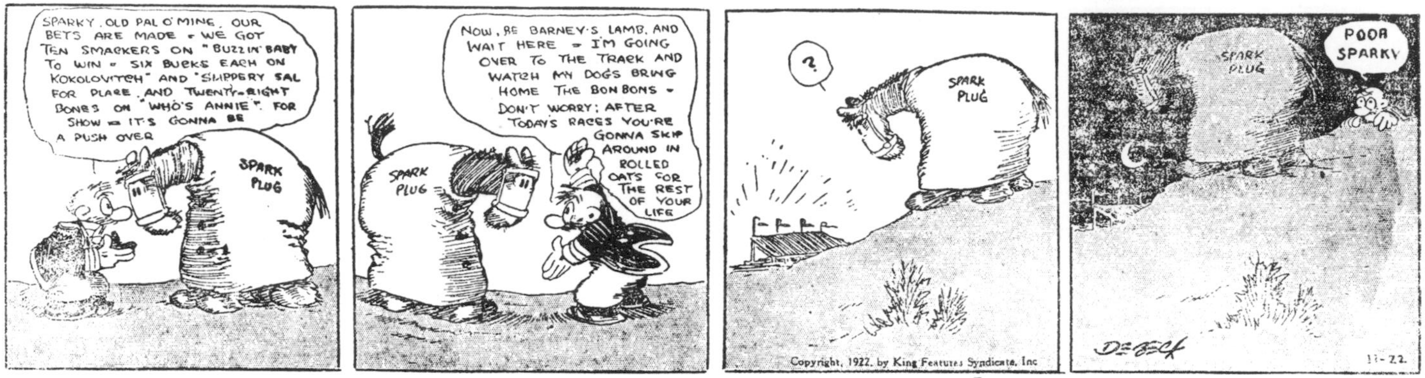
SPARKY, OLD PAL O' MINE, OUR BETS ARE MADE - WE GOT TEN SMACKERS ON "BUZZIN' BABY" TO WIN - SIX BUCKS EACH ON KOKOLOVITCH" AND "SLIPPERY SAL FOR PLACE, AND TWENTY-EIGHT BONES ON "WHO'S ANNIE", FOR SHOW - IT'S GONNA BE A PUSH OVER
SPARK PLUG
NOW, BE BARNEY'S LAMB, AND WAIT HERE - I'M GOING OVER TO THE TRACK AND WATCH MY DOGS BRING HOME THE BON BONS - DON'T WORRY; AFTER TODAYS RACES YOU'RE GONNA SKIP AROUND IN ROLLED OATS FOR THE REST OF YOUR LIFE
SPARK PLUG
?
SPARK PLUG
Copyright, 1922, by King Features Syndicate, Inc
SPARK PLUG
POOR SPARKY
DE BECK
11-22.

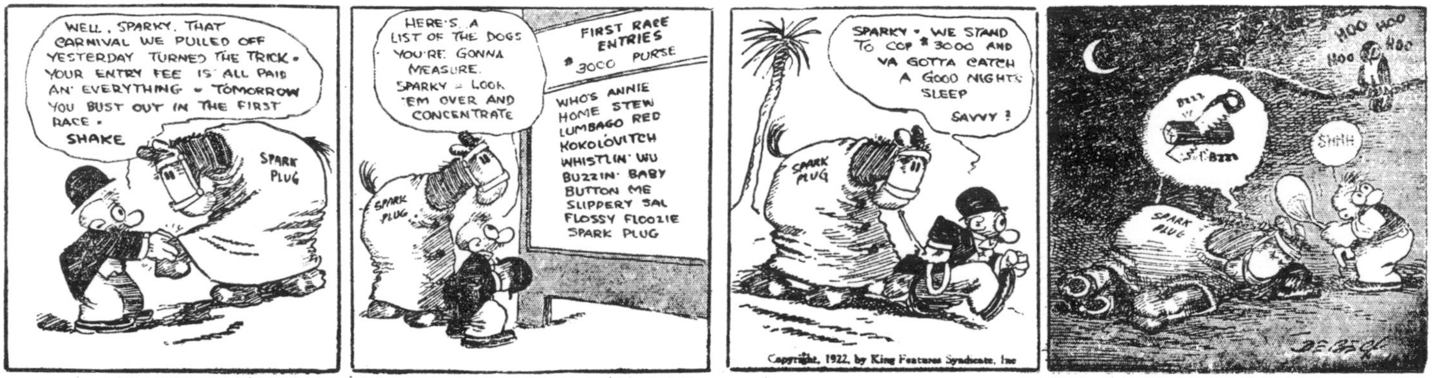
WELL, SPARKY, THAT CARNIVAL WE PULLED OFF YESTERDAY TURNED THE TRICK - YOUR ENTRY FEE IS ALL PAID AN' EVERYTHING - TOMORROW YOU BUST OUT IN THE FIRST RACE -
SHAKE
SPARK PLUG
HERE'S A LIST OF THE DOGS YOU'RE GONNA MEASURE. SPARKY - LOOK 'EM OVER AND CONCENTRATE
FIRST RACE ENTRIES
$3000 PURSE
WHO'S ANNIE
HOME STEW
LUMBAGO RED
KOKOLOVITCH
WHISTLIN' WU
BUZZIN' BABY
BUTTON ME
SLIPPERY SAL
FLOSSY FLOOZIE
SPARK PLUG
SPARK PLUG
SPARKY - WE STAND TO COP $3000 AND YA GOTTA CATCH A GOOD NIGHT'S SLEEP
SAVVY ?
SPARK PLUG
Copyright, 1922, by King Features Syndicate, Inc
HOO HOO
HOO HOO
SHHH
SPARK PLUG
DE BECK

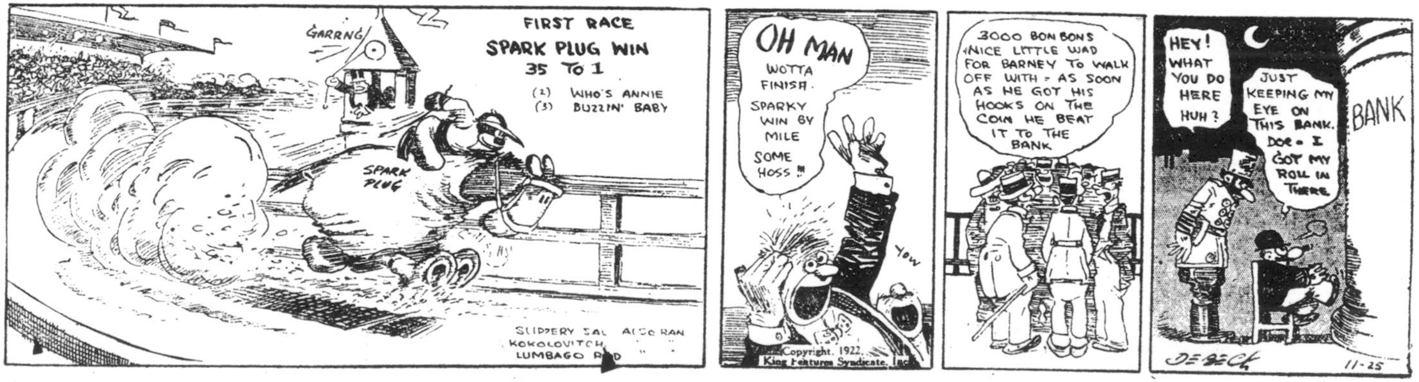
FIRST RACE
SPARK PLUG WIN
35 TO 1
(2) WHO'S ANNIE
(3) BUZZIN' BABY
GARRNG
SPARK PLUG
SLIPPERY SAL ALSO RAN
KOKOLOVITCH " "
LUMBAGO RED " "
OH MAN
WOTTA FINISH
SPARKY WIN BY MILE
SOME HOSS !!
YOW
Copyright, 1922, King Features Syndicate, Inc
3000 BON BONS - NICE LITTLE WAD FOR BARNEY TO WALK OFF WITH - AS SOON AS HE GOT HIS HOOKS ON THE COIN HE BEAT IT TO THE BANK
HEY! WHAT YOU DO HERE HUH ?
JUST KEEPING MY EYE ON THIS BANK. DOC - I GOT MY ROLL IN THERE
BANK
DE BECK
11-25

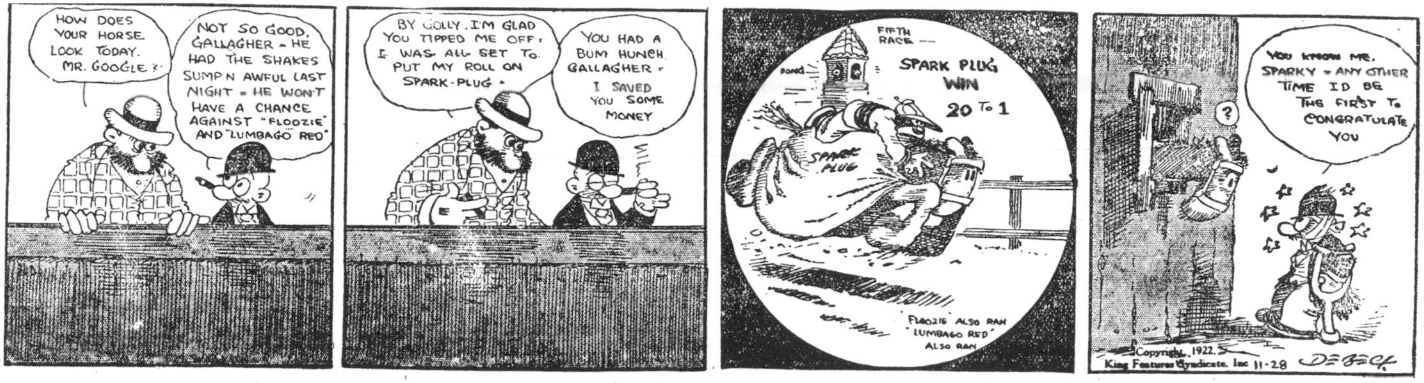
HOW DOES YOUR HORSE LOOK TODAY. MR. GOOGLE ?
NOT SO GOOD. GALLAGHER = HE HAD THE SHAKES SUMP'N AWFUL LAST NIGHT = HE WON'T HAVE A CHANCE AGAINST "FLOOZIE" AND "LUMBAGO RED"
BY GOLLY. I'M GLAD YOU TIPPED ME OFF. I WAS ALL SET TO PUT MY ROLL ON SPARK-PLUG.
YOU HAD A BUM HUNCH. GALLAGHER = I SAVED YOU SOME MONEY
FIFTH RACE —
SPARK PLUG WIN 20 TO 1
SPARK PLUG
"FLOOZIE" ALSO RAN "LUMBAGO RED" ALSO RAN
?
YOU KNOW ME. SPARKY = ANY OTHER TIME I'D BE THE FIRST TO CONGRATULATE YOU
Copyright, 1922, King Features Syndicate, Inc 11-28
DEBECK
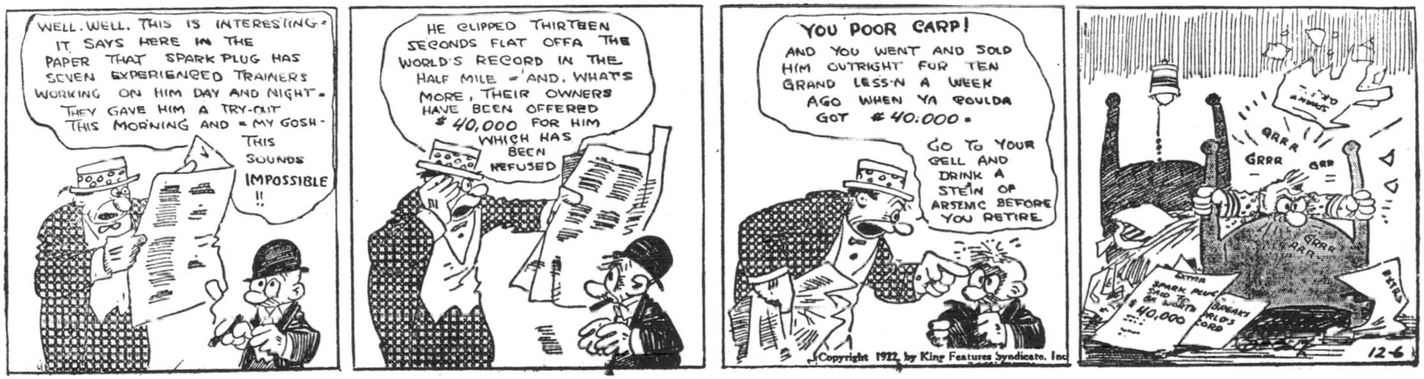
WELL. WELL. THIS IS INTERESTING. IT SAYS HERE IN THE PAPER THAT SPARK PLUG HAS SEVEN EXPERIENCED TRAINERS WORKING ON HIM DAY AND NIGHT. THEY GAVE HIM A TRY-OUT THIS MORNING AND = MY GOSH - THIS SOUNDS IMPOSSIBLE !!
HE CLIPPED THIRTEEN SECONDS FLAT OFFA THE WORLD'S RECORD IN THE HALF MILE = AND. WHAT'S MORE, THEIR OWNERS HAVE BEEN OFFERED $40,000 FOR HIM WHICH HAS BEEN REFUSED
YOU POOR CARP!
AND YOU WENT AND SOLD HIM OUTRIGHT FOR TEN GRAND LESS'N A WEEK AGO WHEN YA COULDA GOT $40.000.
GO TO YOUR CELL AND DRINK A STEIN OF ARSENIC BEFORE YOU RETIRE
Copyright 1922, by King Features Syndicate, Inc
GRRR
GRRR
GRR
12-6
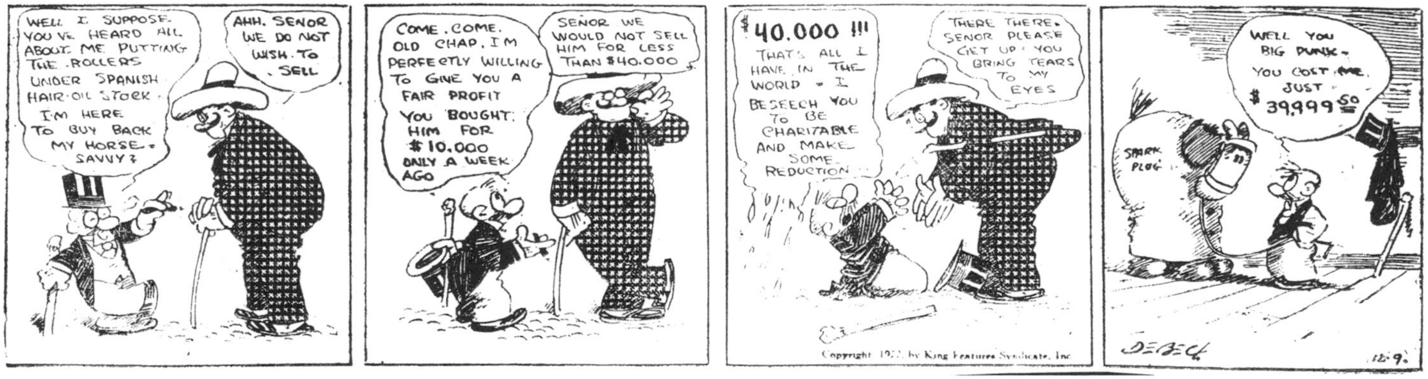
WELL I SUPPOSE. YOU'VE HEARD ALL ABOUT ME PUTTING THE ROLLERS UNDER SPANISH HAIR-OIL STOCK. I'M HERE TO BUY BACK MY HORSE. SAVVY?
AHH. SENOR WE DO NOT WISH TO SELL
COME. COME. OLD CHAP. I'M PERFECTLY WILLING TO GIVE YOU A FAIR PROFIT
YOU BOUGHT HIM FOR $10,000 ONLY A WEEK AGO
SENOR WE WOULD NOT SELL HIM FOR LESS THAN $40.000
$40.000 !!! THAT'S ALL I HAVE IN THE WORLD = I BESEECH YOU TO BE CHARITABLE AND MAKE SOME REDUCTION
THERE THERE. SENOR PLEASE GET UP. YOU BRING TEARS TO MY EYES
SPARK PLUG
WELL YOU BIG PUNK - YOU COST ME JUST $39,999.50
DEBECK
12-9.

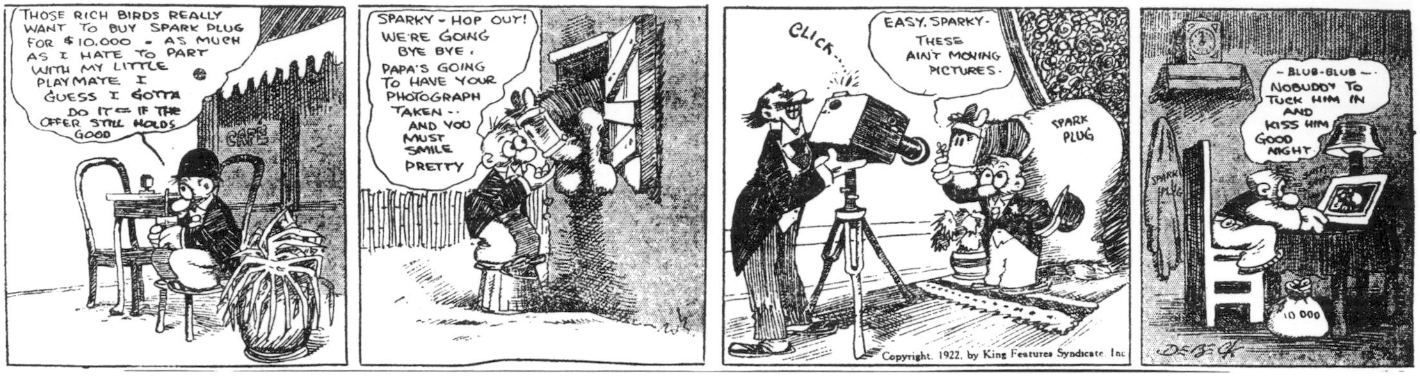
THOSE RICH BIRDS REALLY WANT TO BUY SPARK PLUG FOR $10,000 – AS MUCH AS I HATE TO PART WITH MY LITTLE PLAYMATE I GUESS I GOTTA DO IT = IF THE OFFER STILL HOLDS GOOD
CAFE
SPARKY – HOP OUT! WE'RE GOING BYE BYE. PAPA'S GOING TO HAVE YOUR PHOTOGRAPH TAKEN -- AND YOU MUST SMILE PRETTY
CLICK....
EASY, SPARKY – THESE AIN'T MOVING PICTURES.
SPARK PLUG
Copyright, 1922, by King Features Syndicate, Inc
– BLUB-BLUB – NOBUDDY TO TUCK HIM IN AND KISS HIM GOOD NIGHT
10 000
DE BECK

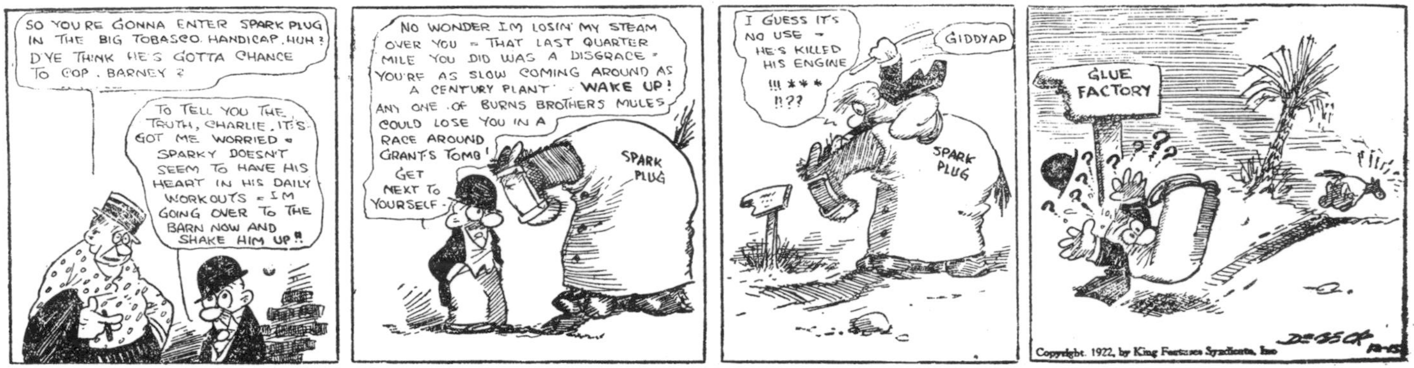
SO YOU'RE GONNA ENTER SPARK PLUG IN THE BIG TOBASCO HANDICAP, HUH? D'YE THINK HE'S GOTTA CHANCE TO COP, BARNEY ?
TO TELL YOU THE TRUTH, CHARLIE, IT'S GOT ME WORRIED = SPARKY DOESN'T SEEM TO HAVE HIS HEART IN HIS DAILY WORKOUTS = I'M GOING OVER TO THE BARN NOW AND SHAKE HIM UP!!
NO WONDER I'M LOSIN' MY STEAM OVER YOU = THAT LAST QUARTER MILE YOU DID WAS A DISGRACE = YOU'RE AS SLOW COMING AROUND AS A CENTURY PLANT – WAKE UP! ANY ONE OF BURNS BROTHERS MULES COULD LOSE YOU IN A RACE AROUND GRANT'S TOMB! GET NEXT TO YOURSELF –
SPARK PLUG
I GUESS IT'S NO USE – HE'S KILLED HIS ENGINE !!! * * * !!??
GIDDYAP
SPARK PLUG
GLUE FACTORY
Copyright, 1922, by King Features Syndicate, Inc
DE BECK

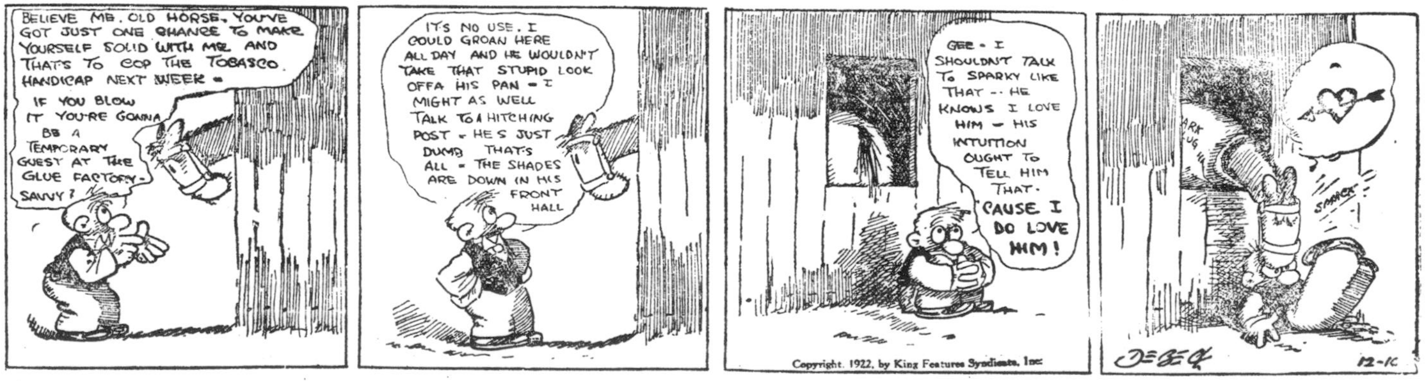
BELIEVE ME, OLD HORSE, YOU'VE GOT JUST ONE CHANCE TO MAKE YOURSELF SOLID WITH ME AND THAT'S TO COP THE TOBASCO HANDICAP NEXT WEEK = IF YOU BLOW IT YOU'RE GONNA BE A TEMPORARY GUEST AT THE GLUE FACTORY – SAVVY?
IT'S NO USE. I COULD GROAN HERE ALL DAY AND HE WOULDN'T TAKE THAT STUPID LOOK OFFA HIS PAN – I MIGHT AS WELL TALK TO A HITCHING POST – HE'S JUST DUMB THAT'S ALL – THE SHADES ARE DOWN IN HIS FRONT HALL
GEE – I SHOULDN'T TALK TO SPARKY LIKE THAT -- HE KNOWS I LOVE HIM – HIS INTUITION OUGHT TO TELL HIM THAT. 'CAUSE I DO LOVE HIM!
Copyright, 1922, by King Features Syndicate, Inc
SMACK
DE BECK
12-16

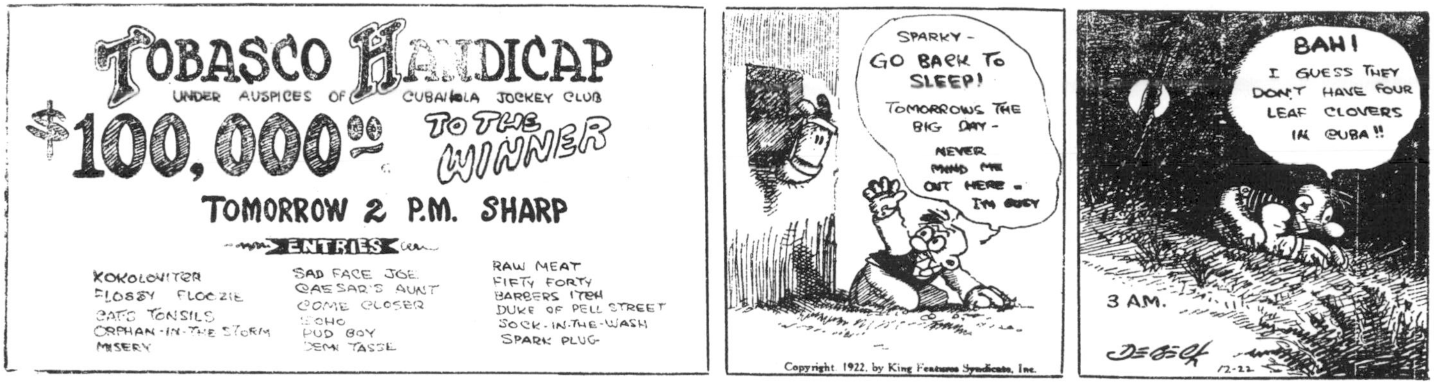
TOBASCO HANDICAP
UNDER AUSPICES OF CUBAHOLA JOCKEY CLUB
$100,000.00 TO THE WINNER
TOMORROW 2 P.M. SHARP
ENTRIES
KOKOLOWITCH
FLOSSY FLOOZIE
CAT'S TONSILS
ORPHAN-IN-THE-STORM
MISERY
SAD FACE JOE
CAESAR'S AUNT
COME CLOSER
ECHO
PUD BOY
DEMI TASSE
RAW MEAT
FIFTY FORTY
BARBERS ITCH
DUKE OF PELL STREET
SOCK-IN-THE-WASH
SPARK PLUG
SPARKY - GO BACK TO SLEEP! TOMORROWS THE BIG DAY - NEVER MIND ME OUT HERE - I'M BUSY
Copyright 1922, by King Features Syndicate, Inc.
BAH! I GUESS THEY DON'T HAVE FOUR LEAF CLOVERS IN CUBA!!
3 AM.
DEBECK
12-22

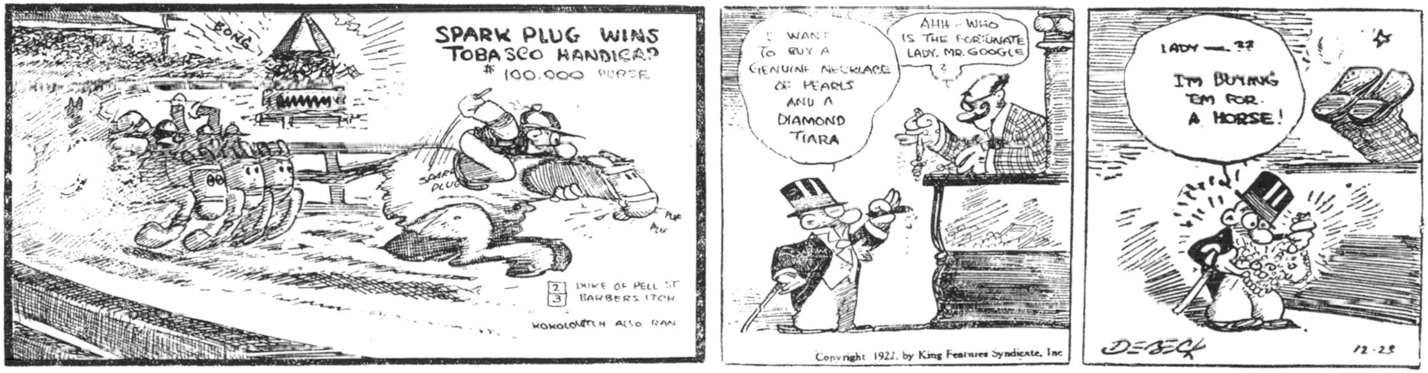
BONG
SPARK PLUG WINS TOBASCO HANDICAP
$100,000 PURSE
SPARK PLUG
PUF PUF
2 DUKE OF PELL ST
3 BARBERS ITCH
KOKOLOWITCH ALSO RAN
I WANT TO BUY A GENUINE NECKLACE OF PEARLS AND A DIAMOND TIARA
AHH - WHO IS THE FORTUNATE LADY, MR. GOOGLE?
Copyright 1922, by King Features Syndicate, Inc
LADY — ??
I'M BUYING 'EM FOR A HORSE!
DEBECK
12-23

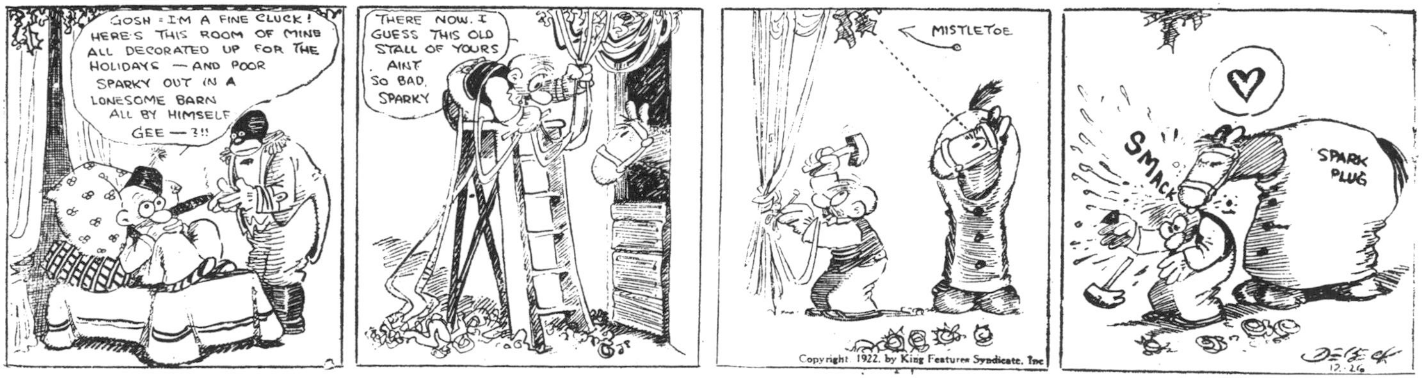
GOSH - I'M A FINE CLUCK! HERE'S THIS ROOM OF MINE ALL DECORATED UP FOR THE HOLIDAYS — AND POOR SPARKY OUT IN A LONESOME BARN ALL BY HIMSELF GEE — ?!!
THERE NOW. I GUESS THIS OLD STALL OF YOURS AINT SO BAD, SPARKY
MISTLETOE
Copyright 1922, by King Features Syndicate, Inc
SMACK
SPARK PLUG
DEBECK
12-26

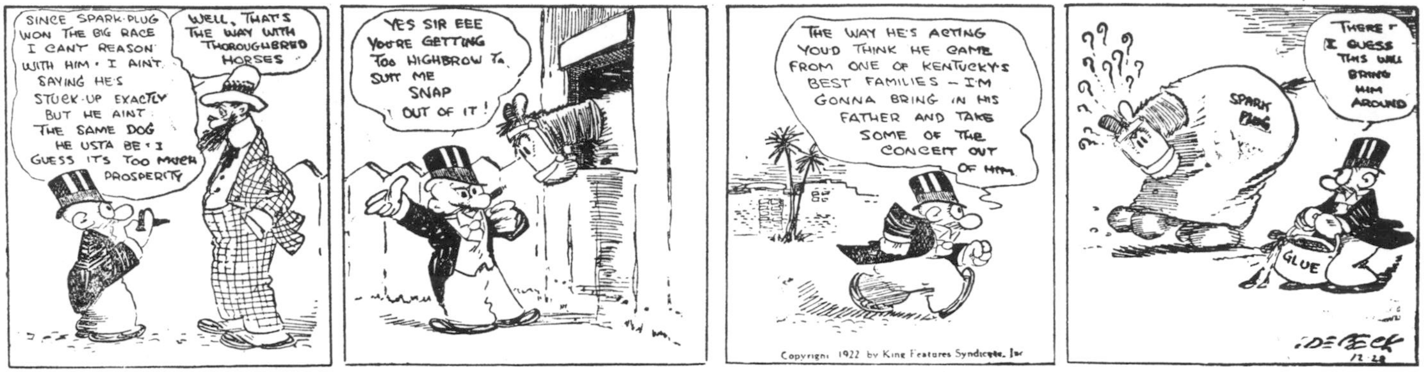
SINCE SPARK-PLUG WON THE BIG RACE I CANT REASON WITH HIM. I AINT SAYING HE'S STUCK-UP EXACTLY BUT HE AINT THE SAME DOG HE USTA BE. I GUESS ITS TOO MUCH PROSPERITY
WELL, THAT'S THE WAY WITH THOROUGHBRED HORSES
YES SIR EEE YOU'RE GETTING TOO HIGHBROW TA SUIT ME SNAP OUT OF IT!
THE WAY HE'S ACTING YOU'D THINK HE CAME FROM ONE OF KENTUCKY'S BEST FAMILIES - I'M GONNA BRING IN HIS FATHER AND TAKE SOME OF THE CONCEIT OUT OF HIM
Copyright 1922 by King Features Syndicate, Inc
THERE - I GUESS THIS WILL BRING HIM AROUND
SPARK PLUG
GLUE
DE BECK
12-28

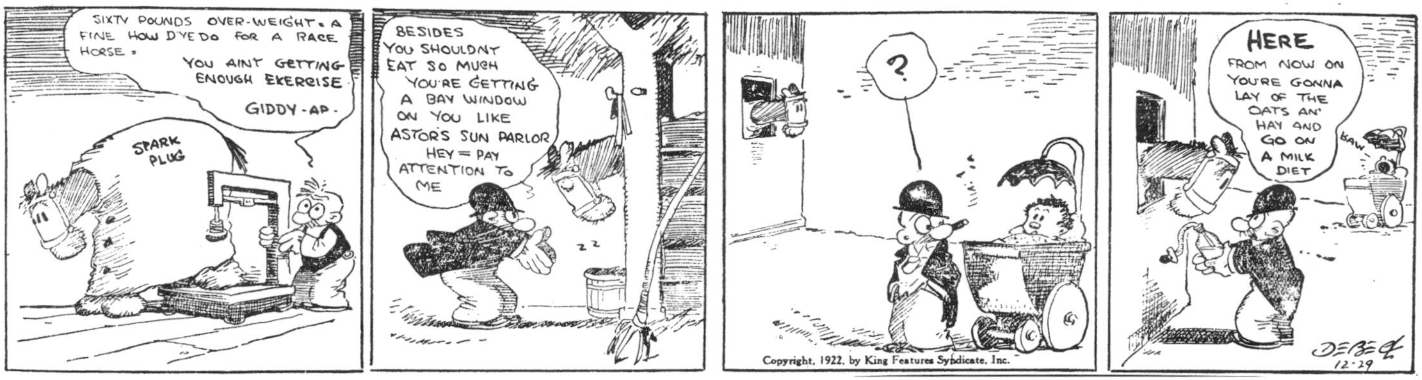
SIXTY POUNDS OVER-WEIGHT. A FINE HOW D'YE DO FOR A RACE HORSE. YOU AINT GETTING ENOUGH EKERCISE GIDDY-AP.
SPARK PLUG
BESIDES YOU SHOULDN'T EAT SO MUCH YOU'RE GETTING A BAY WINDOW ON YOU LIKE ASTOR'S SUN PARLOR HEY = PAY ATTENTION TO ME
?
Copyright, 1922, by King Features Syndicate, Inc.
HERE FROM NOW ON YOU'RE GONNA LAY OF THE OATS AN' HAY AND GO ON A MILK DIET
KAW
DE BECK
12-29

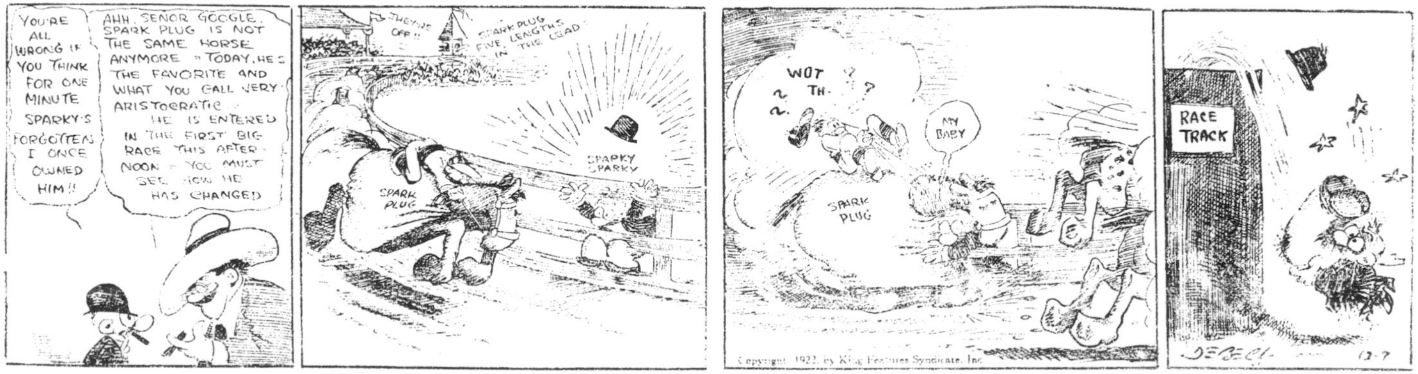
YOU'RE ALL WRONG IF YOU THINK FOR ONE MINUTE SPARKY'S FORGOTTEN I ONCE OWNED HIM!!
AHH, SENOR GOOGLE, SPARK PLUG IS NOT THE SAME HORSE ANYMORE = TODAY, HE'S THE FAVORITE AND WHAT YOU CALL VERY ARISTOCRATIC - HE IS ENTERED IN THE FIRST BIG RACE THIS AFTER-NOON = YOU MUST SEE HOW HE HAS CHANGED
THEY'RE OFF!!
SPARK PLUG FIVE LENGTHS IN THE LEAD
SPARK PLUG
SPARKY SPARKY
WOT TH - ? ?
MY BABY
SPARK PLUG
Copyright 1922 by King Features Syndicate, Inc.
RACE TRACK
DE BECK
12-?

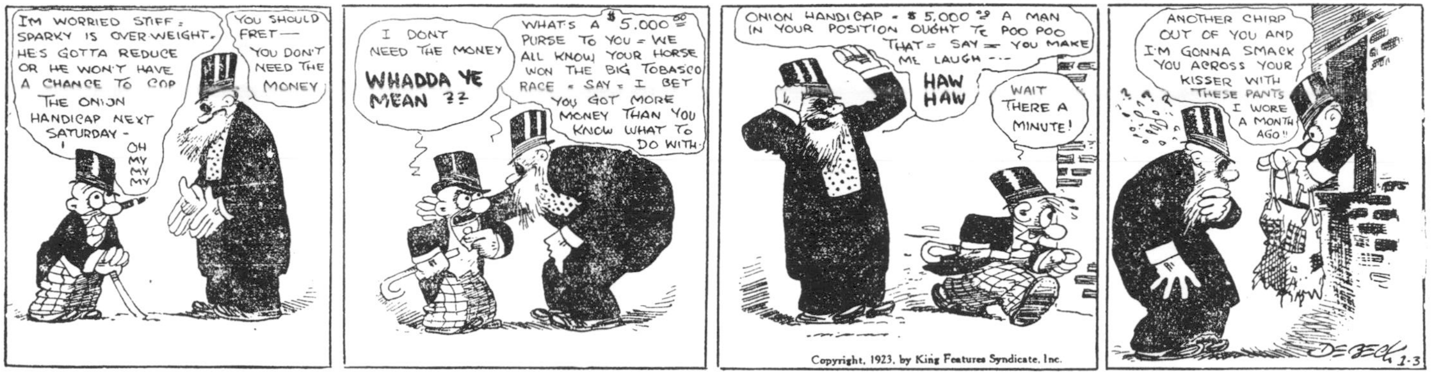
IM WORRIED STIFF = SPARKY IS OVER-WEIGHT. HE'S GOTTA REDUCE OR HE WON'T HAVE A CHANCE TO COP THE ONION HANDICAP NEXT SATURDAY -
OH MY MY MY
YOU SHOULD FRET — YOU DON'T NEED THE MONEY
I DONT NEED THE MONEY
WHADDA YE MEAN ??
WHATS A $5.000 PURSE TO YOU = WE ALL KNOW YOUR HORSE WON THE BIG TOBASCO RACE = SAY = I BET YOU GOT MORE MONEY THAN YOU KNOW WHAT TO DO WITH.
ONION HANDICAP = $5,000 ?? A MAN IN YOUR POSITION OUGHT TO POO POO THAT = SAY = YOU MAKE ME LAUGH ---
HAW HAW
WAIT THERE A MINUTE!
ANOTHER CHIRP OUT OF YOU AND I'M GONNA SMACK YOU ACROSS YOUR KISSER WITH THESE PANTS I WORE A MONTH AGO!!
Copyright, 1923, by King Features Syndicate, Inc.
DE BECK 1-3

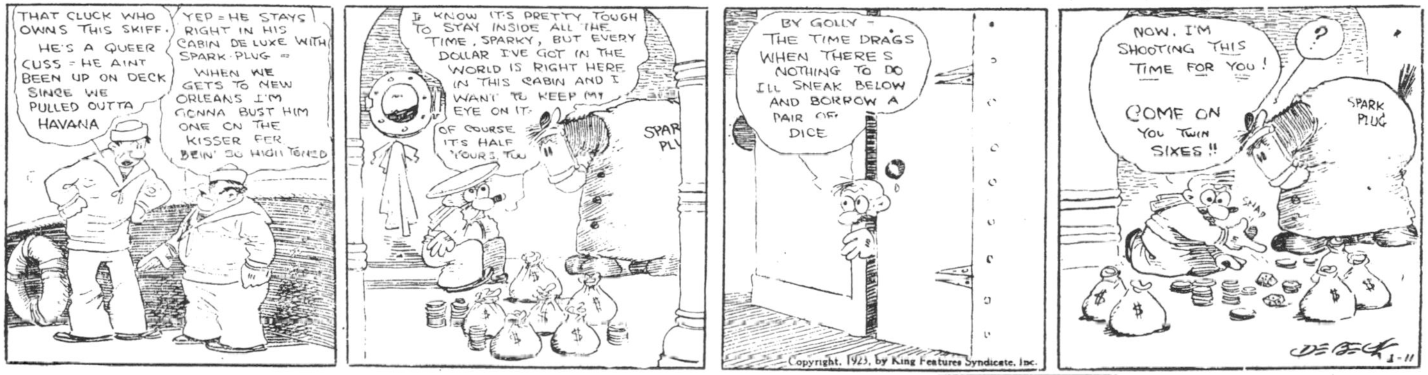
THAT CLUCK WHO OWNS THIS SKIFF. HE'S A QUEER CUSS = HE AINT BEEN UP ON DECK SINCE WE PULLED OUTTA HAVANA
YEP = HE STAYS RIGHT IN HIS CABIN DE LUXE WITH SPARK-PLUG = WHEN WE GETS TO NEW ORLEANS I'M GONNA BUST HIM ONE ON THE KISSER FER BEIN' SO HIGH TONED
I KNOW IT'S PRETTY TOUGH TO STAY INSIDE ALL THE TIME, SPARKY, BUT EVERY DOLLAR I'VE GOT IN THE WORLD IS RIGHT HERE IN THIS CABIN AND I WANT TO KEEP MY EYE ON IT.
OF COURSE IT'S HALF YOURS, TOO
SPARK PLUG
BY GOLLY - THE TIME DRAGS WHEN THERE'S NOTHING TO DO I'LL SNEAK BELOW AND BORROW A PAIR OF DICE
Copyright, 1923, by King Features Syndicate, Inc.
NOW, I'M SHOOTING THIS TIME FOR YOU!
COME ON YOU TWIN SIXES!!
?
SPARK PLUG
SNAP
DE BECK 1-11

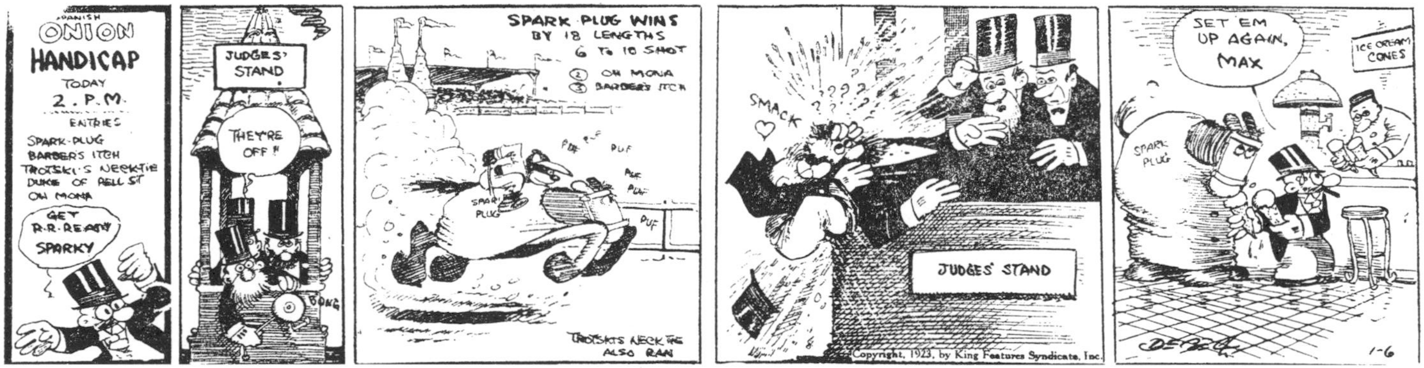
SPANISH ONION HANDICAP TODAY 2. P. M.
ENTRIES
SPARK-PLUG
BARBER'S ITCH
TROTSKI'S NECKTIE
DUKE OF BELL ST
OH MONA
GET R.R. READY SPARKY
JUDGES' STAND
THEY'RE OFF!!
BONG
SPARK PLUG WINS BY 18 LENGTHS 6 TO 10 SHOT
2 OH MONA
3 BARBER'S ITCH
SPARK PLUG
PUF PUF PUF PUF PUF PUF
TROTSKI'S NECKTIE ALSO RAN
SMACK
????
JUDGES' STAND
Copyright, 1923, by King Features Syndicate, Inc.
SET EM UP AGAIN, MAX
ICE CREAM CONES
SPARK PLUG
DE BECK 1-6

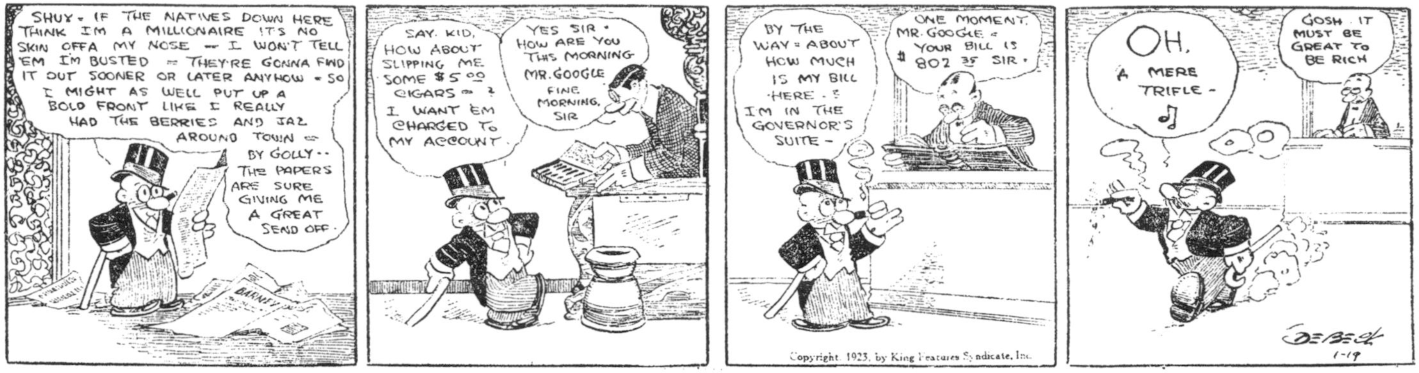
SHUX - IF THE NATIVES DOWN HERE THINK I'M A MILLIONAIRE IT'S NO SKIN OFFA MY NOSE — I WON'T TELL 'EM I'M BUSTED = THEY'RE GONNA FIND IT OUT SOONER OR LATER ANYHOW - SO I MIGHT AS WELL PUT UP A BOLD FRONT LIKE I REALLY HAD THE BERRIES AND JAZ AROUND TOWN = BY GOLLY - - THE PAPERS ARE SURE GIVING ME A GREAT SEND OFF -
SAY, KID, HOW ABOUT SLIPPING ME SOME $5.00 CIGARS = ? I WANT 'EM CHARGED TO MY ACCOUNT
YES SIR - HOW ARE YOU THIS MORNING MR. GOOGLE
FINE MORNING, SIR
BY THE WAY = ABOUT HOW MUCH IS MY BILL HERE - ? I'M IN THE GOVERNOR'S SUITE -
ONE MOMENT, MR. GOOGLE = YOUR BILL IS $ 802.35 SIR -
Copyright, 1923, by King Features Syndicate, Inc.
OH, A MERE TRIFLE -
GOSH, IT MUST BE GREAT TO BE RICH
DE BECK
1-19

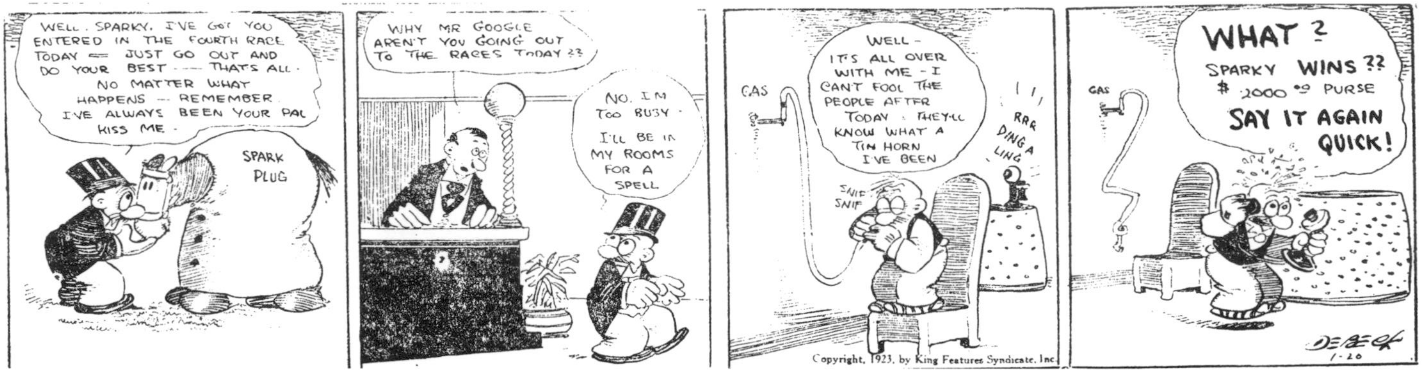
WELL, SPARKY, I'VE GOT YOU ENTERED IN THE FOURTH RACE TODAY = JUST GO OUT AND DO YOUR BEST --- THAT'S ALL - NO MATTER WHAT HAPPENS — REMEMBER, I'VE ALWAYS BEEN YOUR PAL KISS ME -
SPARK PLUG
WHY MR GOOGLE AREN'T YOU GOING OUT TO THE RACES TODAY ??
NO, I'M TOO BUSY - I'LL BE IN MY ROOMS FOR A SPELL
GAS
WELL - IT'S ALL OVER WITH ME - I CAN'T FOOL THE PEOPLE AFTER TODAY - THEY'LL KNOW WHAT A TIN HORN I'VE BEEN
SNIF SNIF
RRR DING A LING
Copyright, 1923, by King Features Syndicate, Inc.
GAS
WHAT ? SPARKY WINS ?? $ 2000.00 PURSE SAY IT AGAIN QUICK!
DE BECK
1-20

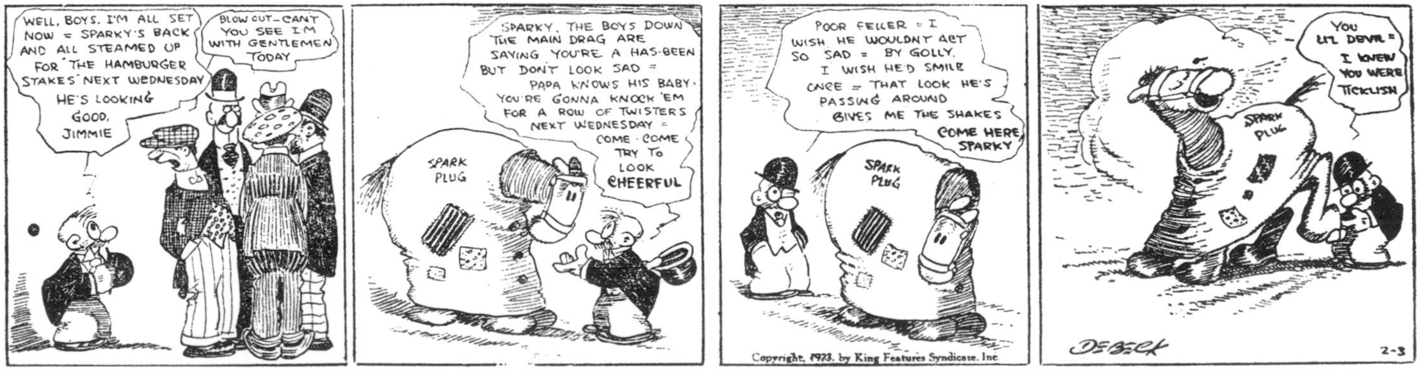
WELL, BOYS, I'M ALL SET NOW = SPARKY'S BACK AND ALL STEAMED UP FOR THE HAMBURGER STAKES NEXT WEDNESDAY HE'S LOOKING GOOD, JIMMIE
BLOW OUT - CAN'T YOU SEE I'M WITH GENTLEMEN TODAY
SPARKY, THE BOYS DOWN THE MAIN DRAG ARE SAYING YOU'RE A HAS-BEEN BUT DON'T LOOK SAD = PAPA KNOWS HIS BABY - YOU'RE GONNA KNOCK 'EM FOR A ROW OF TWISTERS NEXT WEDNESDAY = COME - COME TRY TO LOOK CHEERFUL
SPARK PLUG
POOR FELLER = I WISH HE WOULDN'T ACT SO SAD = BY GOLLY, I WISH HE'D SMILE ONCE = THAT LOOK HE'S PASSING AROUND GIVES ME THE SHAKES COME HERE, SPARKY
SPARK PLUG
Copyright, 1923, by King Features Syndicate, Inc.
YOU LI'L DEVIL = I KNEW YOU WERE TICKLISH
SPARK PLUG
DE BECK
2-3

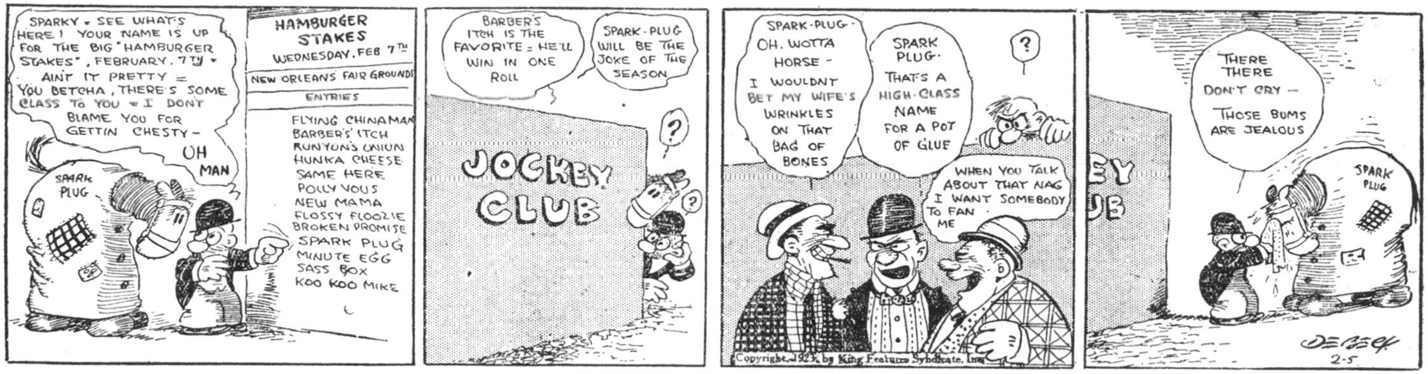
SPARKY - SEE WHAT'S HERE! YOUR NAME IS UP FOR THE BIG "HAMBURGER STAKES", FEBRUARY. 7TH - AIN'T IT PRETTY = YOU BETCHA, THERE'S SOME CLASS TO YOU - I DON'T BLAME YOU FOR GETTIN CHESTY -
OH MAN
HAMBURGER STAKES
WEDNESDAY. FEB 7TH
NEW ORLEANS FAIR GROUNDS
ENTRIES
FLYING CHINAMAN
BARBER'S ITCH
RUNYON'S ONION
HUNKA CHEESE
SAME HERE
POLLY VOUS
NEW MAMA
FLOSSY FLOOZIE
BROKEN PROMISE
SPARK PLUG
MINUTE EGG
SASS BOX
KOO KOO MIKE
SPARK PLUG
BARBER'S ITCH IS THE FAVORITE = HE'LL WIN IN ONE ROLL
SPARK-PLUG WILL BE THE JOKE OF THE SEASON
?
JOCKEY CLUB
?
SPARK-PLUG - OH. WOTTA HORSE - I WOULDNT BET MY WIFE'S WRINKLES ON THAT BAG OF BONES
SPARK PLUG - THAT'S A HIGH-CLASS NAME FOR A POT OF GLUE
?
WHEN YOU TALK ABOUT THAT NAG I WANT SOMEBODY TO FAN ME
Copyright, 1923, by King Features Syndicate, Inc
THERE THERE DON'T CRY - THOSE BUMS ARE JEALOUS
SPARK PLUG
DEBECK
2-5

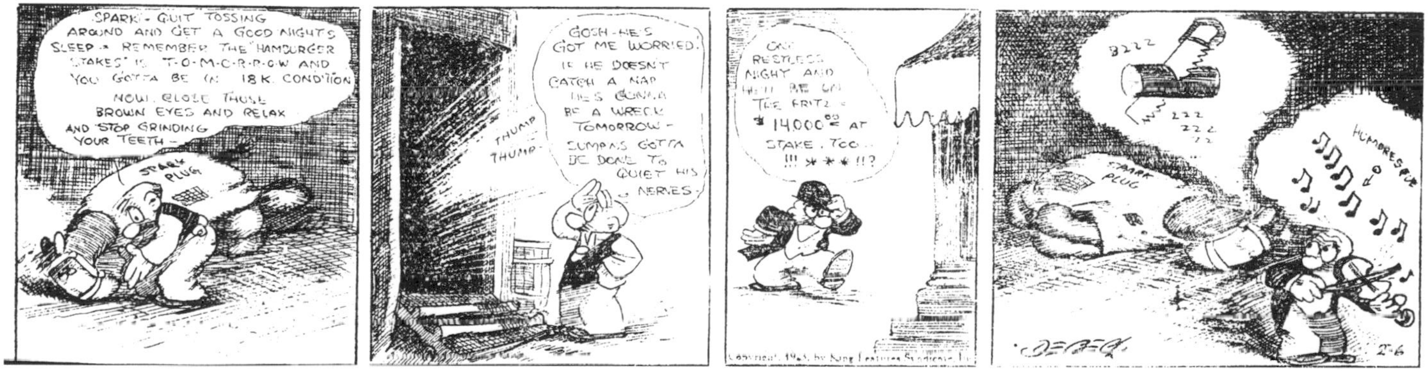
SPARK - QUIT TOSSING AROUND AND GET A GOOD NIGHT'S SLEEP - REMEMBER THE "HAMBURGER STAKES" IS T-O-M-O-R-R-O-W AND YOU GOTTA BE IN 18K CONDITION
NOW CLOSE THOSE BROWN EYES AND RELAX
AND STOP GRINDING YOUR TEETH -
SPARK PLUG
THUMP
THUMP
GOSH - HE'S GOT ME WORRIED. IF HE DOESN'T CATCH A NAP HE'S GONNA BE A WRECK TOMORROW - SUMPIN GOTTA BE DONE TO QUIET HIS NERVES
THE FRITZ -
$14,000.00 AT STAKE, TOO -
!!! * * * !!?
SPARK PLUG
HUMORESQUE
DEBECK
2-6

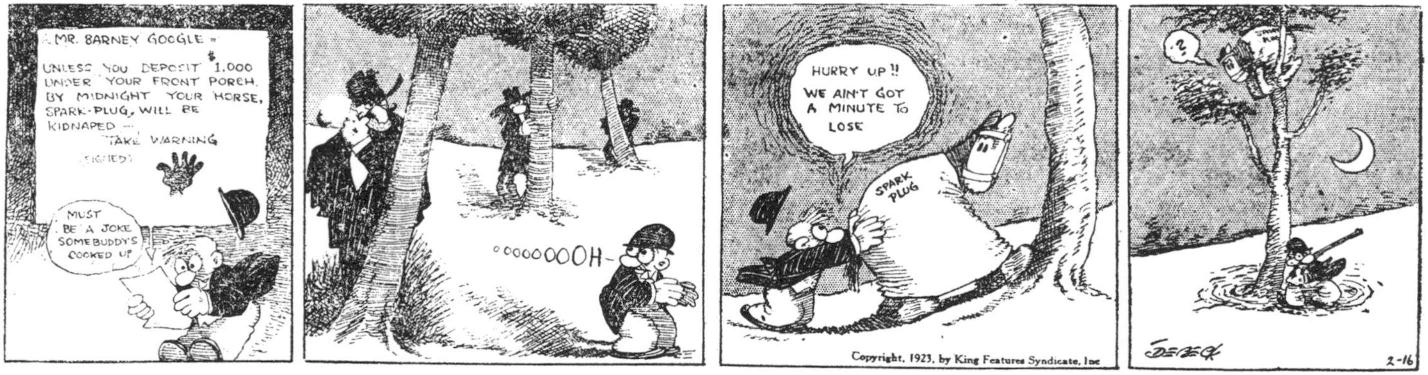
MR. BARNEY GOOGLE -
UNLESS YOU DEPOSIT $1,000 UNDER YOUR FRONT PORCH, BY MIDNIGHT YOUR HORSE, SPARK-PLUG, WILL BE KIDNAPED -
TAKE WARNING
(SIGNED)
MUST BE A JOKE SOMEBUDDY'S COOKED UP
OOOOOOOOH -
HURRY UP!! WE AIN'T GOT A MINUTE TO LOSE
SPARK PLUG
Copyright, 1923, by King Features Syndicate, Inc
?
DEBECK
2-16

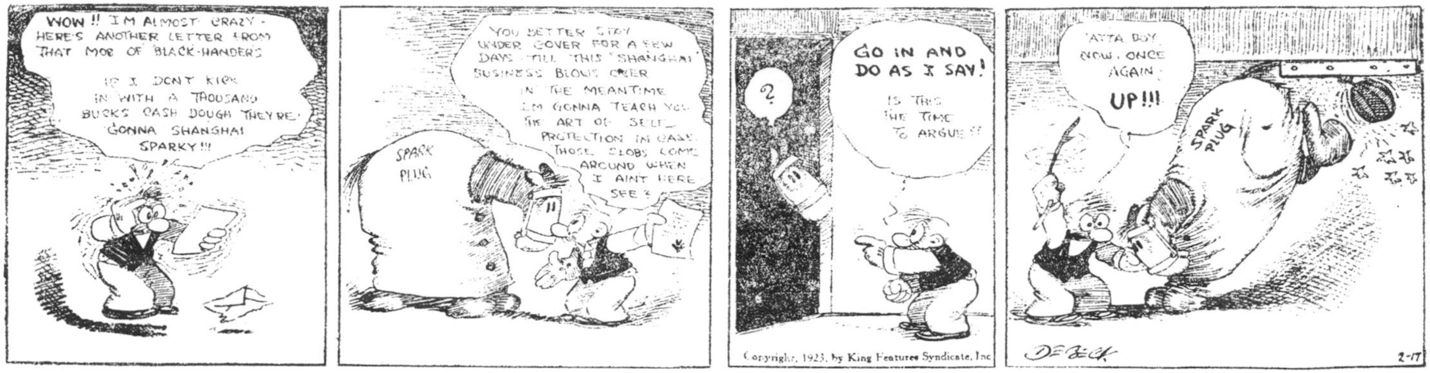
WOW!! I'M ALMOST CRAZY - HERE'S ANOTHER LETTER FROM THAT MOB OF BLACK-HANDERS
IF I DONT KICK IN WITH A THOUSAND BUCKS CASH DOUGH THEY'RE GONNA SHANGHAI SPARKY!!!
YOU BETTER STAY UNDER COVER FOR A FEW DAYS TILL THIS SHANGHAI BUSINESS BLOWS OVER
IN THE MEANTIME I'M GONNA TEACH YOU THE ART OF SELF-PROTECTION IN CASE THOSE SLOBS COME AROUND WHEN I AINT HERE SEE?
SPARK PLUG
?
GO IN AND DO AS I SAY!
IS THIS THE TIME TO ARGUE??
Copyright, 1923, by King Features Syndicate, Inc
ATTA BOY NOW, ONCE AGAIN -
UP!!!
SPARK PLUG
DE BECK
2-17

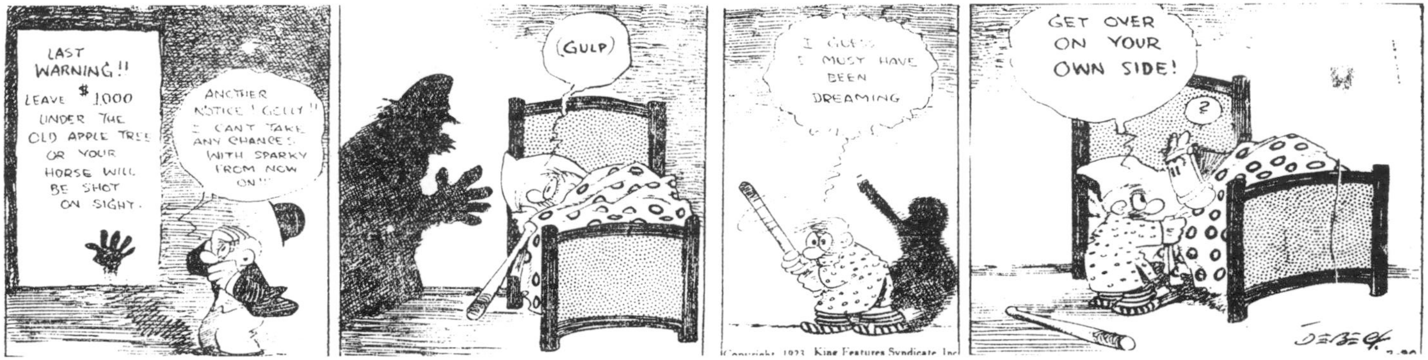
LAST WARNING!! LEAVE $1000 UNDER THE OLD APPLE TREE OR YOUR HORSE WILL BE SHOT ON SIGHT.
ANOTHER NOTICE! GOLLY!! I CAN'T TAKE ANY CHANCES WITH SPARKY FROM NOW ON!!
(GULP)
I GUESS I MUST HAVE BEEN DREAMING
GET OVER ON YOUR OWN SIDE!
?
DE BECK

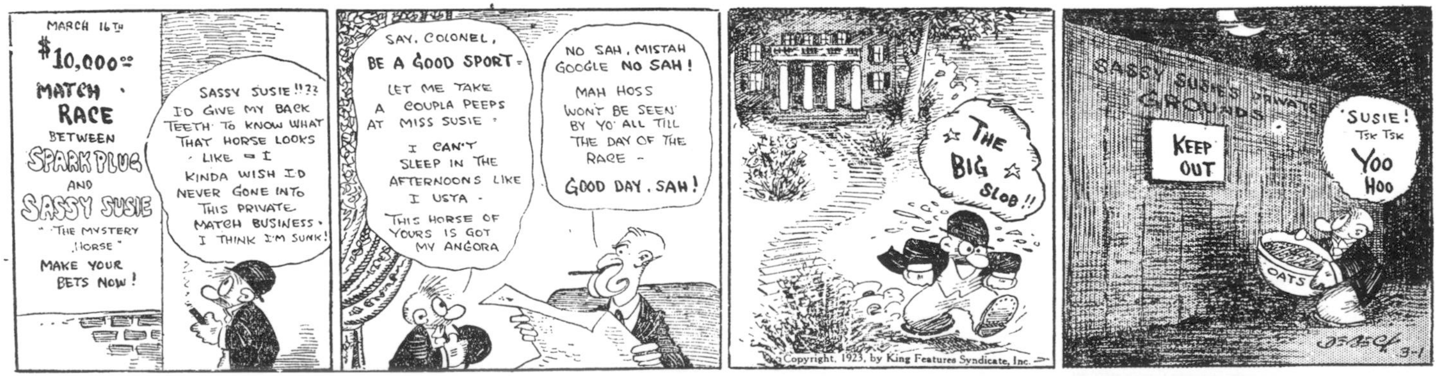
MARCH 16TH $10,000.00 MATCH RACE BETWEEN SPARK PLUG AND SASSY SUSIE "THE MYSTERY HORSE" MAKE YOUR BETS NOW!
SASSY SUSIE!!?? I'D GIVE MY BACK TEETH TO KNOW WHAT THAT HORSE LOOKS LIKE - I KINDA WISH I'D NEVER GONE INTO THIS PRIVATE MATCH BUSINESS - I THINK I'M SUNK!
SAY, COLONEL, BE A GOOD SPORT - LET ME TAKE A COUPLA PEEPS AT MISS SUSIE - I CAN'T SLEEP IN THE AFTERNOONS LIKE I USTA - THIS HORSE OF YOURS IS GOT MY ANGORA
NO SAH, MISTAH GOOGLE NO SAH! MAH HOSS WON'T BE SEEN BY YO' ALL TILL THE DAY OF THE RACE - GOOD DAY, SAH!
THE BIG SLOB!!
Copyright, 1923, by King Features Syndicate, Inc.
SASSY SUSIE'S PRIVATE GROUNDS
KEEP OUT
SUSIE! TSK TSK YOO HOO
OATS
DE BECK 3-1

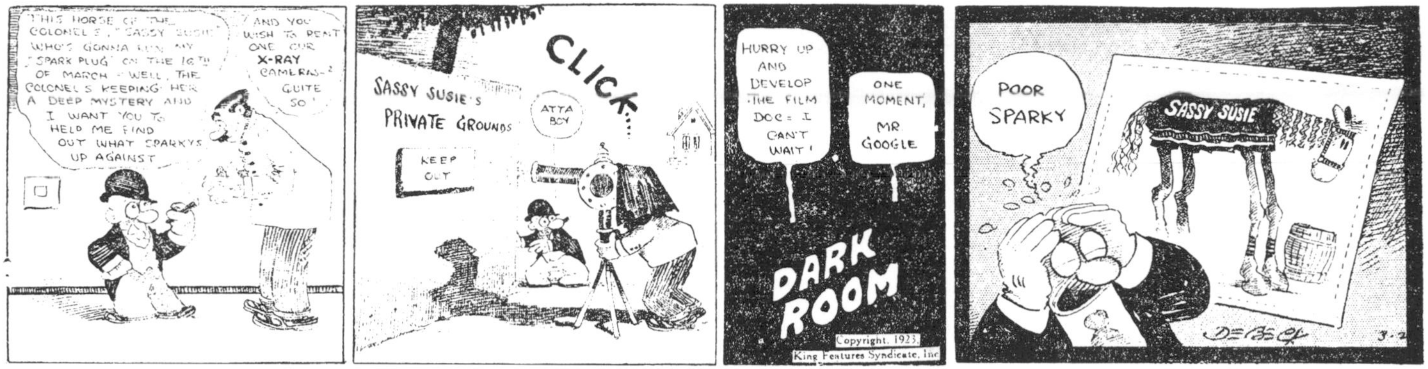
THIS HORSE OF THE COLONEL'S, "SASSY SUSIE" WHO'S GONNA RUN MY "SPARK PLUG" ON THE 16TH OF MARCH - WELL, THE COLONEL'S KEEPING HER A DEEP MYSTERY AND I WANT YOU TO HELP ME FIND OUT WHAT SPARKY'S UP AGAINST
AND YOU WISH TO RENT ONE OUR X-RAY CAMERAS? QUITE SO!
SASSY SUSIE'S PRIVATE GROUNDS
KEEP OUT
CLICK....
ATTA BOY
HURRY UP AND DEVELOP THE FILM DOC = I CAN'T WAIT!
ONE MOMENT, MR. GOOGLE
DARK ROOM
Copyright, 1923, King Features Syndicate, Inc
POOR SPARKY
SASSY SUSIE
DE BECK
3-2
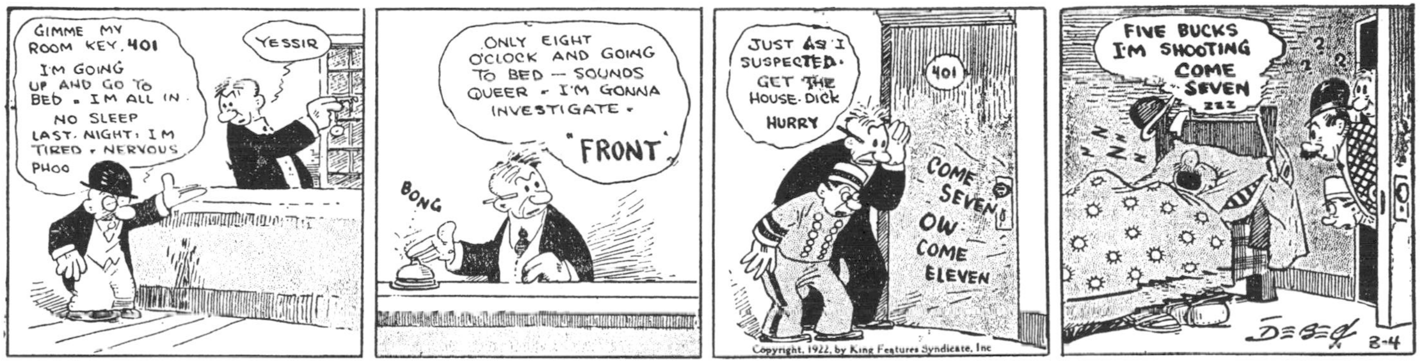
GIMME MY ROOM KEY. 401 I'M GOING UP AND GO TO BED = I'M ALL IN. NO SLEEP LAST NIGHT: I'M TIRED - NERVOUS PHOO
YESSIR
ONLY EIGHT O'CLOCK AND GOING TO BED — SOUNDS QUEER - I'M GONNA INVESTIGATE -
"FRONT"
BONG
JUST AS I SUSPECTED. GET THE HOUSE DICK HURRY
401
COME SEVEN OW COME ELEVEN
Copyright, 1922, by King Features Syndicate, Inc
FIVE BUCKS I'M SHOOTING COME SEVEN ZZZ
DE BECK
3-4
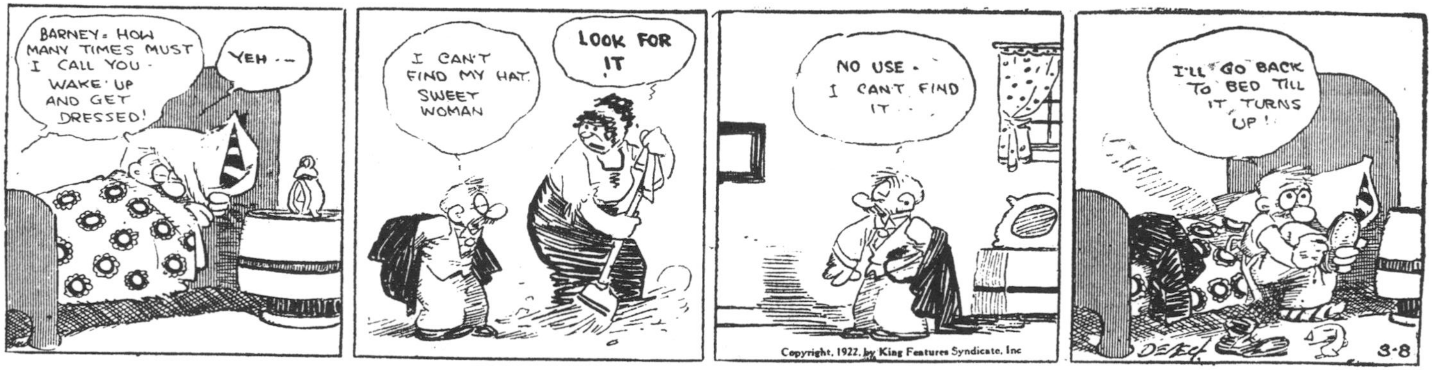
BARNEY = HOW MANY TIMES MUST I CALL YOU - WAKE UP AND GET DRESSED!
YEH - -
I CAN'T FIND MY HAT SWEET WOMAN
LOOK FOR IT
NO USE - I CAN'T FIND IT - -
Copyright, 1922, by King Features Syndicate, Inc
I'LL GO BACK TO BED TILL IT TURNS UP!
DE BECK
3-8

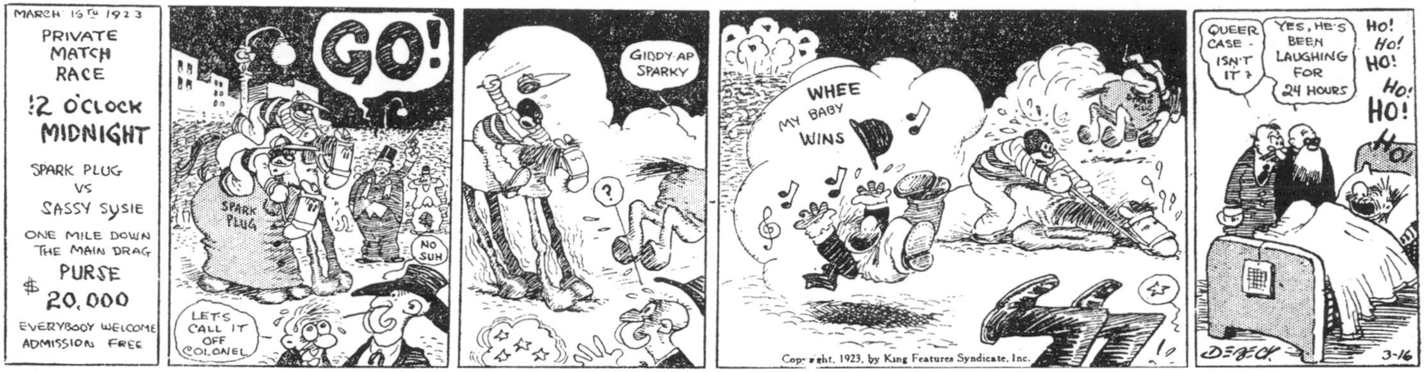
MARCH 16TH 1923
PRIVATE MATCH RACE
!2 O'CLOCK MIDNIGHT
SPARK PLUG VS SASSY SYSIE
ONE MILE DOWN THE MAIN DRAG
PURSE $ 20,000
EVERYBODY WELCOME ADMISSION FREE
GO!
SPARK PLUG
NO SUH
LET'S CALL IT OFF COLONEL
GIDDY-AP SPARKY
?
WHEE MY BABY WINS
QUEER CASE - ISN'T IT ?
YES, HE'S BEEN LAUGHING FOR 24 HOURS
HO! HO! HO! HO! HO! HO
DEBECK 3-16
Copyright, 1923, by King Features Syndicate, Inc.

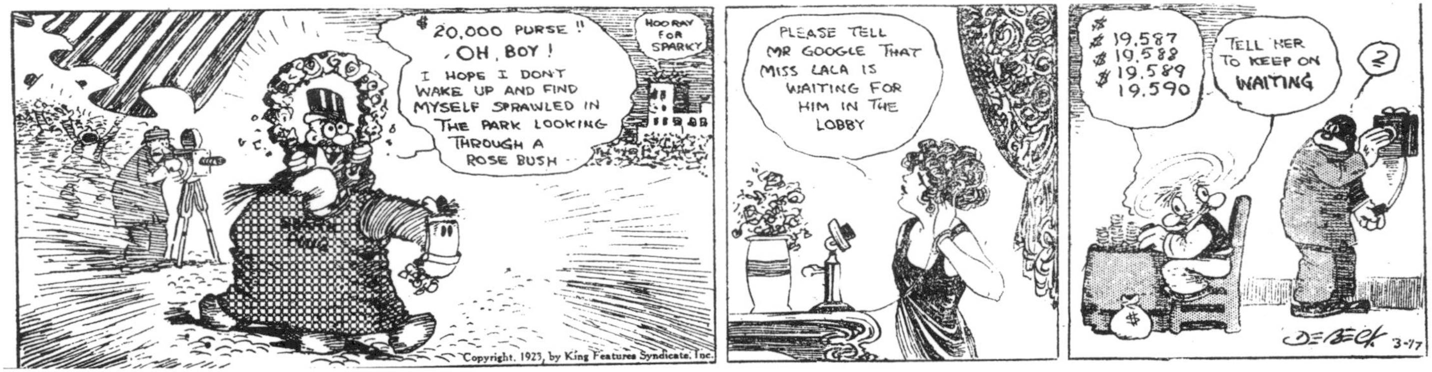
$20,000 PURSE !! , OH, BOY ! I HOPE I DON'T WAKE UP AND FIND MYSELF SPRAWLED IN THE PARK LOOKING THROUGH A ROSE BUSH
HOORAY FOR SPARKY
PLEASE TELL MR GOOGLE THAT MISS LALA IS WAITING FOR HIM IN THE LOBBY
$19.587 $19.588 $19.589 19.590
TELL HER TO KEEP ON WAITING
?
DEBECK 3-17
Copyright, 1923, by King Features Syndicate, Inc.

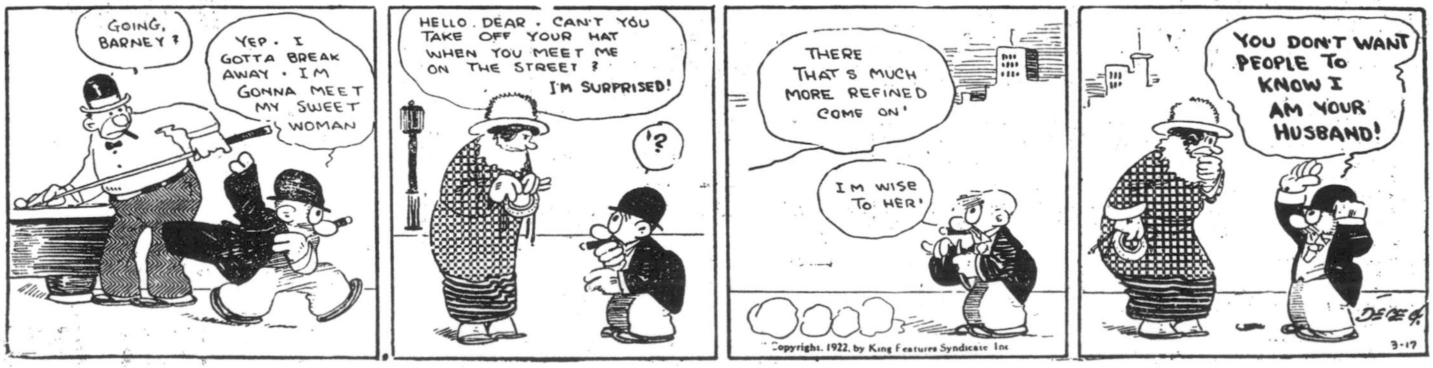
GOING, BARNEY ?
YEP. I GOTTA BREAK AWAY. I'M GONNA MEET MY SWEET WOMAN
HELLO. DEAR. CAN'T YOU TAKE OFF YOUR HAT WHEN YOU MEET ME ON THE STREET ? I'M SURPRISED!
!?
THERE THAT'S MUCH MORE REFINED COME ON'
I'M WISE TO HER'
YOU DON'T WANT PEOPLE TO KNOW I AM YOUR HUSBAND!
DEBECK 3-17
Copyright, 1922, by King Features Syndicate Inc

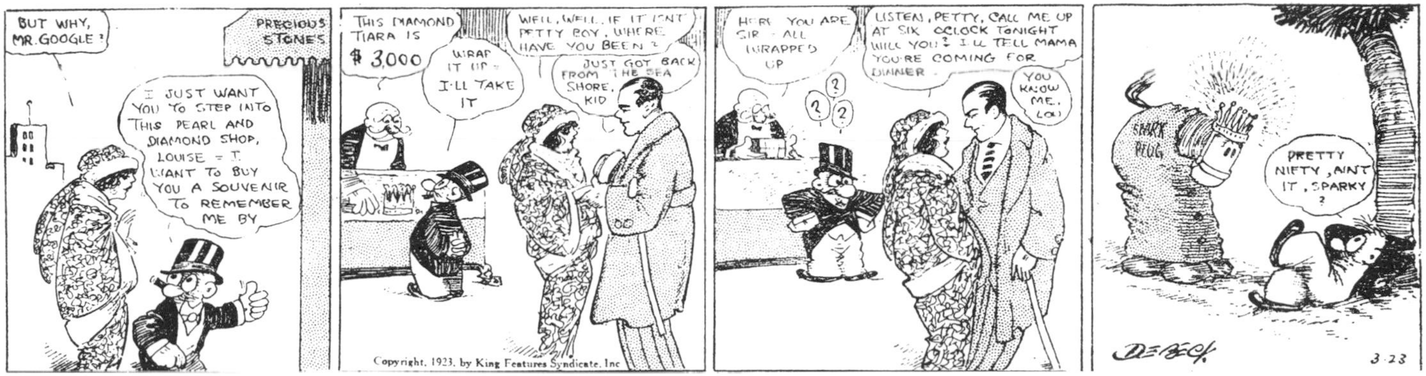
BUT WHY, MR. GOOGLE?
PRECIOUS STONES
I JUST WANT YOU TO STEP INTO THIS PEARL AND DIAMOND SHOP, LOUISE = I WANT TO BUY YOU A SOUVENIR TO REMEMBER ME BY
THIS DIAMOND TIARA IS $ 3,000
WRAP IT UP = I'LL TAKE IT
WELL, WELL, IF IT ISN'T PETTY BOY, WHERE HAVE YOU BEEN?
JUST GOT BACK FROM THE SEA SHORE, KID
Copyright, 1923, by King Features Syndicate, Inc
HERE YOU ARE SIR - ALL WRAPPED UP
? ? ?
LISTEN, PETTY, CALL ME UP AT SIX O'CLOCK TONIGHT WILL YOU? I'LL TELL MAMA YOU'RE COMING FOR DINNER
YOU KNOW ME, LOU
SPARK PLUG
PRETTY NIFTY, AIN'T IT, SPARKY ?
DEBECK
3-23

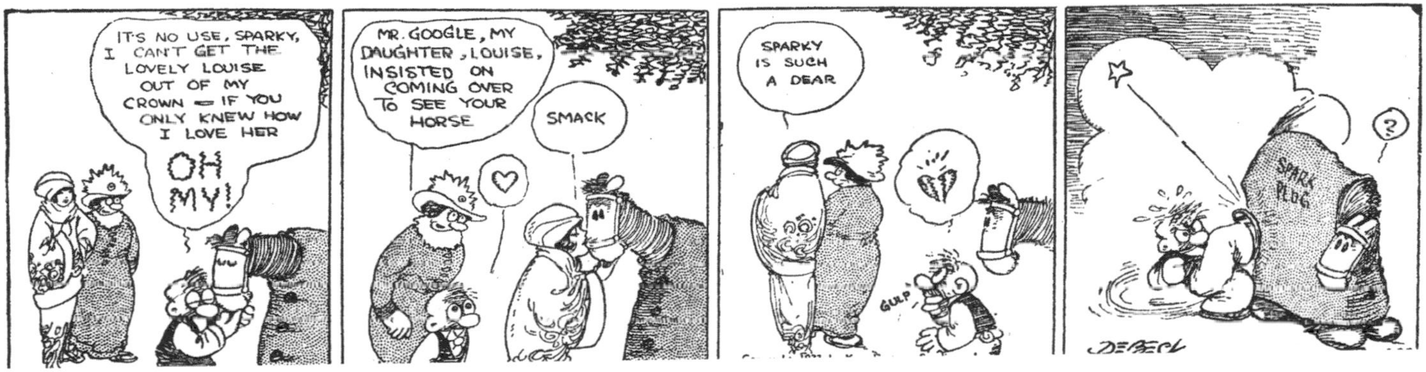
IT'S NO USE, SPARKY, I CAN'T GET THE LOVELY LOUISE OUT OF MY CROWN = IF YOU ONLY KNEW HOW I LOVE HER
OH MY!
MR. GOOGLE, MY DAUGHTER, LOUISE, INSISTED ON COMING OVER TO SEE YOUR HORSE
SMACK
SPARKY IS SUCH A DEAR
GULP
SPARK PLUG
?
DEBECK

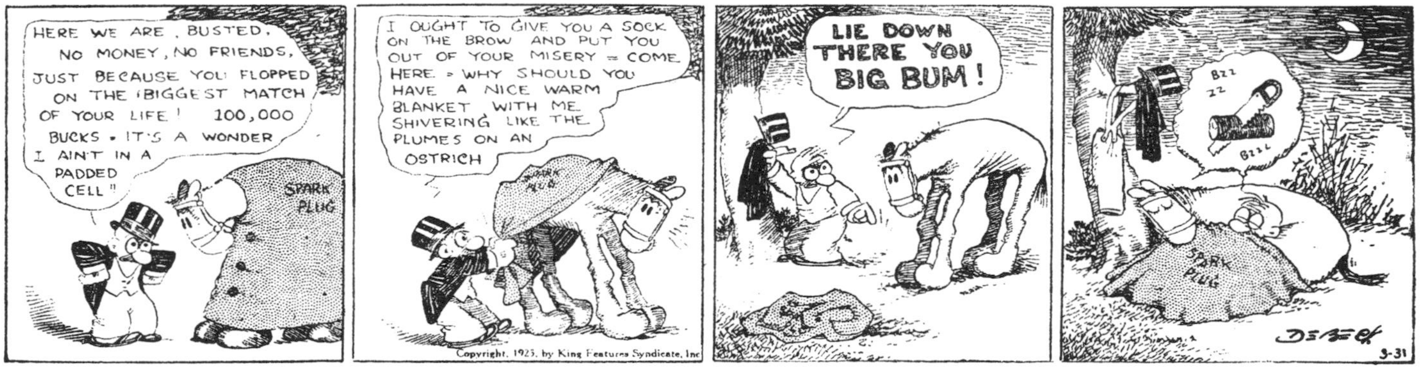
HERE WE ARE, BUSTED, NO MONEY, NO FRIENDS, JUST BECAUSE YOU FLOPPED ON THE BIGGEST MATCH OF YOUR LIFE! 100,000 BUCKS - IT'S A WONDER I AIN'T IN A PADDED CELL"
SPARK PLUG
I OUGHT TO GIVE YOU A SOCK ON THE BROW AND PUT YOU OUT OF YOUR MISERY = COME HERE = WHY SHOULD YOU HAVE A NICE WARM BLANKET WITH ME SHIVERING LIKE THE PLUMES ON AN OSTRICH
SPARK PLUG
Copyright, 1923, by King Features Syndicate, Inc
LIE DOWN THERE YOU BIG BUM!
BZZ ZZ BZZZ
SPARK PLUG
DEBECK
3-31

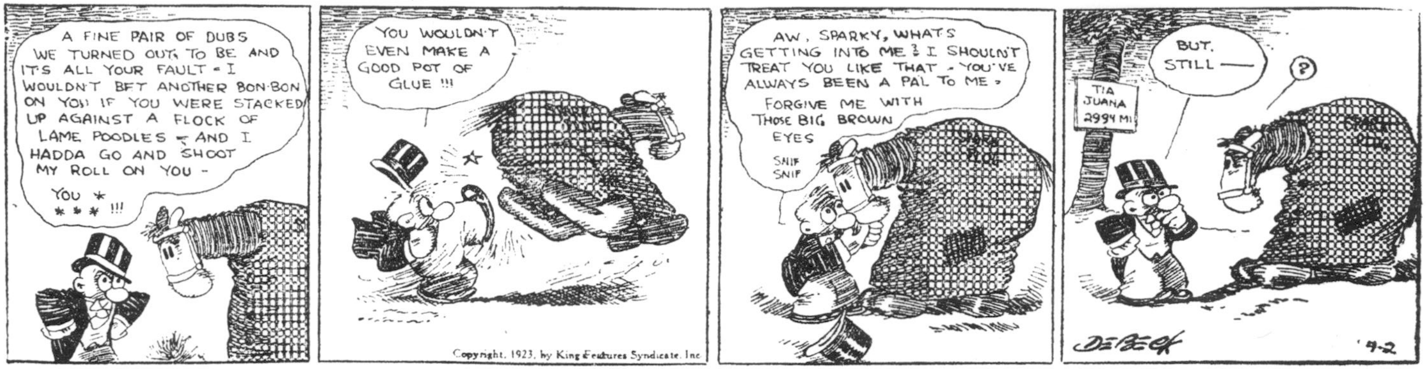
A FINE PAIR OF DUBS WE TURNED OUT TO BE AND IT'S ALL YOUR FAULT - I WOULDN'T BET ANOTHER BON-BON ON YOU IF YOU WERE STACKED UP AGAINST A FLOCK OF LAME POODLES - AND I HADDA GO AND SHOOT MY ROLL ON YOU -
YOU * * * * !!!
YOU WOULDN'T EVEN MAKE A GOOD POT OF GLUE !!!
AW, SPARKY, WHAT'S GETTING INTO ME? I SHOULN'T TREAT YOU LIKE THAT - YOU'VE ALWAYS BEEN A PAL TO ME -
FORGIVE ME WITH THOSE BIG BROWN EYES
SNIF SNIF
TIA JUANA 2994 MI
BUT, STILL —
?
DE BECK
4-2

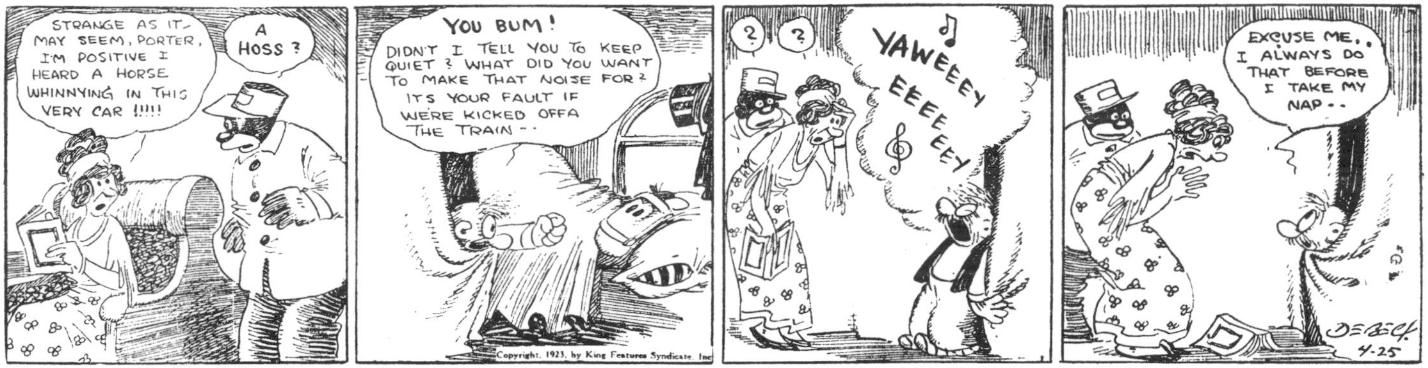
STRANGE AS IT MAY SEEM, PORTER, I'M POSITIVE I HEARD A HORSE WHINNYING IN THIS VERY CAR !!!!!
A HOSS ?
YOU BUM!
DIDN'T I TELL YOU TO KEEP QUIET ? WHAT DID YOU WANT TO MAKE THAT NOISE FOR ? IT'S YOUR FAULT IF WE'RE KICKED OFFA THE TRAIN - -
? ?
YAWEEEEY EEEEEEY
EXCUSE ME, I ALWAYS DO THAT BEFORE I TAKE MY NAP - -
DE BECK
4-25

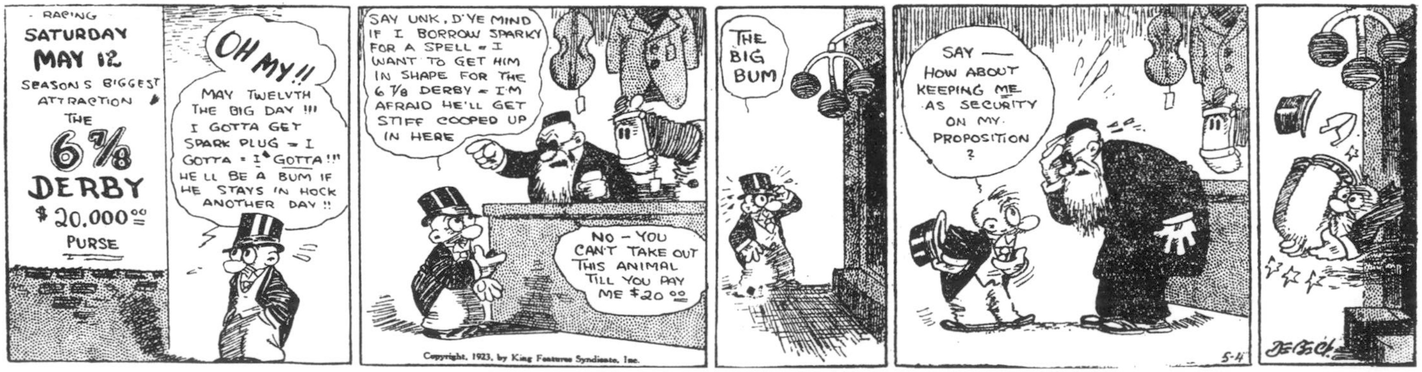
RACING
SATURDAY MAY 12
SEASON'S BIGGEST ATTRACTION
THE 6 7/8 DERBY
$20,000.00 PURSE
OH MY!!
MAY TWELVTH THE BIG DAY !!! I GOTTA GET SPARK PLUG - I GOTTA - I GOTTA !!! HE'LL BE A BUM IF HE STAYS IN HOCK ANOTHER DAY !!
SAY UNK, D'YE MIND IF I BORROW SPARKY FOR A SPELL - I WANT TO GET HIM IN SHAPE FOR THE 6 7/8 DERBY - I'M AFRAID HE'LL GET STIFF COOPED UP IN HERE
NO - YOU CAN'T TAKE OUT THIS ANIMAL TILL YOU PAY ME $20.00
THE BIG BUM
SAY — HOW ABOUT KEEPING ME AS SECURITY ON MY PROPOSITION ?
5-4
DE BECK

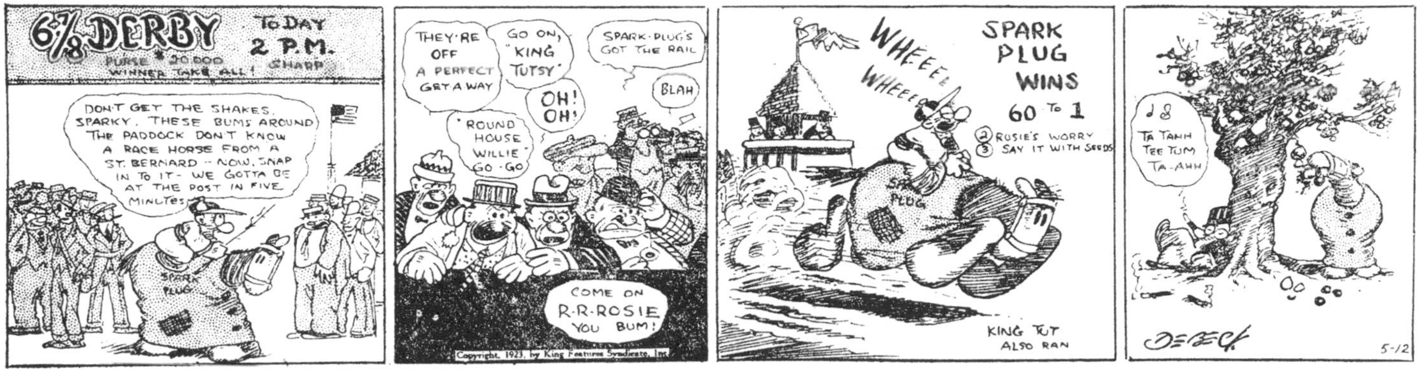
6 7/8 DERBY
TO-DAY 2 P.M. SHARP
PURSE $20,000 WINNER TAKE ALL!
DON'T GET THE SHAKES, SPARKY, THESE BUMS AROUND THE PADDOCK DON'T KNOW A RACE HORSE FROM A ST. BERNARD - NOW, SNAP IN TO IT - WE GOTTA BE AT THE POST IN FIVE MINUTES
SPARK PLUG
THEY'RE OFF A PERFECT GET A WAY
GO ON, "KING TUTSY"
OH! OH!
SPARK-PLUG'S GOT THE RAIL
BLAH
"ROUND HOUSE WILLIE" GO-GO
COME ON R-R-ROSIE YOU BUM!
Copyright, 1923, by King Features Syndicate, Inc.
WHEEEEE
WHEEEE
SPARK PLUG WINS 60 TO 1
② ROSIE'S WORRY
③ SAY IT WITH SEEDS
SPARK PLUG
KING TUT ALSO RAN
TA TANH TEE TUM TA-AHH
DEBECK
5-12

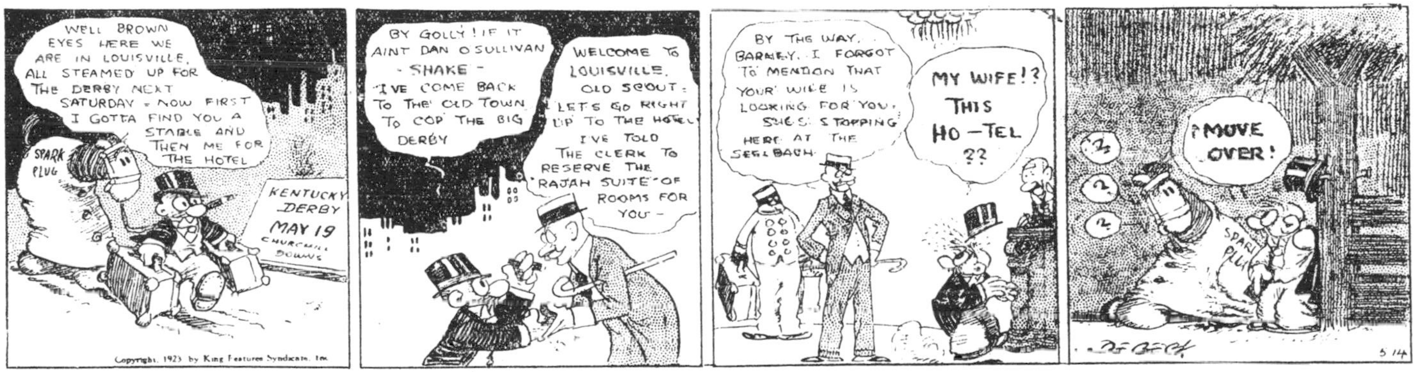
WELL BROWN EYES HERE WE ARE IN LOUISVILLE, ALL STEAMED UP FOR THE DERBY NEXT SATURDAY - NOW FIRST I GOTTA FIND YOU A STABLE AND THEN ME FOR THE HOTEL
SPARK PLUG
KENTUCKY DERBY MAY 19 CHURCHILL DOWNS
Copyright, 1923, by King Features Syndicate, Inc.
BY GOLLY! IF IT AINT DAN O'SULLIVAN - SHAKE - I'VE COME BACK TO THE OLD TOWN TO COP THE BIG DERBY
WELCOME TO LOUISVILLE, OLD SCOUT: LET'S GO RIGHT UP TO THE HOTEL I'VE TOLD THE CLERK TO RESERVE THE "RAJAH SUITE" OF ROOMS FOR YOU -
BY THE WAY, BARNEY, I FORGOT TO MENTION THAT YOUR WIFE IS LOOKING FOR YOU, SHE'S STOPPING HERE AT THE SEELBACH
MY WIFE!? THIS HO-TEL ??
MOVE OVER!
SPARK PLUG
DEBECK
5-14

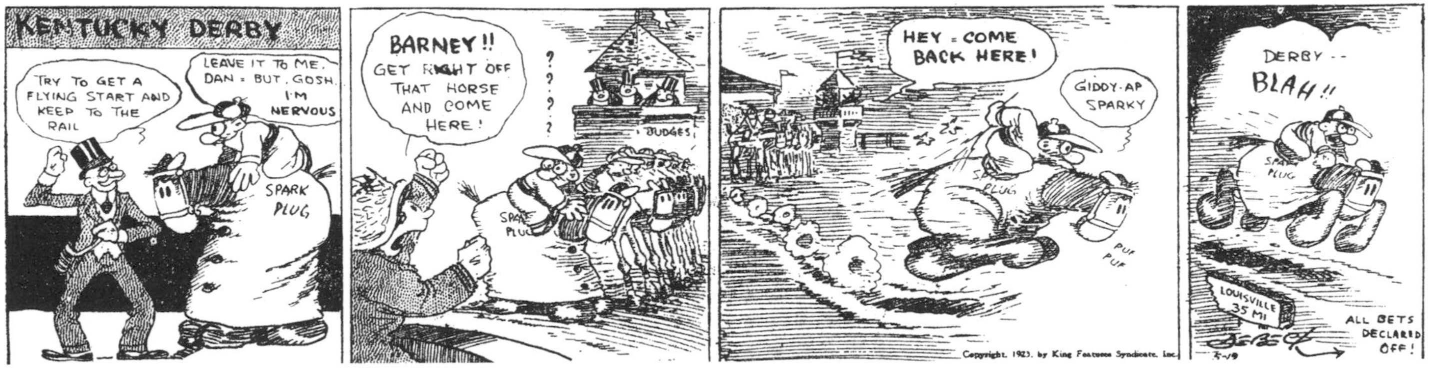
KENTUCKY DERBY
TRY TO GET A FLYING START AND KEEP TO THE RAIL
LEAVE IT TO ME, DAN - BUT, GOSH, I'M NERVOUS
SPARK PLUG
BARNEY!! GET RIGHT OFF THAT HORSE AND COME HERE!
? ? ? ?
JUDGES
SPARK PLUG
HEY - COME BACK HERE!
GIDDY-AP SPARKY
SPARK PLUG
PUF PUF
Copyright, 1923, by King Features Syndicate, Inc.
DERBY -- BLAH!!
SPARK PLUG
LOUISVILLE 35 MI
DEBECK
5-19
ALL BETS DECLARED OFF!

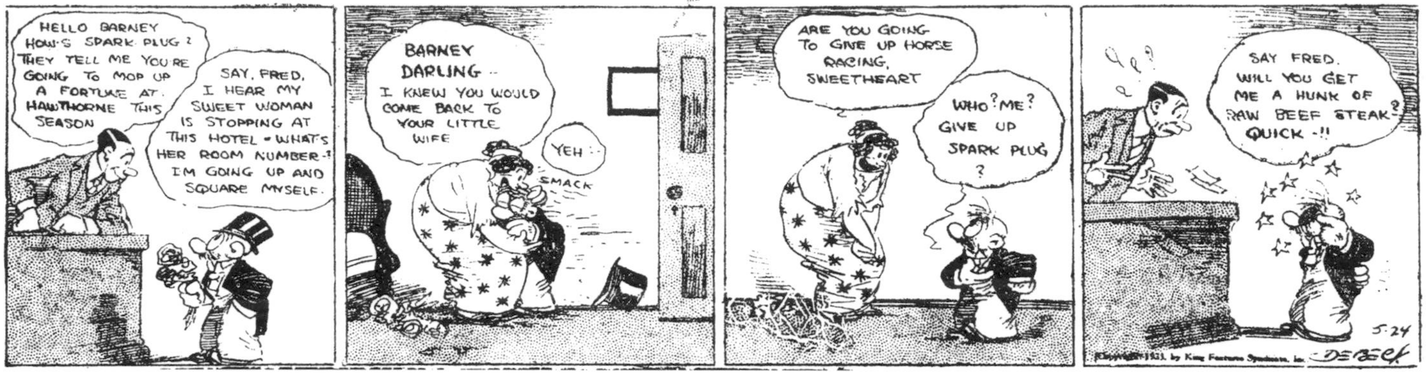
HELLO BARNEY HOW'S SPARK PLUG? THEY TELL ME YOU'RE GOING TO MOP UP A FORTUNE AT HAWTHORNE THIS SEASON
SAY, FRED, I HEAR MY SWEET WOMAN IS STOPPING AT THIS HOTEL - WHAT'S HER ROOM NUMBER -? I'M GOING UP AND SQUARE MYSELF.
BARNEY DARLING -- I KNEW YOU WOULD COME BACK TO YOUR LITTLE WIFE
YEH --
SMACK
ARE YOU GOING TO GIVE UP HORSE RACING, SWEETHEART
WHO? ME? GIVE UP SPARK PLUG ?
SAY FRED. WILL YOU GET ME A HUNK OF RAW BEEF STEAK? QUICK -!!
5-24
Copyright 1923, by King Features Syndicate, Inc.
DEBECK

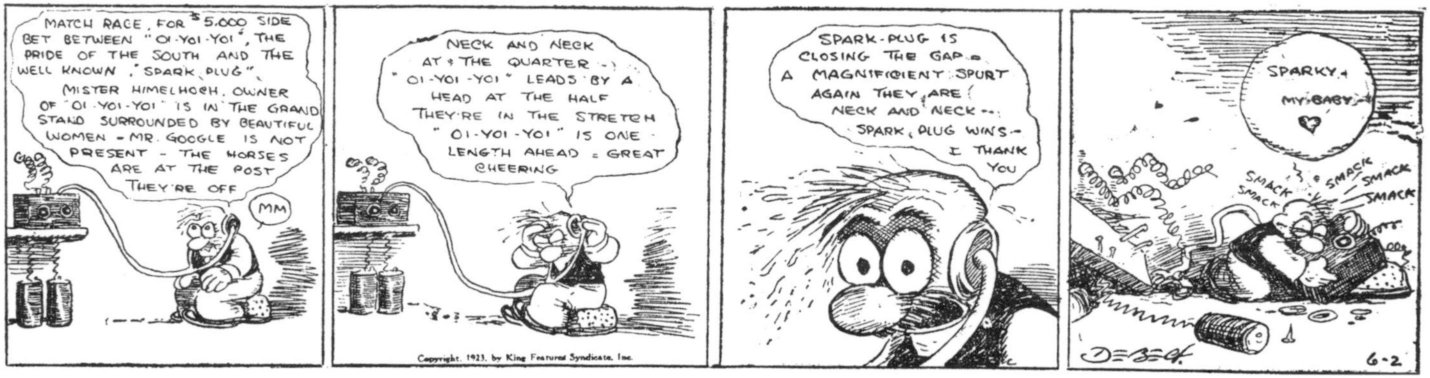
MATCH RACE, FOR $5,000 SIDE BET BETWEEN "OI-YOI-YOI", THE PRIDE OF THE SOUTH AND THE WELL KNOWN, "SPARK PLUG". MISTER HIMELHOCH, OWNER OF "OI-YOI-YOI" IS IN THE GRAND STAND SURROUNDED BY BEAUTIFUL WOMEN - MR. GOOGLE IS NOT PRESENT - THE HORSES ARE AT THE POST THEY'RE OFF
MM
NECK AND NECK AT THE QUARTER -- "OI-YOI-YOI" LEADS BY A HEAD AT THE HALF THEY'RE IN THE STRETCH "OI-YOI-YOI" IS ONE LENGTH AHEAD - GREAT CHEERING
Copyright, 1923, by King Features Syndicate, Inc.
SPARK-PLUG IS CLOSING THE GAP - A MAGNIFICENT SPURT AGAIN THEY ARE NECK AND NECK -- SPARK PLUG WINS - I THANK YOU
SPARKY - MY BABY
SMACK
SMACK
SMACK
SMACK
SMACK
DEBECK
6-2

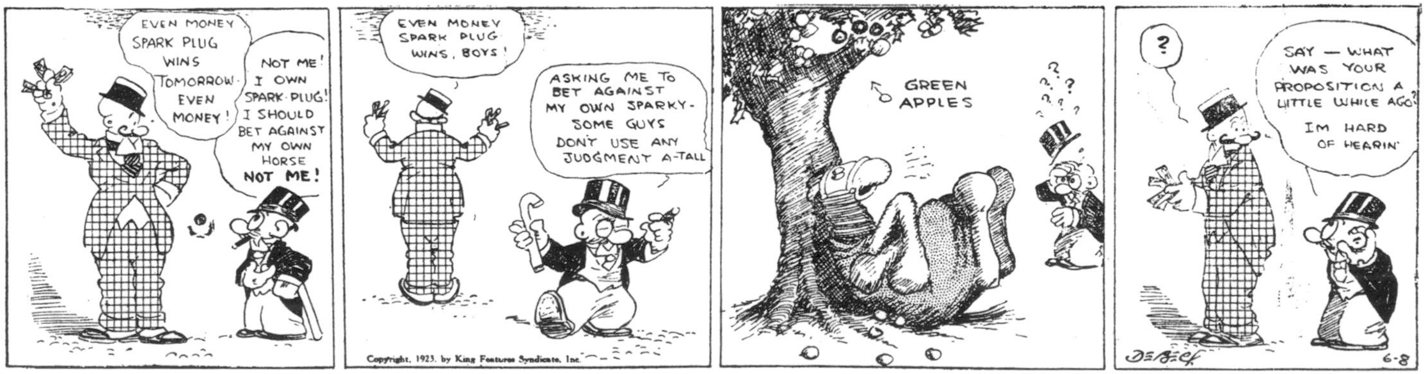
EVEN MONEY SPARK PLUG WINS TOMORROW - EVEN MONEY!
NOT ME! I OWN SPARK PLUG! I SHOULD BET AGAINST MY OWN HORSE NOT ME!
EVEN MONEY SPARK PLUG WINS, BOYS!
ASKING ME TO BET AGAINST MY OWN SPARKY - SOME GUYS DON'T USE ANY JUDGMENT A-TALL
Copyright, 1923, by King Features Syndicate, Inc.
GREEN APPLES
?
SAY — WHAT WAS YOUR PROPOSITION A LITTLE WHILE AGO? I'M HARD OF HEARIN'
DEBECK
6-8

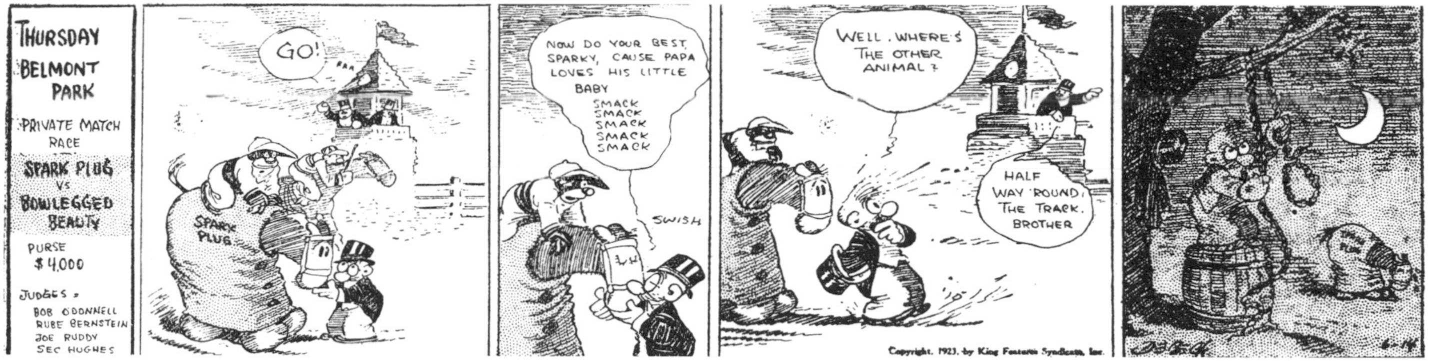
THURSDAY
BELMONT PARK
PRIVATE MATCH RACE
SPARK PLUG VS BOWLEGGED BEAUTY
PURSE $4,000
JUDGES =
BOB O'DONNELL
RUBE BERNSTEIN
JOE RUDDY
SEC HUGHES
GO!
SPARK PLUG
NOW DO YOUR BEST, SPARKY, CAUSE PAPA LOVES HIS LITTLE BABY
SMACK SMACK SMACK SMACK SMACK
SWISH
WELL, WHERE'S THE OTHER ANIMAL?
HALF WAY 'ROUND THE TRACK, BROTHER
Copyright, 1923, by King Features Syndicate, Inc.
DEBECK

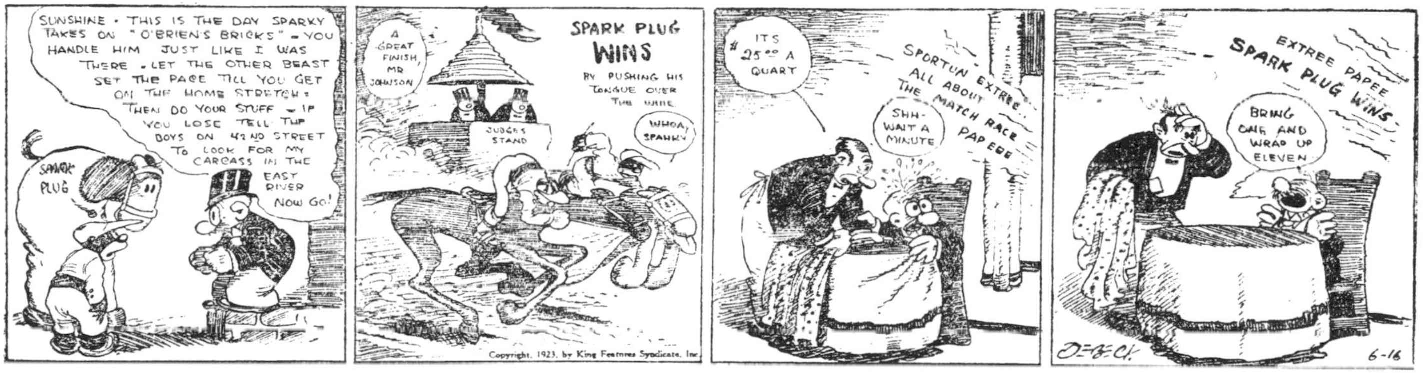
SUNSHINE - THIS IS THE DAY SPARKY TAKES ON "O'BRIEN'S BRICKS" - YOU HANDLE HIM JUST LIKE I WAS THERE - LET THE OTHER BEAST SET THE PACE TILL YOU GET ON THE HOME STRETCH = THEN DO YOUR STUFF - IF YOU LOSE TELL THE BOYS ON 42ND STREET TO LOOK FOR MY CARCASS IN THE EAST RIVER NOW GO!
SPARK PLUG
A GREAT FINISH, MR JOHNSON
SPARK PLUG WINS
BY PUSHING HIS TONGUE OVER THE WIRE
JUDGES STAND
WHOA, SPARKY
Copyright, 1923, by King Features Syndicate, Inc.
ITS $25.00 A QUART
SPORTUN EXTREE. ALL ABOUT THE MATCH RACE PAPEEE
SHH-WAIT A MINUTE
EXTREE PAPEE SPARK PLUG WINS.
BRING ONE AND WRAP UP ELEVEN
DEBECK
6-16

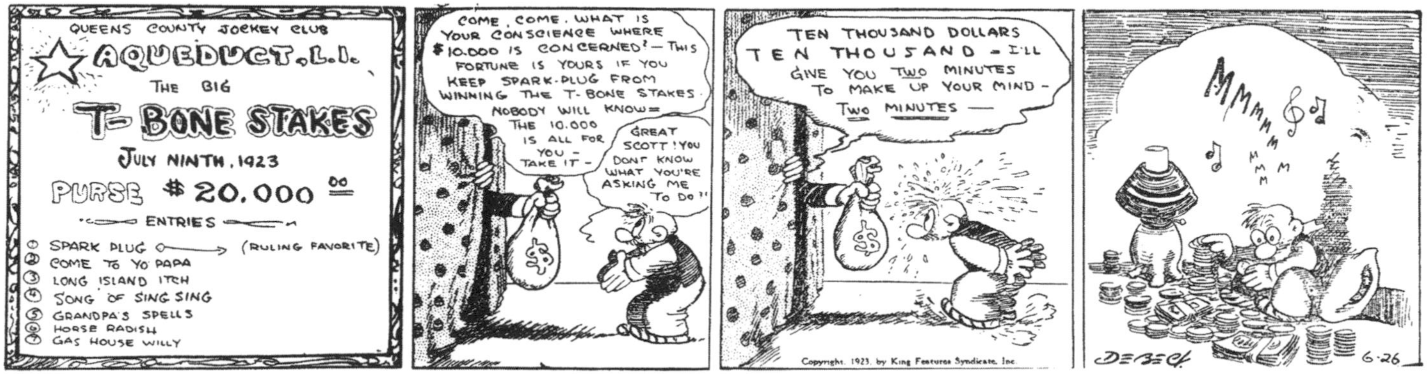
QUEENS COUNTY JOCKEY CLUB
AQUEDUCT, L.I.
THE BIG
T-BONE STAKES
JULY NINTH, 1923
PURSE $20.000.00
ENTRIES
① SPARK PLUG (RULING FAVORITE)
② COME TO YO PAPA
③ LONG ISLAND ITCH
④ SONG OF SING SING
⑤ GRANDPA'S SPELLS
⑥ HORSE RADISH
⑦ GAS HOUSE WILLY
COME, COME, WHAT IS YOUR CONSCIENCE WHERE $10,000 IS CONCERNED? - THIS FORTUNE IS YOURS IF YOU KEEP SPARK-PLUG FROM WINNING THE T-BONE STAKES. NOBODY WILL KNOW = THE 10,000 IS ALL FOR YOU - TAKE IT -
GREAT SCOTT! YOU DONT KNOW WHAT YOU'RE ASKING ME TO DO?!
TEN THOUSAND DOLLARS TEN THOUSAND - I'LL GIVE YOU TWO MINUTES TO MAKE UP YOUR MIND - TWO MINUTES —
Copyright, 1923, by King Features Syndicate, Inc.
MMMMM MMMMM
DEBECK
6-26

Defending the Indefensible
by R. Fiore

The Ten Cent Plague: The Great Comic-Book Scare and How it Changed America
David Hajdu
Farrar, Straus & Giroux
448 pp., $26.00
Hardcover
ISBN: 9780374187675

Fredric Wertham and the Critique of Mass Culture
Bart Beaty
University Press of Mississippi
238 pp., $22.00
Softcover
ISBN: 9780374187675

When history becomes folklore, one construction often put on events is "It Never Would Have Happened If It Wasn't For That Lousy Guy." Popular configurations include "If it wasn't for Charles Darwin, everybody would still believe in God," or "If it wasn't for Alfred Kinsey there wouldn't have been a sexual revolution," or "If it wasn't for Dr. Spock these kids wouldn't be running wild," or the case in point here, "If it wasn't for Dr. Fredric Wertham we never would have had the Comics Code." As memory of the facts faded, the idea that Wertham singlehandedly concocted a witch hunt against comics out of thin air had a strong appeal to those of us who wanted to see it simply as a matter of freedom of expression crushed by the forces of repression. In *The Ten Cent Plague* of David Hajdu (a prepared mind that fortune has favored), Dr. Wertham comes across for all his prominence as a dispensable character in the comic-book pogrom of the '50s. As Hajdu informs us, the anti-comics campaign was a broad-based movement, encompassing the government, the press (daily, weekly and monthly; lowbrow, middlebrow and intel-

lectual), churches, civic groups and individual activists, a movement that had a full-scale dry run, including a Senate Judiciary Committee investigation before Wertham came to the forefront. Because Wertham emerged as their most effective spokesman, the movement used him; if he hadn't been there, they would have gotten along without him, and the outcome would have been the same. To the extent Wertham's agenda differed from the movement as a whole it was ignored. If there was an indispensable man it was Senator Estes Kefauver. Or William M. Gaines. Hajdu makes the telling point that the *New York Times* account of the 1954 subcommittee hearing before which they both appeared devoted one paragraph to Wertham's testimony and 13 to Gaines'.

The Ten Cent Plague leapt to the covers of the nation's book-review sections faster and more prolifically than any book about comics since, well, I imagine, *Seduction of the Innocent*, an outcome I doubt anyone involved could have guessed. Speaking from the perspective of Nerdistan I looked in vain for something to object to in it. It represents the opposite end of the spectrum from the typical journalistic treatment of comics. Instead of superficiality under cover of either glib cynicism or obeisance to the hot subject of the day, you find a reporter's zeal for separating fact from legend and getting to the primary source. For example, in recounting the anecdote of Charles Biro being inspired to invent true crime comics by a newspaper story, Hajdu tracks down the newspaper story Biro referred to and notes that it was printed 10 years too late. (It no doubt helped that the story was in *The New York Times*, but still.) It's the medium's good fortune that the one book about comic books the general reader is most likely to read is not only an exhaustive history of the immediate subject but a well-informed and conscientiously researched history of the medium from its beginnings. The one fault I found was that it perpetuates the miscon-

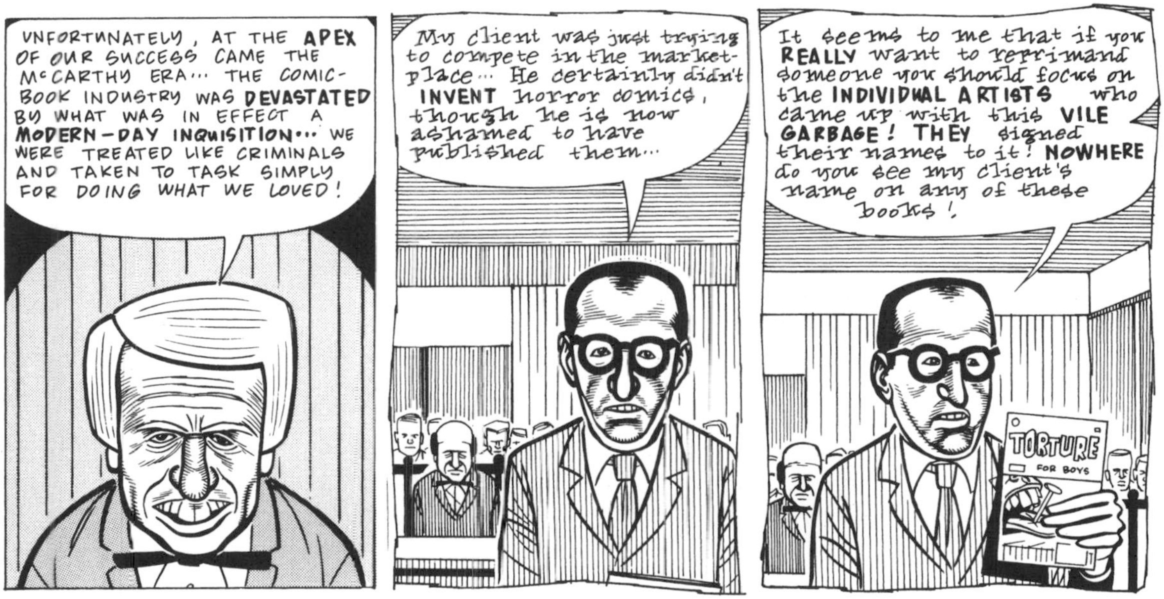
UNFORTUNATELY, AT THE APEX OF OUR SUCCESS CAME THE McCARTHY ERA... THE COMIC-BOOK INDUSTRY WAS DEVASTATED BY WHAT WAS IN EFFECT A MODERN-DAY INQUISITION... WE WERE TREATED LIKE CRIMINALS AND TAKEN TO TASK SIMPLY FOR DOING WHAT WE LOVED!
My client was just trying to compete in the market-place... He certainly didn't INVENT horror comics, though he is now ashamed to have published them...
It seems to me that if you REALLY want to reprimand someone you should focus on the INDIVIDUAL ARTISTS who came up with this VILE GARBAGE! THEY signed their names to it! NOWHERE do you see my client's name on any of these books!
TORTURE
FOR BOYS

From *Pussey!* by Dan Clowes. [©2006 Daniel G. Clowes]

ception of the role of humor in early comic books, which was far more significant than people imagine it was, not only in comics devoted to gags but humorous backup strips in adventure comics. In this, Hadju may just be reflecting the biases of the many cartoonists he interviewed who come mostly from the adventure end of the business. This is, in any case, a disappointment of rising expectations engendered by the unexpected breadth and depth of the book. I would also note the list of individuals who never worked in comic books again after the purge is impressive in its length but perhaps a bit padded with people who were on their way to better things (H.L. Gold, who was going to become one of the most influential science-fiction editors) or were somewhat tangentially involved with comic books (Otto Messmer).

Hajdu's point that the suppression of horror comics was based more on mainstream taste than any legitimate proof that they did harm is true but beside the point. Horror comics were genuine outlaw art, and when you're producing genuine outlaw art you shouldn't be surprised if the cops come after you. Wertham's pseudoscience was ultimately beside the point, because the content of horror comics was so far into the red zone that nobody had to look at the instruments. You imagine an average person of the time having his opinion solicited ...

"Sir, I wonder if you'd take a look at this comic book and tell me ..."

"OH MY GOD, THAT'S THE MOST DISGUSTING THING I'VE EVER SEEN IN MY LIFE!"

"But the question I really wanted to ask was ..."

"WHAT KIND OF SICK, DISEASED MIND COULD HAVE CONCEIVED OF SUCH FILTH ..."

"No, this is one of the better ones, this is *Haunt of Fear* ..."

"THAT MAN HAS AN AXE STICKING OUT OF HIS HEAD!"

"Leaving aside questions of taste, do you believe children reading this would ..."

"CHILDREN! THEY SELL THIS TO CHILDREN? WHO THE HELL IS BEHIND THIS, THE MAFIA?"

The insurmountable problem that faced the defenders of horror comics was that while the charges against them exaggerated to an absurd degree, when you stripped away the exaggeration the reality was hardly more acceptable to mainstream morals. I'm going to discuss EC and William M. Gaines primarily in part because I've read all of the EC comics and none of the others, in part because they were the ones that truly mattered. EC fans will sometimes claim that it wasn't really EC that brought down the wrath of God but his less scrupulous imitators. This, I believe, is a reassuring myth. Not only were EC comics enough to bring out the torches by themselves, but, from what I've seen in the others, the execution doesn't match the depravity. In my book, Johnny Craig made them all look like amateurs.

The position of Gaines and the lesser horror-comics

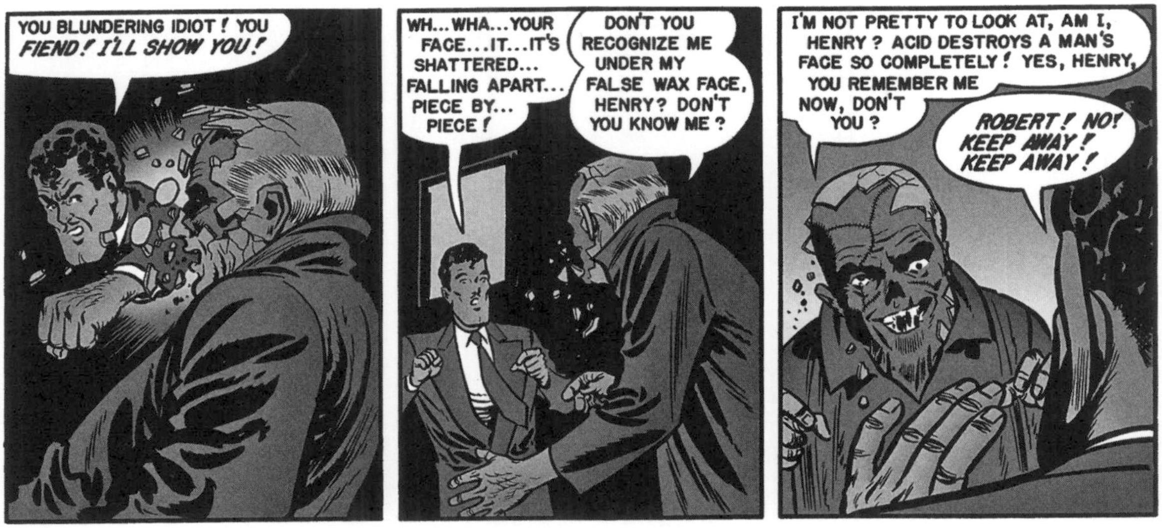
YOU BLUNDERING IDIOT! YOU FIEND! I'LL SHOW YOU!
WH...WHA...YOUR FACE...IT...IT'S SHATTERED... FALLING APART... PIECE BY... PIECE!
DON'T YOU RECOGNIZE ME UNDER MY FALSE WAX FACE, HENRY? DON'T YOU KNOW ME?
I'M NOT PRETTY TO LOOK AT, AM I, HENRY? ACID DESTROYS A MAN'S FACE SO COMPLETELY! YES, HENRY, YOU REMEMBER ME NOW, DON'T YOU?
ROBERT! NO! KEEP AWAY! KEEP AWAY!

This sequence is from Johnny Craig's "Portrait in Wax!" in *The Vault of Horror* #12 (April-May 1950). [©2007 William M. Gaines, Agent, Inc.]

publishers was indefensible because their business depended on freely selling their goods to children. The necessary first step in overthrowing the censorship regime was to get children out of the picture. In the political and social context of the 1950s it's irrelevant whether any children were ever actually harmed or juvenile delinquency was caused by horror comics. Parents have authority over their children, and for a time are granted the privilege of making decisions for them. Given their authority the standard a parent will apply for what is appropriate for children is mostly a common-sense judgment call not subject to proof. If you believe that some things should be forbidden to children, as almost everybody does, then EC-style horror comics would almost certainly fall within the area of things you forbid. I myself am happy to leave the question of what is to be forbidden to children to people who have them. It's not a duty I relish. I think one reason the suppression of horror comics took place is that parents genuinely do want their children to be able to choose their own amusements, and they don't want to have to monitor everything they bring into the house. They expect the producers of children's entertainment to assume parental responsibility. I also think one reason the campaign against comics became so hysterical was frustration at its initial failure of the first impulse. It must have come as quite a shock to discover they were living in a free country.

Gaines did not assume parental responsibility. Gaines instead became a collaborator with his young readers in their momentary escape from the sheltered existence they were enjoying. Contrary to the folk belief, there are ways in which children are less sensitive than adults. When you're young and you're not suffering, yourself suffering in an abstraction. As you begin to understand that suffering is real the macabre comedy of EC horror becomes distasteful. (As the comedian Steve Martin pointed out, you lose your ability to make jokes about cancer when you've seen people you know die from it.) Seeing the material from an adult point of view, parents imagined the comic books were robbing their children of their innocence; in reality the children's response came from their innocence, and it was experience that would make them grow out of it.

I think we have to allow that Gaines must bear a large portion of the blame for the pogrom. It's hard to believe that a reasonably prudent businessman, knowing the general mores of his time and the willingness of his society to apply censorship, observing the level of censorship in every form of commercial entertainment around him, having seen a much milder product inspire book burnings, government investigations, the passing of anti-comics legislation and the arrest of newsdealers, would not realize that something as morbid and grotesque as EC's New Trend was going to bring down the wrath of the nation. The Seduction of the Innocent was followed by the Suppression of the Naïve. In contrast, the publishers of crime comics comported themselves as if they knew they were doing something illicit. They emblazoned every page with a disclaimer along the lines of CRIME DOES NOT PAY, as if they were already preparing their defense statement.

("As will soon become crystal clear to the members of the jury, when my client walked into the First National Bank with a sub-machinegun in his hands, robbery was the last thing on his mind …") You can see in Gaines' testimony a premonition of the trials of Lenny Bruce. Like Lenny, beating the rap wasn't enough for him; he wanted to be exonerated, and it cost him dearly.

So, granting Gaines' share of the blame, granting that the result was in effect the infantilization of the medium and the end of the possibility that commercial comics might grow up with its readership, was this short-lived exercise of freedom worth it? The comic book in its early days was a mountain of dross with veins of gold running through it. Most of those veins were, if the truth were known, in the kid's-humor segment of the industry that was least affected by the Code. Commercially, comic books were a perfect combination of an undemanding audience and an industry with the lack of talent required to satisfy it. Pick 10 comic books at random off the rack and in all likelihood all 10 would be lousy — or not quite good enough. The greatest weakness was writing. The major problem was that a writer good enough to write a good comic book was good enough to get work that was more prestigious and rewarding, such as just about anything else. In most cases, you got good comic books when a good cartoonist also happened to be a good writer. The baseline level of writing in EC comics was head and shoulders above the ordinary level of comic books, perhaps because the baseline writing was being done by a cartoonist who was a decent writer. Therefore the artists, who were excellent on their own terms, had their work buoyed by compelling stories rather than dragged down by listless ones, as

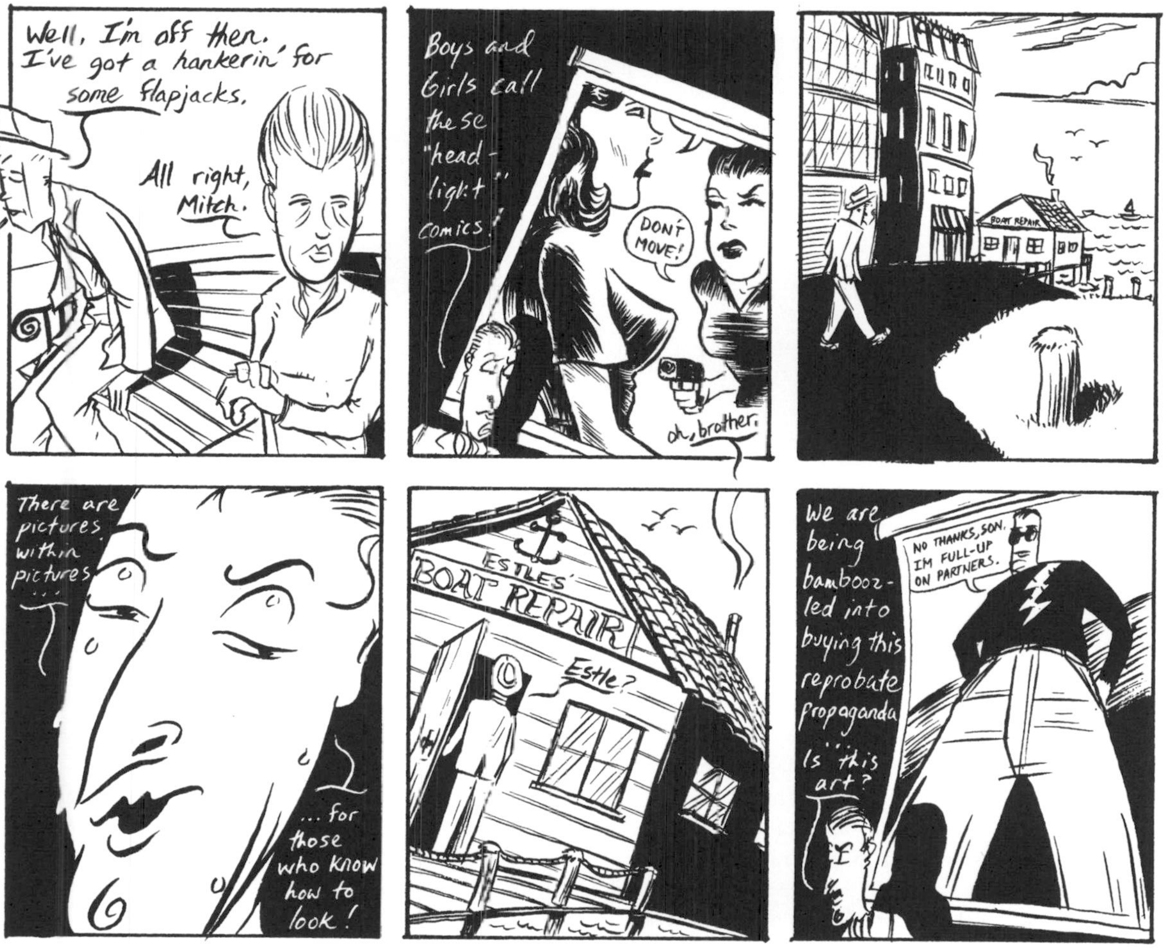
Well, I'm off then. I've got a hankerin' for some flapjacks.
All right, Mitch.
Boys and Girls call these "head-light" comics!
DON'T MOVE!
oh, brother.
BOAT REPAIR
There are pictures within pictures...
... for those who know how to look!
ESTLES' BOAT REPAIR
Estle?
We are being bamboozled into buying this reprobate propaganda.. Is this art?
NO THANKS, SON. I'M FULL-UP ON PARTNERS.

From *Pistolwhip: The Yellow Menace*, written by Jason Hall and drawn by Matt Kindt. [©2002 Jason Hall and Matt Kindt]

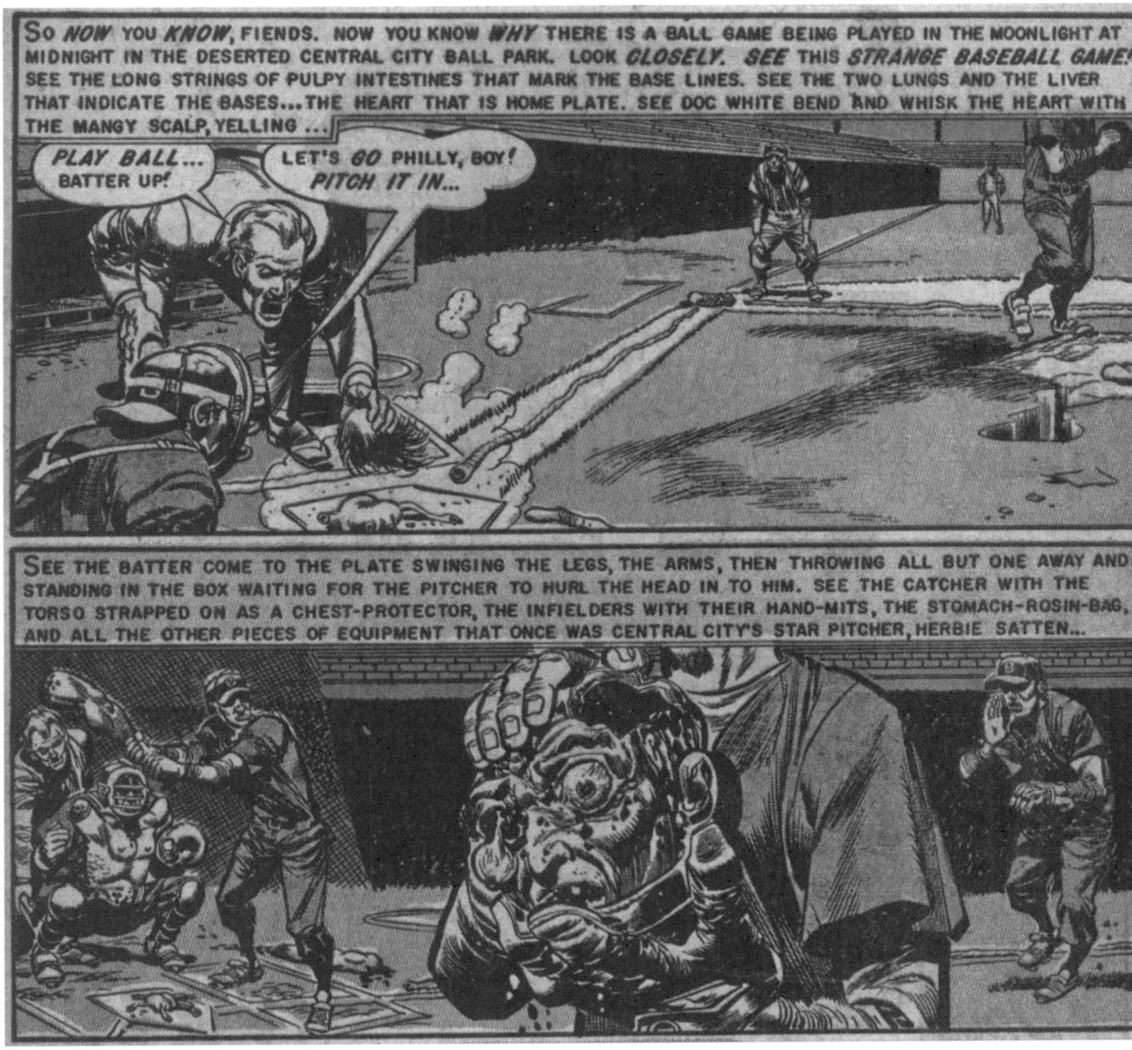
SO NOW YOU KNOW, FIENDS. NOW YOU KNOW WHY THERE IS A BALL GAME BEING PLAYED IN THE MOONLIGHT AT MIDNIGHT IN THE DESERTED CENTRAL CITY BALL PARK. LOOK CLOSELY. SEE THIS STRANGE BASEBALL GAME! SEE THE LONG STRINGS OF PULPY INTESTINES THAT MARK THE BASE LINES. SEE THE TWO LUNGS AND THE LIVER THAT INDICATE THE BASES...THE HEART THAT IS HOME PLATE. SEE DOC WHITE BEND AND WHISK THE HEART WITH THE MANGY SCALP, YELLING ...
PLAY BALL... BATTER UP!
LET'S GO PHILLY, BOY! PITCH IT IN...
SEE THE BATTER COME TO THE PLATE SWINGING THE LEGS, THE ARMS, THEN THROWING ALL BUT ONE AWAY AND STANDING IN THE BOX WAITING FOR THE PITCHER TO HURL THE HEAD IN TO HIM. SEE THE CATCHER WITH THE TORSO STRAPPED ON AS A CHEST-PROTECTOR, THE INFIELDERS WITH THEIR HAND-MITS, THE STOMACH-ROSIN-BAG, AND ALL THE OTHER PIECES OF EQUIPMENT THAT ONCE WAS CENTRAL CITY'S STAR PITCHER, HERBIE SATTEN...

This sequence is from "Foul Play!" in *The Haunt of Fear* #19 (May-June 1953): written by Bill Gaines and Al Feldstein, and drawn by Jack Davis. [©2005 William M. Gaines, Agent, Inc.]

many of their sometimes very talented contemporaries were (it was one of the great creative tragedies that Alex Toth couldn't work with Harvey Kurtzman). I have to say at this point I really don't think the classic Al Feldstein EC story is good comics. They are generally overwritten in a way that constricts the artist from using the sequential medium (as opposed to single images) creatively, and the stories tend to become servants of their own gruesomeness. Take that emblematic EC horror story "Foul Play!," in which a baseball player kills a rival with poisoned spikes in order to win a championship and the murdered player's team takes its revenge by luring the murderer to a ballpark at midnight and playing a ballgame with his dismembered body parts. Leaving aside the question of taste, it's really difficult to see what satisfaction could be derived from this kind of revenge. Its purpose is not to achieve any goal of the characters but to titillate the reader.

Kurtzman is of course Exhibit 1 for the defense. It's not just that *Mad* was probably the best commercial comic book ever published, and that his war comics are undeniably in the top 10, and that EC is the only company that would have given him the autonomy to do that work. It is that only in the pages of EC comics can you see a significant portion his work unmediated by collaborators, and Kurtzman was one of the greatest visual storytellers in the history of comics, and only EC would have ever given him the autonomy he needed to do his best work. Beyond Kurtzman, it's all gravy. The horror comics themselves produced one cartoonist of the first rank in Johnny Craig, then there's Bernie Krigstein, who never came near fully realizing his talent as a cartoonist in any other venue, and the adaptations of Ray Bradbury's stories, and all the other stray bits of inspiration that happen when they're encouraged. None of this happens without the horror comics, which are what made the company a going proposition, and the horror comics themselves are not without interest. There wouldn't have been horror comics if kids couldn't buy them. Leaving aside the wisdom of giving up real existing art for art that might have been, it is an open question whether in 30 years the adventure/thriller side the industry without the encumbrance of the Code would have produced as much good comics as EC published in five. Comic books were one of those bolt holes in a draconian censorship regime through which this kind of thing could escape. I believe having this freedom at this time was worth the risk to children, which I find negligible, and in the end I don't believe any children were harmed in the reading of these comic books.

What we see in *The Ten Cent Plague* is the censorship coalition firing on all cylinders, even as the engine was about to start breaking down. A key vulnerability is reliance on the Harm Principle as a rationale for censorship. The Harm Principle is not a neutral idea; rather, it is an idea conceived to create the widest freedom of expression possible. The censor who utilizes it stands the Harm Principle on its head, but even stood on its head, it's the wrong tool for the job. Just as blood sacrifice devolved into a cracker and a mouthful of wine, stringent self-censorship by producers devolved into rating systems enforced by retailers, and then into advisories enforced by no one. Through it all is the equivocal role played by commerce, a force I once personified as your waiter, Pierre Laissez-Faire. Pierre does not consider consequences or pass judgment, he merely raises an eyebrow as he says, "But of course, sir." A society might think long and hard about treating children as consumers. Here we don't; we just do it. For my own part, I feel blessed to live in a time of almost total freedom of expression, and if it has to end, I hope it doesn't end until the day after I die.

It is a perversity of history that if it weren't for the infamy he acquired, the many undeniable good works of Dr. Fredric Wertham would have been forgotten. He was a genuine altruist and when the art was not commercial, not a proponent of censorship. If as I contend you have to make allowances when commonplace racial attitudes are expressed in the art of the past, you have to give all the more credit for someone who was ahead of his time and championed the rights of minorities when it couldn't do you a bit of good. I think it likely that his obsession with comic books as a cause of violence and mental-health threat had much to do with a desire to find a way to account for his patients' troubles unrelated to race or their upbringing. Particularly now that the Comics Code is a dead letter and the censorship coalition he did such service to a tattered remnant, it's easy to say that there's no ill he contributed to that wouldn't have happened without him, and so one need only give him credit for the good. The truth remains, however, that on its merits *Seduction of the Innocent* was a shameful performance, overreaching in its claims, hysterical in its tone, shoddy in its arguments and unscrupulous in exploiting the credence his credentials gave his pronouncements among the uninformed. Like a mirror image of the crank cancer cure that also turns out to be a crank AIDS cure, Wertham saw comics causing any social ill imaginable, from crime to

HE·MAN ADVENTURE
TWO-FISTED TALES
ENEMY SOLDIER!
No. 19
JAN-FEB.
10¢
HOLD IT KID! HE'S BEEN DEAD FOR HOURS!
THESE ROOKIES SURE GET NERVOUS FIRST TIME UNDER FIRE!

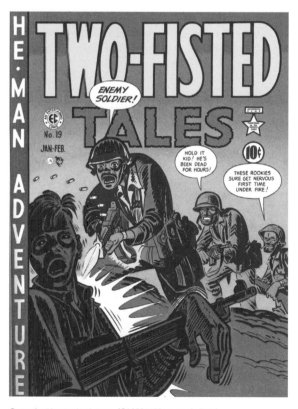

Cover by Harvey Kurtzman. [©1980 William M. Gaines]

segregation to fascism. That he made his arguments with complete conviction in their correctness is an extenuating circumstance, not a justification. An absolute conviction that windmills are giants doesn't give you the right to demolish windmills. You'd think it was the last thing you'd make a centerpiece to your attempt to rehabilitate Wertham, but it's not only history that's perverse. Bart Beaty, associate professor of communications at the University of Calgary, has chosen to base his case for Wertham, *Fredric Wertham and the Critique of Mass Culture*, on his least defensible point.

We can glean much of the quality of Beaty's thinking from his conclusion, which reads in part: "Ultimately, Fredric Wertham aligned himself with the most defenseless portion of postwar American society, children. His critics have aligned themselves with an industry that targeted racist, sexist and imperialist propaganda at minors. He was one man, operating out of a free clinic in Harlem, facing a multimillion-dollar-per-year-industry organization that hired private detectives to intimidate his staff. And yet comic-book fans, cultural commentators, and social scientists have sought to portray Wertham as the reckless destroyer of a powerless cottage industry."

Let's unpack this point by point:

Wertham aligned himself with the most defenseless portion of postwar American society … (1) In reality the helpless children were about as grateful to Dr. Wertham as the Polynesians were to the missionaries who freed them from immodesty. He wanted to take away the one form of entertainment that was shaped by their tastes. (2) Children were hardly at this time defenseless. They were the most sheltered generation in American history, with legions working full time for their purported welfare. (3) To "align" yourself with somebody is not the same thing as actually doing them any good. Comic-book publishers were aligned with children who wanted to read comic books and children were aligned with the comic-book publishers who provided them. (4) What "multimillion-dollar-per-year-industry organization" are we talking about? OK, I can field that one: It's a figment of Beaty's fact-mangling syntax. What he seems to mean is an organization backed by a multimillion-dollar industry, which one I'm not sure. If it's the Association of Comics Magazine Publishers, that wasn't backed by the entire industry but by EC, Lev Gleason, Hillman Periodicals, Harold Moore of *Famous Funnies* and Orbit Publications, not exactly the giants of the field. The giants of the industry only joined forces to capitulate.

His critics have aligned themselves with an industry that targeted racist, sexist and imperialist propaganda at minors. (1) This implies that one cannot find fault with Wertham's methods without endorsing those he opposes. See if you can find the hidden flaw in this logic. (2) What a comfort it must have been for the parents of America to know that thanks to Dr. Wertham they could listen to *Amos 'n' Andy* without fear that comic books were turning their children into racists. (3) The word "propaganda" implies a conscious effort to promote an agenda. To use this term to characterize racism, sexism and "imperialism" — I believe this is the radical word for "patriotism" — is, to use a term of art in the social sciences: bullshit. (In *Wikipedia* we find "Propaganda often presents facts selectively (thus lying by omission) to encourage a particular synthesis, or gives loaded messages in order to produce an emotional rather than rational response to the information presented." There's a picture of Fredric Wertham next to it.) Comic relief characters and Ooga Booga natives do not constitute a propaganda campaign for racism. The racism,

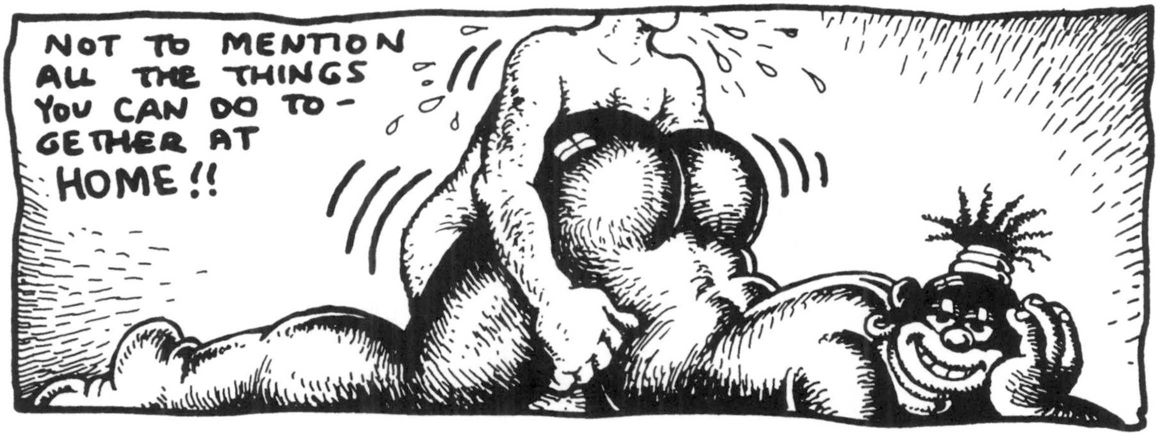
NOT TO MENTION ALL THE THINGS YOU CAN DO TO-GETHER AT HOME!!

Robert Crumb's Angelfood McSpade: from *Zap* #2 (June 1968). [©2004 Robert Crumb]

sexism and "imperialism" in comic books (though not the violence) were incidental to their agenda, which was to make a buck. Propaganda is a loaded word, used here because when you're committing emotional blackmail you want to go armed. (4) The usual excuse about "the standards of the times" is not quite accurate in this case. To say that comic books had an antisocial agenda is to suggest that comic books originated things. Comic books didn't originate things. Comic books stole.

He was one man, operating out of a free clinic in Harlem, facing a multimillion dollar per year industry ... (1) And I thought we'd just put the Wertham monomyth to rest. It's like an EC horror story. (2) He wasn't alone, he was one of a legion of activists that went from individuals to the highest levels of the government, who ultimately adopted a formal strategy of harassing, fining and imprisoning comics-selling newsdealers, and an informal personal campaign of socially ostracizing the people who created them. The comics industry was fragmented and its fragments turned against each other. (3) To identify one party as David and the other as Goliath is not to make any meaningful judgment on the relative merits of their positions.

Other chestnuts to be found in the conclusion: "*Ironically the 'adult age' of comic books arrived as comic book publishers adopted Wertham's suggestions. Wertham never advocated censorship but repeatedly called for age-appropriate labeling of comic books . . . In the 1960s artists such as Robert Crumb took exactly this route.*" This is a little like saying concentration-camp survivors who emigrated to Israel after the war were adopting Adolf Hitler's suggestion that the Jews be relocated out of Germany. Wertham's agenda was keeping comic books out of the hands of children, not to have even dirtier comic books (I can hardly imagine him relishing the idea that he made Angelfood McSpade possible), and the agenda of the cartoonists was to protect their work from the likes of Wertham, who didn't let the Adults Only label stop them. Or this: "*[T]he majority of comics produced in this period were overtly racist and sexist as well as gory and violent.*" I would like to know exactly what portion of his ass he pulled this figure out of. Is he seriously expecting us to believe that he has reviewed all of the 600-odd comics published per month and ascertained their content? Is he expecting us to believe this is even possible? Are we talking here by circulation or by title? And you would have to exclude EC comics, which while gory were not racist and, while displaying the kind of misogyny commonplace when marriage was a life sentence, were more generally misanthropic than sexist per se.

Repeated throughout the book is Beaty's belief that in some universe Wertham's claims have been proven. He is aided in this assertion by a near complete ignorance of what science is. For example, on page 199 he proclaims "Indeed there was — and is — no scientifically based counterargument to *Seduction of the Innocent*." There's a simple reason for this: It's not science. It does not state a hypothesis, make predictions based on this hypothesis, make a good-faith effort to filter out the biases of the researcher, which are staggering, and test the predictions in a way that can be replicated by others. At most, Wertham gathered data to form a hypothesis. *Seduction* can't be refuted because there's no science to refute. It is rather a polemic that operates in the sphere of politics (in which sphere it could hardly have been more successful). Even if *Seduction* had been a legitimate study, no single study proves anything; the results must be repeated independently. Wertham is in fact condemned out of his own mouth, in Beaty's own book, at page 133: "Wertham revealed that he wrote *Seduction of the Innocent* as 'a non-

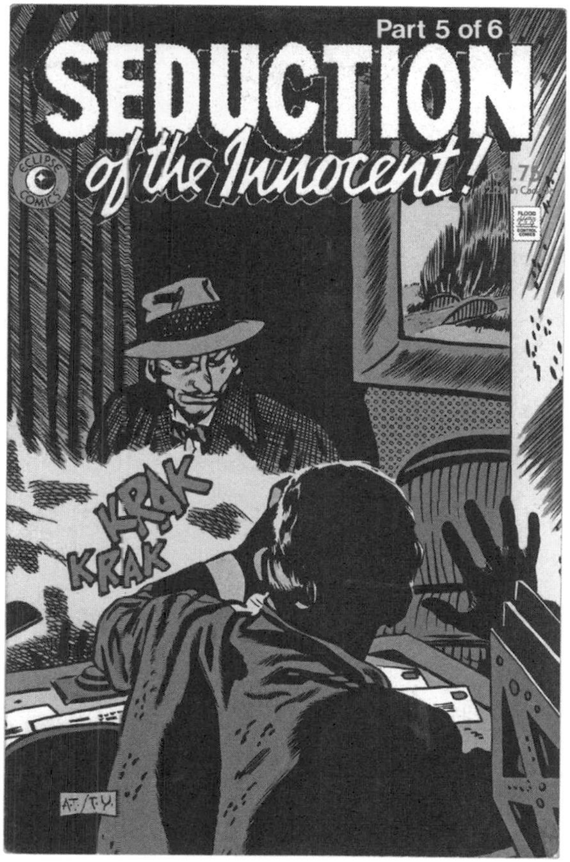
Part 5 of 6
SEDUCTION
of the Innocent!
ECLIPSE COMICS
KRAK
KRAK
An '80s Eclipse series: cover by Tom Yeates. [©1986 Tom Yeates]

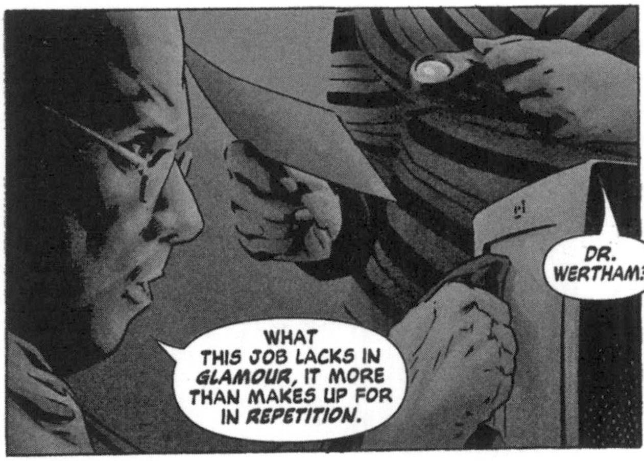
DR. WERTHAM?
WHAT THIS JOB LACKS IN GLAMOUR, IT MORE THAN MAKES UP FOR IN REPETITION.
From *Bad Planet* #1, written by Thomas Jane and Steve Niles and illustrated by Lewis Larosa and Tim Bradstreet. [©2005 Raw Studios]

technical book because I knew I could not budge the psychiatrists anyhow.'" Budging your peers is what science is about. On top of that, Beaty is simply wrong, and Hajdu cites several legitimately conducted studies that contradict Wertham. Wertham knew that once he was addressing people who weren't impressed by his lab coat the jig was up. And since when does the burden of proof fall on the defendant? In any case, there was no defense because the industry surrendered. It emasculated itself and offered its testicles as a sacrifice to the gods of censorship in return for the privilege to continue doing business.

As apologists for crackpots often will do, Beaty attempts to distill a moderate position from an extremist view. We are reassured repeatedly that what Wertham said was not that comic books caused delinquency but that they were merely a factor in delinquency. This distinction is, as far as I can tell, meaningless, and only serves as a smokescreen for Wertham's failure to prove his contentions. If he is saying that there would be less juvenile delinquency if this factor were removed then he's saying that comic books cause delinquency. If you're not saying that then what are you saying? For all of Beaty's evasions the fact remains that he believed that even the most innocuous comic books were damaging, and his prescription was a law that would have forbidden the sale of any kind of comic book to anyone under the age of 15. This is a remedy far more harsh than the Comics Code; the comic book could not have survived it. It would have been tantamount to abolishing an industry by government decree. And it seems crystal clear to me that this was not a byproduct of Dr. Wertham's prescription, but the intention.

Given the state of Wertham's reputation Beaty is compelled to spend something like 100 pages explaining why expert after expert and critic after critic (led by the dreaded "New York Intellectuals") were corrupt, wrongheaded or just plain hated children. I will take as an example his treatment of Dr. Lauretta Bender. Bender, a child psychiatrist at Bellevue Hospital from 1930 to 1956, where she was an expert on, among other things, childhood aggression, treated thousands of children, did pioneering work on autism and childhood developmental disorders, and devised a motor skills test that's still used today. In other words, she had a rather more distinguished career in treating children than Fredric Wertham, observed none of the effects of comic books that Wertham claimed, and wrote articles about the positive effects of comic-book reading on her patients. As a result of this work National Comics engaged her as an occasional editorial consultant, sending her books to review and consulting her on the advisability of products and storylines. (You might construe engaging a renowned child psychiatrist to review your product as responsible behavior if you weren't intent on demonizing comics publishers.) Wertham and Kefauver, whose political dreams would be crushed as part of God's Occasional Justice program, used this association to characterize her as a paid shill for the industry, a bit of churlishness that Beaty endorses. But Beaty treats her worse than that:

> Bender's conclusion that comic books did not harm children was an extreme version of the "blame the child" school of media effects, and it echoed her earlier findings about the impact of incest on children. "The history of the relationship in our cases usually suggested at least some cooperation of the child in the activity ... [A] most striking feature was that these children were distinguished as unusually charming and attractive in their outward personalities. Thus, it is not remarkable that frequently we considered the possibility that the child might have been the actual seducer rather than the one innocently seduced."

Here Beaty conflates two entirely unrelated papers, a 1944 essay entitled "The Psychology of Children's Reading and the Comics" and "The Reaction of Children to Sexual Relations with Adults," a 1937 study of childhood sexual assault written in collaboration with Abram Blau, in order to demonstrate a "pattern" of blaming children for media effects. This argument is weakened by the fact that only one of these articles is concerned with media effects, and that article isn't blaming children for anything. The 1944 essay says that the effects of reading comic books were primarily positive, and that the purported negative effects were grossly overstated. The 1937 study was not a general study of incest as Beaty implies but an in-depth study of 16 children, only four of them cases of incest (but Beaty knows his hot buttons). Bender and Blau were not saying the children were to blame for the sexual assaults but that complicity had to be considered as a possibility. The purpose of the study was not to allot blame to patients but to determine the proper way to treat them. Beaty grossly misrepresents Bender's beliefs, but it gets grosser than that. By the end of the paragraph, he has spun this spurious pattern into "her insistence that the 'normal' child was unharmed by social forces as diverse as incest and comic books, seeking to suggest that if a correlation existed between comic books and juvenile delinquency, the fault lay not with the media but with the children who consumed the media, because those children were 'abnormal' or 'maladjusted.'" 1) She wasn't making the absurd and garbled if-statement Beaty tries to put into her mouth; she was saying the purported correlation didn't exist at all. Here Beaty is begging a question that wasn't even asked. 2) She never said children were unharmed by incest. To the contrary, Bender and Blau found that the four incest cases in the 1937 study were among those where the victims showed immediate harmful effects, and her 1952 follow-up study showed that of the four, one was suffering chronic psychosis while the other three had attained "moderately successful adjustment." "Moderately successful" doesn't sound like unharmed to me. 3) Neither of these papers concern juvenile delinquents. These are tactics unworthy of Karl Rove.

Wertham's views are treated rather differently. A typical example is found on page 176, where Beaty notes, "Wertham argued that television coverage of the war in Vietnam was hardening Americans to the war, not turning them against it." We then get a paragraph of exegesis explaining how this fits into Wertham's general ideas about media violence. What we do not get is any discussion of the fact that Wertham's argument is completely, spectacularly wrong. But then, everyone else disagreeing with Wertham is par for the course, and to Beaty it only proves Wertham right.

It's hard to understand why with over 50 years of legitimate research on violent entertainment to draw on, anyone would waste their time and credibility on someone as discreditable on this subject as Wertham. It is reminiscent of those hard-line anti-communists who can't resist the temptation to periodically try to rehabilitate Joseph Mc-

Carthy, if not the UFO enthusiast's belief that false sightings are evidence of true ones. Or it might simply be that only someone as loose with proof as Wertham could produce the results Beaty wants. The problem with connecting violent entertainment to violent behavior has always been the extreme difficulty if not impossibility of separating these hypothetical effects from other factors. The legitimate lesson an advocate might take from Wertham is: Forget about science. It's not going to help you. You are going to have to argue that the proposition can't be proven scientifically even if it is true, and you're going to have to convince people politically to accept your common sense. Another is: Don't try to pass off pseudoscience as genuine research, for be sure your sin will find you out.

The idea that imaginary violence breeds genuine violence has a certain intuitive appeal, and never more so than when violence in the media increased and the level of violence increased. Then the level of violence in the media increased even more, and the level of violence went down. Which could mean that imaginary violence doesn't cause genuine violence, or it could mean that societies adjust to these things. In terms of comic books before the Code, we engaged in an experiment with poor controls but a huge sample, as every kid who could organize a dime seemed to be reading them. So what happened to this cohort, the children who grew up reading comic books from the '30s to the '50s, and were subjected to this ruthless propaganda campaign for racism, sexism and imperialism? They were the most politically liberal such cohort in American history. They were the people who overthrew white supremacy. They saw through a more broad-based effective feminist movement than the suffragists. They were the first Americans who, when ordered off to war by their government, said no. For a while there, they were even opposed to the death penalty. I guess you'd have to call it a close call.

As for Dr. Wertham, if he was an altruist without ego or concern in any matter but the well-being of children, you can assume he left this life well satisfied with his achievements. If on the other hand there was an element of vainglory to his character, a thirst for the limelight, his later years must have been bitter: To become the center of attention, leading a national and nationally televised crusade and making the wicked tremble and beg his mercy … and then to have it go the way of all politics, never to return, all the while watching his nemesis grow in wealth and public regard, even as his own reputation grew only in infamy. If he had a comeuppance coming, he got it. ∎

Typos
by Tom Crippen

Comic Books: How the Industry Works
Shirrel Rhoades
Peter Lang Publishing Inc.
406 pp., $32.95
Softcover
ISBN: 978-0820488929

A Complete History of American Comic Books
Shirrel Rhoades
Peter Lang Publishing Inc.
353 pp., $39.95
Softcover
ISBN: 978-1433101076

Our Gods Wear Spandex:
The Secret History of Comic Book Heroes
Christopher Knowles, Joseph Michael Linsner
Weiser Books
233 pages, $19.95
Softcover
ISBN: 978-1578634064

Some may see *The Comics Journal* as dedicated to the art of making typos, but a man named Shirrel Rhoades has expanded the form. He was publisher during Marvel's rough years, the ownership wars of the 1990s, and he helped keep the comics line going. He reports starting Marvel Knights and hiring Joe Quesada. Quesada's pretty much all right, and the Marvel Knights *Black Panther, Daredevil* and *Spider-Man* were better than fine. So I'm ready to take Shirrel Rhoades seriously. It's just that if you open either of these books that bear his name, you'll find that on any given page most of the text got there by being cut and pasted and slapped onto a screen. Based on my reading of the footnotes, a total of 1,053 sentences,

paragraphs or sections were lifted (with credit, I should note) from sites on the Web. The word count got high enough and Rhoades had a book — two books. "My first draft proved to be so long we had to subdivide it into two volumes," he tells us.

You picture Mr. Rhoades at work. He's in his study at Key West, beard trim, a glass of ice tea on the desk. He scrolls content and flips suitable items into a file; his wrist keeps going four hours straight. We're not talking about plagiarism — the 1,964 footnotes rain on the eye, paragraph by paragraph, until your soul learns a little about death. But even bad writing requires some thought; cutting and pasting requires less, a lot less. The Rhoades books were not written and they weren't compiled. Google cruised along, its jaws filling with copy, and ctrl-c/ctrl-v excreted the results somewhere two book covers could find the mess. Floating between the Internet chunks, keeping them from scraping, is a thin fluid of originally authored prose. Bobbing alongside the chunks are quotes from author interviews with industry figures. The quotes and Internet chunks and author prose are pretty hard to tell apart; they all slop together.

In one spot the lumps and fluid coalesce into a workable text. I mean pages 127 through 186 of *History,* the section on the Marvel ownership wars and what came after. This stuff isn't great, but the paragraphs do cooperate to put across a coherent sequence of information. Rhoades, most often in floating paragraphs stationed next to the main text ("Flashback," with a little word balloon as part of the heading), lobs in some personal observations: the dumb thing the square Marvel president said to him about his tie; the sight of a Marvel president, a different one, talking an artist through the caricature he wanted of himself. But then the slab tips under the surface; the slop's film closes again. You're back with the random chunks, which produce splendid typos, tropical beauties: "Laura Croft" as the heading, in extra-big type, for a section about Lara Croft; "writer Len Win" two pages before "writer Len Wein." The books themselves are typos. Essentially, a typo is what happens to copy when absolutely no one is paying attention to its production. In the past, the resulting glitch could only be a letter, a word, maybe a word clump. Now we have software and it can be *A Complete History of American Comic Books* and *Comic Books: How the Industry Works.*

A creepy effect, a sign of the books' essential condition, is the way the word clots masquerading as paragraphs pay so little attention to each other. Let me describe a section called "Mass Market." It opens by saying Wal-Mart is a big magazine retailer and maybe it could sell comics too. Then a quote: "'Emotionally everyone thinks comicsbooks should be in Wal-Mart,' says Stephanie Fierman, a former DC marketing exec, 'but rationally that's hard to do with your business hat on. It may not make sense yet.'" OK, I'll bite. Why not? But we don't find out. Fierman moves sideways and tells us what a great "emotional connection" DC and Marvel have with Target. Which rubs up your impatience to know, sure, but why not Wal-Mart. But now she's gone and we have "blogger Matt Maxwell" saying that "Mr. Buckley" figures newsstands are dead for Marvel and he's looking more at "chain stores like Target and Wal-Mart." Mr. Buckley also feels that movies make a big difference when it comes to getting chain store customers to buy comics. And there the discussion ends.

Nobody is home here. You get Robert Crumb being explained with a quote from CBS.com: "His work was 'striking for its grotesque, cartoon style satirizing American culture.'" Maybe Rhoades doesn't care about Underground stuff, but he also has nothing to say about Jim Steranko, Stan Lee or Jack Kirby. When their names come up, so does boilerplate loaded in from more websites. I'm not against Wikipedia or Lambiek.net or even TCJ.com, but an author should do some authoring.

I mentioned creepiness. Reading these books you start feeling like the only person at a party, like a stranded explorer in a lost city. No one else has read this text: You've zigged where the rest of the world has zagged. Your mind starts to fret. How did the text get here — why? The words, look how their formations resemble paragraphs. And each sentence begins with a capital letter, ends directly against a question mark, an exclamation point, two exclamation points, sometimes a period. It's as if some sort of shaping intelligence ... "With Weisinger's retirement, the Silver Age Superman was given a sendoff in 'Whatever Happened to the Man of Steel?'— a two-part

SHIRREL RHOADES
FORMER PUBLISHER OF MARVEL COMICS
COMIC BOOKS
HOW THE INDUSTRY WORKS
AFTERWORD BY STAN LEE
Cover design Clear Point Designs. [©2008 Peter Lang Publishing Inc.]

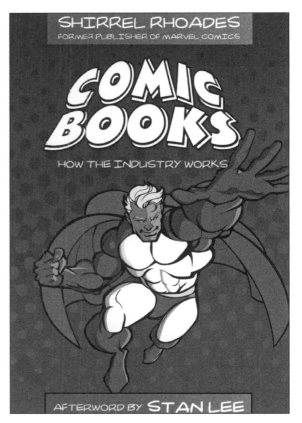

story written by Alan Moore and drawn by Curt Swan." Or maybe not — considering that it was Julius Schwartz who retired at that time and the story was called "Whatever Happened to the Man of Tomorrow."

I feel like a schmuck just for thinking Shirrel Rhoades would've done the work involved in these lousy books. Maybe it was a kid making $8.50 an hour and studying journalism at Florida Keys Community College. Mr. Rhoades did talk a lot with Dan DiDio and Stan Lee and others who've done things in the industry ("74. Paul Levitz, DC Comics, personal interview, Fall 2006"), and the face time's byproduct is scattered through the pages. He has anecdotes about his friend Jim Sokolowski, or "Ski," formerly Marvel's vice president of editorial planning. These are scattered, too: The first shows up on p. 14, 19 pages before we're told who "Ski" is. The appearance takes place in one of those "Flashback" paragraphs, and right next to it the text is talking about magazine publishing in the 1920s. So the flashback is irrelevant and also, because it's about comic books in the 1990s, a flash forward. The books use the rectangles — also labeled "Speaking Up!"

Fans re-enact ancient rites at the San Diego Comic-Con.

and "True Fact" and "Looking Back" — to give itself a *Comics Business for Dummies* kind of feel. The pages start looking like supermarket shelves, with labels everywhere and no consistent reason for the eye to be anyplace particular. When it does land, in the case of the Rhoades books, the eye finds out it's first on the scene: "The modern Aquaman is more angrier and more righteous as the ruler of Atlantis, a darker superhero in keeping with the times." OK, sure. "More angrier."

In a way, the Rhoades experience set me free. Last Christmas, or a few days after, I sat and pondered the back cover of *Our Gods Wear Spandex*. "Fresh insights," the blurbs said, and "exciting" and "could hardly do better." I had a lost-city moment: How could those words have wound up here? Having just finished *Spandex,* I knew it was a dud. Instead of facts logically arranged to support a point of view, it had nothing but wide margins and "Paul-is-dead clue picking." This last phrase is me quoting myself from my column before last ("Big Red Feet, Mighty Chest," issue 289, April 2008), which discusses the book but doesn't give its title or author. The comics community is a fairly decent place, and in *Spandex* the author says he suffers from a "perpetual state of hyper-awareness and agitation." That sounds funny, but in my view the condition does occur and can be debilitating. Sitting by the Christmas tree, I thought that maybe the blurbs represented some sort of humanitarian crisis response. Now I look at the Rhoades books and see "crystal-clear" and "invaluable tool."

So all right, forget it. Here's my review of *Our Gods Wear Spandex*. The book, written by Christopher Knowles, expands upon two notions. The first is that superheroes are modern-day manifestations of age-old mythological forerunners. The second is that creators of various superheroes had their intellectual roots in various occult movements that first sprang up during the 19th century. The first notion is pursued mainly by repeating the phrase "new gods" and by using the term "archetype" instead of "cliché," "gimmick" or "stock figure." The second notion pretty much lies there. The book's standards of proof aren't standards at all. The section on Steve Englehart might at least have mentioned his recurring use of the "celestial Madonna" theme; instead it keenly notes that a young Englehart moved to New York City, where a circle of occultists met who included Chris Claremont's wife. Well, well! Instead of demonstrating that, say, Jerry Siegel or Jack Kirby read about the occult or talked about it, the book settles for showing that every now and then relevant bits of business showed up in their work. Of course, many other bits surfaced as well. Superheroes have their roots in all sorts of goofy shit, including mythology and the occult. To argue that those two influences are crucial just because they're there makes as much sense as claiming that the civil rights movement was Communist-inspired.

Speaking of which, Knowles believes that the civil rights movement occurred in the 19th century. Also, he is confused as to the meaning of "odyssey" and "epic," and he misses the point of the modern-day superhero scene. His book claims that, after 9/11, we need heroes again and therefore the characters are being treated more seriously than during the 1990s. But the day's biggest superhero phenomenon, Spider-Man in the movies, plays up the character's endearing dorkiness. Meanwhile, comics like *Civil War* and *Identity Crisis* have made the heroes less heroic and more fallible, not to say scuzzy and disagreeable.

My favorite part is when Knowles argues that convention costume shows are the same as ancient rites where people dressed up as the gods they worshipped. And in the same way, we celebrate a mass for our silverware every time we have a candlelit dinner. To paraphrase Dorothy Parker, this is not a book to be tossed aside lightly. It is a book to be beaten with a shovel and then buried in wet earth so it will rot faster. That being said, the illustrations are a bit stiff but still a lot of fun. ■

Us and Them Political Cartooning

Political Guerrilla Throws Fez in the Ring

by R.C. Harvey

As we all know by now, we've been told often enough, this is a Historic Presidential Election. One aspect of its historicity is that, for the first time ever, an African American is the candidate of one of the major political parties. Another reason is that the other party nominated the oldest man ever to run for president.

This year's presidential contest is also historic because, for the first time, a woman was a viable and, for a while, even the inevitable, candidate of one of the parties. It's also the first time that a former contestant in a beauty pageant has run for vice president, thereby giving the Grand Old Pachyderm ticket a dignity it didn't otherwise enjoy, and it's the first time that Ralph Nader has run for a third time (or is it the fourth?) although perhaps these latter achievements are too precious to be historic.

But we can't quarrel with another landmark in the annals of American politics: A nationally known Muslim is running for the White House. In yet another first for this election season, Khalil Bendib announced his candidacy in August 2007 (not quite as early as has been fashionable of late) at the Mudrakers Café on Telegraph Avenue in Berkeley, Calif, vowing to turn not only swords into ploughshares but "box cutters, machetes, Ginsu knives — any sharp cutting implement" he would convert to "organic-food-cultivating equipment."

Bendib, who has achieved national repute by drawing scathing editorial cartoons for a suspicious variety of small, usually weekly, newspapers — 1,700 subscribe through MinuteMan Media, a progressive syndicate — aspires to be, as he says, with a nod to Dr. Seuss, the Prez in the Fez. Adopting the campaign slogan "The pen is funnier than the sword," Bendib declared, "Ours will be the funniest, most hilarious administration in American history."

In a press release announcing his candidacy, Bendib acknowledged that some skeptics claim that the current administration, having turned the United States of America into the world's laughing stock over the past seven years, may be a tough act to follow, comedically speaking. How does Bendib propose to outdo the clowns currently occupying the White House? The key, according to candidate Bendib, will be to "make the rest of the world laugh with us, rather than laugh at us, as has been the case for the past decade or so."

Here are a few planks from the candidate's presidential platform:

* On Government waste and pork-barrel spending: "As a self-respecting Muslim, you can guess how I feel about *pork:* I'm not exactly wild about it!" Bendib declared.

* On Education: "Pens not guns, books not bombs, Math Instruction not Mass Destruction."

* On the Patriot Act: "Once elected, I will act like a patriot — and repeal the Patriot Act!"

* On the Use of Torture: In the candidate's own words, "If you absolutely ***must*** obtain information? Tickle, don't torture! Amuse, don't abuse!"

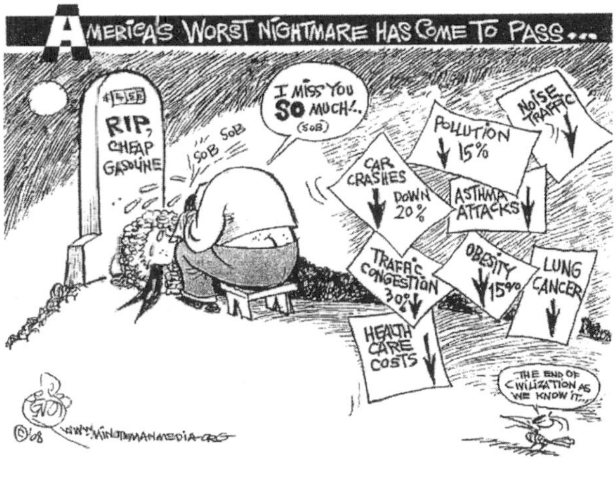
AMERICA'S WORST NIGHTMARE HAS COME TO PASS...
RIP, CHEAP GASOLINE
SOB SOB
I MISS YOU SO MUCH!.. (SOB)
POLLUTION 15%
NOISE TRAFFIC
CAR CRASHES DOWN 20%
ASTHMA ATTACKS
TRAFFIC CONGESTION 30%
OBESITY 15%
LUNG CANCER
HEALTH CARE COSTS
THE END OF CIVILIZATION AS WE KNOW IT...

[© 2008 Khalil Bendib]

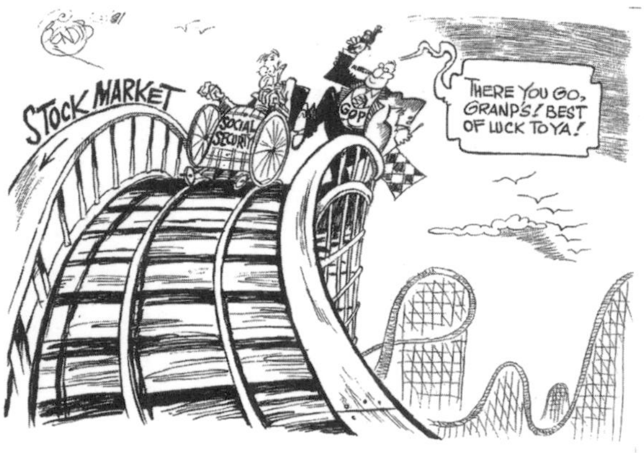
STOCK MARKET
SOCIAL SECURITY
GOP
THERE YOU GO, GRANPS! BEST OF LUCK TO YA!
[© 2008 Khalil Bendib]

* Finally, on Guantanamo Bay, the candidate says: "Render unto Fidel what belongs to Fidel, have the Cubans tear down the torture center and put in something more positive there — like a dental school or something."

"Mirth makes right, not might," Bendib says repeatedly, adding, "Disarming the enemy through the power of laughter and good cheer" is the best defense. "The enemy" in this case is Bendib's satiric target — Islamophobic stereotypes.

Tongue no longer in his cheek, Bendib said, "Sadly, Islamophobia runs deep in America today and it has been cultivated as an excuse for preventive wars, domestic spying, torture, the suspension of habeas corpus and the erasure of so many of our most treasured constitutional freedoms. What better way to bring back our precious liberties and to rid us once and for all of the exaggerated fear of Islam than to elect America's first Muslim president? In 1960, President Kennedy did not bring the Vatican into the white House, as initially feared, and in 2008, the Prez in the Fez will not bring Mecca into the Oval Office!"

To paraphrase another great president before him, the Muslim candidate concludes: "The only thing we have to fear is the fear of Islam itself! God bless America and peace be upon you!"

In his cartoons, Bendib has been campaigning against stereotypical thinking about the Arab world for years. Born in Paris of war-refugee Algerian parents who had fled their native country during the French colony's war for independence, Bendib returned to Algeria with his parents at the age of 6, and when he was 20, he came to California to complete his studies and to escape the political censorship his cartoons experienced in Algeria. He's been lurking noisily around here ever since.

His cartoons, he says, are "hard-hitting, myth-shattering, platitude-mocking cartoons [that] rarely shy away from the truth, as they seek to expose the crude racial stereotypes, 'dis-information' and info-tainment pabulum offered as gospel by our mass media. In the proud tradition of genuine watchdog journalism," he continues, "I aim to comfort the afflicted and afflict the comfortable — and to give a voice to the voiceless."

After digesting a few dozen of his cartoons, I'd disagree with only one of these assertions, his use of the word *rarely:* I don't think Bendib *ever* shies away from the truth as he sees it.

With his North African roots, Bendib has a non-Eurocentric view of the shenanigans in American political and cultural life.Martin Rowson, a Brit writing for the *New Humanist* in late 2003, saw Bendib's drawing style as distinctively American.

Bendib's visual styling partakes zestfully of Seussian mannerisms, from the bulbous-nosed visages and sharp-elbows to the rubbery anatomy of the good doctor's vintage years.

As a political cartoonist, Bendib heaps up pictorial metaphors until every cartoon is a smorgasbord of images, a gluttonous revel of labels and symbols, a groaning board overflowing with implication and import, stuffed with outrage and indignation.

Bendib's drawing style may be American, but his perspective is aggressively not. Rowson continues: "As a skeptical Old European, I agree with almost everything he says, and find none of it objectionable. In the U.S., however, post-9/11, post-The Patriot Act and all the rest, this stuff is genuinely incendiary. I know cartoonists who have been sacked, had their doors beaten down by the FBI in the middle of the night and even fled into exile. All power to his pen, then."

Michael Ramirez was accosted by the humorlessly bu-

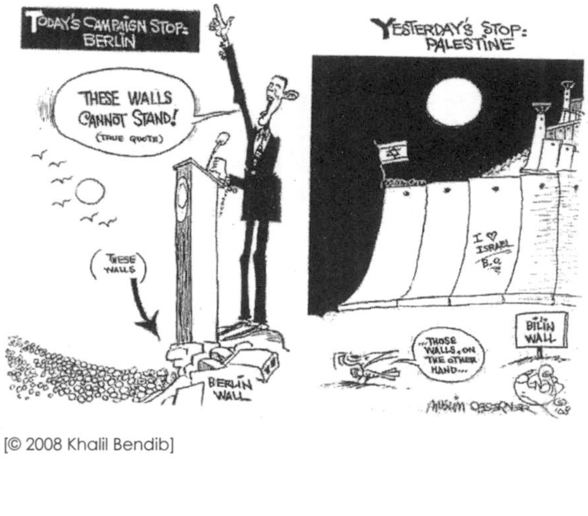
TODAY'S CAMPAIGN STOP: BERLIN
THESE WALLS CANNOT STAND! (TRUE QUOTE)
THESE WALLS
BERLIN WALL
YESTERDAY'S STOP: PALESTINE
I ♥ ISRAEL B.O.
...THOSE WALLS, ON THE OTHER HAND...
BILIN WALL
[© 2008 Khalil Bendib]

reaucratic FBI when it failed to see the satiric comedy in one of his cartoons, which — ironically, for a conservative cartoonist — seemed to advise, as I recall, the assassination of GeeDubya. But even Ramirez escaped with his freedom and his pen.

Rowson, however, is right about Bendib's cartoons being skeptical and non-American (as distinct from un-American) in their inflammatory assaults on the received wisdom of American cultural biases. Bendib's cartoons remind us unflinchingly that in all our policies for the Mid-East, we harbor a bias against Palestinians and for Israelis — with only the slightest regard for facts, history or the possible validity of an opposing point of view.

At a convention of the Association of American Editorial Cartoonists in 2002, Bendib's presentation about this American bias was interrupted by a Jewish cartoonist, Hy Rosen, who, having heard enough about the American prejudice against Palestinians, demanded that Bendib do a few cartoons attacking the Palestinian educational system, which preaches virulent anti-Semitism in schoolrooms and textbooks. Bendib was taken aback momentarily, but continued his presentation without much acknowledging Rosen's complaint.

Bendib is doubtless right about our anti-Arab bigotry; but Rosen is right, too, about Muslim anti-Semitism. An effective political cartoon, however, does not permit the nuance of admitting that an alternate point of view exists. Effective political cartoons are black-and-white statements: there is good and there is evil, and nothing in between.

Bendib epitomizes this unequivocal approach in his editorial cartooning. But he could, for the pure sake of evening the score, have taken a shot at the anti-Semitic bile of the Islamic schoolroom without diluting his attack on American xenophobia.

Compared to Bendib's cartoons, most other American political cartoons are poetic rather than ponderous: needles rather than sledgehammers, they jab and pun and poke fun while Bendib attacks with club and claw. His metaphorical images are vivid and unmistakable. In Bendib's cartoons, corporate America is a bloated villain, a rapacious and unrepentant despoiler of natural resources and civilization. The fat greedy capitalist has long disappeared from the gallery of caricatures in the cartoons of other American editoonists (although not from American life and government, which, for the most part, is run to suit fat greedy capitalists). Politicians in Bendib's cartoons are invariably giants of hypocrisy, greed and self-delusion. Government is always ignorant and unethical. America is self-absorbed and uninformed about the world beyond its borders.

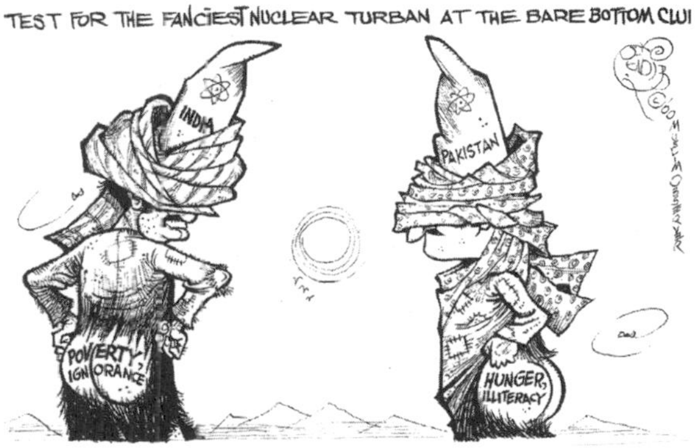
TEST FOR THE FANCIEST NUCLEAR TURBAN AT THE BARE BOTTOM CLU
INDIA
PAKISTAN
POVERTY, IGNORANCE
HUNGER, ILLITERACY

[© 2008 Khalil Bendib]

But Bendib is scarcely blind to the faults of the Arab world as is amply demonstrated by his "Contest for the Fanciest Nuclear Turban" cartoon in this vicinity. Still, Bendib's audience is the American public, not Indians or Pakistanis, so he seldom levels one of his broadsides toward that part of the world. Besides, as he explained when we exchanged e-mails, "Mine is an underdog sensitivity: Whoever happens to be picked on unfairly, I identify with."

Understandably, then, he identifies with cultures and attitudes about which Americans remain obstinately ignorant — thanks, mostly, to a myopic news media dominated by "artificial fog and lethal hypocrisy," according to Norman Soloman in his foreword to Bendib's 2007 compilation of cartoons, *Mission Accomplished: Wicked Cartoons from America's Most Wanted Political Cartoonist* (208 5x8-inch pages, paperback; $17).

Says Solomon: "Bendib will never snuggle into (as he puts it) 'an embedded media ... putting America to sleep.' In the best traditions of political art, his creations offer vantage points with lines-of-sight that contradict the favorite angles of mass media. ... From ground level, Khalil Bendib helps us to see — and, in the process, cuts through hazy illusions."

Lately, Bendib has given his cartoons a subtext, a diminutive beaked and feathered sharp-shooter, who, like Pat Oliphant's penguin Punk, occupies a corner and comments on the principal action transpiring above.

"He cracks me up," Bendib told me. "He just showed up one day on the page, sort of volunteered. He's my alter ego (most of the time), making sarcastic quips to complete the joke or to add to it another layer in another dimension. It gives me one more chance to make readers laugh and think. There's always a P.S.; my mind works that way."

Unlike Oliphant, Bendib hasn't given his mascot a name. In the earliest collection of his cartoons in 2003, *It Became Necessary to Destroy the Planet in Order to Save It* (160 5x8-inch pages, paperback; from Plan Nine Publishing, $15.95), the bird appears in only the latter pages of the book, but in *Mission Accomplished,* the feathered footnote is a constant presence.

In his sharply either/or vision, Bendib reminds me of similarly uncompromising "us vs. them" editoons that can be found, these days, only in labor-union magazines and newspapers. Typically, the labor side of any dispute is championed, and management — or big business, or Congress in the pay of big business — is damned.

The only practitioners of this brand of editorial cartooning I know of these days are Gary Huck and Mike Konopacki, who published a collection of their cartoons, entitled *Them* (112 8x11-inch pages, paperback), in 1990; still available at Amazon.com, as are their other three titles: *Bye! American, Working Class Hero* and *Two-headed Space Alien Shrinks Labor Movement.*

More recently, in 2005, Ben Yomen, a stalwart pro-labor editoonist from the ancient 1930s and 1940s, published *In Labor's Corner* (174 8x11-inch pages, paperback; $20 from Yomen, 1073 Barton Drive, Apt. 102, Ann Arbor, MI 48105), a collection of his cartoons for a host of labor publications over a lifetime.

In mainstream American journalism, perhaps the issues have become too complicated for such simplistic cartoons (although I'd say Bendib proves that it can be done); but we can find the same kind of unflinching assault approach in collections of special-issue cartoons like

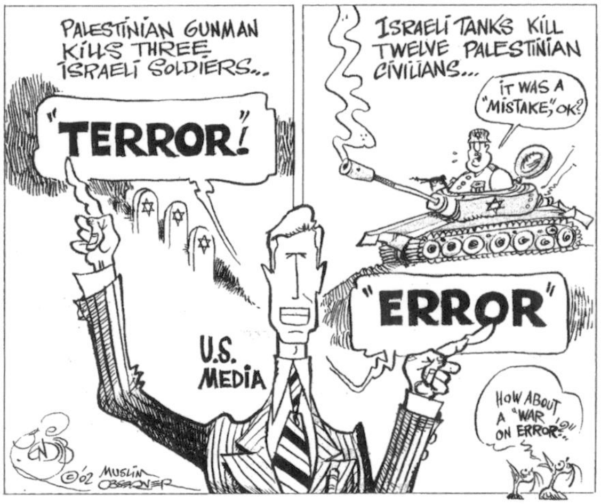
PALESTINIAN GUNMAN KILLS THREE ISRAELI SOLDIERS...
"TERROR!"
U.S. MEDIA
ISRAELI TANKS KILL TWELVE PALESTINIAN CIVILIANS...
IT WAS A "MISTAKE," OK?
"ERROR"
HOW ABOUT A "WAR ON ERROR?"

[© 2008 Khalil Bendib]

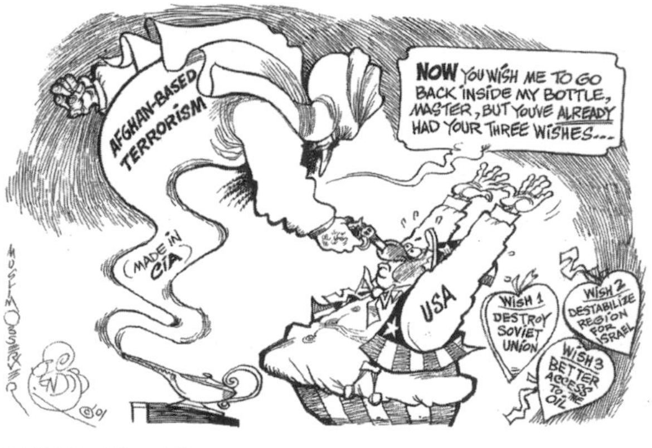
NOW YOU WISH ME TO GO BACK INSIDE MY BOTTLE, MASTER, BUT YOU'VE ALREADY HAD YOUR THREE WISHES...
AFGHAN-BASED TERRORISM
(MADE IN CIA)
USA
WISH 1 DESTROY SOVIET UNION
WISH 2 DESTABILIZE REGION FOR ISRAEL
WISH 3 BETTER ACCESS TO OIL

[© 2008 Khalil Bendib]

Cartooning AIDS Around the World (123 8x11-inch pages, 1992 paperback; available for a pittance at Amazon.com) published under the auspices of Jerry Robinson's Cartoonists and Writers Syndicate. Edited by David Horsey, editoonist at the *Seattle Post-Intelligencer*, and Maury Forman, a former health care administrator, the book collects the work of 61 cartoonists from 21 countries, all promoting the fight against AIDS and lambasting governmental inertia and public apathy.

Public-spirited crusading like this might change a few minds by simply raising consciousness in the body politic, but apart from achieving such modest successes, most editoonists, generally speaking, don't believe their cartoons change minds and hearts. The late Doug Marlette, asked if his cartoons had any effect on the world around him, famously quipped: "I ended the Vietnam War." But the extravagance of his claim betrayed his lack of conviction.

Most editoonists see their work chiefly as cheerleading for like-minded readers or, perhaps, stimulating debate without necessarily changing minds, but, like Ted Rall, they expect to exert some subliminal influence. "I don't think any [political cartoons] change readers' decisions," he was quoted as saying in *Medill Reports*, March 6, 2008. "But I think that in the mix of everything that goes into election coverage, cartoons are a part of that."

Bendib, however, is not content with so piddling an impact. He forges on through the campaign jungles, cutting a swath as he goes. As of July, he had appeared at over 50 campuses and community groups, "and I'm just getting warmed up," he said. "It's a come-from-behind campaign. Obama won't know what hit him." ■

The Potholed Road to Artistry for Cameroonian Cartoonist Issa Nyaphaga

by John A. Lent

Cameroonian cartoonist Issa Nyaphaga has a knack for surviving, even prospering, despite adverse conditions. Hailing from a small village of the Tikar tribe in the heart of Cameroon's equatorial forest — where villagers thought Westerners were dirty for having toilets *inside* their house — Nyaphaga now straddles two continents, doing his art and holding exhibitions, workshops and shows in Paris, New York City, Washington D.C., and elsewhere. In between, he was severely punished by his father who tried to dissuade Nyaphaga from being an artist, beaten by police and imprisoned because of his cartoons, and forced to leave his homeland and find a place in highly competitive Western metropolises.

Now residing in Paris and the U.S., Nyaphaga has expanded on what he learned in that remote village, in the process, developing his own style of artistry. From watching his mother, who painted walls, he learned which soils yielded different colors, explaining in one of our interviews, "She used volcanic ash for her black, white clay for white, and red, yellow and orange came from ground soil. We had no green as there was no green soil."

At age 6, Nyaphaga was drawing pictures using mud as paint and his finger as a brush, much to the annoyance of his Muslim father, himself a calligrapher. Nyaphaga explained:

Photo courtesy of John A. Lent.

> My father did not approve of my cartooning because he was Muslim. I read and drew cartoons and hid them. When he found the cartoons, he'd punish me. For each book I read or drawing I did, I had to support myself on the floor on my left foot and one finger of my right hand or vice versa. Five minutes for each book and drawing. If hundreds [of books, drawings], I would be punished for hours. If I made a mistake in supporting myself, I had to do it for another hour. My father drew signs, letters on paper professionally. He used burned corn, which he mashed and added water to, making it like charcoal. I did that with my drawings too. I love my father, because he made me combative and strong, so I endured prison later on.

At 14, when he went to Douala to pursue his studies, he was introduced to "modern" painting techniques by Kangangang Viking, a painter who, Nyaphaga said,

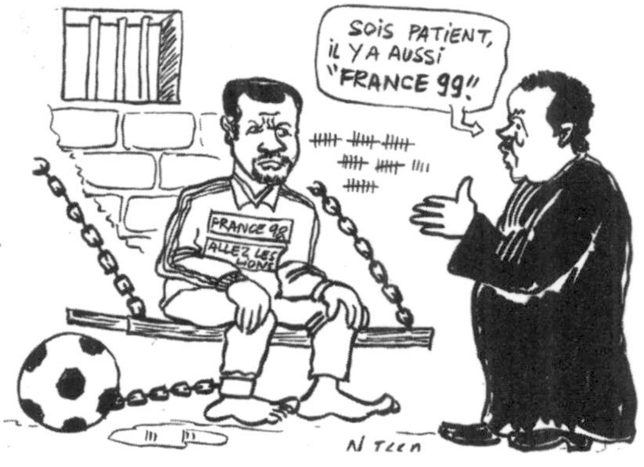
SOIS PATIENT, IL Y A AUSSI "FRANCE 99"!
FRANCE 98
ALLEZ LES LIONS

[©2008 Issa Nyaphaga]

"showed me this stick with hair on it is a brush; this is a wall that moves, which was actually a canvas board." This "spiritual artistic father" told Nyaphaga that he could not always paint with his finger; he also advised, "Don't let anyone in between you and your work; just put such a person on paper and he will disappear." Kangangang exposed the budding artist to the works of Picasso, Van Gogh and others, which Nyaphaga imitated until later, he found his own style, one part of which was dubbed "capillarism" and he, the "ragman of painting."

Nyaphaga said he tried different working materials — sand, sugar, corn and rice — but they had all been used. Then, one day, brush hair fell on his canvas, and he decided to let it become part of the art. Nyaphaga then cut his dreadlocks and pasted that hair on a painting. Capillarism is a procedure where Nyaphaga covers the canvas with hair, paints over it until the paint is absorbed, and then varnishes the entire work. He said the process allows for two views of the same picture — one without the graphic but with the design of the hair; the other with the graphic and minus the hair design. Nyaphaga has tried all types of hair — Indian, other Asian, Caucasian and African, the latter difficult to obtain because of superstitions about hair. "I used my sister's hair," he explained, but adding that in Paris, "everyone sent me hair."

Another aspect of his contemporary art practices that emanates from his African village days is his working primarily with salvaged objects, which Nyaphaga describes as turning "disused objects away from their first use and giving them a new birth." Many of his caricature-esque sculptures were made with objects he found while rummaging through garbage cans — a car bumper, empty toothpaste tube, half-eaten sandwich, and so forth. Nyaphaga is unique among those cartoonists who left Africa partly because of the paucity of artists' materials; he brought with him knowledge of traditional processes learned out of necessity in the village and forged them into new artistic styles.

The first newspaper Nyaphaga drew cartoons for in 1990 was *The Combatant*, which had a satirical called *Moustique Dechainé* (The Freed Mosquito). Nyaphaga learned two realities about African cartooning early on: that it is a low-paying job and that it is dangerous. For four large tabloid drawings, he received what he said was the "equivalent of 30 beer bottles in the local market for one month's work." Concerning the dangers of drawing cartoons, he said, "Everything was quite compromised and so the press found itself as the first force of opposition to the existing regime [that of Paul Biya, in office since 1982]." He added that not only did he and his colleagues produce *The Freed Mosquito*, but they also had to "bring it to the censorship offices, then to the printers. … And often, since the printing press was guarded by the police, they shot at us and some people died."

After *The Freed Mosquito*, Nyaphaga drew for *Galaxie*, a satirical paper with "hard speech," and then for *Sentinelle*, a general newsweekly with a full page of cartoons, before he joined *Le Messager Popoli*. The latter had continuing run-ins with the Biya government, partly because of the biting cartoons of Nyemb Popoli, who on one occasion had fled for his life to equally oppressive Chad, where he stayed a short time until it was safe to return. The

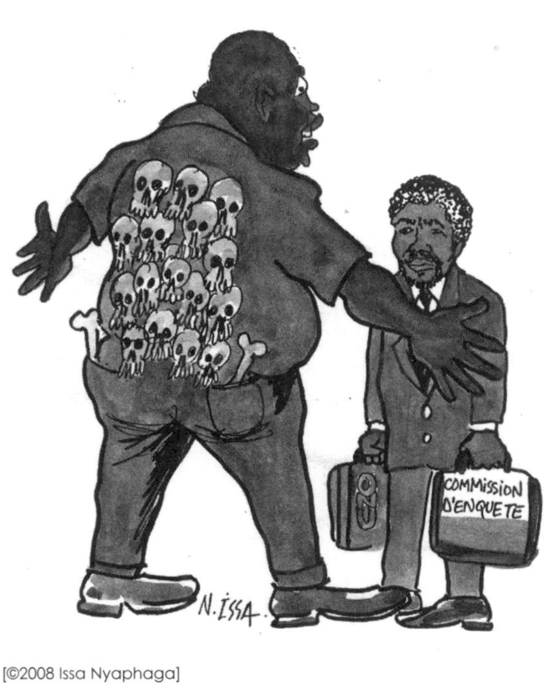
COMMISSION D'ENQUETE
N.ISSA.

[©2008 Issa Nyaphaga]

government kept *Le Messager Popoli* under close scrutiny, requiring that it be pre-censored by three officials. Nyaphaga said writers and cartoonists for the twice-weekly newspaper used pseudonyms although this strategy did not work for him, as he related:

> One day [in 1995], a cop stopped me and demanded to see my ID. He took me to the police station. He said, "We know who you are" and insisted I give him names of others under pseudonyms. I felt I could not give names. I said, "If I do that, it means I work for you. You don't pay me or anything." I could hear people screaming, being tortured. I was in jail two weeks. Usually, you are delayed for two days, 48 hours, but me, two weeks, and no one knew where I was. They beat me, shocked me. They said they were going to send me to New Bell Prison for three years; they said a lot of diseased people are there, with TB, etc.

Nyaphaga said the many beatings he received did not bother him as much as being among killers, rapists and other hardened criminals. He described the ordeal to his friend, Italian documentary filmmaker Nicoletta Fagiolo:

> Since I arrived wounded, because I had already been beaten at the police station due to my profession, I arrived very tired. You could not recognize me, and in the prison like in prisons all around the world, the people ask each other in confidence, "Why are you here?" And I heard people say, "Oh, I am here because I killed two people." "I am here because I raped a woman. We arrived at her house around midnight. I took my gun out and pointed it like this and said, 'Come here woman.'" While he was pissing, I heard terrible things, and then they ask me, "Issaa, why are you here?" And I said, "I did a drawing," and everyone lowered their eyes ....

After 4-5 months at New Bell Prison, Nyaphaga was being taken to trial when a lawyer, there to defend prisoners who did not have legal counsel, recognized him and asked why he was there. Nyaphaga told her he had insulted the government, "made fun of prison." Thereupon, according to Nyaphaga, "She said to give her the number of my file. It was 52. She looked in the file and said there was nothing in it. No charges. She defended me, saying I had a kid and if I stay in prison, my kid would be wronged in society."

Nyaphaga was given a provisional release but had to return to the tribunal in a month and to pay 50,000 CFR (two persons' salaries for a month). He was not permitted to draw any cartoons for three years. Because he had no job, he decided to resume doing his own page in *Le Messager Popoli*, rationalizing, "The people need me," and tempting his fate. Shortly after, an anonymous policeman, who said he and his wife admired Nyaphaga's cartoons, called him, warning, "They are going to get you back." Nyaphaga, who had a show coming up in France, hid out until he could obtain a tourist visa. He said he was able to leave on Feb. 18, 1996, because he bribed the chief of police, knowing that his name was in the computer [at immigration] and many police were at the airport who could prevent him from boarding his flight to Paris.

Life in Europe presented its own set of frustrations and anxieties for African cartoonists such as Nyaphaga, the main ones being the thought that they would not be able to return home for a long time and that the families they

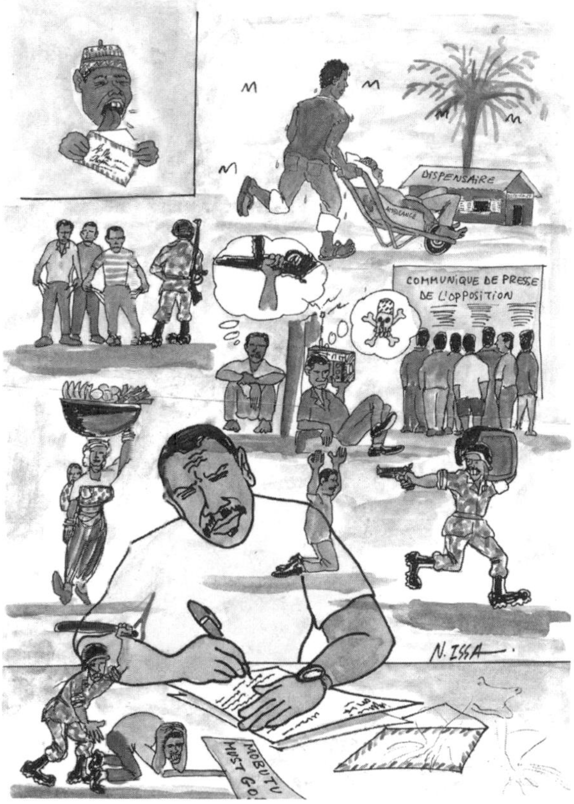
DISPENSAIRE
COMMUNIQUE DE PRESSE DE L'OPPOSITION
MOBUTU MUST GO
N. ISSA

"Writing Home from Exile:" art courtesy of John A. Lent. [©2008 Issa Nyaphaga]

Photo courtesy of John A. Lent: from one of Nyaphaga's art demonstrations/performances.

left behind might be victimized by retaliatory government officials. Nyaphaga, who expected to be abroad only a few months, said because the French "do not open up," he wanted to return home soon after he arrived in Paris. He was dissuaded by one of his 15 brothers [his father has 20 children and four wives], "who told me I should not come home because it would defeat everything they had done to help me out of Cameroon. He asked me, 'Don't you think the other exiles feel like you? And, also, the police are still looking for you.'"

In Paris, Nyaphaga drew cartoons regularly for *Charlie Hebdo*, where he took pleasure in meeting famous cartoonists such as Cabu, Wolinski and Cavanna. He also drew color cartoons for the political magazine *L'Autre Afrique* and illustrations for ad agencies. Always the developer of new ventures, Nyaphaga, with others, started *Gri Gri International*, a satirical periodical touching on voodooism, and with fellow Cameroonian Eyoum Nganguè, JAFE (African Journalists in Exile). JAFE, which defends and protects journalists in danger, was established, according to Nyaphaga, because, "We had to struggle with the administration in France. We felt we had to provide resources for cartoonists and journalists in exile. We start with little things — like always having a couch available for an exile to sleep on, transportation, etc."

Nyaphaga stayed in Paris until 2004 when he began

to travel and do shows, workshops, and exhibitions in the U.S. He teaches his painting techniques in universities, cultural centers, and social institutes, conducts therapeutic workshops for children at risk and teenagers in collaboration with La Source, and oversees Creativen, an organization he founded to contribute to the health and education needs of rural Cameroon. For example, at one point, Nyaphaga sold his artwork to buy a custom-designed three-wheeled bicycle to enable a polio victim "to get around and lead his life in a productive way."

He continues to draw cartoons and satirical works, some of which are part of a philosophical concept he is nurturing called "Urban Way," where he publicly paints his body and stages performances that include live music and his artwork. In these shows, Nyaphaga paints lines and dots on his body that, like animation, leap and dance when he moves. He said these symbols have meanings within stories and traditions of his culture, that one hand of dots represents people, the other of rows of white lines, the interactions among people. All of this is done, he said, as an act of protest against not being able to return home freely. ∎

John Lent is a world-renowned comics scholar, the author of multiple books, and the editor of the *International Journal of Comic Art*.

Modest Riches
The Quaint Charm of Certain Artists
by Donald Phelps

The governing, underlying charm of "quaintness," I suspect, lies in the stable universe the word suggests a manifest willingness to abide, albeit in some obscure nook or oddly shaped frame — to which another widely disdained word, "cozy," may be applicable. "Quaintness" suggests a residence that is stable, even static; it suggests, too, a heritage of peacefully disposed experience.

How often does one encounter the word today? Much less, with (even gently) approving overtones. "Outdated," "folksy," slightly moldy? Disdain for, impatience with, a sort of strangeness that is noncompetitive and nonaggressive. Even in the field of children's art and literature. Take two leading names in this country: Dr. Seuss (aka Theodore Giesel) and Maurice Sendak.

The fizzy, alliterative, swarming, sprawling fables and reveries of Dr. Seuss are too widely known and cherished, I presume, to warrant any extensive dilations from this erratically informed quarter. "Erratically" means here that my first acquaintance with Dr. Seuss was probably the sight of a Seuss-designed, giant mosquito or moth, in one of those illustrated outcries: "Quick, Henry! The Flit!" — an ad for a popular insecticide, that I glimpsed on the subway while my mother was hauling me toward the purchase of new clothes, or a visit to Santa at Macy's. Dr. Seuss mined his juvenile fantasy-projections from the stuff of juvenile nightmares: a wisdom that Victorian illustrators, say, cherished and cultivated, producing memorable art (that grownup children might treasure). The imminent generations, however, would come to brand such perception as criminal, or, at very least, lamentably ill-enlightened. Columbia Workshop. The presentation for that Sunday evening was *The Five Hundred Hats of Bartholomew Cubbins*. Bartholomew was a young boy in a faraway kingdom (the King was jovially bellowed by Howard Lindsay) to reach his epigone some years later, as Clarence Day, Senior, in the Broadway hit *Life With Father*.

Bartholomew's multiple headgear was early (though, likely, not first) in a long procession of jovial vandals, fantasized by Seuss: The Cat in the Hat, with his harum-scarum sorcery; the parade of unlikely critters who sauntered or lumbered down Mulberry Street; that mini-citizenry, the Who people, noticed and defended only by Horton, the Samaritan Elephant; Sam-I-Am, who eventually persuaded his unwilling host to sample Green Eggs and Ham. Whimsical invaders of staid respectability, usually accompanied by avalanches of preposterous plenty, like the mysterious Oobleck, that Bartholomew Cubbins confronted in Giesel's sequel to "The Five Hundred Hats," many years later. Seuss's was a menagerie of garishly hued creatures, often adorned with fantastical crests; striding and capering on gangly, knobby-kneed legs; peering with somewhat eerie, double-circled eyes. Save for the frequent child characters — drawn with tender accuracy — Seuss's was a cast of amicable nightmares: ridiculous monstrosities, onslaughts that engulfed with friendly waves, never smothering.

The values of adult decorum, especially as regarded space, were held at naught. Giesel's ongoing Mardi Gras was never, to my knowledge, seen within a frame. Not, that is, within the books.

There was, however, a comic strip, c. 1934, I would reckon, in Hearst's Sunday *Journal* comics section, immediately preceding the debut of Rose O'Neill's long-running *Kewpies*. I can attest only that Dr. Seuss's appeared to be a pseudo-*Arabian Nights* account, with a young lad, in the bloomers and decorated vest of Eastern fantasy, as its hero. As depicted within the conventional grid sequence of panels, the yarn or reverie appeared (to my admittedly none-too-patient eyes) as an incoherent, stiflingly jumbled phantasmagoria; teeming with hooded figures, veiled maidens, possibly a couple of genii. Indigestible and, pretty certainly, unwelcome to the bewildered eyes of Giesel's kid audience.

An object lesson, I might suggest, in the liabilities of kindergarten chaos as practiced *ad infinitum* by Giesel. It involves the jettison of form, embodied, in the example just cited, in those ubiquitous panel boundaries: expandable (as Hal Foster and Billy DeBeck variously demonstrated) but very, very seldom, if ever, dispensable or, challengeable, at least, as obtusely as Seuss challenged them. Form: that which delimits, that which demarks, that which identifies, in children's art especially — like that of Dr. Seuss and Maurice Sendak. Form entails a sense of the imagination's geography and its component laws.

Such a geographic sense, along with the commitment it would appear to involve, has never been evident for me in the fantastical outpourings of Theodore Giesel. One recalls once more — somewhat querying — the little homilies embodied in some of the later books: *How the Grinch Stole Christmas, Horton Hears a Who, Horton Hatches the Egg*. Aren't such sermonettes the occasional warning or symptom that the author, albeit with whatever benign and public-spirited sentiments — recognizes (make that: rerecognizes) the work of his hands as a Marketable Commodity. And one might observe: a symptom of the deficiency of form, one might say, the integrity of the artist's work, as manifested in laws, not homilies.

I have no wish to detract from the endearing foolery, the humorous bounty of Dr. Giesel's output. I merely, as in a whisper, suggest that in bypassing the realities of form — that form so patent in the work of my other subject, Maurice Sendak — he may have bypassed possibilities of growth, and of advances for his zestful brilliance. Irresistibly, perhaps, I recall the Marx Brothers in their declining years, especially the short-breathed, sentimental inanity of that misfired tribute to Harpo: *Love Happy*.

But — notwithstanding the vicissitudes of their joint career, in later years — I don't perceive the same kind of enfeebling in the work of Laurel and Hardy — who continued to honor, to the last, the music-hall format, with its set-piece routines and rhythms that Stan Laurel, decades before, had brought with him from his London origins. And the guiding principles: precision, deliberation, the certainties of vaudeville identity.

And the people came shouting, *"What's all this about . . .?"*
They looked! And they stared with their eyes popping out!
Then they cheered and they *cheered* and they CHEERED more and more.
They'd never seen anything like it before!
"My goodness! My gracious!" they shouted. "MY WORD!
It's something brand new!
IT'S AN ELEPHANT-BIRD!!

And it should be, it *should* be, it SHOULD be like that!

Because Horton was faithful! He sat and he sat!

He meant what he said

And he said what he meant. . . ."

From Dr. Seuss' *Horton Hatches an Egg*. [©1991 Theodor S. Geisel and Audrey S. Geisel]

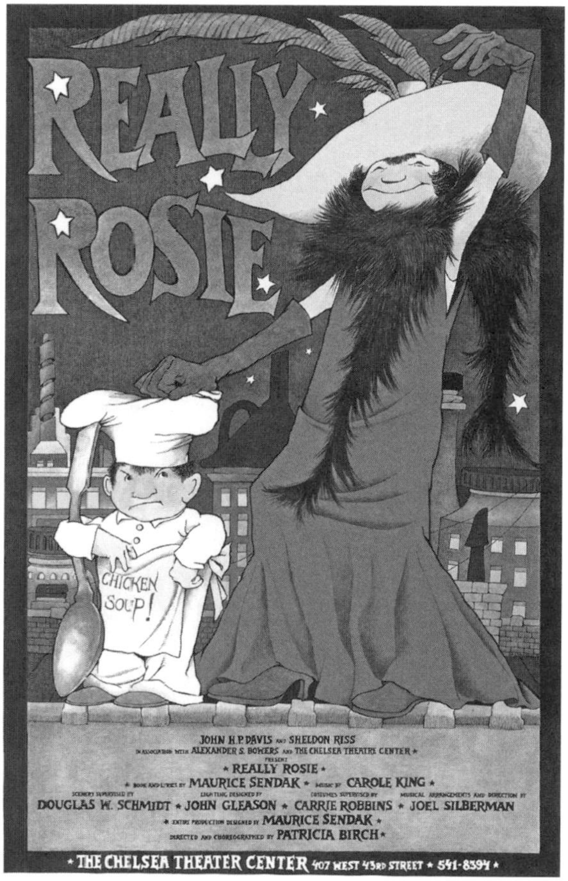
REALLY ROSIE
CHICKEN SOUP!
JOHN H.P. DAVIS AND SHELDON RISS
IN ASSOCIATION WITH ALEXANDER S. BOWERS AND THE CHELSEA THEATRE CENTER ★
PRESENT
★ REALLY ROSIE ★
★ BOOK AND LYRICS BY MAURICE SENDAK ★ MUSIC BY CAROLE KING ★
SCENERY SUPERVISED BY DOUGLAS W. SCHMIDT ★ LIGHTING DESIGNED BY JOHN GLEASON ★ COSTUMES SUPERVISED BY CARRIE ROBBINS ★ MUSICAL ARRANGEMENTS AND DIRECTION BY JOEL SILBERMAN
★ ENTIRE PRODUCTION DESIGNED BY MAURICE SENDAK ★
DIRECTED AND CHOREOGRAPHED BY PATRICIA BIRCH ★
★ THE CHELSEA THEATER CENTER 407 WEST 43RD STREET ★ 541-8394 ★
[©1980 Maurice Sendak]

Such an honoring of form very much reminds me of Maurice Sendak, whose preferred mode was the intimate yet discreet enclosure of fable and low-keyed reverie. His visual language was precise and modestly earthy yet decorous. Some of his works, like "Hector Protector," were adaptations of old nursery rhymes; others, like the tale of Brave Hilda, her baby sister and the goblins, were pastiches of typical tales from, say, Hans Christian Andersen, an author Sendak has acknowledged in print, warmly and acutely.

His stories are locations and habitations for dreamlike accounts that generate waves of subtle energy. The children in the yarns of Dr. Seuss tend to function as consumers, occasionally, as fantasizers, and heroes of their fantasies (like the young inventor of "Scrambled Eggs Super," or the hero, played by young Tommy Rettig, of that rare large-screen Seuss film: *The 5000 Fingers of Dr. T*). Sendak's juvenile protagonists, however, confront and overcome the non-human, sometimes monstrous, occupants of their dream countries through steadfast serenity, fortified with art, usually, music. Brave Hilda invokes the irresistible Muse of Dance to bespell the goblins who have kidnapped, and intend to marry off, her baby sister. (The goblins, themselves, are chortling boy-babies.) By similar means, the hero of *Where the Wild Things Are* pacifies and makes rapport with the fanged and horned denizens of his Nightmare Island.

The stories of Sendak unfold themselves in gravely exact segments of action, by soberly defined anatomies, enacting the fables in compact but soberly graphic pantomime. The pictures as a rule are not enclosed save by the pages' white margins, the concentrated imagery suggesting a dream's flickering vignettes. Yet, I can not sufficiently mark the tone of earthy, almost prosaic reality that Sendak bestows on his visions. A favorite heroine of his earlier past work, "Really Rosie" was an Irish-American miss of about 10. She functioned in what appeared to be a New York tenement setting; where, attired in grownup housedress and shawl, she would officiate at outdoor theatrics. Rosie was featured in the only Sendak animated cartoon I am aware of: I saw it years ago, probably in the '50s, at a presentation by Cinema 16, exhibitors of avant-garde films, at the now-extinct Paris Theater in Manhattan.

Rosie and other Sendak characters (especially alligators, presented with the whimsical affection shared by Walt Kelly's Albert) figured in a group of miniature volumes that I sent as birthday gifts to my young niece (now a young matron with two teenage sons) in California. I can scarcely imagine Dr. Seuss producing any such miniatures amid his spacious luxuriance. Sendak's work, however, is guided by his modest veneration of form, one definition of which might be: the judicious awareness of locality. That he was well capable of expansion when it seemed warranted is illustrated by the (relatively) huge pages of *In the Night Kitchen*. The descent of his small hero among the demonic Night Bakers (resembling slenderized Oliver Hardys in chefs' whites) is rendered in towering compositions that highlight the agoraphobic terror of his nightmare. All, at no sacrifice of Sendak's typical fluid discipline of figures, compositions,

Although my preference for Sendak's work over that of Seuss is probably apparent by now, I cannot sufficiently stress that it is largely relative: The eminence and love accorded both men's work have been richly earned. I have, however, endeavored to evaluate a single factor — form — that, to me, accounts for the all-but-unique tone and appeal of Sendak's work. That plus a scope that, perhaps, still awaits sufficient recognition. ■

The Crypto-Revolution of Our Age
XXIV. Conclusions:
(B) "Soulcraft" As Soulless *Techne* (First Part)
by Kenneth Smith

America is the only nation in history which miraculously has gone directly from barbarism to degeneration without the usual interval of civilization.
— Georges Clemenceau

The problem is, everybody has his reasons.
— Jean Renoir, *Rules of the Game*

For he to whom the present is the only thing that is present, knows nothing of the age in which he lives.
— Oscar Wilde

In spite of its *de jure* "universalist" or uniformitarian/abstractivist ethos of "rational will," modern society is shot through *de facto* with anomalous forms of psyche or character, that is, heterologous personalities driven in extreme degrees by abnormal/unnatural/inhuman principles (and yet others by "superhuman" ones), and marked phenotypically by modernly incomprehensible differences in perspective and purpose. Tragically, we have a supposedly scientific i.e. abstractivist "psychology" when more profoundly we need a *psychology of* the abstractivist impulse, what Freud once termed a "metapsychology": how is "science," how is "psychology," how is "capitalism" or the entire tacit landscape of "modern alienation," how is our banal and self-unconscious abstractivism *concretely* and *humanly* possible, and at what untold and imperceptible psychic costs? Historically and indisputably, *one psychic species'* "noetic" or "rational" utopia can prove a brutal and horrific dystopia *for all other* types, even an outright slaughterhouse.

The modern Babel has been driving itself, ever since the death of Hegel, deeper and deeper into a state of cultural divorce or *Kulturkampf*: massively and wholly incommunicant with one another are our abysmal two enclave-uni-verses, with a no-man's-chasm separating the domain of *noesis*-architected "reality" or *banausic* "objectivity" (what science, economics and technology are obsessed with) and the domain of self-disorienting, rationally and critically defenseless *doulic*-subjectivist *idiotia* or the *pathos* of private appetites and fantasies. In late-modernity, the former has come strategically to *engulf* and *dictate terms to* the latter for the more perfect harmonization of a universalized logicist or Apollonianizing dementia or dysculture of pseudoscience and pseudoreason. The cultural strife of this era is turning more and more from wars *between banausoi and douloi* into *wars of banauseia with its own* incoherent and self-destructive *self*, its *more-radicalized* with its *less-radicalized* forms. *Douloi* in their idiotism have become a wholly occupied and pacified populace, a camp of clueless *castrati*: peasants under a catastrophe-wreaking, faceless and absentee-czar.

In their lives and circumstances, humans diversify into radically different types of composed existences or subcultures, "lifestyles" or *modi vivendi*. This heterogeneity in taste, activities and social relations is alas no proof that humans are truly "individuals" any more than it demonstrates that they freely, deliberately, self-consciously *wanted to want what they want* and were not in truth extraneously conditioned or driven to express and gratify their "selves" in their "own" mass-replicated, generic way. It is modern heresy to see and to say such a thing — and *lèse majesté* against the sovereign Ego to rupture its delusions by insisting on it — but humans are *rarely individuals*, virtually always *types*, and specifically they are types in such a way as to be wholly bereft of all resources for recognizing their typicality. Their thinking no less than their living is a hackneyed script, a clutch of stereotypes and footless abstractivisms stewed together with seasoning trivia to form a meatless and insipid broth. If most people's lives were served up to them as an item in a fast-food joint, they would wonder not only why there was an apparent law against sapor and sapience but also who in his right mind would patronize such a place trafficking in commodified *ennui*. For that is not an existence but a *subsistence*, a mode of availability for other people's exploitative purposes that is designed to put one's feeble higher faculties to sleep. And we observe again, repeatedly and pointedly, the structural significance of this society's obliteration — in education, in the cultural arts, in politics, etc. — of the very species of psyche once called the redeeming "salt of the earth," without whom life in general loses its savor for all forms of psyche: the incandescent cognoscenti who dare to demand an accounting of this world.

Regardless of its one-sidedness in primal constitution or in self-development, every dysdaimonic type of psyche (i.e. all but the truly self-conscious and self-directing *aristos*) is, ironically, profoundly *self-contented to be what* and *as* it is, indeed, relates to itself "as if" it *could not possibly imagine* being otherwise: This is the natural effect of overweening psychic immediacy, which, as the basis underlying ego-formation, makes every psyche seem to itself the "ultimate," the nearly *obsessively important* and often the *divinely self-righteous* "center of all existence." *All actuality* whether of nature, history or society — all cultural accomplishments of transcendent order or *aristeia* — counts utterly for nothing to *banausoi* as well as to *douloi*, but for profoundly different characterological reasons. In *banausoi*, immediacy or self-absorption or self-centeredness takes the form of a *negative immediacy*, a *self-alienative abstractivity* that can leave nothing in its own self as it naturally is, i.e. that is the *negation of* all that is concrete or intuitive or erotic or esthetic, etc.; it is the very *converse of inertializing doulic immediacy* but it is still immediate enough to attach *banausoi* "naively" or fideistically to their apparatus of "doubt" and sophistication and their "scientific" consensuses. *Banausic* thinking and action are all for the sake of an abstracted or symbologically processed "self," quite unlike the natural/psychological (crude or naïve) "self" of *douloi*. In Freudian terms, *banausoi* actually live and draw basal motivation from their egological structures; what to *douloi* is a merely conventional or factitious, adventitious and extrinsic "ego-ideal" is to *banausoi* a successful and profound *self-sublimation*, a self-transfiguration like a visceral religion or cult. As *douloi* are *true believers* in the regime of their own most profoundly habituated feeling-world (social demands, language etc. digested into *emotionalisms*), so *banausoi* are with respect to the regime of rhetoric, conventionalisms, abstractivisms and "idealities." Anomalies or mixed types certainly occur but the *archetypal forms* of psyche are what cohere and endure and dominate the world of organized social life.

What seems external and artificial or exogenously imposed to *douloi* is to *banausoi* a "second nature" that eclipses and overrides primal nature, an order that is utterly coincident with and implicit in their own abstractive and "autonomous" egos: Among *banausoi* the natural self is more utterly paved over and subjected to the geometrisms of modernity. The artificial and conventional world of social constructs — the more systemic languages and manipulable verbalisms, codes of coordinated behavior and perspectives, the symbolic rewards for playing symbological games, the relentless wielding of surgical abstractivisms against one's own subjective self, the enveloping controlled domains of institutions and organizations with their invented and evolved subcultures, the "metaphysics" and "theology" of abstractivism — all of this unnaturalness is precisely *"natural" to banausoi*: If it were not for their distinctively and regularizably *contra naturam* natures, this domain of *artifacts and artifactual humans* would never have been generated and stabilized as a world-logic. *Banausoi* long ago devised a "more rational" mode of existence and relationships, but this mode was, of course, only made circularly to *seem* more rational by *banausic* standards, needs and preconceptions; its massive and profound shortcomings have been recognized by thinkers from Heraclitus and Aristotle onward, but it has consolidated and "totalized" itself into a universe *in spite of* its spectrographic deficiencies or outright insanity.

Banausic or bourgeois ego by its very mode of self-comprehension and integration into society seems extremely abstractable or even atomistic, asocial and solipsistic by contrast with *doulic* self-immediacy that is naturally immersed within its fellows or "peers": but *banausoi* are far more intimately integrated with the social structures and cultural code of abstractivism that holds them all together as their code of "identity." Their intellectualizing process ("rationalization" or "modernization") has appropriately transfigured society's historical base of *Gemeinschaft* or community into a *Gesellschaft* or alienative-"individuated" mode of willful and organized association. The millennial mineralization — the materialism and mechanization — of Western society that built up its physical culture at the expense of its moral or personal culture has correlatively fulfilled the modal characterological imperatives that animate *banauseia*. What is "external" or merely "objective" to *douloi* is for structural reasons not evaluated that way by *banausoi*: The *doulically* "external" is *the internal* to *banausoi*, and the "objective" the "subjective" — an alienating world-order that other types struggle to subsist in is the nourishing and very comfortable home for self-alienative psyches, personalities that are in a significant sense *denaturalized* psyches (in part by modern culture, in part by their own latently rigorist characters). By the same token however, the threat of utter impoverishment and an imminent Depression will thus drive *banausoi* to suicide because they are *utterly invested* psychically in their material extensions of self and their *banausic*-bourgeois status, as their most abysmal reasons for existing (economic collapse also stands as the most stark unmasking of the artificiality, incompetence and systemic fraud within all *banausic* order: Economic depressions are for many a *massive loss of faith* in the earthly God of *banausic* genius). The "code" of the (intrinsically valueless and meaningless) game of management and finance is all the "values" that a *banausos* typically has. The end of a particular conventional "dispensation" or historical *saeculum* — the "dealing of a hand" or distribution of authority and advantages — is for *banausoi* the end of the "world itself," for this is the "natural" architectonics of their character and culture, that is, all that they can ever perceive, comprehend or care about within the infinitude of what actually exists (an infinitude that in principle can mean nothing to *banausoi*).

To *banausoi,* by virtue of this absorption into symbological and abstractivist rules, criteria and games, the domain of hypothetical-conventional intellectualisms (idealities, ideologies and other noetic imperatives and contrivances) is as psychically pervasive and fetishistically compulsive as appetites, emotions, and libidinal conditioning are for *douloi.* That sublimated or "alienated immediacy" (more truly, a psychically perverse "immediacy *of* alienation" which is largely also an "alienation *from* immediacy" within itself and within others) makes even *banausoi* still a *form of ego*, albeit a stripped-down or skeletalized one, devoid of or immune to the many ways that *douloi* are porous to heteronomous forces but open of course to other ways of being guided or influenced. Ego in the case of *banausoi* is sublimated certainly into something "contrary to [*doulic*] human nature," something that lives and thrives among the solvents and volatile spirits of abstractivist culture; and it evolves into something even stranger yet in the case of *aristoi*, namely, a synthesis or marriage of immediacy and alienation, of integral or organismic *gnosis* and *noesis.* There is no uniform structure or metabolism of egology from one species of psyche to another; these heterogeneities are precisely why the varieties of human natures inherently strive toward different economic functions, social contexts, educations, cultures, circles of friends, religions, vocabularies, etc. Existence and the world — and one's own self — as such speak diverse kinds of languages to the different species of char-

acter: the world reflects and refracts the psyche's own *idia*, its natural and preferred specificities, its familiar needs and biases and associations, back to it.

What is distinctive of *aristoi* is a "coolness" or distance *from one's own operative, living or energetic self*, a cultivated and *stoical immunity* to the self-hypnotic, self-intoxicating, primal cohesive powers of the psyche's own raw psychic energy (whether positive *or* negative, immediate *or* alienated) with which all other types are too besotted and in which they are too immersed to be capable of any self-mastery. Unlike *banausoi, aristoi* are in principle resistant against even the seductions of their own egos, not just against the forms specific to *other types'* egologies; and the aristic coolness is necessarily (for this very reason) a nimble and protean art, not just a conventional and conformist or collectivist code, much less an habituated attitude or extrinsically obligated posture. What humans "want" or crave or are convinced of is clearly decisive for most of the species: *self-infatuation* or self-coincidence is the *natural norm*, i.e. what St. Thomas took for granted as *amor propria*, not just love *of* oneself but the kind of love *naturally appropriate to* being a self — but *aristoi* viscerally demand more from themselves than such transiently powerful or psychedelic "seemings" and illusions, and therefore and thereby *aristoi make the profoundest forms of self-criticism* and *self*-agon *necessary* for themselves, which are overwhelmingly and for the most part not possible ("*contra naturam*") much less desirable for other types. Immediacy in every kind of psyche is the magic aura that invests *de facto* energies, accomplishments and habituations with *de jure* rightness, authority, ultimacy, incorrigibility, i.e. normative potency or cogency; immediacy imbues what exists with a sense of coherent or organismic meaning, of being potentially elaboratable into an explicit *logos* or a evocative-fluent *mythos*, i.e. a pregnant gestalt accessible either to *noesis* or to *gnosis*.

In truth there is for humans no "neutral" or "factual" mode of relating to the world, such a thing is merely a figment of *banausic* ideology; no human, not even the most solipsistic *banausos*, ever lived or thought in an absolute or utter axiological *anomie*, although *banauseia* can indeed make it totalitarianly *unthinkable for values* actually to exist and for humans actually to possess discriminating value-intelligence to interpret their meaning and authority. Ideologies, like dogmatisms and cults, have specious or fallacious logics that can make even the most contranatural and fantastic beliefs seem cogent and inescapable, and all that is necessary for this is the scrupulous policing and censoring of any contrarian resources for *gnosis* to critique those ideological-noetic effects from unaccustomed

perspectives. What a rigorist code defines as unthinkable or absurd is imperative indeed not to take even provisionally seriously, for all those whose intelligence, ego and judgment are constituted viscerally by that code; primal self-duties and subrational norms are nothing to be joked about or experimented with, or even perceived, by *banausoi* or by *douloi*. Immediacy, coupled with the constraints of culture or ideology, makes *what we presently are* seem to us a kind of imperious *law*, even an eternal necessity (a tacit fatedness or something "meant to be" by divine Will), but indiscriminately it also includes in its aura all manner of accidents, customs, rhetoric, etc., making it impossible for a mind so self-enthralled to distinguish what is true as a matter of *Logos* or principle and what is merely contingently so (determined by a scheme of variable seeming that holds an impermanent power over us), and thus too what is merely parochially, naïvely and credulously believed in (uncritically or pathetically "taken for granted").

To other, necessarily uncomprehending forms of psyche, *aristoi* seem to bear a contra-natural self-contempt rather than a normal self-enchantment: This self-distanced air of rhetorical "unreachableness" makes them notoriously "difficult to work with," by setting them outside the bourgeois world's games of mutual delusion and manipulation, and its formulaic perspectives and generic motivations. But in spite of their rather stony or Olympian self-distance (not to mention their "inhuman" disdain for others' self-infatuations as well), *aristoi* are *more far-sightedly* in love with what they have inklings that they can *become*: Their future, the whole of their lives-to-come, outweighs every particular here-and-now of what to *douloi* and even to *banausoi* is an "eternal present" anchored in a never-mutating ego. For *douloi* and *banausoi*, albeit for very different reasons, *the part ineluctably trumps the whole*, and that is why dysdaimoniacs suffer the self-concocted and self-incurred conflicts and *pathoi* that they do. *Aristoi's* remoter, icier possibilities are to them something viscerally enthralling and passionate but in a more sublime or sublimated way, as an internal muse of autonomous inspiration, an Argus-eyed conscience where other types hardly have any true conscience of any sort, even one-eyed. *Aristoi* understand primally that "the child is father to the man" and they love their selves as accomplishments of *eukosmia*, as orchestral virtuosities of self-synthesis or -sublimation; they are structured to *esteem their "selves" as pregnant possibilities* rather than as presently cloying and miasmal psychic "sedimentations" or "settlements," the compounded liability that they just happen currently to have become. ∎

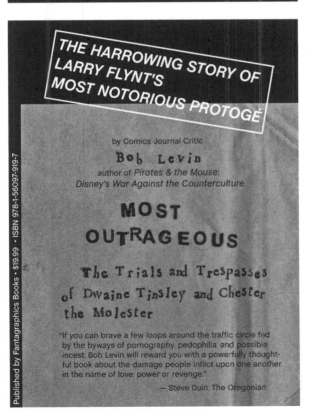

January, 2009 – February, 2009

ALTERNATIVES

AdHouse distributes Scott Morse's *Tiger! Tiger! Tiger!*, which is about Morse balancing work and parenthood (January, $14.95, 48 pp.). Harvey Pekar teamed up with DC/Vertigo and artists such as Darwyn Cooke and Dean Haspiel to create the collection of autbio tales in *American Splendor: Another Dollar* (1/9/09, $14.99, 136 pp.). *Monologues for Calculating the Destiny of Black Holes* is Anders Nilsen's new collection of surreal scribbles: coming from Fantagraphics in January ($22.99, 400 pp.). Julie Wertz edited *I Saw You: Comics Inspired by Real-Life Missed Connections* for Three Rivers Press: it's an anthology of comics in which cartoonists interpret Craigslist "missed connection" ads. Contributors include Gabrielle Bell, Aaron Renier, Keith Knight and many more (2/3/09, $12.95, 192 pp.).

CLASSIC STRIPS/COMIC BOOKS

Sergio Aragonés wrote the introduction to *Al Williamson's Flash Gordon: A Lifelong Vision of the Heroic*, a collection of the most significant of the titular artist's work on the titular title: edited by Mark Schultz (Flesk Publications, $29.95, 256 pp.). *James Robinson's WildC.A.T.S.* showcases the writer's work on the series: coming from DC/WildStorm in January ($19.99, 224 pp.). Trina Robbins expands the Nell Brinkley section from *TCJ* # 270 into *The Brinkley Girls: The Best of Nell Brinkley's Cartoons from 1913-1940* (Fantagraphics, January, $29.99, 128 pp.), which includes a selection of art from one of the earliest female American cartoonists. DC is repackaging Moore's seminal *Saga of the Swamp Thing Book One*, drawn by Stephen R. Bissette (January, $24.99, 176 pp.). At Marvel, Frank Miller and John Romita, Jr., are the creators behind *Daredevil: The Man Without Fear Premiere* (January, $24.99, 224 pp.). Another *Art Out of Time* alumnus gets the Fletcher Hanks treatment in *Boody: The Bizarre Comics of Boody Rogers* from Fantagraphics in February: edited by Craig Yoe ($19.99, 124 pp.).

INTERNATIONAL

Drawn & Quarterly publishes Pascal Blanchet's *Baloney* in January, a tale about a butcher, his daughter and her tutor battling a governor/monopolistic-utility businessman in a small Russian town: Music of the '30s and '40s is evoked ($16.95, 80 pp.). Hot on the heels of his successful *Monster* series, Viz releases *Naoki Urasawa's 20th Century Boys,* Vol. 1: *The Prophet* in February: It's about a gang of musicians who save the world ($12.99, 216 pp.).

MAINSTREAMY

Chris Claremont wrote *Genext Premiere* for Marvel because fans voted it to be his next project: Drawn by Patrick Scherberger, it's set in the future and asks whatever happened to the X-Men and their teenage kids (January, $15.99, 120 pp.). Yen Press releases the first volume of the OEL manga adaptation of best-selling author James Patterson's *Maximum Ride* Vol. 1, which is drawn by NaRae Lee (January, $10.99, 192 pp.). In the '90s, Millar and Morrison each wrote some of *The Flash: Emergency Stop*, which was drawn by Paul Ryan (January, DC, $60.00, 144 pp.). Speaking of Grant Morrison, the second volume of *All Star Superman*, drawn by Frank Quitely (DC, $19.99, 160 pp.) is slated for February: a dying Superman must battle both a super-powered Lex Luthor and Luthor's genetically enhanced clone Solaris, as Metropolis is under attack. Vol. 1 collects the six-issue Chuck Dixon adaptation of *Dean Koontz's Frankenstein: Prodigal Son*, drawn by Brett Booth (February, Del Rey/Dabel Brothers Publishing, $22.95, 176 pp.): Dr. Frankenstein has made it into modern times as a biotech magnate, and his creations run amuck. ■

Have you recently discovered a new favorite cartoonist and want to read an in-depth interview with him or her? Are you doing research for a book or a paper, or do you just want to catch up with the comic industry's magazine of record? Below is a sampling of *TCJ* back issues available from our warehouse for your perusal. For the full backlist of in-print issues, please visit www.tcj.com.

40: JIM SHOOTER interviewed, Spiegelman's BREAKDOWNS reviewed. ($3.50)

48: A 140-page partial-color Special, featuring interviews with JOHN BUSCEMA, SAMUEL R. DELANY, KENNETH SMITH AND LEN WEIN! ($6)

72: NEAL ADAMS interview. ($3.50)

74: CHRIS CLAREMONT speaks; plus RAW with SPIEGELMAN and MOULY. ($3.50)

89: WILL EISNER interview; EISNER interviews CHRIS CLAREMONT, FRANK MILLER & WENDY PINI! ($3.50)

124: JULES FEIFFER interviewed; BERKE BREATHED defends his Pulitzer. ($5)

127: BILL WATTERSON interviewed! Limited Quantity! ($10)

131: RALPH STEADMAN interviewed! ($5)

142: ARNOLD ROTH and CAROL TYLER. ($5)

152: GARY GROTH interviews TODD McFARLANE! ($6)

154: DANIEL CLOWES interviewed; HUNT EMERSON sketchbook. ($6)

156: GAHAN WILSON! ($6)

157: BILL GRIFFITH; special KURTZMAN tribute. ($6)

158: ED SOREL; R. CRUMB discusses life and politics. ($6)

162: Autobiographical cartoonists galore! PEKAR, EICHHORN, NOOMIN, BROWN, MATT, SETH! ($6)

169: NEIL GAIMAN and SOL HARRISON interviewed. ($6)

172: JOE KUBERT interview. ($5)

180: ART SPIEGELMAN; R. CRUMB. ($7)

187: GILBERT SHELTON; GIL KANE. ($6)

206: PETER BAGGE and MILLIGAN, SPAIN II, TED RALL interviewed, JACK KATZ profiled. ($7)

209: FRANK MILLER, SAM HENDERSON! ($6)

213: CAROL LAY interview, Kitchen Sink autopsy! ($6)

215: JOHN SEVERIN pt. 1, TONY MILLIONAIRE! ($6)

216: KURT BUSIEK, MEGAN KELSO, SEVERIN II. ($8)

225: MAD issue. JAFFEE, DAVIS and FELDSTEIN! ($6)

227: CARL BARKS tribute, C.C. Beck's *Fat Head* pt. 2 ($6)

231 : GENE COLAN, MICHAEL CHABON, ALAN MOORE interviewed; Moore's ABC line of comics reviewed! ($6)

241: JOHN PORCELLINO, JOHN NEY RIEBER! ($6)

242: GIL KANE chats with NOEL SICKLES! ($6)

244: JILL THOMPSON, MIKE KUPPERMAN! ($6)

247: Our 9/11 issue: RALL, RUBEN BOLLING interviews. ($7)

248: STEVE RUDE ! ANDI WATSON interviewed! ($7)

250: 272-page blowout! HERGÉ, PANTER, CLOWES and RAYMOND BRIGGS interviewed! CARL BARKS and JOHN STANLEY chat! NEIL GAIMAN vs. TODD McFARLANE trial transcripts! Brilliant manga short story NEJI-SHIKI translated! Essays on 2002-In-Review, EC, racial caricature, post-9/11 political cartooning, Team Comics, etc. and a rare essay by the late CHARLES SCHULZ on comic strips! ($14)

251: JAMES STURM! Underground comix panel ($7)

252: JOHN ROMITA SR., RON REGÉ interviewed. ($7)

253: ERIC DROOKER, JOHN CULLEN MURPHY, JASON! ($7)

254: WILL ELDER, Kazuo Umezu interviews! ($7)

256: KEIJI NAKAZAWA; FORT THUNDER! ($7)

257: A suite of four never-before-published interviews with the late, great comix artist RICK GRIFFIN! Hardworkin' writer JOE CASEY interviewed! ($7)

258: A comprehensive look at the work of STEVE DITKO, and a conversation with GILBERT HERNANDEZ and CRAIG THOMPSON! ($7)

259: 2003 Year in Review: Comics and Artists of the Year! Youthquake! A new generation emerges! ($7)

260: DUPUY and BERBERIAN! JEAN-CLAUDE MÈZIÉRES! They're foreign! ($7)

261: PHOEBE GLOECKNER! JAY HOSLER! ($7)

262: NEW FORMAT! ALEX TOTH profiled, with a generous color selection of his 1950s crime comics, plus an interview with STEVE BRODNER! ($10)

263: ED BRUBAKER interviewed! CEREBUS examined! George Carlson's JINGLE JANGLE TALES in color! ($10)

264: IVAN BRUNETTI interviewed, Underground Publishers, Harold Gray's LITTLE JOE in color! ($10)

265: Essays on WILLIAM STEIG, ERIC SHANOWER interviewed. Harry Anderson's Crime Comics! ($10)

268: CRAIG THOMPSON! BOB BURDEN! TINTIN AT SEA! WALT KELLY'S "OUR GANG" in color! ($10)

269: SHOUJO MANGA ISSUE! MOTO HAGIO interviewed and her short story "HANSHIN" in english! ($10)

270: JESSICA ABEL and LALO ALCARAZ! NELL BRINKLEY comics in color! ($10)

271: JERRY ROBINSON interviewed! RENÉE FRENCH! 50 pages of pre-Popeye THIMBLE THEATRE! ($10)

273: EDDIE CAMPBELL interviewed! JUNKO MIZUNO interviewed! ART YOUNG goes to HELL! ($10)

274: MIKE PLOOG interviewed! SOPHIE CRUMB! Early HARVEY KURTZMAN comics in COLOR! ($10)

275: 2005 YEAR IN REVIEW! DAVID B. interviewed! BOODY ROGERS comics in COLOR! ($10)

276: TERRY MOORE interviewed! BOB HANEY pt. 1! Early B. KRIGSTEIN comics in COLOR! ($10)

277: 30 YEARS OF THE COMICS JOURNAL! THE STATE OF THE INDUSTRY! IT RHYMES WITH LUST! ($13)

278: BILL WILLINGHAM interviewed! BOB HANEY pt. 2! ORESTES CALPINI comics! JAXON tribute! ($10)

279: JOOST SWARTE interviewed! JOHNNY RYAN! LILY RENÉE comics! ($10)

280: FRANK THORNE interviewed! CARLA SPEED McNEIL! CRIME DOES NOT PAY comics! ($10)

281: THE BEST COMICS OF 2006! YOSHIHIRO TATSUMI and MELINDA GEBBIE interviewed! ($10)

282: ALISON BECHDEL! FRED GUARDINEER! Andru & Esposito's GET LOST comics! ($10)

283: LEWIS TRONDHEIM! DAVID SANDLIN! THE 39 STEPS comic adaptation! ($10)

284: ROGER LANGRIDGE! GENE YANG! Frederick Burr Opper's HAPPY HOOLIGAN in color! ($10)

285: DARWYN COOKE! ERNIE COLÓN! KEITH KNIGHT! John Buscema WANTED comics! ($10)

286: POSY SIMMONDS! GAIL SIMONE! Otto Soglow's THE AMBASSADOR in color! ($10)

287: JEFFREY BROWN! GREG RUCKA! Non-Krazy Kat comics of GEORGE HERRIMAN! ($12)

288: NEW FORMAT! THE BEST COMICS OF 2007! Tarpé Mills MISS FURY in color! ($12)

289: ROBERT KIRKMAN! SHAUN TAN! A gallery of MINUTE MOVIES strips! ($12)

290: SCHULZ AND PEANUTS ROUNDTABLE! MATT MADDEN! A gallery of '50s horror comics by BOB POWELL! ($12)

291: TIM SALE! JOSH SIMMONS! A gallery of DAN GORDON comics! ($12)

292: THE DEITCH ISSUE: GENE, KIM, SIMON and SETH all interviewed by Gary Groth! ($12)

293: S. CLAY WILSON! ALEX ROBINSON! ($12)

Libraries and Specials:

TCJ SPECIAL I: WINTER 2002: JOE SACCO interviewed! ($24)

TCJ LIBRARY VOL. I: JACK KIRBY: All of The King's Journal interviews! ($23)

TCJ SPECIAL II: SUMMER 2002: JIM WOODRING interviewed! ($27)

TCJ SPECIAL III: WINTER 2003: BILL STOUT interviewed! ($27)

TCJ LIBRARY VOL. II: Frank Miller: All of FM's Journal interviews and more! ($23)

TCJ LIBRARY VOL. III: R. CRUMB: All of Crumbs Journal interviews! ($23)

TCJ SPECIAL IV: WINTER 2004: Profiles of and interviews with four generations of cartoonists — AL HIRSCHFELD, JULES FEIFFER, ART SPIEGELMAN and CHRIS WARE! ($23)

TCJ LIBRARY VOL. IV: DRAWING THE LINE: Lavishly illustrated interviews with JULES FEIFFER, DAVID LEVINE, EDWARD SOREL and RALPH STEADMAN! ($23)

TCJ SPECIAL V: WINTER 2005: Almost half of this volume is devoted to MANGA! Also features Vaughn Bodé, Milt Gross, and a comics section! ($25)

TCJ LIBRARY VOL. V: CLASSIC COMICS ILLUSTRATORS: A full-color celebration of the work of FRANK FRAZETTA, RUSS HEATH, BURNE HOGARTH, RUSS MANNING, and MARK SCHULTZ! ($23)

TCJ LIBRARY VOL. VI: THE WRITERS: Interviews with ALAN MOORE, CHRIS CLAREMONT, STEVE GERBER and more! ($20)

TCJ LIBRARY VOL. VII: KURTZMAN: Interviews with HARVEY KURTZMAN! ($23)

The *Utne* Independent Press Award Winner for Arts & Literature coverage just keeps getting better. Subscribe now to get these issues:

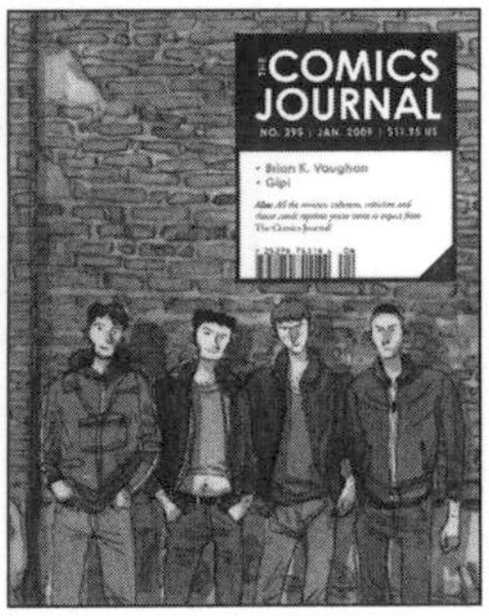
COMICS
JOURNAL
• Brian K. Vaughan
• Gipi

THE COMICS JOURNAL #295

Brian K. Vaughan, writer of *Y: The Last Man*, will take readers behind the scenes of the upcoming *Y* film, TV's *Lost*, the award-winning *Pride of Baghdad*, *Deus Ex Machina* and *Buffy Season 8*, as well as upcoming comics projects. Paul Karasik talks with Italian cartoonist Gipi about his Santa Maria video and animation studio, *They Found the Car*, *Garage Band* and *Notes for a War Story*.

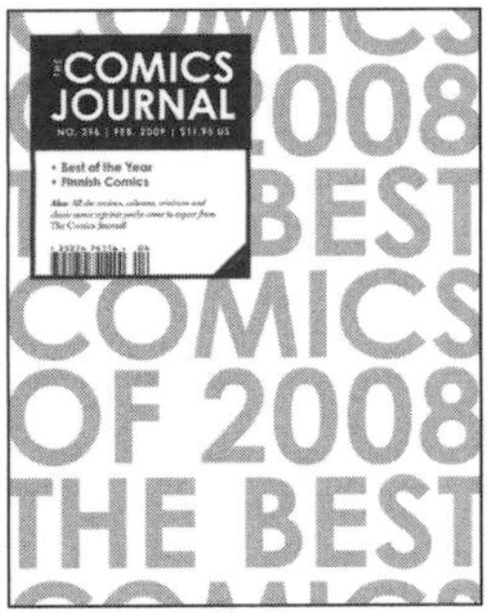
COMICS
JOURNAL
• Best of the Year
• Finnish Comics
2008
BEST
COMICS
OF 2008
THE BEST

THE COMICS JOURNAL #296

Our annual Best-of the-Year issue, featuring interviews with the best cartoonists of the year about their work.

Plus, *TCJ* explores the international comics scene with a sampling of edgy works by contemporary Finnish cartoonists that have never before been published in English.

"Still the best and most insightful magazine of comics criticism that exists."
— Alan Moore

"You ignore it at your peril."
— Neil Gaiman

"The good is always in conflict with the better. *The Comics Journal* attempts to explain the difference."
— Gil Kane

"All in all, *The Comics Journal* is a stand-out inspiration to me."
— Kim Deitch

Read *The Comics Journal* the way the professionals do:
by SUBSCRIPTION.

Please Send Me: (fill in issue # or check option below) Note: All subscriptions include online access to back issues from #277 forward.

- ☐ **5-issue sub — $36 (Can. $64/ Int. $96)**
- ☐ **10-issue sub — $72 (Can. $128/ Int. $193) and our CD Sampler*!**

*Featuring audio interviews with Gil Kane, R. Crumb, Jack Kirby, Charles Schulz and Walt Kelly!

☐ **SPECIAL OFFER!: Subscribe for 10 issues and get a free copy of any TCJ Special or TCJ Library volume listed on the facing page!**

ONLINE ONLY: The complete magazine accessed online: ☐ **5-issue sub — $18** ☐ **10-issue sub — $30**

TCJ Special or TCJ Library volume selected: ____________________

Back Issues: #_______ **QTY.**_____ **#**_______ **QTY.**_____ **#**_______ **QTY.**_____ **#**_______ **QTY.**_____ **#**_______ **QTY.**_____

Method of Payment: ____________________ Amount Enclosed (WA residents add 8.8% sales tax): ____________________

Name: ____________________

Address: ____________________

City: ____________________ State: __________ Zip: ____________________

Visa/MC#: ____________________ Exp. Date: ____________________

Signature (for credit card orders): ____________________

Daytime phone (for credit card orders): ____________________

E-mail (required to access special website features): ____________________

Order toll free with Visa or MasterCard: 1-800-657-1100 or mail to: 7563 Lake City Way NE, Seattle, WA 98115 or visit: http://www.tcj.com